ARCHAEOLOGY

ARCHAEOLOGY

SECOND EDITION

DAVID HURST THOMAS

American Museum of Natural History

Illustrations by Dennis O'Brien

HOLT, RINEHART AND WINSTON, INC.
Fort Worth   Chicago   San Francisco   Philadelphia
Montreal   Toronto   London   Sydney   Tokyo

ABOUT THE COVER: These prehistoric **petroglyphs** were pecked into the walls of a narrow box canyon leading to Mouse's Tank, in the Valley of Fire (twelve miles SE of Overton, Nevada). The four human figures **(anthropomorphs)** probably represent hunters surrounding and dispatching bighorn sheep, which often came to drink at this natural game trap.

COVER PHOTO CREDIT: © Philip Hyde, 1989. Petroglyph photo reprinted by permission from *Drylands: The Deserts of North America*, 1987, Harcourt, Brace, Jovanovich, A Yolla Bolly Press Book.

Library of Congress Cataloging-in-Publication Data

Thomas, David Hurst.
   Archaeology.

   Bibliography: p.
   Includes index.
   1. Archaeology. I. Title.
CC165.T48   1990   930.1   88-34706
ISBN : 0-03-022728-3

Address orders: 301 Commerce Street, Suite 3700, Ft. Worth, TX 76102

Address editorial correspondence: 301 Commerce Street, Suite 3700, Ft. Worth, TX 76102

Printed in the United States of America

1 2 3 4 016 11 10 9 8 7 6 5 4

Holt, Rinehart and Winston, Inc.
The Dryden Press
Saunders College Publishing

This book is dedicated to LSAP(T)—I wouldn't have started and couldn't have finished it without you.

PREFACE

People who like this sort of thing will find
this the sort of thing they like
Book review by Abraham Lincoln

What This Book Is

Most archaeology textbooks strive to impart an encyclopedic, dispassionate perspective on the subject. And more often than not, the author successfully attains that objective, in an erudite, if impersonal, style. This mode of presentation is fine, often enlightening and certainly a matter of individual taste and style.

But I can't do it that way. Little about archaeology is impersonal to me, and my biases are reflected here. In the Prologue, I'll tell the tale of how Gatecliff Shelter was discovered, a fairly subjective sketch designed to tell you something of what archaeology really feels like. Later, in Chapter 7, I'll take you along on our more recent search for the lost sixteenth-/seventeenth-century Mission Santa Catalina de Guale. This search not only will illustrate the growing importance of remote sensing in everyday archaeology, but it also will impart something of the flavor of getting out there and actually doing the archaeology. Despite what some might tell you, archaeology is more than concepts, theory, methods, and typology. It is also dust and discouragement.

Archaeology should be fun, and throughout these pages, I shall stay on a relatively personal level. Archaeological "literature" has an unfortunate tendency to use a stilted narrative as dry and stuffy as the caves we excavate. I don't like that, and so I try to write more or less as I speak.

Given this perspective, it seems inevitable that this work will reflect something of my own personality. In the first chapter, for instance, I narrate the history and development of Americanist archaeology. Individual archaeologists can be as revealing as the archaeology itself, and so I present a history of archaeology in terms of eight well-known American archaeologists. The selection is idiosyncratic, reflecting my own mind-set and background. Other archaeologists would doubtlessly choose others to personify different values. This is what I mean about the largely personal slant.

Why A Second Edition?

Writing a textbook can be much like a childhood disease; a single episode is unpleasant, but usually provides lifetime immunity
—David J. Weber

The first edition of this book was published a decade ago, and since then much has changed in archaeology. Perhaps because of the book's personal narrative style, I have discussed its general approach and specific presentation with dozens and dozens of students and working archaeologists who got their start in archaeology by reading these pages. We also commissioned a number of formal reviews of the first edition, in hopes of improving it the second time around. In sum, whereas the direction and organization remain intact in the second edition, I have made some significant changes, to sharpen the presentation and also to respond to new developments in the field over the past ten years. I also have eliminated outdated and moribund sections that did not work in the classroom. The surviving examples are updated, and dozens of new illustrations have been introduced to demonstrate current archaeology in action.

Historical Archaeology Is Now Prominently Featured

Ten years ago, I wondered whether historical archaeology was sufficiently "anthropological" to warrant inclusion. Today, all my doubts have been erased, and accordingly, I have integrated historical archaeology with the rest of archaeology. Archaeologists working on historic-period sites have propelled themselves into the anthropological mainstream.

Cultural Resource Management Is More Important Than Ever

It has always been important that those working to conserve archaeological resources be familiar with the basic theoretical and practical tenets of their profession. Otherwise, how can they judge the efficacy and relevance of the research they oversee? Today, a considerable portion of **applied archaeology** in America involves archaeological sites of the **protohistoric** and historic periods. Thus anybody seeking employment as an applied archaeologist should be thoroughly familiar with the assumptions, protocols, and basic tenets of historical archaeology.

We Specifically Confront the Role of Women in Archaeology

A recent, alarming survey by Janet Spector and Mary Whelan (1988) found a significant gender bias in archaeology's introductory-level textbooks. As they emphasized, this may be students' only exposure to how contemporary archaeologists work and how their data are projected into the past. Surprised by their findings, I took a hard look at the first edition of *Archaeology* and had to agree. My first edition too often fostered the erroneous impression that archaeology was still dominated by cowboys, adventure seekers, and other macho men. This is surely not true of the discipline today, and I now attempt to provide a more balanced picture. Recognizing that I was skating on thin ice, I solicited and received the gracious assistance of many female archaeologists in framing my approach.

Beyond simply employing gender-neutral language, I have addressed this complex issue by asking two questions: (1) To what degree is contemporary archaeology biased against participation by women, and (2) to what extent is this bias reflected in our perception of the past?

Over the last three decades, women have become increasingly involved in archaeology and currently comprise a significant and influential segment of the archaeological profession. This fact is reflected throughout these pages in researcher-specific sketches, bibliographic citations, and photographs. The career of Dr. Kathleen Deagan is used as a case study, not simply to illustrate what women are doing in today's archaeology, but in the larger sense to illustrate what contemporary archaeology is.

Still, we must not minimize the obstacles facing women entering the profession of archaeology. In Chapter 4, we explicitly look at the barriers that traditionally kept women out of the archaeological marketplace, how women have participated in the archaeological enterprise, and, more important, what the future holds for women in this previously male-dominated profession.

The second, related issue concerns our view of the human past. Many Americanist archaeologists are working to overcome the erroneous, if widespread, "man-the-hunter" stereotype vision of evolution. The so-called feminist perspective on the past is by no means restricted to women, and several examples of this developing direction are incorporated in the later portions of the text.

We Now Include Field Methods

An entirely new part (Chapters 6, 7, and 8) addresses the nature of the archaeological record and how archaeologists generate their data. Special attention has been given to remote sensing, not only as a more efficient way to conduct traditional research, but also as a focus for enhancing the conservation ethic in field studies.

You'll Find a Radically Expanded Bibliography

In this edition, I also changed my approach to the archaeological literature. This shift was prompted by a look back at the introductory text I used when breaking into archaeology, the first edition of *An Introduction to Prehistoric Archaeology* by Frank Hole and Robert F. Heizer (1965). I first took archaeology courses as an undergraduate, and although forced to sell most of my textbooks to keep afloat, I never let go of my Hole and Heizer; I still have it. It was a good-enough overview of mid-1960s archaeology, but the most valuable part was the bibliography. Pedantic, to be sure, but those seemingly endless references helped me out for years. When writing a research paper in grad school or even studying for my doctoral qualifying exams, I always seemed to stop first at my dog-eared copy of Hole and Heizer. Somehow, it always provided just the right reference to the appropriate literature.

Encyclopedic discourses still leave me cold, but I do think that a comprehensive, annotated bibliography can provide a tremendous advantage to those just learning about archaeology. This time around, therefore, I spent considerable effort building up the bibliography of this second edition of *Archaeology*.

Rather than engage in a hackneyed competition over I-can-cite-more-references-by-rote-than-you-can, I've tried to integrate bibliographic information into the presentation. Early on, I discuss what the archaeological literature is, why it is important, and how to use it. Each major section ends in Where to Go from Here?, a selective guide to both classic and contemporary sources in archaeology. Where appropriate, I have annotated and rank-ordered the list. Throughout, I sprinkle short introductions to key scientific journals appropriate to each topic (noting editorial policy, history of publication, and subscription information), should you be interested in pursuing this particular issue in more detail.

I hope the end result will provide the same useful guideposts to the literature that my well-worn copy of Hole and Heizer once gave me.

The Scope Is Defined As Americanist Archaeology

My objective is to explain what is going on in contemporary Americanist archaeology. The term *contemporary* poses few problems—by it, I mean right now, today. By **Americanist archaeology** (a term borrowed from Robert Dunnell), I mean the brand of archaeology currently taught and practiced at major American universities and museums. Americanist archaeology is, of course, practiced around the globe, as scholars will always reflect their intellectual origins, regardless of where they ply their craft.

Certain concepts apply throughout the discipline. But because this is not an encyclopedia, I am selective in my treatment. Although I draw examples from around the world, this remains a first-person textbook. Many of the lessons are taught in terms of my own experiences. Not only are these data the most familiar to me, but I also wish to impart a sense of what modern archaeology feels like.

The Bias Is Explicit

Obviously, I feel perfectly free to interject my own views on the condition of contemporary theory and practice in archaeology. I believe that archaeology can, and should, be a science—that is, archaeological inquiry should proceed according to canons of established **scientific methods:** We set out a framework of what science is and how such procedures are applied to specific archaeological problems. But to me, the philosophy of science is not a particularly lofty and abstract issue; I see science as a standard operating procedure used every day by practicing archaeologists. Accordingly, to illustrate the scientific method, I shall present Heinrich Schliemann's search for Homer's Troy as an extended case study. Schliemann is, I am well aware, an unorthodox choice for demonstrating the workings of scientific archaeology. After all, wasn't he a pothunting treasure seeker and a first-rate scoundrel? Schliemann's archaeology has, to be sure, its unsavory aspects, but it remains true that he did use the fundamentals of scientific inquiry in his search for Troy (even though he didn't realize it).

> **Science is nothing but developed perception, integrated intent,**
> **common sense rounded out and minutely articulated.**
> **George Santayana**

But having said this, I must point out that some archaeologists are now framing alternatives to the "scientific" approach in archaeology. Some have turned to critical theory for the answer, and others are looking toward symbolic anthropology for enlightenment (discussed in detail in Chapter 3). At the heart of such approaches is not whether scientifically derived archaeology is good or bad but whether ethical values have a place in archaeological interpretation. Although science purports to be value neutral, it seldom is. As we discuss in Part One, some archaeologists are challenging the value-free premise of the scientific approach and are deliberately bringing politics into their arena of analysis.

What Comes Before What?

Unlike an encyclopedia, this book is organized to provide a certain flow, and I hope that you will read the chapters in order. In a sense, we follow the old biological principle of "ontogeny recapitulates phylogeny"—the notion that an organism's evolutionary history can be retraced ("recapitulated") by looking at its early developmental stages.

Archaeology works in the same way. The early discipline concentrated largely on ordering artifacts in time and space, and this is still its first task. At mid-century, Americanist archaeology began reconstructing past **lifeways;** this still remains the archaeologist's intermediate goal. Finally, over the last three decades, archaeologists have been searching for the processes that underlie and explain human behavior: Processual studies are today's ultimate objective.

You will also find in these pages a rather heavy dose of anthropology, more than is customary in an introductory archaeology textbook. But one simply cannot understand the trends and directions of contemporary archaeology without a solid grounding in the specifics of contemporary anthropology. The practical archaeologist needs to understand the major questions in modern anthropology before attempting to answer these questions. Current anthropology contains diverse perspectives. Some are essential to the development of contemporary archaeology; other mainstreams remain practically irrelevant.

I still believe in the old adage that "archaeology is anthropology or it is nothing." But archaeology is not all kinds of anthropology, and we must understand how major anthropological strategies operate before we can place archaeology in its proper anthropological perspective. For this reason, then, I stress anthropological theory to a much greater degree than do most writers of archaeological textbooks.

Who Helped Out?

Despite the personal flavor of these pages, no book is completed by a single pair of hands. Many people have helped me, and it could not have been otherwise. I thus close this preface with some appropriate words of thanks.

The overall presentation was vastly improved by a contingent of top-notch colleagues and friends who provided advice and critical reviews of the manuscript: Marcus Arguelles, Mary Beaudry, Jane Buikstra, Margaret Conkey, Cheryl Claassen, C. William Clewlow, Jay Custer, Kathleen Deagan, Kent V. Flannery, Don Fowler, Joan Gero, Donald K. Grayson, Marvin Harris, William Haviland, Robert L. Humphrey, Cynthia Irwin-Williams, William Kelso, Clark Spencer Larsen, Robert Leonard, Mark Leone, Joyce Marcus, Michael J. O'Brien, James O'Connell, Christopher Peebles, Stephen Plog, William Rathje, Elizabeth Reitz, John Rick, Nan Rothschild, Irwin Rovner, Payson Sheets, Stanley South, Janet Spector, and Mary Whelan. Each contributed trenchant suggestions, which I was sometimes too opinionated to follow. Although the finished product remains my own, I gratefully acknowledge the help of these people for improving the ideas and sharpening the focus.

Several others in the American Museum of Natural History also deserve thanks. Margot Dembo handled innumerable editing chores, and my confrere Lorann S. A. Pendleton spent endless hours helping with the background research. The library staff at the museum—particularly Richard Storrow, Marc Epstein, Carol Tucher, and Martin Shapiro—performed extraordinary feats with interlibrary loans, and I am also most grateful for assistance from the people in the photographic collections and studio at the museum: Carmen Collozo, Barbara Methe, Adam Anik, and Jackie Beckett. And as always, my own research staff—Jose Jimenez, Laura Lundenberg, and Debra Peter—helped out in a hundred ways.

I am also grateful to the crew at Holt, Rinehart and Winston—Kristen Olson who initially proposed that we resuscitate the textbook and especially Mary Glenn who allayed thousands of day-to-day concerns.

The singular Dennis O'Brien generated most of the artwork illustrating this volume, and I also gratefully acknowledge the contributions of the late Nicholas Amorosi, who prepared several of the original artifact illustrations.

New York City
July 1988

D. H. T.

TABLE OF CONTENTS

Part Two
Encountering The Archaeological Record   155

Part Three
Archaeology's Initial Objective:
Construct Cultural Chronologies   **251**

Part IV
**Archaeology's Intermediate Objective:
Reconstruct Extinct Lifeways**   **355**

LIST OF FIGURES AND TABLES

Figures

Tables

Prologue

This book considers the major methods, theory, and pragmatics that constitute today's Americanist archaeology. But all too frequently, methodology–theory–practice discourses are too abstract, in danger of becoming divorced from reality altogether, drifting too far afield. So we shall keep this discussion more firmly grounded, more down to earth.

Tales of Two Sites

Our ruminations on method, theory, and practice take place only in the context of real archaeological objects. Accordingly, throughout the text, I emphasize specific objects recovered in my own excavations. Two sites in particular—Gatecliff Shelter and Mission Santa Catalina—crop up frequently. **Gatecliff Shelter** (Nevada) is a **prehistoric** cave in the American Desert West, and people have gathered beneath this shallow shelter over the past seven thousand years. I discovered Gatecliff in 1970, and throughout the 1970s, our interdisciplinary team excavated the microstratigraphic deposits.

The second archaeological case study, **Mission Santa Catalina de Guale,** is located in the fabled Sea Islands off the coast of Georgia. Here, a Franciscan mission was founded among the Guale Indians in the late 1500s, and for more than a century, Santa Catalina defined the northern Spanish frontier along the eastern seaboard. An outpost of St. Augustine, the oldest European-style city in the United States, Mission Santa Catalina was overrun by British troops in 1680. I began searching for this lost mission site in 1978, the same year we finished digging at Gatecliff. Three years later, we discovered Santa Catalina and have been digging there ever since.

In one sense, these two sites are as different as they can be. Gatecliff is a pre-contact, prehistoric site, and Santa Catalina dates to the historic period. Gatecliff is a

Gatecliff Shelter as it appeared in 1970. (Photograph by the author)

high-altitude rockshelter in the western desert, and Santa Catalina is a site by the southeastern seashore. Only a handful of Native Americans made their seasonal home at Gatecliff, but Mission Santa Catalina was the permanent residence for hundreds of Guale Indians. The sediments at Gatecliff Shelter span the last seven thousand years, whereas Santa Catalina lasted only a century. Gatecliff was discovered by old-fashioned, dogged fieldwork; we found Mission Santa Catalina using modern sampling theory and "hi-tech" remote sensing. The Gatecliff excavations were "vertical"—in some places nearly forty feet deep—but nowhere at Santa Catalina have we dug deeper than six feet. The cultural deposits at Gatecliff were stacked up within a floor area of about three hundred square feet, whereas Mission Santa Catalina sprawled across a dozen acres. Buried within Gatecliff Shelter were several thousand stone tools, weighing more than a ton; all the stone artifacts from Santa Catalina would easily fit in a single shoe box. Only three pieces of pottery turned up at Gatecliff, but ten thousand sherds so far have been catalogued from Santa Catalina.

The list of contrasts grows indefinitely, but my point is simple: Having dug at Gatecliff and Mission Santa Catalina for two decades, I have yet to excavate any important data from either. In fact, I have found no data at all.

What Are Archaeological Data?

Why would any right-thinking archaeologist waste half a career digging holes that produced no archaeological data? Am I feebleminded or just unlucky?

Neither, I hope. I found no data at Gatecliff or Mission Santa Catalina because archaeologists do not excavate data—anywhere. Rather, they excavate objects. Gatecliff Shelter and Mission Santa Catalina surrendered overwhelming artifact collections, thousands upon thousands of archaeological objects. But neither the physical sites nor the archaeological objects they contained are data.

Data arise only from observations made on such objects. Each observation is specifically designed to answer one or more relevant questions: How old is this part of the site? Who were the people? What language did they speak? Was the ancient climate similar to that of today? Why did they choose to live in this particular spot? What did they eat? What kinds of social groups were present? Where did they go? Each question may require a different set of observations, giving rise to several batches of dissimilar data. But remember that quite different observations can often be made on exactly the same objects. The hallmark of today's archaeology is the precept that the objects of the past can (and must) be viewed from multiple perspectives. Gatecliff and Mission Santa Catalina provide recurring points of reference, and we use the objects from these two sites—plus many, many others—to illustrate differing perspectives on the past.

More than anything else, today's archaeology is flexible and broad based. Sometimes we ask questions about time; we also consider cultural ecology; we may ask about religion and social organization; sometimes we might inquire about mind-set and cognitive structure; we might even compare vastly different areas, such as the prehistoric Desert West of Nevada with the Australian desert. The theoretical perspective may vary wildly, but the objects often remain the same.

Before dissecting the inner workings of today's archaeology, let me briefly introduce the first of our two case studies, Gatecliff Shelter (Mission Santa Catalina surfaces a bit later).

I can evade questions without help: what I need is answers.
—John F. Kennedy

Full-scale excavations at the *convento* (friary) of Mission Santa Catalina de Guale. (Courtesy of the American Museum of Natural History; photograph by Dennis O'Brien)

How Do You Know Where to Dig?

Every archaeologist who addresses general audiences will, sooner or later, be asked the same question: How do you archaeologists find your sites? How do you know where to dig?

There are as many answers as archaeologists. Some sites have been known for centuries, "discovered" by early explorers like Coronado, de Soto, and Pizarro. The locations of other sites have been handed down through the generations, preserved in oral and written traditions. For example, the site of Tula in northern Mexico was finally identified as the prehistoric Toltec capital by tracing and testing Aztec traditions. Sites are sometimes deliberately discovered in large-scale systematic surveys, during which entire valleys or islands are scanned for the refuse of previous habitation. But some of the best archaeological sites in the world were found by simple accident. Hard work and luck help, too.

My experiences at Gatecliff Shelter are probably typical of contemporary Americanist archaeologists. While a graduate student at the Davis campus of the University of California, I supported my doctoral fieldwork by conducting archaeological field schools. We offered green, untrained students the chance to work in the **Reese River Valley** in central Nevada. It was a trade. The students paid for the summer's research through their enrollment fees. They also supplied the physical labor. In return, I taught them what I could about archaeological fieldwork. The trade seemed fair enough. I progressed in my doctoral research, and they acquired training and credits toward graduation.

Twenty-three students were accepted the first summer at Reese River to conduct a regional random sample as part of the field school sponsored by the University of Nevada. We wanted to see whether the cultural ecology of the prehistoric Reese River Indians was similar to that of the historic **Shoshone** Indians. Although Shoshone still reside here, they deserted their hunting-gathering lifeway long ago in favor of ranching or farming. Because we could no longer observe that ecological system in action, we did the next best thing. We tried to program a computer to reconstruct late prehistoric **Great Basin** cultural ecology.

In the late 1960s, the computer hardware was complicated and cumbersome, and we were only beginning to think about applying computers to archaeological problems. We marshaled all the data we could find regarding the behavior of wild plants and animals and fed them into the campus mainframe computer. We then wrote a FORTRAN program with our interpretation of how the historic-period Shoshone collected wild plants and hunted animals. The computer then constructed imaginary (mathematical) archaeological sites. The computer told us that if the weather were just so, if the plants responded in a certain way to this weather, if the Shoshone gathered certain plants and killed certain animals, then their archaeological sites should look like this. In effect, because there were no Shoshone who still practiced the old ways, we grilled a computer about the extinct Shoshone cultural ecology, ultimately translating these findings into things that archaeologists could recover in the field.

Thus the computer gave us some hypotheses, and now we needed to test these notions against some fresh archaeological data. This is where the twenty-three University of Nevada students came in. We spent six weeks climbing twelve-thousand-foot mountains and walking along saltbrush flats looking for archaeological objects. We were anxious to see whether our computer had indeed succeeded in forecasting where the archaeological objects would be. Could computers really "predict the past"?

It was a hot, dusty chore. But by the end of August we had located more than a hundred prehistoric archaeological sites, some of them loaded with artifacts. Our fieldwork was wrapped up for the year, and I wanted to thank the students for their efforts.

So, expending the last dollars of our slender food budget, I treated my crew to steak dinners in the nearby town of Austin (Nevada). Even though the dusty ride took more than an hour, the push seemed worth it. We relaxed, gnawed our T-bones, drained bottomless brews, and spun rattlesnake and stuck-truck stories into the morning hours.

Austin is a pocket-sized Nevada mining town with fewer than 250 citizens. It is a picturesque little desert dive, which has attracted its share of attention. In his epic journey across backroads America, *Blue Highways* author William Least Heat Moon wrote, "I liked Austin . . . a living ghost town: 40 percent living, 50 percent ghost and 10 percent not yet decided."

But above all, Austin is small-town America, and when two dozen grubby archaeologists come to town for steaks and beer, word soon gets around. When our waitress politely inquired who was in charge and somebody pointed to me, she told me about her husband, a mining geologist who had prospected the western mountains for forty years. There are few places Gale Peer has not been. So when we met, I asked Mr. Peer about the archaeological sites he might have seen. We were hoping to find a local cave or rock shelter with some stratified cultural deposits, in order to check our Reese River findings.

Mr. Peer allowed as to how, indeed, he knew of such a cave—over in **Monitor Valley**, a dozen miles east of Austin. He had not been there in years, but the details were fresh in his mind. "You take the main dirt road south in Monitor Valley, then turn west, up one of the side canyons. I don't remember which one. As you drive along, oh, let's see, maybe ten or fifteen mile, there's a large black chert cliff. It goes straight up. A thousand feet or so. At the bottom of the cliff is a cave. Some time, a long time ago, the Indians painted the inside of the cave. There are pictures of people and animals, plus a lot of writing I don't understand. Then the top of the shelter caved in. Maybe in an earthquake. There's not much of the cave left. Drive out there when you get a chance. I'd like to know what's in that cave." Mr. Peer sketched a map on his business card. He remembered exactly where the cave was relative to the canyon, but he was not sure exactly which canyon. I stashed the card in my shirt, and thanked him for the tip.

Many archaeologists find their sites this way. My colleague Jim O'Connell calls this "gumshoe survey," just hanging out in bars and gas stations, listening to those who know the land best. I hoped that Mr. Peer's advice was as good as his memory seemed to be. Maybe this was the deep cave site I'd been looking for. But of course I had heard of a dozen similar caves, all of which proved uninteresting when investigated.

That was the last night of the field season. We wrapped up dinner, drained the last beer, and headed for our tents. We broke camp the next day and returned to civilization.

The students went their various ways, and I resumed my graduate studies. But throughout that academic year I kept remembering Mr. Peer's cave. Sometimes I felt like dropping everything, hopping into a pickup truck, and taking off for Monitor Valley. But sometimes the classroom seems to get in the way of education, and my graduate student commitments kept me from breaking away, even for a weekend. Besides, I consoled myself, the mountains of Monitor Valley tower eleven thousand feet, and the October snowfall can last until late spring. Even if I knew where it was, the cave would probably be snowed in until May. So I plodded on at my local computer center, every now and again reflecting on a make-believe cave somewhere in the Nevada backwoods.

Summer finally arrived, and once again I rounded up undergraduates to help out at Reese River. Before the field school started, Trudy Thomas and I escaped to central Nevada, scouting out new campsites and hoping to find the cave that Mr. Peer had spoken of nearly a year before. We knew that the rock shelter must be in a canyon—but which one? We had fifteen canyons to choose from.

With the necessary state and federal excavation permits in hand, we started out. Beginning at the southern end of Monitor Valley, we drove up and down each side canyon, working our way slowly northward. The roads were rough, and we sometimes spent a whole day joggling up one canyon, jiggling down another. The weather was no ally. We were snowed into one campsite for three days—and it was already June. Then the sun showed up and melted the snow, washing out the only road. At times it took all our concentration to remember why we were there.

Still, there was this cave. . . . Mr. Peer seemed too astute a geologist and observer of nature simply to have imagined a shelter covered with prehistoric paintings, and we kept looking. Each canyon had potential. We would see something, stop the truck, skitter up the hillside. But each time, it turned out to be a shadow, an abandoned mine shaft, or just a jumble of boulders. The cave with its rock art eluded us.

After a week of this we came to Mill Canyon, just the next one on the list, with no greater potential than the previous ten canyons we had combed. The road was a little worse than most, and we had to inch down a steep ridge into the rocky canyon. Even in four-wheel drive, our truck lurched downslope, on a path so steep it seemed barely glued to the mountainside. Finally, as we started up the flat canyon bottom, a brooding black cliff loomed ahead. The scarp was riddled with small caves and rock shelters. I commented that if we were in Arizona, each cave would be walled with Pueblo masonry and connected by wooden ladders. But this was Nevada, and Shoshone ancestors never built such structures.

And sure enough, the caves were empty, unless you counted the occasional coyote scat, owl pellet, or packrat midden. The cliff face was nearly a half-mile long, and we became more and more discouraged as we moved upcanyon, scanning each small alcove for pictographs. Finally, only one section remained to be inspected, where the black cherty formation was swallowed up beneath the alluvial Mill Canyon bottomland. We saw a dim shadow near the bottom, but a dozen similar shadows had been just that. Shadows.

The paintings were obscured until we crawled into the mouth of the cave. There they were, just as Mr. Peer had said a year before: small human figures, painted in red and yellow pigments. On the other wall were cryptic motifs in white and black. And, yes, the cave had caved in years before. Half the floor was buried beneath tons of chert. One boulder dwarfed the pickup we had left in the canyon.

Archaeologists react to discovery in different ways. Trudy scurried back to the truck for the cameras to photograph the **rock art**. **Pictographs** were her speciality. Being more inclined to dirt and rocks, I scoured the shelter floor, looking for artifacts, animal bones, pieces of basketry. Anything. But no matter how hard I looked, there was nothing remotely suggesting that prehistoric people had lived here. We had the rock art, of course, but pictograph caves sometimes have no habitation debris at all.

Our digging gear was stowed away in the truck, so first we ate lunch and then started digging a small test hole in the floor of the cave. Old World archaeologists term such exploratory excavations **sondages**. I always liked the ring of that word. What class! In Nevada, we just called them **test pits.** Anyway, we set out a small square, fifty centimeters on a side, and I scraped away the rocks and rat dung with my favorite Marshalltown trowel. An old-time archaeologist once told me about digging in a cave just like this. "It smelled brown," he recalled.

We dug through the afternoon, stopping armpit deep when I could no longer reach the bottom of the test pit. It was a pretty meager haul: several pieces of broken bone, a few of them charred, and a dozen stone **flakes**, probably debris from resharpening stone knives or **projectile points**. Not exactly treasure, but we knew that at least one prehistoric flintknapper had paused here to ply his craft. Still we were disappointed. The rock art already spoke of the occasional prehistoric visitor. We were looking for something more.

Across the sagebrush campfire that night we assayed our finds. The rock art was neat; only two similar sites were known in the central Great Basin. The stones and bones were suggestive enough, but the shelter seemed hardly the deep site we had hoped for all year. The **midden** was maybe two or three feet deep, and the **strata** probably jumbled. Hunter-gatherers would often dig storage pits, clear bedding areas, and scoop out fire hearths. The stratigraphy of some desert caves is so jumbled that they look as though they had been rototilled. At best, our test pit results were borderline.

We traveled to Reese River the next day to join the forty-two students enrolled in the summer field course. We spent the first month finishing my doctoral fieldwork. Once I was sure we would fulfill those objectives, I dispatched a small crew over to Monitor Valley. By that time we had rumors of two or three additional caves, and so I assigned some students to do more testing. If they had the time, they were to return to Mill Canyon and sink a larger test pit. A fifty-centimeter square is not much of a sample from any archaeological site.

I commuted. Survey for sites three days in Reese River, drive four hours to Monitor Valley, and spend three days digging there; then back to Reese River again. The Monitor Valley excavations were ahead of schedule, and so I asked one of my young crew chiefs, Brian Hatoff, to take a couple of people to work the Mill Canyon cave. He had finished the test units by my return the next week, and he proudly laid out the findings for me. It looked like a flea market.

I was pleased to hear that their meter-square test pit had penetrated two meters down. The site was twice as deep as I thought. They had to stop because the excavators could no longer climb out of the square hole. They had found four broken arrowheads, hundreds of bone fragments including a bighorn sheep skull, several bifacially chipped stone knives, dozens of flakes, a **grinding stone**, and three small, enigmatic flat rocks with faint scratchings on them. Although these tests were encouraging, we had run out of time. The summer was over. This shelter was added to the list of "possibles" for next summer's excavations. Not bad for a webfoot, I told Brian.

Hatoff's notes refer to "the Mill Canyon site." Discussing the find with a friend at the U.S. Geological Survey, I learned that the precipitous black cliff, called the *Gatecliff formation,* was well known in geological circles. Marshall Kay, a renowned Columbia University geologist, had worked there several years before, clambering over the endless outcrops of chert and dolomite. Kay coined the term Gatecliff to describe how the chert cliff constricted the canyon into a bottleneck, or "gate."

One of archaeology's minor thrills is getting to name your discoveries, and "Gatecliff Shelter" had a decidedly more exciting ring to it than did "the Mill Canyon Shelter." We recorded the site in the archives of the Nevada State Museum as 26Ny301: "26" means Nevada (because it places twenty-sixth in the alphabetical order of

Robert Bettinger excavating in the first test trench at Gatecliff Shelter. (Photograph by the author)

the forty-eight continental states); "Ny" is the first two letters of Nye County; and "301" is the specific site number. The site was now official; it had a name and number.

Gatecliff Shelter dominated my archaeological life during the 1970s. The prehistoric deposits are not five or six feet deep, as I had initially thought. Rather, Gatecliff turned out to be forty feet deep, maybe the deepest rock shelter in the Americas.

Excavating the basal strata at Gatecliff Shelter using the bucket brigade method. (Courtesy the National Geographic Society; photograph by Gary Friedman)

The strata are also not mixed as I first feared. Over the millennia, the shelter had been inundated every so often by flash floods. The surging waters laid down thick layers of mud, forming an impenetrable cap of rock-hard silt. This flooding occurred at least a dozen times, stratifying the deposits into horizontal "floors." Gatecliff had what textbooks—including this one—describe as "layer-cake stratigraphy." The shelter had been occupied for much longer than the last few centuries, as I had thought at first. Gatecliff was old, at least seven thousand years old, as **radiocarbon dating** later established. Prehistoric **pollen analysis** spoke of the past environments in Monitor Valley. A massive "bone bed" of bighorn sheep lay strewn across the shelter's floor some six hundred years ago.

The American Museum of Natural History ultimately dispatched five major field expeditions to Gatecliff Shelter, and more than two hundred people helped excavate the site. In addition to supporting part of the fieldwork, the National Geographic Society prepared an educational film about the site. They also wrote a book about our excavations at Gatecliff. The *New York Times* and *The New Yorker* magazine published stories about Gatecliff. Then there was television and radio. Even a United States congressman became involved in the struggle to preserve the site. Gatecliff was decidedly on the map.

What Exactly Is Gatecliff Shelter?

Gatecliff is antlers, **anvil stones**, **arrowheads**, **atlatls**, **awls**, baskets, beads, **bifaces**, blankets, **blanks**, bones, bows, **burins**, **caches**, **cairns**, ceramics, charcoal, chisels, **choppers**, **coprolites**, **cores**, **crescents**, **denticulates**, dice, digging sticks, drills, **effigies**, **endscrapers**, and **eoliths**.

(*Hint:* For better or worse, archaeology is loaded with such technical terms. Every word appearing in **boldface** is defined in the Glossary, and it's a good habit to look up the unfamiliar words.)

Gatecliff is also feathers, feces, **fetishes**, fire hearths, **flakers**, **flints**, **foreshafts**, **gastroliths**, gouges, **gravers**, **grinding stones**, **Haliotis**, **hammerstones**, hearths, heirlooms, **hematite**, **horncores**, **incised slates**, insects, jars, **jasper**, jewelry, jugs, knives, knots, lances, living floors, **manos**, **manuports**, mats, **metates**, **microblades**, **mortars**, needles, nets, **nocks**, nuts, **obsidian**, **ocher**, **Olivella**, **ollas**, ornaments, paint palettes, pendants, **pestles**, **phytoliths**, **pictographs**, pine nuts, pipes, pollen, potsherds, **projectile points**, **Promontory pegs**, quartz crystals, **quids**, rabbit robes, rattles, reeds, rock art, ropes, **roughouts**, **scapula saws**, scrapers, seeds, **shaft straighteners**, **shaman's bundles**, sherds, **sidescrapers**, **sinew**, silt, snail shells, snares, soil, **spokeshaves**, stones, **strata**, tablets, **talismans**, **talus**, teeth, thongs, tools, twine, turquoise, **ungulates**, **unifaces**, **utilized flakes**, **varves**, vessels, **warps**, **wefts**, **whetstones**, **wickerwork**, **xerophytes**, yarn, and **zoomorphs**.

Gatecliff is a collection of archaeological objects. The cultural objects are made of chipped or ground stone, bone, plant fibers, tanned hides, shells, and turquoise. Archaeologists have a name for such objects: **artifacts**. Archaeological sites contain other objects not made by humans, those relating to the natural environment, and archaeologists term such things **ecofacts**. Prehistoric pollen grains are ecofacts; so are food bones and piñon pine hulls. Corncobs are borderline: To dirt archaeologists, cobs are ecofacts simply because they aren't artifacts; but to specialists in ethnobotany, corn is decidedly an artifact because it was produced by deliberate domestication.

So Gatecliff Shelter is a collection of archaeological objects. But it is more than that. We see collections of archaeological objects in every small-town saloon in the West.

One of the deep stratigraphic sections at Gatecliff. The excavators are mapping the sidewalls in strata deposited roughly seven thousand years ago; they are standing about forty feet below the original ground level. (Courtesy the National Geographic Society)

Sometimes the assortment is no more than a bunch of arrowheads in a cigar box. More aesthetically minded collectors arrange their brightly colored arrowheads in decorative shadow boxes. Sometimes the pictures are of Indian chiefs, with turquoise beads for eyes.

These frames are filled with prehistoric artifacts, but the gin mills are not prehistoric archaeological sites. The reason for this is simple: The artifacts are merely isolates, objects displayed without context. When we dug Gatecliff, we discovered prehistoric implements and ecofacts where they were discarded by their makers. The artifacts were **in situ**—in place. The artifacts had context.

As an archaeological site, Gatecliff Shelter had two critical attributes:

1.   Gatecliff contained objects of the past.
2.   The objects of the past were found in meaningful context.

This is all that matters in archaeology: objects and meaningful contexts. All else is secondary.

Now I understand everything.
—Saul Bellow

Robert L. Kelly puzzling over field notes at Gatecliff Shelter.
(Courtesy the National Geographic Society)

PART ONE

Anthropology, Science, and Archaeology

The principle of culture already gives anthropology a viewpoint of enormous range, a center for coordination of most phenomena that relate to man. And we anthropologists feel that this is only a beginning.
—Alfred L. Kroeber

Archaeological objects vary. So do archaeological contexts. Deciphering meaning from such objects in context is the business of archaeology. In fact, today we have so many complex techniques for doing so, that it has become impossible for anybody to know and understand all of them. No matter how hard each of us might study, we will never learn all there is to know about archaeological theory and technique. New techniques appear each year, and—alas—with each advance in such knowledge, every individual archaeologist becomes relatively less knowledgeable. In truth, archaeologists are learning more and more about less and less.

The same is true of field techniques. Archaeological fieldwork is becoming so rarefied that many of us now regret portions of our earlier research: We threw too much away. This is nothing new. Archaeologists in 1923 did not save charcoal. Why should they? Who knew that in 1949 a physicist named Libby would perfect a method of dating lumps of charcoal? Archaeologists did not collect pollen samples in the 1930s because nobody knew how to reconstruct extinct past environments from microscopic pollen grains. In my first field class, I was told to chuck out all the animal bone that was not "identifiable" (whatever that meant). Today, by trying to save all bone, we are learning about hunting strategies, butchering patterns, seasonality, and even the sex–age characteristics of the past animal populations. Soil from archaeological sites is now a gold mine of information: Seeds can be obtained by **flotation**; **pH tests** tell us about the intensity of prehistoric habitation; and **pedology** tells us about the the geological processes that create our archaeological sites.

Traces of blood thousands of years old can now be detected on stone tools. We had always thoroughly scrubbed our artifacts before cataloguing them in the laboratory. We now realize that important clues—such as the blood residues, can literally go down the drain. Today's archaeologists are beginning to settle for studying dirty artifacts.

Archaeologists are justly proud of their microscopic techniques. No clue from the past is too minor to escape scrutiny. We are now afraid to throw away anything; indeed, entire sites are occasionally brought back to the university or museum and actually "excavated" in the laboratory.

But there is a danger lurking in these procedures, and that danger is *myopia,* losing sight of the forest for the trees. This book does not view archaeology through a microscope; rather, it uses just the opposite: a macroscope. Instead of magnifying the minutiae of archaeology, our macroscope will merge particulars in search of overall patterning.

Archaeology consists of hundreds, maybe thousands, of tiny pieces. Although sometimes the pieces seem so varied that they no longer fit together, there still remains a single picture. The trick is to stand back far enough to see it.

That is one problem: fitting the diversified techniques, concepts, and strategies of archaeology into a meaningful whole. There is a second problem: What does this framework tell us? Can it stand alone, or does it somehow tie into a yet larger whole?

Part One will consider both questions: What are archaeologists? What are scientists? What are anthropologists? When each question has been answered, we will be in a position to assess what contemporary archaeologists are up to. Then we shall find out how they do it.

CHAPTER 1

What Is Archaeology?

1. Binford on, Focuses on Understanding underlying cultural processes

This book explains two things: what archaeologists want to learn and how they learn it.

These objectives are more complex than they might appear. Over the past two decades, Americanist **archaeology** has been a house divided against itself. A great deal of emotion has been vented and copious ink spilled. Part of the conflict came from the so-called **new archaeology.** Some archaeologists praised it to the skies; others rejected it from the start; still others accepted initially the so-called **processual** aims of the new archaeology, but feel that we have now moved into a so-called **post-processual** phase of archaeology. I cannot begin my story of archaeology without taking a stand on recent events in the field. What is the new archaeology, and is it new or not?

uses ideational strategy

Another source of conflict has been the relationship between the sometimes separate fields of **historical archaeology** and **prehistoric archaeology.** Despite early beginnings, the discipline of historical archaeology did not gain formal status until the mid-1960s, when the field entered what some have called its "crisis of identity," vestiges of which remain visible today. Some believe that historical archaeology functions mostly to supply the lesser details of the parent discipline, history. Others assert that contemporary historical archaeology is anthropology's newest branch. Still others contend that historical archaeology must always be a field unique unto itself. So what is today's historical archaeologist up to: anthropology, history, or architecture?

Resolution of these archaeological dilemmas can only come, quite naturally, from examining the past. To what other direction could an archaeologist turn? This initial chapter begins by looking at how contemporary archaeology evolved. This done, we can explore the meaning of today's archaeology and how each part articulates.

"The Literature" of Archaeology and How to Use It

There seems to be no study too fragmented, no hypothesis too trivial, no literature citation too biased or too egotistical, no design too warped, no methodology too bungled, no presentation of results too inaccurate, too obscure, and too contradictory, no analysis too self-serving, no argument too circular, no conclusions too trifling or too unjustified, and no grammar and syntax too offensive for a paper to end up in print.

—Drummond Rennie (senior editor at the *Journal of the American Medical Association*)

In this book, I attempt to provide a succinct, up-to-date synthesis, drawing from my own experience where possible. But no single archaeologist knows more than a fraction of what's significant through firsthand involvement.

This is why we have "the Literature"— the books, journals, bulletins, essays, reports, and newsletters that contain our collective wisdom about the past. Each of us learns by reading what others have done (as you are doing right now). This is why scholars are told to "publish or perish." This is why my museum tells me, "It's not science until it's published." This is why to accuse an archaeologist of "not knowing 'the Literature' " is to deliver a telling blow indeed.

"The Literature" of science can be overpowering, and even veteran scholars despair at the avalanche of new journals and alternative publication outlets springing up each year. The *New York Times* estimated recently that 40,000 scientific journals roll off the presses annually, inundating the scientific readership with more than a million new articles annually. The *New Republic* magazine—using the term *publishing mania*—estimates that sociologists alone generate more than 2400 articles each year. Recent surveys show that the majority of scientific articles go virtually unread. Even more alarming are signs that time-honored quality controls in science are breaking down as tales of research fraud and deception haunt the current headlines.

As in the scientific world at large, contemporary archaeologists face a dilemma: Whereas we all rely on the printed word, none of us can read everything (or even most things). The problem is doubly difficult for students, who must learn not only archaeology but also how to learn archaeology. But anybody serious about understanding contemporary Americanist archaeology must soon leave the relative comfort of the textbook to encounter "the Literature," and I have tried to structure this bibliography to make the transition as painless as possible.

Rather than clutter the text with endless

citations, I have placed the key references at the end of most major sections, in a brief bibliographic review entitled Where to Go from Here? Here, I acknowledge the key sources on which my discussion is based and provide a selective guide to additional relevant material, both classic and contemporary. Where appropriate, I have annotated and rank-ordered the list. At times, I also mention some of the key scientific journals appropriate to each topic (noting editorial policy, history of publication, and subscription information), should you be interested in pursuing this particular issue in more detail.

WHERE TO GO FROM HERE?

Key Journals in Americanist Archaeology

American Antiquity, published by the Society for American Archaeology, is the primary scholarly publication dealing with the archaeology of the Western Hemisphere and archaeological theory, method, and practice worldwide; first published in 1935.

Subscription information: Society for American Archaeology, 808 17th Street N.W., Suite 200, Washington, D.C. 20006.

American Archaeology publishes three topical issues annually, dealing with such diverse subjects such as applied archaeology, pre-Columbian research, dating methods, historical archaeology, predictive site modeling, and survey methodology; first published in 1980 (formerly called *Contract Abstracts and CRM Archaeology*).

Subscription information: American Archaeology, 81 West Mountain Road, Ridgefield, Conn. 06877.

Antiquity is an international journal that occasionally presents important contributions to the archaeology of the Americas; first published in 1927.

Subscription information: Antiquity, c/o The Black Bear Press, King's Hedges Road, Cambridge, England CB4 2PQ.

Archaeology, a widely distributed magazine published by the Archaeological Institute of America, publishes nontechnical articles written by professional archaeologists. Issues cover international travel to archaeological sites, reviews of exhibits, books, news, and films; first published in 1948.

Subscription information: Archaeology, Subscription Service, P.O. Box 928, Farmingdale, N.Y. 11737.

Journal of Anthropological Archaeology "publishes articles on the theory and methodology of archaeology as they relate to the understanding and explanation of the organization, operation, and evolution of human societies." Topics include theoretical modeling, archaeological and historical analyses, and contemporary ethnoarchaeological studies, as well as those with an interdisciplinary focus; first published in 1982.

Subscription information: Journal of Anthropological Archaeology, Academic Press, 1 East First Street, Duluth, Minn. 55802.

Journal of Archaeological Science disseminates a variety of technical discussions dealing with global applications of paleobiology, geomorphology, chronometrics, technology, and materials science; first published in 1973.

Subscription information: Academic Press Inc., 4805 Sand Lake Road, Orlando, Fla. 32819.

Journal of Field Archaeology, published by the Association for Field Archaeology, "serves as an instrument for the discussion of and action concerning the recovery, restoration, and primary interpretation of excavation material, and the protection of antiquities, including opposition to the dealing and illicit traffic in such materials." Most articles are reports of survey and excavation; also important is the Public Archaeology commentary and the Archaeometric Clearinghouse; first published in 1974.

Subscription information: Boston University Scholarly Publications, 985 Commonwealth Avenue, Boston, Mass. 02215.

North American Archaeologist publishes papers on all aspects of Americanist archaeology. Theoretical and methodological articles, provided their database is North America, are acceptable, and research based on cultural resource management by state and local societies are solicited, along with the more traditional academic-museum projects; first published in 1979.

Subscription information: Baywood Publishing Company, Inc., 26 Austin Avenue, Amityville, N.Y. 11701.

Quarterly Review of Archaeology consists of article-length critical reviews of major books and papers; first published in 1980.

Subscription information: Quarterly Review of Archaeology, Inc., 10 Liberty Street, Salem, Mass. 01970.

World Archaeology organizes each issue thematically: with a range of archaeological interpretations. Examples of recent issues include ethnoarchaeology, mines and quarries, quantitativemethods, early humans, urbanization, and rock art; first published in 1970.

Subscription information: Routledge & Kegan Paul, Ltd., 11 New Fetter Lane, London, England EC4P 4EE.

The Western World Discovers Its Past

Most historians ascribe the honor of "first archaeologist" to **Nabonidus** (d. 538 B.C.), the last king of the neo-Babylonian Empire. A sincerely pious man, Nabonidus's zealous worship of his gods compelled him to rebuild the ruined temples of ancient Babylon and to search among their foundations for the inscriptions of the earlier kings. For this reason, Nabonidus is known to modern history more as an antiquarian than an administrator. In fact, we are indebted to the research of his scribes and the excavations by his subjects for much of our modern picture of the Babylonian Empire. Though it stretches the point to call Nabonidus an archaeologist in the modern sense of the term, he is an important figure because he looked to the physical residues of antiquity to answer questions about the past. A simple step but a sharp contrast with the beliefs of his contemporaries, who regarded tradition, legend, and myth as the only clues to the past.

Purists can quibble with labeling Nabonidus as the first archaeologist. When the famous Sphinx of Gizeh was excavated, a small inscribed slab was found between the paws. The slab related a tale of how Thutmose IV (ca. 1425–1398 B.C.) had once fallen asleep at the foot of the Sphinx and dreamed that he would be made king if he first cleared away the sand dunes that had encroached on the Sphinx. Thutmose dutifully did so and later became pharaoh. Cleator (1976, p. 19–20) suggested that this episode entitles Thutmose IV to be considered the first archaeologist because "not only was an ancient site carefully excavated, but an account of the undertaking was subsequently published—two important requisites of archaeological activity in the field." Taylor (1948, p. 10) also claims that the Irish were collecting antiquities as early as 700 B.C.

Archaeology's family tree has an unsavory branch as well, because the looters and grave robbers of antiquity also contributed to the archaeological legacy, and plenty of them are still around. Unlike Nabonidus and Thutmose IV, untold generations of mercenaries were attracted by the promise of easy riches through the looting of tombs.

The early-twentieth-century **Egyptologists** often found, to their dismay, that they had been "beaten to the punch" by looters and vandals. Sometimes the bodies were barely cold before the grave goods were purloined. H. E. Winlock, then director of New York's Metropolitan Museum expedition to Dier el Bahri, found episode after episode in which the ancient Egyptians had rifled the graves of their own rulers. When the Twenty-first Dynasty (ca. 1090 B.C.) mummies of Hent-Towy and Nesit-Iset were discovered, for instance, Winlock and his associates thought they were perfectly intact. But closer examination revealed that the mummies had been unwrapped before interment and the valuable metal pectoral hawks and finger rings stolen. This deceit could only have been the work of the very undertakers commissioned to prepare the mummies for the hereafter (Winlock 1942, pp. 110–114). The pilfering of Egypt's royal tombs has continued for millennia, and in fact, much of the popular appeal of Egyptology is matching modern wits with those of the ancient architects of the tombs, who tried every trick imaginable to outfox looters, both ancient and modern.

Despite their contributions in other fields, the classical Greeks did little to further the aims of modern anthropological archaeology. As we shall see in Chapter 3, one premise of the anthropological world view is that to understand ourselves, we must first understand others. As John Rowe (1965, p. 2) pointed out, "The ancient Greeks for the most part held that the way to understand ourselves is to study ourselves, while what others do is irrelevant." Socrates, for instance, was concerned primarily with his own thoughts and those of his contemporaries; he showed marked disdain for the languages and customs of "barbarians" (by whom he meant all non-Greeks). The Romans, of course, traced their intellectual ancestry to the heroes of Greek legend; they imitated Greek protocol; and they shared in the pervasive Greek **ethnocentrism**. The **ethnographies** of Herodotus and Tacitus stand virtually alone in their concern with non-Greek and non-Roman customs and values.

The legacy of pre-Renaissance writings did little to foster the development of either archaeological or anthropological inquiry, but the Renaissance changed all of this. It has been suggested that the major contribution of the Renaissance—particularly in Italy—was the distinction between the present and the past. Classical Greeks and Romans recognized only the most remote past, which they reified in myth and legend. Because the Europeans of the Middle Ages likewise failed to distinguish between themselves and the ancients, it fell to Renaissance scholars to point up the differences between classical and medieval times.

Petrarch (1304–1374), perhaps the most influential individual of the early Renaissance, is considered to be the first humanist. Beyond his talents as poet and linguist, Petrarch also provided strong impetus for archaeological research. To him, the remote past was an ideal of perfection, and he looked to antiquity for moral philosophy. But in order to imitate classical antiquity, one must first study it. In a real sense, Petrarch's humanism led to a rediscovery of the past by those in the Western European intellectual tradition. Petrarch's influence can best be seen in the work of his close friend Boccaccio, who wrote extensive essays on classical mythology, and also in Giovanni Dondi, who is generally credited with the first systematic observations on archaeological monuments.

But it remained for **Ciriaco** (1391–ca. 1449) to establish the modern discipline of archaeology. After translating the Latin inscription on the triumphal arch of Trajan at Ancona, he was inspired to devote the remainder of his life to studying ancient monuments, copying inscriptions, and generally promoting the study of the past. His travels ranged from Syria to Egypt, throughout the islands of the Aegean, and finally to Athens. When asked his business, Ciriaco is said to have replied, "Restoring the dead to life," which today remains a pretty fair statement defining the everyday business of archaeology (see Rowe 1965, p. 10).

Scholars of the Italian Renaissance viewed antiquity as a world apart, remote yet accessible through literature and ruins. One such scholar, Peter Martyr, considered the European discovery of America to be the most profound event of his lifetime, and although he never visited the New World, he chronicled the discoveries of Columbus and others for his European contemporaries.

The antiquarian spirit was also alive and well in Great Britain. In fact, a group of eminent British historians and students of the classics formed an antiquarian society as early as 1572. The emphasis of this and later societies was to record and preserve the national treasures, rather than indiscriminately to acquire curios and **objets d'art.** Of course, many private collectors were still concerned only with filling their curio cabinets, but the goal of British antiquarianism was to map, record, and preserve archaeological ruins. By the late eighteenth century a healthy interest in classical antiquities was perceived as an important ingredient in the "cultivation of taste" among the European leisured classes, hence the term **antiquarian**.

Archaeological research to this point proceeded mostly within the **humanistic** tradition of Petrarch, concerned primarily with clarifying the picture of the classical civilizations. This lore was readily digested by the eighteenth- and early-nineteenth-century mind because it was in basic agreement with prevalent religious teachings. The Bible had, after all, discussed the classical cultures in some detail.

But a problem arose with the discovery of very crude stone tools among the ancient gravels of England and continental Europe. In 1836 or 1837, **Jacques Boucher de Perthes,** a controller of customs at Abbeville, began to find axeheads in the ancient gravels of the Somme (see Figure 1–1). Along with those tools, he also found the bones of mammals long extinct.

The implication to Boucher de Perthes was obvious: "In spite of their imperfection, these rude stones prove the existence of [very ancient] man as surely as a whole Louvre would have done" (cited in Oakley 1964, p. 94; see also Grayson 1983a). But few contemporaries believed him, in part because of Christian scruples. That is, in the early nineteenth century the prevalent opinion was that human beings had been on earth for roughly six thousand years. Theological scholars, who had studied the problem of The Creation in marvelous detail, simply refused to recognize sufficient time for people to have coexisted with animals of extinct form. Paley's *Natural Theology* (1802) explained the matter something like this: The earth was created according to a splendid design, not unlike a fine watch; God was the ultimate watchmaker, and he had deliberately placed people on his earth in about 4000 B.C.

Actually, this chronology had been suggested before. In 1642, **Dr. John Lightfoot**, master of St. Catharine's College and vice-chancellor of Cambridge University, published

FIGURE 1–1   Boucher de Perthes found stone tools like this in the river gravels of France. (Negative no. 1747; courtesy Department of Library Sciences, the American Museum of Natural History)

a treatise with the delightful title *A Few and New Observations on the Book of Genesis, the most of them certain, the rest probable, all harmless, and rarely heard of before.* Lightfoot's later, slightly refined **chronology** concluded that "heaven and earth, centre and circumference, were created all together in the same instant and clouds full of water . . . this took place and man was created by the Trinity on October 23, 4004 B.C. at nine o'clock in the morning." Glyn Daniel (1962, p.19) irreverently suggested that the vice-chancellor showed a certain understandable prejudice for the beginning of an academic term and the beginning of an academic morning.

This reckoning, of course, simply discounted the possibility of an extensive human antiquity; there simply wasn't enough time. Therefore, almost by definition, Boucher de Perthes must be incorrect; his rude implements must be something other than human handiwork (Grayson 1983a). Some suggested that the "tools" were really meteorites, and others felt that the stones must have been produced by lightning or elves or fairies. One seventeenth-century scholar even suggested that the chipped flints were "generated in the sky by a fulgurous exhalation conglobed in a cloud by the circumposed humour."

Customs officials, however, are not known for their timidity, and Boucher de Perthes refused to admit defeat. More finds were made in the gravel pits of St. Acheul in France, and across the Channel similar discoveries were made in southern England. The issue was finally resolved when British paleontologist Hugh Falconer visited Abbeville to examine the disputed evidence for himself. A procession of esteemed scholars followed Falconer's lead, and in 1859 a paper was presented to the Royal Society of London supporting the claims of de Perthes. In no time, several influential natural scientists proclaimed their support.

The year 1859 proved to be a turning point in the history of human thought: Not only had human antiquity and evolution been accepted by many, but **Charles Darwin** published his influential *On the Origin of Species,* which suggested the process by which that change had occurred.

The floodgates now open, British archaeology followed two rather divergent courses. One direction became involved with the problems of geological time and *in situ* human **evolution**. Many scholars, following in the tradition of Petrarch, continued their course of classical studies, focusing particularly on ancient Greece and Rome. This philosophical split continues into modern times. Today, the education of an Old World prehistorian differs greatly from that of a **classical archaeologist**.

The European discovery of the Americas opened yet another option for prehistoric studies. Rather early in the game it became abundantly clear that in sheer antiquity, American archaeology would never rival the European finds. The New World was indeed new. Beginning with Columbus's triumphant return to Europe in 1493, several vexing issues cropped up. When did people first arrive in the New World? Where had these migrants come from, and how did they get there? How could regions such as the Valley of Mexico and Peru boast fantastic riches, while many other areas such as the American West seemed so relatively impoverished and even primitive?

Enormous confusion and speculation immediately arose. There was, for instance, the "Lost Tribe of Israel" scenario, which pointed up alleged Native American–Semitic similarities. And the fabled Island of Atlantis was seriously proposed by some as the ancestral homeland of the Native Americans. Finally, voyaging Egyptians and even the Vikings were cited as hypothetical proto-Americans.

The mystery thickened with each new discovery of American ruins. How, for instance, does one account for the thousands of prehistoric earthen mounds that dot North America east of the Mississippi? Then-prevalent racist theories generally assumed that the ancestors of the Native Americans were incapable of constructing such monuments, and much debate during the eighteenth and nineteenth centuries centered on the mythic Mound Builders, who had somehow vanished before the arrival of Columbus.

Investigators gradually came to realize the considerable continuities that existed between the unknown prehistoric past and the Native American population of the historic period. As such knowledge progressed, these profound differences between European and American archaeology became more apparent. While the Europeans wrestled with their ancient flints—without apparent modern correlates—American scholars came to realize that the living Native Americans were indeed relevant to the interpretation of archaeological remains. In the crass terms of the time, the Native Americans became to many "living fossils," a relic of times past.

Nearly from the outset, **New World** archaeology was inextricably wed to the study of living Native Americans. While Old World archaeologists began from a baseline of geological time or classical antiquity, their American counterparts began to develop the anthropology of Native America. Native American ethnology not only evolved into a formidable domain of study as such, but it also helped unravel questions such as the peopling of the New World.

Let me stress another important point here. As Europeans studied the archaeology of Europe, they were digging up their own ancestors (Balts, Slavs, Huns, whatever). In the New World, Euro-Americans were often digging up somebody else's ancestors (Native Americans). This difference goes a long way in explaining some of the racist theories common in nineteenth-century Americanist archaeology, and it also explains why the European governments enacted antiquity legislation decades before North American governments did so (see Chapter 4).

WHERE TO GO FROM HERE?

Some General Histories of World Archaeology: The most succinct overall treatment is by Glyn Daniel and Colin Renfrew (1988) *The Idea of Prehistory*; Donald K. Grayson's (1983a) *The Establishment of Human Antiquity* is a powerful treatment of the changing Western perception of its own past; see also Braidwood (1959), Daniel (1981), Oakley (1964), Phillips (1964), Rowe (1965), Taylor (1948, Chapter 1).

Some Histories of Americanist Archaeology: Willey's and Sabloff's (1980) history remains the single most important source; Chapter 9 in Daniel and Renfrew (1988) is a perceptive overview of the "new archaeology"; the papers in Meltzer, Fowler, and Sabloff (1986) present a balanced, if diverse purview; the Fiftieth Anniversary Issue of *American Antiquity* (1985) also contains a selection of historical overviews. See also Fitting (1973), Gorenstein (1977), Griffin (1959), Haag (1959), Schwartz (1968), Silverberg (1968), Stewart (1973), Taylor (1948, 1954), Willey (1968).

Founders of Americanist Archaeology

High time it is, that the younger generation
stops sneering at its predecessors.
—Carleton S. Coon

Now it is time to explain how Americanist archaeology is currently practiced. The last section supplied the foundation, with a whirlwind consideration of the European precursors. Now, to define a workable framework, I borrow Robert Dunnell's (1979) useful term *Americanist* to denote the kind of archaeology that has been developed in association with anthropology in North America. Although many other terms have been used—"scientific archaeology," "anthropological archaeology," and, too often, just "archaeology"—I prefer the phrase Americanist archaeology because it is the least pejorative. I also caution that archaeologists working in the Americanist tradition can (and do) practice their craft around the world.

I shall change modes of exposition as we focus on the Americas. If you want to learn about the history of Americanist archaeology through a blow-by-blow narrative, take a look at some of the excellent discussions listed in Where to Go from Here? What follows is a tale of Americanist archaeology as told through the careers of eight important archaeologists. I will be reducing history to biography.

The history of Americanist archaeology (all history, really) is a commingling of tradition and change. We shall begin with the more traditional figures, who illustrate how archaeology was practiced during their lifetimes. This section is evolutionary, providing a view of how archaeology developed. Then we shall discuss two people who helped define contemporary archaeology; in a sense, that section is revolutionary. We shall finally arrive at today and look at one of our better contemporary archaeologists. All of these ingredients are necessary to understand how archaeology is being practiced today.

But first a warning: These eight archaeologists were deliberately selected to make some specific points. Each is taken to represent the tenor of the time. Other narrators would undoubtedly choose different people. But provided you understand that my selections were made arbitrarily—and largely for effect—I make no apologies. Each person represents a critical stage in the growth of Americanist archaeology, and the career of each has a message to tell.

Thomas Jefferson (1743–1826): America's First Prehistoric Archaeologist

I think that this is the most extraordinary collection of talent, of human knowledge, that has ever been gathered together at the White House— with the possible exception of when Thomas Jefferson dined here alone.
—John F. Kennedy (to his Nobel Prize–winning guests)

The European Renaissance began in the fourteenth century and lasted well into the 1700s. In addition to providing historians with a suitable separation between medieval and modern times, the Renaissance produced a breed of scholars known for their prowess across a prodigious range of topics. Aptly known as *Renaissance men,* these cultivated gentlemen embodied the essence of intellectual and artistic excellence for their time.

Although **Thomas Jefferson** postdates the Renaissance period in a chronological sense, his varied accomplishments place him well within the tradition of the Renaissance thinkers. Not only did the author of the Declaration of Independence later become the third president of the United States, he was also described by a contemporary as "an expert musician (the violin being his favorite instrument), a good dancer, a dashing rider, and proficient in all manly exercises." Jefferson was an avid player of chess (avoiding cards), a fearless and accomplished horseman, and a connoisseur of fine French cooking.

When not designing his famous home, Monticello, Jefferson maintained an impressive correspondence with friends and colleagues. In fact, it has been estimated that he wrote some eighteen thousand letters throughout his lifetime. Jefferson founded the University of Virginia, and his personal library ultimately formed the nucleus for the Library of Congress.

These accomplishments aside, it is one of Jefferson's lesser-known achievements that interests us here. Often labeled the "father of American archaeology" (Willey and Sabloff 1980, p. 29), Thomas Jefferson conducted "the first scientific excavation in the history of archaeology" (Wheeler 1954, p. 58). A leading intellectual force of his time, Jefferson's curiosity about the Native Americans' origins illustrates the initial stage of Americanist archaeology.

Jefferson's education was typical of that of the eighteenth-century colonial gentry. The son of a wealthy tobacco planter, Jefferson formally studied a broad spectrum of subjects, embracing the arts, science, and literature. He specialized in law and decided to enter politics. By the age of twenty-six he had been elected to Virginia's House of Burgesses.

Throughout his life, Jefferson maintained a deep-seated curiosity about the colonies' Native American tribes. Fascinated by Indian lore since boyhood and trained in classical **linguistics**, Jefferson believed that the Native American languages held valuable clues to the origins of the people (see Figure 1–2). Jefferson personally collected linguistic data from more than forty tribes and wrote a long treatise on the subject. His linguistic

FIGURE 1–2   Thomas Jefferson and a highly imaginative artist's conception of an "ancient battle mound." (Courtesy the American Museum of Natural History)

data were never published; unfortunately, the manuscript apparently lost somewhere between Washington and Monticello in 1809.

Reasoning largely from his linguistic studies, Jefferson sensed an Asiatic origin for the Native Americans. But unlike his contemporaries, he was not content to restrict his speculation to armchair theorizing. Always a man of action, he tested his notions on some hard data.

Jefferson's contribution to Americanist archaeology was discussed in the only book he ever published. The project began in 1780, when he (then governor of Virginia) received a questionnaire from the French government requesting information about his state. The French, attempting to acquaint themselves with the newly formed United States of America, sent similar inquiries to leading figures in other states. The request arrived at an opportune time for Jefferson, as he had just begun a self-imposed exile from politics. He labored hard on his questionnaire, eventually writing an elaborate treatise covering such diverse topics as topography, geography, economics, zoology, botany, geology, politics, and, of course, the Native Americans. The manuscript was revised and enlarged from time to time and was eventually published in a limited French edition in 1784 and in a widely distributed American edition in 1787.

Notes on the State of Virginia was structured as a series of replies to queries, the chapter headings reading "Query I," "Query II," and so forth. Query XI dealt with the aborigines of Virginia, in which Jefferson listed the various Virginian tribes, relating their histories since the settlement of Jamestown in 1607 and incorporating a census of Virginia's current Native American population. Concerned primarily with the origins of Virginia's natives, this discussion precipitated a consideration of the available archaeological evidence.

The origin of the Native Americans had been a compelling topic of speculation since the time of Columbus and probably even before. Hundreds of prehistoric Indian **mounds** survived in every state east of the Mississippi River, and theories arose by the score to explain them. The Spanish explorer de Soto correctly surmised that many of the mounds served as foundations for priestly temples, but his astute observation was soon lost in a flood of fanciful reconstruction. Whereas some scholars theorized that the Native Americans had a biblical origin—perhaps they were the descendants of the Ten Lost Tribes of Israel—others suggested a Mexican origin for the ancient monument builders. The racist attitudes prevalent in late-eighteenth-century America had fostered the conception of the mythical Mound Builder People, who allegedly constructed the impressive monuments throughout the Americas before they either mysteriously vanished or underwent a profound degenerative process, rendering them smaller and less intelligent than modern Europeans.

Notes on the State of Virginia confronted this issue directly. To Jefferson, solving the problem of the Native Americans' origins required a dual strategy: to learn as much as feasible about contemporary Native American culture and also to examine the prehistoric remains. He argued emphatically that contemporary Native Americans were in no way mentally or physically inferior to the white races and rejected all current racist doctrines explaining their origins. He correctly reasoned that Native Americans were wholly capable of constructing the prehistoric monuments of the United States.

At this juncture, Jefferson took a critical step in the story of Americanist archaeology. Shovel firmly in hand, he proceeded to excavate a burial mound located on his property. Today, such a step seems obvious, but few of Jefferson's contemporaries would think of resorting to bones, stones, and dirt to answer intellectual issues. Contemporary eighteenth-century scholars preferred to rummage through libraries and archives rather than to dirty their hands with the hard facts from the past.

Written in the flowery style of the time, Jefferson's account provides quite an acceptable report of his investigation. First he describes the data—location, size, method of excavation, stratigraphy, condition of the bones, artifacts—and then he presents his conclusions: Why did prehistoric peoples bury their dead in mounds? He first noted the absence of traumatic wounds, such as those made by bullets or arrows, and also observed the interment of children, thereby rejecting the common notion that the bones were those of soldiers who had fallen in battle. Similarly, the scattered and disjointed nature of the bones militated against the notion of a "common sepulchre of a town," in which Jefferson would have expected to find skeletons arranged in more orderly fashion. The **stratigraphy** indicated to Jefferson that the mound represented several distinct burial episodes, each burial group being covered with rocks and earth. Jefferson surmised, quite correctly, that the burials had accumulated through repeated use and saw no reason to doubt that the mound had been constructed by the ancestors of the Native Americans encountered by the colonists. To Jefferson, the mythical race of Mound Builders was just that: a myth. Today, nearly two hundred years after Jefferson's excavations, archaeologists would modify few of his well-reasoned conclusions.

Thomas Jefferson Describes His Excavation of a Burial Mound in Virginia (1787)

I know of no such thing existing as an Indian monument: for I would not honour with that name arrow points, stone hatchets, stone pipes, and half-shapen images. Of labour on the large scale, I think there is no remain as respectable as would be a common ditch for the draining of lands: unless indeed it be the Barrows, of which many are to be found all over this country. . . . There being one of these in my neighbourhood, I wished to satisfy myself whether any, and which of these opinions were just. For this purpose I determined to open and examine it thoroughly. It was situated on the low grounds of the Rivanna, about two miles above its principal fork, and opposite to some hills, on which had been an Indian town. It was of a spheroidical form, of about 40 feet diameter at the base, and had been of about twelve feet altitude, though now reduced by the plough to seven and a half, having been under cultivation about a dozen years. Before this it was covered with trees of twelve inches diameter, and round the base was an excavation of five feet depth and width, from whence the earth had been taken of which the hillock was formed. I first dug superficially in several parts of it, and came to collections of human bones, at different depths, from six inches to three feet below the surface. These were lying in the utmost confusion, some vertical, some oblique, some horizontal, and directed to every point of the compass, entangled, and held together in clusters by the earth. Bones of the most distant parts were found together, and, for instance, the small bones of the foot in the hollow of a scull, many sculls would sometimes be in contact, lying on the face, on the side, on the back, top or bottom, so as, on the whole, to give the idea of bones emptied promiscuously from a bag or basket, and covered over with earth, without any attention to their order. . . . I proceeded then to make a perpendicular cut through the body of the barrow, that I might examine its internal structure. This passed about three feet from its center, was opened to the former surface of the earth, and was wide enough for a man to walk through and examine its sides. At the bottom, that is, on the level of the circumjacent plain, I found bones; above these a few stones, brought from a cliff a quarter of a mile off, and from the river one-eighth of a mile off; then a large interval of earth, then a stratum of bones, and so on. At one end of the section were four strata of bones plainly distinguishable; at the other, three; the strata in one part not ranging with those in another. The bones nearest the surface were least decayed. No holes were discovered in any of them as if made with bullets, arrows, or other weapons. I conjectured that in this barrow might have been a thousand skeletons. Every one will readily seize the circumstances above related, which militate against the opinion, that it covered the bones only of persons fallen in battle, and against the tradition also, which would make it the common sepulchre of a town, in which the bodies were placed upright, and touching each other. Appearances certainly indicate that it has derived both origin and growth from the accustomary collection of bones, and deposition of them together; that the first collection had been deposited on the common surface of the earth, a few stones put over it, and then a covering of earth, that the second had been laid on this, had covered more or less of it in proportion to the number of bones, and was then also covered with earth, and so on. The following are the particular circumstances which give it this aspect.

1. The number of bones. 2. Their confused position. 3. Their being in different strata. 4. The strata in one part have no correspondence with those in another. 5. The difference in the time of inhumation. 6. The existence of infant bones among them.

Thomas Jefferson's legacy to archaeology is the fact that he dug at all. By his simple excavation, Jefferson elevated the study of America's past from a speculative, armchair pastime to an inquiry built on empirical fieldwork. As a well-educated colonial gentleman, Jefferson understood the importance of exposing speculation to a barrage of facts. The "facts" in this case lay buried beneath the ground, and that is precisely where he conducted his inquiry.

Jefferson also introduced archaeology's foremost methodological tool—**stratigraphy.** Noting that several distinct strata were embodied in the **sidewalls** of the excavation, he correctly inferred a complex sequence of mound construction.

Unlike his contemporaries, Jefferson did not dig to obtain exotic curios for his mantel but initiated his excavations to answer specific, well-formulated problems. He collected his data in as systematic a manner as possible and then drew carefully reasoned inferences from his fieldwork. Jefferson thereby pioneered the basics of archaeological reporting: recording his finds in meticulous detail, which ultimately are published for scrutiny by interested scholars.

It's not what you find, it's what you find out.
—David Hurst Thomas

WHERE TO GO FROM HERE?

Jefferson on Archaeology: Notes on the State of Virginia (1787).

Archaeologists on Jefferson: Willey and Sabloff: *A History of American Archaeology;* (1980, pp. 28–31); Kelso: "Jefferson's Garden: Landscape Archaeology at Monticello" (1982), "Mulberry Row: Slave Life at Thomas Jefferson's Monticello" (1986); see also Chapter 11, this volume.

C. B. Moore (1852–1936): A Genteel Digger

Clarence Bloomfield Moore was born into an affluent family of Philadelphia socialites. After receiving his B.A. degree from Harvard University in 1873, he traveled across Latin America, over the Andes, and down the Amazon. His father died shortly thereafter, and Moore was astonished to learn that his estate allowed him ample means for life. For the next several years, Moore followed the socialite circuit, rambling throughout Europe and joining safaris into exotic Africa (see Figure 1–3).

As a man of leisure, unconcerned with earning a living, Moore felt wholly free to follow his whims and fancy. But by 1892, Moore found the well-to-do socialite life-style to be shallow, meaningless, and boring. Moore had also suffered serious injury

Figure 1–3 C. B. Moore's graduation picture from Harvard University in 1873. (Courtesy Harvard University and Robert Neuman)

to his eye, apparently by an errant tennis ball, and so he began seeking more consequential (and less hazardous) pursuits.

So it was that at age forty, C. B. Moore was transformed from gentleman socialite into gentleman archaeologist. Smitten by his new pastime, he purchased a specially equipped flat-bottomed steamboat, which he christened the *Gopher*. Moore set off to explore the seemingly endless waterways of America's Southeast, excavating the major archaeological sites he encountered. Particularly drawn to the hundreds of burial and **temple mounds**, Moore enlisted the services of Dr. Milo G. Miller as secretary, physician, colleague, and friend.

From the outset, Moore's annual archaeological campaigns were models of organization and efficiency. Aboard his *Gopher,* Moore and Miller conducted preliminary investigations so that likely sites could be located and arrangements could be contracted with landowners; actual excavations began in the spring. Moore hired and supervised the workmen and kept the **field notes**. As human skeletons were located, Dr. Miller conducted a **paleoautopsy** on the spot, examining the bones in the field to determine sex, age, probable cause of death, and any unusual pathologies. The summers were spent cleaning and repairing the finds and then photographing and analyzing the collection.

Moore prepared detailed excavation reports for publication in the fall, distributing the more unusual artifacts to major archaeological institutions such as the Peabody Museum at Harvard, the Smithsonian, and the American Museum of Natural History in New York City. The bulk of the collection, however, was entrusted to the Philadelphia Academy of Natural Sciences, but was later sold to the Museum of the American Indian, in New York City. The transfer, initially conducted in secrecy, was quickly publicized by H. Newell Wardle, then assistant curator at the Philadelphia Academy, who resigned her position in protest.

Moore's winters were normally spent preparing for the next campaign of archaeological fieldwork. His first investigations concentrated on the shell middens and the sand burial mounds sprinkled along the Gulf Coast of Florida. Gradually, year after year, Moore worked his way around to Florida's eastern shore and eventually to the Sea Islands of coastal Georgia and South Carolina. In 1899, Moore returned to the Gulf Coast, traveled up the Alabama River, and examined the coast of northwest Florida. Moore excavated literally dozens of **archaeological sites** on each expedition.

Finally, in 1905, Moore paused on the Black Warrior River, Alabama, to excavate intensively the ruins appropriately known as Moundville. Working with several trained assistants and a crew numbering ten to fifteen, Moore explored the large temple mounds to examine the human burials and unearth spectacular pieces of pre-Columbian art.

In 1905, when Moore found a copper fishhook, ceremonial axes, and ornaments, he concluded that the mounds must have been dwelling places for royalty because they possessed the more-valued objects, and chiefs were evidently buried beneath their residences. The 1906 expedition located objects of sheet copper and copper-coated wood from the flat country surrounding the mounds. The copper artifacts were apparently modeled after implements of stone, pottery, and shell, carrying motifs such as the open hand, the eye, the swastika, forms of the cross, and birds' heads. Today, archaeologists recognize these artifacts as part of the so-called **Southern Cult**, widespread across the Southeast after about A.D. 1200.

Moore concluded that Moundville had been a prominent regional center, thereby rejecting his earlier notion that the mounds had been the residences of the chiefly class; they were simply too big. Moore surmised from the varied art forms that the ancient people of Moundville worshiped the sun, and motifs such as the plumed serpent and eagle suggested to him strong ties with contemporaneous Mexican civilizations (more recent investigations at Moundville are discussed in Chapter 13).

Moore followed his Moundville excavations with trips to Arkansas, Mississippi, Louisiana, Kentucky, and Tennessee. One of his main contributions to archaeology is his work at Poverty Point, Louisiana (Moore 1913), a series of remarkable concentric earthworks initially described by Samuel Lockett in an 1872 Smithsonian Institution report. Moore piloted the *Gopher* up the Bayou Macon in 1912 and spent the winter painstakingly mapping and describing the unique mounds.

Poverty Point was later excavated by James Ford, archaeologist with the American Museum of Natural History (and another of archaeology's "forebears"). Ford described Moore's earlier work as "really quite adequate in so far as can be determined from observation made on the ground. His map . . . is quite good, if the meager instrument work on which it was based is considered . . . if air photographs were not now available, it probably would be unnecessary to amend Moore's description" (Ford and Webb 1956, p. 14). Archaeologists can ask no higher praise from later generations.

By 1916, Moore concluded that the *Gopher* had explored every southeastern river then navigable by steamer. In fact, once a sandbar was removed in northern Florida, Moore promptly piloted the *Gopher* up the newly navigable Chocktawatchee River. He had truly exhausted the resources available for riverboat archaeology. In his twenty-five years as explorer and excavator, Moore catalogued an impressive array of archaeological sites. Of course, archaeological techniques have improved markedly since Moore's times, and many a contemporary archaeologist wishes that Moore had been somewhat less thorough: He left so little for the rest of us.

WHERE TO GO FROM HERE?

Moore on Archaeology: Moore published twenty-one large volumes (mostly in the *Journal of the Academy of Natural Science of Philadelphia*, e.g., Moore 1905, 1907). These monographs were amply illustrated, often by detailed photographs (Moore himself being an award-winning photographer). Even today, these publications remain valuable references to archaeologists working on the mortuary complex of the prehistoric American Southeast.

More on Moore: Wardle (1929): "Wreck of the Archaeological Department at the Academy of Natural Sciences of Philadelphia"; Davis (1987): *Field Notes of Clarence B.*

Moore's Southeastern Archaeological Expeditions, 1891–1918; see also Brigham (1937), Neuman (1984, pp. 38–40), Stoltman (1973), Wardle (1956).

Nels Nelson (1875–1964): America's First-Generation "Working" Archaeologist

The career of **Nels Nelson** stands in marked contrast with that of C. B. Moore. Whereas Moore was the scion of a wealthy family, Nelson was born on a poor farm in Jutland, Denmark. The eldest of many children, Nelson (born Nels Nielson) was first a farmhand, a student only in his spare time; he later claimed that as a youngster he went to school "just enough to read the catechism." Nevertheless, he stumbled onto the James Fenimore Cooper novels while still quite young and became fascinated with the lore of the Native Americans. Several of his relatives had already emigrated to America, and in 1892 Nelson's aunt in Minnesota sent him a steerage ticket to New York.

When young Nels arrived in New York harbor, he was caught up in the monumental wave of European immigration into America. He later recalled that as his ship entered the Narrows, he flung his old clothes out the porthole and vowed to start his young life afresh. His initial experiences in America, however, differed little from his life in Denmark, as the Danish colony in Minnesota closely guarded its European heritage. Determined to become truly Americanized, Nelson deserted his Danish relatives and hired himself out to a farmer near Marshall, Minnesota. Beginning the American first grade at age seventeen, Nelson finally graduated from high school as he turned twenty-one.

Shortly thereafter, Nelson encountered a family returning from California by way of Minnesota. Singing the praises of the West "as only Californians can," they encouraged Nelson to head westward himself. He obtained free transportation west by tending stock in a livestock railroad car. After working at a number of odd jobs (including driving a six-mule team and butchering hogs), Nelson saved enough money to enroll in Stanford University, where he studied philosophy by day and took odd jobs at night to pay his expenses. Not long after, following his professor across the bay to Berkeley, Nelson became disenchanted with his philosophical speculations. Years later, he claimed that his philosophy professor admitted reading Kant twenty-six times without achieving anything beyond frank bewilderment. Concluding that the perplexities of the universe had confounded greater minds than his, Nelson gradually abandoned his philosophical inquiries.

Quite by accident, somebody invited Nelson to attend an archaeological excavation in Ukiah, north of San Francisco, and he was hooked. The dig apparently rekindled the same fascination with Indian lore he had first found in the pages of James Fenimore Cooper. Permanently smitten by archaeology, Nelson immediately enrolled in all the archaeological courses available at the University of California (see Figure 1–4).

Nelson's M.A. thesis was an archaeological survey of the shell middens surrounding San Francisco Bay (Nelson 1909). He later boasted that according to his pedometer, he had walked more than three thousand miles during his reconnaissance, and had

FIGURE 1–4   Nels Nelson with an assortment of Danish archaeological artifacts.
(Negative no. 117658; courtesy Department of Library Sciences, the American
Museum of Natural History)

recorded 425 prehistoric shell mounds. His report discussed the location of these sites
relative to available natural resources, listed the animal bones found in the shell heaps,
and pondered the ecological adaptation implied by such a bayside lifeway. Urban sprawl
has today destroyed all but a handful of these once obvious sites, and Nelson's map,
originally published in 1909, remains an irreplaceable resource to modern archaeologists
interested in central California prehistory.

While pursuing his graduate education, Nelson was employed as a curatorial
assistant at the University's Museum of Anthropology. Still, Nelson was forced to keep a
nighttime job as a janitor and office boy "doing everything from dusting the president's
desk to picking up the money that was left scattered about the tellers' booths after a busy
day." Although Nelson became a leading American archaeologist, he began his career
when the field was largely an avocation of the independently wealthy, a profession poorly
suited to the resources of young immigrant scholars.

Everything changed for Nelson in 1912. The American Museum of Natural History
in New York was launching an archaeological campaign in the American Southwest, and
Nelson was imported to oversee this influential research program. As we shall see in

Chapters 8 and 9, Nelson's stratigraphic excavations in New Mexico proved to be a breakthrough in archaeological technique. In his next few years at the American Museum, Nelson broadened his experience by excavating caves in Kentucky and Missouri, and more shell mounds in Florida.

In 1925, Nelson accompanied an American Museum expedition to Central Asia. Nelson later admitted that while traveling through the Gobi desert, he forestalled menacing Mongols by pretending to be a magician, able to remove his (artificial) eye, brandish it at the potential assailants, and then put it neatly back in place. The Central Asiatic expedition took Nelson throughout mainland China, culminating in a four-humdred-mile trip up the Yangtze River in a Chinese junk. Nelson's fieldwork also continued throughout North America and Europe until his eventual retirement in 1943.

The career of Nels Nelson typifies the state of Americanist archaeology during the first quarter of the twentieth century. Although receiving infinitely better archaeological training than did predecessors such as C. B. Moore, Nelson still learned largely by firsthand experience. Archaeology remained in a pioneering stage, and no matter where Nelson turned—be it the shell mounds of San Francisco Bay, the **pueblos** of New Mexico, or the caves of the Yangtze River—he was the first archaeologist on the scene. In large measure, his first responsibility was to record what he saw, then to conduct a preliminary excavation where warranted, and finally to proffer tentative inferences to be tested and embellished by subsequent investigators.

Nelson also typified the new breed of early-twentieth-century museum-based archaeologists. Tracing his own fascination with archaeology to an exhibit of prehistoric tools at the Omaha Exposition in 1898, Nelson strongly believed that the message of archaeology should be brought to the public in the form of books, popular magazine articles, and, most of all, interpretive displays of archaeological materials.

Today, Nels Nelson is best remembered in archaeology for for his contributions to stratigraphic technique. Nelson's 1912 excavations in the Galisteo Basin of New Mexico are generally acknowledged as the first significant stratigraphic archaeology in the Americas. At that time, the cultural chronology of the American Southwest was utterly unknown, and Nelson's painstaking excavations and analysis of the pottery recovered provided the first solid chronological framework.

WHERE TO GO FROM HERE?

Nelson on Archaeology: Nelson's most important publications include *Shellmounds of the San Francisco Bay Region* (1909), *Pueblo Ruins of the Galisteo Basin, New Mexico* (1914), and "Chronology of the Tano Ruins, New Mexico" (1916).

Archaeologists on Nelson: For critical discussions of Nelson's stratigraphic technique, see Spier (1931), Willey and Sabloff (1980, pp. 85–89), and Woodbury (1960); Nelson's experiences with the Central Asiatic expedition are discussed by Preston (1986, Chapter 8).

A. V. Kidder (1886–1963): Founder of Anthropological Archaeology

Although born in Michigan, the life and career of **Alfred V. Kidder** revolved about the academic community of Cambridge, Massachussets. Kidder's father, a mining engineer, saw to it that young Alfred received the best education available. First enrolled in a private school in Cambridge, Kidder then attended the prestigious La Villa, in Ouchy, Switzerland, after which he registered at Harvard in the premed program. During his junior year, Kidder finally admitted that he would rather be an archaeologist than a "real" doctor, a decision reflecting both difficulties with the required chemistry curriculum in the premed program and also his passionate boyhood interest in archaeology. Writing a few years before his death, Kidder fondly recalled his father's private library, which contained complete sets of the Smithsonian, National Museum, and Bureau of Ethnology annual reports as well as Catlin's famous *North American Indians*.

Kidder soon joined an archaeological expedition to northeastern Arizona, exploring territory then largely unknown to the Anglo world. Working under the direction of Edgar Hewett of the University of Utah, Kidder mapped ruins at Mesa Verde and assisted in excavations at Puye, on the Pajarito Plateau of New Mexico (see Figure 1–5). The southwestern adventure sealed his fate. When Kidder returned to Harvard, he enrolled in the anthropology program and in 1914 was awarded the sixth American Ph.D. specializing in archaeology—and the first with a focus on North America.

In his dissertation, Kidder examined prehistoric Southwestern ceramics, assessing their value in reconstructing culture history. As was Nelson's stratigraphic technique for excavation, Kidder's dissertation was a breakthrough in Americanist archaeology. Relying on scientific procedures, Kidder demonstrated ways of deciphering meaning from archaeology's most perplexing debris, the lowly potsherd. Urging accurate description of ceramic decoration, he explained how such apparent minutiae could be used to determine relationships among the various prehistoric groups. Kidder argued that only through controlled excavation and correlative analysis could inferences be drawn about such anthropological subjects as acculturation, social organizations, and prehistoric religious customs.

In 1915, the Department of Archaeology at the Phillips Academy in Andover, Massachusetts, embarked on a multiyear archaeological project. It was seeking an appropriate site large enough and of sufficient scientific merit to warrant such a research commitment. Largely because of his anthropological training, Kidder exemplified the new breed in archaeology, and he was selected to direct the excavations.

After evaluating the possibilities, Kidder decided on Pecos Pueblo, a massive prehistoric and historic period ruin located southeast of Santa Fe, New Mexico. A bitterly disappointed Coronado, seeking the rumored wealth of the "Seven Cities of Cibola," had stopped at Pecos in 1540, and the ruins were also described in a detailed report published by Adolph Bandelier in 1881. Hewett had briefly studied the seventeen survivors from Pecos, then still living at the Pueblo of Jemez. Kidder was impressed by the great diversity of potsherds scattered about the ruins and felt certain that Pecos

FIGURE 1–5   A. V. Kidder (right) and Jesse L. Nusbaum conducting an archaeological survey at Mesa Verde (Utah) in 1908. (Courtesy Faith Kidder Fuller and
the School of American Research)

contained enough stratified debris to span several centuries. In all, Kidder excavated at
Pecos for ten summers, publishing fifteen short technical reports and five major monographs describing his findings.

The excavations at Pecos were consequential for several reasons: Kidder was the
first archaeologist in America to test Nelson's stratigraphic method on a large scale.
Kidder went beyond pottery to make sense of the artifact and architectural styles preserved
at Pecos. Working before the advent of radiocarbon dating or a tree-ring chronology, his
intensive artifact analysis established the framework of southwestern prehistory, which
remains intact today.

Kidder's work at Pecos so stimulated the field of southwestern archaeology that
archaeologists soon found it difficult to keep up with current finds. In 1927, Kidder
sponsored a convention at which the major southwestern archaeologists were invited to
Pecos in order to exchange information and help establish a more uniform terminology.
Kidder's **Pecos Conference** has been called the major archaeological milestone of the

A. V. Kidder on the Pan-Scientific Approach to Archaeology

Archaeologists are often portrayed in the media as latter-day hermits who trudge off into the wilderness to conquer the secrets of the past. But in fact, contemporary archaeologists never work alone, as archaeological sites contain information too diverse, too varied for any single scholar to analyze. Teamwork is a requirement of all modern archaeology, but the team approach to archaeology is hardly new. Kidder fully anticipated modern trends with his "pan-scientific" approach at Chichén Itzá, Yucatán, in the 1920s:

> In this investigation the archaeologist would supply the Prehistoric background, the historian

Reprinted by permission of M. W. Conkey and J. Spector and Academic Press.

would work on the documentary record of the Conquest, the Colonial and the Mexican periods; the sociologist would consider the structure of modern life. At the same time studies would be made upon the botany, zoology, and climate of the region and upon the agriculture, economic system, and health conditions of the urban and rural, European mixed and native populations. It seems probable that there would result definite conclusions of far-reaching interest, that there would be developed new methods applicable to many problems of race and culture contacts, and that there would be gained by the individuals taking part in the work a first-hand acquaintance with the aims of allied disciplines which would be of great value to themselves, and through them to far larger groups of research workers. (Kidder 1928, p. 753)

1920s, reflecting the need to share information and to seek a preliminary synthesis of the rapidly growing archaeological record of the American Southwest. The Pecos Conference continues today and remains both the social and intellectual focal point of southwestern archaeology.

In a way, the first Pecos Conference signaled the end of Kidder's first career and the beginning of a second. Shortly thereafter, the Carnegie Institution of Washington created its Division of Historical Research, appointing Kidder as the director. Attracting several of his southwestern colleagues to work with him, Kidder launched an aggressive archaeological program to probe the Mayan ruins of Central America. Following on the successes of his Pecos Conference, Kidder convened a tête-à-tête of specialists at Chichén Itzá on the Yucatán peninsula of Mexico, to take stock of Mayan research and define future research directions (see also Chapter 14).

Promulgating his master plan for Mayan explorations, Kidder directed the Carnegie's campaigns for the next two decades, arguing that a true understanding of Mayan culture would require a broad-based plan of action with many interrelated areas of research. Relegating himself to the role of administrator, Kidder amassed a staff of qualified scientists with the broadest possible scope of interests. His plan is a landmark in archaeological research, stressing an enlargement of traditional archaeological objectives to embrace the wider realms of anthropology and allied disciplines. Under Kidder's direction, the Carnegie program supported research by ethnographers, geographers, physical anthropologists, geologists, meteorologists, and, of course, archaeologists.

Kidder even proved the potential of aerial reconnaissance, by convincing Charles Lindbergh, already an international figure, to participate in the Carnegie's Mayan program. Early in 1929, Lindbergh flew Kidder throughout British Honduras, Yucatán, and the Petén jungle of Guatemala. Beyond the new ruins discovered, the Lindbergh flights also generated a wealth of previously unavailable ecological data, such as the boundaries of various types of vegetation. Today, the interdisciplinary complexion of archaeology is a fact of life. But when Kidder proposed the concept in the 1920s, the prevailing attitude still reflected the one person-one site mentality.

Although largely occupied with bureaucratic details for the remainder of his life, Kidder insisted on conducting his own archaeological research, this time at the formidable site of Kamanaljuyu, in Guatemala. He also continued his career-long interest in Pecos, and in 1958—three decades after he had begun digging there—he published the final Pecos volume. When A. V. Kidder died at the age of seventy-eight, it was suggested that he, more than anyone else, was responsible for transforming archaeology from "antiquarianism to a systematic discipline" (Willey 1967).

Beyond his substantive Mayan and southwestern discourses, Kidder helped shift Americanist archaeology toward more properly anthropological purposes. Unlike many of his contemporaries, Kidder maintained that archaeology should be viewed as "that branch of anthropology which deals with prehistoric peoples," a doctrine that has become firmly embedded and expanded in today's Americanist archaeology. To Kidder, the archaeologist was merely a "mouldier variety of anthropologist." Although archaeologists continue to immerse themselves in the nuances of potsherd detail and architectural specifics, the ultimate objective of archaeology remains the statement of anthropological universals about people.

WHERE TO GO FROM HERE?

Kidder on Archaeology: A complete bibliography is published in Wauchope (1965), and selected writings by Kidder appear in Woodbury (1973); some of the most significant publications are "Basket-Maker Caves of Northeastern Arizona" (Kidder and Guernsey 1921); *An Introduction to the Study of Southwestern Archaeology* (Kidder 1924); *The Present State of Knowledge of American History and Civilization Prior to 1492* (Kidder 1928); "Excavations at Kaminaljuyu, Guatemala" (Kidder, Jennings, and Shook 1946).

Archaeologists on Kidder: Woodbury's (1973) biography remains the best single source; Taylor's (1948) monograph takes a decidedly less positive tone; see also Taylor (1954) and obituaries by Wauchope (1965) and Willey (1967).

James A. Ford (1911–1968): A Master of Time

James A. Ford is the last archaeological forefather to be considered here. Born in Water Valley, Mississippi, Ford's major research interest centered on the archaeology of the American Southeast. He began his career at the Mississippi Department of Archives and History. The director, a southern historian of the old school, set Ford to work digging up "Indian relics" from various mounds throughout the state. In truth, such relic collecting would be considered little better than (illegal) **pothunting**. But even as a teenager, Ford's innate sense of order required that he devise rough procedures to control the excavations and generate appropriate field notes. Ford eventually studied anthropology at the University of Michigan and belatedly received his Ph.D. from Columbia University in 1946. While Ford was attending Columbia, Nels Nelson retired from the Department of Anthropology at the American Museum of Natural History, and Ford was chosen as the new assistant curator of North American archaeology.

James Ford came of age during the Great Depression, part of an archaeological generation literally trained on the job. As the Roosevelt administration came to realize that jobs must be created to alleviate the economic conditions, crews of workmen were assigned labor-intensive tasks, including building roads and bridges, and general heavy construction. One obvious make-work project was archaeology, and literally hundreds of the unemployed were set to work excavating major archaeological sites. This program was, of course, an important boost to Americanist archaeology, and data from WPA-sponsored excavations poured in at a record rate. In fact, materials from the 1930s excavations are still being analyzed and published.

Such leviathan gangs of untrained workmen required close supervision, and an entire generation of archaeologists received their training as WPA supervisors. James Ford was one of these archaeologists, working with federal relief–supported crews in Louisiana and Georgia. Following the Depression, Ford graduated to archae-

FIGURE 1–6   James A. Ford surveying the site of Boca Escondida, north of Veracruz (Mexico). (Courtesy Junius Bird)

James Ford on the Goals of Archaeology

The study of archaeology has changed considerably from a rather esthetic beginning as an activity devoted to collecting curios and guarding them in cabinets to be admired for their rarity, beauty, or simple wonder. Students are no longer satisfied with the delights of the collector and are now primarily interested in reconstructing culture history. In recent years methods and techniques have progressed rapidly, and there are indications which suggest that some phases of the study may develop into a truly scientific concern with general principles. This trend seems to be due more to the kinds of evidence that past human history offers than to any planned development. For centuries the perspective of the study of history was narrowed to a listing of battles, kings, political situations, and escapades of great men, an activity which is analogous to collecting curios and arranging them in cabinets. Such collections are fascinating to those who have developed a taste for them, but they contribute little towards the discovery of processes which are always the foremost interest of a science. The evidence that survives in archaeological situations has made it impossible to study prehistory in terms of individual men, or even in terms of man as an acculturated animal. When the archaeologist progresses beyond the single specimen he is studying the phenomena of culture. . . .

I join a number of contemporaries in believing that archaeology is moving in the direction of its establishment as a more important segment of the developing science of culture than it has been in the past. This does not mean that such objectives as discovering chronological sequences and more complete and vivid historical reconstructions will be abandoned; rather these present aims will become necessary steps in the process of arriving at the new goal. (Ford 1952, pp. 317–318)

ological projects in Alaska, Peru, and Mexico (see Figure 1–6). But southeastern archaeology remained his passion.

We noted earlier that Ford had excavated at Poverty Point, the Louisiana site explored forty years earlier by C. B. Moore. Ford's investigation at Poverty Point was fairly typical of mid-1950s archaeology. After completing his initial mapping and reconnaissance—mainly refining details from Moore's previous observations—Ford launched a series of stratigraphic excavations designed to define the prehistoric sequence.

Ford's overall objective was to read in human terms the meaning of the Poverty Point site, a goal considerably more ambitious that that of, say, C. B. Moore, who dug primarily to unearth outstanding examples of artwork. Ford continually asked, What does archaeology tell us about the people? Trying to reconstruct the appearance of the puzzling site, Ford estimated that roughly 530,000 cubic yards of fill had been used to construct the earthworks at Poverty Point, some thirty-five times the volume of the pyramid of Cheops in Egypt. From this figure, he computed that more than three million labor-hours were required to build just one of the Poverty Point mounds. This suggested that a population of several thousand probably cooperated to create these formidable earthworks. Ford finally concluded that the Poverty Point community must have been organized according to fairly rigid and stratified political structures. The splendid geometrical arrangement of the town and ceremonial precinct further implied a central authority exercised by full-time architects and project directors. To Ford, Poverty Point represented more than a fossilized ceremonial center, and he attempted to recreate the social and political networks responsible for this colossal enterprise. In this regard, Ford's approach typified the overarching anthropological objectives of mid-century Americanist archaeology.

The unprecedented accumulation of raw data during the 1930s created a crisis of sorts among Americanist archaeologists: What was to be done with all these facts? Ford and his contemporaries were beset by the need to synthesize and classify and by the necessity to fabricate regional sequences of culture chronology. Unlike Nelson, Kidder, and the others working in the American Southwest, Ford did not have access to deep, well-preserved refuse heaps; southeastern sites were more commonly shallow, shorter-term occupations. To create a temporal order, Ford relied on an integrated scheme of surface collection and classification.

In so doing, Ford refined the techniques of **Sir Flinders Petrie**, the noted nineteenth-century Egyptologist. While excavating predynastic graves at Diospolis Parva, Petrie devised a way to order sequentially the various stages of pottery development, thereby enabling him to date the numerous grave assemblages. As subsequently modified by Ford and others, this technique of sequential ordering is known as **seriation** (see Figure 1–7). Chapter 10 develops the principles behind seriation in some detail, but the central idea is simple: By assuming that cultural styles (fads) tend to change gradually, archaeologists can chart the relative popularity of pottery decoration through time. Generally, a given pottery style is introduced at one specific locality. Its popularity gradually spreads throughout the region until the first type is successively replaced by another style. Thus, at any particular time, the available ceramic assemblage reflects the relative proportions of the various available pottery styles. By fitting the various short-term assemblages into master curves, Ford developed a series of regional ceramic chronologies. Although sometimes overly simplistic, Ford's seriational technique was sufficient to establish the baseline prehistoric chronology still in use in the American Southeast.

Ford then synthesized his ceramic chronologies into patterns of regional history. When C. B. Moore was excavating the hundreds of prehistoric mounds throughout the Southeast, he lacked a system for adequately dating his finds. Using seriation along with other methods, Ford helped bring temporal order to his excavations, and he rapidly moved to synthesize these local sequences across the greater Southeast. Ford proposed the basic division between the earlier **Burial Mound Period** and the subsequent **Temple Mound Period**, a distinction that remains in use today (see Chapter 13). Toward the end of his career, Ford attempted to tie the historical developments of the southeastern cultures to happenings in Central and Latin America. Although contemporary archaeologists tend to scoff at Ford's sweeping generalizations, Gordon Willey (1969, p. 67) predicted that "a good part of what he [had] advanced will one day be accepted."

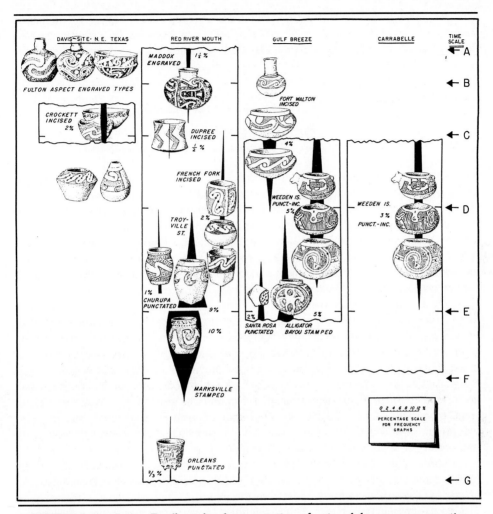

FIGURE 1–7 James Ford's stylized presentation of unimodal curves representing pottery type frequencies, with illustrations of vessels of each type also on the chart. Here, Ford attempted to correlate the ceramic sequences from northeast Texas, Louisiana, and Florida (see Ford 1952, Figure 15). (Courtesy the American Museum of Natural History)

WHERE TO GO FROM HERE?

Ford on Archaeology: "An Interpretation of the Prehistory of the Eastern United States" (Ford and Willey 1941); "Cultural Dating of Prehistoric Sites in the Virú Valley, Peru" (Ford 1949); "The Type Concept Revisited" (Ford 1954); "Poverty Point, a Late Archaic Site in Louisiana" (Ford and Webb 1956); "A Quantitative Method for Deriving Cultural Chronology" (Ford 1957); *A Comparison of Formative Cultures in the Americas: Diffusion or the Psychic Unity of Man?* (Ford 1969).

Archaeologists on Ford: Ian Brown (1978) prepared a short biography; obituaries were written by Evans (1968), Haag (1968), Webb (1968), Willey (1969); see also Stoltman (1973); Willey and Sabloff (1980, esp. Chapter 5)

Americanist Archaeology at Mid-Century

The biographies of these five forebears provide a sense of Americanist archaeology's past. Thomas Jefferson's archaeology was drastically different in manner from that of, say, James Ford. Still, each person made a distinctive contribution to contemporary archaeology, and subsequent chapters will highlight the major innovations of each: Nelson's stratigraphic method, Kidder's southwestern research, Ford's thoughts on artifact classification and seriation, and so forth. Specifics aside, each archaeologist was clearly one of the very best among his contemporaries, and these five careers define a colorful continuum. Americanist archaeology has evolved dramatically over two centuries, and some meaningful trends are evident.

Perhaps the most striking contrast is that brought out by comparing the scholars as individuals. Americanist archaeology began as a pastime of the genteel rich. Thomas Jefferson, a prominent world figure, was born into the best of families and educated as a true colonial gentleman. Even as late as the beginning of this century, archaeologists were still mostly men of inherited wealth (remember C. B. Moore, who purchased the *Gopher* and personally financed his own fieldwork). Not until the days of immigrant Nels Nelson could a "working-class" scholar hope to penetrate the archaeological establishment. You will also note, of course, the virtual invisibility of women in Americanist archaeology by mid-century (a topic addressed particularly in Chapter 4).

Through the years, archaeology developed into a professional scientific discipline. C. B. Moore was among the first generation of full-time professional archaeologists. As practicing specialists, archaeologists from Moore's time and later have affiliated with major museums and universities. This institutional support not only encouraged a sense of professionalism and fostered public funding, but such public repositories also were required to care for the bulky, yet valuable, archaeological artifacts recovered. The twentieth-century Americanist archaeologist is not a collector of personal treasure: All finds belong in the public domain, available for exhibit and study.

We can also see a distinctive progression toward specialization in our five target archaeologists. So little was known about archaeology in the eighteenth century that it was possible for a single scholar to control all the relevant data. Thomas Jefferson's interest in archaeology was stimulated by the existing confusion surrounding the Native Americans' origins, and his curiosity led him to excavate a Virginian burial mound. But his concerns and speculations embraced the entire New World.

By the late nineteenth century, so much archaeological information had already accumulated that no single scholar could hope to know everything relevant to Americanist archaeology. Although C. B. Moore became the leading authority on southeastern archaeology, he knew relatively little about the finds being made by his archaeological contemporaries in Peru, Central America, and even the American Southwest. Because Nels Nelson was affiliated with a major museum, he was able to travel throughout Asia and Europe to keep abreast of archaeological developments; but to do so, he was forced to cease his own fieldwork early in the 1930s. A. V. Kidder pursued two careers, in southwestern and Mayan archaeology. But by mid-century, archaeologists like Ford were forced to specialize in specific localities within limited cultural areas. Today, it is rare to find archaeologists with experience in more than a couple of specialized fields.

But possibly the greatest change has been the quality of archaeologists' training. As a Renaissance man, Jefferson was broadly educated in science, literature, and the arts. His archaeology was wholly self-taught and largely a matter of common sense. Although Harvard-educated, Moore was untrained in archaeology; his fieldwork was still based on personal trial-and-error methods. Nelson and Kidder, among the first professionally trained Americanist archaeologists, studied under America's most prominent archaeologists. From Nelson's time on, Americanist archaeologists were almost without exception well versed in anthropology. The humanist tradition lingers among classical archaeologists, whose training often emphasizes philology and art history rather than anthropology, and is making something of a comeback in Americanist archaeology as well (see Chapters 2 and 3).

In their *A History of American Archaeology*, Willey and Sabloff (1980) characterized archaeology's major periods of growth, and our five "forefather" archaeologists illustrate the major trends. Thomas Jefferson belonged to the "speculative period" which began with Columbus's 1492 voyage. The pressing concern of the time was to explain the origins of the Native Americans and with the exception of Jefferson's rather sophisticated work, archaeology remained the province of the leisured armchair set. The subsequent "classificatory-descriptive period," from about 1840 to 1914, is characterized by the work of C. B. Moore. Archaeological research flourished during this period, with intensive exploration and excavation throughout the Americas. The simultaneous stratigraphic excavations of Nels Nelson in New Mexico and Manuel Gamio in the Valley of Mexico ushered in the next major period, which accentuated issues of cultural chronology. In a sense, Nelson initiated the period, and Kidder personified its culmination. In addition to Nelson's "stratigraphic revolution," the technique of seriation (Chapter 10) was introduced at that time, as was the refinement of artifact typology and ceramic classification. The goals of this period emphasized synthesis, such as that attempted by Kidder for the Maya and the cultures of the American Southwest.

As chronological problems were solved, archaeologists such as James Ford, taking to heart their anthropological training, began to transcend mere chronology to explicate cultural contexts and functions. Although Ford personally contributed to the refinement of local chronologies, he also participated in research programs designed to define **settlement patterns** and to reconstruct prehistoric social environments. Such was the state of Americanist archaeology at mid-century.

Revolution: Archaeology's Angry Young Men

Only dead fish swim with the stream.
—Anonymous

The previous section chronicled the development of traditional Americanist archaeology. A succession of hardworking, intelligent men—the Moores, Kidders, and Fords—symbolize the mainstream archaeological thinking of their day. The technology, assumptions, explanations, and speculation of Americanist archaeology evolved along an unbroken progression. Individual archaeologists came and went, each contributing something, each advancing a few ideas to the cumulative body of archaeological thought. This became mainstream Americanist archaeology.

But archaeology also grew by revolution. A succession of "angry young men" challenged the orthodox archaeological thinking, urging explosive change and demanding instantaneous results; two such crusaders have been particularly influential in shaping modern archaeological thought. We shall now contrast their indignant words with the more traditional reflections just discussed.

W. W. Taylor (1913–): Moses in the Wilderness

Educated at Yale and Harvard, **Walter W. Taylor** completed his doctoral dissertation late in 1942 and then spent the next few years overseas, as he put it, "not a little incommunicado" (Figure 1–8). Taylor found, on returning to the states, that his former professors had arranged a Rockefeller Foundation fellowship, which allowed him to expand his dissertation for publication.

A Study of Archeology, published in 1948 as a memoir of the American Anthropological Association, was a bombshell. Greeted with alarm and consternation by the archaeological community, the book was no less than a public call for revolution. Bourgeois archaeologists—the orthodox fat cats—were blasted, assailed, and berated by this wet-behind-the-ears newcomer. Few liked Taylor's book, but everybody read it.

Taylor first diagnosed a host of disorders afflicting Americanist archaeology and prescribed radical surgery. Early in his book, he launched a frontal attack on the elders of Americanist archaeology. This assault was particularly plucky, as Taylor was himself a rank beginner, having published too little to establish his credentials as an archaeologist, much less a critic. Undaunted, he lined up the archaeological establishment in his sights and then let them have it between the eyes.

A Study of Archeology blasted A. V. Kidder, among others. Taylor considered Kidder to be "the most influential exponent of archeology in the Western hemisphere" (1948, p. 44); Kidder, therefore, was declared to be fair game. What offended Taylor

FIGURE 1–8   Walter W. Taylor during his survey of Coahuila (Mexico) in 1937. (Courtesy Walter W. Taylor)

most was Kidder's alleged two-faced attitude, saying one thing yet doing another. Kidder repeatedly maintained that he was an anthropologist who had specialized in archaeology; Kidder's advanced degree was in anthropology; Kidder had taught anthropology; Kidder headed the Carnegie Institution's stellar team of anthropologists; Kidder was, by definition, an anthropologist. Beginning from this baseline, Taylor then probed Kidder's end products to determine how well his deeds conformed to his stated anthropological objectives.

Boldly Taylor concluded that there was no conformity. He could find in Kidder's research no cultural synthesis, no picture of life at any site, no consideration of **cultural processes**, no derivation of cultural laws—no anthropology at all. This was a heady critique: Here was a novice, barely out of graduate school, assaulting the most distinguished archaeologist of the decade. And not only did Taylor accuse Kidder of bad archaeology; Taylor also claimed that Kidder did not practice what he preached.

These were serious charges, considered to be blasphemy by most archaeologists of the time. But Taylor supported his case with a vivid dissection of Kidder's published record. Kidder's research at Pecos, New Mexico, and elsewhere in the American Southwest was said to be full of "apparent contradictions," merely "description . . . for its own sake." Kidder was scored for failing to supply the details of artifact **provenience**, for concentrating on highly specialized facets of the archaeological record, for ignoring fragmentary specimens, and for failing to generate more culturally relevant data. In fact, Taylor claimed that Kidder was incapable of preparing a proper site report, much less of writing the anthropology of the prehistoric Southwest.

These evaluations were momentous, but Taylor was just warming up. He next focused on Kidder's prestigious research into the archaeology of the Maya and, once again, accused him of failing to live up to his own goals. Data were generated for their own sake: "We have descriptions of Maya artifacts, of Maya buildings, of Maya **epigraphy**, together with comparative data designed to determine their derivation or inspiration . . . but we have no discussion of the place of all these objects within Maya culture, or even within the culture of any one site or part of one site" (Taylor 1948, p. 48). To Taylor, these motivations were antiquarian not anthropological. Moreover, as the powerful chairman of the Division of Historical Research of the Carnegie Institution, Kidder enjoyed unrivaled power to define the horizons of Mayan research. To hear Taylor tell the story, Kidder not only botched his own research but also misdirected the explorations of literally dozens of archaeologists working under his aegis. In 1948, Taylor was indeed archaeology's angriest young man, and his articulate tirade could hardly have been more damning.

Taylor spent page after page chronicling Kidder's failure to consider anthropological issues. Granting that Kidder began his investigations with anthropology in mind, Taylor concluded that somewhere along the line Kidder went astray. Commenting that "the road to Hell and the field of Maya archeology are paved with good intentions," Taylor deduced that the Carnegie Institution, under Kidder's direction, "has sought and found the hierarchical, the grandiose. It has neglected the common, the everyday." Kidder had been blinded by the "pomp and circumstance" of Classic Maya archaeology, disregarding the pedestrian world of real people.

Taylor was, in effect, panning the "comparative" or "taxonomic" approach to archaeology. Kidder—and several other luminaries—were accused of classification and description for their own sake. Claiming to be anthropologists, they failed to do anthropology. Though careful not to deny the initial usefulness of a comparative strategy, Taylor urged archaeologists to get on with the proper business of anthropology: finding out something about people. Chronology, to Taylor, is merely a stepping-stone, providing a foundation for more anthropologically relevant studies of human behavior and cultural dynamics.

W. W. Taylor's prescription was his so-called **conjunctive approach** to archaeology. By conjunctive, Taylor emphasized the interconnection of archaeological objects with their cultural contexts. Whereas comparative scholarship emphasizes relationships among archaeological sites, the conjunctive perspective would shift the emphasis to a particular cultural entity. Taylor attacked Kidder's Mayan research on this basis: Kidder, you're preoccupied with comparing things—temples, glyphs, fancy potsherds—among sites; you've failed to decipher what goes on within any single Maya site. According to Taylor, Kidder merely skimmed off the sensational, the spectacular, the grandiose. A conjunctive approach would scrutinize the minutiae of a single Maya center, attempting to write a comprehensive ethnography of the Maya people who once lived there. In effect, Taylor urged archaeologists to forsake the temples for the garbage dumps. Messy business, this conjunctive archaeology, but Taylor contended that this was the only way for archaeologists to achieve their anthropological goals.

Going beyond the specifics of Maya archaeology, Taylor proposed reforms by arguing for a conjunctive approach in archaeology. Archaeologists must quantify their data (trait lists are rarely useful); they must test hypotheses and progressively refine their impressions (too often initial observations were taken as gospel); they must excavate less extensively and more intensively (too many sites were just "tested" then compared with other remote "tests" with no effort to detect patterning within sites); they must recover and decode the meaning of unremarkable food remains (the bones, seed hulls, and rubbish heaps were too often shoveled out); they must embrace more specialties in the analysis of finds (zoological, botanical, and **petrographic** identifications were too often made in the field and never verified); and they must write more effective site reports (too often only the glamorous finds were illustrated, with precise proveniences omitted).

In perusing Taylor's propositions some four decades after they were written, I am struck by how unremarkable they now seem. Where is the revolution? Today's archaeologists do quantify their results; they do test hypotheses; they do excavate intensively; they do save food remains, they do involve specialists in analysis; and they do write detailed site reports.

But archaeologists did not do these things routinely in 1940, and this is what Taylor was sputtering about. Taylor's suggestions of 1948 embody few surprises for today's student, testimony to just how far archaeological doctrine and execution have matured since Taylor wrote his *A Study of Archeology*.

How, one might wonder, did young Taylor get away with all of this? In one sense, he did not get away with it. When Richard Woodbury reviewed Taylor's book in *American Antiquity*—America's most prominent archaeological journal—he noted that even six years after publication, Taylor's book had rarely even been mentioned in print.

> It is in verbal, and generally informal, comments that archaeologists have been most out-spoken concerning *Study of Archeology*, and it is my impression that such comments have been preponderantly disapproving and rarely favorable. Some comments have been in the nature of outraged resentment that such "disagreeable" things should have been said in print . . . ; others, and perhaps especially those more nearly Taylor's contemporaries, have expressed disappointment that the soundness of some of his comments should be completely vitiated by association with such highly opinionated views, and the whole decked out in grandiose language. (Woodbury 1954, p. 292)

Woodbury went on to chastise Taylor for "crusading for a cause" and displaying a "patronizing attitude." Although *A Study of Archeology* was never reviewed in *American Anthropologist*, an omission that itself tells us something, Taylor was roundly criticized in a letter to the editor by Robert Burgh (1950).

Taylor had an unfortunate habit of illustrating the "good" archaeology with examples from his own unpublished field studies in the American Southwest and Coahuila, Mexico. Archaeologist Paul Martin's reaction was fairly typical:

I think Taylor's ideas would have been far more favorably received and more widely accepted if he had first put out an archaeological report embodying his ideas. . . . To me a concrete example is more easily grasped than an abstraction or a theory; and we who teach could then point to the applications of his principles. I still await with pleasure Taylor's publications of his archaeological work in Mexico. (1954, p. 571)

Today, some forty years after publication of *A Study of Archeology*, much of Taylor's field investigation remains unpublished, unavailable for scrutiny by other archaeologists, who ask him: "When will you publish your work on Coahuila? You attacked Kidder for saying one thing yet doing another. If your ideas are so great, why didn't you ever publish the archaeology to back them up?" Taylor responded, rather lamely, to these charges, suggesting that he had "provided enough pertinent material for critics to chew on for quite a spell. . . . I cannot see that my default explains or condones the lack, in the literature of American archeology, of any objective, thorough, critique of *A Study of Archeology*" (Taylor 1972, p. 30). Americanist archaeologists since Thomas Jefferson have acknowledged the necessity—in fact the obligation—to publish their own findings. Taylor's critique suffered because of his failure to do so.

WHERE TO GO FROM HERE?

Taylor on Archaeology: His classic is, of course, *A Study of Archeology* (1948); see also "Southwestern Archeology, Its History and Theory" (1954); "Old Wine and New Skins: A Contemporary Parable" (1972).

   Archaeologists on Taylor: Burgh (1950): "Comment on Taylor's *A Study of Archeology*"; Woodbury (1954): "Review of *A Study of Archeology*; and Martin (1954): "Comments on *Southwestern Archeology: Its History and Theory* by Walter W. Taylor." See also Binford (1972a, p. 541), Willey and Sabloff (1980, Chapters 5 and 6).

Lewis R. Binford (1930–): Visionary with a Message

> Taylor had the aims but not the tools.
> —Lewis R. Binford

American archaeology's second angry young man is **Lewis R. Binford**. After a period of military service, Binford enrolled in 1954 at the University of North Carolina, wanting to become an ethnographer. But when he moved on for graduate education at the University of Michigan, Binford was a confirmed archaeologist.

   As a young professional, Binford was a man on the move, literally. He first taught a year at Michigan, moved on to the University of Chicago, to the University of California at Santa Barbara, down the coast to UCLA, and finally to the University of New

Mexico in Albuquerque. During his travels, Binford came into contact with the brightest of an upcoming generation of archaeologists (and we will meet many of them later in this book).

The mid-1960s was a hectic time for archaeology. Waves of alienation and confrontation were rolling across the nation, and archaeology was firmly embedded in the intellectual climate of the times. This revolutionary spirit derived in part from the general anxiety that permeated university campuses during the Vietnam War era. Things must change: not just war and poverty and racism and oppression, but also the academic edifice itself. Scholarship must become relevant; older concepts must give way to fresh perceptions. Such was the social environment in which Binford's ideas took hold. Without the revolutionary spirit and social upheaval of the mid-1960s, Binford's archaeology would have taken on a rather different, perhaps less aggressive configuration.

An extraordinary lecturer, Binford rapidly assumed the role of messiah. His students became disciples, spreading the word throughout the land. Binfordians preached a gospel with great appeal in the 1960s. Archaeology does have relevance; archaeology must transcend potsherds to issues of **cultural evolution**, **cultural ecology**, and

Lewis Binford and His Archaeology

As I was riding on the bus not long ago, an elderly gentleman asked me what I did. I told him I was an archaeologist. He replied: "That must be wonderful, for the only thing you have to be to succeed is lucky." It took some time to convince him that his view of archaeology was not quite mine. He had the idea that the archaeologist "digs up the past," that the successful archaeologist is one who discovers something not seen before, that all archaeologists spend their lives running about trying to make discoveries of this kind. This is a conception of science perhaps appropriate to the 19th century, but, at least in the terms which I myself view archaeology, it does not describe the nature of archaeology as it is practiced today. . . . I believe archaeologists are more than simply discoverers.

Archaeology . . . cannot grow without striking a balance between theoretical and practical concerns. Archaeologists need to be continuously self-critical: that is why the field is such a lively one and why archaeologists are forever arguing among themselves about who is right on certain issues. Self-criticism leads to change, but is itself a challenge—one which archaeology perhaps shares only with palaeontology and a few other fields whose ultimate concern is making inferences about the past on the basis of contemporary things. So archaeology is not a field that can study the past *directly,* nor can it be one that merely involves discovery, as the man on the bus suggested. On the contrary, it is a field wholly dependent upon inference to the past from things found in the contemporary world. Archaeological data, unfortunately, do not carry self-evident meanings. How much easier our work would be if they did! (Binford 1983a, pp. 19, 23)

social organization; archaeology must take full advantage of modern technology; archaeology must become more systematic, using uncompromising logic and more sophisticated, quantitative techniques; archaeology must be concerned with the few remaining preindustrial peoples in order to scrutinize firsthand the operation of disappearing cultural adaptations. As Binford's movement gained momentum, nothing was considered sacred in the traditionalist **paradigm** of archaeology. As Binford himself characterized these early years, he and his colleagues were "full of energy and going in all directions at once" (Binford 1972a, p. 125).

Binford and his students—and their students—became the primary agents of change in Americanist archaeology during the 1960s (see Figure 1–9). The phrase *new archaeology* became associated with their way to interrogate the past. The battle plan for the new archaeology was set forth in a seminal series of articles published through the 1960s and early 1970s. Binford's first major paper was entitled "Archaeology as Anthropology" (Binford 1962b). In it, he asked why archaeology had contributed so little to general anthropological theory. His answer was that in the past **material culture** had been simplistically interpreted. Too much attention had been lavished on the artifacts of shared behavior, as passive traits that "blend," "influence," and "stimulate" one another.

FIGURE 1–9 Lewis R. Binford while excavating at Mission Santa Catalina in 1984. (Courtesy the American Museum of Natural History; photograph by Deborah Mayer O'Brien)

Somewhat later, Binford ridiculed this attitude as the "aquatic view of culture": "Interpretive literature abounds in phrases such as 'cultural stream' and in references to the 'flowing' of new cultural elements into a region. Culture is viewed as a vast flowing stream with minor variations in ideational norms" (1965, p. 205). Echoing Taylor, Binford proposed that artifacts be examined in terms of their cultural contexts. Some tools (so-called **technomic artifacts**) articulate mainly with the physical environment, and variability must be understood in largely ecological terms. Other artifacts (termed **sociotechnic artifacts**) function primarily within the social subsystem and so must be analyzed differently. The third artifact category (the **ideotechnic**) reflects most clearly the mental, **cognitive** component of culture. In other words, the same artifact takes on different archaeological meaning depending on which question the archaeologist poses.

Critical here is the perception of the **cultural system**. Following anthropologist Leslie White (see Chapter 3), Binford argued that archaeologists must perceive **culture** as the nonbiological mechanism for relating the human organism to its physical and social environments.

Binford underscored the importance of precise, unambiguous scientific methods. Archaeologists must stop acting like passive receptors, waiting for the artifacts to speak up. Archaeologists must formulate pointed questions (**hypotheses**) to the archaeological record; these hypotheses must then be tested on the remains of the past. Binford (1967) argued, for instance, that contemporary preindustrial peoples can serve as **analogies** for archaeological exploration. The analogues provide a basis for hypotheses, which can then be confirmed (or rejected) on the basis of the archaeological record.

If, as Binford suggested, archaeologists must be more clinical, capitalizing on more logical forms of reasoning, then archaeological field procedures must also be refined to deliver higher-quality data. Binford argued that because archaeologists always work from samples, they should acquire data that make the samples more representative of the populations from which they were drawn. Binford urged archaeologists to stretch their horizons beyond the individual site to the scale of the region; in this way, an entire cultural system could be assessed. And these regional samples must also be generated from **research designs** based on the principles of probability sampling. **Random sampling** is commonplace in other social sciences, and Binford insisted that archaeologists apply these procedures to their own specific research problems.

Binford's strictly methodological contributions were gradually amplified by projects designed to demonstrate how the approach fosters the comprehension of cultural processes. Intricate statistical techniques were applied to a variety of subjects, from the nature of Mousterian (some fifty thousand years old) campsites to the patterning of African Acheulian (hundreds of thousands of years old) assemblages. These investigations were critical because they embroiled Binford in factual, substantive debate. Not only did he advocate different goals and new methods, but he also related to field archaeologists through these substantive controversies—he argued about specifics not just theory. Binford presented an extended consideration of post-Pleistocene human adaptations (1968b) and conducted his own ethnoarchaeological fieldwork among the Nunamiut Eskimo, the Navajo, and the Australian aborigines. The contributions of Binford, his students, and disciples crop up throughout this text. For now, we are concerned more with the role of Binford as one of archaeology's angry young men.

In true Taylor-like fashion, Binford lambasted archaeology's principals, accusing them of retarding progress in the discipline. And yet his reception was quite different. Why was the response to Taylor so muffled, whereas Binford was hailed as "the father of the new archaeology"? Why was Binford's work so rapidly disseminated throughout the world, whereas *A Study of Archeology* languished on the shelf for nearly two decades?

One clue lies in the respective plans of attack. Taylor was always the loner, a pup yipping at archaeology's heels. By contrast, Binford moved into the heart of the archaeological establishment, teaching a vocal cadre of students at several major universities throughout the American West. Binford's leadership was rapidly transmitted across an entire archaeological generation, whereas Taylor's influence remained obscure and rarely acknowledged. Binford thus had numbers on his side. While Taylor was still defending his lack of application of the "conjunctive method," the new archaeologists could point to the triumphs of Binford's dozens of students and cohorts.

The field of anthropology had itself changed during the two decades of the new archaeology. The anthropology of Taylor's time was a rather exclusive discipline. Theoretical programs such as cultural and human ecology were still treated with skepticism, the prevailing feeling being largely one of particularism: Culture is too complex to be explained by far-reaching theories. In fact, Taylor's own professor at Harvard, Clyde Kluckhohn, had roundly criticized his anthropological colleagues for narrow-mindedness. Change was hard to come by in the 1940s.

The 1960s were a time of momentous change in popular music, hair length, dress codes, degree requirements—to say nothing of the pervasive social and economic upheavals felt across the nation. The archaeological-academic establishment opened up. Postwar enrollments had expanded the campuses and provided hundreds of new jobs for archaeologists. Contemporary perspectives on racial, sexual, and age discrimination forced changes in the hiring practices on campus as elsewhere. Careers no longer were controlled by the "good old-boy" network, and women became a viable force in mainstream archaeology. Professional archaeology matured during the 1960s, allowing plenty of room for mavericks, rebels, freethinkers, and nonconformists.

The 1960s were also a time of great change within anthropology. With theorizing once more acceptable, a **nomothetic** revival took place. Moreover, many anthropologists themselves woke up to the relevance of archaeological research to the comprehensive study of people. One anthropologist, Marvin Harris, urged his colleagues to reject the unnecessary conditions they had previously placed on the archaeological subdiscipline: Archaeological units are every bit as real and acceptable as those used by ethnographers (see Chapter 3). Archaeologists gained a new respectability in anthropology in the 1960s, an attitude that was both the cause and the result of Binfordian archaeology.

But perhaps the most important factor in Binford's success was timing. Although Taylor's efforts in the 1940s were, on the surface, unsuccessful, they had a tremendous, if undeclared, effect on archaeology. Many archaeologists were offended by Taylor's needlessly dogmatic and bombastic assessment of his contemporaries. Few directly disputed his motives, but few likewise appreciated his methods. The archaeology of the 1950s was in large measure a reaction to Taylor's suggestions, although he was rarely credited. Taylor paved the way for Binford, who freely acknowledges the influence of *A Study of Archeology* on his own thinking: "I have frequently avoided citing Walter Taylor in my writings except in a positive way because his work was inspiring to me. Clearly I disagree with many of his arguments, yet in print I have avoided these issues on more than one occasion" (Binford 1972a, p. 541). Taylor was the harbinger of impending change; Binford was the architect of that change.

Binford and his students set off a fire storm that quickly spread throughout the archaeological community. A 1970s generation of new graduate students and young professionals was greeted with the admonition: Are you a new archaeologist, an old archaeologist, or what? Make up your mind!

Today, if you are not confused,
you are just not thinking clearly.
—Irene Peter

WHERE TO GO FROM HERE?

Binford on Archaeology: His important books include *New Perspectives in Archeology* (Binford and Binford 1968); *For Theory Building in Archaeology* (Binford 1977); *Nunamiut Ethnoarchaeology: A Case Study in Archaeological Formation Processes* (Binford 1978b); *Bones: Ancient Men and Modern Myths* (Binford 1981); *In Pursuit of the Past: Decoding the Archaeological Record* (Binford 1983a); *Faunal Remains from Klasies River Mouth* (Binford 1984). Fortunately, Binford has collected his scientific papers into two additional books (valuable not only for the articles but also for his retrospective comments about each): *An Archaeological Perspective* (Binford 1972a) and *Working at Archaeology* (Binford 1983b). See especially "Archeology As Anthropology" (Binford 1962b); "A Consideration of Archaeological Research Design" (Binford 1964); "Archaeological Systematics and the Study of Cultural Process" (Binford 1965); "Smudge Pits and Hide Smoking: The Use of Analogy in Archaeological Reasoning" (Binford 1967); "Some Comments on Historical Versus Processual Archaeology" (Binford 1968c); "Interassemblage Variability—The Mousterian and the 'Functional' Argument" (Binford 1973); "Willow Smoke and Dogs' Tails: Hunter–Gatherer Settlement Systems and Archaeological Site Formation" (Binford 1980); "The Archaeology of Place" (Binford 1982).

Archaeologists on Binford: A comprehensive listing of what archaeologists have to say about Binford would fill an entire chapter. For some positive assessments, see the overviews by Daniel and Renfrew (1988, Chapter 9), Flannery (1967a), Willey and Sabloff (1980, Chapters 6–8), Leone (1987), Renfrew (1983). For some less enthusiastic appraisals, see Bettinger (1987), Gould (1985), Hodder (1982b, 1986), Schiffer (1980).

The New Archaeology: What's in a Phrase?

Scientists have the annoying habit of indiscriminately throwing around the word *new*. We have been treated to the new systematics (Huxley 1940), the new biology (Birdsell 1972, pp. 534–535), and, somewhat closer to home, the new ethnography (Sturtevant 1964, pp. 99–101) and the new physical anthropology (Washburn 1951).

So it comes as little surprise that we have a new archaeology. Although the term is most commonly associated with Lewis Binford and his followers, the actual phrase predates the Binford era. In 1917, Wissler referred to colleagues using stratigraphic excavation techniques as "the new archaeologists" (Wissler 1917). In 1954, Richard Woodbury discussed a "new archaeology," as did Haag somewhat later (1959). But the modern usage stems primarily from an article by Joseph Caldwell, published in *Science* in 1959, entitled "The New American Archaeology."

> **New archaeology . . . that precious and prissy phrase.**
> **—Glyn Daniel**

The term caught on in the late 1960s and throughout the 1970s. For a while, one could hardly scratch the recent archaeological literature without being ambushed by the new: "Koster Site: The New Archaeology in Action" (Struever and Carlson 1977); "Working with the 'New Paradigm' " (Whallon 1974b); "The 'New Archaeology' of the 1960s" (Watson 1972). BBC Science correspondent David Wilson (1974) even wrote a book entitled (what else?) *The New Archaeology.*

The term new archaeology has always been troublesome, used by many and agreed upon by few. Ten years ago, to find out what was really going on in Americanist archaeology, I took an informal poll of 640 archaeologists, asking them if they were "new," "traditional," or something else. Responses ranged from the enthusiastic to irate. I was told that this was "probably the silliest questionnaire I have ever received," and my inquiry was called "foolish" and "a particularly loathsome example of simplistic reductionism." One very senior archaeologist berated me for not providing return postage, admitting that "the 13 cents almost prevented my reply." One colleague wrote simply: "Just leave me alone and let me do my own research!"

Even at the zenith of the new archaeology, fewer than than one in five Americanist archaeologists felt comfortable with the term. Most of my colleagues could not characterize themselves as new or traditional, suggesting that the categories were "out-dated," "misleading," "oversimplified," "a crock of shit," or simply "dumb." Though many expressed sympathy for the objectives of the new and the traditional in archaeology, they objected to their separation: "You can't do one without the other." Clearly, archae-

The Difference between History and Evolution

Are major events in history to be explained as the actions of geniuses, or are geniuses the result of the forces of history? This topic has been a major concern of psychologists, historians, and sociologists. Anthropologists, too, have argued the point. Here is what Leslie White, a premier anthropologist, had to say about the role of the genius in history:

Culture does not grow or change at uniform rates; there are periods of intense activity and periods of stagnation and even retrogression. A culture may exhibit little change or progress over a long period and then suddenly burst forth with vigorous activity and growth. An invention or discovery such as metallurgy, agriculture, the domestication of animals, the keystone arch, the alphabet, microscope, steam engine, etc., may inaugurate an era of rapid change and progress.

But are not inventions the work of genius? The answer is of course "Yes," if by genius you mean "someone who makes a significant discovery or invention." But . . . to appeal to "genius" to explain the invention or discovery is an empty redundancy since genius is here defined in terms of the event, and the appeal to exceptionally great native endowment is unwarranted or at least misleading.

. . . An invention or discovery is a synthesis of already existing cultural elements, or the assimilation of a new element into a cultural system. . . . Just as the discoveries of Pasteur would

have been impossible in the time of Charlemagne, so was agriculture impossible in the days of Cro-Magnon. Every invention and discovery is but a synthesis of the cultural accumulation of the past with the experience of the present.

Two significant conclusions can now be drawn: (1) No invention or discovery can take place until the accumulation of culture has provided the elements—the materials and ideas—necessary for the synthesis, and, (2) when the requisite materials have been made available by the process of cultural growth or diffusion, and given normal conditions of cultural interaction, the invention or discovery is bound to take place.

. . . . The significance of the Great Man in history has been obscured by a failure to distinguish between history and evolution. . . .[History] is characterized by chance and is therefore unpredictable to a high degree: no one, for example, could have predicted that Booth would kill Lincoln—or whether or not his pistol would have misfired when he pulled the trigger. [Evolution] however is determinative: prediction is possible to a high degree. In the decomposition of a radioactive substance one stage determines the next and the course and rate of change can be predicted. In short, we can predict the course of evolution but not of history.

The significance of the distinction between history and evolution and its relevance to the Great Man in history is brought out nicely in the debate between Kroeber and Sapir on the "superorganic." Kroeber argues that had Darwin died in infancy the advance and course of development of biological theory would have been much the same as it has been. Sapir counters by asking if the administration of law in New Orleans would have been the same today had it not been for Napoleon. Both disputants are wholly justified in their claims. Unfortunately, however, they are talking about two different things. One is dealing with a deterministic developmental process, the other with the fortuitous course of history. In the evolutionist process, the individual is, as Kroeber maintains and as the phenomena of multiple and simultaneous but independent discoveries and inventions clearly demonstrate, relatively insignificant. But, in the succession of chance occurrences that is history, the individual may be enormously significant. But it does not follow at all that he is therefore a "genius" or a person of exceptional ability. The goose who saved Rome was more significant historically than many an emperor who ruled it. (White 1949, pp. 201, 203, 204–205, 229–230)

ologists seem to experience at least as much trouble analyzing their own culture as they do the cultures of others.

So what do I think? I suggest that the new archaeology is best used to describe a commanding development within the history of Americanist archaeology. I relegate the new archaeology to historical contexts, for it describes a movement within archaeology that began in the early 1960s with the work of Lewis Binford; much of this agenda has been absorbed into mainstream archaeology. Those people who actually called themselves new archaeologists were really affirming that they liked what Lewis Binford said. I like what he said too, but I also liked several things that the "traditionalists" had said decades before and a number of things people have said more recently.

I have discussed the development of Americanist archaeology in terms of some individual archaeologists because it is more interesting to deal with real people—their quirks, their idiosyncracies, their motivations. Biographical history makes a better story, and that is why I wrote Chapter 1 in this fashion.

But there is a danger in this approach, the risk of overemphasizing the role of the individual. I do not subscribe to the Great Man theory of history. We must distinguish between history and evolution. History is a sequence of time-specific events, and people like Thomas Jefferson and Lewis Binford dramatically conditioned the history of Americanist archaeology, which would not have been the same without them.

But let us be sure to distinguish the history of archaeology from the evolution of archaeological thought. The evolution of important ideas is independent of the individuals who proposed them. Somebody had to go out and excavate the first archaeological site in America, and history tells us that that person was Thomas Jefferson. But had Jefferson died in childhood, nineteenth century archaeology would have followed roughly the same course. Similarly, stratigraphic methods would have been adopted in America without Nels Nelson, and so would have seriation without James Ford.

This also applies to today's archaeology, although the distinction is harder to make because we are so much closer to the events. The new archaeology was an important event in the history of Americanist archaeology, but we must restrict the phrase new archaeology to an event-specific, historical usage. New archaeologists are specific scholars who made specific proposals, and these proposals made a great impact on the specific history of Americanist archaeology between about 1960 and 1975.

New archaeology was an important historical entity, as was the Whig party or the Emancipation Proclamation. But these events only signified more far-reaching trends of the time.

There is no new archaeology in the sense of evolution. There is only contemporary archaeology. Note, for example, how few modern archaeologists even want to be called new. The condition of contemporary archaeology evolved from a number of inputs, some of them from the new archaeologists; but many of the contributions came from elsewhere. We must recognize that the thrust of Americanist archaeology today would be almost identical even had Lewis Binford and his students opted for careers in, say, pharmacy.

Kathleen A. Deagan (1948–   ): Neither Angry nor a Young Man

Struggles twixt new and old make interesting history indeed, but this is not a history book. This book is about the methods, the techniques, the assumptions, and the goals of contemporary archaeology. But before grappling with these issues, let me introduce one more archaeologist, somebody who embodies the diversity and animation that is archaeology today.

To my way of thinking, no archaeologist represents contemporary Americanist archaeology better than does **Kathleen Deagan**, currently a Curator and Chair at the Florida State Museum (University of Florida). A historical archaeologist specializing in Spanish colonial studies, Deagan (like Lewis Binford) was born in Norfolk, Virginia; she attended twenty-four different schools before receiving her doctorate in anthropology from the University of Florida in 1974.

Historical archaeologists are to some the most esoteric of the breed, spending their lives rooting about in pursuit of trivia, researching the definitive history of the three-tined fork. There is a grain of truth in this stereotype: documenting detailed change in artifacts—what Noël Hume termed the "signposts to the past"—remains a critical, early-stage component of today's historical archaeology.

Deagan has certainly paid her dues on this score. She may know more than anybody else about Spanish colonial artifacts of the New World, and she spent a dozen years researching her most recent book *Artifacts of the Spanish Colonies of Florida and the Caribbean, 1500–1800* (1987). Already hailed as a masterpiece, this comprehensive synthesis is an indispensable reference for anybody conducting the archaeology of the period.

But to Deagan, historical archaeology is considerably more than monitoring temporal change through artifacts; it is just the first step. Like her mentor, Charles H. Fairbanks, Deagan is pushing the frontiers of traditional historical archaeology, pioneering the archaeological investigation of disenfranchised groups.

Kathleen Deagan on the Potential of Historical Archaeology

Historical archaeology today is actively contributing to a variety of problems and disciplines. From its emergence as a recognized area of research in the 1930s, the field has advanced from being essentially a set of techniques providing supplemental data for other disciplines, through being an anthropological tool for the reconstruction of past lifeways and the study of cultural process, to being a means of discovering predictable relationships between human adaptive strategies, ideology, and patterned variability in the archaeological record.

Certain aspects of historical archaeology should be particularly noted as having the potential for making contributions not possible through any other discipline. The contributions result from historical archaeology's unique ability to simultaneously observe written statements about what people said they did, what observers said people did, and what the archaeological record said people did. Inconsistencies and inaccuracies in the records of

the past provided by written sources may be detected and ultimately predicted. Insights into past perceptions of human conditions provided by such written sources may be compared to the more objective archaeological record of actual conditions in the past in order to provide insight into cognitive processes. The simultaneous access to varied sources of information about the past also allows the historical archaeologist to match the archaeological patterning of a given unit against the documented social, economic, and ideological attributes of the same unit in order to arrive at a better understanding of how the archaeological record reflects human behavior. The unique potential of historical archaeology lies not only in its ability to answer questions of archaeological and anthropological interest, but also in its ability to provide historical data not available through documentation or any other source. The inadequate treatment of disenfranchised groups in America's past, excluded from historical sources because of race, religion, isolation, or poverty, is an important function of contemporary historical archaeology and one that cannot be ignored. (Deagan 1982, pp. 170–171)

Reprinted by permission of K. Deagan and Academic Press.

Kathleen Deagan is best known for her long-term excavations at St. Augustine, continuously occupied since its founding by Pedro Menéndez in 1565. As accentuated by raucous signs sprinkled throughout town, St. Augustine is the oldest European enclave in the United States (complete with the "oldest pharmacy," "oldest house," "oldest church," and so on). Deagan's research here dates back to her graduate student days, her doctoral dissertation—entitled "Sex, Status and Role in the *Mestizaje* of Spanish Colonial Florida"—neatly straddling the traditionally discrete studies of historical archaeology, **ethnohistory**, and anthropology.

Deagan addressed the processes and results of Spanish-Indian intermarriage and descent, a topic dear to the hearts of many anthropologists and ethnohistorians; the fact that people of such mixed descent (**mestizos**) constitute nearly the entire population of Latin America brought this issue to the forefront long ago. Similar processes took place in Spanish Florida, but the Hispanic occupation left no apparent *mestizo* population in **La Florida**, what Deagan calls "America's first melting pot". Accordingly, when she commenced her doctoral research, virtually nothing was known about such early race relations in North America.

Deagan hypothesized about how *mestizaje* must have operated in this colonial setting. Given the nature of the unfortunate interactions that characterized eighteenth-century Florida, she expected the burdens of acculturation to have fallen most heavily on the Indian women living in Spanish or *mestizo* households. Because no *mestizo* people survive here, the tests for her hypothesis were necessarily archaeological. If her hypothesis is true, then acculturation should affect mostly the Native American women's activities visible in the archaeological record (food preparation techniques, equipment, household activities, basic food resources, child-related activities, and primarily female crafts such as pottery manufacture). Moreover, male-related activities (house construction technology and design, military and political affairs, and hunting weapons) should show less evidence of Indian infusion.

To explore these processes, Deagan began in 1973 a series of archaeological field schools at St. Augustine. This long-term, diversified enterprise generated an impressive database, excavating sites with varying income, occupation, and ethnic affiliation, selected to represent the known range of variability from within the community. Hundreds of students have learned their first archaeology at St. Augustine, where a saloon still sports an aging placard celebrating the years of "Digging with Deagan."

Seeking to explore still earlier episodes of Hispanic–Native American interaction, Deagan was, quite naturally drawn to the Caribbean, where between 1980 and 1985, she headed interdisciplinary excavations at Puerto Real, the fourth oldest New World city (established in 1503). As she steadily moved back in time, Deagan's research eventually led her literally to the doorstep of Christopher Columbus.

In northern Haiti, Deagan has apparently discovered La Navidad, the earliest well-documented point of contact between Spanish and Native American. On Christmas Eve, 1492—following two nights of partying with local Taino Arawak Indians—Columbus's flagship *Santa Maria* ran aground. He abandoned ship, moved to the *Nina*, and appealed to the local Native Americans for help. They assigned him the best two houses in their village and Columbus named this tiny settlement La Navidad to celebrate the birth of the infant Christ child (see Figure 1–10).

This disaster left the explorers one boat short. When Columbus sailed home with his world-shattering news, he left thirty-nine unfortunate compatriots behind, protected by a small stockade built from the timbers of the wrecked *Santa Maria*. Returning a year later, Columbus found the settlement burned, his men killed and mutilated.

Columbus soon established the more permanent settlement of La Isabela and Puerto Real—sites of the first sustained contact between Europeans and Native Americans—and Deagan is also conducting field excavations there. Having a population of nearly fifteen hundred people, La Isabela was home to soldiers, priests, stonecutters, masons, carpenters

FIGURE 1–10   Kathleen Deagan digging at Bas En Saline (Haiti), thought to be the site of La Navidad, established by Christopher Columbus on Christmas, 1492. (Photograph by Bill Ballenberg)

warriors. Although this first Columbian town lasted only four years, an instant compared with the entire period of Hispanic–Native American contact, several critical events took place here: the first intentional introduction of European plants and animals; the first expedition into the interior; and the first Hispanic installation of urban necesssities like canals, mills, streets, gardens, plazas, ports, ramparts, roads, and hospitals.

The biological effects of the Columbian exchange soon overtook La Isabela. European and Native American alike suffered from dietary deficiencies, an excessive work load, and contagious disease. Influenza struck during the first week, affecting one-third of the population. When Columbus ordered the settlement abandoned in 1496, fewer than three hundred inhabitants were left.

Deagan is currently extending her Puerto Real research to La Isabela, to investigate daily life in the initial colonial period, including the ways in which European colonists coped with their new and largely unknown New World environment. The team is looking closely at how the new landscape was altered by Europeans; the degree of exchange between them and the Native Americans; the economics and inequities of such colonial enclaves; the demography, health, and nutrition of the population; the decline of the indigenous population; and the disintegration of traditional cultural patterns.

With all this going on, Deagan still found time to pioneer yet another unknown aspect of early race relations in America. Fort Mose—the first free black community in the United States—was established by the Spanish Crown just outside St. Augustine in 1738 as a haven for African slaves who had escaped from the English colony of South Carolina. Like so many episodes in black history, the Fort Mose story is incompletely known, simply forgotten by conventional American history.

Deagan relocated the lost site of Fort Mose in 1986, and her excavations provide an opportunity to reexamine the role of blacks in colonial history: One recent newspaper proclaimed Fort Mose Florida's "castle of freedom." According to Deagan, "The stereotypical image of Blacks in Colonial history has been that of servitude alone. In fact, free Blacks had a very active role in La Florida's Colonial history. Fort Mose is a symbol of Black freedom in Colonial America, and that's an image we don't get much of in the history books" (*Northeast Florida Advocate,* March 16, 1987). Her research is focused on the degree to which the blacks of Fort Mose revived their African heritage after regaining their freedom and whether they picked up Spanish ways.

Beyond the new directions in historical archaeology, Deagan's research demonstrates other important trends. For one, contemporary Americanist archaeology is played out in the public arena. Deagan creates headlines wherever she works. Newspapers around the world chronicle her success, and her research was featured in consecutive years in the pages of *National Geographic* magazine. Deagan has shown extraordinary patience with the onslaught of well-meaning reporters. Some are apparently intimidated or confused by their first visit to an archaeological dig; they just don't know where to look first.

Media types seem astonished that such a successful archaeologist can also be female: "Kathleen Deagan balanced on one foot in the parking lot. . . .'You lose all pride in this profession, changing your clothes in a parking lot,' she said with a wry grin. . . . Wind swirled through the parking lot and tousled her blond hair . . . it would be Archaeology A-Go-Go" (*The Florida Times-Union,* March 18, 1987). Melodramatic coverage like this plagues archaeology these days (although perhaps Deagan has suffered more than most).

But she overlooks the chatter because such reporting has a far more serious side. Archaeologists can no longer afford isolationist ivory-towerism. One way or another— whether through federal grants, state-supported projects, tax laws, or private benefaction—archaeology depends on public support for its livelihood.

Decades ago, Margaret Mead recognized the importance of taking the work of anthropologists to the public, and she spent considerable effort keeping anthropology alive in the print and electronic media. Today, archaeology enjoys unprecedented press coverage, and archaeologists like Deagan know that without such publicity, Americanist archaeology will have no future.

Publicity can pay off in concrete terms. The Fort Mose research, for instance, is directly supported by the state of Florida. State Representative Bill Clark, who sponsored the bill financing the archaeology, called Deagan's discovery of Fort Mose "a major historical find for Black people." To Clark, the excavations show that "blacks were never content to be slaves"; these are "America's first freedom fighters."

Deagan is more than good newspaper copy. Her research and publications have helped establish historical archaeology as a viable subdiscipline in the field of anthropology. Although awash in the time-specific details and artifacts of Columbus, the blacks of Fort Mose, and the Timucua Indians, she is ultimately addressing the general processes behind the particulars: the sexual and social consequences of Spanish-Indian intermarriage, the demographic collapse and biological imbalance resulting from Old World/New World interchange, and the processes behind the disintegration of traditional cultural patterns. Although her data are documentary and archaeological, Deagan is confronting issues of anthropological relevance.

We should point out how much the structure of Americanist archaeology has changed since the days of James Ford and W. W. Taylor. Women have taken archaeology by storm over the past three decades, and Deagan provides a first-rate role model for women thinking of entering archaeology as a profession. Female archaeologists still face an uphill battle in many ways (and we discuss these biases in Chapter 4). But Deagan's visibility in the academic and public arena should give pause to anybody still mistakenly viewing archaeology as a profession reserved for the good old boys in pickup trucks.

WHERE TO GO FROM HERE?

Deagan on Archaeology: "Mestizaje in Colonial St. Augustine" (1973); "Cultures in Transition: Assimilation and Fusion Among the Eastern Timucua" (1978a); "Spanish St. Augustine: America's First 'Melting Pot' " (1980); "Downtown Survey: The Discovery of 16th Century St. Augustine in an Urban Area" (1981); "Avenues of Inquiry in Historical Archaeology" (1982); *Spanish St. Augustine: The Archaeology of a Colonial Creole Community* (1983); *Artifacts of the Spanish Colonies of Florida and the Caribbean, 1500–1800. Volume 1* (1987).

Summary

The origins of archaeology can be traced to Nabonidus, the sixth-century B.C. Babylonian king who looked at the physical residues of antiquity to answer his questions about the past. Since then, archaeologists have continued (as Ciriaco put it in the thirteenth century) "to restore the dead to life." New World archaeology has been inextricably wed to the study of Native Americans, who provided endless clues for those concerned with America's more remote past. Americanist archaeology evolved in the work of scholars such as Thomas Jefferson and C. B. Moore who, though lacking formal anthropological training, applied sound principles of scientific research to problems of America's past. No longer the pastime of genteel rich males, twentieth-century Americanist archaeology has become a specialized discipline, requiring intensive training not only in techniques of excavation but also in ethnology, classification, geology, and the philosophy of science. The gradual evolution of Americanist archaeological thought has been stimulated by a few revolutionary archaeologists, most notably W. W. Taylor in the 1940s and Lewis R. Binford in the 1960s. Archaeology's "angry young men" urged their colleagues to stick by their anthropological guns, to attempt to define the processes operative behind the specifics of the archaeological record. Although once distinct, historical and prehistoric Americanist archaeology are today proceeding within the overall anthropological tradition.

CHAPTER 2

WHAT IS SCIENCE?

Scientists are Peeping Toms at the keyhole of eternity.
—Arthur Koestler

The year was 9268 B.C. The man was trying to make a **Clovis spear point**. He crouched on a flat spot at the foot of the chalk cliffs, near Rattlesnake Buttes in northeastern Colorado. "Coughing twice, rubbing his fingertips on his chest, he lifted the heavy rock and studied it for the last time." His tools had been purposefully selected. The hammerstone was ovoid and of a grainy texture: "It was the possession he prized most in his life." Carefully flaking through the **cortex**, he struck flake after flake, until the core was exhausted. "He dropped his hammerstone, threw back his head and winked at his helper: 'Good, eh.' " Then he reached for his boomerang-shaped soft hammer, fashioned of antler. Gradually, the amorphous flake was "roughed out" into the unmistakable shape of a spear point. Using the elk antler, he pressure-flaked the edges, fashioning "a scimitar-sharp edge around the entire point." Finally, he used his chest-crutch to force off a flake running half the length of the point. The fluting complete, the craftsman stood back and admired his finished Clovis point.

Once the point had been mounted on a sturdy wooden shaft, the craftsman summoned his friends to ambush a mammoth at the neighborhood waterhole. "The mammoth took one faltering step and dropped dead. Not once in a hundred times could a hunter reach a vital point with his spear; usually death was a long-drawn process of jabs in the side and chasing and bleeding, requiring two or three days. But this was a lucky blow, and the men howled with delight." So novelist James Michener described incidents in the life of a Clovis man in his best-seller *Centennial*.

Science Is Sciencing

Human reality is too important to leave to novelists.
—Henry Glassie

To Michener, the Clovis spear point is not an inanimate artifact made of gray-brown stone (see Figure 2–1). Rather, it is "the finest work of art ever produced in the Centennial region . . . a prime fact of our intellectual history." The Clovis craftsman was not a brow-ridged, apelike knuckle dragger; he was "indistinguishable from other men who would occupy this land ten thousand years later. . . . He had considerable powers of thought, could plan ahead, could devise tactics for hunting. . . . He did not take himself too seriously."

This description is imaginative to be sure but probably not too far from the mark. Though not facts, Michener's inferences are credible, given what we now understand about the archaeology of the prehistoric Clovis culture. As a literary artist, James Michener grappled with a segment of human experience and attempted to render it intelligible to others. Through his craft, he attempted to assist modern humans in adjusting to their present environment by understanding their past.

FIGURE 2–1   A Clovis spearpoint (maximum length 114.7 mm.).

Like Michener, all artists initially confront human reality and then explain that feeling to others through illustration. Specifics symbolize generalities; particulars exemplify universals. Michener wanted to convey what (he thought) it was like to be a Clovis hunter, and he did so by considering one particular hunter in 9268 B.C. at Rattlesnake Buttes, Colorado.

Strange as it might seem, scientists share the novelist's objective, to render the human experience intelligible to modern people. But scientists approach this goal from the opposite direction. To them, particulars are important only for what they transmit about the universal. Scientifically, Michener's mammoth, his Clovis point, and the prehistoric flintknapper are relevant only for what they can tell us about the Clovis culture in general. But individually, each is irrelevant.

Science strives to abstract universals from particulars, but so does religion. What distinguishes **science** from religion is the scientist's commitment to explaining things in naturalistic terms, without recourse to supernatural beings and forces. The methods of science and religion also differ. The next section deals with the methods of science in some detail, but for now, we shall assume that science is the search for the universal in nature, using the established canons of the scientific method.

A scientist is a person who practices science. The title of this section, appropriated from Leslie White's *Science of Culture* (1949), tells it all: Science is sciencing. Scientists are not people who wear white lab coats, have offices in science buildings, or subscribe to *Science* magazine. Rather, they use scientific methods to abstract universals from the world of particulars. It is that simple.

The Laws of Science: Predicting the Past

Science is what science does. That is what we have decided. Scientists systematically search for universals in nature, and these universals are called **laws**. But if archaeology is a science—and I think it is—then what are the laws of archaeology? Would any of us recognize a law if we stumbled on it?

The term *law* is itself ambiguous because, in a legal sense, laws are strictures that can be (and are) broken. Legal laws are formal prohibitions of acts that people are prone to commit anyway and can be expected to continue to commit, if on a reduced scale. For example, many cities have laws prohibiting jaywalking. The mere fact that such a law exists suggests that someone, somewhere, actually may cross a street illegally. Why else would we need the law?

By contrast, the ultimate laws of science are inviolable. Laws in nature are statements of what has been, what is, and what—we have every reason to think—will be. A scientific law is no more or less than an unabridged statement of what actually happens. The more completely that scientific laws are understood, the better they will describe actual phenomena. To imply that a law of this sort could somehow be violated is absurd.

How can anybody disobey what actually happens? John Kemeny (1959, p. 38), a distinguished philosopher of science, was right when he stated that the laws of nature do not prescribe, they describe.

But this is a tricky business, as the actual laws—or better, lawlike generalizations—in science are modified or rejected all the time by scientists. This happens because we so imperfectly understand the laws we are after. So even though the ultimate laws of nature may be inviolable, many of the lawlike generalizations that scientists talk about only poorly approximate these ultimate laws: The worse the approximation is, the less satisfactory the lawlike statement will be.

Scientific laws are appealing not just because they describe the past and present but also because they divulge the future. Laws predict events that have yet to occur. Newton's law of gravity, for example, portrays the deportment of apples that have fallen and of apples that are falling and also the behavior of all apples that will fall in the future.

Because archaeology deals mostly with past events, an obvious question naturally arises: What is it, precisely, that the archaeologist wishes to predict? Haven't archaeological events already taken place? Is there such a thing as predicting the past?

As the title of this section suggests, archaeologists can (and do) predict the events of the past. Whereas the archaeological record is composed of past events, our perception of this record is a contemporary phenomenon. The prehistoric **Folsom culture** we discuss today is not the same Folsom culture uncovered in New Mexico in 1926, even though we generalize from some of the same artifacts and features. Science as practiced in archaeology predicts events of the past, but these events are new only because they are new to us. Predicting and verifying that a massive drought occurred in 1530 B.C. is no less a scientific breakthrough than is predicting that such an event will occur at a specific time in the future.

All scientists want to synthesize the laws of nature, each specific science dealing with its own theoretical framework and subject matter. Whereas the laws of physics deal mostly with motion and those of chemistry involve molecular reactions, the laws of social science relate to actions and reactions of *Homo sapiens*. The laws of archaeology are colored by parameters unique to the inquiry into the human past. These characteristics can best be understood by example.

Two threads seem to run through the history of anthropology: Darwin's theory of natural selection and the theories describing the progressive evolution of culture. Although modern biology and physical anthropology amply support Darwinism, cultural evolutionists lag far behind. Even today, we still find anthropologists who rebel at the very notion that the human past can be explained in lawlike fashion.

Part of this discord seems terminological, as people often use the same words for different perceptions. We owe much to Marshall Sahlins and Elman Service for their simple clarification of this semantic issue. They believe that cultural evolution is most profitably viewed as a "double-faceted phenomenon."

> Any given system—a species, a culture or an individual—improves its chances for survival, progresses in the efficiency of energy capture, by increasing its adaptive

specialization. This is **specific evolution**. The obverse is directional advance or progress stage by stage, measured in absolute terms rather than by criteria relative to the degree of adaptation to particular environments . . . a man is higher than an armadillo . . . this is **general evolution**. (Sahlins and Service 1960, pp. 94–95; boldface mine)

It is true, of course that "progress" depends heavily on one's perspective. As Robert Leonard pointed out, if a philosophically inclined jellyfish were to rewrite the history of evolution, chances are that the unique capabilities of jellyfish would somehow land them near the top of the evolutionary scale. Likewise, the progress touted by the early evolutionists is heavily tainted with racist and moral overtones inherent in Western civilization's view of itself. Indeed, some cultural evolutionists argue that archaeologists should deal simply with change, relegating progress to the arena of religion.

Nevertheless, Sahlins and Service emphasize the important distinction between *cultures* and *Culture*. Specific *cultures* adapt to a unique cultural and environmental backdrop, sometimes evolving toward increasing specialization and at other times remaining relatively unvarying for thousands of years. But *Culture*—the cumulative, worldwide, nonbiological body of wisdom—is viewed by many archaeologists as evolving from heterogeneity toward homogeneity, particularly as more technologically advanced groups expand globally at the expense of less stalwart cultures. Others prefer to scale *Culture* in terms of absolute magnitude and internal complexity.

With these two types of evolution in mind (global culture and specific cultures), let us scan a particular anthropological law that Sahlins and Service termed the **law of evolutionary potential**: "The more specialized and adapted a form in a given evolutionary stage, the smaller its potential for passing to the next stage. Another way of putting it . . . is: Specific evolutionary progress is inversely related to general evolutionary potential" (1960, p. 97). Sahlins and Service proposed that groups with more generalized adaptations have a greater evolutionary potential (more options for change) than do groups with a highly specific adaptation. The archaeological record abounds with examples of this law, often disguised as the ubiquitous "northern barbarian" invasion. For example, Mexican prehistory is repeatedly punctuated by raiders from the north—the so-called Chichimecs—who time after time overwhelmed the established state. Moving from their homeland on the frontiers of northern Mexico, the Toltecs moved south to found Tula, the city-state that ruled after the fall of classic **Teotihuacán**. Tula later suffered the same fate as Teotihuacán, namely, destruction at the hands of another tribal group. Similar conquests characterize much of human history, such as the relationship of ancient Rome to Greece and the rise of modern China. These case histories have a common denominator in that, all else being equal, the most rapid evolutionary acceleration occurs among the have-nots, not within the establishment. Agriculture did not arise (as we shall see in Chapter 15) among the hunter-gatherer groups in ecologically favored areas but, rather, in areas of stress and competition. Plant domestication appeared initially among those in need, not among people deeply immersed in some stable, yet conservative, productive network.

The law of evolutionary potential—and this is true of any cultural law—is neither purely anthropological nor purely archaeological: It is a mixture of both. As archaeological data are progressively incorporated into general anthropological theory, rigid lines continue to blur, and such laws become amalgamated with the laws of humanity.

Generalizations stated in lawlike fashion will usually be probabilistic in nature. The Sahlins–Service law is one of potential, not strict determinism. Archaeological laws cannot be expected to be exact, for such statements project incompletely understood phenomena. We are dealing only with successive approximations to the laws of nature and can hope only that such predictions will be correct most of the time, at least until we can specify more closely the conditions under which the phenomena will always occur.

All real-world experiments, especially the archaeological ones, are also subject to the errors of observation and interpretation. Although archaeologists have a stalwart method for handling errors—the theory of statistics and probability—we can never be 100 percent sure of our facts. Any given experiment may seem to confirm a theory, but we can never be absolutely positive that this outcome is not in error. Because the laws of nature are always incompletely known and experiments are always subject to error, archaeological-anthropological laws remain statistical, often couched in mediating terms such as "potential," "most likely outcome," "will usually," and "most frequently." Remember that we are not assuming that phenomena are uncertain; we presume that our statement about the phenomena contains the uncertainty.

Stated another way, laws in archaeology are timeless and spaceless generalizations regarding how cultural processes work. In truth, archaeologists spend much of their time working at a considerably "lower" level, using universal principles in more local, situation-specific explanations. But regardless of which level archaeologists happen to be operating on at the time, they remain "scientists" because they advocate and adhere to established, explicit, repeatable methods. Finding the laws of culture is thus the ultimate goal of most archaeologists (even if relatively few such universal principles have been uncovered). At this point, let us forgo considering what laws actually are to see how those laws are found.

How Science Explains Things: The Maize Maze

Aristotle could have avoided the mistake of thinking that women have fewer teeth than men by the simple device of asking Mrs. Aristotle to open her mouth.
—Bertrand Russell

It seems odd, but science in archaeology is better done than discussed. Archaeologists have been performing some pretty fair science, but only recently have they begun discussing their science in any detail. Consider, for example, how scientific methods were used to look for the origins of plant domestication in the Americas. In 1948, Herbert Dick (then a graduate student at Harvard) excavated a site in southwestern New Mexico named Bat Cave. The site yielded the typical prehistoric material culture from that area—projectile points, pottery vessels, shell beads, basketry, sandals, and so forth—and it also served up an unexpectedly primitive form of corn.

Enter Scotty MacNeish

Radiocarbon tests revealed that these stubby little corncobs were between four thousand and five thousand years old—the oldest and most primitive corn yet discovered. Later that same year, another archaeologist, **Richard "Scotty" MacNeish**, discovered similar specimens in the caves of Tamaulipas, not far below the Mexican border. Over the next few years, additional northern Mexican excavations recovered no corn older than about five thousand years (see Figure 2–2). Searching for more ancient evidence of plant domestication, Scotty MacNeish traveled far to the south, into Guatemala and Honduras. Although he found no ancient corncobs, he did stumble on fossil corn pollen in strata also dating about 3000 B.C.

Given these baseline data, MacNeish contemplated his next move. Corn was apparently no older than 3000 B.C. in either the United States or in Guatemala (well to the south of Mexico City). Scotty reasoned that if any older corn existed, it should be found somewhere between the two areas, probably in southern Mexico. This preliminary assumption was supported by intensive genetic studies conducted by MacNeish's colleague, Paul Mangelsdorf, indicating that corn had probably been domesticated from a

FIGURE 2–2 Richard "Scotty" MacNeish digging at the North Mesa site, near Las Cruces, New Mexico. (Courtesy Richard S. MacNeish)

highland grass. Putting these two pieces together, MacNeish decided that the best place to look for early domestication was in the uplands of southern Mexico.

To test his speculative theory, MacNeish made some specific predictions that could be tested in the field. Studying maps of southern Mexico, he narrowed his search to a couple of prime targets. He first explored Oaxaca, which was quickly rejected: no early corn to be found there. MacNeish then turned to his second choice, the Tehuacán Valley of Puebla State, Mexico. Because corncobs generally survive best in deposits protected from moisture, he looked inside dry caves and overhangs. After personally delving into thirty-eight such caves, MacNeish tested Coxcatlán Cave, which had preserved six petite corncobs more primitive than any previously discovered. Subsequent radiocarbon assay placed their antiquity at about 5600 years, a full 500 years older than any other corn yet discovered.

These finds bolstered MacNeish's theory about the origins of corn in southern Mexico and also fostered an understanding of the processes that condition our early relationships to domesticated plants and animals.

The Scientific Cycle in Action

Beyond his contributions to our knowledge of maize domestication, one can isolate in MacNeish's investigation the three essential components of scientific methods as applied to archaeology:

1. Establish the hypothesis.
2. Determine the test implications of that hypothesis.
3. Evaluate these implications by further examination.

Although MacNeish used other terms, in actual practice he followed this scheme rather closely. Such procedures characterized much archaeological research over the past century. Only during the last couple of decades have archaeologists begun to talk about these methods in any detail.

The first step is to frame a hypothesis—a pronouncement designed to transcend the description of known facts. To understand how hypotheses are derived, let us represent "known facts" as simple points drawn on a graph. Hypothesis formation is the process of drawing a single line to describe these points. There are, of course, an infinite number of hypotheses (lines) that can be drawn to account for the facts (the data points). The scientist must first examine the possible theories and select the most likely, that is, the most probable, for actual testing. On the graph, the most credible lines pass through every point, and plenty of such curves could be drawn. Most people feel that if the points tend to fall in linear fashion, then a straight line will form the simplest hypothesis to describe the known data.

Such hypotheses are generated through **induction**, an inductive argument being one in which the conclusions contain more information than the premises do. The facts as known serve as premises in this case, as the resulting hypothesis not only accounts for these known facts but also predicts properties of unobserved phenomena. There are no rules for induction (any more than there are rules for thinking up good ideas). Some hypotheses are derived by enumerating the data, isolating common features, and generalizing to unobserved data that share these common properties. At other times, archaeologists turn to analogies, relatively well understood circumstances that seem to have relevance to poorly understood cases. But equally common is the simple application of good sense. Acumen, imagination, past experience, and guesswork all have their place in science. It does not matter where or how one derives the hypothesis. What matters is how well the hypothesis accounts for unobserved phenomena.

It is, of course, entirely possible that several hypotheses will apply to the same data, just as several lines can be drawn through the points on a graph. In practice, scientists generally work their way systematically through the various possibilities, testing them one at a time. This method of *multiple working hypotheses* has long been a feature of scientific methods (Chamberlin 1890). To distinguish among the various options, most scientists believe that the simplest hypothesis will tend to be correct. Thus they begin with the simplest hypothesis and see how well it holds up against some new data. If it fails the test, they then will try the next least complicated hypothesis, and so on (see Figure 2–3).

Remember MacNeish's hypothesis about plant domestication? He began his research with a careful assessment of the known facts—the finds at Bat Cave and Tamaulipas, the reconnaissance in Guatemala and Honduras, and the available genetic information. These were, in a sense, his graph points to be accounted for. MacNeish could have come up with any number of hypotheses to explain these facts: Corn could have been domesticated simultaneously all over Mesoamerica in 3000 B.C.; corn could have been domesticated independently in both the north and the south at the same time (3000 B.C.); corn was not domesticated in Mesoamerica at all but, rather, traded from somewhere else, such as South America or even Mesopotamia. These are just a few of the infinite number of possible hypotheses that could be cited to explain the archaeological facts. By choosing the hypothesis he did, MacNeish was selecting the simplest of the available possibilities. But regardless of which hypothesis is initially selected, none is accepted until it survives further, independent observations. Mere induction does not lead to scientific acceptance.

Once the hypotheses are defined, the scientific method requires their translation into testable form. Hypotheses can never be tested directly because they are general statements, and one can test only specifics. "The key to the verification of hypotheses is that you never verify them. What you verify are the logical consequences" (Kemeny 1959, p. 96).

In the classical **hypotheticodeductive** procedure, deductive reasoning is required to uncover these logical outcomes. **Deductive** arguments are those in which the conclusions must be true, given that the premises are true. Such deductive arguments generally take the form of "if . . . then" statements: *If* the hypothesis is true, *then* we will expect to observe the following logical outcomes. Bridging the gap from *if* to *then* is a tricky step.

In the "harder" sciences, these bridging arguments derive directly from known mathematical or physical properties. In astronomy, for instance, the position of "unknown" stars can be predicted using a long chain of mathematical arguments grounded in Newtonian physics. The classic deductive method begins with an untested hypothesis and

FIGURE 2–3 Initial excavations at Coxcatlán Cave in the Tehuacán Valley, Mexico (see MacNeish 1967, Figure 188). (Courtesy Richard S. MacNeish and the University of Texas Press)

converts the generalities into specific predictions based on established mathematical and/or physical theory (the **bridging arguments**).

But how do archaeologists bridge this gap? Where is the "well-established body of theory" that allows us to transform abstract hypotheses into observable predictions?

When MacNeish translated his general hypothesis into testable propositions, he was assuming that several bridging arguments existed (although these assumptions were not explicit). Experience told MacNeish that unburned corncobs can be preserved for millennia in an arid cave environment but rapidly decompose when exposed to moisture. So, MacNeish figured, we should concentrate the search on dry caves and skip the **alluvial** riverbanks. Reasoning like this provided a "bridge" between the logical expectations and the archaeological record. Similarly, the geneticists surmised that maize had been domesticated as a highland grass; accordingly, MacNeish decided to confine his search

James Deetz on Scientific Humanism and Humanistic Science

Throughout these pages, I have taken a relatively "hard" view of science in archaeology. This perspective, shared to a certain extent by most prehistoric archaeologists, draws on the established canons of scientific procedures as a guide to understanding the human past.

But Americanist archaeology is not today a strictly scientific endeavor. Several contemporary archaeologists are increasingly drawn toward "softer" (less scientific, more humanistic) research methods. Subsequent chapters (particularly Chapters 3, 14, and 15) contain several examples employing this humanistic posture, and as a partial counterpoint to my own "scientific" slant, it is useful to consider the appeal of James Deetz for a more humanistic approach to the archaeological record, particularly that from historic-period sites.

> It should come as no surprise that historical archaeology today suffers from a split personality. Unlike prehistoric archaeology, the archaeological study of the historic period in America is done by historians as well as anthropologists. Each discipline, bringing its own methods to bear on the same data as the other, claims its approach to be the right and proper one. Historians, called particularistic by scientific archaeologists, in turn express concern that the many-splendored aspects of humankind cannot be reduced to predictability without doing violence to the complexities of the human experience, dehumanizing it and reducing it to columns and rows of numbers that become an end unto themselves. . . .
>
> On the one hand, we encounter the view, in its most extreme form that archaeology is but a handmaiden to history, and that events unique in

By permission of J. Deetz and *Geoscience and Man*. Reprinted by permission of the Smithsonian Institution Press from "Material Culture and World View in Colonial Anglo-America" by James Deetz in *The Recovery of Meaning: Historical Archaeology in the Eastern United States* by Mark Leone and Parker Potter, editors. © 1988 Smithsonian Institution, Washington, D.C.

> place and time have their material correlates that must be explained in terms of the same unique circumstances. At the opposite extreme is the position that all human behavior is ultimately understandable in the manner in which it is an expression of laws much akin to those formulated by physical scientists. To discover these laws we are told that we must be ever sensitive to the existence of pattern in the artifactual data and use the recurrence of this pattern from case to case to drive deeper to the underlying cause of its expression. Pattern recognition, of course, is dependent on quantification, so we must count.
>
> Mediating between these opposed positions is by no means easy, but each in its own way seems to have a certain deficiency, if not in principle, in practice. I truly am not under the impression that the course I have chosen to steer between these two poles is precisely the correct one. It may well lead to shipwreck on either set of shoals, or worse, rudderless drifting on a sea of idle speculation. Yet the shortcomings in the other courses seem serious enough to require attention. (Deetz 1983, p. 27)
>
> . . . In the last analysis, the study of material culture holds great promise, and happily is young enough to accommodate a diversity of approaches. The particularism of those who labor long and hard to relate objects to individuals and to instill an honest respect for the complexities of the archaeological record, the scientific archaeologists who rightly insist on the importance of controlled quantification, and the humanists who know that numbers can at times burden the soul—all have their place in our collective efforts. I hope that historians will be tolerant of our beginning efforts, although we are sometimes pompous, sometimes wildly off the mark, and all too often dull and pedantic, for the stakes are high, and from these efforts will emerge a more human, democratic view of the American experience. To know where we have been may not only help us in where we are bound, but to know where *all* of us have truly been cannot be a bad thing to know. (Deetz 1988, p. 232).

to the highlands. Here is another bridge into the archaeological record, based this time on genetic theory.

In truth, modern archaeology is almost bereft of explicit theory. The bridging arguments necessary for determining the logical outcomes of hypotheses are generally seat-of-the-pants statements, and archaeological inference is hampered by this lack of precision. Today, the development of **middle-range research** is a significant direction, and Chapter 5 discusses these developments in detail. We should add, somewhat parenthetically, that test implications can also be derived through induction, based on known prior probabilities of the various hypotheses (Salmon 1976, p. 378). But for now, we shall keep things simple and consider only the deductive case.

The final operation in the scientific cycle is actually to test the implications. For MacNeish, this step required additional reconnaissance in archaeologically unknown regions of southern Mexico. These new data were evaluated, and had his projections not been verified, his hypothesis would have been rejected. As it turned out, excavations in the Tehuacán Valley failed to reject MacNeish's particularistic hypotheses. Hence, MacNeish's preliminary notions on plant domestication survived an empirical test.

No such simple experiment can ever completely validate any hypothesis, and more intensive inquiry is generally required to increase credibility. Scientific methods are not really designed to prove anything; instead, the idea is more to eliminate the untenable hypotheses. MacNeish's work at Tehuacán generated new data, ready for synthesis into new, more refined hypotheses (which in turn had to be tested as before). Scientific progress actually requires a pyramiding of verified hypotheses into a hierarchy of more generalized laws.

The process that we sketched is commonly called the *scientific method*. But I prefer the more accurate designation the *scientific cycle* because it emphasizes the reiterative, repetitive nature of the inquiry (see Figure 2–4). Cycle 1 begins in the world of facts. Through the process of induction, these facts are probed, and hypotheses are invented to account for what is already known. But because hypotheses are general declarations, they cannot be tested against further facts until they are translated into their logical consequences, through the judicious use of bridging arguments. The final step reverts to the world of facts during the process of verification.

The scientific cycle thus begins and ends with facts. But these new facts themselves will suggest new hypotheses, and once again, the inductive reasoning will lead from the world of facts to the world of abstraction, thereby initiating a new cycle of investigation. As a method, science implies a continuing upward spiral in knowledge.

WHERE TO GO FROM HERE?

Some Approaches to Scientific Methods in Americanist Archaeology: Patty Jo Watson's (1986) thoughtful synthesis analyzes the state of archaeological interpetation in Americanist archaeology. Merrilee Salmon's *Philosophy and Archaeology* (1982) is a relatively painless overview on the subject (see also Salmon and Salmon 1979). M. Salmon has also published several important papers, especially "Confirmation and Explanation in

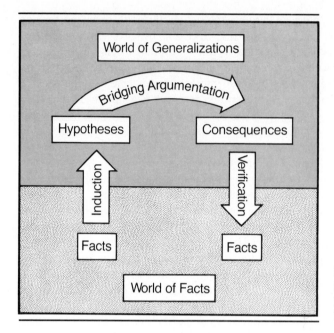

FIGURE 2–4   The scientific cycle (see Kemeny 1959, p. 86). (Courtesy Van Nostrand Reinhold Company)

Archaeology" (1975) and " 'Deductive' Versus 'Inductive' Archaeology" (1976). In one interesting interchange, Bayard (1969) denounced the new archaeology for its lack of precise categories, arguing that archaeology is a discipline, not a science, and challenged somebody to come up with a "law"; Carneiro (1970a) responded to the challenge. Other useful treatments include Bamforth and Spaulding (1982), Binford (1977), Clarke (1968, 1972), Dunnell (1982a), Flannery (1973a), Fritz and Plog (1970), S. J. Gould (1980), Gould and Watson (1982), Grayson (1986), Raab and Goodyear (1984), Schiffer (1976, esp. Chapter 2), South (1977a, esp. Chapters 1, 2, and 8), Spaulding (1968), Thomas (1986), R. A. Watson (1976a, 1976b), Watson, LeBlanc, and Redman (1971, 1984).

Early Plant Domestication in the New World: Barbara Stark (1986) presents an important overview; see also Asch and Asch (1985), Beadle (1977), Bender (1975, 1985), Braun and Plog (1982), Flannery (1973b, 1986), Green (1980), MacNeish (1964, 1978, esp. Chapter 5), Mangelsdorf (1974), Roosevelt (1984a, 1984b), Wright (1977). Chapter 15 also presents a more extensive discussion of this topic.

Heinrich Schliemann
and the New Siege of Troy

Unfortunately, some archaeologists think that scientific methods are new, even revolutionary in archaeology. This is mistaken. Science in archaeology cannot be equated with "contemporary," "modernistic," or "hi-tech." The scientific cycle has been an important, if implicit, method of inquiry in archaeology for a long time. In the following section, we shall see how such systematic thinking was used more than a century ago to locate the lost city of Troy.

In 1875, **Heinrich Schliemann** captured the imagination of the world by announcing that he had discovered Troy, the fabled city in Homer's *Iliad*. Dispelling two millennia of doubt, Schliemann announced that not only had Homer been a marvelous epic poet—which everyone already knew—but also that he had been a reliably accurate historian. Schliemann's claim has since been subjected to a century of scientific scrutiny, and most contemporary archaeologists believe that he was correct. Schliemann really did find ancient Troy.

And yet Heinrich Schliemann remains an enigma in archaeology. Biographers and psychologists see a strong element of neurotic compulsion in Schliemann's work at Troy, an almost feverish drive to vindicate Homer's *Iliad*. The Turkish officials who administered his excavations considered him a swindler and a scoundrel. Greek officials distrusted him, and nineteenth-century academics throughout the world accused him of shoddy scholarship. Frank Calvert, the American vice-consul at the Dardanelles, who owned much of Troy, accused Schliemann of fakery and denied him further access to the site. In his brief yet colorful career, Schliemann earned a remarkable assortment of epithets: egotist, hypochondriac, megalomaniac, dilettante, gold seeker, privateer, and treasure hunter of the lowest order.

But Schliemann earned one other title: father of modern archaeology. Despite his mercurial manner and a compulsion to overstate his theories, Schliemann's historic work at Troy truly established the scientific protocols now standard at thousands of contemporary archaeological excavations.

We shall next examine the Trojan excavations in some detail, because they illustrate how scientific methods actually work in archaeology. Although archaeologists are becoming more explicit about their use of scientific explanations, the basics have been with us for a long while. In fact, we can see every element of proper scientific investigation in Schliemann's Trojan excavation of the 1870s.

Homer Was Putting Us On, Right?

The confusion began with **Homer**, considered the world's first and perhaps greatest poet. Homer was born shortly before 850 B.C. (although some suggest as early as the tenth or eleventh centuries B.C.). Although many of the works traditionally ascribed to Homer have been lost, surviving are his two famous epics, the *Iliad* and the *Odyssey,* some thirty hymns, and some scattered short pieces. Was Homer a real person or a composite of several anonymous epic poets? We will probably never know.

But we do think there was a real **Trojan war**. It took place sometime during the twelfth century B.C., when Troy was an affluent regional capital. It was located just east of the Aegean Sea near the Dardanelles, facing the tiny island of Tenedos. The Trojan horizon was defined on one side by Samothrake, a lofty snow-capped peak from which, according to Homer, Poseidon watched the epic siege of Troy. So magnificent were the towers and walls of the citadel that Greek tradition ascribed their construction directly to the hands of Poseidon and Apollo. On the summit of the Acropolis stood the palace of King Priam, and nearby were those of Hector and Paris. A single road led from the Trojan plain through the Scaean Gate into the heart of Troy.

The Greeks invaded Troy to recover Helen, wife of the Spartan king Menelaus. It seems that Paris, son of King Priam, had carried Helen off to Troy. It happened like this: Peleus and Thetis were getting married, and Eris—the only goddess not invited to the ceremony—was angry, and so she flung a golden apple among the wedding guests. On the apple was inscribed "For the Fairest." This of course caused a furor among the vain goddesses. They finally referred the decision to young Paris, as to which of them was truly the fairest. He decided in favor of Aphrodite, thereby securing Helen for his own. In so doing, however, he also secured the enduring wrath of the slighted Greek goddesses. It was then that Agamemnon pledged to avenge the Trojan insult. He first assembled the greatest Greek heroes—Achilles, Patroclus, the two Ajaxes, Nestor, Odysseus, and Diomedes—and then sailed to Troy with 100,000 men in 1186 ships.

The siege began when the Trojans refused to return Helen, and tradition tells us that the Greeks held Troy under siege for a decade. The blockade was finally broken by Greek treachery: The Greeks retreated, leaving only a giant wooden horse, which the Trojans triumphantly hauled inside their walled city. The wooden horse was, of course, packed with Greek soldiers who, once inside the walls, opened the gate to let in more Greek soldiers, and they all proceeded to sack and incinerate a defenseless Troy.

Homer's *Iliad*, a chronicle of the siege, has become a landmark in classic literature, and scholars have speculated for millennia about the location of the Trojan fortress. Ancient Greek tradition suggested that the ruin at **Hissarlik** was the actual site of Troy. The classical Greeks believed that Hissarlik had been periodically reoccupied, burying all traces of Troy beneath dense layers of later debris.

Demetrios and Strabo Look Askance

The Greek historian Demetrios, who was born about 190 B.C., questioned this prevailing theory. Homer had described Troy's setting in some detail: "As often as [Agamemnon] looked towards the Trojan plain [from the Greek camp], he wondered at the many fires which were burning before [Troy], the sound of flutes and pipes, and the tumult of men" (10.10–13). [Note: This quotation, and all the others from the *Iliad* are taken from Buckley (1873).]

The ruin at Hissarlik fronted a large plain, to be sure, but Demetrios felt that the modern Scamander Plain had been a bay during Trojan times, gradually filled in a successive buildup of post-Trojan alluvial (flood) deposition. Only recently had this large bay become so badly silted in that it became a low, rolling plain. Demetrios thought it impossible for the Greeks to have landed on the Aegean shore and then to have crossed the Scamander Plain to do battle at Hissarlik. The modern shore had been submerged in Trojan times (Figure 2–5).

Demetrios saw a second problem with Hissarlik. In book 22 of the *Iliad*, Homer described the final day of fighting at Troy. With Troy under siege, the Trojan warriors

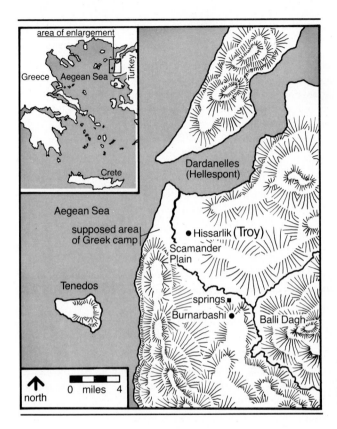

FIGURE 2–5 Map showing the location of Hissarlik (see McDonald 1967). (Courtesy the Macmillan Company)

were confined behind the locked walls of the city. Only Hector, son of the Trojan leader Priam, remained outside to meet the feared Greek warrior Achilles. "Thus [Hector] pondered, remaining; but near him came Achilles, like unto the helmet-shaking warrior, Mars, brandishing upon his right shoulder the dreadful Pelian ash; but the brass shone around, like unto the splendor either of a flaming fire, or of the rising sun" (22.132–136). Yet for all his good intentions and bravery, Hector finally fled before the awesome Achilles: "Then, as tremor seized Hector, he perceived him, nor could he remain there any longer, but he left the gates behind him, and fled affrighted. . . . Hector fled in terror under the wall of the Trojans, and moved his fleet limbs. . . . A brave man, indeed, fled before, but a much braver swiftly pursued him" (22. 132–159).

The Trojans watched helplessly as Achilles chased Hector about their besieged capital. "And as when prize-winning solid-hoofed steeds run very swiftly round the course, and a great reward is proposed . . . so they thrice made the circuit of the city of [Troy] and all the Gods beheld" (22.162–167). Face to face, they crossed swords. "There noble Achilles, eager, drove into him with the spear and the point went quite through his tender neck" (22.326–328). As Hector fell, the Greeks ran forth and "admired the stature and wondrous form of Hector; nor did any stand by without inflicting a wound" (22.370–371). Achilles then

> perforated the tendons of both his feet behind, from the heel to the instep, and fastened them in leather thongs, and bound him from the chariot; but left his head to be trailed behind. Then ascending his chariot, and taking up the splendid armour, he lashed [the horses] to go on, and they, not unwillingly, flew. But the dust arose from them while trailing along, and [Hector's] azure locks around approached [the ground], and his entire head, once graceful, lay in the dust. (22.395–404)

Thus ended the life of noble Hector, dragged into the sunset, head bobbing, from behind the chariot of Achilles. Thus also ends the *Iliad*.

As a steadfast Greek historian, Demetrios refused to believe that Homer would have fabricated such a critical moment. Particularly crucial is the assertion that Achilles pursued Hector thrice about the city of Troy. Demetrios apparently traveled to Hissarlik and personally judged the topography to be unsuitable for such a chase. Demetrios thus rejected Hissarlik as ancient Troy on two grounds: Achilles could not have chased Hector around Hissarlik three times, and the modern Plain of Scamander had been a deep-water bay during Trojan times. Demetrios's conclusion was endorsed two centuries later by the influential Greek historian Strabo.

The ruins of Hissarlik in disrepute, Greek scholars soon began to question the historical veracity of Homer's epics. Is the *Iliad* fact or poetic fiction? Through the next fifteen centuries following Demetrios's evaluation, Greek scholars increasingly suspected that Troy was merely a convenient myth, created for poetic effect. Skepticism during the eighteenth and early nineteenth centuries grew until few scholars accepted the reality of Troy, the Trojan War, and even Homer himself.

Those few nineteenth century enthusiasts who still believed in Troy were divided on the precise location. Most distinguished scholars and travelers of the day—those, that is, who believed in Troy at all—favored a small ruin on the summit of Balli Dagh, near the town of **Burnarbashi**. Although the ruins at Burnarbashi were unpretentious, these scholars felt that Homer had, through poetic license, transformed a nondescript mountain community into the royal city of Troy. The palaces of Priam and Hector, the magnificent Scaean Gate, and the fabled Trojan wealth were seen as concoctions of Homer's poetic mind. The facts of Troy seemed considerably less impressive.

The Burnarbashi theory gained considerable support in 1802 when the French scholar Le Chevalier discovered two freshwater springs near the base of the Burnarbashi ruins. Homer had written:

> Under the wall along the public way . . . two springs of the eddying Scamander rise. The one, indeed, flows with tepid water, and a steam arises from it around, as of burning fire; whilst the other flows forth in the summer time, like unto hail, or cold snow, or ice from water. There, at them, are the wide, handsome stone basins, where the wives and fair daughters of the Trojans used to wash their splendid garments formerly in time of peace, before the sons of the Greeks arrived. (22.146–155)

Le Chevalier reported that both hot and cold springs issue forth near the base of the Burnarbashi ruins. Because springs were unknown near Hissarlik, many influential nineteenth-century savants—Moltke, Welcker, Kiepert, and Curtius—announced their support of Burnarbashi as the true site of Homer's Troy.

Such was the situation when Heinrich Schliemann first tackled the problem of locating Troy. As a boy, Schliemann's father had read to him of the Trojan War, and the ancient heroes captivated Schliemann from the start. He eventually taught himself ancient Greek so that he might enjoy Homer in the original. The more he read, the more he came to believe that Troy, the Trojan War, and the episodes chronicled by Homer must be true in every detail. But what had become of Troy? Surely it was too breathtaking, too monumental simply to have evaporated.

Schliemann began his quest for Troy in 1860, and in his search we can trace the development of scientific methods of archaeology. Next I shall recount the excavations of Schliemann in the idiom of modern science, not because Schliemann thought in these terms (for surely he did not), but, rather, to emphasize the logical structure of his explorations, which mirror today's scientific guidelines almost to the letter.

Heinrich Schliemann and the Scientific Cycle

Although scientific methods are designed to uncover general, universal, lawlike statements, archaeologists use these same procedural principles in their everyday, location-specific research as well. Remember that the scientific cycle begins with hypothesis formation, inducing a tentative conclusion sufficient to account for the known, specific facts. At this stage, there are no rules; induction is the province of the genius, of the creative mind. In the search for Troy, the inductive process evolved over two thousand years. Three hypotheses had come to dominate mid-nineteenth-century scholarship:

Hypothesis A: Burnarbashi is the authentic ruin of Troy.
Hypothesis B: Hissarlik is the authentic ruin of Troy.
Hypothesis C: There is no authentic ruin of Troy because the *Iliad* is poetic fiction.

Keep in mind that the scientific method is not designed to prove anything; it only eliminates untenable hypotheses.

Hypotheses A and B can be tested outright; that is, the sites of Burnarbashi and Hissarlik can be physically scrutinized for Trojan ruins. The third hypothesis—that Troy never existed—cannot be tested because no observations can ever verify or disprove this theory. Hypothesis C thus becomes attractive only after all the other possibilities become untenable on the basis of the data at hand.

The second step of the scientific cycle deduces explicit and testable outcomes from each alternative hypothesis. Such outcomes are commonly stated as "if . . . then" statements: *If* Burnarbashi is the true site of Troy, *then* we should find. . . . *If* Hissarlik is the true site of Troy, *then* we should find. . . . Each declaration is followed by a series of logical outcomes, test implications to be verified or rejected by independent physical evidence.

Here we have multiple working hypotheses. The first hypothesis (Burnarbashi) has precisely the same logical consequences as does the second hypothesis (Hissarlik), because all the hypotheses derive from a single source, Homer's *Iliad*. The site conforming best to these outcomes should be the actual location of Troy. If neither site conforms, then Hypothesis C will become more tenable; maybe Troy is poetic fiction after all. It is, of course, also possible that a third (unknown) site is really Troy; in this case, all three hypotheses would be incorrect. This is why scientists never really prove anything.

Schliemann worked out in great detail the test implications for ancient Troy from specific passages in the *Iliad*. We can summarize Schliemann's expectations for ancient Troy in the following eight propositions:

I.   *Troy was a spacious, opulent city.* Schliemann expected to encounter this wealth in the form of precious metals. (This is why he was so often accused of treasure hunting.)

II.   *Troy should provide ample evidence of imposing temples and other royal architecture.* "But when now [Hector] had arrived at the very beautiful dwelling of Priam, built with well-polished porticoes; but in it were fifty chambers of polished marble, built near one another, where lay the sons of Priam with their lawful wives" (6.244–248). "The most skilful artificers in fruitful Troy . . . made for him a chamber, a dwelling-room, and a hall, in the lofty citadel, near the palaces of Priam and Hector" (6.316–318).

III.   *The Trojan citadel must be surrounded by substantial fortifications.* Homer wrote that so extraordinary were these ramparts that their construction was ascribed not to mortals but, rather, to the deities Neptune and Apollo. "Neptune, the earth-shaker, thus began to speak. . . . The fame of [Troy] will certainly be wherever light is diffused: but they will forget that [wall] which I and Phoebus Apollo, toiling, built round the city" (7.445–455).

IV.   *It must have been possible for Achilles to chase Hector thrice around the city* (22.163-167).

V.   *Troy had two springs—one hot, one cold—located near the former Scaean Gate, the only exit from the city.*

VI.   *Troy was located near the Aegean Sea.* In Book 7, Homer observed that each night after battle, the Trojans returned to Troy, the Greeks to their seaside camp. Messengers were said to be able to leave the city at sunset, travel to the Greek ships, and easily return before sunrise.

VII.   *Troy was erected on a lengthy plain, site of the former Trojan battlefield.* Nearby was the island of Tenedos, and the plain itself was bounded by Mt. Samothrake and Mt. Ida. "Cloud-compelling Jove indeed first begat Dardanus. And he built Dardania, for sacred [Troy], the city of the articulate-speaking men, was not as yet built on the plain, and they still dwelt at the foot of the many-rilled Ida" (20.215–218). "King Neptune . . . sat aloft upon the highest summit of the woody Thracian Samos, admiring the [Trojan] war and the battle. Far from thence all Ida was visible, and the city of Priam [Troy] was visible, and the ships of the Greeks" (13.10–14).

VIII.   *The Scamander River (and tributaries) must flow between Troy and the Aegean coast.* "But when [Hera and Athena] reached Troy, and the two flowing rivers, where Simois and Scamander unite their streams . . ." (5.773–775). Several other passages imply that the Scamander, chief river of the area, flowed from its origin on Mt. Ida between Troy and the Greek camp.

In effect, these hypotheses rested largely on two criteria: (1) the actual ruins of the Trojan citadel (Implications I–III) and (2) the precise topographic setting surrounding the ruins (Implications IV–VIII). The final step in the scientific cycle is verification— bringing new evidence to bear upon the test implications—not necessarily pronouncing one hypothesis correct but, rather, rendering competing hypotheses untenable. In the search for Troy, such independent facts must derive from physical proof: Homeric poetry nurtured the hypotheses, not the data against which to test these ideas.

Schliemann journeyed to Turkey in 1868 to examine firsthand the various ruins and to look over the Trojan landscape. Arriving at the village of Burnarbashi, he climbed to the summit of Balli Dagh, where so many scholars placed the ancient ruins of Troy. He also visited Hissarlik, a one-hundred-foot-high ruin rising above the Scamander Plain. From the outset, he agreed with the ancient Greeks that Hissarlik must indeed be the Trojan ruin. His initial, gut-level hunches arose not from hard scientific evidence but from his intuitive grasp of the situation. Such insights are reserved for the finest fieldworkers of any generation. Good intuition cannot be taught.

Schliemann was hardly the first to visit the Scamander Plain searching for Troy. Many other scholars had carried their dog-eared copies of Homer through Turkey trying to read clues from the landscape. Sixty-five years before, Le Chevalier had located the springs of Burnarbashi, evidence that tipped the balance against Hissarlik.

What set Schliemann apart from earlier travelers was his demand for a more intensive review than merely touring the countryside. Schliemann visited Turkey to uncover the bona fide physical remains of Troy. He wanted to walk through the Scaean Gate, to exhume the palace of Priam, to discover where Achilles had slain Hector. Schliemann was enamored with Trojan lore, and Homer's descriptions were not enough. Schliemann was determined to locate these historic scenes and physically possess the genuine swords, pottery, and gold that had been Homeric Troy. He was a romantic, to be sure. But Schliemann's step-by-step, methodical guidelines propelled him far beyond his contemporaries, to establish the modern canons of scientific thinking in archaeology.

Most mid-nineteenth-century scholars considered it sufficient to read the ancient sources, ponder the critical passages, and perhaps even meander around the region to nurture a feel for the land. This done, they felt free to pontificate on one theory or another. In more contemporary terms, academic investigators of the mid-nineteenth century viewed hypothesis testing—induction, bridging argumentation, and verification—in only the most slipshod fashion.

What is notable about Schliemann was his insistence on verification. Not content simply to amble across some ancient ruins, he intended to excavate these ruins systemati- cally. He planned to catalogue all finds according to stratum and to draw and map the temple ruins as they were unearthed. Photographers would document his excavations to provide proof to a skeptical world.

Schliemann is the progenitor of modern archaeological methods because of his hardheaded appreciation of real data. He elevated the research of the past from speculative fancy to the realm of solid fact. Schliemann felt one could not—and should not—argue theories without finding the physical proof.

Schliemann began digging at Burnarbashi. Although personally favoring Hissarlik, he felt obliged to address the Burnarbashi theory first. After scrutinizing the mountainous landscape, Schliemann undertook limited excavations at Burnarbashi in 1868 and 1871. These results, published by Schliemann in *Troy and Its Remains* (1875), can be summarized according to the preceding eight test implications.

Troy must have been a spacious and complex citadel, with tremendous wealth (Implication I) and massive temples and public architecture (Implication II) and surrounded by intimidating fortification walls (Implications III and IV). But Schliemann's excavations at Burnarbashi proved it to be lacking in every respect. The excavations revealed the modest debris of a casual circuit wall. The village debris was thin, implying only a short-term occupation, probably by just a few inhabitants. And the chronology was wrong. Most of the site dated from 400 to 500 B.C., at least six hundred years too late for ancient Troy. These data hinted that Burnarbashi was merely a minor, short-term fortress, the kind common throughout this region. No stretch of Schliemann's mind could escalate the paltry ruins of Burnarbashi into the Trojan palaces and temples extolled by Homer.

Then Schliemann turned to Implication V, the springs found in 1802: "[Burnarbashi] had been almost universally considered to be the site of the Homeric [Troy]; the springs at the bottom of that village having been regarded as the two springs mentioned by Homer, one of which sent forth warm, the other cold water. But, instead of two springs, I found thirty-four . . . moreover, I found in all the springs a uniform temperature of . . . 62.6 [degrees] Fahrenheit" (Schliemann 1875, pp. 68-70).

So much for Le Chevalier's hot and cold running water. Moreover, these springs were over half an hour's travel from the hilly fortress at Burnarbashi, and they were invisible from the citadel. Schliemann thought it unlikely that Homer would describe these distant springs as "under the wall along the public way" where the "fair daughters of the Trojans used to wash their splendid garments."

The final test implications dealt with Troy's topography: within view of the Aegean Sea (Implication VI), fronting onto the vast plain where the battles took place (Implication VII) and located near the Scamander River (Implication VIII). The ruins of Burnarbashi were not built on a plain at all but on a hill rising some five hundred feet above the surrounding environs. Schliemann thought the battle could hardly have "surged between plain, and city walls"; the hill at Burnarbashi was too steep, rising almost to a peak near the top. Burnarbashi also did not front onto a long, gently sloping plain; in fact it was separated from the Aegean by a steep ridge of hills. How could Agamemnon gaze from the sea, checking the Trojan's watch fires and listening to the sound of flutes and pipes? And even discounting the hills, the ruins were five miles from the Aegean coast. Schliemann thought it impossible that two armies could return over such a long distance to home base each night after battle. Schliemann thus completed this first round of scientific investigation by rejecting the theory that Burnarbashi could be ancient Troy. The ruins were wrong, the dating was wrong, the springs were wrong, the topography was wrong, Burnarbashi was wrong. End of Cycle 1.

What had Schliemann actually proved? Schliemann's preliminary work at Burnarbashi proved exactly nothing. Cycle 1 succeeded only in eliminating one competing hypothesis: Burnarbashi was not likely to have been Troy.

Schliemann's Campaign of 1870–1873

So it was that Schliemann began large-scale excavations at Hissarlik in 1870. Fortified with olive oil to combat the bedbugs and quinine for the malaria, Heinrich and Sophie established their field camp at the base of Hissarlik. Digging in nineteenth-century Turkey was no easy matter. First Schliemann was required to obtain a *firman,* an excavation permit issued rather reluctantly by the Turkish officials. This task alone took Schliemann years of cajoling, intimidating, and bribing officials. He was then required to negotiate the hiring of his crew with the village headman of Renkoi. Skeptical at first, the headman eventually agreed that his workmen would appear at Hissarlik at first light.

It has been said that Schliemann's first seasons at Troy were "more a rape than a scientific examination" (McDonald 1967, p. 17). Though this is no doubt true from the perspective of contemporary excavation technology, we must remember that the Trojan excavations were exemplary for their day. The early work was not without gross blunders, as Schliemann readily admitted later, but that hardly justifies accusing him of ignoring methods that evolved decades later.

The Schliemanns supervised a horde of inexperienced local workmen, the crew averaging 150 men per day. Initially convinced that Homeric Troy lay in the basal stratum of Hissarlik, Schliemann began an enormous north-south trench to bisect the mound and expose Troy. In places, the excavations reached fifty feet deep before penetrating primary soil. This master trench emerged as the heart of Schliemann's strategy, and nothing was allowed to stand in its way. Using picks, shovels, wheelbarrows, and even battering rams and great iron levers, the workmen tore out all walls, structures, and foundations in order to find the earliest occupation. Schliemann detected four distinct strata, which he called "nations," of which the basal stratum was presumably Homeric Troy.

In 1872, however, Schliemann was forced to change his interpretation of the Hissarlik stratigraphy. His aggressive trenching uncovered the base of a well-preserved tower within the second stratum. Beside this tower had once stood a double gateway, with a paved ramp leading inside the fortress. Schliemann immediately assumed this was the Scaean Gate, the fabled entryway to Troy. Now convinced that Homeric Troy lay in the second rather than the first stratum, Schliemann identified the adjacent structure as the palace of Priam because the terra cotta vases found inside the "palace" were so well made. A silver vase was discovered nearby, further convincing Schliemann that he had indeed found King Priam's ancient dwelling.

Hopes were high when Schliemann returned to Hissarlik in the spring of 1873. While probing through the dust and rubble near his Scaean Gate, Schliemann spied a "large copper article of most remarkable form, which attracted my attention all the more as I thought I saw gold behind it" (1875, p. 323) (Figure 2–6). Dismissing the workmen, he and Sophia Schliemann excavated one of archaeology's most famous treasures:

> While the men were eating and resting, I cut out the Treasure with a large knife, which it was impossible to do without the greatest exertion and the most fearful risk of my life, for the great fortification-wall, beneath which I had to dig, threatened every moment to fall down upon me. But the sight of so many objects, every one of which is

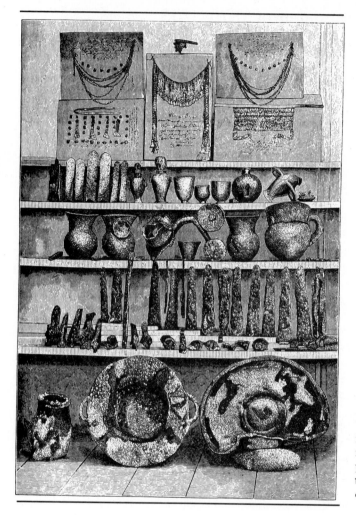

FIGURE 2–6 The "Treasure of Priam" as illustrated in Schliemann's original 1875 publication. (Courtesy the American Museum of Natural History)

of inestimable value to archaeology, made me foolhardy, and I never thought of any danger. (Schliemann 1875, pp. 323–324)

Below the copper "shield" (which proved later to be a basin) lay a copper cauldron, a silver jug, a globular gold bottle, and two gold cups. Further digging revealed more cups and vases of precious metals, lances, daggers, axes, knives, two gold diadems, and four gold earrings. On top of these lay fifty-six more gold earrings and 8750 small gold rings, perforated prisms and dice, gold buttons, six gold bracelets, and more gold goblets. In one of his more eloquent flights of imagination, Schliemann reconstructed the contexts of his treasure in this way:

Cynthia Irwin-Williams on the Contributions of Sophie Schliemann

. . . Within the field of antiquarianism/ archaeology in 19th Century Europe and America, what was the role and contribution of women? To follow the lead of the principal recent chroniclers and historians of archaeology, the apparent answer is "none-at-all." Neither Daniel [1976] in his massive history of archaeology nor Willey and Sabloff [1980] in their treatment of New World archaeology mention a single contribution by a woman archaeologist before World War I.

In fact, however, there were early women pioneers. For the most part they gained entrance to the field and limited public recognition as the wives and daughters of the famous archaeologists of the time. Best known among these was *Sophie Schliemann*, wife of Heinrich Schliemann [Figure 2–7]. Their story reflects something of the climate of the time. . . . In

Reprinted by permission of Cynthia Irwin-Williams.

FIGURE 2–7 Sophie Schliemann, wearing the golden diadem, earrings, and necklace she recovered as the "Treasure of Priam."

1869, at age 47, after amassing a fortune from profiteering during the Civil War, Schliemann decided to divorce his "unsuitable" first wife and to marry a Greek girl specifically to help him in his lifelong passion to find and excavate the lost city of Troy. He selected the photograph of 27 year old Sophie Engastromenos from a collection of photographs presented to him, and proceeded to court and marry the girl in three weeks. He then tutored her rigorously in the arts, history, geography, philosophy and archaeology, so as to prepare her to be his helpmate for his long awaited expedition to Hissarlik in Turkey, which he believed was the site of Priam's Troy. Their work together there . . . led to a tremendous growth of interest in archaeology and prehistory. Throughout, although thoroughly overshadowed by her flamboyant husband, Sophie was recognized as the more diligent, careful and perseverant of the two. What records were made of the excavations were largely the result of her efforts. (Irwin-Williams, in press.)

As I found all these articles together, forming a rectangular mass, or packed into one another, it seems to be certain that they were placed on the city wall in a wooden chest . . . such as those mentioned by Homer as being in the palace of King Priam. This appears to be the more certain, as close by the site of these articles I found a copper key [later identified as a chisel] . . . it is probable that some member of the family of King Priam hurriedly packed the Treasure into the chest and carried it off without having time to pull out the key; that when he reached the wall, however, the hand of an enemy or the fire overtook him, and he was obliged to abandon the chest, which was immediately covered to a height of from 5 to 6 feet with the red ashes and the stones of the adjoining royal palace. (1875, pp. 332–333)

"Priam's treasure," as it became known, further convinced Schliemann that Homeric Troy lay on the second, rather than the basal level of Hissarlik. Schliemann regretted this shift in context, because "unfortunately, in 1871 and 1872, [I] destroyed a large portion of the [second] city, for I at that time broke down all the house-walls in the higher strata which obstructed my way" (1875, pp. 347–348). Then as now, archaeology emerges as a science that destroys its own data, and today's field methods stress the importance of analysis proceeding hand in glove with excavation strategy (see Chapter 6).

The story of Priam's treasure then takes a sordid turn. After recovering the treasure, Schliemann immediately announced that the 1873 field season would terminate in two weeks. The thousands of gold pieces—the necklaces, earrings, buttons, and beads—were hidden from the on-site Turkish guard whose duty it was to inspect all finds. Turkish law at the time required that half of the artifacts remain in the national museum at Constantinople. From its hiding place beneath the Schliemanns' bed, the booty was packed into suitcases, designated as personal possessions, and shipped directly to Athens. In this way, Schliemann avoided the inspection mandated by his Turkish *firman*. Once in Athens, Schliemann hid the treasure in a secret storehouse. Only on selected days, such as Greek holidays, would he risk transporting any of the illicit artifacts. Little by little, the objects were cleaned, repaired, and photographed for publication. Eight thousand gold beads were strung into two necklaces, one of eleven strands, the other of thirteen. Schliemann even photographed Sophia modeling the diadem, earrings, and one of the necklaces from Priam's treasure (Figure 2–7). Contrary to modern protocol among professional archaeologists, Schliemann regarded these priceless artifacts as his personal property, and these underhanded dealings made it easy for Schliemann's enemies to accuse him of looting and privateering.

Schliemann presented Priam's treasure to the Prussian government in 1881, and it went on exhibit in the Berlin Museum for Early History. Tragically, the artifacts disappeared. As the Russian army approached Berlin toward the end of World War II, the curators of the Berlin Museum hastily packed up and hid (or buried) the treasure. To this day, not a single gold bead from Priam's treasure has surfaced. Rumors abound: It was bombed, or melted down, or confiscated, or stolen. Nobody knows. But we do know that even though the objects disappeared, the data did not evaporate. Because data are observations on objects, data remain both fireproof and theftproof.

In his report of the Hissarlik excavations, published in 1875, Schliemann boasted to the world that he had indisputably discovered the ruins of Homeric Troy: "I have excavated two-thirds of the entire city; and, as I have brought to light the Great Tower, the Scaean Gate, the city wall of Troy, the royal palace . . . I have also made an exceedingly copious collection of all the articles of the domestic life and the religion of the Trojans; and therefore, it is not to be expected that science would gain anything more by further excavations" (1875, pp. 349–352). On what did Schliemann base such claims? To examine his reasoning, we must return to the initial eight test implications for Troy.

Implications I through III were overwhelmingly verified. As predicted, Schliemann had discovered fantastic wealth: precious metals, ruined temples, public architecture, and an impressive fortification wall. With regard to Implication IV—that Achilles could have chased Hector thrice around the hill—Schliemann's excavations suggested that Homeric Troy was thirty-seven feet lower than the present surface of Hissarlik. Furthermore, during the continuous occupation, the ridge would have gained in both height and breadth. Thus, even allowing for Homeric hyperbole, Schliemann concluded that the size of Hissarlik would not preclude the epic chase.

The topographic implications (VI through VIII) also seemed to square with the modern Scamander Plain. But in his initial campaign at Troy, Schliemann could not answer the ancient criticism of Demetrios, namely, that the Aegean had once formed a bay on the current alluvial plain. Schliemann also failed to locate a spring near his "Scaean Gate." Schliemann's excavation clearly implicated Hissarlik, not Burnarbashi, as the site of ancient Troy. Not all the predictions were verified, but Hypothesis B fared considerably better than did Hypothesis A (which had been roundly rejected).

Still, Schliemann's publication of the Trojan campaign received mixed reviews. Some, such as C. Schuchhardt, director of the Kestner Museum of Hanover, raved that "the question is now decided forever. On the hill of Hissarlik Dr. Schliemann has uncovered the ancient palaces of Troy, has laid bare its colossal fortifications, and brought to light its treasures of gold and silver" (1891, p. 18). But most scholars, particularly those trained along more traditional lines, thought that Schliemann's work fell far short of his claims. While granting that he had unearthed a significant early civilization, most authorities were critical of his methods and conclusions. At one point, Schliemann was even accused of salting his own site with silver and gold (he was, after all, a well-to-do man). Few scholars would allow any close connection between the artifacts of Hissarlik and the antiquities described in the *Iliad*. The architectural evidence was declared equivocal. In fact, Schliemann's bold correlations between the *Iliad* and archaeology became at times an open joke in both the public press and closed scientific circles (McDonald 1967, p. 26). All in all, the 1875 publication convinced few, and Burnarbashi remained the most fashionable nominee as Homer's Troy (if indeed it existed at all).

Schliemann's Campaign of 1878–1879

Criticism leads to further research and refined hypotheses, and the adverse critiques of *Troy and Its Remains* spurred Schliemann to rise once again in defense of Hissarlik. Schliemann's second Trojan excavations comprise the third loop in his scientific cycle. The first round tested and rejected the Burnarbashi hypothesis. The initial excavations at Hissarlik, the second loop in the cycle, produced ambiguous results, as Schliemann's critics were quick to point out. In order to verify the still untested implications and thereby to respond to his critics, Schliemann commenced his campaign of 1878–1879.

After lengthy political and legal adversity, Schliemann finally convinced the Turkish government to issue him a new excavation permit. By the time he returned to the Scamander Plain in 1878, Schliemann had gained familiarity with the aims and principles of scientific excavation. In the meantime, he had located and excavated the celebrated shaft graves at Mycenae. He thus approached the reexcavation of Hissarlik with a sense of reserve notably absent in his initial campaign.

The new excavations had two clear-cut goals. Schliemann intended first to expose the ruins of the fortifications and of the large building in the second level, near where the treasure had been found. The expedition successfully cleared the entire western half of the mound down to this second, or "Homeric," level.

The stratigraphy was reworked from the initial four "nations" into seven major levels. Schliemann now correlated the Homeric Troy with the third stratigraphic level, superimposed on two previously burned cities. Several additional treasure hoards were found—ten in all—and the collection of ceramics and material culture was dramatically increased. The 1878–1879 excavations showed even stronger support for Implications I through III. There could be little doubt that Hissarlik was rich enough to have been Homeric Troy.

The second goal represented a critical departure from Schliemann's earlier approach. On his return to Hissarlik in 1878, Schliemann brought with him a battery of consulting scientists to conduct a broad-based ecological study of the Trojan plain—its topography, geology, flora, and fauna. One participating scientist, Professor **Rudolph Virchow**, was one of the nineteenth century's premier scholars, and his presence alone lent an air of credibility notably lacking in the earlier Hissarlik excavation.

Virchow made an important contribution during his stay at Hissarlik. While examining the geology of the Plain of Scamander, he excavated test holes to a depth of several meters, but nowhere could he find buried marine sediments. The implications were clear: Demetrios's ancient theory that the Scamander Plain had been submerged during Trojan times was false. This proposition, obliquely subsumed under Implication VII, thus received independent verification.

This broad-based, naturalistic approach to the Trojan Plain culminated in Schliemann's discovery of the much-disputed springs and washing troughs. Lying in an ancient rock channel at the foot of Hissarlik, the springs suggested continuous use from early Mycenaean into Roman times. Schliemann was even able to relocate a "Scaean Gate" in this vicinity. Hence Implication V was also verified by the 1878–1879 fieldwork.

Schliemann summarized his second campaign in *Ilios: The City and Country of the Trojans* (1880), published in German, English, and French. This volume, while still failing to silence his most vociferous critics, conclusively confirmed Schliemann's claim that he had found Homeric Troy. With gusto—tempered considerably by what Virchow termed his "scientific poise and caution"—Schliemann finally established the veracity of his extravagant claims.

Heinrich Schliemann: Scientist in Archaeology?

The shortcomings of Schliemann's excavation technique need not detain us. Of course Schliemann should not have ripped out walls indiscriminately; in fact, he unknowingly dug right through the most likely candidate for Homeric Troy (Level VIIa). Surely he was rash to apply unfortunate and judgmental terms like "Priam's treasure" and the "Scaean Gate." Perhaps we can excuse Schliemann as a "pioneer" who, like all pacesetters, must be forgiven occasional errors in execution and judgment. But he also contributed dozens of innovations to the art of archaeological excavation, creativity that colors our work today. It is amusing to note how many of the recent "revolutions in archaeology" have their roots in the Hissarlik campaigns of the late nineteenth century.

Consider today's highly touted interdisciplinary approach to archaeology, which has received so much attention in the past several years. After his first season at Troy, Schliemann recognized the necessity of taking along consultants to help with clues that Schliemann knew he was untrained to solve: Virchow the naturalist, Emile Burnouf the French archaeologist and scholar, and Dorpfeld and Hofler the architects, cartographers, and photographers. Similarly, in analyzing his finds, Schliemann consulted professional help whenever necessary. In dealing with Priam's treasure, for instance, he consulted Carlo Giuliano, a well-known London goldsmith. Giuliano marveled at the purity of the gold and puzzled as to how primitive goldsmiths could perform such fine work. As with

Will the Real Troy Please Stand Up?

Schliemann's excavation at Hissarlik can be faulted on numerous grounds. But the fact remains that he accomplished precisely what he had set out to do: to apply techniques of scientific excavation to pinpoint the location of ancient Troy. And he succeeded, for few modern scholars dispute the validity of the Hissarlik theory. But in so doing—as the old saw goes—Schliemann raised more questions than he answered. The century of Trojan research that followed Schliemann's lead has obvious historical implications, and it illustrates how hypotheses are progressively revised and refined as part of the continuing scientific cycle.

After Schliemann's second Trojan publication, the focus of research shifted. The debate centered not on the existence and location of Troy—Hissarlik satisfied the Homeric implications all too well—but on the precise level of Homeric Troy in the Hissarlik stratigraphy.

While writing his second volume, Schliemann became progressively more disenchanted with his identification of the "small town, the third in succession from the virgin soil" with Homeric Troy. Compelled to recheck his findings once more, he returned to Hissarlik in 1882 for further excavations. This time working with trained architects, Schliemann changed his mind yet again about the location of Homeric Troy. In *Troja,* published in 1884, Schliemann deleted all references to the third burned city, reverting to his previous correlation of Homer's Troy with the second stratum. Schliemann's thinking thus evolved from Level I to Level II, to Level III, and back to Level II. In the final year of his life, Schliemann would even have changed the correlation to Level VI

(and as we shall see, that correlation is also incorrect). But as McDonald (1967, p. 39) pointed out, such wavering is eloquent example of the self-correcting nature of hypothesis testing in archaeology: "Schliemann no doubt had an embarrassing habit of rushing into print: but no apology is needed in any scholarly field for a change of mind necessitated by new evidence. The unpardonable sin, indeed, is for a scholar to refuse to consider the possibility that a cherished theory may be mistaken."

Schliemann's work at Troy was continued by his young architect, Wilhelm Dorpfeld. Dorpfeld concentrated his 1894 excavations on Level VI, which both he and Schliemann now felt was Homeric Troy. Because of the presence of imported Mycenaean pottery, Dorpfeld concluded that Level VI dated roughly 1500–1000 B.C. Although vague, this was the best evidence available at the time. Also of interest were two "pre-Greek" settlements, labeled VII[1] and VII[2]. Dorpfeld discussed the nature of these settlements in some detail, concluding that VII[1] probably resulted from a reoccupation of Level VI. In fact, many of the VII[1] houses were actually constructed against the ancient city wall. Dorpfeld felt that the newcomers were probably "ordinary people," whereas the Troy VI houses were sturdier, probably belonging to a "leader and dependents."

Transition from Troy VI to Troy VII[1] spurred still further research at Hissarlik (now confidently termed Troy by all). Carl Blegen of the University of Cincinnati led field expeditions to Troy for seven successive years, beginning in the spring of 1932. Applying evolved stratigraphic methods (discussed in

Chapter 5), Blegen learned firsthand how complex the Hissarlik strata really were. Using a nine-part stratigraphic section, Blegen finally recognized forty-nine major and minor catastrophies and reconstructions throughout the occupation of the site—a far cry from the simple four-part scheme first used by Schliemann.

Blegen also applied new techniques of ceramic analysis to demonstrate that Levels I through V represented an essentially continuous occupation spanning a thousand years. Schliemann had correctly interpreted the nature of these levels. The Cincinnati expedition also carefully mapped the location of all animal bone. Judging from the myriad sheep carcasses, the people of Hissarlik had already become major sheep raisers as early as Troy II times. Blegen even suggested that producing woolen textiles was a predominant enterprise at Troy.

A major break occurred in Troy VI, when a distinctive, wheel-made pottery was introduced. Blegen interpreted this as indicative of a full-blown invasion from the Greek mainland. Troy VI was apparently destroyed by a mighty earthquake about 1300 B.C. He found no support for Schliemann's final conclusion that the city had been destroyed by Agamemnon's troops.

So when did the Greek siege take place? Blegen's answer was Level VIIa (Dorpfeld's old Level VII[1]). Blegen believed that the survivors of the Trojan earthquake returned to their ruined home "within a few days" to rebuild their homes on the ruins. The large number of storage jars and the maze of small rooms suggested to Blegen that Troy VIIa was badly crowded (perhaps in expectation of a siege?). The pottery found on the house floors of Troy VIIa suggests perhaps a single generation of inhabitants. Using Mycenaean trade wares, Blegen dated the level as the decade around 1270 B.C. or so.

What about the siege? How was Troy VIIa destroyed? Blegen argued that "the destruction was undoubtedly the work of human agency, and it was accompanied by violence and by fire." The 1930s' excavations uncovered several complete and partial human skeletons, suggesting that the Troy VIIa people had been victims of a violent incursion.

Blegen concluded:

> Here, then, in the extreme northwestern corner of Asia Minor—exactly where Greek tradition, folk memory and the epic poems place the site of [Troy]—we have the physical remains of a fortified stronghold, obviously the capital of the region. As shown by persuasive archaeological evidence, it was besieged and captured by enemies and destroyed by fire, no doubt after having been thoroughly pillaged, just as Hellenic poetry and folk-tale describe the destruction of King Priam's Troy. . . . It is Settlement VIIa, then, that must be recognized as the actual Troy, the ill-fated stronghold, the siege and capture of which caught the fancy and imagination of contemporary troubadours and bards who transmitted orally to their successors their songs about the heroes who fought in the past. (1963, pp. 162, 164)

Did Blegen have the final word about Troy? Probably not. Current researchers are still attempting to unravel mysteries of the Mycenaean civilization. Areas of interest include the linguistic affiliation of the Trojans and their invaders, the presence of horse bones in Troy VI (did the middle Helladic folk ride horses?), the exact nature of Mycenaean economy and trade, and the continuation (or lack of it) from Mycenaean to Homeric times. The problems are never-ending; the more one knows, the more one needs to know.

today's prudent archaeologists, Schliemann knew when to call for help. Then, as now, no single scholar can hope single-handedly to deal with the entire range of complexity encountered in any one archaeological site.

Schliemann must likewise be commended for the meticulous recording and publication of his archaeological finds. He wrote, "Archaeology shall on no account lose any one of my discoveries; every article which can have interest for the learned world shall be photographed, or copied by a skillful draughtsman, and published in the Appendix to this work; and by the side of every article I shall state the depth in which I have discovered it" (1875, p. 219). These are notable statements of principle for the nineteenth century.

Schliemann's self-assertiveness irritated many, past and present, but without such characteristics, he never could have forced himself—or his archaeology—to the attention of the learned world (McDonald 1967, p. 11). I suggest that when modern archaeologists are tempted to label their methods new, or revolutionary, they check the writings of Schliemann. He may have gotten there first.

WHERE TO GO FROM HERE?

Schliemann on Hissarlik (Troy): Troy and Its Remains (1875); *Ilios: The City and Country of the Trojans* (1880); *Troja: Results of the Latest Researches* (1884); see also Schuchhardt: *Schliemann's Excavations: An Archaeological and Historical Study* (1891).

More Contemporary Approaches to Mycenaean Archaeology (including Troy): Blegen: *Troy and Trojans* (1963); McDonald: *Progress into the Past: The Rediscovery of Mycenaean Civilization* (1967); Renfrew: *The Emergence of Civilization: The Cyclades and the Aegean in the Third Millennium BC* (1972); Chadwick: *The Mycenaean World* (1976); Kraft, Kayan, and Erol: "Geomorphic Reconstructions in the Environs of Ancient Troy" (1980); Easton: "Schliemann's Discovery of 'Priam's Treasure': Two Enigmas" (1981).

Heinrich Schliemann As Savant, Scholar, and Fledgling Scientist: Some relatively positive assessments: McDonald: *Progress into the Past: The Rediscovery of Mycenaean Civilization* (1967); Stone: *The Greek Treasure* (1975); Deuel: *Memoirs of Heinrich Schliemann* (1977). A less savory view of Schliemann is summarized by Calder and Traill in *Myth, Scandal, and History: The Heinrich Schliemann Controversy and a First Edition of the Mycenaean Diary* (1986).

Summary

The scientist uses scientific methods to abstract universals from a world of particulars, and it goes almost without saying that contemporary archaeology is a scientific enterprise. Archaeology's scientific laws are timeless and spaceless generalizations that tell how cultural processes work. These laws are found by using a scientific cycle, which consists of three steps: hypothesis formation, bridging argumentation, and verification. Each round in the scientific cycle begins and ends with facts, each new set of facts suggesting new hypotheses that themselves must be tested. As a method, science implies a continuing upward spiral of knowledge. The principles and methods of science have been successfully applied for over two centuries in archaeology, and the scientific cycle provides the backbone for modern archaeological inquiry.

CHAPTER 3

What Is Anthropology?

I went to the University of Chicago for a while after the Second World War. I was a student in the Department of Anthropology. At that time, they were teaching that there was absolutely no difference between anybody. They may be teaching that still. Another thing they taught was that nobody was ridiculous or bad or disgusting.
—Kurt Vonnegut, Jr.

Everyone knows what anthropologists do. They study natives and fossils and chimpanzees. Anthropologists glower from the pages of *National Geographic* magazine and make chit-chat on TV's "Tonight" show. Anthropologists are Margaret Mead, Richard Leakey, Jane Goodall, and Ashley Montagu. Some people think that Stephen Jay Gould is also an anthropologist.

Apparently, few people really know what anthropologists do, what these various scientists share, what makes them all anthropologists. **Anthropology** is an unusual discipline; because anthropologists run in so many different directions at once, it is often difficult to see the common thread. In fact, anthropologists sometimes get so involved with the minutiae of their own deliberations that they themselves forget what they are. What makes an anthropologist an anthropologist?

The answer is deceptively simple: What all anthropologists share is a perspective, an outlook that holds that a true science of humanity can arise only from the holistic, all-encompassing vision. It is not enough to look at any single group—Americans, Chinese, Balinese, or **Australopithecines**—to find the keys to human existence. Every human society, extant or extinct, is declared relevant to the study of people. On this all anthropologists agree.

This is not to say that all anthropologists study the same things: Margaret Mead never excavated an archaeological site and Louis Leakey never interviewed a native Athabascan speaker. Anthropologists, like most modern *Homo sapiens*, participate in a division of labor. The Renaissance anthropologist is dead because one scholar cannot hope to do all things well.

So anthropologists specialize. Before examining how modern archaeology articulates with the rest of anthropology, it is necessary to see just what anthropology is and how anthropologists have carved up the pie of human existence.

Kinds of Anthropology

Anthropologists are highly individual and specialized people. Each of them is marked by the kind of work he or she prefers and has done, which in time becomes an aspect of that individual's personality.
—Margaret Mead

The basic division within anthropology concerns the very nature of human existence. **Physical anthropology** deals with humans primarily as biological organisms; **cultural anthropology** views humans as "the animals of culture." Although these are not wholly independent divisions, they do serve to bisect the range of humanity into manageable domains of study.

Physical Anthropology

The origins of physical anthropology can be traced back to the eighteenth century, when Petrus Camper began measuring human skulls. **Anthropometry** arose as the practice of measuring human morphology, and as anthropologists quickly discovered, human crania are terrific objects to scrutinize. There are so many things to be measured: length, breadth, height, cranial capacity, nasion–basion length, degree of cranial deformation. The list seemed endless. The study of human crania—craniometry—progressed so far, so rapidly, that some physical anthropologists (such as Boyd 1950) have argued that craniometry progressed too far, that the preoccupation with skull measurements retarded the overall development of physical anthropology as a science. Who knows? It is fair to say that craniometry (and anthropometry in general) kept the physical anthropologists off the streets and out of trouble until more relevant domains of study came along.

Physical anthropology has come a long way since the days of Petrus Camper and his cranial calipers. Modern physical anthropologists pursue a number of facets on the biological side of humankind. One major concern is the biological evolution of man. How did the modern species *Homo sapiens sapiens* come into being? An intricate family tree has been pieced together by physical anthropologists over the past century, working largely from fossil evidence and observation of living primates.

A second major focus of modern physical anthropology is the study of human variability. No two human beings are identical, even though we all are members of a single species. The study of inherited—so-called racial—differences has become a strategic domain of scientific investigation and also a matter of practical concern for educators, politicians, and community leaders. To what extent, for example, are IQ scores the result of inherited (racial) differences? The answer has wide-reaching political and social significance.

Cultural Anthropology

Physical anthropologists provide a background against which to consider the workings of cultural anthropology. In the next section, we shall dissect the concept of culture. For now, it is sufficient to conceive of culture as those rules by which human societies operate. **Ethnologists** study the culture of modern groups. By questioning and observing people throughout the world, ethnologists try to evaluate how diverse cultural elements intermesh and change in contemporary human societies. **Anthropological linguists** concentrate on a more specialized cultural component—language—evaluating linguistic behavior in considerable detail: phonological structures, the relationship of language to thought, the way in which linguistic systems change through time, the structural basis of language.

This book is primarily concerned with the third kind of cultural anthropology— archaeology. Archaeologists also attempt to comprehend human culture, but their technology and field methods differ radically from those of the ethnologists and the linguists. Archaeologists usually study extinct cultures, systems that no longer operate. They thus work at something of a disadvantage because there is nobody to talk to. Lacking living, breathing informants, archaeologists have formulated a powerful array of techniques for gleaning relevant information from the material remains of the past. We shall examine dozens of these archaeological methods in later chapters. For now, it is important to see how archaeology articulates with the rest of cultural anthropology. We will find numerous attributes in common but some sizable disparities as well.

WHERE TO GO FROM HERE?

Key Journals in Anthropology

Abstracts in Anthropology provides summaries of major archaeological publications, listed geographically and also according to "theoretical, methodological, and general" headings; first published in 1970.

Subscription information: Baywood Publishing Co., Inc., P.O. Box D, Farmingdale, N.Y. 11735.

American Anthropologist, the primary journal of the American Anthropological Association, publishes technical papers in all areas of anthropology but specializes in articles of significant findings and theoretical analyses. Students will find the book reviews and review articles of particular interest; first published in 1888.

Subscription information: American Anthropological Association, 1703 New Hampshire Avenue, N.W., Washington, D.C. 20009.

Current Anthropology publishes technical articles from around the world in all sub-disciplines of anthropology. The most important articles are accompanied by commentaries by other specialists. Issues also contain review articles, research reports, and accounts of conferences; first published in 1960.

Subscription information: Current Anthropology, Orlie Higgins, Circulation Manager, University of Chicago Press, Journals Division, P.O. Box 37005, Chicago, Ill. 60637.

Ethnohistory, the official journal of the American Society for Ethnohistory, concentrates on historical documentary evidence relevant to the anthropology of the Americas. Students will find the book reviews and special subject issues of particular interest; first published in 1953.

Subscription information: Journals Fulfillment, Duke University Press, 6697 College Station, Durham, N.C. 27708.

Journal of Anthropological Research publishes articles in all branches of anthropology relating to peoples and cultures, past and present, in any region; first published in 1969 (as Volume 24 of the *Southwestern Journal of Anthropology).*

Subscription information: Subscriptions Manager, *Journal of Anthropological Research,* University of New Mexico, Albuquerque, N.M. 87131.

Journal of Quantitative Anthropology contains articles discussing analytical problems and theoretical issues, as well as reviews of the development and application of quantitative and computer methods for anthropological problems, with worldwide coverage; first published in 1989.

Subscription information: D. Reidel Publishing Company, 101 Philip Drive, Norwell, Mass. 02061.

Reviews in Anthropology contains in-depth, synthetic, review essays analyzing a series of articles on a similar topic. Typical titles: "New Information on China's Remote Past"; "Gender, Power, and Traditional Arts"; "Ethnoarchaeology of Pottery-Making"; first published in 1974.

Subscription information: Redgrave Publishing Company, 380 Adams Street, Bedford Hills, N.Y. 10507.

Culture: A Legacy from the Early Days of Anthropology

A dozen distinct academic disciplines purport to study culture (or at least cultural behavior): economics, sociology, linguistics, political science, history, cultural geography, psychology, and so forth. "Classical" historians, for instance, might investigate

Greek culture, Roman culture, or Byzantine culture; their interest centers on the cultural characteristics of each particular society. But one does not expect to find classical historians discoursing on the general nature of culture, for if they did, they would cease to be classical historians; they would have become anthropologists. It is this generalized, overarching conception of culture that forms the central theme melding so many diversified (and sometimes conflicting) concerns into a singular, collective anthropological perspective.

What is Culture?

There is surprisingly little general agreement among anthropologists about just what culture is (Goodenough 1970, p. 101). In a classic study, A. L. Kroeber and Clyde Kluckhohn (1952) compiled over two hundred distinct definitions of culture, proposed by as many anthropologists and social scientists. Since that time, the number of definitions of culture must have tripled.

Fortunately for us all, archaeologists need not be overly concerned with the quest for culture's ultimate definition. But we must recognize something about how human culture works and how anthropologists go about studying it. Suppose we begin with the classic definition offered by Sir Edward Burnett Tylor (the person considered by many as the founder of modern anthropology). Tylor's (1871) definition of culture appeared, interestingly enough, on the first page of anthropology's first textbook: "Culture . . . taken in its wide ethnographic sense is that complex whole which includes knowledge, belief, art, morals, law, custom, and any other capabilities and habits acquired by man as a member of society." Culture in this sense is *learned,* embodied in a society's general body of tradition. Although this definition provides a proper baseline from which to investigate past cultural behavior, Tylor's formulation is too general. We must find a way of pinning down this broad definition by asking precisely how one goes about perceiving cultural behavior, both in the present and in the past.

Language: One Becomes Three

This task is simplified by an analogy to the workings of language, itself a subset of all cultural phenomena (Aberle 1960, p. 14). The rather simple principles involved in language can tell us something about the more complex principles involved in general human culture (see also Goodenough 1970, 1971).

Linguistics consists of three components: the **idiolect**, the **language** (or dialect) per se, and the **system of communication**. No two speakers of a language pronounce every linguistic element in precisely the same way. Each speaker has a personal idiolect, which is how we can identify specific voices on the radio or the telephone. But linguists postulate that an overall manner of speaking—what we call language—transcends and orchestrates all the idiolects within a speech community. Although each individual speaker pronounces the language in a distinctive manner, the pervasive linguistic structure consists of shared speech patterns within a community. Language, in other words, is a generalized model that individuals only approximate to a greater or lesser extent.

The third aspect of linguistics, the system of communication, explains why languages exist at all. People speak because they have some message to communicate: Please pass the oatmeal; go to your wickiup; do you have tickets for the football game? Each is a message communicated by language. Furthermore, an entire repertory of hand gestures, facial expression, body language, and even manner of dress and hair length amplifies the system of purely verbal communication. Most modern languages also rely on a written language to further enhance communication.

So it is that linguists recognize a strategic contrast between language itself and language as a vehicle of communication. Language is shared behavior, and speech communities are defined on the basis of these collective speech patterns. But individual speakers occupy different positions in the chain of communication: People do not share a system of communication; they participate in it. Speakers partake in the system differently. For this reason, we carefully distinguish medium (human language) from the function it serves (human communication). Communication is why language evolved, but the reverse is not true.

The Potlatch: Culture at Three Levels

This linguistic analogy provides some insights into culture in general. Just as linguists define three linguistic components (idiolect, language, and a system of communication), so too can cultural phenomena be said to have three components. The cultural idiolect is an individual's version of his or her culture. Like linguists, cultural anthropologists must sort through apparently chaotic individual behavior in pursuit of common threads.

Nineteenth-century Kwakiutl Indians practiced the potlatch; rural East Indians worship cows; the Tsembaga Maring (a New Guinea clan) nurture massive pig herds for ritual slaughter. Each suite of cultural enterprises and beliefs is part of an enormous corpus of auxiliary rules and prescriptions that forms the cultural whole. Seemingly exotic cultural events such as potlatches, cow worship, and ritual pig slaughters have kept generations of anthropologists busy observing, participating, and describing. These are culture's shared, modal ingredients.

But culture, like language, likewise has a third component, the underlying system. Shared language exists to provide a system of communication among people, and shared culture serves a similar function. Leslie White (a general anthropologist) pioneered the investigation of cultural systems, and archaeologists have reworked White's reasoning to suit the study of extinct cultural systems. Following White's lead, Lewis Binford (1964) defined the cultural system as a set of repetitive articulations among the social, technological, and ideological aspects of culture. These three facets are not genetic—they are, in White's terminology, *extrasomatic,* meaning "outside the body" or learned.

Social, technological, and ideological perspectives together comprise the nonbiological (cultural) mechanisms through which human populations handle their biological and derived needs. This view of the cultural system emphasizes the structural elements basic to human adaptation, and deemphasizes the aggregates of "cultural traits" that happen to be shared.

The point is this: people do not share a cultural system—they participate in it

(Binford 1965). More precisely, one participates in a system of behavior that reflects, and is governed by, the underlying culture that itself constitutes a system. Participation is determined by one's place in the society, often expressed through intricate sets of statuses and roles.

This important point can be illustrated by the well-known case of rivalry **potlatch** practiced by several late-nineteenth-century tribes throughout the northwest Pacific coast of Canada and the United States and best documented for the Southern Kwakiutl of Vancouver Island (see Figure 3–1). The postcontact potlatch consisted of competitive feasting, during which ambitious, status-hungry men battled one another for social approval by hosting massive, often opulent feasts. Kwakiutl protocol dictated that the more food one gave away, the greater the prestige that would be accrued. Potlatch feasts were considered successful only when the guests had "eaten themselves under the table" and crawled groaning into the forest, only to vomit and return for more.

The competitive feasting extended far beyond simple gluttony. Late-nineteenth-century potlatching culminated in the outright destruction of property—not only food but also clothing, money, pieces of art, and even entire houses. The logic was this: The more goods that were destroyed, the greater the host's prestige would be. The guest chief

FIGURE 3–1   The potlatch was performed in Kwakiutl villages like this one at Newittee (British Columbia). The signs on the doors read "Boston. He is the Head chief of Arweete. He is true Indian. Honest. He don't owe no trouble to white man" and "Cheap. He is one of the head chiefs of all tribes in this country. White man can get information." As photographer Edward Dossiter's 1881 journal entry noted wryly, "The two chiefs . . . seem most desirous of cultivating friendships with whites." (Negative no. 328739, courtesy Department of Library Sciences; the American Museum of Natural History)

belittled the host's efforts and eventually held a return potlatch manifesting his own superior means and hence superior status.

Potlatches proceeded according to strict, culturally dictated rules. One person functioned in the role of host, inviting neighbors to his village for the feasting and festivities. The host parceled out gifts of varying degrees of worth: boxes of candlefish oil, baskets of berries, stacks of blankets, animal skins. As each gift was presented, the guests responded with a great degree of (culturally prescribed) dissatisfaction. They were being insulted by the host's generosity. Some guests served in the roles of "speaker" or "artist," and dancers assumed a variety of traditional poses, such as that of cannibal dancer, bear dancer, and food dancer.

The potlatch contains all three cultural components previously defined. The observer would initially be overwhelmed by the cultural idiolects. Each costume and mask is unique; every dancer has his or her own style; each speaker renders a personal touch. This idiosyncratic behavior reflects a degree of culturally prescribed variance from group standards (Goodenough 1970, pp. 101–102).

Viewed in another way, the potlatch is a piece of shared, modal behavior. All Kwakiutl share an implicit belief in the institution of the potlatch, and that is why they participate. By the same token, most Americans share a belief in the ballot box, a knowledge of American English, and the use of cash (Aberle 1960, pp. 14–15). In this sense, the potlatch consists of communally shared cultural beliefs.

The potlatch can also be viewed as not shared at all, but as an adaptive system in which one participates, and that participation is differential. Potlatching exhibits a vast array of culturally prescribed roles and statuses. The host's participation is quite different from that of the insulted guest; the hired dancer's role contrasts with the host's wife. This participation, of course, is not actually culture but, rather, cultural behavior.

The potlatch also served an adaptive function within the fabric of Kwakiutl culture. But what could be adaptive about the wholesale destruction of personal property or the flurry of personal indignities exchanged over potlatch fires? The question "Why potlatch?" has confounded generations of observers. Anthropologists versed only in the shared behavior view of culture could not focus beyond the burning blankets and flaming candlefish oil. These destructive and wasteful cultural practices were viewed as "quaint." Fifty years ago, anthropologist Ruth Benedict termed this culture *Dionysian,* accentuating the violent, frenzied aspects: "The final thing they strove for was ecstasy" (Benedict 1934, p. 175).

A rather different interpretation of the potlatch arose after investigators looked beyond the potlatch's obvious visual effects into its systemic functions. What ecological, technological, and economic purposes were being served by such odd (to us) cultural behavior? Could the potlatch serve any useful function? Some anthropologists think the answer might be yes.

First, the competitive feasting between local groups may have actually increased overall regional productivity. People seem to work harder when personal prestige is at stake, and such regionalized banquets and revelry might have helped distribute goods and services between villages, thereby overcoming the effects of failures in local production

(Piddocke 1965, Suttles 1960). Had each northwest coastal village been totally independent, then the failure of salmon to run up a particular stream could have been locally
disastrous. But through the potlatch system the less fortunate villages were invariably
invited to several potlatches hosted by their more prosperous neighbors. Although the
visitors were required to endure seemingly endless barbs and slights, they departed with
full bellies. In effect, the less fortunate Kwakiutl traded prestige for sustenance. All else
being ecologically equal, this year's luckless should have had ample opportunity to
redeem their lost status when their neighbors fell on hard times.

But what if some villages sustained continued subsistence catastrophe? There is
some suggestion that the potlatch helped shift population from less productive to more
productive villages (Hazard 1960): economically prosperous villages could "boast" of
(and demonstrate) their affluence at the potlatch ceremonies, thereby inducing guests to
leave their impoverished situations and join up with the more wealthy, more ecologically
stable village.

To summarize, human culture can be trisected into three distinct domains of
analysis: the idiolect, the body of modal values, and the underlying cultural system. In the
potlatch we can see all three ingredients. Whereas most anthropologists concede the
existence of all three elements, there is remarkably little consensus on how to conceptualize these complex cultural components. Before narrowing the scope to archaeology, we
shall look more closely at the mainstreams of current anthropological thought.

The Emic Versus the Etic

The art of being wise is the art of knowing what to overlook.
—William James

The concept of culture provides the baseline from which all anthropology begins. But
culture is hardly a monolithic concept, and as you might expect, anthropologists who
investigate culture tend to accentuate one aspect over another.

The dichotomy between **emic** and **etic** approaches is critical. The term *emic* is
applied whenever anthropologists employ concepts and distinctions that are somehow
meaningful, significant, accurate, or "appropriate" to the participants in a given culture
(Harris 1968b, p. 571). The potlatch ceremony, discussed earlier, has a complex series of
emic rules about how individual Kwakiutl persons should act during attendance. Emic
research into potlatching might attempt to identify the categories and rules required to
think and behave like each Kwakiutl of the various stations attending a potlatch. Emic
statements—the "native's point of view"—can be scientifically falsified by demonstrating
that they contradict the mental calculus used by participants in a given culture.

An opposite research strategy uses *etic* categories, calling on concepts and distinctions that are meaningful and appropriate to the community of scientific observers

(Harris 1968b, p. 575). Etic observations of the same potlatch ceremony enumerate participants, their relationship to one another, the quantities and values of goods exchanged and destroyed, and the prevailing ecological and economic conditions at each participating village. Such etic observations would not necessarily be familiar or understandable to the Kwakiutl participants, and such statements could neither be verified nor negated by comparison with native categories. Successful etic statements, expressed in the vocabulary of science, can be verified only when independent observers using similar operations agree that a given event has transpired.

Both emic and etic data are useful, and the comparisons of emic and etic versions of culture provoke some of the most meaningful challenges to anthropological inquiry.

Ideational Versus Adaptive Research Strategies

It is likewise useful to understand a major dichotomy in anthropological thought. Baldly stated, an **ideational strategy** focuses on ideas, symbols, and mental structures as driving forces in shaping human behavior. Alternatively, an **adaptive strategy** isolates technology, ecology, demography, and economics as the key factors defining human behavior.

Neither viewpoint implies "always"; both seek only to discriminate causes that "tend to" produce observed effects. Both ideational and adaptive strategies allow for the interplay and interaction between the mental and the material. The ideational approach maintains that sociocultural phenomena are best understood by mental ingredients; adaptivists feel that these sociocultural differences are better understood by identifying the precise nature of materialistic parameters.

Culture As Adaptation

Several points must be made about the adaptive view of culture. Concern is primarily with "culture as a system," with the cultural idiolect and shared aspects of culture secondary. It is the cultural system that articulates human communities directly with their ecological settings. Especially meaningful in this adaptive sense are technology, modes of economic organization, settlement pattern, forms of social grouping, and political institutions.

Culture can be viewed principally in adaptive terms, in a sense analogous to natural selection: "Man is an animal and, like all other animals, must maintain an adaptive relationship with his surroundings in order to survive. Although he achieves this adaptation principally through the medium of culture, the process is guided by the same rules of natural selection that govern biological adaptation" (Meggers 1971, p. 4). Cultures in this sense function in dynamic equilibrium within their **ecosystems**. When deviations occur in environment, demography, or technology, their effects will spread throughout the cultural system.

Adaptive prime movers are those elements of technology, subsistence economy, and social organization most closely tied to production. This view contrasts sharply with the ideational perspective. Although there is a certain amount of disagreement as to how cultures actually adapt, all cultural adaptationists agree that economics (in its broadest sense) and its social correlates are in most cases primary. Ideational systems are secondary.

Throughout this book, we will explore such strategies largely through the writings of one or two highly influential scholars (with a comprehensive bibliography attached at the end). These writers do not represent the totality of thought in a particular area, but they do tend to be the most vocal, the most zealous advocates for one posture or another.

CULTURAL MATERIALISM

The most coherent adaptive approach in anthropology is termed **cultural materialism**, a movement with roots extending back at least a century. Cultural materialism is largely associated with Marvin Harris, professor of anthropology at the University of Florida. The cultural materialist strategy develops an integrated corpus of theory to explain the evolution of differences and similarities in the global repertory of sociocultural systems.

FIGURE 3–2 Marvin Harris. (Courtesy Marvin Harris)

The Premises of Cultural Materialism

All cultural materialists begin from a scientific premise. As detailed in the last chapter, knowledge in science is acquired through public, replicable, empirical, objective methods. The objective of such scientific research is to formulate theories to explain cultural differences and similarities. Rival theories are selected by the same criteria, based on their power to predict and to admit independent testing. By explicitly embracing a scientific framework for explanation, cultural materialists reject humanist and aesthetic theories that attempt to explain culture on nonscientific grounds.

Cultural materialism focuses on behavioral events, which must be distinguished from mental events because they are observed in such different ways. They cannot be understood using the same set of criteria. Human behavior is available to the scientific community in a form that can be observed, measured, photographed, and objectively described. Human thought, the events of the mind, can be observed only indirectly; that is, scientific observers must communicate what is going on inside their heads. Although there are distinct relationships between behavior and thought, these associations must be demonstrated and not assumed.

Although behavior has its emic component—the native's perception of what has transpired—cultural materialists further narrow their focus to etic behavior, the observable outcome of human behavior. Within these guidelines, cultural materialistic research covers a rich array of topics (see Where to Go from Here?): theories about the origin and evolution of sex and gender roles, explanations of why warfare is so prevalent, origins of dietary patterns and food avoidance, and settlement and demographic trends. We shall also examine numerous archaeological applications in the following pages. Interestingly, a number of anthropologists pursuing research fully consistent with the principles of cultural materialism have been careful not to align themselves explicitly to the cultural materialistic cause (Harris 1988b).

Modern cultural materialistic thought is also closely intertwined with the seminal writings of Leslie A. White. Basic to White's thinking was a division of the cultural system into three major portions: technological, sociological, and ideological (White 1949, p. 364). White's technological subsystem is broad based, consisting of material, mechanical, physical, and chemical instruments, together with the techniques of their use. Technology joins humans to their environment by means of the tools of production, means of subsistence, materials of shelter, and the instruments of offense and defense.

Cultural materialists use the term **infrastructure** to denote those key elements considered most important to satisfying basic human needs: those demographic, technological, economic, and ecological processes—the modes of production and reproduction—that are assumed to lie at the causal heart of every sociocultural system. Specifically, Harris argues that it is the *etic behavioral infrastructure* that mediates a culture's interactions with the natural and social environment.

Put in another way, the infrastructure embraces the etic and behavioral components of production and reproduction modes:

Cultural Materialism: A Thumbnail Sketch

The following is a summary of the basic principles of cultural materialism (see Harris 1987, pp. 107–111):

Cultural Materialism Is Science: By explicitly accepting science as an explanatory framework, cultural materialists reject humanist and aesthetic explanations of culture. Scientific explanations are those that use testable hypotheses that attempt to predict (or retrodict) human behavior against relatively objective, empirical evidence (Chapter 2).

Cultural Materialism Separates Behavior from Thought, "Emics" from "Etics": Behavioral events and mental events cannot be understood through the same set of observable criteria. Behavior (or the direct physical consequences of behavior) can be observed, measured, photographed, and objectively described; events of the mind must be elicited indirectly, by asking questions and recording responses. The relationship between behavior and thought must be demonstrated; it is never assumed. A crosscutting distinction is important:

- Are we using concepts and distinctions that are meaningful and appropriate to the participants in a given culture? If so, then we are using *emic* categories, which can be scientifically verified; such categories correspond to a view of the world that participants accept as real, meaningful, or appropriate.
- Or is the investigator using concepts and distinctions that are meaningful and appropriate to the observer? If so, then these are termed *etic* categories, which derive from the vocabulary of science and are not necessarily familiar or understandable to participants in the culture being studied.

Cultural Materialists Assume Certain Biological and Psychological Givens: Certain empirically observable needs and drives are universal attributes of all people: sex, hunger, thirst, sleep, vulnerability to stress, and the like. These biological and psychological givens are critical to cultural materialism because they provide a way to define "currencies," ways of measuring inputs and outputs of cultural systems: energetic efficiency, nutritional costs and benefits, infant mortality, allocation of sexual privileges, and so forth.

Cultural Materialists Look to the Infrastructure for Causality: Certain key components are more important than others in helping satisfy basic human needs: Demographic, technological, economic, and ecological processes are assumed to be the causal core of culture. More specifically, it is the etics of behavior that constitute the infrastructure through which culture interacts with the constraints of nature. The various theories of cultural materialism give strategic priority to the laws of physics, chemistry, and biology for influencing human behavior.

Cultural Materialists Provide Two Additional Categories of Sociocultural Systems—Structure and Superstructure: Structure consists of the domestic and political systems. *Superstructure* denotes the realms of values, aesthetics, rules, beliefs, religions, and symbols. Each division can be viewed in terms of attendant behavioral/mental and emic/etic criteria.

Cultural Materialists Believe in Infrastructural Determinism: At the heart of the research strategy behind cultural materialism lie two beliefs:

- Optimizing the cost–benefit relationship for the satisfaction of basic human biological needs causes changes in the etic behavioral infrastructure.
- Changes in the etic behavioral infrastructure determine changes in the rest of the sociocultural system.

These principles do not comprise a theory; they comprise a research strategy that, cultural materialists believe, best conforms to the canons of acceptable scientific explanation. Because these principles form a strategy (rather than a theory), they can be disproved only in light of alternative principles that produce better and scientifically acceptable theories.

Mode of Production: Technology and practices employed for expanding or limiting basic subsistence production (especially food and other energy production), given the restrictions and opportunities provided for a specific technology interacting with a bounded habitat.

Mode of Reproduction: The technology and practices employed for expanding, limiting, and maintaining population size (specifically, demography, mating patterns, fertility, natality, mortality, nurturance of infants, medical controls, contraception, abortion, infanticide) (see Harris 1988a, p. 135).

To Leslie White, the sociological subsystem was made up of those interpersonal relationships that emerge as behavior: social organization, kinship, economics, ethics, and military and political organizations. White's sociocultural subsystem is now subsumed by the term **structure**, with the following etic, behavioral components:

Domestic economy: The organization of reproduction and basic production, exchange, and consumption within camps, houses, apartments, or other domestic settings: family structure, domestic division of labor, domestic socialization and enculturation, age and sex roles, domestic discipline hierarchies and sanctions.

Political economy: The organization of reproduction, production, exchange, and consumption within and between bands, villages, chiefdoms, states and empires: political organizations, factions, clubs, associations, corporations, division of labor, taxation, tribute, political socialization and education, class/caste and urban/rural hierarchies, discipline, police/military control, warfare (see Harris 1988a, p. 135).

Superstructure refers to values, aesthetics, rules, beliefs, religions, and symbols. Expressed in etic behavioral terms, superstructure is manifested as art, music, dance, literature, advertising, religious rituals, sports, games, hobbies, and even science (Harris 1988a, p. 135).

The Principle of Infrastructural Determinism

To this point, White's original subsystems are probably acceptable (to one degree or another) to both ideational and adaptive anthropologists. But this is where both White and his cultural materialistic progeny make the break.

The principle of **infrastructural determinism** has two facets. First, human society optimizes the costs and benefits for those genetically derived needs most important to the survival and well-being of human individuals (sex, sleep, nutrition, vulnerability to stress, and so forth); these occur primarily in the etic behavioral infrastructure. Second, such infrastructural changes determine changes in the rest of the sociocultural system. This important principle lies at the heart of cultural materialism.

Though clearly interrelated, the three sectors influence one another differentially (see Figure 3–3), and cultural materialists assign priority to the modes of production and reproduction. Technological, demographic, ecological, and economic processes become the independent variable and the social system is the dependent variable. Domestic and political subsystems (the structure) are considered to be secondary; values, aesthetics, rituals, religion, philosophy, rules, and symbols (the superstructure) all are tertiary. The modes of production and reproduction tend to foster rather distinctive ideological systems. Farmers think differently from hunter-gatherers, who view the world differently from industrialists. To the cultural materialists, infrastructure is the key to understanding the growth and development of all culture.

Such causality is probabilistic. Not every cultural similarity and difference can be explained by infrastructural determinism. Some sociocultural traits in every society arise from arbitrary, idiographic events. But as scientists, cultural materialists look past the exceptions to seek overarching generalities that can be tested and refined.

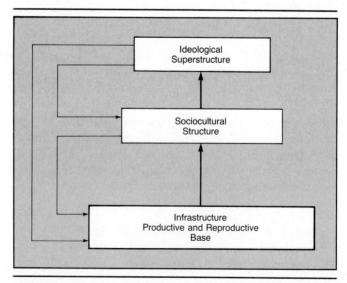

FIGURE 3–3   How the cultural materialist views causality.

Note also that infrastructural determinism allows for feedback between components. Stating that structure and superstructure are causally dependent on infrastructure does not mean that determinations are transmitted in a single direction. No component is a passive recipient. Without input from domestic, political, and ideological subsystems, the observable modes of production and reproduction would have evolved differently.

These principles do not comprise a theory; they comprise a research strategy that, cultural materialists believe, best conforms to the canons of acceptable scientific explanation. Because these are strategic principles (rather than theoretical beliefs), they can be disproved only in light of alternative principles that produce better and scientifically more acceptable theories.

The strategy of cultural materialism has been assailed for invoking simplistic, mechanical, monistic determinism: Infrastructure always determines structure and superstructure. Harris was quick to deny this accusation: Social phenomena are too complex to be explained by any single factor, materialistic or otherwise. People cannot live simply by producing and reproducing at random "without an idea in their heads." Neither can one envision people surviving without an infrastructure—"living on ideas alone." All three subsystems are critical, but cultural materialists argue that the relationships are asymmetrical, with infrastructural variables more causal than the others. But this does not mean that an infrastructure could survive without domestic, political, and ideological support.

This position can be traced back to Friedrich Engels:

> According to the materialist conception of history the determining element in history is *ultimately* the production and reproduction in real life. More than this neither Marx nor I have ever asserted. If, therefore, somebody twists this into the statement that the economic element is the only determining one, he transforms it into a meaningless, abstract and absurd phrase. The economic situation is the basis, but the various elements of the superstructure—political forms of the class struggle and its consequences, constitutions established by the victorious class after a successful battle, etc.—forms of law—and even the reflexes of all these actual struggles in the brains of the combatants: political, legal, philosophical theories, religious ideas and their further development into systems of dogma—all exercise their influence upon the course of the historic struggles and in many cases preponderate in determining their *form*. (cited in Harris 1968b, pp. 244–245)

Cultural materialists underscore that ultimately—"in the first and last instance"—material conditions emerge as causal only given a sufficient number of cases and in the long run (Harris 1968b, p. 245; 1987, p. 110).

Is Cultural Materialism Relevant to Contemporary Americanist Archaeology?

Absolutely.

I would guess that roughly half of the practicing American archaeologists consider themselves to be cultural materialists, to one degree or another (Leone 1972; Schiffer 1983). The others are scattered between particularistic, atheoretical perspectives and the ideational approaches discussed next.

Cultural materialism has appealed to archaeologists for two reasons. The cultural materialistic strategy emphasizes technology, economy, environment, and demography, all aspects of the human existence that survive in the archaeological record. Almost by default, Americanist archaeologists have for decades concentrated on precisely the same factors that cultural materialism holds as primary.

Equally important, cultural materialism needs archaeology. In several of his most important writings, Marvin Harris calls for archaeological support of his theories of human behavior. Harris urges archaeologists to throw off the constraints imposed by current ethnographic theory: Archaeologists "are capable of defining entities whose reality, I assure you, is every bit as well grounded as the entities which are now being discussed at great length by ethnographers" (1968b, pp. 359–360). Although Harris is hardly the first ethnographer to say this, cultural materialism is important to archaeology in part because archaeology is important to cultural materialism.

WHERE TO GO FROM HERE?

Cultural Materialism: Some General Discussions: Marvin Harris has written extensively on the subject; for an introduction, I recommend *The Rise of Anthropological Theory* (Harris 1968a), *Cultural Materialism: The Struggle for a Science of Culture* (Harris 1979), and *Food and Evolution: Toward a Theory of Human Food Habits* (Harris and Ross 1987); see also "Anthropology: Ships That Crash in the Night" (Harris 1988b) and *Culture, People, Nature* (Harris 1988a).

Cultural Materialism: Some Pragmatic Applications: The origin and evolution of sex and gender roles (Divale and Harris 1976), explanations of why warfare is so prevalent (e.g., J. Ross 1980, Morren 1984); origins of dietary patterns and food avoidance (e.g., E. Ross 1980, Harris 1985); settlement and demographic trends (e.g., Abruzzi 1982, Harris and Ross 1987).

Culture As Ideas

The basic theme of the ideational approach to anthropology is simple: "The realm of ideas, the force of symbols is centrally important in shaping human behavior" (Keesing 1976, p. 137). Culture in the ideational sense refers primarily to the complex sets of perceptions, conceptual designs, and shared understandings that underlie the way that people approach life. Culture, in this sense, is principally what humans learn, not what they do or make. This perspective on culture emphasizes cognition: ideas, thought, shared knowledge. Ideational culture does not encompass material belongings or performance.

Ideational views of culture suggest that one cannot comprehend human deportment without postulating a *cognitive code* for behavior. Much of what we perceive in the world, and hence endow with meaning, does not exist in the physical world at all. It exists only in the mind's eye. Robert Murphy (1976, p. 52) chides anthropologists, that by dismissing the ideational perspective of culture, they risk journeys down rivers, where the native women are breaking rocks with their wet laundry. The ideational theorist insists on "getting inside the informant's head."

At the risk of oversimplification, we can isolate three mainstreams of thought in the ideational strategy: critical Marxist theory, structuralism, and symbolic anthropology. Numerous other variants exist, but these three directions demonstate both the utility and the pitfalls of the ideational strategies to understanding the past.

Within anthropology, epic struggles between "materialism" and "idealism," "hard" and "soft" approaches, and interpretive "emics" and explanatory "etics" dominated discussions until well into the seventies; judging from the current literature, such struggles have only just begun in Americanist archaeology.

Critical Theory

> The oppressed are allowed once every few years to decide which particular representatives of the oppressing class are to represent and repress them.
> —Karl Marx

Anthropology in the late 1960s and 1970s became clearly embedded in political events. Radical social movements—the counterculture, the antiwar movement, the women's movement—appeared on a vast scale, affecting the academic world (and to some extent originating in it). Karl Marx became a rallying symbol for much of this new criticism, and "Marxist anthropology" sprang up in several forms.

The Premises of Critical Theory

The Marxist approach emphasizes the impact of economics on industrial society, especially as manifested in the division of labor and mode of production. In less stratified, non-Western societies, the Marxist perspective often focuses on how cultural definitions of sex and age limit dominance in social and political hierarchies.

For our purposes, we shall focus on critical Marxist theory because this variant is having an impact on Americanist archaeology. **Critical theory** refers to a series of attempts to adapt ideas from Karl Marx to an understanding of events and circumstances of twentieth-century life that Marx did not know (Leone, Potter, and Shackel 1987, p. 283). This effort began in the 1920s with the so-called Frankfurt school of philosophy. Such critical theory has been applied to a variety of intellectual endeavors, including law, history, decorative arts, literature, geography, museum studies, and, of course, anthropology.

"Critical" in this sense means that the relations between the assumptions and discoveries of a scholarly discipline and its ties to modern life become a central concern and thus are subject to examination. Such critical analysis automatically subjects the questions, methods, and discoveries of a science like anthropology to questions about the anthropologist's own culture.

Is Critical Theory Relevant to Americanist Archaeology?

A growing number of archaeologists would answer yes. Particularly among historical archaeologists, critical Marxist theory has attracted a vocal following. In Chapter 4, we shall see how critical theory has been used to examine the role of women in contemporary Americanist archaeology. Critical theory also highlights the importance of taking archaeology public, and the inset explains how a critical Marxist perspective is translated to tourists visiting excavations in Annapolis, Maryland. In Chapter 15, we shall return to this topic, examining how Mark Leone and his colleagues have applied the tenets of critical theory to explain the emergence of the "Georgian mind-set" in eighteenth-century Annapolis (see also the references in Where to Go from Here?).

To understand how critical theory works in Americanist archaeology—and how it differs from the other anthropological perspectives—one must understand three important concepts.

1. *Critical Theory Emphasizes the "Reflexive" Aspects of Culture:* The critical theorist views culture from an *interactive* (or *recursive*) perspective. Rather than assuming that people simply bear their culture passively, the critical theorist assumes "that people create, use, modify, and manipulate their symbolic capabilities, making and remaking the world they live in" (Leone 1986, p. 416). Viewed in this reflexive sense, material culture is not merely a reflection of economics, social organization, or ideology; it becomes an instrument to create meaning and order in one's world. Critical theorists recognize a distinctive relationship between the present and the past and assume this relationship to be economic and political. Who owns the artifacts of the past? Who controls their disposition? For what purposes do archaeologists interpret the past?

2. *Critical Theory Emphasizes Meaning:* Critical theory joins the other ideational perspectives in rejecting the doctrine of infrastructural determinism. Whereas ecological, economic, demographic, and technological considerations are not excluded, they are encompassed by and subordinated to an analysis of the social—and particularly political—organization of production. Unlike the cultural materialists, critical Marxists do not dismiss cultural beliefs and native categories as irrelevant to the real or objective operations of a society.

Unlike their symbolic colleagues, critical theorists retain a role for the materialist tradition. Although rejecting the ranked order of causal relationships in Figure 3–3, critical theory welcomes advances in our understanding of the natural environment, economy, demography, and technology and suggests that such conditions lead to social contradictions, conflicts, and exploitation. Ideology, in effect, "hides" or "masks" such internal contradictions, preventing active conflict and ensuring continued operation of the cultural system. Ideology, in this sense, acts within a stratified or class society to

Critical Archaeology in Action:
Working with the Public at Annapolis

Annapolis has always been a small American community. Founded in about 1650, it became the capital of Maryland in 1695, later experiencing a "golden age" of wealth and fame that peaked between about 1760 until the end of the American Revolution. In a move designed to subordinate symbolically the military to civil authority, George Washington came to Annapolis to resign his command of the Continental Army. The Treaty of Paris, officially ending the American Revolution, was also signed there. During the early days of the United States, even though Annapolis remained the state capital, the international commercial and industrial potential of nearby Baltimore attracted many of its wealthiest residents. Although the United States Naval Academy moved to Annapolis in 1845, the nineteenth century signaled the era of "gentile eclipse" for Annapolis (Leone, Potter, and Shackel 1987, p. 286). The 1950s saw the beginning of a commercial revival based on yachting, tourism, and new highways that suddenly defined Annapolis as a suburb of Washington, D.C., less than thirty miles away.

Historic preservation has played a major role in the commercial renaissance of Annapolis, and this thumbnail sketch encapsulates the history of Annapolis to several generations of tourists who bought guidebooks, listened to tour guides, and sauntered through the historic-house museums of Annapolis.

But, using Critical Theory, archaeologist Parker Potter noticed something interesting about the process. As the tourists poured through, they received the history of Annapolis as a collection of disconnected units from different time periods and institutions. History-for-the-tourist was left in the hands of diverse groups and institutions, some overlapping, some in competition. Potter realized that Annapolis thus had no unified history connecting the different parts of the city. Black and white populations were presented as unconnected, as were the histories of the city of Annapolis and of the naval academy.

As written and presented by whites, black history (viewed from the nineteenth century) was considered to be separate from white history (presented from the eighteenth century perspective). Slavery was not seen as antecedent to relationships between contemporary groups. In other words, a series of separations forced history into opposing compartments:

eighteenth century versus nineteenth century

white versus black

historic district versus naval academy

residents versus visitors

Parker Potter, working with Mark Leone and others, designed an on-site program for the five thousand to ten thousand visitors who stopped by each year to learn from the archaeology of Annapolis.

During the summer of 1986, while visiting the research team at Historic Annapolis, I—along with 3800 other visitors—had the opportunity to encounter ongoing excavations in a parking lot on Main Street which, until the 1930s, contained the two-and-a-half-story house of one Thomas Hyde. My guide laid out an argument something like this:

Now that I've told you about who we are and how we dig, I'd like to tell you about why we're digging here.

As I mentioned a few minutes ago, one important class of archaeological finds is ceramics. Most ceramic tableware used in this country was made in England until the first half of the nineteenth century, and since we know when these items were made, we can use fragments of them to help us date archaeological sites.

But ceramics are useful for more than dating. There was a revolution in the manufacture and marketing of English earthenware ceramics led by Josiah Wedgwood in the middle of the 1700s. Wedgwood and others developed materials and techniques that allowed the mass manufacture of relatively inexpensive tableware in matched sets. Before the middle of the 1700s, ceramic items usually didn't come in sets and were generally used communally, several people eating from one vessel and sharing another for drinking. The Wedgwood revolution changed all that. Wedgwood introduced plates that allowed each diner to have his or her own plate identical to those of the other diners. He also created sets of dishes which included many different sizes and shapes of vessels for different courses. A proper set of dishes had soup plates *and* breakfast plates *and* dessert plates *and* butter plates, in addition to regular dinner plates. And so on.

We feel that the use of a fully elaborated set of dishes, then as now, was not simply a matter of manners, unconnected to the rest of life. In the elaboration of sizes and shapes of dishes is a dual process of both segmentation and standardization. Separate plates separate the diners at a table from each other, along with the use of proper manners—using the "right fork" and so on. Manners and dishes provided clear rules and divisions

which told and showed individuals how to relate to each other. The meal became segmented here by 1750, and the rules for eating segmented society by separating people.

Meanwhile, the process of segmented labor and mass production which standardized dishes standardized many other kinds of manufactured goods as well. The plates whose sherds we are digging up here served to regularize the eating behavior of those who used them, and at the same time the regularity was the product of both a regulated manufacturing process and a regulated life for the workers who made them. Much of material culture was being standardized, and much of human behavior. These ideas are worth our attention because, while they were new in the middle of the 1700s, many of them are still with us today and are taken for granted as ways we assume the world has always operated. And if we take these things as givens, we forfeit the opportunity to understand their impact on us or to change them. This is how we think about the ceramics we dig up.

These ideas about segmentation don't just have to do with dishes. Just as individual plates and specialized serving dishes separated foods and diners, houses came to have more and more rooms, with different activities being performed apart from each other in separate rooms. Before 1700 many work-related and domestic activities took place in the same room of the house. By 1750 people were building houses with separate rooms for eating, sleeping, cooking, and working. . . . In the early 1700s work and domestic activities usually all went on in the same place. By 1800 in Annapolis people divided work from home life by using shops, taverns, and offices in separate buildings from their homes. Houses like this one we are excavating were used only for domestic life by 1800. By the time large-scale manufacturing began in Baltimore in 1850, work was located far from home, and the distance got greater and greater. . . .

Vacations and tourism are a major industry and a big issue in Annapolis, as in many other small historic towns. Each year over one million people visit Annapolis, a city of only about 32,000 people, so it is easy to understand the city's interest in paying close attention to tourism here; the city works hard to protect the things about it that attract visitors. . . .

In some very subtle ways, Annapolis attempts to use George Washington to guide visitor behavior. For as long as the town has considered itself historic, local guidebooks and histories have included many references to George Washington and his twenty or so visits to the city. In many of these accounts there is a strong emphasis on the social and domestic aspects of Washington's visits to the city; his trips to the racetrack, the balls he attended, the plays he saw, and the family members and friends he visited. The picture of Washington that emerges is very similar to the profile of the kind of visitor Annapolis has very publicly said it wants to attract, the "quality tourist" . . . , one who spends some money in town without disrupting anyone or anything or leaving a mess behind. The effect of presentations of Washington that make him look like the kind of visitor that Annapolis tries to attract today is that Washington ends up as a model tourist. . . . What makes this subtle and unaware portrayal of Washington as a model tourist so interesting is that tourism and vacations were not even in-

vented until eighty years or more after Washington died. . . .

In the last fifteen minutes I've tried to do two things. By discussing the origins of some taken-for-granted aspects of contemporary life, separations and segmentation, I have tried to show that our way of life is not inevitable; it has its origins and its reasons, and it is open to question and challenge as a result. The second thing that I've tried to do, through the George Washington example, is to show ways in which history is often made and presented for contemporary purposes. The next time you see a presentation of history, visit a museum, take a tour, watch a television show about the past, or whatever, you can ask yourself what that version of history is trying to get you to do. (Leone, Potter, and Shackel 1987, pp. 289–291)

Rather than hearing a pasteurized, white-bread version of Annapolis history, these visitors receive a message directly from Critical Theory. These tours are designed to teach participants how to question and challenge their guides—and anybody else who would create and interpret the past (see also Leone 1983, Potter and Leone 1986).

reproduce inequality without serious resistance, violence, or revolution. "Ideology is what reproduces capitalist society intact" (Leone 1986, p. 418).

Critical Marxism attempts to offer a place for everything, refusing to partition inquiries into material relations and "ideology" (Ortner 1984, p. 140). In a sense, critical theory attempts to mediate between the hard-line etic, "scientific" materialists and the "soft" emic, subjective ideationalists.

3. *Critical Theory Critiques the Function of the Past and Our Knowledge of It:* Critical archaeology asserts the active role of the past in a society that studies it. The past, whether viewed through archaeology, the print and video media, myth, or museums, becomes an active vehicle for communicating and composing meaning. The critical archaeologist argues, in the Marxist tradition, that history will always be produced to serve class interests. Exploring the political uses of archaeology produces a more conscious perception of the social function of archaeology, and requires that archaeologists address the past for the greater social benefit as defined through a materialist critique.

> The philosophers have only interpreted the world;
> the thing, however, is to change it.
> —Karl Marx

WHERE TO GO FROM HERE?

Critical Theory in Archaeology: Some General Discussions: The best overviews are found in Leone (1986) and Leone, Potter, and Shackel (1987); see also Ortner (1984, pp. 138–141), Wylie (1985).

Critical Theory in Archaeology: Some Pragmatic Applications: Joan Gero (1985; see also Chapter 4) uses critical theory to assess the role of women in contemporary Americanist archaeology; Mark Leone and his colleagues use critical theory to explore the "Georgian mind-set" in eighteenth-century Annapolis (Leone 1984, 1988a, 1988b; Leone and Shackel 1987; see also Chapter 15); Russell Handsman (1981, 1982) uses critical theory to study the processes of industrially based urbanism in New England; see also Gero, Lacy, and Blakely (1983), Leone and Potter (1988), Little (1988), Perper and Schrire (1977).

Structural Anthropology

The central figure in **structural anthropology** is **Claude Levi-Strauss**. Virtually all structural writings bristle with quotations from Levi-Strauss, whose publications have almost acquired the status of sacred texts. To the uninitiated, the multitudinous writings of Levi-Strauss seem so diverse and all-encompassing that they are like the Bible: Any position on any issue can be supported by a carefully selected quotation. One critic has quipped that Levi-Strauss has interpreted structure; the task of structural anthropologists is to interpret Levi-Strauss.

The Premises of Structuralism

Structural anthropology views culture as the shared symbolic structures that are cumulative creations of the mind. The objective of structural analysis is to discover the basic principles of the human mind as reflected in major cultural domains—myth, art, kinship, and language. To Levi-Strauss, the real world can always be reduced to mental structure, an important premise implying that the material conditions of the real world—subsistence and economy—serve only to constrain human culture; adaptive considerations cannot explain culture. When discussing the custom of primitive people to select totems, for instance, Levi-Strauss asserts that "natural species are not chosen because they are 'good to eat' but because they are 'good to think'" (1963b, p. 89). He concentrates his research on those areas that are least "constrained" by external, material considerations such as myth and religion.

Levi-Strauss set out to determine, then demonstrate, how the human mind operates on the "raw materials of experience" to produce endlessly elaborated conceptual schemes. To Levi-Strauss, the underlying logic of thought is always binary, containing two-way contrasts (+ or –, white or black, and so on). These symbolic polarities run throughout the fabric of a culture, and in this way, the human mind is like a modern computer. In fact, the fundamental dualism is a constant, not a variable. Binary contrasts operate in all cultures. In this sense, Levi-Strauss is more concerned with the workings of general worldwide culture than with any particular culture.

Structuralism has gone far beyond mere methodological discussion in anthropology, producing a large body of results (acceptable to the structuralists, at least). Prominent among the diversified interests of Levi-Strauss has been the study of myth, the cultural domain least constrained by the external conditions of subsistence, economy, and ecology. Levi-Strauss set forth these theories in his monumental four-volume *Mythologiques*. The first volume, *The Raw and the Cooked* (1969b), deals with a complex of myths among Latin American tribes. His explanations rely heavily on cultural evidence. Subsequent volumes trace mythological thought throughout the Americas, concluding with a "sweeping vision of culture, the mind and the human condition" (Keesing 1976, p. 403).

At least as important to anthropological theory as is the analysis of myths and mythic themes is Levi-Strauss's widely influential theory of marriage, exogamy, and exchange. **Alliance theory** attempts to explain why primitive groups consistently seek their mates from outside the local group. That is, why are most primitive residential groupings exogamous?

Levi-Strauss explictly rejects the adaptive explanation offered in the last century by E. B. Tylor and others, namely, that **exogamy** kept a growing tribe unified by exchanging mates between **clans**. In this way, "savage tribes must have had plainly before their minds the simple practical alternative between marrying-out and being killed out" (Tylor 1889, p. 267). Levi-Strauss rejects the idea that exogamy functions to reduce intergroup competition.

Instead of focusing on descent and kinship, Levi-Strauss sees the exchange of women by groups of men as the key element in a social structure. To Levi-Strauss, exogamous marriage is neither the cause nor the underlying motive for exchange. The situation works the other way, that is, exchange is the central relationship in primitive societies. Exchange, in and of itself, has a positive value and hence is basic to human culture: "It is always a system of exchange that we find at the origin of rules of marriage. . . . But no matter what form it takes, whether direct or indirect, general or special, immediate or deferred, explicit or implicit, closed or open, concrete or symbolic, it is exchange, that emerges as the fundamental and common basis for all modalities of the institution of marriage" (Levi-Strauss 1969a, pp. 478–479). Marriage, exogamy, kinship, and descent all have evolved to facilitate this fundamental exchange. From this base, Levi-Strauss goes on in *The Elementary Structures of Kinship* to analyze incest, dual organization, marriage of cousins, and kinship systems throughout the world.

Critics and converts alike agree that the anthropology of Levi-Strauss is aesthetically elegant and logically coherent. But whether, in addition, his arguments are scientifically defensible has been the subject of considerable debate. Regardless of the outcome, Levi-Strauss emerges as one of the major driving forces in twentieth-century anthropology.

Is Structuralism Relevant to Americanist Archaeology?

Levi-Strauss (1963b) once proposed structural approaches to the archaeology of Poverty Point, a site examined by both C. B. Moore and James Ford (see Chapter 1). According to his interpretation, the octagonal plan and the linear platforms suggest a basic binary mental organization by those living there. Few archaeologists accepted the Levi-Strauss interpretation of Poverty Point, but the example does point up the principal difficulty with such structural hypotheses.

How can one test Levi-Strauss's ideas about Poverty Point? Even if one could establish *empirically* that the Poverty Point people did have eight clans, it would be a drastic jump to conclude that the earthworks symbolize a binary dualism as pervasive as male/female, sacred/profane, raw/cooked, and bride takers/bride givers. Even with contemporary ethnographic evidence, these mental structures remain Levi-Strauss mysticisms. They may or may not have anything to do with the minds of the informants.

This issue of verification goes to the heart of Levi-Strauss's structuralism. In reviewing the empirical critique, Scholte (1973, p. 688) compiled an imposing roster of criticisms already launched at Levi-Strauss in this regard: The procedures on structuralism "are judged to be viciously circular, if not actually false. . . . It is subjective, selective, arbitrary, merely clever, even specious. It is abstract, rigid and dogmatic. It may even be meaningless and incomprehensible. It is certainly unverifiable and unempirical. In sum, structuralism is, at best, an aesthetic experience, at worst, a self-fulfilling prophecy."

When these notions are applied to archaeological phenomena, the problem is compounded many times over, and the problem of verification is also the main stumbling block to full acceptance of structural approaches in Americanist archaeology. Such research is commonly criticized as "impressionistic" (Leone 1977), and Hodder recognized that "structuralism is notoriously linked to unverifiable flights of fancy [and] ungrounded arguments" (Hodder 1986, p. 49).

James Deetz provided a partial answer—quoted at some length in the previous chapter—suggesting that a more humanistic, less "scientific" approach may be required to reap the full benefits of structural principles for Americanist archaeology. But to what extent is archaeology willing to forsake its long-standing commitment to scientific procedures and explicit verification?

WHERE TO GO FROM HERE?

Structuralism in Americanist Archaeology: Some General Discussions: Hodder (1982b, 1986, pp. 34–54), Kent (1987a), Leone (1986, pp. 421–424), Washburn (1983).

James Deetz on Structural Approaches to Archaeology

The causes of the transformation of specific sectors of the physical world—be they gravestones, dishes, clothing, or houses—seem relatively easy to identify but may be difficult to explain. To say that tastes, values, or simple preference changed and produced a new form merely points to a cause and an effect, but does not explain what activated the causes (e.g., why did tastes change?). A more powerful explanatory tool might be found in the still controversial school of structural anthropology, which has incurred the distrust of many social scientists, who charge that it is nonpositivist and cannot be subjected to scientific methods of proof, and that it has little predictive value. Yet structuralism holds the promise of providing an explanation for change in the physical world in toto, of explicating relationships between changes in seemingly unrelated categories of material culture, and of relating these transformations to changes in attitudes and worldview. . . .

In simplest terms, structuralism holds that human thought is organized and functions according to a universally shared complex of

Reprinted by permission of the Smithsonian Institution Press from "Material Culture and World View in Colonial Anglo-America" by James Deetz in *The Recovery of Meaning: Historical Archaeology in the Eastern United States* by Mark Leone and Parker Potter, editors. © 1988 Smithsonian Institution, Washington D.C.

oppositional structures that are mediated differently by different cultures, or by the same culture at different times. Although such a proposition is unprovable—we may or may not think in binary terms—it may provide a model that has heuristic value. As Glassie states, "At least binary thinking has aided in theory building" [1975, p. 20]. . . . These oppositional pairs are believed to structure subconscious thought and thus affect all of human behavior as it is seen at the observable particularistic level. Accordingly, similar changes taking place in the same direction and at the same time in otherwise unrelated sectors of culture are attributable to changes in the nature of the mediation of underlying oppositional structures. For example, the shift from many colors to white seen not only in houses but also in gravestones and ceramics [in New England] at the end of the eighteenth-century might result from the strong mediation of the complex-simple opposition in the direction of simplicity, and the strong mediation of the opposition between artificial and natural in the direction of artificiality. Rather than seek an explanation of why houses, or gravestones, or dishes are made white by the century's end, we should look for an explanation of the underlying shift in mediation of the oppositional structures in question. (Deetz 1988, pp. 221, 222)

Structuralism in Americanist Archaeology: Some Specific Applications: Glassie (1975) uses structuralism to analyze historic, domestic architectural change in Middle Virginia (see Chapter 14); Deetz (1977, 1983, 1988) extends Glassie's work to New England (see also Chapter 14); Conkey (1982) uses structural principles to analyze Paleolithic cave art; Kent (1984, 1987a) uses structuralist-oriented theory to examine spatial organization among the Navajos; see also Fritz (1978); Upham (1982, 1987) and Plog (1984) use the structuralist concept of alliance to understand regional system formation and the connectivity between regions in the American Southwest.

Symbolic Anthropology

Although the term **symbolic anthropology** was never actually applied during the 1960s, it has evolved to denote a major branch of ideational thinking that is enjoying increasing popularity in archaeological theory.

The Premises of Symbolic Anthropology

Symbolic anthropology is closely linked with the work of Clifford Geertz, who uses "culture" in a decidedly shared, ideational sense (1973, pp. 6–7). Consider the distinction between a wink and an involuntary eye twitch, gestures identical as physical behavior. We cannot measure the difference between them. Yet, culturally, the difference is manifest. A twitch is a reflex, an unconscious response without cultural meaning. But a wink is a signal in a code of meanings that all Americans share—a code unintelligible, however, to an Eskimo or an Australian aborigine. Even among winks, there can be enormous subtlety. Consider for example, a second winker, who derides the first for winking badly by producing a burlesque, intentionally inept wink. Such subtle behavior acquires meaning and conveys information only within a universe of shared cognitive significance.

To Geertz, culture is embodied in such symbols, through which members of a society communicate their world view and values—to one another and to anthropologists (Ortner 1984, p. 129). So viewed, culture is more than a private common denominator between individuals; it becomes a public phenomenon transcending the cognitive realization of any single individual. Geertz thus sees culture as a code for communication. Culture has a "collective magic" that cannot be understood from any single participant's perspective. In other words, Geertz views culture as a stage play that has a public significance above and beyond the part of any individual actor. Because this shared consciousness transcends any single individual's experience, the collective understanding between two individuals of the same culture is far more than merely the sum total of their two individual parts. By emphasizing such overt, public symbols, Geertz infused culture with a relatively fixed locus, giving it a certain degree of objectivity. Culture is shared and, in a real sense, public. Like language, culture is viewed as an abstraction, an idealized account, synthesized by the analyst and not wholly represented in the consciousness of any single native actor.

The premise that culture is both shared and public has led symbolic anthropologists to stress the distinction between the culture and the social system within which that culture operates. Geertz (1973) defined culture as "an ordered system of meaning and of symbols, in terms of which social interaction takes place"; the social system is "the pattern of social interaction itself." This focus led Geertz and his disciples to question how symbols shape the ways that individuals see, feel, and think about their world, in other words, how symbols operate as vehicles of culture.

This approach to culture is decidedly emic, attempting to study culture from the participant's perspective. Viewed in this way, culture is a product of social beings' attempting to make sense of their world. Thus if an anthropologist is to make sense of such culture, it is necessary to situate himself or herself in the position from which culture is constructed.

Is Symbolic Anthropology Relevant to Americanist Archaeology?

A small, but increasing number seem to think so.

Symbolic archaeologists reject the tenets of cultural materialism (e.g., Hodder 1985, Leone 1986). Often belittling progress made on studies of the natural environment, domesticated plant and animal foods, and the tools, shelter, and techniques used to supply, support, reproduce, and control a population, symbolic archaeologists also complain that such materialistic studies ignore meaning, the context of daily life, and deliberately attempt to manipulate social relations and the whole world of thought.

The most prominent use of symbolic approaches has been by British archaeologists working on the Bronze Age of northwest Europe (see Where to Go from Here?). Like Geertz, these symbolic archaeologists view culture as shared symbolic thought and ideas. Symbols become the motivating force behind behavior and material culture. This approach also stresses the individual rather than the group, in order to isolate people using symbols to negotiate reality on a moment-by-moment basis.

Such symbolic studies have come under severe fire from both archaeological and anthropological circles. As you might expect, the materialists view symbolic anthropology as unscientific, mystical, even softheaded. "Whereas the cultural ecologists considered the symbolic anthropologists to be fuzzy-headed mentalists, involved in unscientific and unverifiable flights of subjective interpretation, the symbolic anthropologists considered cultural ecology to be involved with mindless and sterile scientism, counting calories and measuring rainfall, and willfully ignoring the one truth that anthropology had presumably established by that time: that culture mediates all human behavior" (Ortner 1984, p. 134).

Symbolic anthropology has traditionally relied on intensive interaction with informants. By understanding "appropriate behavior," anthropologists have learned how informants use symbols to structure their own realities. Such methods were often designed "to get inside the informant's head," to determine the structure of culturally acceptable responses.

Traditional Americanist archaeology has always believed that "getting into an informant's head" results only from the improper use of one's shovel. But most of the information that the symbolic anthropologist seeks disappeared with the informant's death. And the scientific cycle, as we have seen, requires that hypotheses be validated by testing them on independent data. How does one scientifically test the symbolic framework that existed in the past? This problem has long led most Americanist archaeologists to shy away from making symbolic interpretations; there were simply no hard data with which to work.

Today's symbolic archaeologists have responded to the problem by rejecting scientific methods (e.g., Hodder 1982a, Miller and Tilley 1984). The so-called anti-positivist position holds that because the scientific method is itself of cultural origin, it becomes impossible to create or depend on a science of the past to produce any more than "interpretation." Such outright rejection of the canons and methods of scientific inquiry have hindered the acceptance of British symbolic archaeology on this side of the Atlantic.

Although we shall have occasion to refer to such symbolic studies later in this book, the truth is that symbolic archaeology remains largely independent of, and irrelevant to, mainstream Americanist archaeology.

WHERE TO GO FROM HERE?

Symbolic Archaeology: Some General Discussions: Hodder (1985) uses the term post-processual to argue for a more symbolic, more "historical," more individually oriented archaeology; Shanks and Tilley (1987a) add to symbolic archaeology an eclectic blend of critical theory and "post-structural" initiatives; see also Leone (1986) Miller (1982), Tilley (1982).

Symbolic Archaeology: Some Specific Applications: Tilley (1984) discusses ideology in the Middle Neolithic of Sweden; Hodder (1982b) discusses the symbolic meaning of ceramic patterning in the Dutch Neolithic; see also Kristiansen (1984), Pearson (1984).

Summary

Anthropologists believe that the true science of humankind can arise only from a holistic, all-encompassing perspective. The physical anthropologist views people chiefly as biological organisms, whereas the cultural anthropologist analyzes people as the creatures of their culture. Archaeology, as a branch of cultural anthropology, is deeply concerned with the concept of culture, the learned body of tradition that ties a society together. Cultural phenomena can be divided into three major domains of study. The cultural idiolect reflects an individual's version of his or her overall shared, modal culture, and the cultural system is the underlying structural basis for a society's biocultural adaptation. These three aspects of culture are reflected in different ways by various schools of anthropological thought. Contemporary anthropological thinking can be characterized by two major strategies of research. The ideational strategy deals with mentalistic, symbolic, cognitive culture. Critical Marxist theory attempts to adapt ideas from Karl Marx to an understanding of events and circumstances of twentieth-century life that Marx did not know. Viewed in a reflexive sense, material culture is not merely a reflection of economics, social organization, or ideology; it becomes an instrument to create meaning and order in one's world. Structural anthropology attempts to discover the fundamental principles of human cognition, primarily through the analysis of myth, art, kinship, and language. Symbolic anthropology emphasizes the definition and use of symbols as codes of communication.

The contrasting adaptive strategy in anthropology, cultural materialism, emphasizes those aspects of culture that most closely articulate with the environment, technology, and economics. This infrastructure is seen as ultimately conditioning the character of both structure and superstructure.

To date, archaeologists have been most heavily influenced by these adaptive mainstreams, although many contemporary archaeologists are attempting to apply the ideational perspective as a mode of archaeological explanation. Although some are more important than others, no single anthropological school dominates contemporary archaeology.

CHAPTER 4

What Is Contemporary Americanist Archaeology?

The popular image of the archaeologist seems to be an extraordinary cross between a cobwebbed Methuselah and a rather sharp-looking youth with a shovel who is unable to read "No Trespassing" signs.
—Ivor Noël Hume

Having looked briefly at the modern mainstreams of anthropological thought, we shall now narrow our focus to the primary topic of this book, the field of Americanist archaeology.

Americanist archaeology is struggling to escape the myths promulgated by movies and television (Figure 4–1). As everybody knows, Hollywood archaeologists are pistol-packing, hard-drinking professors who circle the globe seeking prehistoric treasure, braving the occult and political intrigue, muttering "To hell with the mummy's curse. . . ." These macho-men are accompanied by buxom yet plucky research assistants—always young, female, and foxy. Together, they are academic but death-defying as they oversee their crew of a thousand sweating, cursing, rebellious natives. They usually have a treasure map.

The history of our field does reveal a glimmer of truth in the stereotype. Archaeologists do, from time to time, carry guns. Fieldwork has sometimes been hazardous. Some archaeologists drink too much. And one or two even have worked as CIA spies.

Although today's reality is quite different, many myths persist. Here, we will explode three of the more common fictions: The truth is that most Americanist archaeologists are not professors; many Americanist archaeologists dig historic-period sites; and plenty of Americanist archaeologists are not men.

FIGURE 4–1   Indiana Jones in *Raiders of the Lost Ark*—played by Harrison Ford—artfully personified a world of stereotypes regarding archaeologists. (© 1988 Lucasfilm Ltd. All rights reserved; photograph by Keith Hamshere)

The First Myth: Americanist Archaeology Is Strictly An Academic Profession

> The destruction of a prehistoric site is permanent.
> Like Humpty Dumpty, it cannot be reassembled.
> —Louis Brennan

Americanist archaeology, it is true, began as a wholly "academic" endeavor, and before 1970 or so, most archaeologists were employed as university professors and museum curators. But an employment revolution of sorts has recently overtaken Americanist archaeology, and the results are far-reaching. Today, perhaps 40 percent of all Americanist archaeologists work as professors and curators. The rest make their living through "applied archaeology." This job profile has changed the operating structure of archaeology.

For decades archaeologists have preached the importance of protecting archaeological sites, but it was not until the new awareness of **ecology** in the 1960s that some real progress was made. In the mid-sixties there were demonstrations such as Earth Day, and thousands of people chanted non sequiturs like "Save the Ecology" or displayed bumper stickers like "I'm for Ecology." The voter appeal of these popular movements was not lost on the legislators, whose ears pricked up, and many of them became "conservationists" too. In fact, sufficient legislative power came down on the side of the ecologists for laws to have been drafted to protect the nonrenewable resources of the nation.

But what are nonrenewable resources? Most people think of redwoods and whooping cranes and baby seals. Others think that energy-related assets like oil, coal, and uranium make up America's nonrenewable resources. But most legislators have a legal background, and in the course of legally defining nonrenewable resources, they realized that properties of historic value must be included as well. After all, they reasoned, how many Monticellos do we have? Are archaeological sites "nonrenewable" or what?

As a result of this legislation, archaeological sites were included in the ecological legislation of the late 1960s and the 1970s. Archaeological sites are now legally nonrenewable resources, just like redwoods, whooping cranes, and shale-oil fields.

The movement became known as **culture resource management**, and a working definition of cultural resources reads like this: "physical features, both natural and manmade, associated with human activity. These would include sites, structures, and objects possessing significance, either individually or as groupings, in history, architecture, or human [cultural] development. . . . Cultural properties are unique and nonrenewable resources" (J. M. Fowler 1974, pp. 1467–1468).

One of the important pieces of legislation is the Archaeological and Historic Preservation Act of 1974, more commonly known as the Moss–Bennett Act. This act requires all federal agencies to consider the dangers posed by their activities on the archaeological sites on the land. And—here is the important part—these agencies are authorized to spend up to 1 percent of their own money for archaeological salvage. Congress thus provided a means for supporting archaeological conservation without having to go through the National Park Service or come to Washington for special congressional authorization. But even more influential than Moss–Bennett is the National Environmental Policy Act (NEPA) of 1969. Combined with two other measures—the National Historic Preservation Act and Executive Order 11593—federal agencies now have guidelines on how to assess the impact of proposed construction on archaeological sites.

This legislation has defined a new philosophy of governmental decision making, requiring that environmental and cultural variables be considered side by side with technological and economic benefits when planning future construction. These new requirements have created thousands of archaeological contracts, which result in reports detailing the nature of the archaeological resources endangered and how the projects' impact should be mitigated.

The immediate result of the federal legislation has been to spotlight the need for accurate information regarding archaeological sites. Sometimes the federal agencies have the resources to undertake such studies, but more commonly the agencies contract with academic institutions, museums, and qualified private individuals to prepare the required reports. In fact, it has been estimated that in a few years 90 percent of all archaeological research in the United States will be contract related.

The nature of **conservation archaeology**, or cultural resource management, has been changing in recent years. Environmental impacts are no longer mitigated merely by finding a few sites that might be nice to dig. Federal agencies are now taking steps to locate *all* archaeological sites of value that are under the agency's control or may be subject to damage. This intensive survey requires more than a preliminary visit to the area in question. Modern legal regulations require the intensive examination of all the federal lands involved. The archaeological sites discovered are then evaluated against a recent set of federal standards known as the Criteria of Eligibility for the National Register of Historic Places (see King, Hickman, and Berg 1977, Appendix A).

Federal procedures have thus created an unprecedented demand for trained archaeological personnel. Not only must conservation archaeologists know the local pottery types and soil zones, but they also must be acutely aware of provisions in the latest federal and state legislation.

Contract work in archaeology is big business. In recent years the Army Corps of Engineers and the Soil Conservation Service have spent considerably more money annually for Americanist archaeology than have the National Science Foundation and other granting agencies combined. Such huge sums of money are still relatively new to archaeology and inevitably raise the question, Who is a qualified professional archaeologist anyway?

One answer comes from the **Society of Professional Archeologists (SOPA)**, incorporated in 1976. SOPA was created largely in response to the rapid growth of contract archaeology in the United States and Canada. As stated in the Articles of Incorporation, the purposes of SOPA are to

1. Strengthen the identification of archaeology as a profession and of qualified archaeologists as professionals;
2. Encourage high standards in the training of archaeologists;
3. Require high standards of performance from practicing professional archaeologists;
4. Communicate to the public the importance of the proper practice of archaeology;
5. Assist governmental and other organizations which use archaeologists in the course of their activities to identify those properly qualified for the purpose.

A major function of SOPA has been to compile and maintain an up-to-date listing of professional archaeologists. By initiating a certification program for professional archaeologists, SOPA recognizes individuals who meet the qualifications of a professional archaeologist. Those accepting such certification must subscribe to SOPA's Code of Ethics, Institutional Standards, and Standards of Research Performance. In essence, SOPA, a self-policing agency, attempts to ensure that individuals claiming professional competence are really qualified. The SOPA directory lists all archaeologists who have been accepted to date and is available to the public.

WHERE TO GO FROM HERE?

Some Landmark Sources on the Conservation of America's Archaeological Heritage: Judd (1929): "The Present Status of Archaeology in the United States"; Brew (1961): "Emergency Archaeology: Salvage in Advance of Technological Progress"; Hester Davis (1972): "The Crisis in American Archaeology"; Lipe (1974): "A Conservation Model for American Archaeology"; McGimsey (1972): *Public Archeology;* see also Dixon (1971), Gumerman (1973), King (1971, 1976, 1977), Lipe and Lindsay (1974).

On the History of Conservation Archaeology: In "Conserving American Archaeological Resources," Don Fowler (1986) shows how the new movement for cultural resource management is not really so new after all; see also Fowler (1982), Haag (1985), Jennings (1985).

Some More Contemporary Consideration of Archaeological Conservation: For discussions of the Americanist conservation movement, see Kelley (1977), King (1977), King, Hickman, and Berg (1977), Schiffer and House (1977). McHargue and Roberts (1977) provide an amateur's guide to the avocational practice of conservation archaeology in North America; also see Brennan (1973) and Feldman (1977). The problem of preserving archaeological resources around the world is addressed in papers edited by H. Cleere (1984): *Approaches to the Archaeological Heritage: A Comparative Study of World Cultural Resource Management Systems;* see also Rahtz (1974).

Our ideals, laws and customs should be based on the proposition that each generation in turn becomes the custodian rather than the absolute owner of our resources—and each generation has the obligation to pass this inheritance on to the future.
—Alden Whitmann

The Second Myth: Americanist Archaeologists Care Only About Prehistoric Sites

Historical archaeology has been a visible force for centuries. The early archaeologists discussed in Chapters 1 and 2 were historical archaeologists, pursuing the classic splendor of historical sites in Greece, Rome, and the biblical lands by relying on both documents and archaeological objects as their tools of research. Heinrich Schliemann (Chapter 2) is a perfect example of this early tradition in historical archaeology. In North America, some of the earliest known excavations took place on historic-period sites. The Plymouth settlers excavated a historic-period Algonquian Indian grave only two years after their arrival.

Despite such early beginnings, historical archaeology did not gain formal status as a discipline until the mid-1960s. For a while, historical archaeologists could not even agree on a name for themselves. Cleland and Fitting (1968) spoke of historical archaeology's "crisis of identity" which remains, to some extent, even today. Interestingly, historical archaeology underwent its crisis during the emergence of the new archaeology, an event largely restricted to prehistorians. What should be the major focus of research: to write cultural history (to particularize) or to understand cultural processes (to generalize)? Although the new archaeology has disappeared as an intellectual cadre, the basic questions persist. Particularly in historical archaeology, the debate still continues regarding the proper focus of inquiry. What are the options?

One group—the Handmaiden-to-History school (after Noël Hume 1964)—argued that historical archaeology should function primarily to supplement the historical record of the past. Writing twenty-five years ago, Noël Hume saw the historic site archaeologist as "a new breed—he is actually a historian with a pen in one hand and a trowel in the other" (1964, p. 215). This perspective is manifested mostly by those involved with large, continuing projects closely connected with historic reconstruction and restoration. At such public centers as Plimoth Plantation, Colonial Williamsburg, Little Bighorn, and Fort Michilimackinac, extensive archaeology has been conducted specifically to recover data necessary to restore and interpret the sites (Deagan 1982, p. 159) (see Figure 4–2). But the benefits of such research often extend beyond simple restoration.

Americanist historical archaeology began in the 1940s and 1950s, concentrating on a very few selected sites, particularly houses of the rich and famous, forts, and other military sites; Colonial Williamsburg served as a model for this early-stage historical archaeology. The initial research there was largely in the hands of architectural historians, with little attention paid to the middens and lesser structures. As historic documents were exhausted for clues to dating, historical archaeologists generally followed their prehistoric colleagues in developing independent, artifact-based methods for dating sites and components (we explore several such techniques in Chapter 10).

Although a few historical archaeologists still believe that writing culture history is an objective—keeping the "handmaiden" imperative alive—most view such research as merely a necessary first step toward more important goals. For one thing, the fruits of culture resource management have created a boom. Historical archaeology has blossomed into a massive program that compares in funding and popularity with that of prehistoric archaeology in many parts of the country. Although this early work was mostly done by those trained initially in history or architecture, more recent research has been conducted largely by those whose major academic ties are to anthropology (Fairbanks 1977, p. 133).

Admitting that the debate about the proper orientation of historical archaeology has not been fully resolved, most historical archaeologists today seem to follow the anthropological perspective. Viewed on this broader scale, historical archaeology may

FIGURE 4–2 Curious visitors experience something of life in seventeenth-century colonial America by visiting Plimoth Plantation (Massachusetts). (Courtesy Plimoth Plantation)

pertain to the entire range of human behavior: spoken word, written word, preserved behavior, and observed behavior (Schuyler 1977). There can be little doubt that historical archaeology is today viewed by most practitioners as a subdiscipline of anthropology (a good thing, as most contemporary historical archaeologists received the bulk of their training in departments of anthropology). But historical archaeology remains to some extent differentiated from its prehistoric counterpart because of the important alignment with nonanthropological disciplines, particularly history per se and architecture.

So what is historical archaeology? Although a profusion of definitions still exists, we follow Kathleen Deagan's (1982, p. 153): Historical archaeology is "the study of human behavior through material remains, for which written history in some way affects its interpretation."

Mainstream historical archaeology tends to deemphasize what Noël Hume (1969, p. 10) once called a "Barnum and Bailey" emphasis on the "oldest," "largest," and "most historically significant" site, looking instead toward reconstructing lifeways in the entire social context, whether or not presently viewed as "historical." There is a distinct parallel to W. W. Taylor's message four decades ago, when he urged Mayan archaeologists to transcend the hierarchical and the grandiose, and to get on with the anthropology of real people.

This emphasis on "backyard archaeology" (Fairbanks 1977) has naturally led historical archaeologists into the anthropological camp, making basic contributions—with their prehistoric archaeological colleagues—to an understanding of **paleoethnography.** One particularly important direction of the "reconstructionist" school has been the focus on so-called historically disenfranchised groups in our own culture, what has been termed "archaeology of the inarticulate," attempting to undercover the archaeological roots of American black culture, Asian-American culture, Native Americans during the historic period, and Hispanic-American Creoles.

The history of the powerless, the inarticulate, the poor has not yet begun to be written because they have been treated no more fairly by historians than they have been treated by their contemporaries.
—Jesse Lemisch

Some of this research has called into question the "melting-pot" interpretation of America's past. Both Deetz (1977) and Schuyler (1976) contend that the evolution of American society was more a systematic exclusion of non-Anglo groups from mainstream Anglo-American society. Such bias is all the more unknown, as conventional historical records are most incomplete and distorted when dealing with racial minorities. Yet in other cases, as at St. Augustine, the "melting-pot" model seems a rather accurate reflection of the way in which Hispanic-American society functioned in the New World (Deagan 1980).

Although many historical archaeologists see generalizing, processual objectives as important to their field as well, most such studies remain rooted in particular times and particular places, "concentrated on cultural processes operating at specific times and places, and are thus, strictly speaking, particularizing in result. They provide, however, the building blocks on which more general processual questions about human culture may be investigated" (Deagan 1982, p. 162).

In one sense, historical archaeologists have an advantage here because they can enhance their shovel work with documentary records: In many cases, the effects of ethnic affiliation, income, religion, occupation, family composition, economic network, and political restrictions can be taken as givens and need not be inferred directly from the archaeological record. One particularly effective result of processual research in historical archaeology has been the study of **acculturation**, emphasizing trading relations, religious conversion, and racial intermarriage. In subsequent chapters, we shall explore several cases in which historical archaeologists are pursuing such timeless, spaceless (processual) questions.

WHERE TO GO FROM HERE?

Important Sources on Americanist Approaches to Historical Archaeology: Deagan (1977, 1982), Deetz (1977a), Noël Hume (1969), Schuyler (1970, 1976), South (1977a, 1977b).

What Should Historical Archaeologists Call Themselves?: For some opinions, see Deagan (1982, p. 153), Deetz (1977b, p. 5), Noël Hume (1969, p. 12), Schuyler (1970, p. 119), South (1977a, p. 1).

Historical Archaeology is the premier American journal devoted to historic-period archaeology in the Western Hemisphere; papers also deal with major issues of relevant archaeological theory and practice worldwide; first published in 1967.

Subscription information: Society for Historical Archaeology, P.O. Box 231003, Pleasant Hill, Calif. 94523.

The Third Myth: Americanist Archaeology Is Only For Macho-Men

> I asked a Burmese why women, after centuries of following their men, now walk ahead. He said there were many unexploded land mines since the war.
> —Robert Mueller

Like all social sciences, contemporary Americanist archaeology is firmly entangled in the web of late-twentieth-century attitudes. Whereas most archaeologists aspire to an impartial, objective science, we shall always remain creatures of our own culture. Archaeology is a social endeavor, and today's methods and interpretations are far from "value neutral" (Gero 1985, p. 342). In subsequent chapters we shall explore how contemporary attitudes toward race, politics, religion, and gender color our specific interpretations of the past.

Right now, we shall focus on archaeology as a profession and the degree to which women participate in that discipline. Traditional Americanist archaeology has, without question, been a male-dominated venture. Chapter 1 sketched the history in terms of eight "forebears," and not until we reached the 1970s could a woman, Kathleen Deagan, be selected to represent the field.

Choosing America's premier archaeologists reflects somewhat my own view of the profession and also the fact that for decades women, (and other minorities) were excluded from Americanist archaeology. And the written histories of the field necessarily reflect this bias.

But the truth is that women—like Sophie Schliemann (Chapter 2)—were there in the early days of archaeology but are not well represented in the written histories because they participated as wives and philanthropists and avocational archaeologists. Access to formal training in archaeology was limited, fieldwork opportunities almost nonexistent (unless you married the dig director), and publication outlets nil. As a result, although women have been a compelling force in Americanist archaeology for a century, they remained almost invisible until the last few decades.

Gender bias was evident everywhere in archaeology's past. The first annual meeting of the Society for American Archaeology (SAA)—still the most conspicuous professional organization representing Americanist archaeologists—was held in Pittsburgh in 1935. Of the forty-two members presented for election as "fellows" of the new society, only four were women (Griffin 1985). The presidency of the SAA remained exclusively male until 1958, when H. Marie Wormington was elected to the office (Figure 4–3). Cynthia Irwin-Williams served as president between 1977 and 1979; at this writing, Dena Dincauze is the president of the Society of American Archaeology. The same is true of the Society for Historical Archaeology. Since its founding in 1967, only three women—Kathleen Gilmore (1978), Kathleen Deagan (1985), and Mary Beaudry (1988)—have been elected president.

H. Marie Wormington (1981) attributes much of the earlier bias against women in archaeology to the mistaken beliefs that "women could not withstand the rigors of the field" or that marriage and childbearing would preclude devotion to an archaeological career. If you think such attitudes are no longer with us, take a look at the examples in Chapter 6 entitled "Watch Out for Popular (Mis)Perceptions of Women in Archaeological

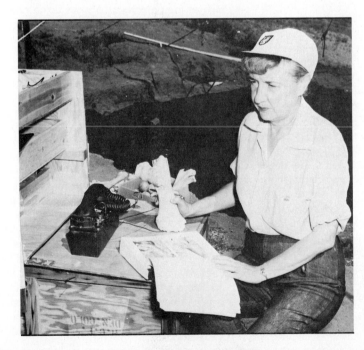

FIGURE 4–3 Marie Wormington working at the Frazier Agate Basin site (Colorado). (Courtesy H. M. Wormington)

Joan Gero on the "Woman-At-Home" Ideology

Although the social climate of Americanist archaeology has changed radically over the past two decades, women still face significant hurdles. Even today, fieldwork opportunities still favor male participants; Irwin-Williams (n.d.) estimates that perhaps half as many opportunities are available to female archaeological students as to males. And as Joan Gero points out, there still lingers a perception—among individual archaeologists and some grant-giving agencies—that men are somehow better suited to fieldwork and women should stick to "stay-at-home" aspects of archaeology.

[Since archaeology is conducted in a thoroughly social world] we can expect archaeologists to conform in their professional roles to the same ideological constructs they adopt to explain the past. We are alerted to certain strong parallels between the male who populates the archaeological record—public, visible, physically active, exploratory, dominant, and rugged, the stereotypic hunter—and the practicing field archaeologist who himself conquers the landscape, brings home the goodies, and takes his data raw! Not only does the public uphold this image of the archaeologist (Gero 1981, 1983), but the archaeologist himself concurs (Woodall and Perricone 1981). Corresponding, then, to the stereotyped male, we expect to find the female archaeologist secluded in the base-camp laboratory or museum, sorting and preparing archaeological materials, private, protected, passively receptive, ordering and systematizing, but without recognized contribution to the productive process. The woman-at-home archaeologist must fulfill her stereotypic feminine role by specializing in the analysis of archaeological materials, typologizing, seriating, studying wear or paste or

Reprinted by permission of J. M. Gero and the Society for American Archaeology.

iconographic motifs. She will have to do the archaeological housework.

[If gender ideology does actually guide the division of labor] in archaeological research, then male archaeologists would be concentrated in field-base research, undertaking projects that include the collection of primary data from excavations or surveys. Female archaeologists, on the other hand, would be involved in non-field projects, projects where the investigator analyzes data that she or he did not collect from an archaeological context, and where data collection is not a significant aspect of the research. . . .

By 1979-1980 . . . all measures demonstrate a significant trend toward a male preoccupation with field-base research and a female involvement with non-field oriented research. In fact, by all measures, the proportion of females doing non-field related research is consistently twice as high as the proportion of males doing non-field research, although males almost completely dominate the high-technology niche of archeometric (non-field) research. Conversely, close to twice as high a proportion of male archaeologists do field-related research as female archaeologists [with minor exceptions]. . . .

As soon as women enter the profession in larger numbers . . . the trend is unambiguous: very close to two-thirds of the female archaeologists base their dissertation research on non-field oriented, analytic projects, while very close to two-thirds of the males undertake field-related research. We can also extrapolate from this sequence that in the last ten years males have dropped from conducting between 92% and 95% (in 1960–1974) to only 75–78% of the field-base dissertation research (in 1974–1984). But this shift is fully accounted for by the swelling of the female doctorate ranks, where consistent proportions of field and non-field research are maintained but larger numbers of females contribute to field research each year. (Gero 1985, pp. 344–345, 347)

Fieldwork." As Wormington (1981, p. v) dryly noted, "Activities by many archaeologists, who are women, have amply demonstrated that this is not the case."

Nevertheless, recognition of women in professional archaeology took a long time, in part because of such hesitation. Most archaeologists get their first taste of fieldwork in academic-based field schools (like the one I described in the Prologue). Although some archaeological field schools admitted women in the 1920s (Gifford and Morris 1985), it was not until the early 1970s that "mixed" digs became commonplace.

No hard figures seem to exist. Linda Cordell estimates that only about 10 percent of currently employed archaeologists are female (Cordell 1986, p. 4). This is curious, as women have assumed a considerably more prominent place in anthropology. The *Anthropology Newsletter* (April 1987) noted that "The average 1985–1986 anthropology Ph.D. . . . is 38 years old, married, white, female and childless. She holds a nonacademic job with a yearly salary of $24,000. Her name . . . is Judith" (Givens 1987). Women now outnumber males receiving Ph.D.s in anthropology, but a smaller proportion of women choose to specialize in archaeology. As Linda Cordell (1986) points out, Judith is still not an archaeologist.

That gender bias persists in Americanist archaeology is no secret. But it is equally obvious that many women are making successful careers in this field. There is no single viewpoint regarding the future for women in archaeology, but here is career advice from some who did make the grade:

> Mary Eubanks Dunn: "After I passed my Ph.D. requirements, one faculty member confided that a lot more had been demanded of me than of the male students because the faculty knew that it is difficult for a woman to get a job in archaeology. Only a woman who can demonstrate truly superior ability has a chance to make it." (Williams 1981, p. 124)
>
> Leslie E. Wildesen: "Being female is an asset in initial hiring because of the emphasis placed on equal opportunity. . . . The more information I learn, and the further along the path from 'recent Ph.D.' to 'grand old *man*' of the profession I get, the more incensed I become at the diminished expectations women are led to have, and at the decreased opportunities women are offered to fulfill even those expectations." (Williams 1981, p. 88)
>
> Cynthia Irwin-Williams: Gender bias "makes for a kind of 'do or die' point of view. The result for me was that I began to do individual independent research much earlier than people who found it easier to join large projects. Exclusion from the mainstream opportunities led to a fierce determination to do it on my own." (Williams 1981, p. 9)

One further point deserves mention. As several archaeologists (including Joan Gero, Mary Whelan, and Margaret Conkey) have recently recognized, the inclusion of female archaeologists in the Americanist mainstream involves more than "just add women and stir." We simply are not seeing women coming in and doing the same thing.

The field of Americanist archaeology is necessarily changing as a result of integrating a distinctive group of people (women) because all of us operate—to one degree or another—within our own cultural experience when we interpret the past. Women's experiences are different from men's because women occupy a different place in American society than men do. The theoretical diversity in Americanist archaeology is closely linked with our ability to encourage diversity among the participants of the field—be they women, Native Americans, black Americans, or other previously disenfranchised ethnic groups.

WHERE TO GO FROM HERE?

The Role of Women in Americanist Archaeology: Gero (1985) provides a thoughtful and influential discussion of the stereotypes plaguing women in archaeology; Irwin-Williams (n.d.) examines the role of women in the development of archaeology, with emphasis on pioneers in the field before the 1960s; Cordell (1986) discusses a similar topic with respect to the American Southwest; Barbara Williams's (1981). *Breakthrough: Women in Archaeology* contains the biographies of six contemporary female archaeologists; Scott (1987) provides a powerful analysis of the role of women within the discipline of American history; see also Wilk (1985).

The Aims of Americanist Archaeology

Despite these disparate constituencies within Americanist archaeology, there is general agreement among contemporary archaeologists on the aims of archaeology. Archaeology's initial objective is to construct **cultural chronologies**, thereby ordering the remnants of past material culture into intelligible temporal segments. The intermediate objective is to breathe life into these chronologies by reconstructing past lifeways. The ultimate objective of contemporary archaeology is to spell out the **cultural processes** that underlie human behavior, past and present. These processes are expressed as lawlike statements, as timeless, spaceless universals.

Note that these objectives are rank ordered, beginning with chronology, proceeding to lifeway, and culminating in process. This sequence reflects both the way in which archaeologists approach their goals and the relative primacy attached to each objective. Chronologies are an essential first step, but understanding past lifeways is more important. Elucidating the cultural processes is the most important archaeological endeavor.

This ordering likewise mirrors the progress of archaeology as a science. The pioneering archaeological investigation in most areas of the world has been chronological, defining the sequence of cultures that have lived there. Once a rudimentary chronological arrangement was crafted, archaeologists tended to branch out, asking questions about how people in these extinct cultures actually lived; this is second-stage research focused on past lifeways. Finally, after some information about lifeway is available, archaeologists can begin to seek the universals behind the adaptations.

Keeping these strictures in mind, we can now examine the actual methods and theories that enable contemporary archaeologists to pursue their three cardinal objectives.

Initial Objective: Construct Cultural Chronology

Chronology is at the root of the matter, being the nerve
electrifying the dead body of history.
—B. Laufer

Chapter 3 emphasized that archaeology's major contribution to anthropological theory is time. Although many ethnologists study cultural evolution and cultural change, if they restricted themselves to ethnographic testimony, their studies would remain shallow, short term, and perfunctory. Only through an archaeological perspective can episodes of both short- and long-term cultural evolution be satisfactorily documented. The same holds true for human ecology. It is marvelous to scrutinize the adaptive nuances of an existing human group, but this study takes on broader significance only when one can determine how such an adaptation came to be, an understanding that generally requires an archaeological perspective.

Paradoxically, time is archaeology's double-edged sword. Before archaeologists can explore the particulars of cultural evolution, ecology, and process, the archaeological record must first be partitioned into appropriate temporal and spatial segments. Ethnographers have it easy because they operate within a single time interval—the present. The time frame is a given in ethnographic investigation.

But consider the difficulties in patroling time at a major archaeological site, such as Gatecliff Shelter (introduced in the Prologue). Radiocarbon evidence tells us that people have lived intermittently at Gatecliff for at least seven thousand years. How many different cultures were there? Five? Ten? Seven thousand? This is no mere exercise in **typology** and classification. Any discussion of a cultural system must necessarily assume that all the so-called components of this system actually existed at the same time. Suppose you're reconstructing a prehistoric trade network. If you suspect a series of interrelated trading stations—Group *A* trades with Group *B*, Group *B* passes goods on to Group *C*, Group *C* returns something to group *A*—you are obviously presuming that Groups *A*, *B*, and *C* must have been contemporaries. How else could they have been trading partners?

One of archaeology's cardinal principles is this: Whatever else you intend to do, you must first have a firm grasp on time. Archaeologists have long realized that you must know the when and the where before contemplating the how, the who, the what, and especially the why. Defining a temporal framework generally involves two related procedures: dating the physical remains and contexts and classifying the archaeological objects to reflect these temporal categories. These techniques are discussed in detail in Part Two.

There is a second, equally important point to remember about chronology: It is a preliminary step (archaeology's "initial" objective), not an end in itself. Remember from Chapter 1 that forty years ago, W. W. Taylor chastized his predecessors for falling in love with chronology and cultural history—and forgetting the rest. Even today, archaeologists must avoid the misguided quest for the ultimate chronology. It does not exist. Chronologies are simply hypotheses either satisfactory for the needs at hand, or not. Period. Chronology is merely a step toward a more meaningful, anthropologically relevant objective; it must not be confused with the goal itself. By comprehending and acknowledging the preliminary nature of chronology, archaeologists are entitled to take certain shortcuts. Because chronology is merely a means to an end, archaeologists are authorized temporarily to discount much of the cultural variability encountered in chronology building.

At the chronological stage, archaeologists use a deliberately simplified definition of culture. Remember from Chapter 3 that culture has three convergent parts: idiolect, shared culture, and cultural system. Taken together, these three components comprise what most anthropologists think of as culture. If archaeologists are serious about their role as social scientists—and if archaeologists are to provide a truly relevant input to social theory—then all configurations of culture must be considered.

But this need not be done all at once. Archaeologists discovered long ago that to establish chronological order, they can concentrate on the shared aspects of culture and set aside the more idiographic or systematic cultural components. Chronology building is grounded in a deliberately simplified, narrowly defined segment of the total cultural picture. This means that a cultural chronology must be approached with due caution. Chronology only tells the archaeologist when. Chronologies do not tell us what or why. The what of culture is a lifeway question, involving the totality of an extinct society. This is archaeology's intermediate objective, and a change in our definition of culture is required to answer the what questions. Moreover, the why of culture—the processes behind human behavior—is an even more complicated topic. Do not make the mistake of using simplified chronological methods (archaeology's initial goal) to answer processual questions (archaeology's ultimate goal).

Grandma's Law: Eat your vegetables and then you can have your dessert.
—Lawrence Peter

Intermediate Objective: Reconstruct Extinct Lifeways

Once established, a workable chronological framework frees the archaeologist to ascend to a second, loftier ambition, that of resurrecting forgotten lifeways. At this intermediate stage, archaeologists seek to recall what Claude Levi-Strauss once called "the ring of bygone harmonies" (1963b, p. 114).

Chronology is only a stepping-stone. Reconstructing past cultural adaptations, by contrast, is directly relevant to and comparable with modern ethnographic observation. Ethnologists pore over adaptations for which firsthand descriptive observations are possible; archaeologists, at this stage, study adaptations that existed only in the past. This stage of archaeological inquiry has been succinctly termed *paleoethnography*, the "anthropology of the dead" (Heizer and Graham 1967).

What is a lifeway? Simply put, lifeways are the what and who of culture, embracing the breadth of human experience: where people live, the population densities, technology, economy, organization of domestic life, kinship, maintenance of law and order, social stratification, ritual, art, and religion. Although all aspects of human lifeways are not equally well preserved, these lacunae are more than compensated for by the perspective of time, the long-term *in situ* evolution visible only in the ground.

The archaeologist must embrace a new mind-set when approaching human lifeways. When building chronology, one is free to pick and choose among cultural particulars, searching out the peculiarities that best reflect the nits of temporal change. But once the archaeologist graduates to paleoethnography, such cavalier treatment becomes grossly inappropriate.

Remember Gatecliff Shelter? As long as chronology was our objective, we could excavate deep, vertical test pits—what Kent Flannery calls "telephone booths." These steep-sided excavation shafts exposed stratigraphic changes; we were looking for artifact forms that changed through time, and we found them. The overall cultural context in each stratum was largely irrelevant to the resulting chronology. All we cared about was that corner-notched dart points were fabricated before side-notched arrowheads. These **time-markers** were critical because they helped us date archaeological deposits at other sites and even infer time ranges at isolated surface sites.

But archaeologists cannot live by chronology alone. Once we pinned down the Gatecliff chronological sequence with sufficient radiocarbon evidence, the excavation strategy changed markedly. We shifted to a "horizontal" perspective in an attempt to expose intact prehistoric campsites. We carefully plotted the artifacts and features and were able to construct the surface appearance of campsites occupied millennia ago.

Once the when and the where queries were satisfied, we could move up to the more pertinent what questions:

What was the population density at Gatecliff Shelter?

What was the prehistoric social organization like?

What time of year did people live at Gatecliff?

What animals did they eat, and what hunting techniques did they use to catch them?

What plants did they collect, and how did their seasonal availability influence human scheduling?

What were the trade networks, and what was traded?

What were the social relationships with neighboring societies?

So-called what questions can proliferate ad infinitum; once one uncertainty is put to rest, five more spring forth to take its place.

Once we began to pursue the past lifeways at Gatecliff Shelter, we realized that the answers to the what questions did not necessarily lie inside the shelter, because these were a nonsedentary people, moving several times each year. Gatecliff was only one link in an intricate chain of settlements that extended fifty miles or more in all directions. To assess the total, year-round picture requires one to shift one's perspective outside the cave toward the region surrounding Gatecliff. Archaeologists reconstructing cultural adaptations of nonsedentary societies can no longer rely on the record contained in single, isolated sites—it's like trying to reconstruct a mainframe computer by looking at a single chip. Isolated components provide some clues, but hardly the total picture.

In Part Four of this book we shall look at the techniques archaeologists use to reconstruct past lifeways. Not only must we go beyond the single site, but archaeologists also must transcend those seductive shared aspects of culture. If you're after past lifeways, you'd better view culture in its total systemic context. Building a chronology encourages the search for the typical, the modal, the normal—what most people did.

Once the archaeologist becomes the paleoethnographer, chronological shortcuts become inappropriate; fleshing out past lifeways does not stop with the average. Variability becomes the watchword, variability due to technology, ecology, economy, demography, social structure, political organization, or ideology. Lifeway transcends the shared aspects of culture to embrace the total systemic matrix in which that culture operated. This shift from the modal to the systemic requires different field strategies and different conceptual frameworks. Although the same archaeological objects are often used for both chronology and lifeway, the data generated from these objects are different indeed.

Ultimate Objective: Define Cultural Processes

An archaeologist's ultimate goal should be to cease doing archaeology.
—David Hurst Thomas

Exploring chronology and past lifeways are particularistic ventures: particular artifacts from particular cultures that existed at particular times in particular places. Shoals of archaeologists have been occupied for decades describing these particulars. Depending on your perspective, culture is either a blend of shared traits or a system that joins a society to its environment. The shared-culture approach is germane to chronology, but little else. To define past lifeways, the archaeologist must perceive culture as a maze of interlocking components.

Yet even the most ingenious reconstruction of an extinct society's ecological niche or its religion or social organization remains mere description. That lifeway remains unique, fixed in time and space. Archaeology's toughest goal is to decode the processes behind these specifics. Components of a cultural system remain static until the processes that propel the system are defined.

Anthropologists learn about such processes by isolating cultural systems at a single point in time. Called **synchronic** analysis, this strategy studies how the various subsystems join to meet society's needs. The synchronic approach is a common ethnographic technique. We know, for instance, that the Nevada Shoshone of the 1850s lived in small groups centered on the biological family. Describing the composition of particular Shoshone families is a particularistic activity. But when he visited the Shoshone, ethnographer Julian Steward wanted to define how the system behind the specifics worked, how their social organization equipped the Shoshone for life in their stern Great Basin surroundings. Steward demonstrated that the family band basically linked two complementary economic totalities. The men spent most of their time hunting game animals; the women gathered wild seeds, dug roots, and collected berries and nuts. Neither sex was ecologically self-sufficient, but when linked by marriage, the male–female dyad produced a remarkably secure ecological unit. In systemic terms, the social subsystem served a critical survival function. The Nevada Shoshone had planted in Steward's mind the initial idea, but when he considered the underlying causes—those general rules that lie behind the specifics—it was clear that his family band was bound by neither time nor space. Steward (1955) suggested that the family bands could be found under similar circumstances throughout the world, citing the North American Eskimo and the Nambicuara, Guato, and Mura in Latin America as examples.

Synchronic cultural processes can also be considered using archaeological data. Although the techniques of inquiry differ vastly, the objectives remain the same. Anthropologists—whether studying extant or extinct societies—attempt to define the dynamic cause-and-effect relationships that operate in ongoing cultural systems.

Ethnographers can define cultural processes only for contemporary or selected recent, historic-period societies. Human societies from the past two million years are available only to archaeologists. At best, ethnographic studies of culture change are calibrated in terms of decades; the archaeologists' perspective on cultural evolution spans the duration of humankind. The synchronic perspective is complemented by a **diachronic** approach that defines the cultural processes controlling the evolution of such systems through time. Diachronic studies analyze how the various subsystems evolved relative to one another and how the overall system changed with respect to the external environment. How did selected societies evolve from simple collectors and hunters into farmers? The same processual question can likewise be reversed to focus on stability rather than change: Why do some systems, such as that of the Nevada Shoshone, appear to remain almost unchanged for millennia?

The search for cultural processes is really the pursuit of regularities that are both timeless and spaceless. Crafting these pan-human consistencies comprises archaeology's ultimate goal. Field archaeologists must initially flesh out the specifics of chronology and lifeway. These data must be explained. and such explanation requires that archaeologists unearth the processes behind the cultural system.

Throughout Part One, we examined the basics of what science and anthropology are. Chapter 2 showed how archaeologists use the so-called scientific cycle as a path to understanding: induction, bridging argumentation, verification. Chapter 3 charted contemporary anthropology and looked at the various ways in which anthropologists view the world.

We can now weave together these diverse threads. The archaeologist tracking chronology and lifeway is a technician exploiting the tools of the trade. In the next several chapters, we shall detail the guidelines and operations suited to resolving difficulties in the physical archaeological record. Why are things buried, and how do archaeologists know where to dig for them? How do we know how old things are? Is there just one proper way to dig an archaeological site? Is it possible to find out what vanished people ate? What did the environments of the past look like?

At this level, archaeological technique is combined with the steps of the scientific cycle to determine the specifics of the past. But the details of radiocarbon dating and the fossil pollen spectrum become increasingly immaterial as archaeologists near their ultimate goal. At the outset, I stated that the culmination of archaeology is to cease doing archaeology altogether. Although this verdict may sound sacrilegious (even blasphemous), it remains true.

Delving into cultural processes demands that archaeologists rise above the minutiae of the past. Processes are timeless and spaceless—archaeologists trying to supersede the temporal and spatial are obliged to gaze beyond the past and try to account for today and also tomorrow. As archaeologists turn to cultural process, they can no longer keep their eyes riveted to the ground. Scholars seeking human process must embrace every possible reservoir of information—ethnography, history, sociology, economics, whatever. Once archaeologists do this, they are no longer just archaeologists; they are social scientists.

Let me explain this thorny point by analogy. My colleague Robert Carneiro is a South American ethnologist, and when he takes to the field—say among the Kuikuru of Brazil—his days are saturated with matters of ethnographic detail: photograph this venture, tape that chant, weigh these victuals, tally how much forest has been burned and when the crops are planted, plot the settlement pattern and evaluate why camps are periodically moved (see Figure 4–4). At this level, Carneiro is wholly preoccupied with the specifics of Kuikuru ethnography, recording events, thoughts, and observations in his field notes. When he returns from the field, he is faced with the staggering task of drawing his field notes into a comprehensive description of contemporary Kuikuru lifeway.

To this point, Carneiro has been generating ethnographic data. But as an anthropologist, he is concerned with more than simple ethnographic narrative. He is also a leader in the study of cultural evolution, and some of his ideas are considered in Chapter 15. One particularly compelling article, published in 1970, set out the so-called **circumscription theory** to account for the derivation of state-level societies. Nearly thirty years ago, Carneiro postulated that state-level organization evolved initially in provinces where an indispensable resource, especially prime agricultural land, was sharply restricted. When warfare breaks out over such scarce resources, the vanquished peoples cannot simply hightail it into the previously "uninhabitable"—or at least unproductive—hinterlands, they must submit to conquest by and amalgamation with their victors. The theory is considerably more involved than this, however, and we shall return to it in Chapter 15. But basically Carneiro argued that circumscription of the social and/or physical environment eventually gave rise to the state level of political organization.

FIGURE 4–4 Robert Carneiro while conducting ethnographic fieldwork among the Amahuaca (Peru). He is wading in the Inuya ("with jaguar") River. (Courtesy Robert Carneiro)

Carneiro's hypothesis attempts to explain how all state-level organizations came into being, regardless of when or where, and it is an excellent example of how processual statements work in anthropology. How does Carneiro support his argument? Cultural evolutionists try to explain phenomena beyond simply the ethnographic present. Carneiro thus is required to look beyond the immediate ethnographic specifics, and so clearly he has surpassed his role of ethnographer to become a cultural evolutionist. As a cultural evolutionist, Carneiro must consider all relevant information, be it ethnographic, historical, sociological, archaeological, or whatever: In fact, archaeological sources comprise more than 50 percent of Carneiro's supportive data, coupled with about 10 percent historical data; less than 30 percent of Carneiro's documentation is drawn from ethnography.

Robert Carneiro is clearly starring in two roles. While sitting in a steamy Kuikuru village writing up his field notes, he is a field ethnographer. But when debating the principles of political evolution, he is a cultural evolutionist. There is no contradiction here. As an anthropologist working in the field, Carneiro promulgated ethnographic data relevant to state-level organization. In fact, without his ethnographic experiences, the idea of the circumscription theory might never have occurred to him. But once he sets out to test that theory, he is not, and cannot be, constrained by his own experience. It is perfectly logical for Carneiro to be a field ethnographer at one level and a cultural evolutionist at another.

Archaeologists have similar split personalities. I personally worked at Gatecliff Shelter for a total of thirteen months (over nine years), with a crew averaging about thirty-five people. To a field archaeologist, the day can seem like a titanic mass of detail: not only minutiae "How old is geological unit 6–74?" and "What's the exact provenience of this Pinto point?" but also pedestrian affairs like "Why is the cook four hours late in getting back from town?" and "What the hell do you mean you ripped the door off the pickup truck?" Workaday archaeologists are dedicated to (1) keeping their crews alive and (2) recovering and recording archaeological objects as painstakingly as possible. When fieldwork is finally completed, archaeologists move to the laboratory, where they analyze their finds and prepare the final research monograph.

Archaeologists laboring at these tasks are analogous to the field ethnographers, although the particulars can differ mightily. Whereas Carneiro might be fidgety about truculent informants, convincing the Brazilian air force to fly him out of the jungle, and the latest rip in his mosquito netting, field archaeologists are troubled by sonic booms that threaten to cave in sidewalls, by level bags improperly labeled, and problems of correlating this year's excavations with last season's field notes. Ethnographers have specific techniques, pressures, and requirements, and so do archaeologists. But these disparities evaporate at the processual level. Cultural evolutionist Robert Carneiro goes beyond the specifics of his ethnographic fieldwork to focus on broader issues of cultural evolution. Analogously, archaeologists working at the processual level rise above the nuances of reconstructing chronology or piecing together extinct lifeways.

The archaeologist tackling the problems of plant domestication, for instance, is really functioning as a human ecologist. Or perhaps a cultural materialist. Or maybe even a cultural evolutionist. Such archaeologists will probably find more in common with a plant geneticist or an agronomist or a nutritionist than with the good old buddies from archaeological graduate school. But one thing is certain. Any archaeologist serious about defining processes that transcend time and space had better gaze far beyond the archaeological. Human ecologists, cultural evolutionists, and cultural materialists cannot restrict their vision to any single source, archaeological or otherwise. This is why the ultimate goal of all archaeologists is to cease doing just archaeology.

Keeping the Priorities Straight

This simple sequence—chronology, lifeway, process—explains both the growth and practice of contemporary archaeology, and this book unfolds along this progression. But let me warn you not to oversimplify this relationship. In legitimate research enterprises, the best archaeologists often pursue a little of each objective simultaneously. Any given excavation might generate, say, some data useful for upgrading the chronology and some additional details about the lifeway, which may someday be synthesized in a related (or independent) investigation of processual relationships. Modern archaeologists almost never encounter a wholly pristine region about which absolutely nothing is known. Throughout today's world one always finds at least an embryonic cultural progression available. As research results snowball, this old chronology will be refined, sometimes through fresh technology, but often simply because more high-quality data emerge. Just because I heuristically divide archaeology's objectives into three parcels, please do not read this as a series of monolithic rules to be slavishly copied. More often than not, archaeologists toil on all three objectives simultaneously.

Here's another caution about research priorities in archaeology: I contend that although chronology is our initial goal, process is our ultimate objective. And this is true. But delving into any specific problem, archaeologists often commence with a processual concern, and then select an appropriate geographic region. Then the fieldwork begins: Chronological questions beg for answers, and multifarious details of lifeway remain to be worked out. Finally, these findings must be incorporated into a series of processual statements. Remember Scotty MacNeish's quest for early maize domestication in Mexico (Chapter 3): He started with a problem, looked over several potential research areas, settled on the Tehuacán Valley as most promising locale, excavated Coxcatlán Cave, and finally answered his initial research problem about the processes of plant domestication. In this case, as in many, good archaeology actually begins and ends with process, refining the particulars of chronology and lifeway along the way.

Summary

Americanist archaeologists are a diverse lot. Whereas some earn their living as academics, most are now "applied archaeologists." Whereas many continue to excavate prehistoric sites, the rapidly expanding field of historical archaeology has now surpassed the scope and level of funding in prehistoric archaeology in some parts of the country. Although many obstacles remain, women are now well integrated into mainstream Americanist archaeology, once a male-dominated profession.

Despite the wide diversity, Americanist archaeologists share three fundamental objectives. Archaeology's initial chronology building—the when and where of archaeology—must precede the more sophisticated inquiry about the past. But chronology is merely a stepping-stone toward more anthropologically relevant objectives; chronology cannot be viewed as an end in itself.

Archaeology's intermediate objective is to reconstruct extinct lifeways, to observe the anthropology of the dead. A lifeway encompasses all of the recoverable aspects of human existence: settlement pattern, population density, technology, economy, organization of domestic life, kinship, maintenance of law and order, social stratification, ritual, art, and religion. At the level of lifeway, the archaeologist's task is to reconstruct as completely as possible the human condition for a given culture at one point in time; this is paleoethnography.

Archaeology's ultimate objective is to elucidate the cultural processes that underlie human behavior, past and present. Investigating chronology and lifeway is a particularistic enterprise: particular artifacts from particular cultures that performed at particular times in particular places. The ultimate objective of archaeology is to expose underlying regularities that are both timeless and spaceless, which requires the archaeologist to rise above the particulars of the past. Because these processes are unconnected to time or space, scholars should seek all plausible scraps of relevant information—be they archaeological or sociological or economic or whatever. Archaeologists operating at the processual level cannot be handcuffed to any single source of information, archaeological or otherwise. This is why the ultimate goal of all archaeologists must be to cease doing just archaeology.

Excavating grave goods at Mission Santa Catalina. (Courtesy the American Museum of Natural History; photograph by Clark Spencer Larsen)

PART TWO

Encountering the Archaeological Record

Before looking at how archaeologists pursue their three primary goals—constructing chronology, reconstructing extinct lifeways, and defining cultural processes—we should first learn something about the physical record from which all archaeological inquiry arises. Although the general public is familiar with many archaeological terms—such as radiocarbon dating, the expression **archaeological record** is new to most people. And yet it is this record that conditions most of what we know about our remote past.

In Part Two we shall examine the archaeological record as both an abstract and a concrete phenomenon: what it is, how it is structured, and the ways in which archaeologists encounter it.

The Archaeological Record: What Is It?

Simply stated, the archaeological record is "the remains of prehistoric or historic cultures that are visible or uncovered by archaeologists today. It is the static remains of past dynamic behavior. Due to a variety of intervening factors, both natural and cultural, it is not usually a direct reflection of past behaviour" (Sabloff, Binford, and McAnany 1987, pp. 203–204). Let us dissect this succinct statement into its three key components.

First, as we have already seen, *the archaeological record is a contemporary phenomenon*. Although the objects and their contexts might have existed for centuries or millennia, observations and knowledge about those objects and contexts remain as contemporary as the archaeologists who do the observing.

The second significant point is that although created through dynamic behavior, *the archaeological record itself is static, dead, lifeless, and non-informative*. Michael Schiffer of the University of Arizona has brilliantly clarified this critical realization (in sources cited in Where to Go from Here?). Schiffer (see Figure II–1 on p. 159) began with the key distinction between archaeological and systemic contexts. The artifacts, features, and residues with which archaeologists deal once were part of an ongoing, dynamic behavioral system. Arrowheads were manufactured, used for specific tasks, often broken, sometimes repaired, and then lost or deliberately discarded. Potsherds were once part of whole pots, which were manufactured and decorated according to prescribed cultural criteria, used for utilitarian or ceremonial functions, and then either broken or deliberately discarded, perhaps as part of a rite or ritual. Food bones are the organic residues resulting from a succession of activities—hunting, butchering, cooking, and consumption. While these materials are being manufactured and used, they exist in their **systemic context**. These items are part of the actual behavioral system.

By the time such materials reach the archaeologist's hands, they have ceased to participate in this behavioral system. The artifacts, features, and residues that the archaeologist deals with were found in their **archaeological context**, interacting only with the natural environment. Although these natural conditions still remain dynamic and interactive, the cultural milieu has become static and noninteractive. It is common, of course, for items to move back and forth between contexts. During the archaeological excavation at Gatecliff Shelter, for instance, artifacts were removed from their archaeo-logical contexts and placed into the systemic contexts of the 1970s. In effect, doing archaeology is part of today's systemic context.

Formation Processes Creating the Archaeological Record

To this point, we have perceived the archaeological record as contemporary, yet static and distinct from the behavioral processes that produced it. Our definition of the archaeologi-cal record contains a third key attribute: *Because of a variety of intervening factors, both natural and cultural, this record is not usually a direct reflection of past behavior.*

These "intervening factors" are what condition the archaeological record as we know it today. Before archaeologists can meaningfully encounter the archaeological record, they must grasp the important transformations that wrenched the objects, features, and residues from their behavioral interactions and deposited them into the static record we encounter today. Once again, we are indebted to Michael Schiffer for defining an appropriate framework for understanding the transformational processes, both cultural and noncultural, that create the archaeological record.

Cultural processes are defined as "the processes of human behavior that affect or transform artifacts after their initial period of use in a given activity" (Schiffer 1987, p. 7). For our purposes, we will distinguish among four distinctive cultural transformations that directly influence the creation of archaeological sites: deposition, reclamation, dis-turbance, and reuse.

Depositional processes: So-called cultural deposition transforms materials from a systemic to an archaeological context, whereas depositional processes are the operations directly responsible for the accumulation of archaeological sites. Cultural deposition processes are relatively easy to study, and they constitute the dominant factor in forming the archaeological record. For example, when a pottery vessel is broken and discarded on the trash heap, it has ceased to function in the behavioral system and becomes incorporated in its new archaeological context: This is cultural deposition. Similarly, when an individual dies and is buried, the physical being has been transformed from a systemic to an archaeological context. Depositional processes need not involve deliberate discard or ritual; one major depositional process is the simple loss of still useful artifacts. In this case, the transformation from systemic to archaeological context is accidental, involving artifacts that are still capable of performing tasks in the behavioral system. Archaeologists are generally quite familiar with cultural deposition processes because they are directly relevant to conventional archaeological interpretation. In Chapter 8, we shall examine the law of superposition, the most general statement governing depositional processes in archaeology.

Other principles governing cultural deposition are more complex. Size, for instance, has been found to have a major influence on the way that items are deposited in the archaeological record. One study (cited in Schiffer 1977, p. 21) of discard behavior was conducted on the campus of the University of Arizona. Small items (those less than four inches in overall dimensions) were discarded almost independently of the location of trash cans, but larger items almost always found their way into trash cans when they were available. A number of specific "transforms" can be related to the deposition of faunal materials, artifacts, and ecofacts (see Schiffer 1987, Chapter 4). In Chapter 13, we shall examine how this size-sorting effect conditioned the archaeological deposits at Gatecliff.

Reclamation Processes: Somewhat more elusive is the process of reclamation. As the name indicates, it is a transition of cultural materials from the archaeological back into the systemic context. It is not uncommon to find evidence that archaeological artifacts have been scavenged for reuse by both nonindustrial and industrial peoples. Whenever a discarded projectile point is resharpened, a potsherd picked up and used to scrape hides, or an old brick reused in a new fireplace, reclamation has occurred. The act of archaeological excavation is itself reclamation: Artifacts are removed from their archaeological contexts and integrated into the functioning behavioral system of the archaeological profession. A common and recurring problem when dealing with surface sites (such as those discussed in Chapter 12) is to recognize and account for previous collecting on the same site.

Robert Heizer and C. William Clewlow (1968) once demonstrated that when the surface of an archaeological site is repeatedly collected, the larger, more complete artifacts are the first to disappear. As both scientific collection and unethical "pothunting" continue, the remaining complete artifacts are removed, along with the smaller, harder-to-find ones. After sufficient collecting pressure, all that is left is a scatter of barely recognizable bits and pieces. Archaeologists oblivious to the ongoing reclamation processes would probably produce differing (systemic) interpretations for the same site, depending on the stage of previous collecting. Unlike cultural deposition, reclamation has received relatively little attention from archaeologists until very recently.

Disturbance processes: The first two cultural formation processes pertain to the transference of materials between archaeological and systemic contexts. But the archaeological record is also heavily conditioned by transformations within the archaeological and systemic context. Disturbance changes the contexts of materials within the archaeological site itself. Examples include such diverse mechanisms as dam building, farming, and heavy construction, as well as noncultural activities such as freeze-thaw cycles, landslides, and simple erosion. Although the disturbance process has few direct implications for systemic contexts, the modification (and, indeed, preservation) of archaeological sites is a major and pressing problem facing modern archaeology.

Reuse processes: The final relevant cultural mechanism is reuse, or the transformation of materials through successive states in the behavioral system. The reuse process moves a single object through a series of different behavioral settings. Potsherds, for example, are sometimes ground up to be used as temper in manufacturing new vessels, and broken arrowheads are occasionally rechipped into drills and scrapers.

A host of noncultural formation processes also influence the archaeological record. The natural environment affects cultural materials, in both systemic and archaeological contexts: microscopic and mechanical decay; churning by rodents and earthworms; geological events such as volcanic eruptions, earthquakes, and flash floods; and so forth.

A complex suite of natural and cultural transformations interact to create each unique archaeological site, and they must be recognized in order to project contemporary meaning onto our observations of the past. Schiffer (1976, p. 42) speaks of the effects in this way: "The structure of archaeological remains is a distorted reflection of the structure of natural objects in a past cultural system." These distortions occur as the result of both cultural and noncultural processes, and the regularities in such processes are a major concern of contemporary scientists studying the archaeological record.

Throughout the rest of this section, we examine the nature of this record and the diverse ways in which archaeologists attempt to assign meaning to their observations of it. In Chapter 5, we shall see how (and why) archaeologists are conducting "actualistic" studies to learn more about the systemic contexts in which the archaeological record is initially formed. From conducting ethnoarchaeological fieldwork to digging up their own garbage, these archaeologists try to define the dynamics that link behavior to the static archaeological record we can observe in the twentieth century.

Once we understand something of these linkages, we shall turn to some strategies and tactics used to examine the static archaeological record. Chapter 6 returns to Gatecliff Shelter to look at some of the principles and controls guiding modern archaeological excavation. But no matter how meticulously one digs, site excavation remains site destruction, and in Chapter 7, we shall investigate some of the newer, "noninvasive" techniques for discovering the archaeological record without destroying it. This done, we shall be ready to evaluate how archaeologists are fulfilling their three primary objectives: constructing chronology, reconstructing extinct lifeways, and understanding the processes that explain cultural similarities and differences.

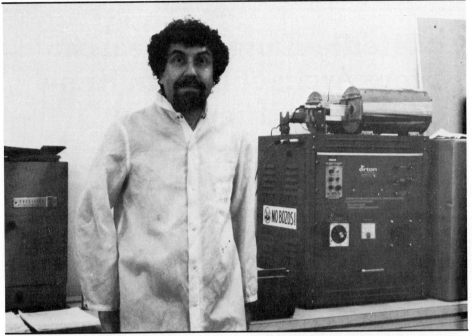

FIGURE II–1   Michael Schiffer in the Laboratory of Traditional Technology at the University of Arizona. The machine behind him is a *dilatometer*, used for estimating the original firing temperature of pottery. (Courtesy of Michael Schiffer)

WHERE TO GO FROM HERE?

Some Basic Sources on Archaeological Formation Processes: Michael Schiffer has been the driving force behind the study of formation processes; his book *Behavioral Archaeology* (1976) remains critical to an understanding of modern archaeology, and a more recent volume (1987), *Formation Processes of the Archaeological Record,* synthesizes the basic principles; see also Schiffer (1972, 1977).

CHAPTER 5

Middle-Range Research: How Archaeologists Know What They Know

Perhaps how it comes to be is really more distinctive . . . than what it is.
—Alfred Kroeber

Archaeologists are increasingly aware of how little they know about how their sites were formed. A series of ongoing research programs is attempting to fill this void. By conducting so-called middle-range research, archaeologists are generating the bridging arguments necessary to interpret the past. We shall consider several ways to do this, using ethnoarchaeology, experimental archaeology, historical documentation, and the heralded "Garbage Project" as examples of how archaeologists study the processes of site formation.

The Linkage Problem

We learned in Chapter 2 that facts never speak for themselves. Facts are known and particular observations, and the mission of science is to transform these facts into universal statements called theories. In reality, the facts of archaeology are contemporary observations made on the material remains of the past. Archaeology requires external input from the behavioral world in order to bridge the gap between these contemporary observations and past behavior.

Geologists face a similar problem. The geological record, like that of archaeology, consists of only two things: the objects and the relationships among them. A "geological fact" is an observation made by a contemporary geologist on objects from the geological record. Because the rocks do not speak, how do geologists advance from their contempo-

160

rary observations to meaningful pronouncements about the remote geological past? This obstacle was addressed long ago by pioneering geologists. The modern science of geology is said to have begun largely through the efforts of James Hutton. An eighteenth-century medical doctor and gentleman farmer, Hutton formulated a simple principle that provided the very cornerstone of modern geology. Hutton's principle, called the **doctrine of uniformitarianism**, asserts that the processes now operating to modify the earth's surface are the same ones that operated long ago in the geological past. It is that simple: The geological processes of the past and the present are assumed to be identical.

We know from modern experiments that as today's glaciers move, they deposit distinctive glacial debris, ranging from microscopic particles to boulders weighing several tons, and much of this glacial rubble is deposited in formations called *moraines*. Moreover, these individual rocks tend to acquire characteristic scratches (striations) as they move. The thorough study of modern glaciers has convinced geologists that moraines and striations are formed only through glacial action.

Suppose a geologist finds moraines and striated rocks in Ohio, California, or New Mexico, where no glaciers exist today. Armed with a knowledge of contemporary glacial processes, the geologist can readily frame and test hypotheses explaining ancient glacial action. In other words, observation of contemporary, ongoing processes provides the bridging arguments necessary to assign meaning to the geological objects of the past.

Precisely the same logical stricture applies to archaeology. Archaeologists recover the material remains of past cultural processes. Like geologists, archaeologists can frame hypotheses that account for the formation and deposition of these physical remains. Input from contemporary anthropological observation supplies the bridging arguments necessary to translate general hypotheses into specific, observable outcomes that can be expected to appear in the archaeological record. Anthropology allows archaeologists to bridge this important gap between contemporary observation and relevant statements about past behavior. This is why archaeology is anthropology or it is nothing.

Some Bones of Contention

Let me illustrate this relationship more fully with an example. As we shall discuss in Chapter 11, archaeologists often study the abundance and distribution of animal bones to learn about past diets, hunting practices, how animals were domesticated, how animals were butchered, the season in which the hunt or harvest was conducted, and a host of other related questions. This is called **faunal analysis**.

Most of these faunal studies begin with a consideration of the relative frequencies of various animal bones in archaeological sites. When analyzing the bones from Suberde, a seventh-millennium B.C. **Neolithic** village in Turkey, Dexter Perkins and Patricia Daly observed that the upper limb bones of wild oxen were usually missing. These static facts—contemporary observations—were then interpreted in terms of past human behavior. In this case, the investigators suggested that the relative frequencies of the bones resulted from the way in which the oxen had been butchered: The animals must first have been skinned; then the meat was stripped from the forequarters and hindquarters, and the upper limb bones thrown away. The investigators presumed that the meat was piled on the skin and the lower limb bones were used to drag the hide bearing the meat back home (Perkins and Daly 1968, p. 104). Calling this the **schlepp effect**, they figured their interpretation explained why the upper limb bones were left at the kill site and the lower limb bones were discarded at the habitation site.

R. E. Chaplin analyzed the bones recovered from a late-ninth-century A.D. Saxon farm in the Whitehall area of London. The facts in this case also suggested a shortage of limb bones, and Chaplin suggested that they (particularly the limb bones of sheep and cattle) disappeared because the carcasses were dressed and exported to market. Chaplin then hypothesized about the marketing and animal husbandry strategies implied by such trade (Chaplin 1971, pp. 135–138).

Investigators working on American Plains Indian sites also discovered that the upper limb bones of food animals were often missing. When Theodore White analyzed these facts, he decided that the bones must have been destroyed during the manufacture of bone grease from the marrow (White 1954, p. 256).

I could cite other examples, but the point is clear. Exactly the same archaeological fact—that habitation sites contain more lower limb bones than upper limb bones—has been construed in three different ways:

1. Perkins and Daly: Upper limbs were discarded at the **kill site**, and lower limbs were hauled with the meat back to the campsite.
2. Chaplin: Upper limb bones were selectively butchered and traded to market.
3. White: Upper limbs were pulverized into bone grease and hence destroyed at the campsite.

The relative frequencies of animal bones comprise some real data—these observations are the "facts" of archaeology. But what do these facts—actually contemporary observations made on the archaeological record—tell us of past behavior? They have been read differently by three teams of archaeologists, each interpretation suggesting dissimilar behaviors that allegedly created these same facts. Which (if any) interpretation is correct?

Consider this deadlock in terms of the scientific cycle (Chapter 2). The first step was *hypothesis formation,* in which one or more hypotheses were generated to account for the observable facts. Hypotheses are general statements, designed to cover the known facts and also to predict facts as yet unobserved. The next step in the scientific cycle is to deduce the *logical outcomes* of one's hypotheses. Because hypotheses are stated in general form, one must translate the generalities into specific outcomes. Such a translation, from general to specific, occurs through *bridging arguments,* logical statements that furnish the necessary test implications. The scientific cycle is complete when these implications have been tested (verified or rejected) by further facts.

Earlier, in outlining the scientific cycle, I admitted that archaeologists have difficulty in supplying these bridging arguments, and the bone frequency examples illustrate why this is so. The initial facts were bone counts at three archaeological sites: Lower limb bones were more common than bones from the upper appendages. On these facts all archaeologists can agree.

Over the years, three different hypotheses were suggested to explain the facts. Some investigators thought that the animals had been butchered away from the habitation area and that some bones were discarded at the butchering locale while others were carried to camp with the meat. Let us term this perfectly reasonable first suggestion H^1. A second hypothesis, H^2, postulates that after butchering, the choice cuts were traded away, which is why the upper limb bones were rarely found at the habitation site. A third proposal, H^3, hypothesizes that the larger bones had been ground into bone grease, thereby increasing the relative frequency of the smaller elements in the archaeological record.

Dozens of additional hypotheses could be framed to explain why upper limb bones were less common than the lower limbs and feet. Perhaps some bones were venerated in a shrine away from the habitation area. Or maybe the larger bones were made into awls and bone pins. Or possibly the largest bones were used as clubs. At this stage in the scientific cycle, one is perfectly justified in using imagination (and genius, if available) to generate worthwhile hypotheses. There are no rules governing how to get a good idea.

But scientific protocol does stipulate how to select among the competing hypotheses. Let us restrict our attention to the three numbered hypotheses (H^1, H^2, and H^3). Each one is a generalized statement about human behavior. A contemporary archaeologist can never hope to observe somebody butchering a Neolithic wild ox. None of us will ever observe firsthand the making of bone grease by a nineteenth-century American Plains Indian. Those opportunities are gone. Instead, archaeologists must concentrate on finding the material consequences of activities like butchering Neolithic oxen or making bison bone grease.

We do this by constructing a series of logical if . . . then statements: If bone grease were manufactured from bison bones, then we should find artifacts X, Y, and Z and physical residues M, N, and O; bones should be distributed in patterns C, D, and E; and specific bone elements (J, K, and L) should be missing. Similarly, to test H^2, we must generate some if . . . then statements regarding the trading of meat and bones. Which are the best cuts to trade? How far can meat be transported to be traded before it spoils? Is meat marketed only in the winter months? Are carcasses butchered in special ways so that certain cuts can be traded? These if . . . then statements are bridging arguments that translate general, untestable hypotheses into specific expectations that can be tested using archaeological evidence.

But—I hope you are wondering—how do we know these things? Why do archaeologists surmise that making bone grease requires artifacts X, Y, and Z? And how do we know which bone elements are destroyed in the process? Hypothesis testing is only as robust as these if . . . then bridging arguments. If we generate incorrect implications, then our hypothesis testing will be worse than useless, because it will lead us to believe in specious conclusions.

In the last section, I introduced the notion of **middle-range research** in archaeology. Because the facts are incapable of speaking for themselves, it is necessary for archaeologists to provide firm bridging arguments to breathe behavioral life into the objects of the past. In an analogy between archaeology and geology, I cited the doctrine of uniformitarianism: The processes that now operate to modify the earth's surface are the same processes that operated in the geological past. It is necessary to understand the ongoing geological processes in order to provide the bridging arguments necessary to assign meaning to the objects of the geological past. One must have, for instance, a knowledge of contemporary glaciers in order to interpret the glacial features of the remote past. Precisely the same issues face contemporary archaeologists when they attempt to interpret the material remains of past cultural processes. Archaeologists also must frame hypotheses to account for the formation and deposition of these physical remains and so require bridging arguments to translate the general hypotheses into specific outcomes that can actually be observed in the archaeological record.

Properly formulated, middle-range research will link our ideas about the world to the world itself, and it will attribute meaning to our empirical observations. Middle-range research dictates the way that we perceive the past and is quite different from the research used to explain that past. In this case, defining middle-range relationships requires that we also define the precise relationships between concepts and an appropriate class of empirically observable phenomena. Such a linkage has been extremely important to both past and contemporary Americanist archaeology. But archaeologists have only begun to direct their efforts toward building middle-range research from data derived through the technology of remote sensing.

Middle-range research did not, of course, begin with Lewis Binford. As Grayson (1986) points out, middle-range linkage has been an important aspect of archaeological inquiry for more than a century. Binford's recent emphasis served largely to focus this research, and even critics of the new archaeology recognized the importance of middle-range research (e.g., Trigger 1984, p. 294).

Archaeologists interested in learning about middle-range processes cannot restrict their attention to the dead. In order to define relevant bridging arguments, archaeologists must observe firsthand the workings of a culture in its systemic contexts. This is why they are turning to living peoples for clues to the interpretation of prehistoric remains. Although people are never considered as data, the insights gained by participation in a functioning society have opened the eyes of modern archaeologists.

In all such research, it is necessary to look around and select the closest available analogies for study. Geologists interested in glacial processes cannot today study firsthand the massive continental glaciers that once draped the North American continent, but they can examine the numerous mountain glaciers that occur at the highest altitudes and the higher latitudes.

Archaeologists are now doing same thing, studying closely the possible analogies in order to understand the processes that condition the archaeological record. Sometimes, it is possible to reconstruct such conditions experimentally (and we shall discuss several such experiments). In other cases, contemporary human societies can be found that continue to function under conditions that—in a limited way—are analogous to specific circumstances of the past.

Archaeologist James O'Connell has been conducting one such study among the Hadza of northern Tanzania, attempting to understand the processes that condition which bones will turn up in the archaeological record (Figure 5–1). When first encountered by Europeans, at about the turn of the century, the Hadza made their living by hunting and gathering. But over the past half century, the Hadza population has been subjected to a

FIGURE 5–1 Ethnoarchaeologist James O'Connell leaving camp with a Hadza hunter on a morning foraging trip during the dry season of 1986 (northern Tanzania). Conducting a "focal person follow," O'Connell will follow along and keep a record of what he does, particularly with respect to time spent on acquiring food, kinds and amounts of food collected, and amounts consumed in the field and brought back to camp. (Courtesy James F. O'Connell)

variety of government- and mission-sponsored settlement schemes encouraging them to enter into full-time farming. None of these plans worked out, and today most Hadza have returned to the bush, continuing to make a living by full-time hunting and gathering. By conducting **ethnoarchaeology**, O'Connell and his colleagues are currently studying the Hadza people to learn specific ways in which human (and nonhuman) activities condition the faunal assemblages and other aspects of the archaeological record (e.g., Hawkes, O'Connell, and Blurton Jones 1987, O'Connell, Hawkes, and Jones 1987). In the next section, we shall consider some methods and results of such ethnoarchaeology.

WHERE TO GO FROM HERE?

The basics of middle-range research were set out by Binford (1977, pp. 2–10; 1981, pp. 21–30; 1983a); a rather different viewpoint is expressed in Binford (1987). Thomas (1986) assesses the role of middle-range research in hunter-gatherer archaeology (see also Thomas 1983a); other perspectives can be found in Grayson (1986), Hayden and Cannon (1984), Raab and Goodyear (1984), Salmon (1982), Willey and Sabloff (1980).

Middle-Range Research and the Lipschitz

It would be easy to assume, mistakenly, that such middle-range research would eventually evolve into a grand edifice, erected on lofty principles and generalizations. Actually, the most useful middle-range research turns out to be fairly prosaic in nature. After all, this research is merely a way of making sense out of empirical chaos, and as such it takes on a decidedly mundane cast.

Consider the case of Tel Yin'am, a late Roman-Byzantine site in Israel (Liebowitz and Folk 1980). The excavators came upon a paved surface of uniformly sized and closely fit basalt cobbles. Locally occurring basalt had been used in 99 percent of all construction at this site and has, in fact, been used for building throughout the eastern lower Galilee area for millennia.

The Tel Yin'am cobbles were slightly worn on the upper surfaces, but nobody had any idea what this wear patterning meant. Although the excavators could obtain endless empirical data from the paved floor cobbles, they lacked any way of assigning a behavioral meaning to these archaeological facts.

Not far away, in the modern kibbutz of Yavne-el, Moshe Lipschitz and his family have walked out of their front door and across the street for the past eighteen years. This modern street is paved, like many in the area, with exactly the same kind of squared basalt cobbles that turned up in the Tel Yin'am excavations. Over nearly two decades the pavement in front of the Lipschitz house had begun to wear in some places but not in others.

This is when Moshe Lipschitz and his paved street became involved in middle-range research. Liebowitz and Folk (1980) studied the modern evidence and came up with an "official unit of scuffle," which they called a *Lipschitz*, defined as the wear produced by one family in two decades. One Lipschitz of wear produces distinctive rounded corners on basalt cobbles, with an apparent radius of curvature of about two meters.

In adopting the Lipschitz, the investigators cautioned that the constant works only on basalt pavements. Limestone, used occasionally for construction materials, wears more rapidly. There are also differential, but unknown, effects of abrasion caused by animal feet, naked human feet, moccasins, sandals, and leather shoes: "This information awaits further research and volunteer scufflers with patience" (Liebowitz and Folk 1980, p. 33).

But once the Lipschitz had been established, they returned to the archaeological pavement. Because the basalt cobbles at Tel Yin'am had only about one-half Lipschitz of wear, the excavators concluded that "the Tel Yin'am pavement was probably made for a private room; obviously it could not have been for a street or public building" (Liebowitz and Folk 1980, p. 32).

This little study illustrates how middle-range research can be derived to deal with the everyday empirical and definitional problems in archaeology. Middle-range research, used for many years in Americanist archaeology, is, after all, where you find it.

Ethnoarchaeology

Ethnoarchaeology had a fairly modest beginning. Richard Gould, for instance, was trained as an archaeologist at the University of California and spent months living with the aborigines of Australia and the Tolowa of northwestern California. Gould was observing the behavior behind the processes that form the archaeological record. Why, he would quiz his informants, are arrowheads made in a particular manner? How does one go about surviving in a harsh environment without benefit of agriculture or industry? Exactly who lives with whom, and what would these houses look like a hundred (or a thousand) years from now?

Gould once asked some Tolowa to look at his ongoing archaeological excavations, hoping they could solve some of the puzzles he had encountered. Gould had started digging under the then-standard assumption that habitation areas are best located by looking for surface concentrations of artifacts and midden deposit. But despite repeated digging, he was unable to locate any prehistoric house remains on an otherwise promising site. Seeing his dilemma, the Tolowa informants were quite amused: "Them old-timers never put their houses in the garbage dump. . . . They don't like to live in their garbage any more than you would" (Gould 1966, p. 43). They pointed, instead, to a steep slope on the edge of the "site." Although this hillside had seemed to Gould an unlikely spot on which to construct a house, he followed their suggestion. After only twenty minutes of digging, he came upon a well-preserved redwood plank house buried only eighteen inches below the surface. Gould's Tolowa informants grinned knowingly.

Do the !Kung Have Tool Kits?

Before the mid-1960s, archaeologists only rarely worked directly with informants (although plenty of them relied on data from ethnographers). Since that time, ethnoarchaeology has become fairly common. Archaeologists have come to realize the importance of establishing a relevant middle-range theory, and the study of living peoples is perhaps the best single way to do so.

As archaeologists reached beyond mere chronology, they began to make assumptions about the behavior behind the static archaeological record. Increasingly such critical assumptions were being tested through ethnoarchaeological research, one being the so-called **tool-kit** concept, an important assumption in the 1970s (see also Chapter 13): "The aim of such analysis is generally to define 'tool kits,' or clusters of artifacts and other items which occur together on occupation floors as a consequence of having been used together in certain activities. It is hoped that inferences concerning patterns of prehistoric human activity can be made by interpreting these 'tool kits' in terms of their contexts and their position on the occupation floors" (Whallon 1973, p. 266).

Note the implicit bridging argument here that allows an inference about dynamics from the static archaeological remains: Under ideal conditions, tools found in spatial association on an occupation surface (archaeological context) reflect a single task (systemic context). In fairness, few archaeologists, especially Robert Whallon, made the bald assumption that tool kits must *always* be found in spatially discrete concentrations *(activity areas)*. Most recognized that multiple factors could intervene between the behavioral and archaeological contexts. But if assemblages did turn up in spatially discrete areas at least some of the time, this pattern could be translated into meaningful statements about the behavior that produced the patterning.

It certainly sounds logical enough to infer that tools found together on a **living surface** must have been discarded from a single or a few related tasks. But how do we know this is necessarily so? Just because the bridging argument sounds plausible is insufficient reason. *"Plausibility does not render the interpretation true or accurate;* it simply emphasizes the utility of investigating such possibilities" (Binford 1983a, p. 75).

Similar reasoning in geology would lead to the interpretation of morainal features as glacial deposits just because the explanation "sounds logical" or "seems plausible." Geologists certainly do not do this. They go out and investigate active glaciers to see whether or not they in fact produce moraines. And if so, exactly what do these moraines look like? In other words, geologists have for centuries realized the importance of relating the "facts" of the geological record to systemic, processual contexts. Archaeologists have only recently arrived at this point.

John Yellen is one who, in the 1970s, began to take a hard look at such "plausible" concepts and assumptions. Although trained at Harvard as an archaeologist, Yellen spent over two years in Botswana, studying the behavior and material culture of the !Kung Bushmen. Although he never became fluent in the language, he did learn enough !Kung so that he could dispense with an interpreter and conduct his own direct interviews. Yellen's goal was to draw plans of !Kung campsites in order to provide fundamental data to be used in middle-range theory formation. He was particularly concerned with recording how long each camp was occupied, exactly what activities occurred there, and how these activities were reflected in the archaeological record (Figure 5–2).

Yellen mapped sixteen !Kung camps and was able to make some generalizations. The !Kung camp is circular in shape, with huts located along the circumference of the circle and entrances facing toward the center. The hut serves primarily as a place in which to store belongings; very few activities actually take place inside it. Only during rainstorms do people sleep in the huts at night. A hearth is located in front of each hut. It provides warmth in winter and a place to cook food and also serves as a focus for domestic activities. In all camps a characteristic amount of debris accumulates around each hearth, including vegetable remains (such as nut shells and fruit and melon skins), bone fragments, and waste products of manufacturing activities (such as bits of ostrich eggshell, bone, wood shavings, and fiber used for making string). A few fist-sized nut-cracking stones are the only items of value left at a campsite when it is abandoned. The staples of the !Kung tool kit—iron knives, axes, and adzes—are never left behind, and Yellen found only one such lost tool in over two years of research.

!Kung camps are thus divided into public and private areas. The public portion includes both the center of the camp circle and the space outside it. The primary, or

FIGURE 5–2   A !Kung village near Gomodino Pan (Botswana).
(Courtesy the American Museum of Natural History).

family, area consists of the hearth, the hut, and the space immediately surrounding it. The individual's space within a !Kung campsite is thus divided into three parts: the area belonging to one's own family, similar spaces belonging to other families, and the communal area shared by all.

These sixteen campsites formed a data base for Yellen to examine the concept of the tool kit. He was impressed with the number of disruptive factors that conspired to mix and jumble the archaeological context of these sites. The exact area being utilized depends on a number of changing factors, such as the continually shifting pattern of sun and shadow. The huts themselves provide some shade, and in some camps, the charcoal and nut scatters tend to lie to the east and north of the huts. In other camps it is more convenient to use the shade provided by trees and shrubs. Thus, the same general areas used for skin drying and the roasting of animal heads are also occupied to take advantage of shade. Children run and play continually, scattering and discarding debris. There are some adults who maintain their own huts and hearths, but they are dependent largely on others for food. At these huts, occupational debris is either scanty or absent.

Nevertheless, a certain pattern of occupation does emerge for all !Kung camps (Figure 5–3). Activities do not occur at random, and the by-products of such cultural activities do indeed tend to cluster across the camp spaces. Yellen defines four basic activity areas. The *communal activity area* is characterized by an absence of evidence: Nothing ever appears in this central area. The *nuclear activity area* includes the hut, the hearth, and associated debris; this is the site of most domestic activities. Outside the hut circle one finds a *shade area* and a *special-use area* for drying skins and so on.

What does this evidence tell us about tool kits? Yellen finds little support for the common assumption that artifacts found in similar archaeological contexts must have been involved in similar systemic contexts. The debris from subsistence activities (cooking and preparing vegetable foods) is found scattered about with debris resulting from manufacturing activities, such as making ostrich eggshell beads or poison arrows. There is no spatial separation in the archaeological record because there is no spatial separation in the systemic context. Similarly, the debris from a single activity, such as cracking nuts, can be found in several different places in the !Kung camp. Nuts are usually cracked in the nuclear family context, but people also crack nuts in the shady area outside the hut circle.

Research such as Yellen's early work among the !Kung points up many fallacies in archaeological interpretation, and his notions of camp patterning among the !Kung have been amplified and refined by parallel studies among similar groups elsewhere in the world (in Chapter 13, we shall have occasion to examine the tool-kit and activity area correlates in much greater detail).

WHERE TO GO FROM HERE?

The Tool-Kit Concept in Archaeology: Whallon (1973, 1974a) conducted the pioneering pattern recognition studies; see also Whallon (1986). Yellen's (1977) critique appeared in

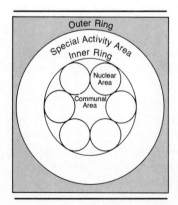

FIGURE 5–3 Schematic interpretation of activity patterning at a !Kung camp (see Yellen 1977, Figure 12). (Courtesy John Yellen and Academic Press, Inc.)

Archaeological Approaches to the Present, which in turn was critiqued by Binford (1983a, esp.pp. 238–239; 1987); see also Schiffer (1972) and Schiffer and Rathje (1973).

Lewis Binford Takes Off for Points North

Such ethnoarchaeological inquiry provides the arguments necessary to bridge the gap between observable archaeological contexts and nonobservable systemic contexts. These propositions, by their nature, will apply to systemic contexts both present and past. Ethnoarchaeology is based on the premise that if generalizations cannot adequately cover the contemporary contexts, they cannot be viewed as adequate.

Why Did Lewis Binford Begin Doing Ethnoarchaeology?

In 1967 I received funds to go to Europe for a year to work more closely with [François] Bordes in Bordeaux. My program for research was the following. If we could not study the chipped stone directly, perhaps we could study faunal remains and the horizontal distributions, on excavated archaeological floors, of both fauna and chipped stone. Then it might be possible to relate variability in the lithics to these other properties of the archaeological sites in question. . . . I worked for a year in France, identifying and plotting all the stone tools and animal bones by anatomical part and by breakage pattern.

Then began the first of a whole series of disillusionments. . . . I performed one correlation study after another—so many, in fact, that I needed a great steel trunk in order to carry all the papers back to the United States. I could tell you cross-correlations between any pair of Mousterian tool-types, between tools and bones, between bones and the drip-lines in cave sites, between almost any type of data you care to name. What I found, of course, was

many new facts that nobody had seen before. But none of these new facts spoke for themselves. . . .

My metal trunk was so big and heavy that I decided to return home by boat and that five-day trip from Le Havre to New York gave me an opportunity for some disconsolate self-reflection. The whole project was obviously a total failure. What had I done wrong? What had I not done that I should have done? Could it really be that archaeologists simply cannot learn anything about the past? Where was I missing the real problem?

. . . By the time we steamed into New York City, just before the New Year of 1969, some of the answers to these problems were suggested, at least in my thoughts. I prepared a research proposal to go to the Arctic in the spring of 1969 to live with a group of Eskimo hunters. My reasons for going there were little more specific at that stage than that it could hardly fail to be a good educational experience. If I was ever to be able to make accurate inferences from archaeological facts, I was convinced that I had to understand the dynamics of living systems and study their static consequences. (Binford 1983a, pp. 98, 100–101)

Reprinted by permission of L. Binford and the Publisher, Thames and Hudson. © 1983.

Lewis Binford conducted significant ethnoarchaeological research in the 1970s among the Nunamiut Eskimo. Binford was introduced to the Nunamiut by John Campbell, who had conducted pioneering research on settlement patterning in Anaktuvuk Pass (Campbell 1968), and this earlier work gave Binford a workable point of departure for his own studies. This Eskimo group was particularly appropriate to Binford's interest because he had studied reindeer bones on Mousterian sites in France and it was a chance to work with people still hunting reindeer. The Arctic environment was also somewhat similar to the **Middle Paleolithic** French occupation sites he had studied. But Binford emphasized that "the focus on fauna and my study of the Nunamiut were not research choices made because of an abiding interest in either fauna or Eskimos. My primary interest was in evaluating the utility of certain concepts commonly employed by the archaeologist" (Binford 1978b).

Binford accompanied the Nunamiut hunters on practically all the various kinds of hunting they practice today. Like Yellen, Binford was concerned with recording what the hunters did at each locality and what debris would be left for the archaeologist. Also like Yellen, Binford (1973, p. 242) was struck by the general lack of correlation between observed activities and the artifacts that were deposited in the archaeological record. Binford characterized the Nunamiut technology as "almost exclusively **curated**," meaning that artifacts are reused and transported so much that they are rarely deposited (lost) in contexts that reflect their actual manufacture and use. The problem for archaeologists is that localities that are demonstrably different in behavioral (systemic) terms produce archaeological sites that are almost identical. Differentiation among activities is possible only by means of artifacts, which are very rare and nearly always broken and heavily modified through use. The more that artifacts are curated, preserved, and transported, the less correspondence there will be between the systemic and archaeological contexts of given sites.

Since then, Binford has expanded his ethnoarchaeological fieldwork across three continents. In Australia, he joined James O'Connell to study site structure and butchering patterns among the Alyawara Aborigines (Figure 5–4). He traveled to South Africa to observe firsthand the effect of hyenas and other scavengers on bone assemblages. Binford also returned several times to the Nunamiut, mapping, collecting, and observing the linkages between modern behavior and the archaeological record it creates.

The Ethnoarchaeology of Highland New Guinea Flintknappers

O'Connell, Yellen, and Binford study how nonindustrial people patterned their sites. Effective middle-range research also requires that archaeologists understand the processes involved at the artifact level. In some ways the artifact level is more difficult to study because Western technology has intruded on most contemporary societies, regardless of how remote they are. The Nunamiut hunters that Binford studied, for instance, conducted most of their hunting using snowmobiles and high-powered rifles. Although these tech-

FIGURE 5–4   Lewis Binford inspecting an abandoned aborigines' camp near MacDonald Downs Homestead, Australia. The melons scattered about are of a type formerly cultivated when the site was occupied by Alyawara-speaking aborigines. (Courtesy James F. O'Connell)

nological advances do not necessarily change the process of site formation, many processes in bow–arrow–spear technology remain unknown.

The problem is that many prehistoric techniques have perished with their practitioners. Consider the manufacture and use of stone tools. Fortunately for the archaeologist, **flintknapping** is a messy business; archaeological sites are commonly littered with broken stone artifacts and waste from stone tool manufacture. As discussed in Chapter 10, the superficial outline of a stone artifact is sometimes sufficient to define a series of temporal types: Side-notched projectile points might, for instance, occur later in one region than do corner-notched points.

But stone tools can provide more than just chronological information if we understand how they were manufactured and used. To be sure, native aboriginal stoneworkers are rare in this modern world, but such groups do exist, and archaeologists have recently recognized their ability to contribute to relevant middle-range research. Not only can these peoples provide information about the physical technology of making stone tools, but questions also can be posed regarding the sociological and idiosyncratic implications of stone artifacts and the debris from their manufacture. For example, do distinctive social groupings, such as parishes or bands, manufacture their tools in characteristic ways? How do group norms condition the finished artifact? Do such artisans tend to think—as do archaeologists—in terms of artifact types? Are individual preferences expressed in stone tool assemblages? Questions such as these can be answered only through research involving informants who have learned the techniques of stoneworking in their native cultural matrix. The following example discusses one such project designed to learn about the sociology of stone tool manufacture.

It was in 1964 as a graduate student at Australian National University that J. Peter White first visited the highlands of New Guinea. Although he was trained primarily as a field archaeologist—his doctoral dissertation was the first ever written on the prehistory of New Guinea—White was delighted to find some local residents who still knew how to manufacture stone tools. Realizing the scientific potential of this situation, White framed a research strategy and returned to New Guinea in 1967 to study this vanishing craft, its social implications, and its correlates. Additional study in 1973 expanded the scope ·to consider more closely the selection made of stone tools.

White worked among the Duna speakers of the western New Guinea highlands who subsist primarily on sweet potatoes and domestic pigs. Some seventeen thousand Duna-speaking people live in three main valley systems around Lake Kopaigo in the western highlands. The Duna live in scattered houses which, before Christian missionaries arrived, were occupied by men, or women and children, but not both. Usually the pigs lived with the women.

Duna people first became aware of European technology thirty to forty years ago. Although adult males now prefer to use steel axes and knives, each was raised by his parents with a working knowledge of stone tool manufacture and repair. During White's visit, a few men still carried stone tools with them, and many would use a stone flake when a steel knife was not handy.

To make a tool, the Duna first collect the proper raw materials, in this case, chert nodules from a nearby stream. Sharp stone chips are then fractured from the raw nodule (the **core**), in basically two ways. The most direct means is by holding the nodule in one hand and striking it with another rock (the **direct percussion** technique). Alternatively, men could exert more control by placing the core on a large platform stone (the **anvil**). The core is then smashed with a stone hammer into dozens of sharp flakes. The considerable amount of lithic debris apparent in Figure 5–5 is quite similar to that found in many prehistoric sites; sometimes the remains have been deposited over thousands of years. Cores are sometimes wrapped in bark so that the resulting flakes tend to be longer and narrower; that is, they are more bladelike. The bark wrapping also keeps the stone chips and waste flakes from scattering about on impact.

After observing this process for some time, White questioned the Duna about the kinds of artifacts they were making. The Duna make no linguistic distinction between the

FIGURE 5–5 Aluni clansman fracturing flakes from a chert core (Highland New Guinea). (Courtesy J. Peter White)

initial core and the flakes driven from it; both are called **aré**. These sharp little tools are used in wood carving, stripping fibers, and drilling shells. Figure 5–6 shows one such *aré* being used to carve barbs on a Duna hunting arrow. Although a steel knife holds an edge better, the lithic counterpart works almost as well.

Some flakes are selected for a more specialized function. These flake tools—called **aré kou** by the Duna—are tied with orchid fibers into a handle of cane or wood and are then used for drilling holes or shredding fibers. Even today, *aré kou* are preferred to any available steel tool for preparing cane for bow and arrow bindings.

The important point for ethnoarchaeology is that White's experiments have allowed the Duna themselves to define two emic types of stone tools, distinct in morphology, function, and cognitive significance. To the Duna, of course, the ethnoarchaeologist is making a fuss about nothing. When asked to arrange some *aré* into whatever groupings he liked, one Duna man responded, "In the old days we didn't do that, we didn't know anything about putting them in different piles, we just looked for the good ones and used them."

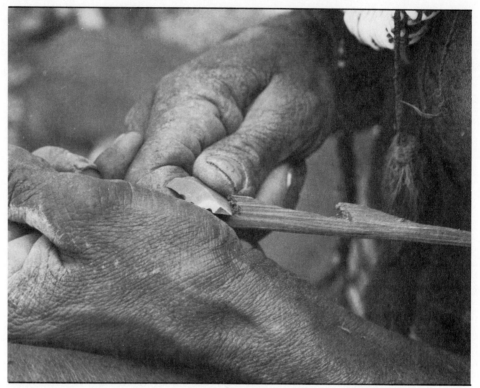

FIGURE 5–6 *Aré* being used to carve barbs into a wooden arrowhead. (Courtesy J. Peter White)

In planning his initial research among the Duna, White elected to examine some previously unexplored social correlates of artifact manufacture. Specifically, given an assemblage of similar stone tools, what can one tell regarding the cultural matrix in which they were manufactured? This amounts to identifying and interpreting the social variables of flintknapping. Functional variables and differences in raw material somehow are related to the technological aspects of stone tool making—method of flaking, selection of flakes for hafting, and so forth—and in turn ought to be observable in the local tool traditions in the parishes. Individual variation also affects the final appearance of the tools. In order to study these aspects in an objective manner, a research design was formed that held all variables constant save the one under immediate study.

The first such variable was the fluctuation of tool morphology in artifacts manufactured by the same worker. Making crude stone tools involves an element of randomness, reflecting both the haphazard nature of stone fracture and the range of tolerance for acceptable tools. Perhaps these tolerances vary from day to day, even for the same worker. Once this variation per individual can be properly isolated, these figures can serve as a baseline against which to compare further, independent variables. Another source of patterned variation is that among workers, as some men are likely to be more consistent in their artifact manufacture or perhaps more skilled in the mechanics of flaking stone. There could also be differences among the local parishes, as daily face-to-face contact could be expected to condition group norms for tool manufacture. What could be considered a decent tool by one group might seem odd or sloppy to their neighbors. On the other hand, group membership is fairly fluid, and extensive residential movement could readily overwhelm the development of local traditions of artifact manufacture.

Three independent variables were isolated in the stone tool complex of the Duna: functional differences, idiosyncratic variations, and group norm patterns. White's project attempted to determine which, if any, of these dimensions of variability could be detected in the stone tools. If patterns could be isolated in the ethnographic sample, which had been collected under strict control, then perhaps similar variability exists in prehistoric assemblages for which no controls are available. This study could also provide some anthropological data about the Duna's contemporary culture. As before, the operational boundary between archaeology and ethnography disappears.

Two parishes were initially selected for study. Hareke, a dispersed grouping of 375 people, is situated about fifteen miles—a five-hour walk—from Aluni, a smaller community with a population of only 160. White initiated his project by observing the overall range of techniques used by the Duna in artifact manufacture. After he understood the basics of Duna technology, he asked several knappers in each parish to prepare batches of tools for him. Eighteen men were selected as informants, ten from Hareke and eight from Aluni. Every day, these men produced between twenty and seventy-five individual tools, both *aré* and *aré kou*. Each individual's daily output was catalogued as a unit, and so the basic element of analysis was a single worker's daily output for each tool type. This analytic unit was termed a *TMD*, a type-man-day. In this manner, tools could be analytically separated in the laboratory; stoneworker output could be sorted by maker to study individual bias, by daily output to examine the worker's variations from day to day, and also by parish to study the relationship of tool traditions in each parish. Through such a priori deductive reasoning, White constructed a research design in which the three variables being analyzed—variation among types, variation among individuals, and variation among parishes—could be held constant relative to other sources.

After a couple of months, over nine thousand artifacts had been procured in this experiment, and the problem became how to analyze effectively so many data. The first step was to measure the individual attributes that seemed to reflect best the variation in each assemblage (TMD). One is limited in quantitative analysis, as there are only a few measurable variables on such crude tools (see Figure 5–6). White selected six attributes: length, width, thickness, edge angle, weight, and length–width ratio. White's attributes are etic categories, consistent with the rules and vocabulary of scientific inquiry. The Duna apparently categorize their stone tools very differently.

These measurements resulted in a tremendous mass of data, which were analyzed by an advanced, **multivariate** statistical technique known as **principal component analysis**. These computations showed that without doubt, the men of Hareke differ from their Aluni neighbors in their standards of tool manufacture. Although the two communities consist of an apparently homogeneous group of individuals (that is, they are of the same culture), the *aré* and *aré kou* from Hareke are generally longer, wider, thicker, and heavier than those of Aluni. This is significant because the workers of both parishes adamantly maintain that there is no difference between the tools of the two groups. In other words, White's etic, "scientific" approach successfully distinguished meaningful differences of which the actual tool makers were unaware. These mathematical results can be interpreted in terms of concrete human behavior.

Figure 5–7 represents a small portion of the computer output, comparing four of the Aluni men. The vertical dimension is the length–width ratio of individual artifacts, and the horizontal axis represents total size. Each numbered point represents a single TMD, a type-man-day. The circled areas represent *aré,* and the uncircled zones depict *aré kou.* From the outset, it is easy to distinguish between tool types, for *aré kou* are always smaller than *aré.*

The statistical analysis of each parish shows a second significant pattern: Individual technicians vary in the way in which they manufacture and classify their stone tools. This is to be expected because of the way in which Duna perceive their world: "Duna men are not intellectuals and do not spend their time discussing the meaning of things. They assume all people think the way they do until faced with evidence to the contrary, in which case they remark: 'well they're other men, their ways are something else' " (White, Modjeska, and Hipuya 1977, p. 381). Individual number five from Aluni—his name is Daka—consistently manufactures and selects more bladelike *aré kou* than does either individual number seven, Agele, or artisan number eight, Tage. Aluni worker number six tolerates a wider range of total size, especially in his *aré.*

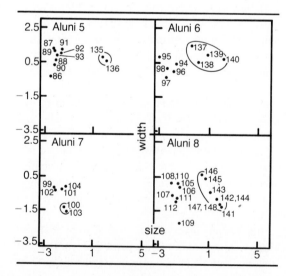

FIGURE 5–7 Statistical analysis of stone tools made by four Duna men, plotting the supervariables size against width. The circled area represents *aré* and the uncircled area depicts *aré kou.* (Adapted from White and Thomas 1972; courtesy J. Peter White and Methuen Co.)

Figure 5–7 demonstrates that people often exhibit parallelisms in their artifact classifications. One fellow makes his tools consistently larger, wider, and sharper than does a colleague who is content to put up with more variability in his tools. Obviously, some degree of variability exists in both workmanship and classification. It is also interesting to note, once again, such differences are insignificant to the workers actually making the artifacts.

In looking at the overall implications of this study, one is first struck by the fact that sociocultural parameters can be accurately defined using metric limits of artifact classes. The use of objective etic attributes, size, length–width ratio, and edge angle components, show differences between groups already defined; but there is some question whether such criteria would be adequate to separate groups when based on archaeologically recovered assemblages

White's initial study left some questions unanswered about why these distinctions exist, and so he conducted follow-up research in 1973. A random sample of *aré kou* was selected and presented to sixty-three Duna men living in five parishes (including Hareke and Aluni). Each man was asked to sort the stone tools into relevant categories, and the results were tabulated. In the first experiment, the exact role of each stone type was unclear. But the second time around, White decided to emphasize selection to a greater degree, presenting a number of men with the same artifact assemblage to classify. In this way, he controlled almost completely the variables of raw material and technical competence. Although cognitive variability certainly includes an appreciation of raw material, which in turn could be influenced by technical competence, the variability in the second experiment could be attributed strictly to personal evaluation rather than factors uncontrollable by the flintknapper.

White found that a few specimens in the sample were highly favored by nearly everybody. These individual artifacts must have been very close to the ideal type. But after the "ideal" *aré kou* were removed, considerable disagreement resulted about how to classify the remainder.

No overall geographic trend emerged in four of the five parishes. The current residential fluidity seemed to prevent the development of locally differentiated artifact traditions. Here is a case in which face-to-face groups exist without developing separate lithic traditions even when such factors as methods of learning and conditions of artifact use and manufacture might appear to favor such development.

But significantly, the tool classification of Duna living in Hareke differed from that of their neighbors. Hareke is some distance away from the others, and residential movement between it and the other four parishes is somewhat restricted. Thus, we are probably viewing the kind of localized variability that could evolve into an archaeologically visible stone tool tradition.

White's work also tells us something about the concept of archaeological type. In past discussions, some archaeologists have suggested that archaeological classifications should always attempt to mirror mental patterns in the mind of the maker (see Chapter 7). That is, regardless of whether one is dealing with temporal or functional types, this argument states that archaeological types are also emic, cognitive types, corresponding to a prehistoric mental template. The Duna experiments show that whereas discrete archaeological types can be defined according to metric attributes, and these patterns vary to some degree across space, the scientific etic types have little correspondence to the maker-defined emic categories. Although various "ideal forms" clearly exist in the Duna mind, at least two kinds of categories are operating—one based on use of *aré* as tools and the other based on *aré* as materials for tools—and neither kind has a corresponding linguistic division. We also note that these "covert categories" are accessible only through ethnoarchaeological research, in which informant interaction can be documented. Further, many archaeologists would be tempted to point out that because there is disagreement regarding "emic" classes among the Duna themselves, how can archaeologists possibly hope to construct emic classifications without informants?

This study also has implications for the study of idiosyncratic variation, discussed in Chapter 3. Stoneworkers, like many other artisans and craftsmen, have characteristic methods of performing their craft. It is therefore conceivable that much of the so-called typological variation that archaeologists note in prehistoric assemblages is no more than variation among contemporary craftsmen.

WHERE TO GO FROM HERE?

The basics of Duna stone tool technology are described in White (1968) and White and Thomas (1972). A follow-up study with additional controls was reported by White, Modjeska, and Hipuya (1977); see also Thomas (1978), White (1985), White and Dibble (1986), White and Modjeska (1978).

Other Ethnoarchaeological Studies of Lithic Technology: Among the Australian aborigines (Binford 1986, Binford and O'Connell 1984, Hayden 1979, Tindale 1985); among contemporary Highland Maya (Hayden 1987).

The Archaeology of Yesterday's Lunch

> Wait a thousand years and even the garbage left behind by a vanished civilization becomes precious to us.
> —Isaac Asimov

> Why wait a thousand years?
> —William L. Rathje

Our final example of ethnoarchaeology is the self-declared Garbage Project. Emil Haury has been the senior archaeologist at the University of Arizona for decades. A specialist in southwestern prehistory, Haury continually taught his students that "if you want to know what is really going on in a community, look at its garbage."

Haury's earthy advice was not lost on his students and colleagues. In 1971 the University of Arizona launched a long-term, in-depth study of just that—garbage. But it must have surprised Haury when he found out which community the Garbage Project decided to study; they were after the garbage of contemporary Tucson.

The Garbage Project—or, as it is often called, Le Projet du Garbage—was started by William Rathje, a Harvard-trained archaeologist who had previously specialized in the Classic Maya (Figure 5–8). Through the Garbage Project, Rathje was attempting to apply archaeological methods to the analysis and description of modern societies. Rathje objects to the traditional injunction in archaeology that the lifeways being reconstructed must be extinct. He contends that we still have a great deal to learn about contemporary lifeways and that a century of archaeological experience with material culture should be brought to bear on relevant issues of modern society.

As now constituted, the Garbage Project has three fundamental goals (see Rathje 1984):

- to develop quantitative measures from artifacts as another source of information about how people manage household resources.
- to use the data from artifacts to build a practical theory of household management based on interactions among artifacts, actions, and attitudes.

FIGURE 5–8 Archaeologist William Rathje, director of the Garbage Project, with a choice array of "data." (Courtesy William Rathje)

- to examine the tangible link between present and past with an eye toward understanding that past and anticipating the future.

We shall examine each objective in order.

Quantifying Material Reality

The archaeology of contemporary society began as a rather bizarre concept, but a considerable amount of such ethnoarchaeological research has been conducted over the past decade (see the references at the end of this section). Rathje was dissatisfied with available research techniques for dealing with contemporary society, particularly the dependence on interviews and questionnaires. The very act of conducting an interview and administering a questionnaire is a foreign element intruding into the social setting under study. Respondents are continually aware of their status as subjects, and the test measure itself can act as an agent of change and bias (Rathje and Hughes 1975, p. 152). Sociology and psychology have become largely the science of administering questionnaires and interviewing informants. Nothing in the training of sociologists or psychologists equips them to deal with the actual physical evidence.

Archaeologists, of course, have been dealing with mute material evidence for over a century. So why restrict ourselves to behaviors that have become extinct? In 1971, Rathje began his search for ways to apply established archaeological methods and theory to the analysis of contemporary behavior.

The key term here is *nonreactive*. Whereas conventional questionnaires condition the nature of the response, material culture is static and relatively easy to quantify. The Garbage Project has been the first large-scale attempt to apply archaeological techniques to ongoing lifeways.

Rathje's Garbage Project focused on Tucson, an urban community with a population of slightly over 360,000. A strict sampling design ensured the proper correlation with relevant socioeconomic variables. Garbage was picked up from randomly selected households with selected sampling tracts. Over three hundred volunteers from the University of Arizona sorted the garbage on special sorting tables provided by the sanitation department's maintenance yard in Tucson. As with all archaeological fieldwork, the student workers were required to take the appropriate inoculations, and were given appropriate field equipment, in this case, laboratory coats, surgical masks, and gloves. Students sorted garbage items into two hundred categories under the larger headings of food, drugs, sanitation products, amusement and educational items, communication, and pet-related products. The data were then recorded on forms for computer processing (see Figure 5–9). The standard principles of archaeological classification provided objective, repeatable categories of data retrieval.

Over a decade, the Garbage Project involved seven hundred students and sixty organizations, recording more than a million items from eight thousand household refuse samples. The initial Tucson project has operated continually since 1973, and satellite projects have been launched in Milwaukee (1978–1979), Marin County, California (1980–1981), and Mexico City (1981, 1983).

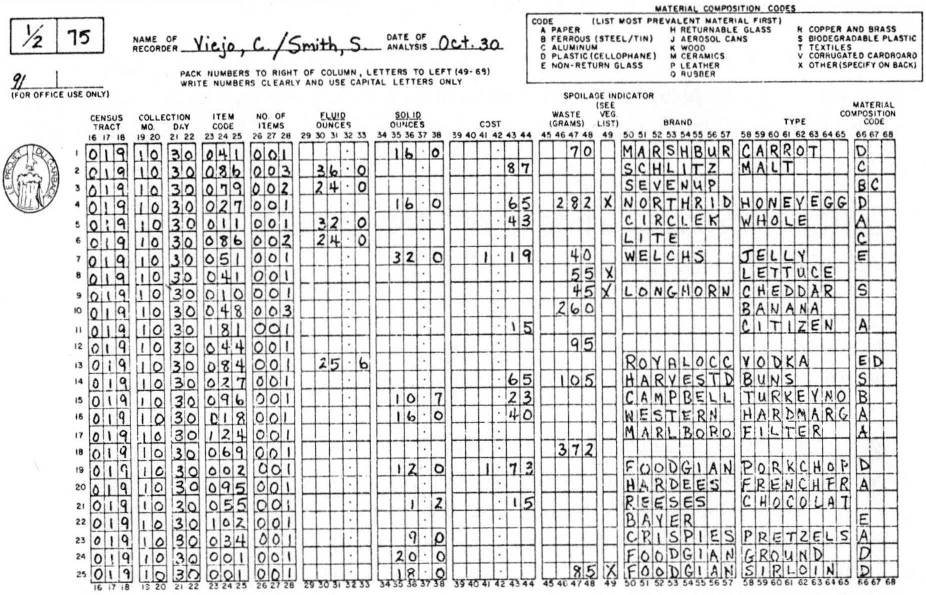

1/2 | 75

NAME OF RECORDER Viejo, C./Smith, S. DATE OF ANALYSIS Oct. 30

PACK NUMBERS TO RIGHT OF COLUMN, LETTERS TO LEFT (49-69)
WRITE NUMBERS CLEARLY AND USE CAPITAL LETTERS ONLY

91 |
(FOR OFFICE USE ONLY)

MATERIAL COMPOSITION CODES

CODE (LIST MOST PREVALENT MATERIAL FIRST)
A PAPER
B FERROUS (STEEL/TIN)
C ALUMINUM
D PLASTIC (CELLOPHANE)
E NON-RETURN GLASS
H RETURNABLE GLASS
J AEROSOL CANS
K WOOD
M CERAMICS
P LEATHER
Q RUBBER
R COPPER AND BRASS
S BIODEGRADABLE PLASTIC
T TEXTILES
V CORRUGATED CARDBOARD
X OTHER (SPECIFY ON BACK)

	CENSUS TRACT 16 17 18	COLLECTION MO. 19 20	DAY 21 22	ITEM CODE 23 24 25	NO. OF ITEMS 26 27 28	FLUID OUNCES 29 30 31 32 33	SOLID OUNCES 34 35 36 37 38	COST 39 40 41 42 43 44	WASTE (GRAMS) 45 46 47 48	SPOILAGE INDICATOR (SEE VEG. LIST) 49	BRAND 50 51 52 53 54 55 56 57	TYPE 58 59 60 61 62 63 64 65	MATERIAL COMPOSITION CODE 66 67 68
1	019	10	30	041	001		16·0		70		MARSHBUR	CARROT	D
2	019	10	30	086	003	36·0		·87			SCHLITZ	MALT	C
3	019	10	30	079	002	24·0					SEVENUP		BC
4	019	10	30	027	001		16·0	·65	282	X	NORTHRID	HONEYEGG	D
5	019	10	30	011	001	32·0		·43			CIRCLEK	WHOLE	A
6	019	10	30	086	002	24·0					LITE		C
7	019	10	30	051	001		32·0	1·19	40		WELCHS	JELLY	E
8	019	10	30	041	001				55	X		LETTUCE	
9	019	10	30	010	001				45	X	LONGHORN	CHEDDAR	S
10	019	10	30	048	003				260			BANANA	
11	019	10	30	181	001			·15				CITIZEN	A
12	019	10	30	044	001				95				
13	019	10	30	084	001	25·6					ROYALOCC	VODKA	ED
14	019	10	30	027	001			·65	105		HARVESTD	BUNS	S
15	019	10	30	096	001		10·7	·23			CAMPBELL	TURKEYNO	B
16	019	10	30	018	001		16·0	·40			WESTERN	HARDMARG	A
17	019	10	30	124	001						MARLBORO	FILTER	A
18	019	10	30	069	001				372				
19	019	10	30	002	001		12·0	1·73			FOODGIAN	PORKCHOP	D
20	019	10	30	095	001						HARDEES	FRENCHFR	A
21	019	10	30	055	001		1·2	·15			REESES	CHOCOLAT	
22	019	10	30	102	001						BAYER		E
23	019	10	30	034	001		9·0				CRISPIES	PRETZELS	A
24	019	10	30	001	001		20·0				FOODGIAN	GROUND	D
25	019	10	30	001	001		18·0		85	X	FOODGIAN	SIRLOIN	D

FIGURE 5–9 Garbage Project data recording form. (Courtesy William Rathje)

The University of Arizona archaeologists are hardly the first to snoop in somebody else's garbage can. The most sensational garbage probe occurred in 1971, when A. J. Weberman—a self-proclaimed garbage guerrilla—investigated the private lives of celebrities as reflected in their garbage. In one sense, Weberman was following up the same discrepancy that bothered the sociologists—that people say one thing yet often do another. Pop singer Bob Dylan, for instance, proclaimed benign disinterest in popular fan magazines, boasting that he never read what they wrote about him. But when Weberman ransacked Dylan's New York garbage pail, "the many rock magazines wasted Bob's claim that he didn't follow the rock scene" (Weberman 1971, p. 114).

Dylan, of course, was outraged and reportedly directed his housekeeper henceforth to deliver his trash directly to the sanitation workers. Weberman conducted similar garbage exposés on other celebrities such as boxer Muhammed Ali, playwright Neil Simon, and yippie Abbie Hoffman.

Rathje terms such tactics "a rip-off . . . a threat to the conduct of garbage research as a means of quantifying the resource management strategies of population segments" (Rathje and Hughes 1975, p. 154). To combat the adverse publicity that resulted from the Bob Dylan and Muhammed Ali cases, the Garbage Project instituted elaborate safeguards in their collection procedure so as to ensure the complete anonymity of particular individuals and households. The sample garbage is collected by the sanitation department foremen, who are not present when the bags are opened, and they are forbidden access to the Garbage Project data. Personal data such as names, addresses, photographs, or financial statements are never recorded and are not analyzed. The Garbage Project field director and/or one senior Garbage Project field supervisor are always present during analysis to ensure that no personal items are examined or saved. Participating students were required to sign pledges against even looking at such personal items. No garbage of any kind was saved; all aluminum was recycled, and the rest of the garbage was used as sanitary landfill.

Building a Practical Theory of Household Resource Management

The Garbage Project has used its accumulated data to study a number of contemporary social issues, one of them being the rate of alcohol consumption. In 1973, the Pima County Health Department conducted interviews with 1 percent of the households in the city of Tucson. Questions were phrased like this: "On the average, how many cans or bottles of beer does————have in a usual week?" The sample was carefully chosen using conventional sociological procedures, and informant anonymity was assured. The health department then published its findings, which were taken by many as an accurate indication of the rate of alcohol consumption in Tucson.

How did the questionnaires stack up against the material evidence? Rathje's garbage volunteers record the presence of beer bottles and cans as part of their routine sorting. They also note the kind and volume of the containers discarded and have even tried to monitor the amount of recycling of aluminum cans.

Rathje points out the discrepancy between front-door answers given to interviewers and back-door behavior as reflected by the actual contents of the trash. Garbage cans don't lie, and the differences from the health department questionnaire were striking. In one tract, only 15 percent of the respondent households admitted to consuming beer, and no household reported drinking more than eight cans in a week. But the Garbage Project data from that same area showed that over 80 percent of the households had beer containers in their garbage cans and that fully 54 percent discarded more than eight cans each week. In fact, those households averaged about two and one-half six-packs each week (Rathje and Hughes 1975, p. 157). Although the details varied among the sampling tracts, the patterning was always the same: significantly heavier beer consumption—in the form of more drinkers and higher rates of drinking—than was reported to the interviewers.

That the interview data are distorted should astound nobody. People simply drink more beer than they own up to. But the degree of distortion is noteworthy, and the analysis of the material remains even provides future interviewers with a means for correcting this inevitable bias. The skewing, it turns out, is also correlated with socioeconomic factors. The low-income Mexican-American households typically distorted their interviews by reporting no beer consumption at all (Rathje and McCarthy 1977, p. 268). By contrast, although the middle-income Anglo respondents admitted to limited beer consumption, they significantly underreported the amount of beer they actually consumed. These preliminary findings point up future directions not only for garbage research but also for the administration of health questionnaires.

One of the most striking findings to emerge from the Garbage Project is evidence showing how people cope with economic adversity. Most economists simply assume that as the economic squeeze gets tighter, people will economize, particularly by using cheaper products more efficiently But the Garbage Project's "First Principle of Edible Food Loss" suggests otherwise (Rathje 1984, p. 17). This pattern, dubbed "crisis buying" suggests that the more redundant and familiar a diet is, the lower the rate of food losses or "waste" will be.

Consider the 1973 beef shortage. Prices increased dramatically, and beef became scarce in many retail stores. Garbage Project data confirmed that purchase behavior changed immediately as shoppers experimented with new cuts of beef. Although some people stocked up, anticipating even higher prices, other shoppers cut down on beef purchases (Rathje 1975). Common sense tells us that when prices go up and a commodity is scarce, people will waste less of scarce, expensive items. But this did not happen with the beef shortage. In the spring of 1973, a time when beef prices were astronomical and there was considerable economic pressure to conserve beef, beef waste hit an all-time high—9 percent of the volume purchased (excluding the weight of bone and fat). For every one hundred pounds of beef purchased, nine pounds of edible and expensive beef was discarded out the back door. A similar pattern of waste showed up during the "sugar shortage" of 1975. Consumers radically changed their shopping patterns, and more waste was the result.

Rathje has also found corollaries to his First Principle. Although the final products of Mexican cuisine are extremely varied—burritos, enchiladas, fajitas, and tacos—they all are made from the same basic ingredients, in contrast with so-called American cooking. The First Principle suggests that Mexican-American households should therefore waste less food, and Garbage Project surveys show precisely this result in both Tucson and Milwaukee.

More recently, the Garbage Project also examined the effectiveness of public awareness programs. The National Academy of Science, the National Cancer Institute, and the American Heart Association all have warned that affluent Western societies ingest too much fat, with direct and measurable costs in human health. But do Americans heed such warnings? Between 1979 and 1985, the Garbage Project tracked the purchase of red meat and the discard of separable fat in Tucson neighborhoods. Between 1979 and 1982, the discard rate of meat fat remained relatively constant. But in 1982, the National Academy of Science released its report, *Diet, Nutrition, and Cancer,* warning of the dangers of meat fat. The next year, the American Heart Association stepped up its campaign to publicize dietary guidelines, urging a decrease in the consumption of saturated fat and cholesterol. At just this time, the rate of discard of meat fat nearly doubled and has remained stable. The purchase of red meat with separable fat (such as steaks, roasts, and chops) declined significantly. Although the causal linkage is not entirely clear, Rathje and Ho (1987, p. 1359) suggest that "perhaps someone is listening to the public dietary recommendations."

But this good news is tempered by another Garbage Project finding. Rather than households purchasing more chicken and fish to replace the red meat, the purchase of red meat with nonseparable fat (hamburger, sausage, and bacon) either remained constant or actually increased. This pattern suggests that whereas separable fat is increasingly being avoided and discarded, people are simply switching to products with "hidden," nonseparable fat products, apparently unaware of the high fat content of hamburgers and hot dogs. Although this trend could also be accounted for by greater convenience, it seems likely that misinformation and misunderstanding were actually leading the public into expanding their consumption of exactly what they were trying to avoid.

Linking Past to Present

The Garbage Project attempted to project perceived patterns of food loss back into time. It gave American householders mixed reviews. On the one hand, the actual waste of food has declined through time. During World War I, the War Food Administration collected large-scale food discard data for United States households (the only known precursor to the Garbage Project). In 1918, households lost between 25 percent and 30 percent of the total amount of solid food acquired (Rathje 1984, p. 20). This compares with only 10 percent to 15 percent in food waste in Tucson during the period of the Garbage Project. The decrease in waste is probably linked to increasingly available technology for processing, packaging, and transporting of foods. But although this represents a significant improvement, Rathje points out that it was achieved in a typically American way: by turning to technology to solve our problems.

The Garbage Project data also disclose some surprises about the effectiveness of recent recycling campaigns. The advertising media have given great coverage to campaigns by beverage companies and aluminum factories to recycle aluminum cans: Boy Scouts sponsor newspaper drives to raise money and to save trees, and more Christmas

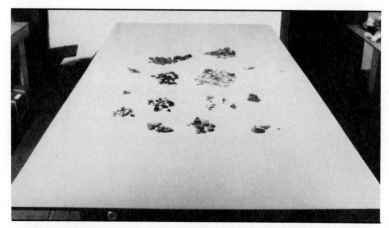

FIGURE 5–10   The total sherd assemblage recovered from the Edward Winslow site, occupied from 1635 to 1650 (Plymouth, Massachusetts). (Courtesy Plimoth Plantation)

FIGURE 5–11   The total sherd assemblage recovered from the
Joseph Howland site, occupied from 1675 to 1725 (Plymouth,
Massachusetts). (Courtesy Plimoth Plantation)

cards are printed on recycled paper each year. As Rathje (1975) puts it, "We think of
ourselves today as ardent recyclers." But the facts are otherwise. In 1975, the households
of Tucson recycled only 19 percent of all wood fiber; this figure stands in marked contrast
with the 35 percent national average that was recycled during World War II. Similarly,
studies in a mid-1800 trash deposit in Magdelena, Mexico, show that only broken bottles
were discarded, and these had apparently been reused extensively before breakage. In the
1970s, the average Tucson household discarded about five hundred whole bottles each

FIGURE 5–12   The total sherd assemblage recovered from a trash
pit used by a single family, 1830 to 1835 (Plymouth, Massachusetts).
(Courtesy Plimoth Plantation)

year; of these, over 10 percent were made of returnable glass and could have—ideally—been used up to forty times had they been returned.

Rathje has projected these findings back in time by drawing upon the excavations at Plimoth Plantation, Massachusetts (Deetz 1973, Rathje 1984). By using the methods discussed in Chapter 10, James Deetz and his colleagues determined that the Edward Winslow site was a farmhouse in Plymouth occupied during the first decades of the colony's existence (1635–1650); Figure 5–10 shows the meager collection of broken ceramics discarded during this interval, arrayed across Deetz's laboratory table. The increase in ceramics by the turn of the eighteenth century is impressive: The Joseph Howland farmhouse, in Kingston, Massachusetts, was occupied between 1675 and 1725, and Figure 5–11 shows the assemblage of sherds from that dump. Finally, Figure 5–12 shows the debris dumped from a single family in Plymouth over just five years (1830–1835). Part of this trend was due to more individualized ceramic use, and part of it resulted from the increasing availability of ceramic products.

The Garbage Project has even begun to conduct its own archaeological excavations. Public landfills were targeted in three places (Tucson, near Oakland, California, and near Chicago). Standard archaeological techniques—such as those discussed in the next chapter—are being used to look at temporal change in material composition (1970–1987) and also to examine both the climatic and geological variability of hazardous waste leakage. The various "strata" can be documented using newspapers, and magazines. Season of deposition can be monitored, for instance, by the presence of pine needles in "Christmastime" deposits. Telephone books are particularly good stratigraphic markers because everybody receives new ones at the same time and most toss out the old with the next day's garbage.

As you might expect, the Garbage Project has received mixed reviews from Americanist archaeologists. Although many applaud this endeavor as "building middle-range theory" and "constructing a science of material culture," others have expressed concern. Bruce Trigger (1978, p. 14) worries that such nontraditional directions may sap the strength of Americanist archaeology. Like many of their colleagues, Willey and Sabloff (1980, p. 258) grant that the Garbage Project is "oft-cited" and "innovative" but ask, "Is their research archaeology?"

The Garbage Project highlights the utility of applying archaeological methods to discern modern, ongoing trends. It is so radical that comparable data are almost nonexistent. Only future research will determine whether Rathje's findings are fluke or fact. But it seems clear that the Garbage Project has firmly established archaeological method and theory on the contemporary social scene.

WHERE TO GO FROM HERE?

Sources on the Garbage Project: The best overview of objectives is provided by Rathje (1984), "The Garbage Decade"; Rathje and Ho (1987) discuss the patterns of meat fat consumption; see also Rathje (1974), Rathje and McCarthy (1977), Rathje and Schiffer (1982).

Experimental Archaeology

The last section discussed how ethnoarchaeologists are generating middle-range research by examining firsthand the workings of functioning sociocultural systems. Such processes can also be studied by recreating the necessary conditions and looking for the linkage between systemic and archaeological context. Known as **experimental archaeology**, this research has the same function as ethnoarchaeology. But whereas ethnoarchaeologists work within a functioning behavioral system, experimental archaeologists attempt to define processes through controlled and directed replication.

Experimental Archaeology Is Not New

One of the earliest studies in experimental archaeology can be traced back to Saxton Pope, in a touching episode of early anthropology. In 1911, a beaten and defeated Indian, later named Ishi, was found crouching in a slaughterhouse corral near Oroville, California. His family either had been murdered or had starved, and Ishi himself had given up the will to live. The local sheriff locked him in the jail, as "wild" Indians were not allowed to roam about freely in those days. Through good fortune, Alfred Kroeber, a young anthropologist at the University of California, learned of Ishi's plight and arranged for his release. Kroeber brought Ishi to San Francisco and secured quarters for him in the university museum. From that time until Ishi's death in 1916, Kroeber and his staff taught Ishi the ways of civilization, and the Indian revealed his secrets of survival in back-land California; clearly Ishi had more to offer.

Ishi soon developed a tubercular cough—which later cost him his life—and was treated daily by Dr. Pope, a surgeon from the nearby University of California Medical Center. Over their short association, Pope and Ishi found common ground in their interest in archery. An odd combination: Pope, the urbane physician/scholar paired with the Yahi Indian, hair singed in tribal custom, together shooting arrows through the parks of downtown San Francisco. Pope was a good student, and after Ishi's death, Pope continued his research into the almost lost art of archery, studying the bows and arrows preserved in museum collections and often test-shooting the ancient specimens.

Pope wrote *Hunting with the Bow and Arrow* (1923) describing his experiments in archery. The book not only provided baseline information for interpreting ancient finds but also quickly became the bible of the bow-hunting fraternity. Apparently, as many urbanites as archaeologists were intrigued by the fine points of this nearly extinct art. Now, of course, archery is big business. This is but a single example of how the techniques of a nearly lost survival art were salvaged by timely observation and experimentation.

Stone Tools: How Were They Made?

Unlike archery, many other prehistoric techniques have perished with their practitioners, and experimental archaeologists have been forced to rediscover the lost technology.

Earlier, we considered Peter White's work among New Guinea flintknappers. The Duna study is unusual, because most native flintknappers perished well before the twentieth century, and with them the trade secrets that might have enabled archaeologists to learn more from the stone tools so commonly found in sites.

Fortunately, a school of dedicated experimentalists has spent years rediscovering the technology necessary to fabricate stone tools. The late Don Crabtree (affiliated with the Idaho State University Museum) began this research by undertaking a series of carefully documented studies to uncover the nature of prehistoric stoneworking. One of Crabtree's many projects was to rediscover the techniques necessary to create the **Folsom projectile points** discovered at the Lindenmeier site in Colorado. Folsom points, some of the world's most exquisite stone artifacts, were originally made between twelve thousand and eleven thousand years ago. Mounted on spear shafts, these artifacts were used for hunting now-extinct forms of American bison. Although the spear points are only about two inches long, Crabtree counted over 150 minute sharpening flakes removed from their surface (see Figure 5–13).

The distinctive property of Folsom artifacts is the **flute** (or channel flake) removed from each surface. Nobody is really sure why these artifacts were fluted in this distinctive

FIGURE 5–13 Folsom spear points replicated by Don Crabtree. Note the two "fluting" flakes removed from the bottom two points. (Courtesy Don Crabtree)

fashion, but everybody agrees that fluting is an extraordinary feat of flintknapping. The technical quality and intrinsic beauty of the Folsom point intrigued Crabtree. Most projectile points can be fashioned in a few minutes. But making the Folsoms must have required hours, assuming that one understood how to do it in the first place. And in the twentieth century, nobody did.

Frank H. H. Roberts, the archaeologist who excavated the Lindenmeier Folsom points (1935, p. 19–21) concluded that the channel flakes must have been driven off by indirect percussion, with a bone or antler punch serving as an intermediary to transfer the blow to the artifact. Interested in flintknapping for most of his life, Crabtree thought about this, tried it out himself, and concluded that Roberts's technique would not work.

So began an experimental period that lasted over forty years. Crabtree tried every way he could think of to manufacture Folsom replicas. In his published account, Crabtree (1966) described the eleven different methods he had tried to remove fluting flakes. Most techniques simply did not work: Either the method was impossible with primitive tools or the flute was different from those on the Folsoms. One method succeeded only in driving a copper punch through Crabtree's left hand.

Crabtree eventually concluded that fluting flakes could be removed in only two ways. In one experiment, he placed an antler shaft on the bottom of the unfinished artifact and then struck the punch with a sharp upward blow. But because placement of the antler punch was critical, this technique requires two workers—not a very satisfactory solution. At one point, Crabtree came across a documentary source describing some long-lost flintknapping techniques once practiced by Native Americans. Particularly interesting were the observations of a Spanish Franciscan friar, Juan de Torquemada, who had traveled through the Central American jungles in 1615:

> They take a stick with both hands, and set well home against the edge of the front of the stone, which also is cut smooth in the front of the stone, which also is cut smooth in that part; and they press it against their brest [sic], and with the force of the pressure there flies off a knife. . . . Then they sharpen it [the tip of the crutch] on a stone using a hone to give it a very fine edge; and in a very short time these workmen will make more than twenty knives in the aforesaid manner (quoted in Crabtree 1968, p. 449).

Torquemada was describing how flakes could be driven off a polyhedral core, but Crabtree wondered whether the method might work to produce meaningful results on his Folsom replicas. Crabtree manufactured a chest crutch following Torquemada's descriptions, padding one end and equipping the other with a sharp antler flaker. He tied an unfinished, unfluted Folsom point into a wood-and-thong vise, which he gripped between his feet. Bracing the crutch against the chest, he successfully detached perfect fluting flakes, time after time. The resulting artifacts were almost identical to the prehistoric Lindenmeier Folsom points.

Crabtree's pioneering research unleashed an avalanche of interest in the fluting problem. Irwin (1968) was able to detach fluting flakes with **direct percussion**, using wood or stone as a "backstop." Flenniken (1978) did it with a modified version of Crabtree's method of **indirect percussion**. Frison and Bradley (1980) discovered a portion of elk antler in some Folsom point–manufacturing debris at the Agate Basin site,

Obsidian Blade Technology: Modern Surgery's Newest Ancient Frontier

All experienced lithic technologists have their battle scars. Should you decide to try your hand at flintknapping, it won't be long until you've sliced, diced, mashed, and otherwise trashed your fingers. In his fifty years of flintknapping, The Master, Don Crabtree, slashed himself in about every conceivable way—across his fingers, through the palm, through a fingernail; one flake zipped right through his shoe. He once termed this regularized blood letting "making a contribution to the lithic blood bank."

One day, while surveying the carnage, he noted that whereas he still had epic scars from jagged-edged flint flakes, the wounds caused by obsidian had healed quickly and were almost invisible. He wondered about that.

Then he saw a friend slice himself while handling some obsidian artifacts Crabtree had just made. The gash bled profusely, and a physician was summoned. But by the time the doctor arrived, some twenty minutes later, the wound had already begun to heal.

A curious soul, Crabtree decided to use an electron microscope to compare some of his obsidian flakes with the sharpest razor blades.

> The platinum plus razor blade is the sharpest thing man has ever developed, far sharper than the old surgeon's scalpel. . . . But this platinum plus [razor] blade had a rounded edge at about 750 diameters. Still the obsidian blade is far sharper even at 10,000 diameters. That platinum plus may be like an aerial view of west Kansas, you know—pretty nearly flat. But the obsidian blade can be magnified so many thousand times more and still have been sharp. It fractures right to the last molecule of the matter. (Crabtree 1979, p. 30)

Immediately recognizing the potential of such supersharp instruments for surgical applications, Crabtree worried that "the surgeon who pioneers the use of such blades may be accused of reverting to caveman tactics."

The breakthrough came in 1975, when Crabtree himself faced major surgery. After some debate, he cajoled his surgeon into using obsidian blades Crabtree himself had fashioned:

> The first surgery was when I had a rib removed and a lung section. The cut goes from right under the breast there, clear around back under the shoulder blade. So it's about an 18" cut. And you know I hardly have a scar. You have to get the light on it just right to see the sutures. And then I've had abdominal surgery four times, from my sternum down to the pelvis—one time was to remove a blood clot. Then I had bilateral femur arteries of woven dacron tubing put in. . . . And there was no problem with sterilization. A fresh blade comes off sterile.

Crabtree's venturesome surgeon, Dr. Bruce A. Buck, was equally enthusiastic, and he wrote up a laudatory article in the *Western Journal of Medicine* (Buck 1982) (see Figure 5–14).

The story of Crabtree's successful surgery was picked up by the Associated Press, and a flood of related popular stories soon appeared in *Omni, Geo, Natural History, Science News,* and *Science '81.* Not long thereafter, more technical assessments cropped up in medical journals, reporting on successful experimental surgeries and speculating about additional applications.

Everyone was impressed with the "exquisitely sharp" obsidian edge. Obsidian blades

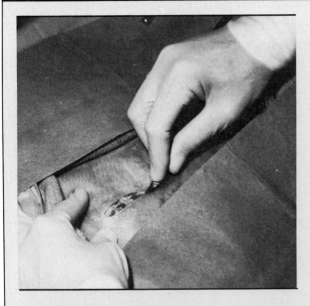

FIGURE 5–14 Most people having kidney stone surgery fear "going under the knife." But when facing this surgical procedure, archaeologist C. William Clewlow decided to "go under the flake," convincing his surgeon to use obsidian flakes that Clewlow himself had manufactured. (Courtesy C. William Clewlow).

are as sharp as the newest diamond scalpels, which, in turn, are one hundred to three hundred times sharper than steel blades. Experiments showed that the size of the steel cut was not only much larger than the glass cut but also very irregular. Moreover, the steel blade caused considerable tissue translocation, drawing "hamburgerized" tissue into the incision area.

Such medical research cannot proceed without the hands-on assistance of flintknapping archaeologists (for somebody must still be skilled enough to create the blades in the first place). Particularly important has been the involvement of Payson Sheets, an archaeologist who began studying obsidian blade technology for his doctoral dissertation in 1969 (Sheets 1987). Acting on a suggestion from Crabtree, Sheets has pioneered research on surgical applications and in 1980, working in collaboration with an eye surgeon in Boulder, presented a paper at the Welsh Cataract Congress.

Sheets and the surgeon have formed a partnership called Fracture Mechanics Limited and have received a patent to protect their manufacturing process. Another Crabtree associate, Errett Callahan, began another company, Aztecnics, to market obsidian blades.

Payson Sheets tells of one operation in Washington D.C., in which a physician planned thoracic surgery using an obsidian blade for half the cut and then his favorite steel blade for the rest, hence creating a control situation to study for cutting and healing. Incredibly, he read the X-rays backwards—performing his operation on the wrong lung; subsequent surgery on the "correct" side was done entirely with steel scalpels. Although this unfortunate patient reported considerable discomfort from the steel-cut side, he experienced virtually no pain during recovery from the obsidian cuts.

Eye surgeons have used obsidian knives to remove cataracts and to assist in cornea transplants. The sharpness allows for extraordinarily accurate incisions, and because less pressure is required, the eye remains more stationary in the orbit when obsidian tools are used. Obsidian implements have also been successfully used for breast biopsies, bilateral vasectomies, facial plastic surgery, and nerve microsurgery.

Using an ancient technology for modern purposes is another case of the far-fetched turned practical. The roots of modern medical science, for instance, can be traced to the curiosity of a few who conducted clandestine (and illegal) autopsies to determine the nature of human physiology and the causes of disease. The same is true in the thriving fields of computer technology and bioengineering: both started as simple inquisitiveness, without any thought of a practical application. Without overstating the point, these episodes illustrate the importance of "pure" research. Who knows the direction from which the next angel of enlightenment may descend?

and after extensive experimentation, they concluded that channel flakes could be successfully removed with a wood-and-antler lever/fulcrum device. Tunnell (1977) used indirect percussion with a grooved anvil-and-backstop arrangement. Gryba (1988) recently reported several experiments in which he detached channel flakes with a simple, hand-generated pressure technique.

What Does Replicative Experimentation Prove?

But what do all these experiments mean? If Crabtree was right, was Irwin wrong? Or maybe Crabtree was wrong and Flenniken was right? But if Gryba is right, does this mean that Crabtree, Irwin, and Flenniken all were wrong? Considerable confusion exists on this point. A widely distributed review article on anthropological flintknapping suggests a series of "formal procedures" by which such replicative experiments are to be judged: The first step is to identify correctly the technique(s) involved, which is then controlled for several variables, ultimately producing a "statistically valid sample." Finally, experimental results are compared technologically with prehistoric controls to assess validity. "If valid, the replicator has reproduced a tangible aspect of prehistoric human behavior and demonstrated the reality of that behavior" (Flenniken 1984, p. 197).

The results of experimental archaeology cannot be judged in this way. Thor Heyerdahl (1950) once argued that Easter Island had been populated from the east, by Peruvians, rather than by Polynesians from the west. When skeptics told him that the ocean currents made a westward voyage impossible, Heyerdahl took up the challenge and launched his famous (and successful) raft trip aboard the *Kon Tiki*. But what did Heyerdahl prove? Did he "reproduce tangible aspects of prehistoric human behavior" by his raft trip? Did he "demonstrate the reality" of the past? Hardly. The voyage of the *Kon Tiki* merely demonstrated to the world that such a westward raft trip was not impossible.

This is an important finding. But no amount of trans-Pacific bravado will ever prove that prehistoric Peruvians had floated to Easter Island. This is an empirical matter, requiring archaeological validation.

So too with lithic experimentation. Crabtree demonstrated that it was not impossible to use a chest crutch to replicate the Lindenmeier Folsom points. Gryba showed that hand-held percussion could be used to recreate channel flaking. But none of these experimental flintknappers demonstrated how the Lindenmeier Folsom points were actually made. Once again, this is an empirical question, requiring considerable archaeological verification. Experimental archaeologists cannot attempt to think in terms of "right" and "wrong." Replicative experiments do not "demonstrate the reality" of anything; experiments demonstrate only the possibility that a given technique could have been used in the past. So long as these objectives are kept in mind, experimental flintknappers can make significant contributions to the growing body of middle-range research in Americanist archaeology.

Stone Tools: What Were They Used For?

Another promising recent direction of experimental study is to determine the function of prehistoric stone tools. As the stone tools were used in their behavioral contexts, the edges often became damaged and dulled. Tools found in the archaeological record often contain such distinctive edge damage. Sometimes stone knives are found to have minute **striations** or scratches, which often reveal the direction of force and the nature of tool use. Sickles used to harvest grain often acquire a characteristic sheen from abrasion by silica contained in the plant stalks. Tools used for piercing or drilling often have small nicks or polishing on the surfaces that protrude. And so on.

The pattern of edge damage (often called **microwear**) on a stone tool is archaeological evidence regarding some previous behavior. But given only the stone tool, how do we know that the edge damage resulted from a specific action? How, for instance, do we know that the sickle sheen came from harvesting plants rather than from scraping hides? How do we know that the striations on a stone knife came from gritty inclusions contained in meat rather than from cleaning it off or from putting it into a sheath? (Figure 5–15)

This is an issue requiring a bridging argument to eliminate ambiguity. Archaeologists who use microwear patterns to infer tool function must in each case demonstrate the relationship between the wear pattern observed (archaeological context) and the act that produced that wear (systemic context). Hundreds of experiments have been conducted to provide precisely this sort of one-to-one relationship between edge damage and tool use. Although microwear studies can be traced well back into the nineteenth century, the trend was established by Sergei Semenov, whose major work, entitled *Prehistoric Technology,* was first published in the Soviet Union in 1957. Semenov documented the results of more than two decades of experimentation with primitive tools, some studies dating back to the 1930s. He experimented with a variety of techniques to replicate prehistoric tools, manufacturing artifacts of both stone and bone. His major contribution was the definition of three kinds of microwear: polishing, coarse abrasion (such as grinding and striations),

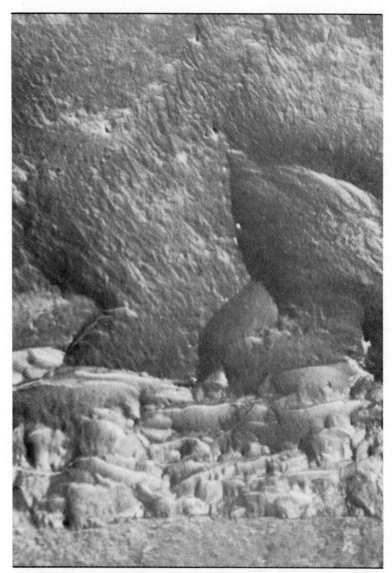

FIGURE 5-15 Photomicrograph of a scraper, dating 400 B.C., from Gatecliff Shelter. The photograph was taken at low power (about 50x magnification) on a scanning electron microscope. The broad, smooth flaking at the top of the picture is retouch, part of the manufacturing process. The small step scars at the bottom result from edge damage during use, probably from scraping a relatively hard surface (such as antler or bone). (Courtesy the American Museum of Natural History)

and rasping of the edge. Semenov argued that the direction of the microscopic striations seems to be the most important key in the discovery of functions of ancient implements.

The translation of *Prehistoric Technology* into English in 1964 spurred a flurry of microwear research throughout the world. One such follow-up study was conducted by Ruth E. Tringham, who studied with Semenov for a year in Leningrad, then moved her experiments to the University College of London and eventually to Harvard University (see Tringham et al. 1974). Tringham and her associates conducted a wide range of experiments in the tradition of Semenov, with some important differences. Although Semenov's work was largely intuitive and unsystematic, Tringham followed rigorous procedures to determine the exact extent and nature of tool wear in a number of different media. She attempted to reproduce working edges and to bring each into contact with a specific material working in a given direction. Experiments consisted of making tools from British flint and systematically applying tools to a variety of media such as antler, bone, wood, skin, flesh, and plant fiber, carefully maintaining constant direction of force and counting the number of strokes needed. Some of the tools were hand held, but others were placed in a haft.

Then the experimental tools were examined under a low-power stereoscopic microscope (the actual "power" varying between 40 and 60X). Photographs were taken to document each stage of wear. Among other things, Tringham found that Semenov's striations were not as universal as he had thought. Striations appear slowly and sometimes not at all. Instead, Tringham concentrated on **microflaking**, the minute edge chipping that occurs as stone tools are used. This approach allowed her to characterize the kind of wear resulting from a variety of functional movements. Cutting, for instance, produced a series of tiny uneven flake scars along both sides of the working edge. Planing, however, produced flake scars only on the surface opposite that in direct contact with the worked material. Boring produced distinct trapezoidal flake scars, especially on the sides of the tool. In addition, the edge damage varied with the nature of the materials being worked. Soft-worked materials such as skin and flesh produced only scalar-shaped scars, whereas hard materials such as antler and bone produced crushing and eventually dulled the edge so that it would no longer cut at all.

Tringham's experiments established the value of functional analysis with low-power microscopy, and numerous investigators have followed in this tradition, taking advantage of the relatively inexpensive equipment and rapid rate of analysis (see Where to Go from Here?)

An alternative approach was pioneered by Lawrence Keeley, who used "high-powered" microscopy (up to 400X) to test the variables of lithic material, worked material, action, use duration, edge angle, and intentional retouch. The Keeley technique focuses on locating specific **micropolishes** rather than damage to tool edges (**microscarring**).

Keeley's work is particularly noteworthy because he employed a series of "blind" experiments to test both the accuracy and the repeatability of his technique. The blind tests were conducted at the suggestion of M. H. Newcomer (University of London) who was skeptical of Keeley's ability to determine tool use from microwear analysis. Newcomer used a red deer antler and quartzite hammerstone to manufacture a set of fifteen tools of fine-grained black flint from the chalk at Brandon, Suffolk. He then worked on a series of materials—ash and pine, bracken, ox bone and hide, rabbit skin and bone, pork fat, raw and frozen lamb—and replicated a range of simple activities known from ethnographic evidence: scraping, slicing, sawing, boring, chopping, and whittling. Newcomer used the fifteen artifacts only in left-handed fashion, being careful not to drop, step on, or use them with gritty hands—"applying this sort of accidental damage would have put the wear analyst at an unfair disadvantage."

Newcomer then turned the artifacts over to Keeley, who knew the ground rules but not the specifics of the experiments. The implements were carefully cleaned using detergent, warm water, warm dilute NaOH, and warm HCl. Sometimes an ultra-sonic cleaning tank was used to remove extraneous material such as finger prints and organic deposit from the flint surfaces. Keeley then proceeded to use his "high-power" method to study each piece. Specifically, he looked at four characteristics: (1) general tool size and shape, (2) type and placement of damage, (3) distribution and orientation of linear wear features (like striations), and (4) location and extent of microscar polish.

How well did Keeley's high-power analysis do in the blind test? Table 5–1 shows some remarkable results. In fourteen of sixteen interpretations—because the right and left edges of Tool 14 seemed different, they were scored independently—he correctly identified the "business end" of the tool. Keeley contends that the only "mistake" should not be held against him: He admits to "simple human error" in the case of Tool 10: "There is no doubt in Keeley's mind that if the used area of this implement's edge had actually been examined, then the correct interpretation of its function would have followed." Tool 5, used to scrape raw pig hide for thirty-one minutes, had no apparent wear, as un-contaminated fat cannot be expected to "damage" flint (Newcomer and Keeley 1979, p. 203).

Keeley's results fell off slightly when he reconstructed tool wear (twelve of sixteen correct); he felt that this degree of accuracy adequately reflected interpretive possibilities on prehistoric implements. However, when identifying the material being worked (ten of sixteen correct), Keeley cried foul. In conducting his butchering experiments, Newcomer had used a wooden cutting board, and Keeley feels that the wood and meat polishes confounded the issue. Similarly, Keeley misread the polish on Tool 7 as bone polish and that on Tool 11 as antler polish. But as it turned out, Newcomer had used extremely well seasoned wood, at least ten years old.

These blind experiments established the validity of the high-power method of microwear analysis in the minds of many archaeologists, and the techniques have become an important tool in the arsenal available to reconstruct prehistoric behavior. Studies such as Keeley's provide direction for a functional analysis of stone tools and also a way to bridge archaeological and systemic contexts. Although microwear analysis continues to be extremely time-consuming, this is an important beginning.

TABLE 5–1—Results of Blind Testing in "High Power" Microwear Analysis

Tool No.	Use by Newcomer	Interpretation by Keeley
1	Whittling seasoned ash sapling (2 cm diameter) for 18 min.	Cutting* wood (branch less than 4 cm diameter).
2	Chopping ash sapling (3 cm) on pine cutting board for 21 min.	Chopping wood.
2	Sawing ash sapling (2.5 cm) for 12 min.	Sawing possibly wood.
4	Cutting raw lamb meat on cutting board (see above) for 44 min.	Cutting unknown material, possibly vegetable matter or meat.
5	Scraping fat from raw pig hide for 31 min.	Unused.
6	Whittling seasoned pine for 14 min.	(1) Whittling wood, (2) graving wood or bone (secondary use).
7	Drilling seasoned pine for 10 min.	Graving, planing, and scraping bone.
8	Cutting raw lamb meat on cutting board for 28 min.	Cutting meat.
9	Unused.	Unused.
10	Cutting ox hide on cutting board for 23 min.	Cutting meat (guess)—wrong area of edge thought to have been used: counts as wrong interpretation.
11	Scraping ash sapling (1.5 cm) for 13 min.	Scraping antler (or possibly wood).
12	Cutting frozen lamb meat on cutting board for 23 min.	Cutting or sawing wood.
13	Cutting bracken fern for 26 min.	Slicing unknown material but probably vegetable matter.
14a	Right edge used to skin off rabbit then cut skin into strips.	Cutting meat.
14b	Left edge used to cut forefeet off rabbit at joint.	Cutting meat, cartilage, bone (i.e., breaking joint).
15	Scraping ox bone for 11 min.	Scraping possibly hide, less likely antler.

*In the sense of slicing rather than whittling.
Source: Newcomer and Keeley 1979, Table 1. Reprinted by permission of M. L. Newcomer and L. H. Keeley and Academic Press.

The last two sections have focused on experimental and ethnoarchaeological research conducted on stone tools. This focus is important to archaeology because in so many cases stone tools are all that survive. But the experimental approach is hardly limited to lithics. Hundreds of experiments have been conducted within the last few decades in order to test the prevailing theories regarding the relationship of culture to the physical world in which it exists. Experiments range from Heyerdahl's daring trans-

Atlantic and trans-Pacific voyages (1950, 1971) to the lesser-known experiments in clearing agricultural fields using stone tools (e.g., Iversen 1956, Saraydar and Shimada 1971). Entire fortifications have been constructed, only to be experimentally burned to the ground and then excavated (see Coles 1973, Chapter 2). In addition, many experiments have been conducted to determine the techniques used in lost crafts such as ancient pottery manufacture (see Mayes 1962, Shepard 1956) and primitive metallurgy (Coghlan 1940, Wynne and Tylecote 1958).

WHERE TO GO FROM HERE?

General Sources on Experimental Archaeology: Coles *Archaeology by Experiment* (1973) provides a useful, if somewhat dated, summary of many other experiments designed to provide insights into how the archaeological record has been formed; see also Coles (1967).

On the Experimental Replication of Stone Tools: Don Crabtree published a series of landmark papers that still command the attention of serious students (1966); see also Flenniken (1981, 1984) and Swanson (1975).

Use–Wear Analysis on Flaked Stone Tools: Perhaps the most informative overall source is Vaughan (1985); see also Hayden (1979), Odell (1982).

Sources Using the "Low-Power" Microscopic Method: Odell (1979, 1981), Vaughan (1985, pp. 19–23); plus other papers in Hayden (1979).

Sources Using the "High-Power" Microscopic Method: The best description of the procedure and the "blind" tests is found in Keeley (1980, pp. 63–82); see also Holly and Del Bene (1981), Keeley (1974), Keeley and Newcomer (1977), Moss (1983), Newcomer and Keeley (1979).

Other Use–Wear Studies Employing "Blind Testing": Bamforth (1986), Knuttson and Hope (1984), Odell and Odell-Vereecken (1980), Shea (1987).

Other Important Directions in Flintknapping and Microwear Studies: Identifying and defining the spatial correlates of stone tool manufacture and use (Binford and O'Connell 1984, Newcomer and Sieveking 1980); developing a regional approach to lithic variability (Camilli 1983, Cross 1983, Kelly 1983, 1985, Magne 1985); establishing "if and only if" linkages between observed behaviors and the traces they produce on stone tools (Greiser and Sheets 1979, Hayden 1979); isolating the role of raw materials in determining lithic variability (Flenniken 1981, Straus 1980, Sussman 1985); distinguishing natural from cultural modification (Grayson 1986, Patterson 1983); defining biases in differential recovery of lithic assemblages (Kalin 1981, Nicholson 1983); determining the role of postdepositional factors that affect stone tools (Flenniken and Haggerty 1979).

Lithic Technology publishes original and significant articles of lithic archaeology, theory, method, and techniques from a global perspective; first published in 1972.

Subscription information: c/o Dr. Eric Gibson, Department of Sociology and Anthropology, Trinity University, 715 Stadium Drive, San Antonio, Tex. 78284.

Historical Documentation: Middle-Range Research's Newest Mandate?

There now are signs that historical documentation may eventually be used in much the same way that ethnoarchaeologists and experimental archaeologists build middle-range expectations. Mark Leone and Parker Potter (1988, p. 11) noted that traditionally the documentary and archaeological records have been linked in two rather unsatisfactory ways. In many cases, the documetary record works like a literary time machine—the archaeologist digs first and then sifts through the documents to see what things mean. Alternatively, one can begin by writing document-based history and then excavate to fill in the gaps and add detail.

But in each case, the archaeological and documentary records are treated as somehow linked, with one field being dependent on the other. Any unexpected findings or inconsistencies between the archaeological and documentary evidence is commonly labeled as "an exception" or "an anomaly" and promptly discarded, thereby quashing any hope of fresh insight. This is the traditional approach in historical archaeology.

But middle-range research approaches a similar dichotomy from a perspective of independence. The ethnoarchaeologist, for instance, uses the "economic anatomy" of a given species to assess samples of bones both observed ethnographically and recovered archaeologically. Neither sample is "correct" or "superior." Each framework has its own biases and frame of reference. Insight is gained by understanding the "ambiguity" between the two independent records.

Leone and Potter suggest that historical archaeologists can generate the same middle-range framework by viewing the archaeological and documentary records as equally valid yet independent lines of evidence. Rather than discarding differences in the record as "exceptions" or "noise," this middle-range approach looks for "ambiguities" between the historical and archaeological evidence, recognizing that the unexpected will continue to expand our knowledge.

Although a few pioneering studies are currently available (e.g., Leone and Crosby 1987, Leone and Potter 1988, Palkovich 1988; see also Chapter 15), not enough research has been conducted to know whether a middle-range perspective in historical archaeological archaeology will prove fruitful. The next few years should tell the tale.

Summary

The "facts" of archaeology are incapable of speaking for themselves; it is therefore necessary for archaeologists to use bridging arguments to breathe behavioral life into the objects of the past, which have actually existed in two discrete contexts. The artifacts, features, and residues, without which archaeologists could not work, were once related to an ongoing behavioral system. While these artifacts were being manufactured and used, they existed in their systemic contexts. But by the time they reached the hands of the archaeologist, the objects had ceased to participate in their behavior system and had passed into archaeological contexts.

The formation of archaeological sites requires four basic processes: cultural deposition, reclamation, disturbance, and reuse. Each process has certain regularities, but archaeologists are only beginning to understand the complex mechanisms involved. One way to supply these bridging arguments between archaeological and systemic contexts is to study firsthand the workings of ongoing societies. As contradictory as it may seem, a number of archaeologists—the ethnoarchaeologists—spend their time studying living societies, observing artifacts, features, and residues while they still exist in their systemic contexts. To date, ethnoarchaeological studies have examined, among other things, the processes determining settlement pattern and intrasite patterning, the reality of the tool-kit concept, the mechanisms of artifact curation and reuse, and the social correlates of stone tool manufacture and use. Ethnoarchaeologists are also examining the relationship of material culture to modern industrial society, as illustrated by the Garbage Project at the University of Arizona.

Archaeological formation processes are also currently being defined by experimental archaeologists. Although sharing a primary interest in middle-range research, ethnoarchaeologists work within a functioning behavior system, whereas experimental archaeologists attempt to derive relevant processes by means of experimental replication. Much of this initial experimental work has concentrated on the manufacture and use of stone tools, although archaeologists are currently experimenting on a wide range of problems, including tool efficiency, processes of site destruction and preservation, and methods of ceramic manufacture. Thor Heyerdahl's epic trans-Atlantic and trans-Pacific voyages can even be considered to be a variety of experimental archaeology.

CHAPTER 6

Sampling Sites: Why Archaeologists Dig Square Holes

Excavated sites are the archaeologist's bread and butter.
—Lewis Binford

Every introduction to archaeological excavation should begin with two stipulations:

- There is no "right" way to excavate a site (but there are plenty of wrong ones).
- Nobody ever learned how to dig properly from a book (including this one).

Despite recent advances, archaeological excavation remains as much art as science. All we can do here is to look at some common techniques, some archaeological standards and conventions, and, perhaps most important of all, what it feels like to be on a dig. I joined my first archaeological excavation as a college junior. From that day on, I was hooked. It is much easier these days to participate in an excavation, and anybody with even a casual interest in archaeology ought to give it a try.

How We Excavated Gatecliff Shelter

In the Prologue, we told you about the discovery of Gatecliff Shelter. Although thrilling—and at times electrifying—finding a site like Gatecliff is only the beginning. Next, I shall

Who Really Dug Guilá Naquitz?

My discussion of Americanist archaeologists tends to focus on the research of isolated personalities. Although this approach is designed to bring archaeology alive, the emphasis on individuals also glosses over the critical role of teamwork in all phases of archaeological investigation. In the following, Kent Flannery imparts some of the cameraderie and harmony that accompanied the excavations at Guilá Naquitz (Oaxaca, Mexico):

Guilá Naquitz (Site OC-43) was discovered on January 26, 1966. Part of the following month was spent converting the old ox cart trail from Mitla to Díaz Ordaz into a road that would allow us access to the Rancho El Fuerte caves by means of our 4-wheel-drive pickup truck. . . . We returned to Guilá Naquitz on April 14 with a larger crew. . . . [I] and [Chris] Moser were joined by Silvia Maranca, and the crew of Mitla workmen was increased to 10. This group of Zapotec-speaking Mitleños was the heart and soul of our project and should be considered the real excavators of Guilá Naquitz. . . . Their patience, intelligence, careful attention to detail [were] indispensable to our success, and their unflagging high spirits and sense of humor kept us continuously entertained [see Figure 6–1].

Somehow our Ford pickup, "El Caballito Blanco," made it up the boulder-strewn slopes of the mountain every morning, and we dismounted in a wind-deflated gully below the cave. Somehow all the equipment made it up the cliff, including the 10-gallon *garrafón* of drinking water that Don Juan would entrust to no one else. Once at the cave, Moser would tether his faithful watchdog on the talus to keep out any stray goats that wandered away from their herders on the slopes below us. . . . Over the sound of trowels and paintbrushes, an interminable shaggy-dog story would

Reprinted by permission of K. V. Flannery and Academic Press.

be told in Zapotec by one of the excavators. Inevitably, the punch line would be in Spanish, but this was little consolation to those of us who had not understood the preceding 1500 words. . . . The frequent inclusion of lines such as, "Confiésame, Padre, porque yo he pecado," made it clear that many stories involved priests and confessionals, but the sins were confessed in Zapotec to the accompaniment of high-pitched laughter. Though we gradually picked up the minimum vocabulary necessary to describe the archaeological deposits, . . . we never really deciphered any of the stories.

Nor did the entertainment cease at lunchtime. Out of the hamper came tortas, fruit, and other goodies prepared by Lupe back at the *Posada La Sorpresa*, along with a dozen hard-boiled eggs. No, make that eleven hard-boiled eggs. The twelfth was "the egg of the day," a raw one indistinguishable from the others, which had been slipped into the basket by Eligio Martínez. Tension mounted as we all began to crack and peel our eggs, and we waited to see who would get the egg of the day. Finally there would come a crack, a sickening squish, and an epithet in English or Zapotec. Eventually, Moser began cracking his egg on Eligio's head as a precautionary measure.

One memorable lunchtime there came an ear-splitting whoop, and seconds later one workman emerged from the shadow of the cliff holding the tattered remnants of what had once been his shirt. Everyone knew what had happened: One of the screen operators had captured a scorpion and cut off the last segment of its tail, leaving it harmless but alive and very angry. Approaching one of the trowelmen as he hunched over his lunch, he had pulled his comrade's collar away from his neck and suspended the creature over the resulting opening by holding its tail between his fingers. As the trowelman looked up, the last he saw was an obviously live scorpion plummeting down between his shoulder blades and his shirt. Now most of the workmen were on the ground, helpless with laughter. "It's the only way," one of them giggled, "we can get him to change that old shirt."

No one ever lost his temper at such times, not even the victim. He simply waited; he knew his turn would come, and probably sooner than his tormenter expected.

Through the long afternoons, our crew of Mitleños became better and better at following the cultural stratigraphy of the cave. They knew each living floor intimately, remembering what had been found in it and in which square, and had their own code name for each. Zone C, with its soft white ash, was referred to as *leche en polvo*, "powdered milk." Zone D, with its granular brown matrix of burned oak leaves, was referred to as *el Nescafé*, "instant coffee." Zone E was simply *yuš* (Zapotec for "sand"). We were constantly amazed at the near-photographic memory our trowelmen displayed for the squares they had dug and the retrospective comments they made that were confirmed by field notes from weeks before.

. . . It was with some sadness that we closed the excavation on May 10, 1966. Guilá Naquitz had been a great site, a joy to excavate, with remarkably clear stratigraphy and excellent preservation throughout. Beyond that, it had been a colorful experience shared with a group of people none of us would ever forget. (Flannery 1986, pp. 65–67)

FIGURE 6–1 The real excavators of Guilá Naquitz Cave (clockwise from lower left): Ambrosio Martínez, Alfredo Sosa, Genaro Luis, Pablo García, Felix Sosa, Don Juan Martínez, Eligio Martínez, Angel Sosa, Carlos Pérez, Ernesto Martínez, and Kent Flannery (see Flannery, 1986, Figure 5.2). (Courtesy Kent V. Flannery)

sketch what happened during the seven field seasons we spent at Gatecliff. Our strategy and tactics evolved dramatically as we learned more about the site and its potential.

Digging Telephone Booths

As recounted, it started with two simple test pits, dug the same year we found the site. From day one, we wanted to learn two things: how long people had used Gatecliff Shelter and whether the buried deposits could tell us about the human chronology of the region. These two questions were clear-cut, and so was our fieldwork. Our earliest excavation strategy was vertical, designed to supply, as expediently as possible, a stratified sequence of artifacts and ecofacts associated with other potentially datable materials. In our first three years at Gatecliff, we excavated deep vertical test pits, what Kent Flannery calls "telephone booths."

Like most archaeologists, I dig "metrically" in test pits typically one meter square. A few colleagues still hang on to feet and inches—mostly because they don't want to replace their equipment—and their telephone booths are often a yard square, never more than five feet on a side. There is, of course, a minimum size in such exploratory soundings: Squares much smaller would squeeze out the archaeologists, and larger units are overly destructive (and too time-consuming).

Test pits tend to be quick and dirty, particularly because they must be excavated "blind," without knowing what stratigraphy lies below. Nevertheless, even in test pits, archaeologists must maintain three-dimensional control of the finds: the X axis (front to back), the Y axis (side to side), and the Z axis (top to bottom). This is why archaeologists dig square holes. Provided the sidewalls are kept sufficiently straight and perpendicular, excavators can use the dirt itself to maintain horizontal control on the X and Y axes by measuring directly from the sidewalls. As test pits deepen, however, the sidewalls may start sloping inward, cramping the digger and biasing the measurements. Field archaeologists call these sloppy pits "bathtubs"—decidedly bad form.

What about vertical control? At Gatecliff, we dug test pits in arbitrarily imposed 10-cm levels. Everything of interest—artifacts, ecofacts, soil samples, and so forth—are kept in separate **level bags**, one for each 10-cm level. The Z dimension for each level is usually designated according to distance below the ground surface: Level 1 (surface to 10 cm below), Level 2 (10 to 20 cm below), and so forth.

Excavation procedures vary widely, depending on the stage of excavation, the nature of the deposit, and the impulse of the archaeologist in charge (remember, digging is an art, not a science). Because they are so small, test pits are often dug by trowel (rather than by shovel), maintaining a horizontal working surface. Deposit is scooped into a dust pan, dumped into a bucket, then carried off-site for a closer look.

Life is just a bowl of pits.
—Rodney Dangerfield

More Permanent Controls

Test Pits I and II told us that Gatecliff Shelter warranted a closer look, and we returned the next year to do just that. The site was divided into a one-meter **grid system**, oriented along the long axis of the shelter. We assigned consecutive letters to each north-south division and numbered the east-west division. By this method, each excavation square could be designated by a unique alphanumeric name (just like Bingo—A–7, B–5, and my favorite K–9) (Figure 6–2). Each excavator was still responsible for digging a single one-meter square unit, but by aligning the units, we created a *strata-trench* one meter

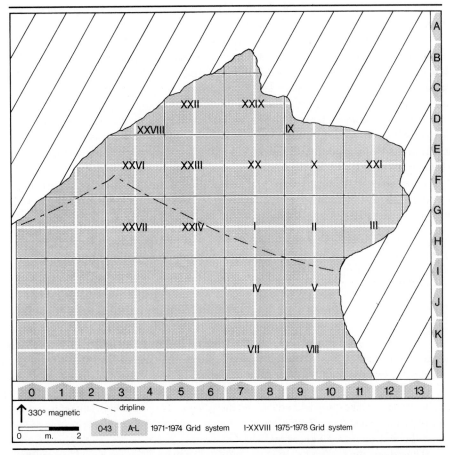

FIGURE 6–2 Plan view of the two grid systems used at Gatecliff Shelter. Alphanumeric system defined one-meter excavation squares between 1970 and 1974. From 1975 on, Roman numerals were used to designate the two-meter excavation squares (see Thomas 1983b, Figure 8). (Courtesy the American Museum of Natural History)

wide and eight meters long. Bulk soil samples were also periodically saved so that microscopic remains could be retrieved in the laboratory.

The east wall of the "7-trench", so named because it contained Units B–7 through I–7—was defined as the **master profile**. All artifacts, features, soil and pollen samples, and radiocarbon dates were correlated with this one particular vertical section (the implications of this stratigraphic section are considered in Chapter 8).

As the 7-trench deepened, the sidewalls grew, and the excavation had to be expanded laterally. The vertical strategy used to this point dictated that a number of central units be excavated to bedrock; surrounding units were "telescoped" to minimize the height of the freestanding walls. The excavation was hampered by the large chert roof fall. Access to the excavation area was by means of portable ladders, and a makeshift ramp constructed across the top of the roof fall.

A **site datum** was established at the rear of the shelter. Using an altimeter and a U.S. Geological Survey topographic map, we determined the elevation of this datum point to be 2319 meters (7607 feet) above sea level. But in on-site operations, this single point defined a horizontal **datum point**, arbitrarily designated as zero. All site elevations from this point on were plotted as "X centimeters below datum."

All archaeological **features**—fire hearths, artifact concentrations, sleeping areas, and the like—were plotted on a master site map, and individual artifacts found *in situ* were plotted in three dimensions. Artifacts found in the screen were bagged by stratigraphic or **arbitrary level**.

Field notes at this stage were kept by individual excavators in bound graph paper notebooks. Good field notes record everything, whether or not it seems important at the time:

Soil conditions: Loose or compact? Dark or light? Charcoal present?
Stratigraphic change: Is the level uniform from top to bottom, side to side?
Artifacts recovered: Exact provenience (when possible); key artifacts drawn.
Other remains: Density of bones, waste flakes, ceramics.
Horizontal plan drawing
Sidewall profile

Depending on the nature of the site (and the stage of excavation), field notes can either be taken "formless" (as in the preceding) or recorded on specific unit-level forms, with precise categories defined for each kind of necessary information.

People often pair up during this kind of excavation, one digger with one screener. The excavator usually takes the field notes, and the screener keeps track of artifact provenience and fills out the level bags. To minimize boredom, we found it useful for people to switch jobs at the end of each 10-cm level.

These were the logistics required to pursue a vertical excavation strategy at Gatecliff Shelter. But each site poses different problems, which must be solved by changing field tactics. At this stage, we were looking primarily for change through time. At Gatecliff, this meant looking for key time-sensitive artifacts to be grouped into temporal types (in Chapter 10, we discuss these time-markers in detail). Such temporal types enabled us to place previously undated archaeological contexts into a temporal sequence as we excavated. Laboratory work (such as radiocarbon dating) subsequently tested these preliminary field hypotheses, what geologists call their "horseback correlations."

The vertical excavation strategy is a deliberately simplified scheme designed to clarify chronology. As emphasized throughout this book, archaeologists concentrate on the shared aspects of culture when attempting to chart culture change along a temporal axis. Although this strategy blurs much of the complexity in the archaeological record, it can be justified for these initial temporal aims.

By the end of our fourth field season, our major strata-trench had reached a depth of nine meters below the ground surface. The master site stratigraphic sequence was well known, and by that time, we had run two dozen radiocarbon dates to pin down the absolute dates of each stratum. We had successfully defined the cultural sequence of Gatecliff Shelter, but our vertical excavation strategy had also left us with a series of extremely steep and hazardous sidewalls. Even though the excavation was telescoped to minimize these sidewalls, the sheer verticality of the site made it dangerous. Change was clearly in order, both conceptually and logistically.

The Horizontal Excavation Strategy

By this time, we realized that Gatecliff Shelter held potential far beyond mere chronology. Remember that establishing cultural chronology is only archaeology's first objective; our early excavations amply demonstrated that Gatecliff could make useful contributions to paleoethnographic objectives as well. Several stratigraphic units contained short-term, intact occupational surfaces, and the remaining excavations at Gatecliff concentrated on the spatial distributions within these key stratigraphic units.

Conducting paleoethnography requires a shift in both perspective and digging strategy. Paleoethnographers look beyond the shared, modal aspects of culture to view things as part of the overall cultural system. In other words, the focus moves from the when and where to the more elusive what. Viewed in this manner, digging mine shafts and telephone booths becomes inappropriate. The vertical strategy implies that the cultural context within each statum is largely irrelevant to the overall chronology. Rather, the vertical strategy is concerned primarily with determining when selected artifacts or ecofacts were deposited relative to the others.

Culture in the systemic sense embraces the structural elements basic to adaptation rather than merely aggregates of functional traits that happen to be shared. The paleoethnographic approach requires looking at the interrelationships among artifacts, waste debris, cultural features, cave walls, and drip line. We must understand what activities took place, not just which artifacts were deposited.

The tactics required to pursue this systemic strategy likewise change, sometimes radically. With the stratigraphy suitably defined, extensive vertical sections were no longer necessary, and we concentrated on opening entire living surfaces simultaneously (see Figure 6–3). To do this, we regridded Gatecliff Shelter into two-meter square units.

These larger excavation units correlated with the previous grid system but were renamed for convenience.

The cultural lenses at Gatecliff were slowly excavated by hand, with thicker stratigraphic units removed in arbitrary 10-cm levels. Exposing living floors proceeded more slowly than had the previous vertical excavations, and excavators were instructed to recover all artifacts *in situ*. Features were screened separately, and flotation samples were retained for laboratory processing. Significant debitage scatters were plotted, as were concentrations of bone and other artifacts. The excavated deposits were then placed in buckets and carried to the screening area where they were passed through 1/8-in. screens, and as before, artifacts missed by the excavators were saved along with all fragments of chippage and bone.

More than one hundred cubic meters of fill had been removed from Gatecliff by this time, and we were well aware of which strata contained cultural debris and which strata were **sterile**. The known sterile lenses—of which there were several at Gatecliff—were rapidly shoveled out as a single unit, without regard to arbitrary level, the deposits placed in wheelbarrows and processed through an ingenious dump sifter, constructed by my late colleague Junius Bird on the southeastern margin of the site. The deposits were dumped

FIGURE 6–3　Artist's reconstruction of the horizontal excavation strategy at
Gatecliff Shelter (see Thomas 1983b, Figure 15).
(Courtesy the American Museum of Natural History)

down a long ramp over a mesh of 1/2-in. screen. The soil not passing through the screen was diverted onto a sorting table, where it was thoroughly examined for artifacts and noncultural remains.

To pursue this horizontal strategy, it was necessary for us to remove the massive chert roof fall, which covered the eastern half of the site. The boulder measured approximately fifty cubic meters and not only covered significant deposits but also posed a threat to the excavators working below. We spent ten days removing this boulder with a jackhammer and pry bar. We did not blast for fear of losing the rock art at the rear of the shelter. Once the roof fall was removed, we began to excavate across the entire interior of the shelter.

The horizontal strategy also required significantly more control within contemporary stratigraphic units. A single crew chief took excavation notes for the entire site at this point (rather than having individual excavators do it, as before). Vertical excavation relied on **line levels** to maintain vertical control, but because the horizontal strategy required more precision, a concrete datum point was established on each living surface, and all vertical measurements were taken using builder's levels and **stadia rods**. These three-dimensional data were transferred to site notebooks, and living floor maps were plotted for each surface at the time of the excavation (see Figure 6–4). A single excavator was assigned to each two square-meter unit, and all artifacts, features, and large ecofacts were plotted on large-scale living floor maps. Since then, sophisticated computer-driven systems have been developed to assist in piece-plotting objects on living surfaces.

Archaeological sites with such deep, stratified deposits are rare, and excavating such middens poses certain problems to the excavator. For example, the profile in Figure 6–5 could not have been excavated in a single vertical cut because of the danger of collapse. In a similar situation, my colleague Don Fowler once cleared a fifteen-foot-high profile at a cave in eastern Nevada. It took two days to clean the section for final drawing and photography, and just as they began to make the final sketch, an air force jet screamed overhead. The resulting sonic boom triggered the collapse of the stratigraphic profile and also a fusillade of angry letters of protest from the archaeologists. But like Humpty Dumpty, there is no piecing together a collapsed stratigraphic profile.

All our excavation units at Gatecliff Shelter were stair stepped, so that no walls stood higher than two meters (until the very last stage of the excavation). Should a collapse occur—as they did from time to time—there would be no danger of excavators being totally buried. The various aspects of the excavations will be discussed in later chapters, but the Gatecliff profile illustrates how the law of superposition—in this case, alternating cultural and natural deposits—facilitates archaeological interpretation.

I emphasize the difference between vertical and horizontal strategies because they represent different assumptions and different objectives. Consider the matter of provenience: Artifact provenience in the vertical strategy means little more than stratigraphic placement. The exact location within a given stratum is analytically irrelevant. Artifacts found in the screen were as useful as those found *in situ*.

The horizontal stategy, however, emphasizes the context of artifact and ecofacts

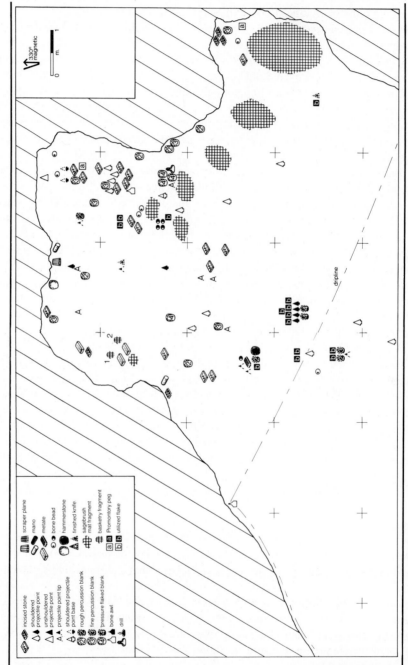

FIGURE 6–4 The spatial distribution of artifacts on Horizon 2 (deposited in about A.D. 1300) at Gatecliff Shelter (see Thomas 1983b, figure 240). (Courtesy the American Museum of Natural History)

FIGURE 6–5 David Rhode exca-
vating the basal stratum at Gatecliff
Shelter, approximately forty feet be-
low the modern ground surface.
(Courtesy the National Geographic
Society)

within excavation strata. Artifacts found *in situ* are carefully plotted relative to one
another on living floor maps. When an excavator misses an artifact—and it turns up in the
screen—a significant piece of information has been lost because it can then be located
only to the nearest one meter square. Therefore, much more attention (and time) is
required for the excavation of the occupational surfaces.

Some Rules and Principles Guiding
Archaeological Excavation

Our Gatecliff Shelter excavations covered the basics of archaeological excavation:
stratigraphy, recovery, provenience. Although the strategies are universal to archaeology,
the tactics are site specific. For example, prehistoric pueblo sites in New Mexico,
containing well-defined room clusters and ceremonial **kivas**, must be excavated very

The Legend of the Marshalltown Trowel

The archaeological record is usually first encountered at the tip of the trowel, an object dear to the heart of field archaeologists. Although archaeologists rarely endorse individual products, trowels are an exception (Figure 6–6).

As every archaeological veteran knows, there is only one kind of trowel, the Marshalltown, named after a town in Iowa. What makes the Marshalltown so legendary? For one thing, the handle is welded, not riveted. Nobody likes a wobbly trowel blade. The steel is also high quality and holds a good edge. It comes in a variety of sizes and lasts a lifetime. There is simply no substitute.

Plenty of folklore surrounds the Marshalltown trowel. When Kent Flannery delivered the Distinguished Lecture to the American Anthropological Assocation in 1981, he called it "The Golden Marshalltown: A Parable for the Archeology of the 1980s."

People often personalize their trowels. Some archaeologists square off the ends, others prefer a rounded point; Bill Rathje and Mike Schiffer (1982, p. 194) recorded seven kinds of "technofunctional, use–wear, and stylistic variability" in Marshalltown trowels. When digging in forested areas, some even cut a notch in the edge, to trim back the roots. And you can always tell whether the owner is left- or right-

FIGURE 6–6   Some well-worn Marshalltown trowels. (Photograph by the author)

handed, just by looking at the wear pattern on the trowel blade. People like to hang onto their trowels, often carving their initials in the handle.

Most archaeologists sharpen their trowels. In fact, I've had crew members who spent more time in trowel maintenance than in excavation. In California, there was once an archaeologist who used juvenile delinquents as excavators. They got so involved with macho trowel sharpening, they'd sneak up and secretly slit their supervisors' Levis, from cuff to belt loop.

Writing for the *National Geographic* in 1967, Emil Haury expands the Marshalltown lore. Returning to reexcavate the Hohokam village of Snaketown, after an absence of three

decades, Haury's seminar class at the University of Arizona presented him with a "good-digging token," a silver Marshalltown bearing the inscription from Shakespeare's *Julius Caesar:* "You are not· wood, you are not stones, but men." Haury unpacked his graven trowel at Snaketown, where "standing in the old village, I hurled the shining trowel into the air. Jones Williams, a 72-year-old Pima who had been with me on Hohokam adventures before, turned the first spade of earth at the place where it landed. And, sure enough—that proved to be the least productive spot in the whole village! I gave up the business of magic and went back to the hardheaded work of excavation."

differently from a high-altitude cave in Nevada. Peeling off sequential levels in a Maya temple in Guatemala differs radically from excavating through seemingly homogeneous shell midden deposits in Georgia. Underwater archaeology uses a host of techniques and equipment totally alien to terrestrial contexts.

Still, certain considerations transcend the site-specific context, and the rest of this chapter addresses the more universal characteristics of archaeological fieldwork.

Sifting the Evidence

Archaeologists agree that Marshalltown makes the only trowel worth owning (see the inset). But when it comes to sifters, all agreement evaporates. Because most archaeologists manufacture their own screens, the design and workmanship vary from dig to dig. Some screens are suspended from tripods; others have two legs; and some are mounted on rollers. When we dug Alta Toquima Village (Nevada), at twelve thousand feet, we invented a "backpacker" design for our screens.

Junius Bird was a crusader in screening archaeological deposits. In the mid-1950s, he and James Ford published two articles in *American Antiquity,* describing their views on how sifters should work. When I first met Junius, he had just returned from visiting a dig in the American Northwest and was livid about the dinky little screens being used on such an important site. He later wrote an article describing how these sifters wasted a million dollars (Bird 1980).

The story went like this:

The sifters utilized while I was at this excavation were the small box type on rollers moving back and forth on a fixed frame. . . . These were set within and at the mouth of the shelter in close proximity to the excavators, subjecting them to windborne dust and dirt as they worked. The capacity of each box was small; sorting for artifacts and other materials had to be done on the wire within the boxes, then these had to be lifted from the frames to be emptied. Later most if not all of the sifted dirt and trash had to be removed to other locations.

This procedure seemed both cumbersome and extremely time-consuming. The excavators were racing against time because a dam was being constructed to flood the entire site. Junius Bird argued that had "proper" sifting and recovery methods been used, the site could have been entirely excavated "with greater accuracy long before there was any risk of flooding" (see Figure 6–7). But the excavations fell seriously behind schedule, and the waters were rising daily. To buy some time, the Army Corps of Engineers constructed a massive (and expensive) coffer dam around the unexcavated deposits. Unfortunately, because the engineers had overlooked the nature of the underlying deposits, the dam failed, actually siphoning in water and flooding the remaining unexcavated site. This, according to Junius Bird, is how the wrong sifters cost the taxpayers a million bucks.

Modern archaeologists spend plenty of time thinking about sifters and how they facilitate archaeological excavation. There is general agreement that sifters of some sort are necessary on all terrestrial sites. Even into the 1970s, the occasional archaeologist in America could be caught simply **troweling** or shoveling the deposit, sorting through the loosened matrix for artifacts and then tossing the dirt on a spoil pile. Today, we recognize that simply too much artifactual and ecofactual material is lost when the deposit is not screened; in fact, some deposits contain such minute remains that even sifting cannot be used.

I am dismayed that even today, some federally funded projects skip this step owing to "high costs." The fact is that all archaeological deposits should be systematically screened unless a more precise recovery technique (such as flotation) is used.

Screen size affects what is recovered. For my M.A. thesis project, I built a three-decker screen with superimposed layers of 1/4-in. over 1/8-in. over 1/16-in. mesh screens (Thomas 1969). The idea was to find out how screen size affects the recovery of animal bones in archaeological sites. We found that the then-standard 1/4-in. mesh is entirely adequate when the midden contains only bones of large animals such as bighorn or bison, but significant numbers of medium-sized animals, such as rabbits and rodents, are lost through the 1/4-in. gauge. A 1/8-in. mesh screen is recommended whenever the faunal assemblage includes these smaller mammals. In fact, even significant amounts of small mammal bones are lost through 1/8-in. screens. When one is concerned with recovering animals the size of, say, pack rats or small birds, a flotation method of recovery is strongly recommended. Casteel (1970, 1976a) showed that standard methods of excavation often completely overlook fish bones (see also Reitz 1982). He recommends that archaeologists dealing with fish remains should not screen their sites at all but, rather,

FIGURE 6–7 A few of the innumerable screen designs used by archaeologists.

take column or core samples, which are then sorted by hand in the laboratory. It is clear that the nature of the archaeological debris must be seriously considered before selecting a method of excavation.

Flotation

In some archaeological sites, like the upper parts of Gateciff Shelter, the deposits are sufficiently protected from moisture so that plant remains simply dry up and can be recovered by screening. But in more humid climates, plant remains generally are preserved only when they have been burned and hence carbonized. The most common method of recovering such plant remains is *flotation,* a technique that has become standard during the last few decades.

There are several procedures for "floating" archaeological samples, but all of them do basically the same thing. Dirt, of course, does not float; but burned seeds, bones, and charcoal do. By using water (or chemical) flotation, archaeologists can float most ecofacts (and even some artifacts) into a "light fraction," and the residual ends up in a "heavy fraction."

In an early application, Stuart Struever (1968a) floated soil samples from two hundred features attributable to the Middle Woodland component at the Apple Creek site, Illinois. The samples were hauled to nearby Apple Creek, where they were placed in mesh-bottomed buckets and then water separated by students who worked midstream. Over forty thousand charred nutshell fragments, two thousand carbonized seeds, and some fifteen thousand identifiable fish bones were collected in this manner. Standard dryland excavation techniques would have missed them all.

While excavating at Salts Cave in Kentucky, Patty Jo Watson (1974) and her associates were not blessed with a nearby stream, and so they improvised. The sediments to be floated were placed in double plastic bags and carried outside the cave (see Figure 6–8). The samples (weighing a total of fifteen hundred pounds) were spread in the shade

FIGURE 6–8   Patty Jo Watson (left) and Louise Robbins operating a flotation device. (Courtesy Patty Jo Watson and the Cave Research Foundation)

to dry. Two fifty-gallon drums were filled with water, and the dry samples were placed in metal buckets whose bottoms had been replaced with window screen. The buckets were submerged in the fifty-gallon oil drums, which had been filled with water. After a few seconds, the investigator skimmed off the charcoal and carbonized plant remains that had floated to the surface, using a small scoop made from a brass carburetor screen. Both light and heavy fractions were placed on labeled newspaper to dry once again. The sediments at Salts Cave yielded carbonized remains of hickory nuts and acorns, seeds from berries, grains, sumpweed, chenopods, maygrass, and amaranth (Yarnell 1974).

Despite a proven track record, flotation is still considered by some to be too expensive or too impractical for everyday application. In part to deflate such arguments, Kent Flannery (1976a, pp. 104–105) described what may be the simplest flotation procedure ever devised:

> Gray ash and black ash are good bets for flotation samples, so is ashy brown earth with visible charcoal flecks. White ash is usually not so good, because the burning is too complete and the oxidation too strong to promote carbonization. Take as big a sample as you can. A 2-kilo sherd bag is good, but a 5-gallon wicker basket lined with newspaper is better. Let the sample dry for a week, very slowly, in the shade; if it dries in the sun, the seed coat shrinks faster than the inner seed, and it cracks.
>
> Now fill a plastic washtub with water, and add a couple of teaspoons of sodium silicate ("water glass") to each liter of water. The silicate acts as a deflocculant, to disperse the clay and bring the charcoal to the surface clean. Pour in some cupfuls of dirt from the sample, stir, and when you think all the carbon is floating, pour it off into a screen before it starts to waterlog. Be generous with the water, and pour only carbon, not mud into your screen. When the screen is full, let it dry for a day in the shade, slowly. And *there* are your carbonized seeds.
>
> Remember, a 5-mm. mesh will only stop avocado pits and corncob fragments. A 1.5-mm. mesh will stop chile pepper seeds. But if you want the chenopods, amaranths, and smaller field weeds, you have to turn to carburetor mesh.

Today, flotation is not an expensive or even a particularly time-consuming process. Kent Flannery's flotation operation required only a couple of buckets and a few minutes. Flotation techniques can (and should) be fitted to the local requirements. At Mission Santa Catalina, we used a converted fifty-five-gallon drum, and one person can process dozens of samples each day. Some elaborate power-driven machines are available for separating specimens by "froth flotation."

But technology is not the issue. What is important is that for decades archaeologists meticulously saved, catalogued, and identified all scraps of bone but ignored the plant remains. The resulting skew led archaeologists to overemphasize the hunting aspects and ignore the gathering component altogether. Now that flotation techniques have come into their own, archaeologists are placing proper emphasis on the gathering of wild and domesticated plant foods. The "man-the-hunter" myth is explored in more detail in Chapter 11.

WHERE TO GO FROM HERE?

Flotation Techniques in Archaeology: Wagner (1982) has tested seed recovery in several different flotation systems, suggesting widely variant results; see also Jarman, Legge, and Charles (1972), Keeley (1978), Munson (1981), Pendleton (1983), Reitz and Scarry (1985, pp. 12–13), Watson (1974, 1976).

Automating the Excavation

From test pit through full-scale excavation, archaeologists must maintain exacting records of the three-dimensional provenience of the objects being recovered. At Gatecliff, we piece-plotted artifacts by removing each item separately and assigning a unique number to the find. Level maps were prepared for each surface, and the artifacts were plotted in each unit. The most time-consuming part of the process is measuring the three-dimensional coordinates. At the beginning of an excavation, the coordinates are measured with levels and tape measures. As excavation techniques increase in complexity, so does control over provenience, generally requiring a transit or builder's level. Measurements are always recorded to the nearest centimeter. Because of human error and the difficulty of keeping straight sidewalls, such measures are probably not more accurate than ± 5 cm.

Fortunately, archaeologists are not alone in their need to measure things, and we are able to apply the increasingly sophisticated complex engineering and computing technology to our excavations. Not only does such automation free archaeologists from much routine drudgery—to spend more time actually excavating—but the increased accuracy is providing an extraordinary degree of quantitative control.

Working at the famous site of La Quina (France), Harold Dibble (University of Pennsylvania) recently developed an automated method of on-site recording. At the heart of the system is a *theodolite*, which functions like a transit but contains a built-in electronic distance meter. At La Quina, artifacts occur in well-defined living surfaces, each littered with thousands of stone tools. Using traditional methods (like those I described for Gatecliff Shelter), Dibble and his team recorded two thousand tools and bones in one field season. But during the next season, by using the theodolite, he cut the measurement time by 60 percent (recording seven thousand items in the same amount of time).

The system works like this. While one excavator works the theodolite, another holds a small prism reflector at various points on the tool or bone. The theodolite's built-in distance meter emits a laser beam that bounces off the prism and returns to the instrument. These measurements are then computed into the familiar *X, Y,* and *Z* coordinate system.

This procedure is fast, simple, and cost effective. The total cost for the system is less than $20,000. Each measurement takes about five seconds, and is accurate within ± 5 millimeters. And because each measurement is independent, there is no danger of cumulative errors' sneaking in (often a problem with the standard transit measurement system). This system is so efficient that the La Quina crew began taking several measurements on each item, and so the *in situ* orientation was also recorded. The same is done for features such as hearths and roof fall, eliminating the need to prepare the tedious "end-of-level" maps that eat up so much time on a dig.

Dibble's theodolite transmits these data to a small computer, together with data on the kind of object being measured, the stratigraphic provenience, and the initials of the excavator. A small printer immediately produces a tag that is attached to the artifact for its trip to the field laboratory.

Dibble has also worked out software allowing him to quickly manipulate and retrieve his data from La Quina. This program graphically displays the color-coded artifacts across the site, from a variety of perspectives. It will immediately produce living surface maps, similar to those from Gatecliff (Figure 6–4), but skip the laborious hand-plotting and drafting stage entirely.

WHERE TO GO FROM HERE?

Automated Means for Archaeological Measurement: Dibble (1987) describes his setup for the La Quina excavations; see also Sanders and Sanders (1986).

Archaeology's Conservation Ethic: Dig Only What You Must

Archaeologists have traditionally protected their excavations to defend their sites from vandals and pothunters. On my first job in archaeology, we were forced to post a twenty-four-hour guard (armed, appropriately enough, with bow and arrow) to protect the open excavation units from looters and treasure seekers. At Gatecliff, we tediously backfilled the site by hand every year, to protect the archaeology from the curious public and the public from the dangers of open-pit archaeology.

On St. Catherines Island, the problem is somewhat different. The only visitors are scientists, who realize the research value of archaeological sites and leave the excavations untouched. It is thus possible to open a few test units on several sites, return to the laboratory to process the finds, and then come back to the more promising sites for more intensive excavation.

But the luxury of research freedom highlights today's added responsibility of site conservation. Archaeology is a destructive science, ruining its sites in the very process of excavation. Sites can be excavated only once, and so it is imperative to do things right. On strictly research projects—like our work at Mission Santa Catalina—the sites are not threatened in any way, and one must adopt an enlightened and conservative strategy of excavation. Many archaeologists vow never to excavate more than half of a site not threatened by development or erosion. Whatever the rule, responsible investigators have a suite of questions that are generally asked by all, plus additional questions specific to each excavation. The trick is to excavate only what is necessary to answer such questions, leaving as much intact as possible for further investigators, who undoubtedly will have better questions to ask and superior techniques with which to find the answers.

How Do People Learn How to Dig?

From the outset, I emphasize the importance of hands-on experience in archaeology. There is no substitute for personal field experience, and no textbook or classroom exercise satisfactorily simulates the field situation. Learning to excavate means getting your hands dirty. It all boils down to going on a dig, and there are three ways to do this.

Most archaeologists get their first taste of fieldwork by enrolling in an organized archaeological field school, like the one I described in the Prologue. The major universities and colleges generally offer such opportunities, sometimes on weekends but more

Watch Out for Popular (Mis)perceptions of Women in Archaeological Fieldwork

In Chapter 4, I warned prospective archaeologists about the gender bias that persists in the public perception. Many still erroneously perceive excavation as "man's work," relegating women to more ladylike pursuits. Anybody thinking about joining a dig should keep an eye open for such outmoded thinking and act accordingly. Here are a couple of examples from archaeology's not-so-recent-past illustrating how this antiquated perspective can still crop up (examples courtesy of Joan Gero and Mary Whelan).

From *How to Travel and Get Paid for It* by Norman D. Ford (1970):

> Besides coming in handy for disarming the suspicions of warlike natives, women are becoming increasingly useful to Archaeologists. . . . On a number of these expeditions, qualified women are taken along to deal with the painstaking cataloging and other highly detailed work which men abhor. . . . Digging is like fishing—it gets in your blood. You'll see remote parts of the world where few men have been. And you'll probably end up by marrying an archaeologist.

From *Historical Archaeology* by Ivor Noël Hume (1969, p. 60):

> I realize that we live in a time when discrimination can land you in jail, but I must risk it and say that you stand a better chance by taking on an inexperienced male volunteer than a female. Digging is, after all, a masculine operation, and while more women than men are likely to do well in the pot-washing shed or in the laboratory, shovel-wielding females are not everyday sights in Western society. If they are to be useful on a site (and the right women can be splendid excavators), they must be prepared to be accepted as men, eschewing the traditional rights of their sex. It is vastly time-wasting for men working in one area to be hopping up and down to push barrows for women working in another. Besides, it is inordinately restricting after clouting one's knee with a shovel to have to look around to see if women are in earshot before commenting on it.
>
> Women volunteers who come along because their husbands are there are unlikely to be of much use in the field; they are best referred to the provisions supervisor or to the conservator for help with the pot-washing. Effective archaeology demands complete concentration on the work in hand, and the more feminine the women the more lax the concentration. One lady volunteer improperly dressed for the occasion can cause havoc throughout the crew as well as damaging the ground on which she walks. High heels and low décolletage are a lethal combination.

often during the summer session. Field schools are conducted on virtually every kind of archaeological site, and living conditions vary from pup tents to relatively plush dormitories. Many instructors require only a passing classroom familiarity with archaeology, whereas others accept only relatively advanced graduate students.

It is increasingly possible to join a dig as a volunteer. Many large research and cultural resource management projects rely on nonpaid participants to supplement the paid staff. A number of overseas excavations rely almost exclusively on volunteers who pay their own transportation, and exchange their on-site labor for room and board. Earthwatch is an organization that pairs selected archaeological projects with motivated volunteers willing to help out. Although somewhat more expensive than the average archaeological field school, Earthwatch excavations provide rare opportunties to become involved in worthwhile (and sometimes glamorous) archaeological fieldwork. Over the years, I have conducted nearly a dozen Earthwatch sessions, including the Gatecliff Shelter and Mission Santa Catalina excavations.

Avocational ("amateur") archaeological societies also offer numerous opportunities to excavate. In many cases, these nonprofessional groups are well trained and adequately supervised. The best ones coordinate their own excavations with ongoing professional-level research. But some caution is advised here. Current ethical standards discourage private collectors from digging up artifacts. In many instances, "pothunting" is illegal, and the courts have recently upheld a number of convictions for such looting activities. Although most archaeological societies discourage illegal and unethical destruction of archaeological sites, a few outlaw groups still sponsor "digs" for the sole purpose of obtaining artifacts. If you have any question about the integrity of an archaeological society, a local university or museum can usually clarify the situation. As a rule of thumb, you might ask a couple of key questions: What professionally trained archaeologists are involved in the excavations, and what happens to the artifacts once they have been dug up? If no responsible archaeologist is involved, and/or if the artifacts end up in private hands, you are advised to steer clear of the dig.

At the end of this chapter, I list some sources for obtaining information on current fieldwork opportunities in archaeology. But a couple of additional warnings are in order. Fieldwork opportunities vary from year to year, and you should obtain the most current information before making plans. And having supervised a dozen such digs, let me enter a personal plea: Before signing on with any expedition or field school, be certain you know what you are getting into. Archaeological excavation is physically taxing, and field camps can be socially intense. Neither you nor the dig will benefit if you are unable or unwilling to participate fully. If you have specific questions, by all means talk to the archaeologist in charge before making a commitment. Do not get in over your head.

WHERE TO GO FROM HERE?

Some General Sources on Archaeological Field Technique: Probably the best single source is *Field Methods in Archaeology* by Hester, Heizer, and Graham (1975). Knut Fladmark's (1978) *A Guide to Basic Archaeological Field Procedures* is little known but

How Do I Join an Archaeological Dig?

Numerous opportunities exist for the novice in archaeology, but people are often puzzled about where to begin. Here are some useful contacts:

Clearinghouses

Archaeology magazine publishes a list of "classifieds" which include entries for archaeological field schools, both domestic and abroad. Other dig possibilities may be advertised elsewhere in the magazine (address: P.O. Box 928, Farmingdale, N.Y. 11737).

"Field Opportunities Bulletin" is published annually by the Archaeological Institute of America; there is a charge (53 Park Place, New York, N.Y. 10007).

"Your Career in Archaeology" is available from the Society for American Archaeology (808 17th Street, N.W., Suite 200, Washington, D.C. 20006).

The American Anthropological Association provides information regarding field school opportunities (1703 New Hampshire N.W., Washington, D.C. 20009)

Archaeology Abroad offers a bulletin listing opportunities (31–34 Gordon Square, London WC1H OPY, England)

For information regarding fieldwork possibilities in Israel: Ministry of Education and Culture, Department of Antiquities and Museums, Box 586, Jerusalem, Israel 91000

Institute of Archaeology
University of Tel Aviv
Romat-Aviv, Israel

Israel Students' Tourist Association
109 Ben Yehuda Street
Tel Aviv, Israel

Pay-As-You-Go Archaeology

Earthwatch helps paying volunteers join two-week archaeological expeditions throughout the world (617–926–8200).

University of California Research Expeditions Program allows the general public to join small University of California research excavations around the world; no experience necessary. Partial student and teacher fellowships available (University of California, Desk K5, Berkeley, Calif. 94720).

Crow Canyon Archaeological Center allows nonexperienced participants to join excavation teams working on thirteenth-century Anasazi pueblos. Adult programs of a week or more are available June through October (800–422–8975).

Several museum and independent travel groups offer specialized travel packages to archaeological sites, often with professional archaeologists as guest lecturers. Although few offer hands-on possibilities, several visit ongoing excavations; be certain to find out the exact itinerary before joining up. A partial listing is available in *Archaeology* and *Natural History* magazines.

Placement Information For the More Advanced

"Employment Opportunities for Anthropology Graduates" is available from the Southwestern Anthropological Association (c/o Dr. R. E. Taylor, Department of Anthropology, University of California, Riverside, Calif. 92502).

probably the best of all to keep in your knapsack when digging: It covers the gamut from map reading and surveying, through using a light meter, to getting a truck into four-wheel drive. Another good general reference is Joukowsky (1980): *A Complete Manual of Field Archaeology;* Wheeler's (1954) *Archaeology from the Earth,* although badly out-of-date, provides the flavor of what digging was like in the good old days of archaeological imperialism. Stanley South (1977a, esp. Chapter 8) draws on his extensive experience to provide some guidelines for excavating historic period sites; Noël Hume (1969) covers the same ground, but with a contrasting emphasis. For other information on field methods, see Dancey (1981).

Summary

Despite recent advances, archaeological excavation remains as much art as science. Here, we look at some common techniques, some archaeological standards and conventions, and, perhaps most important of all, what it feels like to be on a dig. Diverse excavation strategies represent different assumptions and different objectives. In a vertical strategy, designed largely for chronological control, artifact provenience generally means little more than stratigraphic placement; the exact location within a given stratum is analytically irrelevant. But in a horizontal strategy, designed to explore the conditions of past lifeways, the context of artifact and ecofacts within excavation strata becomes critical; artifacts found *in situ* are commonly plotted relative to one another on living floor maps. When an excavator misses an artifact—and it turns up in the screen—a significant piece of information has been lost because it can then be located only within the excavation square. Modern archaeologists spend plenty of time thinking about recovery techniques, and both mechanical sifters and flotation devices are commonplace. From test pit through full-scale excavation, archaeologists maintain exact records of the three-dimensional provenience of the objects being recovered, and computer-assisted equipment is now available for this purpose.

One cannot overemphasize the importance of hands-on experience in archaeology. There is no substitute for personal field experience, and no textbook or classroom exercise satisfactorily simulates the field situation. Learning to excavate means getting your hands dirty. It all boils down to going on a dig. At the end of this chapter are listed sources for information on current fieldwork opportunities in archaeology.

CHAPTER 7

Working Toward a Less Invasive Archaeology

As archaeologists age, they sometimes look back and sigh about the heavy price of doing fieldwork. Some say the back is first to go. Others claim it's the knees. I even knew somebody with "trowel elbow." But regardless of what gives out, it's a cinch that field-oriented archaeologists will eventually show up at the doorstep of the neighborhood orthopedist.

It was not long ago that a slipped disk or blown-out knee meant immediate and sometimes radical surgery. And such surgery was often more painful than the injury. Although your knee joint bounced back pretty quickly after the cartilage was removed, it took months for the muscle tissues and nerves to recover from the ten-inch long incision required to get at the injured area. Here was a classic case of the cure being worse than the disease.

All that has changed in modern medicine. New CATSCAN and ultrasound technology allows the physician to map in detail the afflicted areas without any damage to the patient or nasty "exploratory" surgery. And when surgery is warranted, techniques like arthroscopy and laser microsurgery permit physicians to trim, cut, excise, and repair even gross damage with only the slightest incision. Today's *noninvasive* techniques minimize tissue damage and surgical intervention. Football players are now returning to the fray, in the same season, after what were once career-ending back operations. Quarterbacks now routinely have off-season knee procedures; Dan Marino calls it "changing his oil."

I got the bill for my surgery. Now I know what those doctors were wearing masks for.
—James H. Boren

Americanist archaeology is undergoing a similar revolution. In the days of Schliemann and C. B. Moore, archaeologists simply blasted away at their sites, leaving ruined ruins in their wake. For example, the earliest excavations at Colonial Williamsburg were conducted by architectural historians who used an extraordinarily destructive method known as **cross trenching** (Noël Hume 1969, p. 73), digging parallel trenches a shovel blade in width and throwing up the dirt on the unexcavated space between. The strategy was designed to disclose foundations for restoration, but the workmen paid little attention to the artifacts, and none whatsoever to the stratigraphy encountered. To archaeologists at mid-century, the greatest technological revolution was the advent of the backhoe as a tool of excavation.

Americanist archaeology today views its sites differently. Part of this new conservation ethic reflects the definition of archaeological remains as nonrenewable resources (see Chapter 4). But equally important has been the development of noninvasive technology for doing relatively nondestructive archaeology. Using the archaeological equivalents of CATSCAN and ultrasound, archaeologists can now map subsurface features in detail—without ever excavating them. And when it does become necessary to recover samples, we can, like the orthopedic surgeon, execute pinpoint excavations, minimizing damage to the rest of the site.

In the next section, I shall relate the story of how remote sensing and other exploratory technology helped us discover the site of Mission Santa Catalina. Even fifteen years ago, we lacked the theory and technology to find this lost sixteenth-/seventeenth-century site. At present, we are excavating the mission complex using a variety of pinpoint excavation techniques. The idea is to leave large parts of our sites unexcavated, as a legacy for our archaeological grandchildren, who doubtless will possess technology we cannot even imagine.

How to Find a Lost Spanish Mission

If some unwitting hands have not pulled them down, if they were not built entirely of wood, if the weather has not beaten too fiercely through the centuries, or if the streams have not innundated them, some fortunate hunter may yet stumble upon the mission remains of Santa Catalina de Guale. . . . Although at the time of the coming of the English, Santa Catalina was the most important of the Guale missions, the fierceness of the struggle in this region may have led the Yamasees and the English to treat it as the Romans did Carthage.
—John Tate Lanning

As luck would have it, that "fortunate hunter" turned out to be me. Three hundred years after Mission Santa Catalina disappeared, I led the team of archaeologists that rediscovered Georgia's most important Spanish mission.

First, a word of background about this little-known chapter of American colonial history. At its seventeenth-century zenith, Spanish Florida consisted of three dozen Franciscan missions, each a satellite settlement heavily dependent on the colonial capital at St. Augustine. To the west lived the Timucuan, Apalachee, and Apalachicola Indians, to the north, toward St. Catherines Island, lay the province of Guale. Although a dozen sixteenth-/seventeenth-century missions once existed in the present state of Georgia, not one such mission site could be identified archaeologically when we began our search for Santa Catalina.

Like many historians and archaeologists before us, we felt that the lost mission of Santa Catalina lay along the western margin of St. Catherines Island, a fourteen-thousand-acre tract fifty miles south of Savannah. Unique among the so-called Golden Isles, St. Catherines Island has not been subdivided and suburbanized. The Georgia-based, not-for-profit St. Catherines Island Foundation owns the island and strictly regulates a comprehensive program of research and conservation. This enlightened and progressive land management policy ensured that Mission Santa Catalina was not destroyed beneath the crush of condos and fast-food joints that typify too many of the southern barrier islands.

A Regional Perspective

When I first visited St. Catherines Island in 1974, the combined French, English, and Spanish historic documentation supplied only vague geographic clues; and although several first-rate archaeologists had previously worked on the island, none had successfully located this important mission site.

Virtually uninhabited, St. Catherines Island is today blanketed with dense forest, briar patches, and almost impenetrable palmetto thicket. When we began our search for Santa Catalina, I was overwhelmed by the huge area involved. We knew so little that I could not overlook any portion of St. Catherines Island.

By its nature, archaeological fieldwork is slow and tedious—and nobody could (or should) excavate an entire island—so we began by random sampling. This method required that the archaeological team walk a series of thirty-one east-west transects, each one hundred meters wide. Our crews attempted to follow a specific compass heading without deviating from the survey transect. This randomized approach forced us to look into the most unlikely, inaccessible places (even when we didn't expect to find anything).

It is essential to dig in just the right place. Taking a lesson from statistical survey theory, we began our search by random sampling. In principle, archaeological random sampling should not differ from that of the Harris political polls or TV's Nielsen ratings: One must create a situation in which every element has a known and equal probability of being selected.

We decided that **transect sampling** would be the most appropriate survey method (this, and several other techniques for regional archaeology are introduced in Chapter 12). In effect, over a period of three years, we took a 20 percent randomized sample of the archaeology of St. Catherines Island, looking for, among other things, the lost mission of Santa Catalina de Guale (see Figure 7–1).

Theory is fine, but practical random sampling in archaeology is hardly easy because

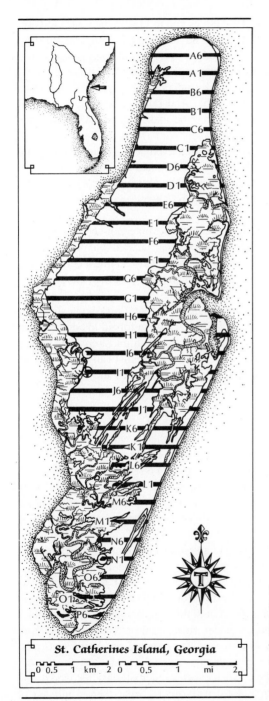

FIGURE 7–1 Systematic transect research design used when conducting a 10 percent regional randomized sample on St. Catherines Island. Occurrences of sixteenth- and seventeenth-century Spanish ceramics have been circled (see Thomas 1987, Figure 22). (Courtesy the American Museum of Natural History)

a "known and equal probability of being selected" forces you to look in the most unlikely, inaccessible places. Such fieldwork is much like the old "beeline hike" I learned in Boy Scouts: Follow your compass heading, and walk through, over, or under any obstacle. If a tree lies across your path, go over it. If you run into a palmetto and briar patch, crawl through it. No need to worry about yellow and black spiders hanging from the live oaks (it's uncool to gag or scream while inhaling a web). And don't give rattlesnakes and cottonmouths a second thought (that's why we gave you the snake guards). And above all, do not divert from your transect.

Our survey turned up 135 mostly unrecorded archaeological sites, ranging from massive shell middens to isolated shell scatters. We investigated each site with two or more one-meter-square test units, in all excavating more than four hundred such test pits. Viewed from the air, the island began to look like a Swiss cheese, except that the holes were square.

Controlled survey sampling told us that sixteenth-/seventeenth-century Spanish period ceramics occurred only at five of the 135 archaeological sites, all but one along the western perimeter of the island. The ruins of Mission Santa Catalina almost certainly lay buried in a target area the size of thirty football fields along the southwestern margin of the island.

But thirty football fields is still a huge area to dig with dental pick and camel hair brush. Moreover, although our confidence was growing, we were forced to admit almost complete ignorance of what we were looking for. Did Santa Catalina survive merely as heaps of sixteenth-/seventeenth-century garbage? Or could we realistically hope to find evidence of buried buildings as well? Clearly it was time to scratch the surface.

Power Auger Sampling

Looking around for better ways to find the needle hidden in this haystack, we fortunately learned of Kathleen Deagan's successful search for sixteenth-century St. Augustine, buried beneath and mixed into four centuries of later debris. Following her example, we purchased a gasoline-powered posthole digger (an **auger**, really) and began excavating hundreds of round holes. With this noisy, nasty machine, two people can dig a three-foot-deep hole in less than a minute. The power auger throws up a neat doughnut of dirt, to be hand-sifted for artifacts (Figure 7–3).

We began the augering procedure by digging a series of systematically spaced test holes; we used a drill bit thirty-two centimeters in diameter, reaching a depth of nearly a meter. Sherds, bone, and shell were recovered when the doughnut of spoil dirt was screened. In all, we dug 615 auger tests while looking for Santa Catalina. Once the grid had been laid in with a transit, a two-person crew could dig approximately 12 auger holes per hour. Two screeners, working behind the auger crew, could sift and sort fill from approximately 4 holes per hour. Had we tried to excavate standard one-meter tests pits, we would still be digging.

Once the field testing was complete, we identified all materials recovered and plotted the distribution in a series of simple dot-density maps. Since then, a number of

Looking for Old St. Augustine

Working with historians and town planners in 1976, Kathleen Deagan set out to find the exact boundaries of sixteenth-century St. Augustine, founded in 1565. The problem was that St. Augustine had been continuously inhabited since prehistoric times, and the presumed sixteenth-century settlement lay sandwiched between prehistoric occupational debris and four centuries of later debris (see Figure 7–2).

By comparing modern street plans with existing sixteenth-century maps, project historians nominated a nine-block area to the south of the town's central plaza as reflecting the original settlement's layout. Some six hundred power auger holes were drilled along a systematic grid throughout downtown St. Augustine to test this hypothesis.

To do this, Deagan used a "modified systematic sampling strategy," in which auger tests were drilled along a five- and ten-meter grid system, tied into existing street corners. The auger proved a particularly efficient tool for digging through driveways, parking lots, and shell middens. The survey technique was a relatively fast, inexpensive, reliable, and fairly nondestructive method of gathering information needed for the long-term inventory of St. Augustine's cultural and historical resources.

One potential problem was that the presumed sixteenth-century town lay in a highly developed downtown section. Fortunately, St. Augustine is acutely aware of its unique history, and residents were intensely interested in helping to learn more about the "oldest city." The power auger technique was pivotal here, for it caused minimal disturbance to both the archaeological record and the modern citizenry. Nonetheless, gardens and lawns were temporarily uprooted; sections of St. Augustine's streets were occasionally removed; and the local schoolchildren had to give up their playground for a season, giving Deagan and her crew time to test their property.

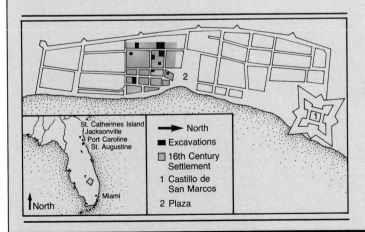

FIGURE 7–2 Location of the sixteenth-century occupation in colonial St. Augustine. The street plan, taken from the 1764 Elizio de la Puente map of the walled eighteenth-century city, remains virtually the same today (see Deagan 1980, p. 23). (Courtesy Kathleen Deagan)

As it turned out, the sixteenth-century artifacts clustered exactly where the historians had predicted. Deagan then initiated a program of excavation to refine these preliminary town boundaries and to probe the households of the early Spanish settlers as they adapted to life in their New World.

WHERE TO GO FROM HERE?

The Power Auger Survey of Downtown St. Augustine: A somewhat nontechnical account is provided in Deagan (1980): "Spanish St. Augustine: America's First Melting Pot"; the more technical details can be found in Deagan (1981).

readily available computer programs have greatly assisted the data conversion process. But even using the hand-plotted maps, the power auger data allowed us to focus further field evaluation on a single 100-by-100-meter square in the overall sampling grid for St. Catherines Island. Although this area contained absolutely no additional surface evidence to distinguish it from the surroundings, it contained the remarkably well preserved ruins of Mission Santa Catalina de Guale.

In effect, the simple and expedient auger testing narrowed our search area from thirty football fields to a target zone smaller than three acres. Although we found broken Guale Indian pottery almost everywhere we dug in that area, diagnostic mission period artifacts—mostly Hispanic **majolica** and **olive jars**—were largely restricted to a single,

FIGURE 7–3 Two archaeologists muscle a gasoline-powered soil auger into the ground to obtain subsurface samples in the search for sixteenth-century St. Augustine (see Deagan 1980, p. 25). (Courtesy Kathleen Deagan)

well-circumscribed area. By 1981, we had defined this 100-meter-square area (prosaically called Quad IV) as the most probable location for the central mission complex.

Now it was time to stop digging and reanalyze.

Space-Age Technology to the Rescue

Quad IV was a totally undistinguished piece of real estate, covered by typical scrub palmetto and live oak forest. The only evidence of human occupation was a little-used field road for island research vehicles. Although aboriginal shell scatters could be seen here and there, Quad IV betrayed absolutely no surface clues of what lay below.

At this point, we shifted our field strategy once again, switching from preliminary subsurface testing to noninvasive, nondestructive remote sensing. Choosing the right method depends on what you expect to find. What, exactly, were we looking for? For more than a century, Santa Catalina had been the northernmost Spanish outpost on the eastern seaboard, and this historical fact implied considerable size and permanence. The seventeenth-century mission must have had a fortified church, some buildings to house the soldiers and priests, plus enough granaries, storehouses, and dwellings for hundreds of Guale Indian neophytes.

We reasoned that the mission buildings were built by a **wattle-and-daub** technique, and the auger tests had indeed turned up a few clumps of fired daub. Freshly cut timbers were probably set vertically along the walls and reinforced with cane woven horizontally between the uprights. This sturdy wattlework was then plastered ("daubed") with a mixture of marsh mud, sand, and plant fibers (probably Spanish moss). Roofs were thatched with palmetto.

So constructed, wattle-and-daub buildings are biodegradable. Left to nature, the roof will go first; if it does not burn off, the thatch will either blow away or simply rot. And once directly exposed to the weather, mud and twig walls will simply wash away. Archaeologists seeking such a dissolved mission would soon be out of business.

But if we were lucky—and many archaeologists would rather be lucky than good—the mission buildings would have burned, firing and hardening the daub walls, like a pot baking in a kiln. Fired daub, nearly as indestructible as the ubiquitous potsherd, thus became a key in our search for Santa Catalina.

But how do you find chunks of fired daub buried beneath a foot of sand? It turns out that the marsh mud used in daub plaster contains microscopic iron particles. When intensely heated, the particles orient toward the magnetic north—like a million tiny compass needles. To pinpoint these magnetically anomalous orientations, we relied upon a **proton precession magnetometer**. The theory behind this device is a bit complicated, but the principle is simple: Magnetometers measure the strength of magnetism between the earth's magnetic core and a sensor controlled by the archaeologist.

Ervan G. Garrison and James Tribble (then both associated with Texas A&M University) directed the first proton magnetometer survey on St. Catherines Island in 1981; after that, we did our own magnetometer work (Figure 7–4). Although some rather sophisticated computer graphic technology is usually required to filter magnetic survey

FIGURE 7–4   Ervan Garrison and Deborah Mayer O'Brien conducting a remote sensing survey at Mission Santa Catalina using a GeoMetrics Proton Magnetometer (see Thomas 1987, Figure 28). (Courtesy the American Museum of Natural History; photograph by Dennis O'Brien)

data, the subsurface patterning at Santa Catalina was so striking that our remote sensing paid off even before the computer plots were generated.

As the Texas A&M team packed up their field equipment, leaving to work up the data in their lab, they shared a couple of hunches, based strictly on their raw magnetometer readings: "If we were y'all, we'd dig in three places: right here, over yonder, and especially right here." We took their advice, exploring each of the three magnetic anomalies in the few days remaining in our May field season. One anomaly—"especially right here"—turned out to be an iron ring. Excavating further, we came upon another ring and more below that. At about nine feet down, we hit the water table. Digging underwater, we finally encountered a well-preserved oak well casing.

Archaeologists love wells because, like privies, they can be magnificent artifact traps. After removing the bones of an unfortunate fawn (which had long ago drowned), we found an array of distinctive Hispanic and Guale Indian potsherds, and a metal dinner plate dropped (or tossed) into the construction pit. All artifacts were typical of the sixteenth and seventeenth centuries. We had indeed found Mission Santa Catalina, and we pressed on to see what else the magnetometer might turn up.

Our second magnetic anomaly—the one "right here"—was a small mound. We thought at first it might be a grave or tomb. But after removing the overburden, we came across a burned daub wall that, as it fell, had crushed dozens of Spanish and Guale domestic artifacts: imported tin-enameled glazed cups, painted ceramic dishes, a kitchen knife, and at least two enormous pots for cooking or storage. Charred deer and chicken bones littered the floor, and dozens of tiny corncobs were scattered about. This time, the magnetometer had led us to the kitchen (or **cocina**) used by seventeenth-century Franciscan friars at Santa Catalina.

Finally, we began digging the "over yonder" anomaly, which proved to be a linear daub concentration more than forty feet long, obviously the downed wall of yet another, much larger mission building. Here excavations turned up none of the everyday implements and debris so common in the scorched kitchen. Instead we found human graves, the first of more than four hundred Christianized Guale Indians buried here.

The search was over. We had discovered the *iglesia*, the paramount house of worship at Santa Catalina de Guale. Our magnetometer survey had given us trustworthy directions to the buried daub walls and iron barrel hoops. Even without computer enhancement, the magnetometer had taken us to the very heart and soul of Mission Santa Catalina.

These important landmarks would, eventually, have been found through wholesale test trenching, but remote sensing was dramatically more cost effective and also nondestructive. As our research unfolded, we used additional remote sensing technology to help define the configuration of these unexcavated mission buildings. In the spring of 1982, Gary Shapiro and Mark Williams conducted a pilot study of the subsurface **soil resistivity** at Santa Catalina. By monitoring the relative resistance to an electrical current passed through the ground, they could project the size, orientation, and configuration of the unexcavated buildings at Mission Santa Catalina. Projections from the resistivity survey were further amplified against independent data from extensive ground-penetrating radar studies.

Since the discoveries of 1981, we have been conducting detailed archaeological excavations at Santa Catalina. To date, we have completely exposed the outlines of the church (*iglesia*) at Santa Catalina. The church was constructed on a single **nave** plan, lacking both **transept** and **chancel**. The lateral church walls were constructed of wattle and daub that, when encountered archaeologically, consisted of a densely packed linear rubble scatter; this is what the magnetometer "saw" in Quad IV.

In the late seventeenth century, the mission compound was surrounded by cleared agricultural fields, extending for miles in each direction. So situated, even a one-story wattle-and-daub church would have been easily visible for miles up and down the nearby intracoastal waterway. The whitewashed walls and shell-covered churchyard were deliberately designed to enhance its visibility.

Beneath the nave and sanctuary of the church we discovered the cemetery, where approximately 400 to 450 Christianized Guale Indians had been interred. In addition to the bones, this **campo santo** contains a truly astounding array of associated grave goods. Roughly one-third of the skeletons were encountered in the original grave pits, usually buried face up, with feet toward the altar and hands across the chest or (less commonly) the abdomen. Because the cemetery was used for more than a century, the people eventually ran short of burial space. Time and time again, the excavators encountered partial interments disturbed by later burials. These bones have much to tell, and technology is becoming available to help unravel their story. In Chapter 11, we discuss how such skeletal materials are being used in a new, *biocultural* approach to the past.

Eastward, across the plaza from the church, stood the Franciscan **convento**, usually translated as "monastery," "convent," or "friary." The *convento* comprised one or more subsidiary buildings in which friars and lay brothers lived their cloistered lives, as regulated by the rules of their order. *Conventos* followed a simple plan, often a single row of rooms, apparently defining the sides of a quadrangle which contained the sacred garden (the *garth*). Inside the *convento* were the refectory, the cells (the friars' rooms), and perhaps some specialized rooms, such as a kitchen, offices, workshops, or granary. Meals were to be taken in silence inside a refectory. Water assumed great significance in Franciscan rite, and a source of fresh water was always a matter of concern when positioning a friary; this is why the well was constructed nearby.

The search for Santa Catalina is one small case of the maturation in Americanist archaeology. Rather than rip into the site with backhoes and front loaders, we drew on today's technological arsenal, which includes a dozen noninvasive, nondestructive techniques to assess the archaeological record. Remote sensing is simply another way to gather archaeological data, in this case data from unexcavated objects, features, and buildings. That these things still lie buried beneath the ground has become irrelevant.

WHERE TO GO FROM HERE?

The Archaeology of Mission Santa Catalina: A general overview of the search for and discovery of Mission Santa Catalina is provided in Thomas (1987); some preliminary results and interpretations appear in Thomas (1988); see also Garrison, Baker, and Thomas (1985).

Power Auger Survey in Archaeology: Deagan (1981), McManamon (1984), Percy (1976), Shapiro (1987), South and Widmer (1977).

Remote Sensing in Contemporary Archaeology

Generations of archaeologists have longed for some metaphysical method of peering beneath the earth's surface, a way of learning from archaeological sites without actually having to dig them. As Lewis Binford once put it: "Ideally, we should have an X-ray machine which would allow us to locate and formally evaluate the range of variation manifest in cultural features" (1964, p. 437). And some significant progress has been made in sampling at the regional level (see Chapter 12).

But over the past decade, many (myself included) have begun to realize that probability sampling and randomization alone will never adequately address variability in archaeological site location and site structure (see Chapter 6). A growing dissatisfaction with rote sampling methodology has led many of us to look more closely at the application of nondestructive technology to archaeology. Recently, Binford's elusive X-ray machine has been used in a series of increasingly sophisticated remote sensing contrivances. This new technology, when appropriately integrated with solid, traditional archaeological objectives, can indeed tell us, before excavation, where the sites are, what they contain, and how these parts are articulated.

The term **remote sensing** is, in its strictest usage, limited to various applications of *photogrammetry,* but in contemporary archaeology, remote sensing has come to embrace the total array of techniques used in geophysical observation: not only visual and infrared aerial sensing but also a broad range of chemical and geophysical techniques, especially **magnetometry, resistivity, ground-penetrating radar**, and even **differential heat analysis** (Benner and Brodkey 1984). Most of these techniques were initially designed to measure geophysical features on the scale of several yards or even miles. Yet to be most effective in archaeology, such operations must be scaled down to the order of inches and feet (Weymouth 1986, p. 313).

Geophysical technology has been used, to date, mostly for defining structure within archaeological sites, being considered too costly and/or time-consuming to help in the initial discovery of such sites. But today, thoughtful strategies of archaeological research can probably render geophysical prospection useful for site discovery as well.

The promise of remote sensing is awesome. But its full potential will be realized only as archaeologists transcend the seductive gadgetry to integrate this technology into the mainstream of archaeological theory. Before considering further the theoretical background of remote sensing, let us examine how a few specific technologies are being applied to solve everyday problems in contemporary archaeology.

WHERE TO GO FROM HERE?

Some General Sources on Remote Sensing in Archaeology: Weymouth (1986) provides the best single overview of the topic, although articles by Ebert (1984), McManamon (1984), and Parrington (1983), and the volumes by Lyons and Avery (1984) and Wynn (1986) are also excellent. For a more analytical view of remote sensing in the overall archaeological context, see also Dunnell (1982b, p. 85; 1984, p. 495).

Remote Sensing of Environment publishes scientific and technical results on theory, experiments, and applications of remote sensing to earth resources and environment. It is useful for archaeologists primarily as a source of current environmental data for large-scale surface surveys.

Subscription information: Out of the price range of all practicing archaeologists—look in the library.

Remote Sensing Newsletter in Anthropology and Archaeology, published under the auspices of Section H, the American Association for the Advancement of Science, provides an informal forum for archaeologists to exchange practical information about recent development in remote sensing theory and practice.

Subscription information: c/o Scott L. H. Madry, Editor, 113 N. Randall Street, Slidell, La. 70448

A Proton Magnetometer Approach

The primary tool in the search for Santa Catalina was the proton precession magnetometer. The receiving part of a magnetometer is about the size of a transistor radio, worn in a reverse backpack so that the operator can see the readout while tramping through underbrush (see Figure 7–4). Attached by an eight-foot cord is the sensor, a white coffee-can-like device on an aluminum tent pole. The sensor is filled with a hydrocarbon-charged fluid, usually kerosene or alcohol.

Protons in this fluid act like tiny spinning magnets, and they can be temporarily aligned (polarized) by applying a uniform magnetic field from a wire coil inside the sensor. When this current is removed, the spin of the protons causes them to "precess" in the direction of the earth's magnetic field, much like a spinning top rotates about a gravity field. An atomic constant (the "proton gyromagnetic ratio") converts the frequency emitted by the spinning protons to a measurement of the earth's magnetic intensity at that spot.

The theory may be complex, but the principle is simple: Magnetometers measure the strength of magnetism between the earth's magnetic core—the North Pole—and the sensor. If hundreds of these readings are taken across a systematic grid, a computer plotter can generate a magnetic contour map reflecting both the shape and the intensity of magnetic anomalies beneath the ground surface.

Many subsurface anomalies are archaeologically irrelevant magnetic "noise"—interference from underlying rocks, AC power lines, or hidden iron debris. The earth's magnetic field fluctuates so wildly on some days that the readings are meaningless, and electrical storms can hopelessly scramble magnetometer readings. Even minor interference such as the operator's wrist watch or eyeglasses can drive a magnetometer crazy.

But when everything works just right, the magnetometer provides the equivalent of an areal CATSCAN, telling archaeologists exactly what is going on beneath the earth's surface (see Figure 7–5). Many archaeological features have characteristic magnetic signatures, telltale clues that hint at the size, shape, depth, and composition of the archaeological objects hidden far below. Shallow graves, for instance, have a magnetic profile vastly different from, say, a buried fire pit or a wattle-and-daub wall.

WHERE TO GO FROM HERE?

On Using Proton Magnetometers in Archaeology: Weymouth (1986) provides the best general treatment; von Frese and Noble (1984) provide a good discussion in the context of historic sites archaeology; see also Johnston (1961), Scollar (1969), Steponaitis and Brain (1976).

A Soil Resistivity Approach

Soil resistivity is a way to monitor the electrical resistance of soils in a restricted volume near the surface of an archaeological site. Perhaps because of its relatively low cost, soil

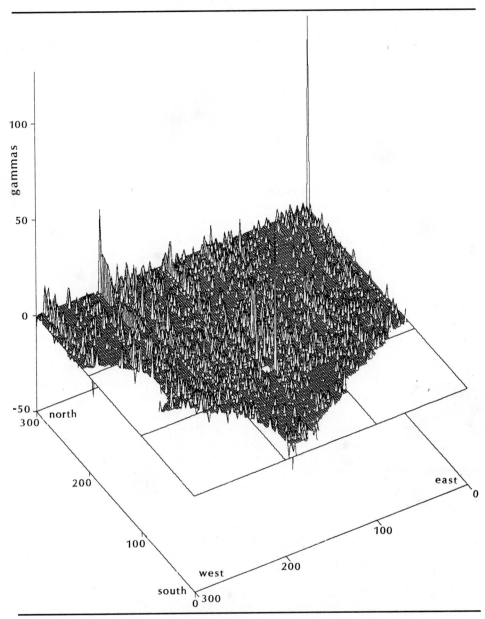

FIGURE 7–5   Three-dimensional magnetometer map of the Mission Santa Catalina area (see Garrison, Baker, and Thomas 1985, Figure 8). (Courtesy Ervan Garrison and the American Museum of Natural History)

resistivity has become a popular technique of geophysical prospection over the past three decades.

The degree of soil resistivity depends on several factors, the most important of which is usually the amount of water retained in the soil. Moisture is inversely related to the degree of resistivity. Compaction such as occurs in house floors, paths, and roads tends to reduce pore sizes and hence potential to retain water, thereby registering as high resistance. In effect, buried features can often be detected and defined by their differential retention of groundwater.

The aggregation of fill in pits, ditches, and middens will also alter resistivity. Foundations or walls, particularly those in historic-period sites, generally have greater resistivity than that of the surrounding soil, and the generation of humus by occupation activity increases the ion content of the soil, thereby reducing resistivity.

To illustrate how soil resistivity survey actually works in archaeology, let us return to our search for Mission Santa Catalina, sketched at the outset of this chapter. After the initial discovery and pilot resistivity survey, Gary Shapiro and Mark Williams returned to St. Catherines Island to conduct a more comprehensive resistivity study. They used a Williams Model 103 Resistivity Meter, personally designed and built by Mark and his father, Marshall Williams. This device, specifically designed for archaeological applications, incorporates a number of technical advantages over most commercially available resistivity devices (see Williams 1984).

The soil resistance was measured by setting four probes in line at one-meter intervals, each probe inserted to a depth of twenty centimeters. When an electrical current was passed between the probes, the electrical conductivity was recorded between the two center probes. In this way, readings were consistently taken on east-west grid lines at one-meter intervals (each twenty-meter line resulting in twenty-one readings). The line was then advanced one meter north or south, and another twenty-one readings were taken. This procedure resulted in a gridded array of resistance values, recorded in the field on graph paper and eventually transferred to magnetic disks. Locations of trees, backdirt piles, roads, and other features that might influence earth resistance were also charted.

One of the preliminary resistivity surveys was conducted in a test square straddling a five-by-five meter test of "Structure 2" at Santa Catalina, initially located by the proton magnetometer survey. From our test excavations, we knew that this building was probably the *cocina* (kitchen), but we had no idea of the building's configuration. Figure 7–6 shows the resistivity diagram of this area, clearly identifying the margins of this unexcavated building. Our recent excavations have conclusively confirmed the accuracy of the soil resistivity diagram.

WHERE TO GO FROM HERE?

Some Sources on Soil Resistivity: Carr's (1982) handbook has become a standard reference; Weymouth (1986) is good on this topic as well; see also Bevan (1983), Carr (1977), Shapiro (1984), Weymouth and Huggins (1985).

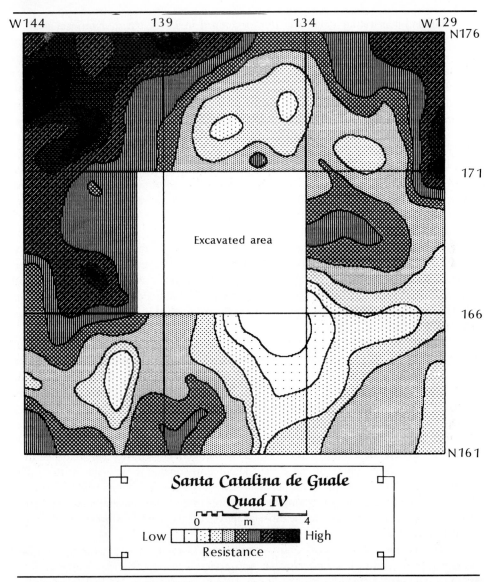

FIGURE 7–6   Soil resistivity contour map of Structure 2 at Mission Santa Catalina (see Thomas 1987, Figure 39). (Courtesy the American Museum of Natural History)

A Ground-penetrating Radar Approach

Another "active" method of geophysical prospection, ground-penetrating radar, is a rather expensive technique, but the cost is offset to some degree by its speed. But neither radar equipment nor the interpretation of the results is simple, and the assistance of trained specialists is always required.

Ground-penetrating radar was first developed in 1910, but a significant peak in relevant articles coincides with the Apollo 17 lunar sounding experiment in the early 1970s. Today, ground-penetrating radar techniques are commonly employed by environmental engineering firms to aid in selecting routes for proposed rights of way; finding buried rock or deep swamp deposits; investigating foundations; making mineral studies; searching for peat, lignite, and coal; making siltation studies; locating and identifying caverns in limestone; making groundwater studies; and investigating ground pollutants.

Impulse radar operates as an echo-sounding device, transmitting energy over a frequency band. Radar pulses directed into the ground reflect back to the surface when they strike targets or interfaces within the ground (such as a change of stratum, interface between soil and rock, presence of groundwater or buried objects, and void areas). As these pulses are reflected, their speed to the target and the nature of their return are measured. The reflection time of the signal can provide useful information about the depth and three-dimensional shape of buried objects.

By using transducers of various dimensions, it is possible to direct the greatest degree of resolution to the depth of specific interest. A pulsating electric current is passed through the bow-tie shaped antenna, inducing electromagnetic waves that radiate toward the target and return in a fraction of a microsecond to be recorded. The dimensions of this transducer influence the depth and detail that can be expected in any specific archaeological application.

As the antenna is dragged across the ground surface, a continuous profile of subsurface electromagnetic conditions is printed on the graphic recorder. The location and depth of subsurface targets can be inferred from, and tested against, this graphic record.

Groundwater can pose a problem in such studies because it changes the relative permeability of most soils. Soils are good reflectors when they are associated with steep changes in soil water context, as occurs in coarse materials. Unsorted soils, such as moraine deposits, will have a broad and varying capillary zone, and thus no clear reflection. Ground-penetrating radar is generally ineffective over saltwater, in penetrating some clays, and at depths of more than about thirty meters below the surface. The maximum depth of penetration is dependent on the conductivity of the overlying deposit. Deep profiling by ground-penetrating radar requires more expensive equipment and more highly trained personnel than do the other geophysical prospecting technologies currently used in archaeology.

The method seems to work best when the soil resistivity is high, as in well-drained soils and those with a low clay content. Subsurface wells, foundations, cellars, voids, cavities, and well-defined compacted zones, such as house floors, are known to provide clear radar echoes. Ground-penetrating radar equipment is relatively portable, and it may be transported on a handcart as the transmitter/receiver is dragged across the earth's surface; this is what we did at Santa Catalina.

Even though comprehensive, substantive archaeological applications of ground-penetrating radar remain somewhat limited, this technique has extraordinary potential for archaeological remote sensing; however, the theory behind this technique is not simple. We conducted an intensive radar study at Mission Santa Catalina in 1984. By this time, we had completed the magnetometer and soil resistivity surveys, and excavations were being conducted in the church, kitchen, and friary. We were also using shallow test trenching to determine the extent and configuration of the associated Guale Indian *pueblo* area.

Historical documents suggested that Santa Catalina had been fortified as a precaution against British attack, and so we thought that a stockade and moat complex might have been constructed to protect the Spanish buildings immediately adjacent to the central plaza. Yet, despite three years of remote sensing prospection and excavations, we had failed to locate any trace of defensive fortifications at Santa Catalina. Thus, our immediate objective for the ground-penetrating radar survey was a search for fortifications, such as palisades, bastions, or moats encircling the central mission zone.

We used the existing grid system, having cleared transect lines of brush and palmetto before our survey. Initially, a number of systematic north-south transects were run at twenty-meter intervals, followed by a series of east-west transects. Obvious anomalies were hand plotted on the basis of the gray scale output, and additional transects were run across these target areas. The trajectories of significant anomalies were plotted on the ground by means of pin flags. We then ran a third set of transects at a forty-five-degree angle, to intercept buried anomalies in a perpendicular fashion.

One final concern guided our radar survey. By this point, we had become such great believers in, and advocates of, remote sensing technology, that we worried about extending our excavations into areas not first surveyed geophysically. Remote sensing is not very effective in partly excavated areas, and we were troubled about the potential information loss when sites are excavated "blind," without benefit of a remote sensing survey. It will not be long before preliminary remote sensing will be required as baseline documentation before the destruction of sites through excavation. The complete ground-penetrating radar survey of Santa Catalina had thus become mandatory simply to stockpile potential information lost during the excavation process.

Figure 7–7 shows a typical radar profile from Mission Santa Catalina. It reads like a stratigraphic profile, with the ground surface at the top and the water table at the bottom. Horizontal distance is indicated by dashed lines, manually induced by the antenna

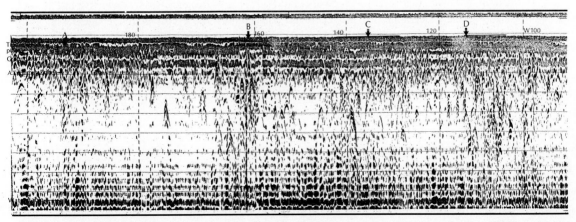

FIGURE 7–7   Printout from one of the dozens of ground-penetrating radar transects at Mission Santa Catalina (see Thomas 1987, Figure 46). (Courtesy the American Museum of Natural History)

operator to denote each twenty-meter stake. Figure 7–7 has two dark bands at the top of the profile, representing the transmitting radar pulse leaking into the receiver. All patterning below these lines represents echo reflecting from subsurface characteristics.

The dark, irregular bands (denoted as A1 on Figure 7–7) represent the radar signs reflected from the near-surface humic A1 **soil horizon**. This horizon is where most living organisms are active, and it is characterized by an extensive buildup of organics. At Santa Catalina, the A1 horizon ranges in depth from ten to twenty centimeters. The hyperbolic echoes evident here result from radar contact with relatively small objects buried beneath the line of traverse.

Below the irregular A1 horizon is the loose, sandy, weathered C horizon, represented on Figure 7–7 by an area of sparse radar echoes. In this culturally sterile control zone, the haphazardly dispersed parabolic returns probably result from small roots and naturally occurring iron concretions. The variegated regular banding at the base of Figure 7–7 represents returns reflected by the water table, at a depth of about two meters.

So far, all these features could be found in most sterile, noncultural areas near the site of Santa Catalina. But anomaly C is clearly a cultural feature, which turned out to be our missing fortification wall, cleanly dividing the mission compound itself from the aboriginal pueblo areas to the northwest. The radar seemed to reflect the presence of an indistinct backfilled wall trench. The sharp radar echo D occurs in an untested zone of Santa Catalina. Independent radar and magnetometer surveys suggest the presence of a structure in this area.

The general objective of the ground-penetrating radar research was to establish a baseline library of radar signatures for Santa Catalina. We now have comprehensive sets of such profiles, suitable for comparison with both the results of excavation and the projections obtained from other means of geophysical survey.

We also accomplished our specific objective: The test excavations, guided by radar profiles, led directly to the discovery of the palisade and bastion complex encircling the central buildings and plaza at Santa Catalina. Excavations proceeded according to these features. Although this defensive network could surely have been located by extensive test trenching, the radar approach proved to be considerably more cost effective and less destructive than conventional archaeological exploration.

In effect, we saturated a 2.6-acre area with several methods of remote sensing. Then we began extensive excavations to compare the efficacy and results of each method against in-the-ground archaeological evidence. Once the excavations are finished, we can comprehensively compare magnetometer, resistivity, and ground-penetrating radar methods against the facts as defined by excavation.

WHERE TO GO FROM HERE?

Some Sources Discussing Ground-penetrating Radar in Archaeology: Bevan and Kenyon (1975) provide a detailed discussion for archaeologists, outlining the theory behind ground-penetrating radar surveys; see also Bevan, Orr, and Blades (1984); Weymouth (1986); and for a more technical discussion, see Ulricksen (1983).

Archaeology Is More Than Just Digging Sites

Relatively little archaeology had been done in the central Great Basin when we began working there in the 1960s because archaeologists had not yet come to grips with the predominantly nonsite character of such regions. True, we spent a decade digging Gatecliff Shelter in this area, but even this forty-foot-deep site had very little potential based on its surface appearance. Spectacular dry caves and Early Holocene lakeside occupations are rare, and the multiroom pueblo is absent. In part because of this, some of archaeology's most desirable artifacts—basketry, fluted points, and painted pottery—are almost nonexistent in this area. By mid-century standards, this area seemed to have very little archaeological potential, particularly because archaeologists were trapped in the pervasive site-specific mind-set.

Still, this area is extremely rich in prehistoric archaeological remains. But these assemblages rarely occur in buried contexts, and they are rarely concentrated in convenient "sites." Most artifacts are simply lying on the surface, and until recently, archaeologists thought they were important only as signposts for places to dig, as a way to prospect for the "real" archaeology.

Precisely the same assemblages can be considered from a site-specific context, a nonsite context, or (preferably) from both perspectives. Only the research framework differs. Gatecliff Shelter—an archaeological "site" in the conventional sense—illustrates this point. Following established procedure, we nominated Gatecliff Shelter to the National Register of Historic Places, assigning it the Nevada State Museum trinomial 26Ny301; Gatecliff is clearly a site in cultural resource management terms. When it came time for the final analysis of materials recovered from Gatecliff, we asked the National Science Foundation for funds to write up our "site report." During the 1970s, when my colleagues asked me where I was working, it was convenient for me to tell them that I had a "neat" site, which I called Gatecliff Shelter.

And yet for many purposes, Gatecliff Shelter is not a site at all. More realistically, Gatecliff is a composite of sixteen relatively independent sites that happen to be stacked one on top of another, inside a chert and dolomite overhang in Mill Canyon, Nevada. Had each horizon been deposited as a surface scatter, several—but not all—would undoubtedly have qualified as sites by the traditional definition.

So what is Gatecliff Shelter: one site, ten sites, or sixteen sites?

Today, we realize that the archaeological record need not simply be viewed as Easter eggs, scattered about the landscape awaiting discovery. For administrative purposes, Gatecliff can be viewed as a single site. In terms of cultural chronology, it is convenient to think of Gatecliff as one site within which six millennia of human prehistory is recorded. But in spatial analysis on a regional scale, it is much more useful to isolate horizontal segments of Gatecliff Shelter as analytical units. It is irrelevant whether or not these subsegments are themselves sites.

The problem was the concept of the archaeological site. For years, "sites" remained unchallenged as primary existential entities. They had always been archaeology's "proper" units of observation. But over the past couple of decades, several archaeologists have begun to question seriously whether the site is really a useful abstraction. **Surface archaeology** has become a respectable venture, and archaeologists have developed a body of powerful techniques to cope with this record. Correspondingly, the concept of nonsite archaeology is now widely used around the world.

In much of our central Great Basin research, we found it quite feasible to conduct fieldwork totally unencumbered by archaeological sites. We considered sites to be little more than a necessary analytical evil; we needed sites only when the time came to assign numbers for the Nevada State recording system.

Nonsite archaeologists did not invent a new archaeological record—the objects and their contexts remained the same. What distinguished nonsite archaeology from its more traditional site-specific counterpart was the modification of the archaeologist's perspective. Rather than recovering archaeological objects from ten-centimeter levels inside one-meter excavation squares, the **nonsite** perspective started to perceive pattern and process on a scale of kilometers and hectares. As we shall see in Chapter 12, quadrat and transect survey, sampling fractions, and stratified random samples suddenly became the tools of archaeology on a regional scale.

Nonsite archaeology has also radically modified the way that we perceive surface remains. Previously, **surface sites** were commonly viewed as merely another way of "predicting" subsurface distributions. But more recently, archaeologists have come to realize that the surfaces can indeed be a critical source of data. Surface archaeology has become meaningful in its own right.

Archaeologists have also come to realize that plow zones can contain significant spatial information, even after repeated plowing. Archaeological data generated from surface and plow-zone assemblages can (and do) provide systematic, quantifiable information at both local and regional levels. As we shall see in later chapters, such data can point to growth patterning within sites, identify discrete areas of activity, and distinguish places where people live from places used only during daytime. As Robert Dunnell has noted, "The full potential of these developments will not be realized until their results are treated as independent bodies of information, some of which may duplicate traditional objects and features, but many of which are new kinds of archaeological information" (Dunnell 1985, p. 594). Combined with excavation-derived data, "surface" materials can contribute to our understanding of changing land use patterns through time, dating components across entire regions and determining intrasite relationships.

WHERE TO GO FROM HERE?

Nonsite Archaeology: Binford (1980, p. 9), Dunnell and Dancey (1983), Foley (1981), Tainter (1983), Thomas (1975, in press).

On the Growing Importance of Surface Materials in Archaeology: Dunnell (1985), Lewarch and O'Brien (1981).

The Potential of Noninvasive Archaeology

There is a striking parallel between remote sensing in today's archaeology and the birth of nonsite, surface archaeology two decades ago. In both cases, the nature of meaningful data has changed, as is vividly illustrated by recent developments in the field of Maya archaeology. After years of debate about the foggy relationship between urbanism and Classic Maya subsistence, investigators tried using airborne synthetic aperture radar to penetrate the forest cover. Adams, Brown, and Culbert (1981) mapped and spot-verified the extensive systems of previously unknown canals that drained a truly impressive segment of the lowlands. An entirely new avenue of inquiry was opened. Although the issues of Classic Maya susbsistence can hardly be settled by remote sensing, such technology without question generated a fresh perspective on a traditional problem, creating data inherently different from that obtained through more conventional techniques of excavation and terrestrial survey.

Remote sensing can lead us to new ways of defining traditional concepts in archaeology, provided that we work out unambiguous relations between the things still buried and the reasons we know they are there. Doing this requires that we construct the requisite middle-range linkages between the more traditional archaeological concepts—walls, structures, and features—and the way that they are perceived ("remotely") by the sensors of geophysical machinery.

Remote sensing technology can give archaeologists a cost-effective means of making a noninvasive, nondestructive assessment of the archaeological record. In this early developmental stage, the emphasis has necessarily been on technology, but for such technology to pay off in archaeology, the hardware must be thoroughly integrated into the mainsteam theoretical fabric of working archaeology. This has not happened, and there remains an unfortunate tendency to extol the virtues of remote sensing studies simply as "cheaper and more efficient surrogates for traditional kinds of evidence" (Dunnell 1985, p. 594). Newer developments in geophysical technology and field technique cannot be viewed merely as refined ways of generating traditional archaeological data.

At this more general level, remote sensing can act as a bridge between the empirical record of geophysical technology and theory building in archaeology. Archaeologists are now building a baseline library of geophysical signatures for key archaeological sites. Looking at the Mission Santa Catalina, example, one can ask:

- What is the diagnostic resistivity signature for a daub pit?
- How do palisade walls show up on a magnetometer survey?
- What does a cemetery look like on a ground-penetrating radar survey?

Archaeologists are not only comparing the results between geophysical survey and actual excavation; they are also examining the efficiency of the various geophysical media. Although preliminary, such exercises should ensure that in the future, at places like Santa Catalina, destructive exploratory groping can be avoided. Subsurface research designs can be guided instead by a sequence of unambiguous, nondestructive geophysical signatures.

Constructing a crosscutting compilation of remote sensing signatures is another instance of middle-range research in archaeology, another way to assign meaning to empirical observations.

The use of such remote sensing technology also makes archaeologists look once more at the nature of their data. "Empirical observation" in yesterday's archaeology was conducted by "tactile sensing"—you-know-what-something-is-after-you've-dug-it-up-and-can-hold-it-in-your-hand. This is archaeology by capture; the physical artifacts were viewed as comprising the "hard data" of archaeology.

Although archaeologists working in this framework soon fill up their empty museum cases and storerooms, they are often confused about what archaeological data really are. As we discussed in Chapter 3, archaeological data are not the objects or things that archaeologists acquire. Rather, archaeological data are the counts, measurements, and observations made on these recovered objects. There can be no archaeological data in this sense until an archaeologist observes them. Data cannot exist passively. Archaeological data are deliberately generated (sometimes decades after the objects were recovered). Remote sensing is simply one more way of generating archaeological data. But in this case, archaeologists are making their counts, measurements, and observations on objects and features that have not yet been excavated.

Summary

Americanist archaeology is undergoing a revolution. In the days of Schliemann and C. B. Moore, archaeologists simply blasted away at their sites, leaving ruined ruins in their wake. To archaeologists at mid-century, the greatest technological revolution was the advent of the backhoe as a tool of excavation. Americanist archaeology today views its sites in a radically different manner. Part of this new conservation ethic reflects the definition of archaeological remains as nonrenewable resources. But equally important has been the development of noninvasive technology for doing relatively nondestructive archaeology. Using the archaeological equivalents of CATSCAN and ultrasound, archaeologists can now map subsurface features in detail without ever excavating them. And when it does become necessary to recover samples, we can, like the orthopedic surgeon, execute pinpoint excavations, minimizing the damage to the rest of the site.

We discussed our search for Mission Santa Catalina (Georgia), one small example illustrating how Americanist archaeology has matured. Rather than rip into the site with backhoes and front loaders, we drew on today's technological arsenal, which includes a dozen noninvasive, nondestructive techniques to assess the archaeological record.

The proton magnetometer allows archaeologists to measure the strength of magnetism between the earth's magnetic core and a surface sensor. If hundreds of these readings are taken across a systematic grid, a computer plotter can generate a magnetic contour map reflecting both the shape and the intensity of magnetic anomalies beneath the ground surface. When everything works just right, the magnetometer provides the equivalent of an areal CATSCAN, telling archaeologists exactly what is going on beneath the earth's surface. Many archaeological features have characteristic magnetic signatures, telltale clues that hint at the size, shape, depth, and composition of the archaeological objects hidden far below.

Soil resistivity is a way to monitor the electrical resistance of soils in a restricted volume near the surface of an archaeological site. Perhaps because of its relatively low cost, soil resistivity has become a popular technique of geophysical prospection over the past three decades. Another "active" method of geophysical prospection, ground-penetrating radar, is a rather expensive technique, but the cost is offset to some degree by its speed. However, neither radar equipment nor the interpretation of the results is simple, and the assistance of trained specialists is always required.

Such remote sensing is simply another way to gather archaeological data, in this case data from unexcavated objects, features, and buildings. That these things still lie buried beneath the ground has become irrelevant.

Archaeologists are also learning to transcend the "site" concept, viewing the archaeological record instead from a more regional perspective. For years, sites remained unchallenged as primary existential entities. But over the past few decades, several archaeologists have begun to question seriously whether the site is really a useful abstraction. Surface archaeology has become a respectable venture, and archaeologists have developed a body of powerful techniques to cope with this record. Archaeologists have also come to realize that plow zones can contain significant spatial information, even after repeated plowing. Combined with excavation-derived data, "surface" materials can contribute to our understanding of changing land use patterns through time, by dating components across entire regions and determining intrasite relationships.

David Hurst Thomas pointing to the Mazama ash at the base of Gatecliff Shelter deposits (see Thomas 1983b, Figure 35). (Courtesy the American Museum of Natural History; photograph by Susan Bierwirth)

PART THREE

Archaeology's Initial Objective: Construct Cultural Chronologies

Because archaeology is a subdiscipline of anthropology, Americanist archaeologists rely heavily on the concept of culture. In one sense, archaeologists deal with culture as would any other social scientists: Culture has three components (cultural idiolect, shared culture, cultural system), and each constitutes a necessary domain of study. But in another sense, the problems confronting archaeologists differ markedly from those facing anthropologists who specialize in, say, ethnographic or linguistic scholarship. Archaeologists lack living informants, making certain aspects of cultural belief and behavior of the past inaccessible. But—almost as if to compensate for this void—archaeologists have access to a world of material remains, adding a time depth and overarching perspective inconceivable in synchronic ethnographic or linguistic inquiry.

This diversity in data requires that archaeology derive some innovative tactics to conduct the social science of humanity's past. Each of culture's three domains requires specialized treatment to bridge the gap between lofty concepts and practical guidelines for use in actual archaeological research. Here, we shall consider in detail two of the three cultural components, shared culture and the cultural system.

The Modal Concept of Culture

> Simplicity, simplicity, simplicity! I say, let your affairs be as two or three, and not a hundred or a thousand; instead of a million count half a dozen, and keep your accounts on your thumbnail.
> —Henry David Thoreau

You're an archaeologist assigned to research a potentially enlightening yet archaeologically unexplored territory. You are instantly besieged by a bewildering spectrum of objects

251

produced by societies ranging in complexity from simple to industrial. Dozens of cultural behaviors and noncultural factors are manifested in the archaeological objects: temporal and spatial variability, differing tool functions, a diversity of technologies, differential preservation, vandalism, and on it goes. The cultures you are dealing with—modern, historical, and prehistoric—are multivariate, enigmatic mystifying phenomena, with all conceivable sources of human variability simultaneously directing input into the archaeological record you are asked to unravel.

The first responsibility of every archaeologist is to simplify. Generations of our archaeological forebears have found it unrealistic, even preposterous, to try to cope simultaneously with all variability inherent in any set of archaeological objects. Cultural items are just too multifarious. The first assignment facing archaeologists thus is to reduce cultural variability to manageable proportions, to control the variability across a few consequential variables, and then to move on to the more elusive inputs in the archaeological record. How does such elementary simplification take place? As in many complex situations, compromise is required.

We know that human culture consists of three related components—individualistic cultural idiolect, the shared facets, and the underlying cultural system—but because archaeology has a gargantuan database, nobody can deal simultaneously with these three aspects of culture. All archaeological assessment commences with twin difficulties: (1) Archaeological data must first be controlled for time, and (2) all aspects of culture cannot be studied simultaneously.

Over the years, archaeologists have chosen to begin their inquiry by provisionally adopting a simplified, purposefully streamlined concept of culture. Some time ago, archaeologists stumbled upon a powerful postulate: Temporal variability is best reflected by the shared, modal aspects of culture. It is difficult to overemphasize how important this simple conclusion has been to practicing archaeologists.

It means that when archaeologists set out to monitor chronological change, most of the cultural complexity can, provisionally, be skipped. As long as one merely attempts to partition the archaeological record into manageable segments of time and space, both the cultural idiolect and the cultural system can be momentarily overlooked. Temporal and spatial divisions are most clearly reflected in shared, modal cultural behavior.

Why, you might ask, should time be more readily deciphered through the shared aspects of cultural remnants? Perhaps one answer is that archaeologists must start somewhere, and shared aspects are among the most conspicuous elements of the archaeological record. But a more satisfying explanation derives from the fundamental characteristics of time and space as rudimentary variables.

I keep six honest serving men
They taught me all I knew:
Their names are What and Why and When
And How and Where and Who.
Rudyard Kipling

Time is a linear dimension. Time flows. Following archaeological convention, Figure III–1 renders time vertically. The horizontal axis symbolizes the presence of some shared cultural characteristic: the kind of pottery, the method of manufacturing stone tools, the way houses are built, the motifs painted on cave walls. Once we arbitrarily elect to fix on temporal variation, we are free to disregard the why and what in favor of the when and where. Never mind, for the moment, why a particular cultural ingredient becomes more or less popular or what its function was. At this point, it is sufficient to recognize that things change through time. Ignoring the why and what allows archaeologists to nominate any aspect of material culture for analysis, regardless of how it articulates with the cultural system.

For precisely this reason, archaeologists often highlight seemingly trivial aspects of cultural behavior: what kind of temper people add to clay in their pottery, how people notch their spear points, whether they sew their moccasins along the side or along the top. Archaeologists at this rudimentary stage are seeking only a method of monitoring change through time. Why these cultural items transmute can be answered later.

Let me show you how this modal concept of culture actually serves archaeology. The most ancient pottery in North America occurs in the southeastern United States, mostly along the coasts of Florida, Georgia, and South Carolina, and also inland up the principal waterways such as the Savannah River (Stoltman 1966). These ceramics are distinctive and readily recognizable, consisting generally of bowl-shaped vessels with thick walls and flaring lips. Although some of the later vessels are decorated by impressions from sticks or fingernails, they were never painted.

The most distinctive aspect of the earliest North American ceramic tradition is **temper**, foreign materials introduced into the moist clay to keep the vessels from cracking when fired. Prehistoric potters had a variety of tempering materials from which to choose—sand, coarse grit, seashells, even ground-up potsherds. The earliest North American potters chose to use plant fibers, usually grass or shredded palmetto. Why they chose organic fibers over sand or seashells we may never know. But we do recognize that this was a cultural decision followed almost without exception for a specific period of time.

On the basis of radiocarbon evidence, we now know that these earliest pots were first made about 2500 B.C. and seemed to die out about 1000 B.C., when potters started tempering ceramics with coarse grit and sand. Put another way, whenever this distinctive fiber-tempered pottery is found in undisturbed primary contexts, the age of these deposits can be guess-dated between 2500 and 1000 B.C., based strictly on the ceramic association.

By looking at other attributes, it is possible to refine this elementary chronology a bit further. The earliest fiber-tempered wares are plain pots, without surface decoration. But about 1500 B.C. potters started decorating their vessels with simple designs applied before firing. Common motifs include small circles (probably made with a reed), cross-hatching, and interlocking frets. As before, we will never know why the first design was added or exactly what the design signified to the potter. But we can be fairly certain when these pots were manufactured. Whenever a decorated fiber-tempered pot (or, for that matter, even such a potsherd) is found in primary undisturbed archaeological contexts, we can justifiably hypothesize that the contexts date between 1500 and 1000 B.C.

Fiber-tempered pottery of the prehistoric American Southeast has thus been defined as an archaeological time-marker. Plotting the relative frequency of fiber-tempered sherds against time generates a graph like Figure III–1. Plain, undecorated sherds were rare in 2500 B.C., but as time went by, such pottery became increasingly widespread, and the sherds were found more frequently in archaeological sites. About 1500 B.C., decorated sherds start showing up, increasing in frequency until about 1100 B.C., after which such ceramics become progressively rarer, finally disappearing from the archaeological record altogether.

This is the kind of temporal change that the archaeologist initially seeks to isolate: Time has been effectively segmented, using the details of material culture as a guide. As we shall see, time-sensitive objects like potsherds are generally grouped into temporal types. Such time-markers enable archaeologists to fit previously undated archaeological contexts into an established time sequence. The next step of investigation synthesizes several such temporal types into larger divisions called cultural phases. These basic archaeological concepts will be discussed in some detail in Chapter 10; for now it is sufficient for you to keep in mind the importance of placing cultures securely in time

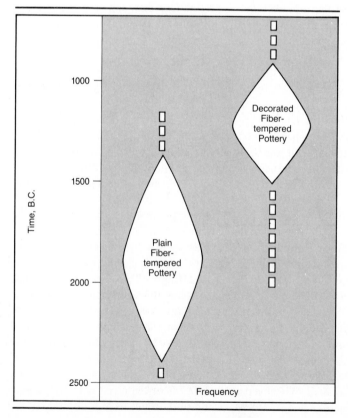

Hypothetical changes in frequency of fiber-tempered pottery in archaeological sites along the Georgia/Florida coast.

before trying to conceptualize the extinct cultural system from which they came. It is senseless to compare components of a dynamic cultural system before making certain that those subsystems were actually contemporary.

Fiber-tempered ceramics also demonstrate how archaeologists use the modal concept of culture. Even a single potsherd reflects a variety of cultural inputs, and this is where the modal concept of culture is strategic. Looking at the pottery of, say, the Georgia coast, one can ask simply, What changes across time? That is, we eliminate the constants in order to search for variety. All pottery is made of clay, and so that is a constant. All pots have been fired, and so that is another. But by examining enough archaeological collections, one begins to perceive sometimes subtle dissimilarities. The earlier pots, we notice, are tempered with vegetable fiber, whereas the later ones use sand, grit, or smashed potsherds. Temper thus seems to be a useful variable. Because the earlier fiber-tempered pots are plain and the later ones are ornamented, surface decoration becomes a second variable well suited to partitioning time. And so on.

But why do pots made after 1500 B.C. tend to be decorated? Why wasn't quartz grit used for temper before 1000 B.C.? Why don't fiber-tempered pots have outcurving rims? Do certain decorative motifs occur only in ceremonial contexts? All are provocative questions that may tell us of the cultural milieus that once operated on the prehistoric Georgia coast. But these questions must be ignored for the moment because they arise from more sophisticated goals of archaeology and are not germane to the initial probing steps of analysis.

The important point here is to begin with a deliberately simplified scheme and gradually build the approach to deal with multivariate cultural complexity. It is sufficient at the outset to isolate time-markers and to define some tentative cultural phases. These initial phases are not inviolate; they are working hypotheses that will probably be modified in light of additional information.

The modal concept has a simplified view of reality. People began making plain fiber-tempered pots about 2500 B.C. We do not know why; we only know when. About 1500 B.C. potters began decorating their pots. We do not know why they did that either, but the change furnishes a way of monitoring temporal context in our archaeological sites. Once the sites are suitably ordered, using such basic criteria, we can begin to explain why these changes occurred. But we cannot explain before we explicate, and the modal concept of culture is the path toward temporal explication.

To summarize, time varies in linear fashion, progressing from before to after. By restricting focus to modal behavior—the shared aspects of culture—archaeologists chart cultural changes along a temporal scale. These changes can then be plotted on a map to determine spatial variability. This is how archaeology derives its basic analytical units.

Not all culture changes, of course. Culture change is an extremely complicated business, and the modal conception temporarily ignores the question of why. Initially, it is enough to document that a change has occurred. The chances are that the change will be apparent only across a restricted range of archaeological objects. Suppose you did a site with one hundred classes of objects: potsherds, chipped-stone dart points, grinding slabs, bone awls, and so on. Ninety-five of these items remain constant through time. The modal concept of culture—defined by what most people do or believe—allows you to ignore the 95 percent of the stable cultural inventory to concentrate on the critical 5 percent that has deviated. Keep in mind that the modal concept of culture is only a heuristic, and not an explanatory, device.

Culture Chronology Versus Culture History

Archaeology's initial chronological aim makes two assumptions:

1. All variability not attributable to time (and/or space) is irrelevant.
2. Temporal variability is best isolated by monitoring only shared cultural behavior.

In chronological analysis, the archaeologist addresses only the isolated segments of the archaeological record that differ across time and/or space. This assumption is simplistic, to be sure, for the archaeological record is rife with nontemporal, nonspatial variability. But it is precisely this complexity that leads us to simplify. For chronological purposes, any source of variability other than temporal or spatial is random noise and temporarily irrelevant.

Consider the case of Shoshone pottery. Ceramics appear suddenly in about A.D. 1300 in the archaeological record, and the historic Shoshone people are known to have ceased manufacturing pottery by about 1860. Shoshone brownware pottery thus implies certain limits: time—A.D. 1300–1860, space—the Desert West. Note that the early boundary (A.D. 1300) is only an estimate derived from radiocarbon dating, whereas the late constraint (1860) is based on historical documentation. The initial 1300 date is thus subject to considerably more error than is the termination date. Such is often the case with time-markers, and this disproportionate error will cause no particular difficulties so long as we recognize it.

Its temporal parameters suitably established, Shoshone pottery is a useful time-marker in the chronology of the Desert West. Sites exhibiting a significant number of these potsherds can be tentatively assigned to the A.D. 1300–1860 interval (subject, of course, to independent verification by suitable dating techniques).

But Shoshone pottery, taken as a time-marker, leaves many more questions unanswered. What about the origins of the Desert West ceramic complex? Was this post-1300 pottery introduced as the result of a migration of Shoshone-speaking peoples? Did the idea of pottery simply spread across the Desert West? Or did the peoples of the Desert West independently invent the idea of pottery?

These are deceptive questions, and their answers require a thorough understanding of the local cultural history. Is it possible to document a population movement across the Desert West at A.D. 1300? If so, where did these newcomers come from? And what happened to the pre-1300 inhabitants of the Desert West? What conditions allow the replacement of one group of hunter-gatherers by another group? Are there signs of warfare in A.D. 1300? Did the climate change to render the pre-1300 adaptation untenable, thereby enabling the Shoshone to invade the Desert West? Could it be that a ceramic-using population moved into the Desert West and intermarried with the previous inhabitants? Did the ecological adaptation somehow change to make ceramic vessels more efficient after A.D. 1300? Were the vessels actually manufactured in the Desert West, or were they traded in from neighboring ceramic-manufacturing areas? If so, what did Desert West peoples trade for the ceramics, and why did this exchange begin only after A.D. 1300?

Data-free questions like this can proliferate *ad nauseam*. The point here—and a compelling point indeed—is that the mechanics of cultural change cannot be understood strictly from the exploration of time-markers. By definition, we base our time-markers on selected aspects of shared culture; time-markers deliberately ignore most of the cultural system. Obviously, questions such as diffusion, migration, and independent invention are complex, reflecting changes in the underlying cultural systems. Time-markers, grounded only in shared behavior, are patently inadequate for unraveling the mechanics of cultural systems.

We must thus distinguish between cultural chronology and cultural history: A cultural chronology documents a temporal and spatial change in shared aspects of culture; a cultural history provides a sketch of what people actually did. Cultural chronology thus does not equal cultural history. Chronology strictly documents changes in selected objects, with the most convenient chronological summary being the familiar seriation chart (Chapter 7). By contrast, cultural history attempts to explain how and why specific cultural systems change or remain stable.

The time-marker Shoshone pottery tells us that distinctive potsherds occur in archaeological deposits dating from A.D. 1300 to 1860 across the Desert West. But viewed as a time-marker, Shoshone pottery tells us nothing about why pottery was introduced in 1300. For some reason, one segment of the Desert West cultural system changed, and people began using (if not manufacturing) pottery. This complex issue can be studied only by pursuing related shifts in the lifeway, drawing evidence from the settlement pattern and demography, cultural ecology, social organization, and religion. If one posits that the pottery was introduced through the people's physical migration, then a second cultural system must be examined, the system operative in the area from which the newcomers migrated.

Cultural history is not explicated by using time-markers or through the modal definition of culture. A systematic perspective is required. Time-markers document only changes in shared material culture; they do not tell us why such changes have occurred.

This warning is repeated several times throughout the text. It is a critical point that speaks to the very objectives of archaeology. You cannot study cultural systems before having a chronology, and your chronology must be based on the modal concept of culture. You must then redefine the units of analysis to reflect their ultimate, systemic content. These two complementary objectives must be kept separate, because to confuse the two is to commit a lamentable archaeological sin.

WHERE TO GO FROM HERE?

The Theory of Chronology in Contemporary Archaeology: Schiffer (1972): "Archaeological Context and Systemic Context"; Hammond (1974): "Archaeometry and Time: A Review"; Dean (1978a): "Independent Dating in Archaeological Analysis."

Some Good General Sources on Chronological Methods in Archaeology: Brothwell and Higgs (1970): *Science in Archaeaology,* Fleming (1977): *Dating Techniques in Archaeology,* Michael and Ralph (1971): *Dating Techniques for the Archaeologist,* Michels (1973): *Dating Methods in Archaeology,* Oakley (1968): *Frameworks for Dating Fossil Man,* Orme (1982): *Problems in Case Studies in Archaeological Dating,* Taylor and Longworth (1975): "Dating: New Methods and New Results", Taylor and Meighan (1978): *Chronologies in New World Archaeology.*

Archaeometry is a technical research journal emphasizing the role of physical science in archaeology and art history. Authors are encouraged to write with the nonspecialist in mind; first published in 1958.

Subscription information: Research Laboratory for Archaeology and the History of Art, Archaeometry Manager, Oxford University, 6 Keble Road, Oxford, England OXI 3QJ.

MASCA Journal publishes articles on archaeometallurgy, dendrochronology, and computer applications. Worldwide in scope, it covers theoretical and practical applications of archaeological science as well as book reviews; first published in 1984.

Subscription information: Subscriptions Manager, *MASCA,* University Museum, University of Pennsylvania, 33rd and Spruce Streets, Philadelphia, Pa. 19104.

CHAPTER 8

Stratigraphy

Civilization exists by geological consent, subject to change without notice.
—Will Durant

Archaeology is a parasitic discipline, relying heavily on results from other sciences. Archaeologists are forever borrowing methods, techniques, and theories from their nonarchaeological colleagues. In the chapter on dating in archaeology, for instance, we shall draw on the expertise of physicists, botanists, and molecular biologists. Geology has been another useful mine for ideas. Geologists crystallized the principles of the stratigraphic method, only to have archaeologists pirate these concepts wholesale. Two such stratigraphic principles have been especially important to penetrating the archaeological record, the concepts of superposition and index fossils.

Nicolaus Steno (1638–1687) initially formulated the **law of superposition**. Simply stated, Steno's law tells us that in any pile of sedimentary rocks undisturbed by folding or overturning, the strata on the bottom must have been deposited first. On a broader scale, this principle, almost preposterously simple, holds that—all else being equal—older deposits tend to be buried beneath younger ones. This canon facilitates the correlation of various geological exposures such as cliffs, stream valleys, and drill cores.

But geological correlation has its limits. It is impossible, for instance, to correlate geological exposures at the Grand Canyon directly with the White Cliffs of Dover in England. Ever resourceful, our geological colleagues dreamed up a second principle, the **index fossil concept**, which assisted worldwide correlation.

This second concept is a bit more involved. In the early nineteenth century, a British surveyor named **William Smith** (1769–1839) began collecting data from geological strata throughout England. Smith gradually became enraptured by the fossils he found in various canals and vertical exposures. As he grew to understand the regional geology, he recognized that different exposures of the same stratum contained comparable fossils.

Smith eventually became so knowledgeable that when somebody showed him a fossil, he could guess the stratum from which it had come.

Smith's French contemporaries were making similar discoveries. While mapping the fossil-rich strata surrounding Paris, **Georges Cuvier** (1769–1832) and **Alexandre Brongniart** (1770–1847) discovered that certain of their fossils were restricted to specific geological formations. After applying the law of superposition to arrange the strata in the proper chronological sequence, they then organized their fossil collection into the appropriate stratigraphic order. French fossil assemblages, it turned out, varied systematically according to the age of the parent strata. Cuvier and Brongniart then compared their fossils with modern species and discovered, as expected, that fossils characterizing later strata more closely resembled modern forms than did those of more ancient strata.

Fossils contained in a geological stratum thus became a clue to the relative age of the deposit. This is the **index fossil concept**: Rocks containing similar fossil assemblages must be of similar age. Obviously there are exceptions to both the index fossil concept and the law of superposition, but these two principles enabled geologists around the globe to correlate their stratigraphic sections into master chronologies. Both principles are likewise important as archaeological guideposts for interpreting the human record of the past.

Archaeology's Law of Superposition

Chapter 1 examined Thomas Jefferson's excavation of a Virginia burial mound, generally acknowledged as the initial application of stratigraphic principles to archaeological deposits (e.g., Wheeler 1954, p. 58). Jefferson's firsthand stratigraphic observations enabled him to reconstruct the various stages of construction of the site, thereby suggesting its probable use as a burial feature. Stratigraphic techniques for analyzing burial mounds have changed very little since Jefferson's time, as my own excavations on the Georgia coast illustrate.

McLeod Mound: Interpreting Stratigraphy Is Easy

McLeod Mound is located on St. Catherines Island, not far from Mission Santa Catalina (Thomas and Larsen 1979). This small sand mound stands only one meter high and covers about three hundred square meters. When first examining the mound in 1974, we noted a small depression in the northeastern corner, probably the result of much earlier vandalism. Several oyster shells, presumably unearthed by the vandals, littered the surface of the mound.

We excavated only about 40 percent of the entire mound in a series of two-meter-square excavation units, simultaneously exposing a contiguous section of the premound surface and creating a continuous east-west profile of the mound stratigraphy. In this way, we could examine not only the sequence of mound construction but also the horizontal patterning of the ceremonial area beneath the mound.

Once we finished digging, we drew a stratigraphic profile (Figure 8–1) and photographed each section. Table 8–1 shows the standardized descriptions of each primary depositional unit, recording the thickness, texture, and general character of each stratigraphic unit. The number in parentheses, such as (10 YR 4/5: moist) is a soil description from the **Munsell Color Chart.**

This stratigraphic profile and measured section became part of our basic data from McLeod Mound. (Remember: data are not the objects but the observations we make on the objects.) Up to this point, any competent field archaeologist digging at McLeod would have produced comparable data. The field strategy might have been different, but the records would, somewhere, contain these same basic observations. The canons of archaeological description require that such primary data be published in detail to allow archaeologists to compare a profile with others excavated elsewhere.

Now comes the interpretation. Although most archaeologists would have generated similar primary data, the interpretation of those basics is not mechanical. Our task is to translate this observable stratigraphic record into a meaningful interpretation of the prehistoric behavior that produced the stratification. This is where the law of superposition, pirated from geology, comes to the immediate aid of archaeology.

Steno's law holds that, all else being equal, older deposits lie at the base of the stratigraphic profile. So we work from the bottom up. Unit I is a sterile yellow sand, and we know from coring near McLeod that these yellow Unit I sands underlie the entire area.

Table 8–1—Measured Stratigraphic Section of McLeod Mound

Unit	Thickness	Description
IV	10 cm	*Secondary humus,* dark grayish brown sand, fairly dense root mat (10 YR 4/2: moist), formed as A horizon of Unit IIIc. Contact gradual over 4–5 cm.
IIIc	30–40 cm	*Upper mound fill,* brownish yellow sand (10 YR 6/6: moist). Radiocarbon date: A.D. 130–110 ± 75 (UGA-1256). Contact distinct.
IIIb	50–65 cm	*Lower mound fill,* dark brown sand (10 YR 3/3: moist), charcoal flecks throughout. Contact abrupt.
IIIa	4–5 cm	*Shallow lens,* brownish yellow sand (10 YR 6/6: moist), occasional charcoal flecks present. Contact very abrupt.
II	90 cm	*Primary humus,* very dark grayish brown sand (10 YR 3/2: moist), slightly mottled with abundant charcoal present, apparently disturbed with lens of shell embedded near center of mound, formed as A horizon of Unit I. Radiocarbon dates: 1600–1640 B.C. ± 70 (UCLA-1997E); 850–890 B.C. ± 65 (UGA-1557). Contact gradual.
I	30+ cm	*Sterile substratum,* yellow sand (10 YR 7/8: moist), slightly mottled, uncompressed occasional charcoal flecks present near top. Bottom not exposed.

Thomas and Larsen, 1979, Table 8.

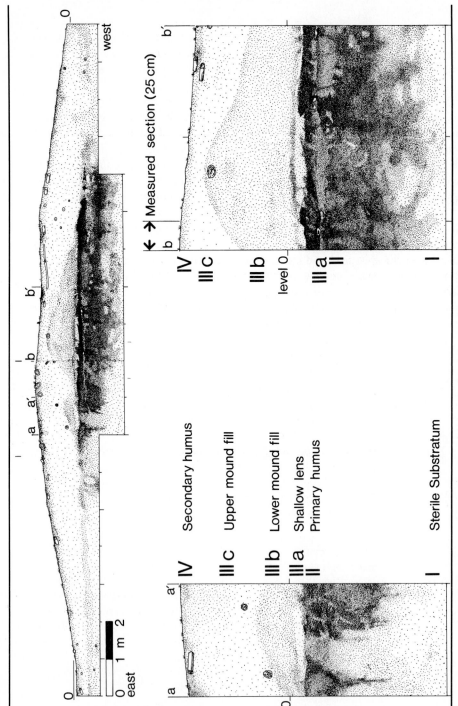

west

east

0   1 m   2

IV   Secondary humus

III c   Upper mound fill

III b   Lower mound fill

III a   Shallow lens
II   Primary humus

I   Sterile Substratum

Measured section (25 cm)

level 0

IV

III c

III b

III a

II

I

FIGURE 8–1   Stratigraphic section of McLeod Mound (see Thomas and Larsen 1979, Figure 9). (Courtesy the American Museum of Natural History).

Unit I was laid down during the Silver Bluff submergence of the **Pleistocene** period, 40,000 to 25,000 years ago. Pleistocene glaciers had built to a maximum then, capturing enormous volumes of water and consequently lowering sea levels as much as 330 feet below current levels. The Georgia coastline at that time extended seventy to eighty miles eastward of the present beach. The chain of Sea Islands, including St. Catherines, was formed first as extensive onshore dune ridges, which became isolated into islands when the glaciers melted, beginning 18,000 years ago. Thus Unit I at McLeod is a dune formation more than 25,000 years old and has nothing to do with people.

Soil cores also indicate that in undisturbed stratigraphic contexts, Unit I will always be capped by a rich organic layer, formed by weathering, which appears as a black horizontal stain across the McLeod profile. This primary humus, stratigraphic Unit II, formed after the deposition of Unit I, but before human involvement with the area. Charcoal and charred stumps from Unit II have been radiocarbon dated to about 1700 B.C. The fire that produced them was almost certainly set deliberately to clear the land. The blaze may have been localized and controlled, as charcoal concentrations are restricted to the mound proper and are absent from soil samples taken in the undisturbed forest surrounding McLeod.

Unit III, subdivided into three subunits, poses a greater interpretive problem. A large central pit was dug through Units II and I sometime after the burning. Five human burials were laid out inside and then buried beneath the burned humus and a fine lens of oyster and clam shell. These shells have been radiocarbon dated to about 500 B.C., telling us that considerable time elapsed between initial burning of the area and the excavation of the central pit. By means of techniques discussed in Chapter 11, we decided that these shells were collected between November and May of the same year. The shallow yellow lens (Unit IIIa) is reworked sand from Unit I, piled up as a ring of backdirt during the excavation of this central tomb.

Stratigraphic Units IIIb and IIIc represent the actual mound-building episode, after the tomb was closed. Three large "barrow" areas show up on the topographic map. The McLeod mound builders dug these pits to obtain construction fill. The color variation between IIIb and IIIc reflects differing parent materials. The prehistoric excavator's backdirt from the burned Unit II was a dark gray. But once the barrow pits reached Unit I, the mound fill became the light yellow sand characteristic of the sterile substratum.

A secondary humus zone then enveloped the entire mound. This humus (Unit IV) is lighter than that of the Unit II because it had so little time to build (less than 2500 years) and because it was not charred to clear the undergrowth.

This sequence of construction, inferred entirely from the stratigraphic column and profile—plus a working knowledge of the local geology—turned up in eight additional mounds we dug on St. Catherines Island (Thomas and Larsen 1979). In each case, the law of superposition was the key that unlocked the stratigraphic sequence. Nothing in our interpretation departs radically from that made in 1784 by Thomas Jefferson. Though it is true that modern excavators dig more systematically, document more completely, and have recourse to increasingly sophisticated technology for absolute dating, I am confident that had he been there, Thomas Jefferson would have interpreted the McLeod Mound stratigraphy in exactly the same way that I did.

Gatecliff Shelter: Stratigraphic Interpretation Is Not As Easy As It Looks

Mortuary sites such as McLeod were wholly constructed by people. But some archaeological sites are more complicated because their stratigraphic profile reflects considerably more than human activity. At Gatecliff Shelter, we ran into an extremely complex situation, with stratigraphy considerably more subtle than at McLeod Mound.

During our first three seasons at Gatecliff, I recorded and interpreted the Gatecliff stratigraphy myself. Drawing upon my somewhat limited classroom training in geology, soil science, and microstratigraphy, I prepared schematic and pictoral descriptions of gross stratigraphy. This master profile—the so-called cowboy stratigraphy—continued to serve as the major descriptive device throughout the excavations (Figure 8–2).

As the 1973 field season wound down, it became clear that Gatecliff was too complex for me to continue the geological interpretation. This is not unusual in archaeology. On small-scale digs, archaeologists must often cover all the bases, from stratigrapher to photographer, from engineer to camp cook. But as the operation expands, specialists must be recruited to take over selected aspects. The trick is for an archaeologist to recognize the critical line separating flexibility from recklessness. So I arranged for some experienced Great Basin geologists to join the team. Bill Melhorn (Purdue University) and Dennis Trexler (Nevada Bureau of Mines and Geology) joined us in 1973, and Jonathan O. Davis (Desert Research Institute), three years later. Although each had somewhat different ideas—and some rather heated debates took place—the diversity fostered a better overall interpretation of the stratigraphic column.

Over a decade, we had exposed a remarkably well stratified profile, more than forty feet deep, spanning the last 7000 years. Gatecliff Shelter has textbook stratigraphy, and that is why I discuss it here.

The Gatecliff profile resulted from a complex interplay of natural and cultural factors. The cowboy stratigraphy demonstrates how two very different kinds of deposits resulted from each set of processes. The thin dark levels (such as those numbered 9, 11, and 13) are living surfaces, or cultural horizons. Each dark horizontal band represents a single campsite. The sixteen cultural horizons occurred as the result of human habitation, and these surfaces contain the fire hearths, broken stone tools, grinding slabs, flakes, food remains, and occasional fragments of basketry and cordage. In Chapter 10, we discuss how material culture from each horizon at Gatecliff can be used to define time-markers, which in turn are useful for dating other sites. Chapter 13 discusses how the patterning of these artifacts on each floor allows the reconstruction of the activities that occurred on each living surface.

But what makes Gatecliff so unusual is that living surfaces were capped by sterile, noncultural layers of purely geological origin. After the excavation was finished, we divided up the Gatecliff profile into a sequence of fifty-six geological strata: layers of more or less homogeneous or gradational sedimentary material, visually separated from adjacent layers by a distinct change in the character of the material deposited (see Table 8–2).

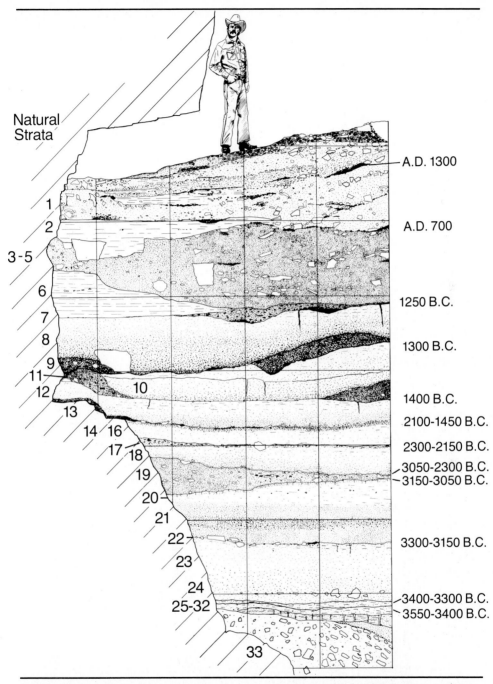

Natural Strata

1
2
3-5
6
7
8
9
11
12
13
14 16
17 18
19
20
21
22
23
24
25-32
10
33

A.D. 1300

A.D. 700

1250 B.C.

1300 B.C.

1400 B.C.
2100-1450 B.C.
2300-2150 B.C.
3050-2300 B.C.
3150-3050 B.C.

3300-3150 B.C.

3400-3300 B.C.
3550-3400 B.C.

FIGURE 8–2 The cowboy stratigraphy—more formally termed the *master profile*—at Gatecliff Shelter. The standing figure is exactly six feet tall (and the grid system is metric). Only the upper thirty-three of the fifty-six stratigraphic units are evident in this cross-section (see Thomas 1983b, Figure 22). (The American Museum of Natural History).

Table 8-2—Physical Stratigraphy of Gatecliff Shelter

Stratum	Soil	Nature of Deposit	Field Designation	Cultural Association	Age (C-14 yr. B.P.)	Date (C-14yr. A.D./B.C.)
1	S-1	Rubble	GU 14	Horizons 1–3	0–1250 B.P.	A.D. 700–present
2		Sand and silt	Upper GU 13	—	1250 B.P.	A.D. 700
3	S-2	Rubble	Part of GU 12	Part of Horizon 4	1250–1350 B.P.	A.D. 600–700
4		Sand and silt	GU 13 &GU 12 Silt		1350 B.P.	A.D. 600
5	S-3	Rubble	Part of GU 12	Parts of Horizons 4, 5, 6	1350–3200 B.P.	1250 B.C.–A.D. 600
6		Sand and silt	GU 11	—	3200 B.P.	1250 B.C.
7		Rubble	GU 11 & GU 10R	Horizon 7	3250–3200 B.P.	1300 B.C.–1250 B.C.
8		Sand and silt	GU 10	—	3250 B.P.	1300 B.C.
9		Rubble	GU 9R	Horizon 8	3300–3250 B.P.	1350 B.C.–1300 B.C.
10		Sand and silt	GU 8 A&B		3300 B.P.	1350 B.C.
11		Rubble	GU 7R	Horizon 9	3400–3300 B.P.	1450 B.C.–1350 B.C.
12		Sand and silt	GU 7	—	3400 B.P.	1450 B.C.
13		Rubble	6 Living Floor	Horizon 10	4050–3400 B.P.	2100 B.C.–1450 B.C.
14		Sand and silt	GU 5 Silt	—	4050 B.P.	2100 B.C.
15		Rubble	Part of GU 5	—	4100–4050 B.P.	2150 B.C.–2100 B.C.
16		Sand and silt	Part of GU 5	—	4100 B.P.	2150 B.C.
17		Rubble	GU 4	Horizon 11	4250–4100 B.P.	2300 B.C.–2150 B.C.
18		Silty sand	GU 3	—	4250 B.P.	2300 B.C.

					B.P.	B.C.
19		Sand and rubble	GU 2	Horizon 12	5000–4250 B.P.	3050 B.C.–2300 B.C.
20	S-4	Silt and clay	GU 1A	Horizon 13	5100–5000 B.P.	3150 B.C.–3050 B.C.
21		Sand and silt	GU 1 & GU 7–74	—	5100 B.P.	3150 B.C.
22		Rubble	GU 6R–74	Horizon 14	5250–5100 B.P.	3300 B.C.–3150 B.C.
23		Gravel, sand, and silt	GU 6–74 & GU 5–74	—	5250 B.P.	3300 B.C.
24		Rubble	GU 4R–74	Horizon 15	5350–5250 B.P.	3400 B.C.–3300 B.C.
25		Silt	GU 4–74	—	5350 B.P.	3400 B.C.
26		Rubble	GU 3R–74	Horizon 16	5500–5350 B.P.	3550 B.C.–3400 B.C.
27–29		Silts	GU 3A–74	—	5500 B.P.	3550 B.C.
30		Sand	GU 3B–74	—	5500 B.P.	3550 B.C.
31		Rubble	GU 2R–74	—	5700–5500 B.P.	3750 B.C.–3550 B.C.
32		Fine sand and silt	GU 2–74	—		
33		Fine sand and silt	GU 12–76, GU 1–78 & GU 1–74	—		
34		Silt and very fine sand	GU 2–78	—		
35		Rubble	GU 3R–78	—		
36		Silty medium sand	GU 3–78	—		

Thomas, 1983b, Table 3.

Some strata, such as 2, resulted from small ponds that occasionally formed at the rear of Gatecliff Shelter. The pond water acted as a sink for windblown dust particles, which settled out as finely laminated silts. Other strata, such as 8, consist of coarser sediments grading from gravels at the bottom to fine sand silts at the top. Apparently, the ephemeral stream flowing in front of Gatecliff Shelter occasionally flooded and coursed through the shelter. The water of such flash floods would first deposit coarse sediments such as pea-sized gravels. As the water's velocity diminished, its carrying capacity decreased, and smaller particles were deposited. Finally, when the water slowed, the tiniest silt particles would cap the stream deposits. Such floods occurred several times throughout the seven thousand years of deposition at Gatecliff, and each time the previous occupation surface was immediately buried. When the inhabitants returned to Gatecliff, they thus lived on a new campsite, separated from the previous one by as much as two feet of sterile alluvial sediments.

Fifty-six such depositional strata were stacked up inside Gatecliff. Here is how we described one stratum at Gatecliff (evident at the bottom of the cowboy stratigraphy):

Stratum 32, Fine Sand and Silt

In alternating layers; silt is dark grayish brown (10 YR 4/2D), platy, micaceous, strongly calcareous; 2 cm. granules at base. As much as 10 cm. thick in places, though discontinuous over rubble piles; top was at −6.27 m. in the Master Profile, about −6.70 m. in the southwest pile and in the 1978 excavation; bottom was at −6.80 m. in 1978 excavation and −6.90 m. in 1976 excavation. Stratum 32 was called GU 2-74 in the field, and there are no radiocarbon dates available. This layer was deposited by a single flood about 5700 years ago and apparently very little time passed between the deposition of this layer and 33 below. (Davis et al. 1983, pp. 58–59).

Several important points can be made with reference to Stratum 32 at Gatecliff.

Note the detail of description. Exact depths are given relative to a central-site datum point, arbitrarily assigned a zero value of 0.0 m. (Actually, the Gatecliff datum is 2319 meters [7606 feet] above sea level.) When paired with our horizontal grid system, these arbitrary elevations document the exact configuration of each geological stratum. As at McLeod Mound, the soil color is documented by Munsell chart readings. Each geological term is sufficiently well defined so that geologists who have never visited Gatecliff can still understand what Stratum 32 looked like. Note also how we separate such descriptions from our interpretation. This way, others can use our data to make their own assessments (disagreeing with us, if they wish). Geoarchaeologists sometimes use the term *stratification* to refer to the physical layers in a site, reserving *stratigraphy* for the geoarchaeological interpretation of the temporal and depositional evidence.

Get your facts first, then you can distort them as you please.
—Mark Twain

You can also see how we dated Stratum 32. Although forty-seven radiocarbon dates were processed on materials from Gatecliff, no date was available from this particular stratum. But this level was only 20 cm below Stratum 30, with an associated radiocarbon date of about 5500 years. The law of superposition allowed us to estimate that Stratum 32 was laid down about 5700 years ago.

Other strata at Gatecliff provided different clues to help date the site. Stratum 55, near the very bottom of the site, contained an inch-thick lens of sand-sized volcanic ash (or **tephra**), fragments of crystal, glass, and rock once ejected into the air by a volcanic eruption. Not discovered until the last week of the last field season, the tephra was indistinct, mixed with the cobbles and rubble of Stratum 55. In the laboratory, Davis confirmed that this ashy deposit was the **Mount Mazama Ash** (Davis 1983). When this mountain in the Oregon Cascades blew up 6900 years ago, it spewed out eleven cubic miles of pumice and related materials; the caldera formed by the Mazama explosion now contains Crater Lake. The Mount St. Helens eruption in 1980 was a cherry bomb in comparison. The prevailing winds, coupled with the force of the explosion itself, carried Mazama ash across the western United States. Wherever the ash settled out, it created a "marker-bed" (see also the discussion in Chapter 11 of pollen grains included in the Mazama ash). **Tephrachronology** has become a valuable tool for dating sites in volcanically active areas. When Davis found the Mazama ash at the bottom of Gatecliff, we had a critical, independent check on the largely radiocarbon-derived chronology at Gatecliff, and so we knew that Stratum 55 must be 6900 years old.

In truth, I am not certain whether I would have recognized the volcanic ash at the bottom of Gatecliff. At Mummy Cave (Wyoming), near Yellowstone National Park, the excavators confused the thin layers of Mazama ash with wood ash; fortunately, the important tephra lens was later recognized under the microscope (see p. 250). Fortunately, the Mazama tephra at Gatecliff was instantly recognized by Jonathan Davis (not coincidentally, a leading expert on the volcanic ashes of the Great Basin). Both cases highlight the importance of having specialists work on-site, during excavation.

Gatecliff is like a giant birthday cake. The sterile strata are the layers and the cultural horizons are the icing capping each layer. Both strata and horizons contained datable artifacts and ecofacts that could be used to reconstruct the human events and environmental background. Several of these studies will be introduced in subsequent chapters. But the important point is that such objects would be relatively useless in archaeology had it not been for the stratigraphically controlled contexts in which they were recovered.

WHERE TO GO FROM HERE?

Geoarchaeology: Archaeological Geology by Rapp and Gifford (1985) is a diverse collection, with several important articles and a valuable selected bibliography on geoarchaeology; Stein (1987) reviews the relationship between archaeology and geology in the examination of site-specific sediments; see also Butzer (1982), Dimbleby (1977).

Using Volcanic Ashes to Date Archaeological Sites (Tephrachronology): Steen-McIntyre (1985) has prepared a comprehensive review article; Sheets and Grayson (1979) have assembled a diverse range of data dealing not only with dating but also the ecological effects of vulcanism on human ecology. For specifics about the Mount Mazama eruption, see Davis (1978, 1983), Mehringer (1986), and Mehringer, Blinman, and Peterson (1977).

Geoarchaeology is a relatively new journal exploring the interface between archaeology and the earth sciences: geology, paleontology, geography, oceanography, and soil science, with articles reporting on the environmental setting of archaeological sites, providing materials analysis of artifacts, synthesizing the broader aspects of geoarchaeology, and describing new techniques and equipment; first published in 1986.

Subscription information: John Wiley & Sons, Subscription Department, 605 Third Avenue, New York, N.Y. 10158.

The Index Fossil Concept

Geologists proposed the law of superposition rather early in the game, in 1669 (when Franciscan friars were still preaching to the Guale at Mission Santa Catalina!). But fossils did not become a worthwhile tool for geological correlation until much later, during the early nineteenth century. So whereas an archaeologist like Thomas Jefferson could apply principles of superposition to his excavations, his successors had to wait nearly two centuries to learn—once again from geologists—how the index fossil concept might make human artifacts useful tools in dating archaeological sites.

Nelson's Phony Stratigraphy at San Cristobal

Nels Nelson, one of archaeology's forefathers extolled in Chapter 1, is generally credited with first using the index fossil concept in stratigraphic archaeology. In 1912, the president of the American Museum of Natural History, Henry Fairfield Osborne, sent Nelson on a tour of European archaeological sites to bone up on the most recent methodological innovations (and also, not coincidentally, to round up collections of artifacts to be displayed in New York). While at Castillo Cave in Spain, Nelson participated for several weeks in excavating tightly stratified Paleolithic remains. Like Gatecliff Shelter, the Castillo grotto held deposits roughly forty-five feet thick, the thirteen archaeological strata ranging from Paleolithic times through the Bronze Age. Nelson was staggered by the fine-scale stratigraphic divisions possible at Castillo, and he eagerly sought similar sites on his return to the American Southwest the next year.

But Nelson's initial stratigraphic excavations in the Galisteo Basin, south of Santa Fe (New Mexico) were disappointing (Figure 8–3). Trash heaps in the Southwest tend to be badly jumbled, not at all like the crisp strata of European caves. Although he tested several sites, the middens contained either too brief a time span or had been riddled by prehistoric grave digging.

Ironically, Nelson finally came across the stratigraphy he was seeking at Pueblo San Cristobal, where he had been working for three years. When he returned to San Cristobal in 1914, he was determined to try out a new stratigraphic method. Selecting an area with minimal disturbance, Nelson isolated a block of debris measuring three by six feet wide and nearly ten feet deep. Clearly the midden had accumulated over a long interval, and several discrete kinds of pottery were buried here. But there was still a problem because the greasy black midden lacked the sharp stratigraphic divisions Nelson had seen in the Paleolithic caves of Europe. How do you dig stratigraphically without perceptible strata?

Not one to be easily deterred, Nelson did the next best thing: He created his own stratigraphy. First dividing his test block into one-foot vertical sections, Nelson dug each level in the way he had learned to dig the strata in Europe, accurately cataloguing the sherds recovered by level (Figure 8–4). To Nelson, the only difference was that the Castillo Cave strata were readily discernible, whereas the "stratigraphy" at San Cristobal was arbitrarily imposed as twelve-inch levels. Apparently mistrusting his workmen to

FIGURE 8–3   General view across Nelson's early excavations at the San Cristobal ruins (New Mexico). (Courtesy the American Museum of Natural History)

maintain proper controls, Nelson later noted, "I performed this work with my own hands, devoting fully three days to the task" (1916, p. 165). Imposing arbitrary levels on nonvisual stratigraphy seems almost pedestrian today, but in 1914, Nelson's stratigraphic method was a dazzling and revolutionary innovation, immediately seized by New World archaeologists as a fundamental of excavation.

Given these arbitrarily imposed divisions, Nelson could apply the principles of superposition to look for culture change within a midden column (Figure 8–4). All else

FIGURE 8–4   Nelson's initial excavation by arbitrary levels in Refuse Heap B, San Cristobal Pueblo. (Courtesy the American Museum of Natural History)

being equal, the oldest trash should lie at the bottom, capped by more recent accumulations. Even though the dense midden lacked tangible stratigraphy, Nelson began to search for time-markers in the form of diagnostic pottery types. The concept is precisely that of the index fossil, developed a century before by geologists Cuvier and Brongniart. Just as geologists learned to distinguish certain extinct life forms as characteristic of various rock strata, so too could archaeologists use diagnostic artifact forms to characterize (and hence date) strata across archaeological sites.

So it was that Nels Nelson applied the index fossil concept to the prehistoric ceramics of San Cristobal. Pottery was a natural choice, as sherds were the most common cultural debris and Nelson knew that ceramic styles varied considerably across the American Southwest. More than two thousand sherds turned up in the ten-foot test section at San Cristobal. First grouping the sherds into obvious stylistic categories, Nelson then plotted their distribution according to depth below the surface (see Table 8–3). Column 1 contains the frequency of corrugated pottery, the most common everyday cooking ware. Because the relative frequency of corrugated sherds remained fairly constant throughout the occupation of San Cristobal, Nelson rejected Column 1 as a potential index fossil. Column 2 tabulated the frequencies of "biscuit ware," a dull whitish yellow pottery that Nelson felt was traded into San Cristobal from someplace else. But these frequencies did not change markedly throughout the stratigraphic column either, and so biscuit ware also was rejected as a potential time-marker.

Nelson then turned to the three remaining columns—which he termed Types I, II, and III—and discovered, just as Cuvier and Brongniart had with their French fossils, that certain forms were associated with specific stratigraphic levels. The most ancient levels at San Cristobal contained a predominance of black-on-white painted pottery (Nelson's Type I). Type I sherds were most numerous below the eight-foot mark and only rarely

Table 8–3—Potsherd Frequencies from Pueblo San Cristobal, New Mexico

Depth Below Surface	Corrugated Ware (1)	Biscuit Ware (2)	Type I (black-on-white) (3)	Type II (2-color glaze) (4)	Type III (3-color glaze) (5)
1st foot	57	10	2	81	5
2nd foot	116	17	2	230	6
3rd foot	27	2	10	134	3
4th foot	28	4	6	93	0
5th foot	60	15	2	268	0
6th foot	75	21	8	297	1?
7th foot	53	10	40	126	0
8th foot	56	2	118	51	0
9th foot	93	1?	107	3	0
10th foot	84	1?	69	0	0
Total	649	83	364	1283	15

Nelson 1916, p. 166.

recovered above seven feet. Type II pottery—red, yellow, and gray sherds ornamented with a dark glaze—occurred most commonly above the seven-foot mark.

This evidence meant that Type I sherds are "diagnostic" of the eight-foot and below strata and the Type II sherds characterized the upper deposits. The Type III pottery (three-color glazed ware), though rather rare at San Cristobal, appeared only in the uppermost levels of Nelson's column. This made sense, as three-colored wares were still being made when the Spaniards arrived in New Mexico in the sixteenth century.

Creating ersatz stratigraphy was a brilliant stroke, and remains today the preferred method of excavation whenever visible stratigraphic units are absent. Nelson's arbitrary levels made possible the definition of three important time-markers (archaeology's equivalent to index fossils). Not only did he document the specific ceramic changes at San Cristobal, but the presence of these pottery types elsewhere provided clues to the age of undated archaeological deposits (Chapter 10 discusses further how pottery types function as time-markers).

Kidder Does Nelson One Better

Nels Nelson thus blazed the trail, but it remained for A. V. Kidder to put Nelson's stratigraphic method on the map. Kidder visited the San Cristobal dig and shortly thereafter adapted the technique for use at his large-scale excavations at Pecos Pueblo, less than twenty-five miles to the east. From his earlier research, Kidder surmised that, like San Cristobal, the early Pecos sequence was characterized by black-on-white pottery, followed by a later phase in which glazed ceramics predominated. The last of these, the Glaze 5 period, arose sometime before the Spanish conquest and survived until nearly 1680.

By 1915, Kidder had located several rich deposits laid down during the later phases, but the early black-on-white period was poorly represented. Kidder resolved the next year to uncover the earliest Pecos occupation. Unlike modern searchers—who can call on nondestructive, noninvasive remote sensing techniques—Kidder followed Schliemann's lead by digging a series of lengthy exploratory trenches, cut at intervals of one hundred feet or so. Finding almost no refuse on the gaunt west slope of Pecos—probably owing to the fierce prevailing west winds that still buffet the Pecos valley—Kidder shifted his trenching to the leeward side of the ruin. Just inside the defensive perimeter, Kidder located a series of chambers with razed walls rising less than eighteen inches (Figure 8–5). When only black-on-white rubbish was found stacked against these walls, Kidder knew he had found the earliest dwelling at Pecos. Here indeed lay the founding settlement, the nucleus of the Pecos pueblo. Burials interred in the black-on-white rubbish comprised the first Pecos cemetery. As shown in Figure 8–5, the succeeding Glaze 1, 3, and 4 walls were built south of this early occupation, and they in turn were swamped by tons of Glaze 5 and 6 rubbish.

Kidder's Pecos investigations verified Nelson's techniques again and again. By carefully following the course of the various trash heaps, characterized by the time-marker sherds, Kidder reconstructed the several centuries of habitation at Pecos Pueblo. And

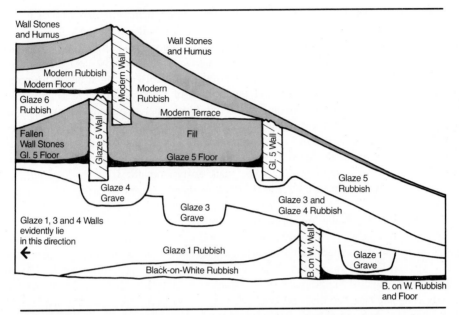

FIGURE 8–5   Cross section of Pecos Pueblo, showing walls, burials, and ceramics (see Kidder 1924, Figure 8). (Courtesy Yale University Press)

when walls or burials were encountered, they could be dated by applying the index fossil concept to the associated midden.

WHERE TO GO FROM HERE?

The Index Fossil Concept in Archaeology: Spier (1931): "N. C. Nelson's Stratigraphic Technique in the Reconstruction of Prehistoric Sequences in Southwestern America" (see also Spier 1917); Woodbury (1960): "Nels C. Nelson and chronological archaeology"; see also Dunnell (1986a, pp. 26–28), Grayson (1983a, esp. Chapter 4), Haag (1986), Kidder (1924, pp. 94–129), Nelson (1914, 1916), Taylor (1948, pp. 122–140), Willey and Sabloff (1980).

Horizontal Stratigraphy

The overriding concern of geologists like Steno, Smith, and Cuvier was verticality—how sedimentary beds stack up on one another. But more recent geological investigation has also looked at diversity within a single stratum. The paleogeography of certain stratigraphic units is extraordinarily well known. The oil-rich Permian Basin of west

instance, is known to have formed, in part, as stream deposits, elsewhere as back-reef, quiet-water lagoons. Stratigraphy obviously has a horizontal dimension.

Archaeologists are also aware of "flat stratigraphy," and this is why temporal variability can sometimes be expressed horizontally. Archaeology's most dramatic example of horizontal stratigraphy can be found at Cape Krusenstern, a beach formation northeast of Nome, Alaska. An aerial photograph of Cape Krusenstern (Figure 8–6) discloses that the cape is not a single beach at all but, rather, a hundred secondary dune ridges that merge to create a peninsula extending far into the Chukchi Sea. The modern shoreline, designated as Beach 1, is a protracted, relatively flat surface made of coarse sand and gravel. Behind this most recent beach is an older shoreline (Beach 2), which has become stranded and landlocked. As you walk away from the Chukchi Sea, you will encounter 114 such relic beach terraces, most of them covered by a protective rind of grassy sod.

J. L. Giddings began investigating the archaeology of Cape Krusenstern in 1958, and he spent four seasons excavating beneath the frozen sod. Eventually, he dug up house pits, human burials, artifact caches, tent sites, and entire settlements of the peoples who once lived on Cape Krusenstern. The Krusenstern ruins are as tightly stratified as the sediments of Gatecliff Shelter or the trash heaps of Pueblo San Cristobal. But rather than finding campsites stacked one on top of another, Giddings discovered that Cape Krusenstern sites are stratified side by side. One important corollary to the general canons of vertical stratigraphy thus applies to beach terraces such as Krusenstern.

The principle of horizontal stratigraphy is not complex: On any series of uneroded beach surfaces, the younger stratum will be seaward, the older inland. The modern Krustenstern beach contains house pits of very recent Eskimo who camped there within the past century. Five beaches or so inland are multiple-roomed, deeply entrenched house ruins of an ancestral pre-Eskimo culture called Western Thule. The artifacts and distinctive pottery found inside these houses pinpoint the Western Thule sites to an age of about A.D. 1000. Farther inland, about Beach 35, are the large square pit houses and clusters of shallow summer lodges constructed by the Ipiutak peoples, a society known for their expertise in carving ivory. Some fifteen beaches behind the Ipiutak sites, nearly a kilometer from the modern sea, are the hearths and tent sites of the Choris peoples, characterized by large spear points remarkably like those used to hunt extinct forms of bison on the western American Plains.

Beach 35 also contains a ruined settlement of deep, multiple-roomed winter lodges, along with a few scattered summer settlements. Giddings coined the term "Old Whaling" culture to emphasize the profusion of whale bones scattered in and about these houses. Farther back, on Beach 78, are the hearths of the culture known as the Denbigh Flint complex, and even more ancient tent sites were found on Beach 104.

In all, the Cape Krusenstern archaeological sequence spans at least five thousand years. Not only is the archaeology enlightening, but it also provides valuable clues to interpreting the geological processes evident there. Studies of the ocean sediments indicate that the modern beach is built of gravels that slowly shift southward along the coast, moved along by persistent long-shore currents. But the beachfront of Krusenstern

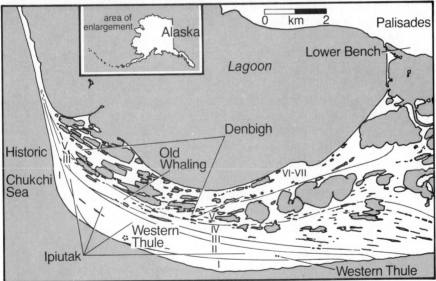

FIGURE 8–6   Aerial photograph and sketch map of beach ridges at Cape Krusenstern, Alaska. The most recent beaches are in the foreground, and the oldest beaches are back toward the lagoon. Segment numbers I to VII correspond to Beaches 1 to 104 (see Giddings 1966, Figures 3 and 4). (Courtesy the National Oceanic and Atmospheric Administration and the American Association for the Advancement of Science)

has switched direction at least six times, changing some twenty to thirty-two degrees each time (Giddings 1966, p. 131). Some geologists attribute this change to the prevailing wind's shifting directions, coupled with a slight rise in sea levels. Giddings, however, argues that because the early Denbigh Flint sites have never been washed over by water, sea levels could not have risen more than a meter or so over the past five thousand years.

This is one case, finally, in which archaeologists can begin to pay back their enormous debt to the geological profession, because archaeological sites provide the best fine-scale chronological control for geological research. The horizontal stratigraphy evident on the beach ridges of Cape Krusenstern holds promise as an ideal laboratory for future geological studies of shifting sea levels and sea currents.

The principle of horizontal stratigraphy has also been applied in the continental United States by archaeologist Chester DePratter and his geological colleague James Howard. Together, they have been using archaeological dating (primarily of ceramics) to document rates of growth and erosion on the Georgia coastline. Unlike Gidding's work at Krusenstern, the challenge here is basically geological: How did the Georgia Sea Islands originate, and to what extent are they being modified by ongoing erosion? Both deposition and erosion have formed a number of beach dunes along the margins of islands such as St. Catherines. Geologists have long wished to document how these islands change but lack a reliable method of dating the beach lines.

Here again, archaeology returns a favor to geology. Native Americans prospered on the Georgia Sea Islands for the past four thousand years, their ecological adaptation closely linked to the shallow marine habitat. Shell heaps dot the beach lines of coastal Georgia, just as Eskimo and earlier sites accumulated on the Alaskan shorelines. Ceramic styles changed rapidly during this interval, and archaeological sites can be dated with some accuracy from the potsherds contained in the shell middens. The two independent factors—(1) growing shorelines and (2) rapidly changing pottery styles—result in a fine-grained chronology that permits geologists to measure the growth of the Georgia Sea Islands.

This island chain is progressively growing seaward. When the aboriginal occupation commenced four thousand years ago, the shoreline must have been several hundred meters from the modern beaches. As on Cape Krusenstern, people adapted to the sea tend to leave archaeological sites clustered along the then-current shoreline. As younger beach ridges develop, people move. The oldest archaeological sites are, of course, found on the oldest beaches, and the more recent dunes contain the more recent archaeological sites.

To find old sites, you must look in old dirt.
—Jonathan O. Davis

The distribution of prehistoric pottery thus dates the antiquity of sand dunes. In a pilot study on Tybee Island (near Savannah, Georgia; see Figure 8–7), DePratter and Howard

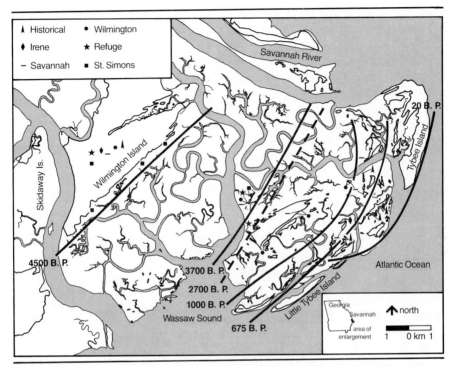

FIGURE 8–7   Distribution of archaeological sites and inferred prehistoric beach lines on Wilmington and Tybee Islands, Georgia (see DePratter and Howard 1977, Figure 2). (Courtesy Chester B. DePratter)

demonstrated that their methods work. You will remember from the Introduction to Part Three that the earliest pottery on the coast, and also in North America, is fiber-tempered St. Simons ware, a pottery type found on Tybee Island only some three miles from the modern shoreline. Because the archaeologists are certain that St. Simons pottery is more than three thousand years old, geologists can safely conclude that the shoreline was about three miles inland at 1000 B.C. St. Simons pottery cannot be found any closer to the modern shoreline because the seaward beaches had not yet formed. The next oldest kind of pottery, known as Deptford, occurs up to two miles off the present beach line, but no closer; therefore, the 500 B.C. shoreline must have been about two miles inland from the current beach. During the Wilmington–St. Catherines phases (some 850 years ago), the shoreline was about a mile inland, and the pottery of the protohistoric Irene phase is found much closer to the present beach. The geological processes still continue, of course, and future archaeologists will be able to date the late-twentieth-century shoreline from the Coke bottles and beer poptops that litter today's beaches.

This is an excellent use of the principle of horizontal stratigraphy. It is necessary, of course, to have a detailed cultural chronology, for without a radiocarbon-dated ceramic sequence the beaches could not be dated. It is also fortunate that the Georgia coastline was heavily populated in the past. Furthermore, the coast has been tectonically inactive (a good thing, as earthquakes would have disrupted the gradual development of beach dunes). Finally, because the Sea Islands are relatively undeveloped, most archaeological sites remain undisturbed and, in fact, undiscovered. Remember also that horizontal stratigraphy is fallible. One can never rule out the possible reoccupation of ancient beaches and terraces by later cultures.

These last two studies underscore the shifting relationship between archaeological and geological science. Archaeology began as a parasitic science, borrowing concepts, techniques, and methods from the "hard" sciences. But thanks to research at places like Cape Krusenstern and the Georgia Sea Islands, the borrowing has now become reciprocal. Geophysics gave birth to radiocarbon dating; archaeologists use C-14 dating to establish ceramic chronologies; geologists can now employ C-14-verified pottery types to date previously undatable geological surfaces. Archaeology still has its scientific debts to repay, but pioneer studies such as these suggest that the balance may soon be redressed.

WHERE TO GO FROM HERE?

Geoarchaeology of the Georgia and Southeastern Atlantic Coastline: Bigham 1973, DePratter and Howard (1977), Griffin and Henry (1984), Hoyt and Hails (1967), Hoyt and Henry (1971).

Summary

Archaeologists are notorious for pirating useful techniques and concepts. When dealing with stratigraphy, they have relied on two essential geological principles. The law of superposition holds that (all else being equal) older geological strata tend to be buried beneath younger strata, and the index fossil concept states that strata containing similar fossil assemblages must be of similar age. Exceptions exist, but these principles have enabled geologists around the world to correlate individual stratigraphic sections into master chronologies.

Archaeologists commonly use the law of superposition to unravel complex sequences of stratification within archaeological sites. Most of the stratigraphic record in sites, such as burial mounds, results from deliberate cultural activities; people have systematically deposited strata as cultural features. But in many habitation sites, stratigraphy results from accidental accumulation, often a complex interplay between natural and cultural deposition. The law of superposition is an organizing principle through which such diverse archaeological sites can be interpreted and correlated.

Archaeologists have modified the index fossil concept for use in archaeological contexts. Changing ceramic patterns, for example, become clues for stratigraphic interpretation and correlation. The methods of establishing and monitoring such cultural change were discussed in Chapter 7.

A final means of correlation, horizontal stratigraphy, can be applied whenever successive cultural occupations are spaced along a systematically changing landscape. Beach lines are particularly good candidates for horizontal cultural stratigraphy. Whenever a shoreline is progressively growing, archaeological sites tend to array along a spatial (and hence temporal) continuum: Older sites occur on inland beaches, and the later sites cluster along more recent (seaward) surfaces. Horizontal stratigraphy not only establishes the validity of cultural sequences but also is an independent way to determine absolute rates of beach deposit and erosion.

Chapter 9

Establishing Chronological Controls

A stitch in time would have confused Einstein.
—Anonymous

The Fourth Egyptian Dynasty lasted from 2680 to 2565 B.C. The Roman Colosseum was constructed between A.D. 70 and 82. In the seventeenth century, Dr. John Lightfoot proclaimed that God created the entire earth in 4004 B.C., at precisely 9 A.M. on October 23. Each date represents the most familiar way of expressing chronological control—the **absolute date.** Such dates are expressed as specific units of scientific measurement: days, years, centuries, or millennia, but no matter what the measure—Lightfoot computed his estimate by projecting biblical life spans—all absolute determinations attempt to pinpoint a discrete, known interval in time.

Archaeologists also measure time in a second, more imprecise manner by establishing the **relative date.** As the name implies, relative duration is monitored not through specific segments of absolute time but, rather, through relativistic relationships: earlier, later, more recent, after Noah's flood, prehistoric, and so forth. Although not as precise as absolute dating, relative estimates are sometimes the only dates available. Taken together, both forms of dating, absolute and relative, give archaeologists a way of controlling the critical dimension of time.

Archaeologists have plenty of ways to derive both absolute and relative time, but in this brief overview, we can consider only a few dating techniques. We shall ignore some important techniques—such as counting annual varves in geological deposits, dating through decoding the Maya calendar, and using many of the chemical methods such as the fluorine test, used in exposing the infamous **Piltdown hoax**—but you can get information about these by looking up the appropriate references in the various Where to Go from Here? bibliographies sprinkled throughout.

Dendrochronology

Like many of archaeology's dating techniques, **tree-ring dating (dendrochronology)** was developed by a nonarchaeologist. The first systematic dendrochronologist was A. E. Douglass, an astronomer inquiring into how sunspots affect the earth's climate. Douglass began with the knowledge that trees growing in temperate and arctic areas remain dormant during the winter and then burst into activity in the spring. In many species, especially conifers, this cycle results in the addition of well-defined concentric growth rings (Figure 9–1). Because each ring represents a single year, it is, in theory, a simple matter to determine the age of a newly felled tree: Just count the rings. Douglass took this relatively common knowledge one step further, reasoning that because tree rings vary in size, they may preserve information about the environment in which individual trees grew. Because

FIGURE 9–1 Cross section of ponderosa pine, showing record of 108-year life span. Note particularly the evidence of fire scarring: Four scars can be seen around the growth center, another is isolated by sound wood in the left center, and four others are evident at the far left. (Courtesy the American Museum of Natural History)

environmental patterning affects all the trees maturing there, these regular patterns of tree growth (that is, ring width) should fit into a long-term chronological sequence.

Douglass began his tree-ring chronology with living specimens, mostly yellow pines near Flagstaff and Prescott, Arizona. He would examine a stump (or a core from a living tree), count the rings, then overlap this sequence with a somewhat older set of rings from another tree (Figures 9–2 and 9–3). But the dead trees and surface snags went back only five hundred years or so. Beyond this point, dendrochronology had to rely on the prehistoric record. Fortunately for him, Douglass was working in the American Southwest, where arid conditions enhance preservation. By turning to archaeological ruins, Douglass began mining a vast quarry of tree-ring data. Sampling ancient beams and supports, he slowly constructed a prehistoric "floating chronology," spanning several centuries but not tied into the modern samples. Douglass could use his floating sequence to date various ruins relative to one another, but the hiatus between prehistoric and modern sequences meant that his chronology could not be correlated with the modern calendar.

Douglass was therefore forced to work with two separate sequences. The absolute sequence permitted him to date with precision those ruins later than about the fourteenth century A.D. The second, relative sequence dated archaeological sites only in relation to one another, and this older sequence was expressed in purely arbitrary numbers followed by the designation R.D. (relative date).

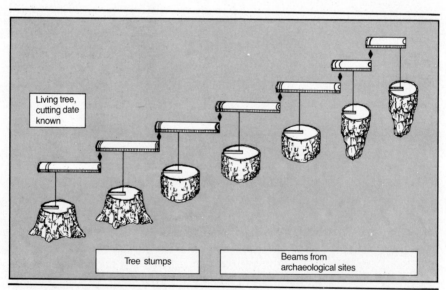

Living tree,
cutting date
known

Tree stumps

Beams from
archaeological sites

FIGURE 9–2   Schematic representation of how a tree-ring dating chronology is built, starting from a sample of known age and overlapping successively older samples until the sequence extends back into prehistoric times.

FIGURE 9–3 Robert Bettinger using an increment borer to remove a sample suitable for tree dating. The tree, incidentally, is not injured in the process. (Courtesy Robert L. Bettinger)

Gap Hunting: Where Is America's Rosetta Stone?

Thus arose "the gap," an unknown span of time separating the ancient, prehistoric sequence from the known, historically grounded chronology. At this point the National Geographic Society, the American Museum of Natural History in New York, and the Carnegie Institution of Washington joined in, launching ambitious expeditions to locate logs from the pesky undated interval. The "gap hunters," as they were known, experienced little initial success. Each sequence was occasionally extended a year or two, but the void persisted. The problem was that Pueblo peoples had built their substantial sites at Mesa Verde, Chaco Canyon, and elsewhere during the relative part of the sequence and then took off for parts unknown. The trail became clear again only in "postgap" sites, occupied after the Spanish arrived in the Southwest.

Perhaps the contemporary Hopi towns could help, as people had resided there during gap times. Striking a deal with the Hopi, the gap hunters started poking holes in the roof beams at Old Oraibi. Although stretching the historic sequence back to A.D. 1260, the gap lingered.

Finally, in 1929, the Third National Geographic Society Beam Expedition came across the ruins at Showlow, a modern village in east-central Arizona and an unappetizing place to dig, amidst a disarray of pigpens and corrals. Morale sagged; the laborers were offered a bonus of $5 to anybody finding a specimen with a hundred rings or more. At last, the excavators happened on a charred log fragment, routinely preserved in paraffin and labeled HH-39. Only later did Douglass realize that nasty little HH-39 neatly bridged the gap. It has since been termed the **Rosetta stone** of American archaeology.

All that work, and here was the answer: The last year of the relative sequence was A.D. 1284. The sequences were united, creating blinding headlines in the pages of *National Geographic*. Almost overnight, Douglass was able to tell southwestern archaeologists when their most important sites had been built: Mesa Verde was erected between A.D. 1073 and 1262, Pueblo Bonito in Chaco Canyon between A.D. 919 and 1130, the Aztec ruin between A.D. 1110 and 1121, plus dozens of others.

Ironically, when HH-39 was added to the picture, the gap hunters discovered that the former absolute and relative sequences actually overlapped by forty-nine years. Apparently a long period of drought during the thirteenth century had formed rings so minute that they had been previously overlooked. There had been no gap at all! The data had been there since the earlier expedition to the Hopi town of Oraibi, but it took a specimen like HH-39 to clarify the sequence.

Since then, the dendrochronological sequence has been extended back millennia, and many other areas are building their own sequences, including Alaska, the American Arctic, the Great Plains, Germany, Great Britain, Ireland, Turkey, Japan, and Russia.

Year-by-Year Chronology: An Archaeologist's Reverie Becomes Reality

Not only did tree-ring dating spread worldwide, but the methods also have became increasingly sophisticated. In August 1927, Douglass traveled to Betatakin, an extensive cliff dwelling in northeastern Arizona (Figure 9–4). The gap was still open at the time, but the Betatakin readings were subsequently joined to the Pueblo Bonito and Aztec sequences, helping set the stage for the dramatic fusion at Showlow. Douglass collected two dozen samples that placed the construction of Betatakin within a decade of A.D. 1270. Accuracy to this degree was stunning sixty years ago—and still is, compared with most other techniques.

But contemporary archaeology requires even more from its dating techniques. Jeffrey Dean of the University of Arizona's Laboratory of Tree-Ring Research spent two months stockpiling further samples from Betatakin in 1962. The total collection now represents 292 individual beams, and modern tree-ring technology literally documents the growth of Betatakin room by room.

Betatakin Cave was first occupied about 1250 by a small group that built a few structures that were soon destroyed. The occupation was probably transient, the cave serving as a seasonal camping spot for men traveling to plant fields at some distance from their home.

The actual village site at Betatakin was founded in 1267, when three room clusters were constructed; a fourth cluster was added in 1268. The next year, a group of maybe twenty to twenty-five people felled several trees, cut them to standardized length, and stockpiled the lumber, presumably for future immigrants to the village. Additional beams were stockpiled in 1272, but none was used until 1275, which signaled the beginning of a three-year immigration period during which more than ten room clusters and a kiva were added. Population growth at Betatakin slowed after 1277, reaching a peak of about 125 people in the mid-1280s. The village was abandoned sometime between 1286 and 1300 for unknown reasons.

Tree-ring dating obviously has tremendous potential to provide absolute dates for archaeological sites, subject to one important limitation (shared with all other dating methods): There must always be a clear-cut association between the datable specimen and the definable cultural behavior. At Betatakin, Dean was required to assume that the wood was timbered during site occupation, as using dead trees or beams from abandoned structures provides erroneously ancient dates.

Tree-ring dating can be applied to many, but not all, species of trees. The most commonly dated species is piñon pine, followed by ponderosa pine, Douglas fir, juniper, and white fir. Limber pine, bristlecone pine, and the giant sequoia have also been extensively studied. Even sagebrush is (sometimes) datable.

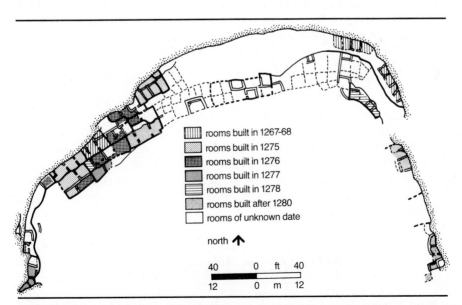

FIGURE 9–4   Floor plan of Betatakin, Arizona, and the construction sequence as inferred from tree-ring evidence (see Dean 1970, Figure 13). (Courtesy Jeffrey S. Dean and the School of American Research)

Matching unknown specimens to the regional master key has been a slow, laborious process requiring an expert with years of experience. Gradually, more automated means such as correlation graphs have been devised, and computer programs have been attempted (based on the statistical theory of errors). To date, no truly successful computer program is available because they are unable to handle the problem of false and missing rings. Today's skilled dendrochronologist can still date samples much faster than any computer.

Dendrochronology also had potential for providing climatic data. Assuming that tree-ring width is controlled by environmental factors such as temperature and soil moisture, one should be able to reconstruct past environmental conditions by examining the band widths. But tree metabolism is complex, and progress in ecological reconstruction has not provided as many answers as might be desired. Perhaps the more sophisticated means of automated tree-ring analysis will provide more satisfying results.

WHERE TO GO FROM HERE?

Some Classic Studies of Dendrochronology: Bannister (1970): "Dendrochronology," Bannister (1962): "The Interpretation of Tree-Ring Dates," Stallings (1939): *Dating Prehistoric Ruins by Tree-Rings.*

More Contemporary Discussions of Dendrochronology: Baillie (1982): *Tree-Ring Dating and Archaeology;* Bannister and Robinson (1975): "Tree-Ring Dating in Archaeology"; Dean (1978a): "Independent Dating in Archaeological Analysis"; Fritts (1976): *Tree Rings and Climate;* Stahle and Wolfman (1985):"The Potential for Archaeological Tree-Ring Dating in Eastern North America"; Ward (1987): *Applications of Tree-ring Studies.*

What Was It Like to Hunt the Gap?: Douglass (1929): "The Secret of the Southwest Solved by Talkative Tree Rings"; Haury (1962): "HH-39: Recollections of a Dramatic Moment in Southwestern Archaeology"; Morris (1933): *Digging in the Southwest.*

Tree-Ring Bulletin publishes original research on applications, new techniques for data acquisition or analysis, and regional or subject-oriented reviews and syntheses dealing with tree-ring growth and the application of tree-ring studies to problems in archaeology, geology, ecology, hydrology and climatology; first published in 1966.

Subscription information: Laboratory of Tree-Ring Research, University of Arizona, Tucson, Ariz. 85721.

Obsidian Hydration

Obsidian—volcanic glass—has been fashioned into stone tools for millennia. As anyone who has ever fractured an obsidian nodule is well aware, these razor-sharp flakes can be chipped into a host of handy artifacts: knives, scrapers, drills, projectile points, and so forth. Obsidian artifacts are found in archaeological sites on every continent except

Australia and one day may rival ceramics as archaeology's most useful artifact for controlling time.

Two geologists working for the U.S. Geological Survey, Irving Friedman and Robert Smith, first started looking into the potential of obsidian as a time-marker in 1948. Friedman and Smith knew that obsidian is a fairly "dry" rock, containing only about 0.2 percent water. But when a piece of obsidian is fractured and the fresh surface is exposed to the environment, water is absorbed into the new surface. The absorption, or *hydration*, process continues until the obsidian reaches approximately 3.5 percent water, the saturation point. These zones, or rims, of hydration are denser than is the unhydrated inside, and the hydrated zone has different optical properties. Whenever obsidian is broken, the hydration process begins from scratch on the fresh surface. This much is simple geophysics, but Friedman and Smith propelled this knowledge into archaeological relevance by reasoning that the degree of hydration observed on an archaeological artifact could measure how long it has been since that surface was created by the flintknapper.

How Wet Can a Rock Be?

The principle behind **obsidian hydration dating** is as clever as it is austere: The longer the artifact surface has been exposed, the thicker the hydration band will be. By making certain that the datable surfaces were only those exposed by deliberate flintknapping, obsidian hydration can be taken as a direct indicator of age.

To measure how much hydration is present, the artifact must be cut and a thin section prepared. First, a wedge is removed from the edge of the artifact by making intersecting cuts with a diamond-impregnated saw. This section is then ground thin on a lapidary machine and affixed to a microscopic slide with Canada balsam. The obsidian wedge is ground once again, this time to less than fifty microns thick. The slide is finally ready for microscopic analysis, using a polarizing light source. Figure 9–5 shows what the prepared archaeological specimen looks like under the microscope.

Obsidian hydration dating is simple, rapid, and cheap: Ten obsidian hydration dates may be run for the cost of a single radiocarbon determination. Students can be readily trained to prepare obsidian hydration samples, and several laboratories are currently in operation for such dating. But obsidian dating is hardly without difficulty. After examining about six hundred specimens, Friedman and Smith discovered that the rate of hydration is not uniform throughout the world. Of the several variables that seem to influence the hydration rate, atmospheric temperature seemed to be paramount. Once a sufficient number of global samples were analyzed, they constructed a world map describing the correlation between climate and hydration rates.

The origin (and hence chemical composition) of obsidian samples is another major factor in determining hydration rate. Donovan Clark, then a graduate student at Stanford University, analyzed hundreds of obsidian artifacts from five prehistoric California sites and compared the hydration rims with known radiocarbon determinations of the sites. Clark found that central California obsidian hydrates at slightly more than one micron per thousand years. Thus, by comparison with radiocarbon dating, Clark suggested a means of converting obsidian hydration from a relative to an absolute dating technique.

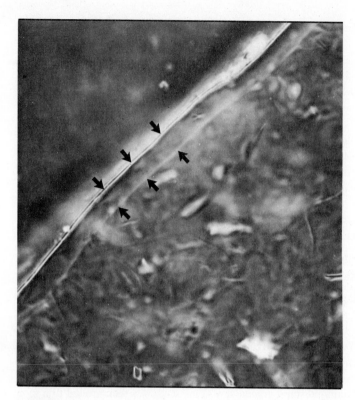

FIGURE 9–5 Photomicrograph of obsidian hydration band, taken at 490X. The specimen is a geological sample from Mono County, California. The band, denoted by arrows, is 4.2 microns thick. (Courtesy Frank J. Findlow)

Absolutes from Relatives?

A study by Findlow and others (1975) illustrates how the obsidian hydration technique is used to date specific flows. The Government Mountain–Sitgreaves Peak obsidian flow is the most heavily exploited in the American Southwest. Obsidian from this area ranges from gray to shiny black in color, and the matrix is free of inclusions. Its excellent fracturing qualities probably account for its wide distribution by trade throughout Arizona and southern Utah.

Obsidian from the Government Mountain–Sitgreaves source was recovered in ten archaeological sites, ranging in age from about 1500 B.C. to historic times. After the samples were prepared for microscopic analysis and the hydration bands were read, the results were synthesized into the following rate of hydration:

$$Y = 43.58 + 158.16 \ (x^2 - x)$$

where Y is the date (in years B.P.) and x is the hydration value in microns.

A few examples will illustrate how this hydration equation is used to date archaeological sites. Awatovi (Arizona) is a large Hopi city abandoned in A.D. 1630 (Brew 1941).

Findlow and his associates dated ten Government Mountain obsidian artifacts recovered from the latest occupation at Awatovi. The hydration rims averaged 1.8 microns thick, leading to an estimated age of

$$Y = 43.58 + 158.16 \ (1.8^2 - 1.8) = 271 \text{ years B.P.}$$

Age converts to a calendar date of about A.D. 1680, in fairly close agreement with the historically dated abandonment of Awatovi.

Findlow and his research group used this same procedure to date Stratum 3 at site CS-184, also in Arizona. The average rim thickness was 5.2 microns, which converts to an absolute age of 3498 years B.P. In this case the obsidian hydration value agrees closely with the date estimated by the radiocarbon method.

The future of obsidian hydration dating remains somewhat clouded because of lingering problems such as artifact reuse, short-term temperature fluctuations, and variable amounts of available moisture.

Michels and Bebrich (1971) have also demonstrated that obsidians of different composition can hydrate at different rates. In studying obsidians from the central Mexican highlands, Michels found that green rhyolitic obsidian hydrated almost three times as fast as did the gray rhyolitic obsidian. That is, even under uniform temperature conditions, the green obsidian hydrates at a rate of 11.45 millimicrons^2 per millennium, whereas the gray obsidian hydrates at a rate of only 4.5 millimicrons^2 per thousand years. Fortunately, this differing composition was obvious by superficial inspection, but the problem of differing rates is compounded when seemingly identical obsidians are of different composition. A number of investigators are currently working on the physiochemical separation of various obsidian sources.

As long as the restrictions are kept in mind, obsidian hydration does provide a useful technique for dating archaeological sites. Michels (1973) considers a number of such potential uses, including testing archaeological stratigraphy, testing for artifact reuse, and defining assemblages in the absence of reliable stratigraphy. There are certainly limitations on obsidian hydration dating, but even the best dating technique cannot be used without some restrictions and caution.

WHERE TO GO FROM HERE?

Some Early Statements About Obsidian Hydration Dating in Archaeology: Clark (1964): "Archaeological Chronology in California and the Obsidian Hydration Method: Part I"; Friedman and Smith (1960): "A New Dating Method Using Obsidian, Part I: The Development of the Method."

More Recent Sources on Obsidian Hydration Dating: Friedman and Trembour (1978) discuss obsidian as "the dating stone," providing an excellent, if somewhat dated introduction to hydration studies; Michels and Tsong (1980) likewise review progress, describing a "coming of age"; see also Ambrose (1976), Ericson (1975), Meighan (1976), Michels (1973, Chapter 13). Related technology now also permits dating manufactured glass (Lanford 1977).

Specific Applications of Obsidian Hydration Dating in Archaeology: Hawaii: Berrera and Kirch (1973), Ecuador: Bell (1977), Arizona (Findlow et al. 1975), Nevada (Layton 1973), California (Johnson 1969, Ericson 1975), Oregon (Johnson 1969), Mexico (Meighan, Foote, and Aiello 1968).

Radiocarbon Dating

In 1949, a physical chemist named **Willard F. Libby** announced to the world that he had discovered a revolutionary new radiocarbon (C-14) dating technique (Figure 9–6). The world apparently agreed and handed Libby the Nobel Prize in chemistry for his breakthrough. The earliest radiocarbon dates worked on organic materials younger than about 30,000 years. But more recently, technical refinements have extended the effective range of the C-14 method to over 75,000 years.

FIGURE 9–6 Willard Libby with the extraction apparatus in the Radiocarbon Laboratory at University of California, Los Angeles. (Courtesy Rainer Berger and the University of California, Los Angeles)

How Many Kinds of Carbon Do You Know?

Like many great thoughts, the basic principle behind radiocarbon dating is deceptively straightforward. Cosmic radiation produces neutrons, which enter the earth's atmosphere and react with nitrogen to produce the "heavy" carbon isotope carbon-14.

$$N^{14} + neutron = C^{14} + H$$

Carbon-14 is "heavy" because its nucleus contains fourteen neutrons, rather than the more common load of twelve. The extra neutrons make the nucleus unstable and subject to gradual (radioactive) decay. Libby calculated that after 5568 years, half of the C-14 available in a sample will have decayed; this is termed the **half-life** of C-14. Whenever a neutron leaves a C-14 nucleus, a radioactive (beta) particle is emitted, and the amount of radioactivity remaining can be measured by counting the number of beta emissions per gram of carbon.

$$C^{14} = B\text{-} + N^{14}+$$

These fundamentals established, Libby proceeded to convert the fact of radiocarbon decay into a chronometric tool. Once again, back to basics: Plants and animals are known to ingest atmospheric carbon in the form of CO_2 (carbon dioxide) throughout their lives. When an organism dies, no more carbon enters its system, and that which is already present starts its radioactive decay. By measuring the beta emissions from the dead organism, you can compute roughly how long ago that organism died.

Radiocarbon decay is, strictly speaking, a random process, as nobody can ever predict exactly which C-14 molecule will decay. It is an actuarial matter, like a life insurance table (nobody knows who will die this year, but it's a dead certainty that a certain number will).

What the Radiocarbon Laboratory Tells You

Forty-seven radiocarbon determinations were processed on charcoal from Gatecliff Shelter, and these samples illustrate how contemporary archaeologists actually use the radiocarbon method. The procedure is fairly simple: Collect appropriate samples in the field, correlate them with the known stratigraphy, and submit selected samples to a commercial radiocarbon laboratory. Radiocarbon dating is not cheap; current rates run about $200 to $250 per sample. Once you come up with the bucks, all that's left is to wait for the results in the mail.

The radiocarbon lab reports a date like this:

UCLA-1926A 5200 ±120 radiocarbon years B.P.

This is an actual date, from charcoal found in Hearth A on Horizon 12 at Gatecliff Shelter (Thomas 1983b, Table 2). The first designation records the laboratory and sample number: the University of California (Los Angeles) Radiocarbon Laboratory sample number 1926A. The second part—5200—estimates the age of the sample in radiocarbon years B.P., the latter an abbreviation for "before present," arbitrarily defined as the year 1950. Keep in mind that the sample was measured in radiocarbon years, not calendar years. As we will see, radiocarbon dating has certain biases, and the laboratory date must be "corrected" to reflect actual calendar years. Thus far, the radiocarbon lab at UCLA has told me that a tree died 5200 radiocarbon years before 1950 and that charcoal from that tree was deposited on Horizon 2 at Gatecliff Shelter.

How to Handle the Uncertainty

So far, so good. But remember that the lab report attaches a "±120" to the age estimate. The standard deviation estimates the consistency (or lack of it) between the various "counting runs" performed at the laboratory. This statistical appendage, read as "plus or minus," is the standard deviation (or "sigma"), a projection of the error in the estimate. Because of their random, statistical nature, radiocarbon dates cannot be precise. Some samples, like this one, generate relatively minor inaccuracy (only 120 years, more or less). But sometimes C-14 determinations involve larger errors—up to several hundred years—and the plus-minus factor warns the archaeologist about this unusually high degree of uncertainty.

The standard deviation expresses the range within which the true date probably falls. In UCLA-1926A, the number "5200 radiocarbon years" estimates the actual age of the sample (which, of course, remains unknown); the standard deviation estimates the range of error. We know from statistical theory that there is a two-in-three (67 percent) chance that the true date falls within one "sigma." Specifically, by both adding and subtracting 120 from the age estimate, we will find the probability to be 67 percent that the true age of UCLA-1926A falls between 5080 (*minus* 120) and 5320 (*plus* 120) radiocarbon years B.P.

Because random probabilities are involved, we can never be absolutely certain that the true age falls into this interval, but the chances are good (two in three) that it does. If you want to be more certain, try doubling the standard deviation. In this case, there is a 95 percent chance that the actual date falls within ±2 sigmas; if you want to know why this is so, take a look at my statistics book (Thomas 1976, Chapter 10). The chances are 95 in 100 that the true age of UCLA-1926A falls within two sigma = 2(120) = ±240 years—that is, between 4960 and 5440 radiocarbon years B.P.

The standard deviation must never be omitted from the radiocarbon date, because without it one would have no idea how accurately the sample was actually measured. Statistical theory provides simple methods to test whether two radiocarbon determinations are the same or different.

How to Submit a Radiocarbon Sample

Despite the cautions about controls, corrections, and assumptions, radiocarbon laboratories can date only the sample submitted. The onus remains on the archaeologist to provide relevant and uncontaminated samples. Extreme care must be taken to date only undisturbed areas of sites. There is also the problem of humic acid, which, once formed in the soil, can contaminate all of the datable organics in that site. But on the other hand, sometimes the humic acid itself can provide useful dates. The nature of the materials submitted for dating is likewise important: Wood charcoal seems the best, followed by well-preserved wood, paper, parchment, and so forth (see Table 9–1).

Particular care must also be taken to prevent contamination of samples after extraction from the site. Samples are generally placed immediately in aluminum foil or adequately labeled sterile jars. Many archaeologists (myself included) prohibit smoking on or near an excavation, lest a future C-14 sample become contaminated. These procedures help guarantee accurate laboratory assay, but the responsibility is always the excavator's to submit only significant samples and to interpret the results in light of other clues of dating.

Tree Rings Incite the Second Radiocarbon Revolution

Radiocarbon dating relies on a number of key assumptions, perhaps the most important being that the radiocarbon level—that is, the ratio between carbon-12 and carbon-14—has remained constant in the earth's atmosphere. Libby assumed this when developing the method, but we now know that this assumption is not valid. That is, levels of atmospheric carbon-14 have shifted somewhat over the past millennia. The first investigator to find fault with the atmospheric assumption was H. De Vries of The Netherlands (De Vries 1958). De Vries cut several beams from historic buildings and determined the exact age of the wood by counting tree rings. When he later dated the known-age specimens by

TABLE 9–1—Sample Size Desired for Common Archaeological Materials

Material	Weight Desired (gm)*	Minimum Weight
Charcoal	8–12	1
Wood	10–30	3
Shell (carbonate date)	30–100	5
Shell (conchiolin date)	500–2500	200
Bone (carbonate date)	100–500	50
Bone (collagen date, less than 5000 years old)	200–500	100
Bone (collagen date, more than 5000 years old)	400–1000	250
Iron (cast iron)	100–150	30
Iron (steel)		150
Iron (wrought iron)	1000–2500	500
Peat	10–25	3

*These refer to dry samples that possess average carbon contents.
Source: Michels 1973.

radiocarbon assay, he found the C-14 contrast to be 2 percent higher than expected for the known-age wood. Scientists at the time generally dismissed the work, as the errors De Vries discovered were relatively small, just barely outside the limits of expected error.

But the specter of error finally inspired radiocarbon specialists to look more closely into the problem. This joint investigation was conducted by laboratories in Copenhagen, Heidelberg, Cambridge, New Haven, Philadelphia, Tucson, and La Jolla. In one landmark study, Hans Suess of the University of California at San Diego (La Jolla) analyzed wood from the bristlecone pine tree. Native to the western United States, bristlecones are the world's oldest living organisms, some living up to 4600 years. Working from live trees to ancient stumps, investigators had already extended the bristlecone tree-ring sequence back nearly 8200 years (by the technique we just discussed). Suess radiocarbon-dated dozens of known-age samples and compared the results obtained by each method. It was clear that there were significant fluctuations in the atmospheric C-14 concentrations. The assumption of C-14 stability was false, rendering the hundreds of previous radiocarbon determinations in error. Although dates younger than about 1500 B.C. were not too far off, comparison with the tree-ring data showed that more ancient radiocarbon dates could be up to 700 years too young.

The fluctuations in carbon-14 appear to be worldwide because the earth's atmosphere is so well mixed. Once a gas is released into the atmosphere, it becomes evenly distributed throughout the entire global surface within a few years. Hence the discrepancy between tree-ring and radiocarbon ages, first noted by De Vries, must be independent of geographic origin.

When radiocarbon dating was first introduced, Egyptologists told Libby that his dates did not square with the historically derived dynastic chronology. Libby attributed this disparity to experimental error, but now that we know that the effect is due to differential production of atmospheric C-14, it is possible to "correct" for these errors. A series of international conferences have been held on the problem, and several correction tables have appeared in recent years. Ironically, the profusion of such calibration tables—and the fact that they become obsolete so quickly—has made some archaeologists (myself included) reticent to correct their radiocarbon dates. I did just this when publishing the forty-seven radiocarbon dates from Gatecliff Shelter (Thomas 1983b)—working instead in the awkward "radiocarbon years, B.P."—holding off the corrections until the specialists could finally agree among themselves.

Such agreement has now been reached (we hope). The Twelfth International Radiocarbon Conference (June 1985) was held in Trondheim, Norway, and the most recent "state-of-the-art" radiocarbon age calibrations appeared in a special issue of *Radiocarbon* (Stuiver and Kra 1986). At the risk of having to recompute down the road, most archaeologists accept the Twelfth International Radiocarbon Conference (Trondheim) results and use these tree-ring correction factors in their research (see inset).

Most regional sequences are unaffected by the correction factors. As long as all dating is by radiocarbon, the various subareas will remain in identical relationships, the only change being in the absolute dating. American cultural sequences, for example, remain intact, although all appear slightly older in absolute time. The Old World, however, is less fortunate because of disparities in dating techniques. In areas where writing was invented quite early, historic records provide firm chronology, extending some five-thousand years in length. Radiocarbon dates for the Fertile Crescent and Egypt were corrected and supplemented by independent historical records. Western European chronologies, however, lacking historical evidence, were arranged strictly according to radiocarbon determinations. Over the years, Old World data have been almost universally interpreted as indicating that the early traits of civilization, such as metallurgy and monumental funerary architecture, were originally developed in the Near East, only later diffusing into the "culturally retarded" European area. The peoples of the Near East were considered the inventors and the barbaric Europeans the recipients.

The bristlecone correction changed much of that. Colin Renfrew (1971, 1973) compared the process to a "temporal fault line." Most European chronologies are now placed several centuries earlier, but the classical Greek and Near Eastern chronologies remain unchanged. Stonehenge, formerly considered to be the work of Greek craftsmen who traveled to the British Isles in 1500 B.C., clearly predates even the Mycenaean civilization; Renfrew (1973, p. 16) now refers to Stonehenge as the world's oldest astronomical observatory. These "corrected" radiocarbon dates suggest that Europe can no longer be viewed as a passive recipient of cultural advances from the Mediterranean heartland. Monumental temples were built on Malta before the pyramids of Egypt. The elaborate British megalithic tombs now appear to date a full millennium before those in the eastern Mediterranean. It is no longer possible to believe that agriculture and metallurgy moved from Asia into Europe, and recent finds in Rumania may prove to be the earliest evidence for writing (Evans 1977). Although diffusion of cultural traits remains an important process, the recalibration in some cases reverses the direction of the arrow. In other instances the whole concept of a "cradle of civilization" seems irrelevant. As Evans put it, "If it is not yet time to write new textbooks on prehistory . . . it is time to discard the old ones" (1977, p. 84). This prophecy has certainly proved true. The impact of the second radiocarbon revolution is clearly evident in recent discussions of European prehistory (e.g., Champion et al. 1984, Renfrew 1979).

Accelerator Dating: The Third Radiocarbon Revolution

Radiocarbon dating is now in the throes of a third revolution. But unlike the second one—which caused some archaeologists to write off the technique entirely—this upheaval has no downside.

Archaeology has a tendency to be viewed as weird science by some because it progresses through unique and unrepeatable experiments (Wendorf 1987). This dismal assessment is partially true. Digging remains our primary "experimental" method, and every excavation destroys the stratigraphic association of archaeological objects. For rare or unique finds, it is simply impossible to confirm the discovery by repeating. Maybe this is why archaeologists are always feuding with one another.

How to Use Tree-Ring Corrections on Your Radiocarbon Dates

Let us explore the correction factors for two radiocarbon dates processed on charcoal recovered from Horizon 4 at Gatecliff Shelter (Thomas 1983b, Table 2):

Example A: (GAK-3611)   1730 ±90 radiocarbon years B.P.

Example B: (GAK-3612)   2020 ±90 radiocarbon years B.P.

In this case, the initial letters tell us that the samples were processed at the Gakushuin Laboratory (Japan).

The Trondheim Proceedings actually provide three different ways to apply the same series of conversions. Because each method illustrates an important principle regarding tree-ring corrections in radiocarbon analysis, I shall work through an example, using the various techniques.

The Graphic Method

The tree-ring calibration curve on Figure 9–7 consists of three curves. The center line is the actual calibration curve, the two outer lines indicating the one-sigma (one standard deviation) uncertainty associated with the radiocarbon estimate.

The conversion from raw radiocarbon years to calendar years is not difficult (see Stuiver and Pearson 1986, p. 808). To find the *central tendency,*

1.   Draw a horizontal line through the radiocarbon age to be converted.
2.   Draw a vertical line through the intercept of

the first line and the calibration curve (the center line).
3.   The tree-ring–corrected calendrical age (expressed in years A.D./B.C.) is read on the bottom axis, and the corrected age B.P. appears at the top.

For Example B from Gatecliff, the raw date of 2020 B.P. corresponds to a corrected calendrical date of about 35 B.C. (read at the bottom of the graph) or about 1985 B.P. (at the top). It's as simple as that.

Example A is a bit more complex because it crosses the tree-ring curve not just once but three times: at A.D. 255, A.D. 280, and A.D. 315. This blip is caused by atmospheric fluctuations in C-14, and so we cannot tell which age is reflected by the raw laboratory result. Accordingly, we must consider all three.

Although tree-ring dating provides absolute results, the derivation of these correction factors involves random errors, and one must also correct the ± factor at the end of the date. This correction could also be done using the graphic method (see Stuiver and Pearson 1986, p. 808), but there are much easier ways to do this.

The Tabular Method

Exactly the same data for Figure 9–7 are incorporated into a series of tables, also published in the Trondheim Proceedings (from Stuiver and Pearson 1986, Table 3–Y). By working through such tables (one is computed for each two-decade interval), it is possible

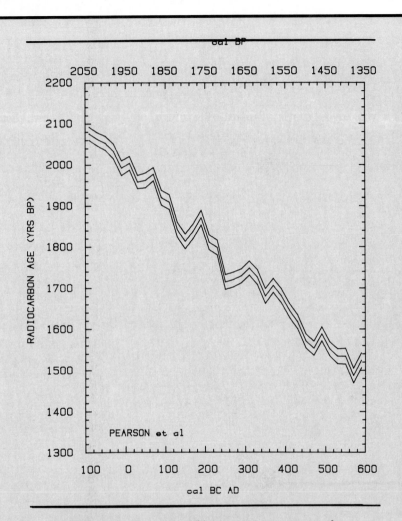

FIGURE 9–7 Tree-ring calibration curve covering the period 100 B.C. to A.D. 600 (see Stuiver and Pearson 1986, Figure 1D). (Reprinted by permission of Minze Stuiver and *Radiocarbon*)

to find the proper, tree-ring–corrected calendrical equivalents, with the error factors already recomputed (see Table 9–2).

In Example B, the radiocarbon age of 2020 B.P. corresponds to a calibrated calendar age of 35 B.C.; the corrected age estimate is 1985 B.P. Note that using the tabular data allows a more precise correction than does fitting the curves to the graph.

The uncorrected date had a ±90 ap-

TABLE 9–2
```
RADIOCARBON AGE BP 1980    CALIBRATED#AGE:    cal AD    15
                                             cal BP 1935

Sample 0 and cal AD(cal BP) ranges:
0 =   20    cal BC 3-cal AD 53(1952-1897)
0 =   40    cal BC 37-cal AD 67(1986-1883)
0 =   60    cal BC 56-cal AD 78(2005-1872)
0 =   80    cal BC 97-cal AD 88(2046-1862)
0 =  100    cal BC 110-cal AD 120(2060-1830)
0 =  120    cal BC 151-149(2100-2098)  cal BC 120-cal AD 130(2070-1820)
0 =  160    cal BC 190-cal AD 210(2140-1740)
0 =  200    cal BC 340-322(2289-2271)  cal BC 200-cal AD 240(2150-1710)
                        -------0-------
RADIOCARBON AGE BP 2000    CALIBRATED AGE:    cal BC    1
                                             cal BP 1950

Sample 0 and cal BC(cal BP) ranges:
0 =##20    cal BC 37-cal AD 16(1986-1934)
0 =   40    cal BC 58-cal AD 28(2007-1922)    cal AD 40-52(1910-1898)
0 =   60    cal BC 97-cal AD 66(2046-1884)
0 =   80    cal BC 105-cal AD 78(2054-1872)
0 =  100    151-149(2100-2098)    cal BC 120-cal AD 90(2070-1860)
0 =  120    cal BC 170-cal AD 120(2120-1830)
0 =  160    cal BC 200-cal AD 140(2150-1810)
0 =  200    353-306(2302-2255)    cal BC 240-cal AD 230(2190-1720)
                        -------0-------
RADIOCARBON AGE BP 2020    CALIBRATED AGE:    cal BC    36
                                             cal BP 1985

Sample 0 and cal BC(cal BP) ranges:
0 =   20    cal BC 65-cal AD 1(2014-1949)
0 =   40    cal BC 97-cal AD 16(2046-1934)
0 =   60    cal BC 105-cal AD 28(2054-1922)    cal AD 42-52(1908-1898)
0 =   80    151-149(2100-2098)    cal BC 117-cal AD 66(2066-1884)
0 =  100    cal BC 170-cal AD 80(2120-1870)
0 =  120    cal BC 190-cal AD 90(2140-1860)
0 =  160    340-322(2289-2271)    cal BC 200-cal AD 130(2150-1820)
0 =  200    362-282(2311-2231)    cal BC 260-cal AD 210(2210-1740)
                        -------0-------
RADIOCARBON AGE BP 2040    CALIBRATED AGE:    cal BC    50
                                             cal BP 1999

Sample 0 and cal BC(cal BP) ranges:
0 =   20    97-34(2046-1983)
0 =   40    cal BC 106-cal AD 1(2055-1949)
0 =   60    151-148(2100-2097)    cal BC 117-cal AD 16(2066-1934)
0 =   80    cal BC 169-cal AD 28(2118-1922)  cal AD 42-51(1908-1899)
0 =  100    cal BC 190-cal AD 70(2140-1880)
0 =  120    cal BC 200-cal AD 80(2150-1870)
0 =  160    353-306(2302-2255)    cal BC 240-cal AD 120(2190-1830)
0 =  200    cal BC 370-cal AD 140(2320-1810)
```

After Stuiver and Pearson, 1986, Table 3–Y. Reprinted courtesy of the author and *Radiocarbon*.

pended to it, and this tabular approach also helps us compute the new error estimate. Table 9–2 is computed in two-decade increments, and so we must round the error up from ±90 to ±100 years (just to be on the safe side). The appropriate error entry is listed as "cal BC 170-cal AD 80(2120–1870)." Reading through the computerese, we find that for a ± factor of one hundred years (one sigma each way), there is a two-thirds probability that the true calendrical age of date GAK-3612 lies between A.D. 80 and 170 B.C.. The most probable age remains 36 B.C. In tree-ring–corrected years B.P., the new error factor is expressed as the range 2120 to 1870. Note that after this conversion, the range of error is no longer symmetrical about the mean.

The Desktop Computer Method

The same conversion can be effected a third way, by applying new computer software, easily installed on IBM-compatible computers (instructions for obtaining this program appear in Where To Go From Here?). Figure 9–8 shows the computer printout for GAK-3611. Note

that such computer processing allows more precise computations than does the curve fitting and also avoids the problem of interpolating between fixed intervals (as we had to do with the ±90 error factor).

The Stuiver–Reimer computer program also allows investigators to average radiocarbon dates across several samples. Remember that the raw determinations for Examples A and B differed by only 290 radiocarbon years. Should—for whatever reason—we wish to collapse these two determinations, it is a simple matter to pool the counting runs. The new, uncorrected composite date is 1875 ±63.6 radiocarbon years B.P. (and the appropriate tree-ring–corrected dates are also appended). By pooling these two dates, the error rate decreases from ±90 to ±63.6 radiocarbon years (reflecting the increased number of counting runs on a "single" sample). Note that such pooling removed the problem of multiple crossings.

Regardless of which method is used, the tree-ring correction factors tell us that the raw dates from Gatecliff Shelter were too old and allow more accurate comparison with absolute calendar age.

Continued p. 302

The "third revolution" in radiocarbon dating puts archaeology on firmer scientific ground. The recent development of the **accelerator mass spectrometric (AMS) technique** for radiocarbon dating drastically reduces the quantity of datable material required. When a Geiger counter is used to monitor the beta-ray emissions, several grams of organics are required (see Table 9–1). But because the new accelerator technology counts the proportion of carbon isotopes directly, the sample size needed is only a few milligrams.

Armed with the new technology of radiocarbon dating, archaeologists have already begun to "redo the experiment." In some cases, this research has fundamentally changed our perception of the human past. As a direct result of AMS determinations, archaeologists must now abandon several models once thought to explain the early domestication of

Continued from p. 301

```
                        UNIVERSITY OF WASHINGTON

                        QUATERNARY ISOTOPE LAB

                  RADIOCARBON CALIBRATION PROGRAM 1987

                              REV. 2.0


   Calibration file(s): ATM20.14C

   Listing file: C14FIL.TXT

   Plot file: C14FIL.PLT



   GAK-3611

    Radiocarbon Age BP  1730.0   90.0                      Reference(s)

     Calibrated age(s) cal AD   261,  288,  327       (Stuiver and Pearson)

               cal BP  1689, 1662, 1623

    cal AD/BC (cal BP) age ranges obtained from intercepts (Method A):

     one Sigma**    cal AD  213- 412(1737-1538)

     two Sigma**    cal AD   80- 540(1870-1410)



     Summary of above ---

     minimum of cal age ranges (cal ages) maximum of cal age ranges:

        one sigma    cal AD  213 (  261,  288,  327)  412

                     cal BP 1737 ( 1689, 1662, 1623) 1538

        two sigma    cal AD   80 (  261,  288,  327)  540

                     cal BP 1870 ( 1689, 1662, 1623) 1410
```

FIGURE 9–8   Sample desktop computer output for the tree-ring conversion of radiocarbon determination GAK–3611 from Gatecliff Shelter. (Computer printout based on program from Stuiver and Reimer, 1986, courtesy *Radiocarbon* and Minze Stuiver)

plants (see Chapter 15). AMS radiocarbon dating allows investigators to date the individual amino acid fractions extracted from partially fossilized bones and has already been used to date the earliest skeletal materials in the New World. For years, George F. Carter has argued from geomorphological evidence that humans have been in the New World for at least 50,000 years. His views sharply contradict the conventional wisdom, which holds that humans crossed the Bering Straits no more than about 25,000 years ago. Carter was particularly vocal about some human skeletal remains found near San Diego, California. He identified five bones that he thought were especially ancient, and Jeffrey Bada (Scripps Institute of Oceanography) processed them using a problematical dating technique based on amino acid, with the following results: 26,000 years; 6000 years; 28,000 years; 44,000 years; and 48,000 years. These dates strongly supported Carter's assertions of humans' long inhabitation in the New World. If accurate, Bada's amino acid determinations would become the oldest direct dates available for New World hominids. These dates at least double the time conventionally assigned to humans in the New World.

However, many archaeologists were skeptical, not only about the extreme age, but also about the accuracy of the amino acid technique. These dates have caused great consternation. Until very recently, the skeletons in question could not be directly dated by radiocarbon because too much bone would be destroyed in the process. But direct AMS radiocarbon dating has conclusively demonstrated that these skeletons are considerably later. Many range between three thousand to five thousand years in age, and the oldest is no more ancient than eleven thousand years old. The technique of amino acid dating has been resoundingly rebuked.

The following is another concrete example of how the dating revolution affects everyday archaeology. In 1924, M. R. Harrington and L. L. Loud excavated a cache of a dozen extraordinary duck decoys, long ago buried in the dusty depths of Lovelock Cave (Nevada) (Figure 9–9). Although they almost certainly were manufactured in prehistoric times, the desert aridity had preserved these singular artifacts in near-mint condition. Cleverly crafted from tule reeds twisted to simulate the body and head of the duck, some had plain tule bodies and others were adorned with paint and feathers. As artifacts, the decoys are striking. Even *Sports Illustrated* extolled the creativity and craftsmanship of these prehistoric duck hunters.

But nobody knew how old the decoys were. The excavators assigned the artifacts to an ill-defined "Late Period," and the over next five decades, various archaeologists studied the unique decoys and guess-dated their age. Although estimates ranged from 500 B.C. to the historic period, conventional wisdom among Great Basin archaeologists held the decoys to be about two thousand years old.

The Lovelock Cave originals were curated at the Museum of the American Indian (Heye Foundation) in New York City. In 1969, L. Kyle Napton (California State University, Stanislaus) and Robert F. Heizer (University of California) secured a large-enough chunk from one of the decoys to submit for conventional radiocarbon dating. Incredibly, the irreplaceable sample was lost by the radiocarbon laboratory (giving a new meaning to the term *laboratory error*). Although Napton tried to obtain additional

**FIGURE 9–9   Cache of duck decoys from Lovelock Cave, Nevada.
(Courtesy Museum of the American Indian–Heye Foundation, N.Y.; photograph
by M. R. Harrington; photo no. 9452)**

samples, he realized that samples adequate for conventional radiocarbon dating would unacceptably damage the unique artifacts.

Then came radiocarbon's "third revolution" to the rescue. Knowing that extremely small samples could be dated, Don Fowler (University of Nevada) obtained permission to remove such samples from the Lovelock decoys. Under watchful curatorial eyes, he gingerly snipped off tule tidbits from inside two decoys. The priceless clippings, each the size of your little fingernail, were hand-carried to the West Coast and submitted for processing by the new University of Arizona accelerator mass spectrometer (AMS) facility.

So far, so good. But AMS dating is still rather expensive, and a conspicuous lack of funds remained an obstacle. Fowler secured a grant from the Nevada State Historic Preservation Office, and Napton personally kicked in some more. But still the coffers were only half-full. Not one to give up easily, Fowler cooked up a scheme for his colleagues to ante up the rest: This was, after all, Nevada. Plenty of Great Basin archaeologists (myself included) were interested in the true age of the Lovelock decoys. So Don Fowler started a lottery: Guess the accelerator date and win a valuable prize. The Churchill County Museum donated the prize, a modern tule duck decoy manufactured by Daven George, a Northern Paiute Indian living not far from Lovelock Cave. At $10 per guess, enough money was finally raised to pay the radiocarbon laboratory.

Guesses ranged wildly. Some took a scholarly approach, scrutinizing the ecological implications of duck decoy technology and then placing these events in Holocene Great Basin prehistory. Others used a table of random numbers. One archaeologist gave up on scholarship: He averaged the twenty-three previously available radiocarbon dates from Lovelock Cave and guessed this mean date. One wag even submitted October 23, 4004 B.C.—the vice-chancellor Lightfoot's infamous 1642 computation for the beginning of the earth (see Chapter 1).

Fowler received the laboratory results in September 1984 (Tuohy and Napton 1986). The two statistically consistent AMS radiocarbon dates came out to be 2080 ±330 and 2250 ±230 radiocarbon years B.P. (Tuohy and Napton 1986, p. 814). Taking into account the plus-minus factor, the dates overwhelmingly confirmed the previous conventional archaeological wisdom: The Lovelock decoys are about two-thousand years old. Curiously, not one archaeologist in the lottery trusted this conventional wisdom; as it turned out, the closest guess was nearly eight hundred years off. And the winner was Mr. Brian Hatoff, now an archaeologist with the Bureau of Land Management and also that webfooted student mentioned in the Prologue who dug the initial test pits at Gatecliff Shelter.

You can readily see the potential for AMS dating. In effect, radiocarbon dating has evolved from a relatively destructive technique to a relatively noninvasive one. As in the Lovelock Cave case, archaeologists are busy devising new applications. Accelerator technology is a product of the 1980s, and since the first such dates became available, this new technology has had a dramatic impact. Antiquarians and musicians, for instance, are turning to AMS technology to detect fakes: Is this really a Stradivarius violin?

The newest radiocarbon revolution recently grabbed headlines around the world when AMS dating was applied to the **Shroud of Turin**, thought by many to be the actual cloth in which Christ's crucified body had been wrapped. Although the Roman Catholic Church never officially proclaimed the shroud to be Christ's burial cloth, neither did it discourage that belief. Three million of the faithful filed past the shroud when it was last displayed in the Cathedral of St. John the Baptist in 1978. Many believed they had looked into the face of Christ. What did they see?

The shroud itself is an unspectacular sheet of twill-woven linen cloth, slightly more than fourteen feet long and a yard wide. On this appears a pale sepia-tone image of the front and back of a naked man about six feet tall. Pale carmine stains of blood mark wounds to the head, side, hands and feet. Believers took the shroud to be a true relic of Christ's Passion. But critics since the fourteenth century have been equally convinced that the shroud is a cruel, if clever hoax. Studying the Shroud of Turin became a scholarly and scientific discipline on its own.

The mystery only deepened when teams of scientists from the Air Force Academy, the Los Alamos laboratory and several other research centers examined the shroud in detail, photographing it under ultraviolet and infrared light, bombarding it with X-rays, peering at it microscopically. To the delight of many, the hi-tech scientists could not come up with a clear conclusion either way. Creationists around the world squealed with delight: Why should the United States government support places like the Smithsonian Institution when scientists cannot even explain how such an "obvious fraud" was perpetrated? The implications for science in general (and archaeology in particular) were enormous, and the debate raged on.

For nearly forty years, scientists had argued that radiocarbon dating could definitively determine whether or not the Shroud of Turin dates to the time of Christ. Unfortunately, conventional radiocarbon methods would have destroyed a handkerchief-sized piece of the shroud, and Church authorities rejected all such requests. But since the new AMS method of radiocarbon dating necessitates destruction of only a minuscule sample of linen—easily removed from unobtrusive parts of the shroud—the Pontifical Academy of Sciences agreed in 1984 to such dating.

After years of squabbling about the ground rules, three laboratories (at the University of Arizona in Tucson, the British Museum in London, and the Swiss Federal Institute in Zurich) finally received a postage-stamp-size piece of the shroud, plus control specimens of various ages. Only British Museum officials, who coordinated the research, knew which specimen was which. When the owner of the shroud, Pope John Paul II, was informed of the outcome, his response was simple: "Publish it."

And publish it they did. In October 1988, a hodgepodge of ecclesiastical and technological specialists hosted a news conference at which Anastasio Cardinal Ballestrero, Archbishop of Turin, solumnly announced the results. All three laboratories agreed that the flax plants from which the linen in the shroud was made had been grown in medieval times—between 1260 and 1390—long after the death of Jesus.

Although a certain degree of mystery still surrounds the shroud, particularly since nobody can explain how such an image was created using Middle Age technology, one thing is clear: Radiocarbon dating's "third revolution" unambiguously resolved this controversy that spanned five centuries. The Shroud of Turin could not possibly be the authentic burial cloth of Jesus.

WHERE TO GO FROM HERE?

Some Classics in the Development of Radiocarbon Dating: Arnold and Libby (1949): "Age Determinations by Radiocarbon Content: Checks with Samples of Known Age," Libby (1955): *Radiocarbon Dating,* Waterbolk (1971): "Working with Radiocarbon Dates;" Willis (1969): "Radiocarbon Dating."

More Recent Discussions of Practical Radiocarbon Dating: The most useful introductory statement is Taylor's (1987b) *Radiocarbon Dating: an Archaeological Perspective,* emphasizing the collaboration between archaeologist and radiocarbon lab. See also Michels (1973, Chapter 9): *Dating Methods in Archaeology,* Ralph (1971): "Carbon-14

Dating;" Stuckenrath (1977): "Radiocarbon: Some Notes from Merlin's Diary." Grootes (1978) describes how the C-14 time scale can be significantly extended by thermal isotopic enrichment; Stuiver, Heusser, and Yang (1978): "North American Glacial History Extended to 75,000 Years." Taylor (1985) reviews the impact of radiocarbon dating, as reflected in the pages of *American Antiquity*.

What About the Statistics Attached to Radiocarbon Dates?: Long and Rippeteau (1974): "Testing Contemporaneity and Averaging Radiocarbon Dates;" Thomas (1976, Chapter 10): *Figuring Anthropology.*

Tree-Ring Correction Factors in Radiocarbon Dating: Browman (1981): "Isotopic Discrimination and Correction Factors in Radiocarbon Dating;" Klein et al. (1982): "Calibration of Radiocarbon Dates: Tables Based on the Consensus Data of the Workshop on Calibrating the Radiocarbon Time Scale;" Michael (1985), Stuiver (1982): "A High-Precision Calibration of the A.D. Radiocarbon Time Scale;" Stuiver and Kra (1986): "The Calibration Issue: 12th International Radiocarbon Conference."

PC-compatible computer software is available to help archaeologists convert radiocarbon determinations to tree-ring–calibrated calendrical dates. A floppy diskette, described in Stuiver and Reimer (1986), can be obtained from the Quaternary Isotope Laboratory, University of Washington, Seattle, Wash. 98195.

Accelerator Dating in Archaeology: Banning and Pavlish (1978): "Direct Detection in Radiocarbon Dating;" Bennett et al. (1977): "Radiocarbon Dating Using Electrostatic Accelerators: Negative Ions Provide the Key;" Berger (1979): "Radiocarbon Dating with Accelerators." Browman (1981), Hedges and Gowlett (1986) provide a particularly readable and up-to-date account of new developments; Muller (1977), Wendorf (1987): "The Advantages of AMS to Field Archaeologists."

Background for Case Studies of AMS Dating: The Lovelock Cave Duck Decoys: Grosscup (1960), Heizer and Napton (1970), Loud and Harrington (1929), Tuohy and Napton (1986).

Early Human Skeletons in the New World: Bada, Schroeder, and Carter (1974); Bada et al. (1974); Stafford et al. (1984); Taylor (1987a); Taylor et al. (1985).

The Shroud of Turin: Dale (1987), Gove (1987), Wilson (1986), Nickell (1983), Tribbe (1983), Zugibe (1982).

Radiocarbon is a technical scientific journal devoted to publishing compilations of C-14 dates produced by various laboratories. *Radiocarbon* also publishes technical and interpretive articles on all aspects of the technique; first published in 1959.

Subscription information: Managing Editor, *Radiocarbon,* Kline Geology Laboratory, Yale University, 210 Whitney Ave., P.O. Box 6666, New Haven, Conn. 06511.

Thermoluminescence

A weak but measurable flash of light is emitted whenever prehistoric ceramics, tiles, bricks, or figurines are ground up and intensely heated. But if you repeat the experiment on the same sample, no flash will occur; the sample will just glow.

This difference is due to *thermoluminesence*. The fabric within ceramics traps energy inside its internal microscopic lattice, and when the sample is heated, the stored energy is released as light. Simplified, it works like this: Nuclear radiation always exists within the ceramic fabric, and radioactivity constantly bombards everything else inside the sherd. Although most of the nuclear energy dissipates as heat, some electrons are knocked away from their parent molecules. Most electrons eventually return home, but a few runaways keep bouncing around inside the ceramic lattice. In their wanderings, the malcontents will eventually encounter imperfections in the lattice. When this happens, they are "trapped." As time passes, an increasing amount of energy is stored in this way.

But heating the lattice to 500° C or so precipitates a jailbreak. Maverick electrons are allowed to slip their bonds, becoming free once again to wander. This release is what creates the flash of light, called the thermoluminescent (or TL) signal. Firing a pot in a kiln creates a *time-point zero,* effectively setting the TL clock at zero. When samples are reheated under laboratory conditions and the intensity of the light emissions is measured, it is possible to gauge the elapsed duration between the two episodes of heating. Figure 9–10 shows how the technique works.

Actually computing the age of ancient ceramics or figurines is considerably more complicated than this, requiring a number of additional procedures, cautions, and assumptions. Still, a number of relatively reliable dates have become available, and TL dating is now extensively used to date archaeological deposits, detect fakes in art collections, even date burned flint artifacts.

Where to Go from Here?

Some General References for Thermoluminescence Dating: Aitken (1985): *Thermoluminescence Dating*, Fleming (1979): *Thermoluminescence Techniques in Archaeology;* see also Mazess and Zimmerman (1966), Ralph and Han (1966, 1969), Rice (1987).

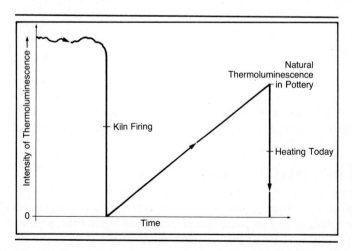

FIGURE 9–10 Schematic representation of the process of "time-zero" setting in the thermoluminescence dating of pottery (see Fleming 1979, Figure 1.1). (Courtesy Oxford University Press)

Archaeomagnetism

When mapping Gatecliff Shelter, we used information from the U.S. Geological Survey (U.S.G.S.) "Wildcat Peak" map. At the bottom of each such topographic map are two small intersecting arrows, denoting the **declination**, the difference between true and magnetic north. Around Gatecliff, magnetic north is 17° east of true north. This means that survey crews taking a compass heading must subtract 17° from the bearing to locate true north. Because of the declination, most of our survey work was done according to a grid system oriented toward magnetic (rather than true) north.

But when we conducted our transect survey looking for Mission Santa Catalina in Georgia, the "St. Catherines Sound" quadrangle map told us that the declination in this area was zero degrees. This made the survey easy, because compass bearings pointed directly toward true north, without any correction necessary.

Actually, the picture is slightly more complicated than this, because the magnetic declination actually changes through time, and the amount of change depends on where you are. At the southern tip of Texas, the declination in 1960 was 8° 50 minutes east of true north. But in 1970, the magnetic declination in south Texas was only 8° 30 minutes east. Although these differences matter little to most field archaeologists, they do illustrate the dynamic relationship between the earth and its magnetic field.

Archaeomagnetism is a dating technique based on just this difference in the earth's changing magnetic configuration. We have already glimpsed how these magnetic parameters are used by archaeologists when, in Chapter 7, we sketched how the proton magnetometer found the buried daub walls at Santa Catalina. The marsh mud used in plastering the mission walls contained particles that, when heated, aligned themselves toward the magnetic north of the time. When the walls collapsed, these previously aligned particles created a "magnetic anomaly," detectable by a magnetometer even when buried beneath a foot of sand.

This same principle has been converted to a dating technique called archaeomagnetism. Its geological cousin, **geomagnetism**, uses the same principles but operates on the vast geological time scale. It works like this. Many materials encountered in archaeological sites contain magnetic particles that can become aligned with the Earth's magnetic field in several ways:

Thermal magnetism: The particles are heated to a critical temperature (over 700° C.).

Chemical magnetization: Chemical changes change the size of the magnetic grains.

Depositional magnetization: Already-magnetized particles reorient while settling out after being redeposited through water or wind action.

The daub walls at Santa Catalina were magnetized by thermal alteration. When the mission was torched in 1680, the flames agitated the particles inside the daub, destroying all previous alignments. When the magnetized grains settled out during cooling, the magnetism associated with electron spin oriented individual grains toward the prevailing magnetic field. This specific alignment was destroyed when the walls collapsed because the orientation of individual particles was disturbed.

Thermoluminescence is usually used to date stable archaeological features, such as kilns, burned floors, and brick footings. In a consolidated matrix, hand samples are removed, and smaller cores are taken to the lab. Less consolidated sediments are sampled in the field by coring or by carving little *in situ* pillars over which plastic cylinders can be placed (this is how we took the archaeomagnetic samples at Gatecliff). Regardless of how the samples are removed, their precise orientation (relative to true north) must first be recorded by leveling the top of the sample and then inscribing true north along the horizontal surface. In this way, data regarding initial orientation are preserved, and each sample can be accurately realigned in the laboratory setting.

Such remnant magnetism is converted to an archaeologically relevant date by comparing the sample's orientation with a master profile of the earth's magnetism in the past. This geomagnetic field, created by the earth's liquid core, is currently changing in direction and intensity at different rates in different areas; this is why each U.S.G.S. map has its individual correction factor for declination and also why the declination must be revised periodically. The accuracy of archaeomagnetism thus depends on both the location and the actual age of the sample.

This record of "secular variation" must be developed independently for each region. It is done by measuring the direction of magnetization for known-age features and then building a composite record, which can be used to date unknown specimens. Archaeomagnetism is an extremely popular dating technique in the American Southwest, and hundreds (if not thousands) of prehistoric fire pits and ovens have been so dated (e.g., Eighmy and Doyel 1987; Eighmy, Sternberg, and Butler 1980). Correlation with dendrochronological samples and tree-ring dated ceramics suggests that the accuracy of such determinations lies between ±20 and ±40 years.

We also used archaeomagnetic dating at Gatecliff Shelter. In this case, we decided to monitor the depositional magnetization by looking at the already-magnetized particles that settled out while being water-deposited inside Gatecliff. To avoid problems of "overprinting," we deliberately avoided fire hearths and other areas of obvious sheet burning (both of which would have destroyed the magnetism we were looking for). We were after "natural," not "cultural," magnetism.

We took a series of seventy-two sediment samples spanning a four-meter section of well-stratified sand and silt lenses (Strata 5 through 22). The exposure was first carefully cleaned and azimuth readings were made across this face with a Brunton compass. Archaeomagnetic samples were taken at five-centimeter intervals using small plastic boxes, pushed into the exposure, and broken off to preserve the magnetic orientation. J. S. Kopper (Long Island University) processed the samples at the Paleomagnetic Laboratory of the University of Edinburgh.

Radiocarbon evidence later showed that although the exposure covered four meters of sediments, the time span represented only about two thousand years (from about 3300 B.C. at the bottom up to about 1250 B.C. at the top). Absolute archaeomagnetic dating of these sediments was not feasible, as the average period of magnetic declination swings in North American sediments is about two thousand years or so, based on sediments in Lake

Michigan (Creer 1977). We simply did not have enough time represented to use this correlation.

But the archaeomagnetic results were helpful as a relative dating technique, confirming the geomorphological interpretation of the sediments. As demonstrated in the preceding chapter, Gatecliff Shelter contains a sequence of graded sediment beds. The geomorphology suggested that each of these strata had been laid down in a geological instant (perhaps a single afternoon). The archaeomagnetic profile confirmed these depositional inferences by showing a consistent declination through such graded beds. (Actually, had we taken samples at two-centimeter intervals [instead of five centimeters], the results would doubtless have been more informative. Oh, well, live and learn.)

WHERE TO GO FROM HERE?

Some General References on Archaeomagnetism: Synthesis articles by Tarling (1975, 1985) and Wolfman (1984) provide the best jumping-off place, and Tarling's (1983) book *Palaeomagnetism: Principles and Applications in Geology, Geophysics and Archaeology* fills in the gaps; see also Aitken (1960).

Specific Examples of Archaeomagnetic Dating: Silt deposits at Gatecliff Shelter (Nevada): Thomas (1983b, pp. 412–416); cave paintings at Tito Bustillo cave (Spain): Creer and Kopper (1974); Hadrian's Wall (England): Heller and Markert (1973); ovens and hearths in the American Southwest (Eighmy, Sternberg, and Butler 1980); Wolfman (1984).

Potassium–Argon Dating

Another absolute dating technique monitors the decay of potassium (K-40) into argon gas (A-40). Rather than estimating the rate of radioactive emissions (as in C-14 dating), the K-A method determines the ratio of potassium to argon particles in a rock. Because potassium decays through time, the more argon that is present, the older the rock is. The initial datum in C-14 dating was the death of the absorbing organism, as C-14 acquisition ceases with death. **Potassium–argon dating** is applied to rocks, and so the age estimate refers to the latest significant lithological change, usually in the form of metamorphism.

K-A dating involves assumptions not unlike those of radiocarbon analysis. There must have been no argon trapped at the time of formation; that is, all argon must be the direct result of potassium decay, and all argon must be retained in the rock structure without absorption by the atmosphere. It is known that some rocks, such as mica, tend to leak argon, and so care must be taken in deciding which rock types to subject to potassium–argon dating.

The archaeological potential of potassium dating is more limited than that of radiocarbon, because the K-A time range is so great (as much as several billion years). Rarely are archaeological deposits so old. But some critically important early sites in Africa have been successfully dated by the K-A method. At Olduvai Gorge, for example, the potassium–argon dates indicated to L. S. B. Leakey that his hominid fossils were roughly 1.75 million years old.

The late Glynn Isaac discovered a mass of broken bones strewn across a twenty-foot area in the badlands of Kenya. Scattered among the bones (mostly hippopotamus) are remains of stone tools, including flakes and a few pebble choppers. The site, termed KBS, is embedded in a volcanic tuff, and pumice cobbles within the tuff have been dated at 2.61 ±0.26 million years by means of the potassium–argon technique (Isaac, Leakey, and Behrensmeyer 1971).

WHERE TO GO FROM HERE?

General References on K-A Dating: Faul (1971), Gentner and Lippolt (1969), and Miller (1969).

A Brief Warning About Arguments of Relevance

We have considered several current methods of obtaining chronometric dates for archaeological sites, but one important issue has yet to be addressed. In the section on dendrochronology, for instance, I said that tree-ring dating provides absolute dates for archaeological sites. Although this is true, it points to an important issue not yet discussed.

Archaeological sites can never be dated by simple equivalences. For example, a tree-ring cutting date provides the year, such as A.D. 1239, that a particular tree died. By itself, this date tells us exactly nothing about archaeology. The event being dated is the death of a tree, an inherently uninteresting event in itself. Trees die daily, and we are not in the business of conducting tree autopsies. Rather, a dead tree assumes archaeological importance only when its death is somehow relevant to a human behavioral event of interest, such as the roofing of a pueblo room. The same argument applies to archaeology's other dating methods, which really only tell us when a clam died, or a piece of obsidian was broken, or a particular rock was heated.

In every case, the event dated must be demonstrated to be contemporaneous with a behavioral event of interest—roofing a pueblo, cooking a meal, or killing a deer (Schiffer 1976, pp. 140–143). The demonstration of association is a key issue in archaeological dating, and the general topic of arguments of relevance will be considered in more detail in Chapter 12.

Summary

Contemporary archaeologists are equipped with a powerful battery of techniques that can be used to date objects of the past. Dendrochronology, or tree-ring dating, enables archaeologists to establish the precise year of death for many species of trees commonly found in archaeological sites. When properly correlated with known cultural events, these "cutting dates" can often pinpoint the exact occupation history of a site. Obsidian hydration is a microscopic technique that measures the amount of water absorbed into the freshly broken surface of an obsidian artifact or piece of waste chippage: The older the artifact is, the greater the degree of hydration will be. Radiocarbon dating is a physiochemical technique that monitors the degree of radioactive emission from organic specimens. During life, all plants and animals ingest atmospheric carbon (including C-14), and after they die, they cannot absorb any more C-14. Through the continuing process of radiocarbon decay, these C-14 molecules break down at a steadily decreasing rate. By determining the current rate of C-14 breakdown, one can estimate the length of elapsed time since the death of a plant or animal. Recently, physicists discovered that the atmospheric level of radiocarbon has changed somewhat over the last several millennia. Many archaeologists thus now "correct" their radiocarbon dates using an absolute chronology based on the radiocarbon dating of bristlecone pine samples of known age. New advances in accelerator-based radiocarbon methods permit archaeologists to use extremely small samples, vastly stretching the potential of the method. Potassium–argon dating, like the radiocarbon method, monitors the rate of radioactive conversion, in this case, the conversion of potassium into argon gas trapped within geological strata. The maximum time range of the radiocarbon method is roughly 75,000 years, whereas potassium–argon dating can extend back several billion years.

These various dating techniques, by themselves, tell us nothing about cultural activities. Dendrochronology, for example, can estimate only when a certain tree died; obsidian hydration tells us only when a certain piece of obsidian rock was fractured. In each case, the event being dated must be demonstrated to be coeval with a behavioral (cultural) event of interest.

CHAPTER 10

Sorting Cultural Things in Time

There is no difference between time and any of the three dimensions of space except that our consciousness moves along it.
—H. G. Wells

All anthropologists recognize certain restrictions in their fieldwork. Ethnologists can work at only a single time level—now; ethnohistorians are restricted to written records; and linguists can study only languages still spoken or the written versions of ancient languages. Archaeologists likewise have limitations, as we can study only those cultural items surviving to the present. Rarely is the contemporary world greeted by the particulars of a Pompeii. More commonly, the archaeological record consists of patterned scatters of stone, bone, pottery, and dirt. Because so few obvious and tangible clues survive, archaeologists have evolved pragmatic and precise techniques to extract the last morsel of information from each site.

Archaeologists excavate two kinds of things: artifacts and ecofacts. Everyone knows what an artifact is—it is the material remains from human activities. At one time, archaeology was almost totally artifact oriented, with archaeological sites viewed as little more than mines in which to prospect for more artifacts. But over the past several decades, archaeologists have shifted objectives, realizing that understanding the person behind the artifact is more compelling than the artifact itself. Contemporary archaeology thus has turned from simply obtaining things to fill museum cabinets to discovering how people of the past actually lived.

This reorientation has required archaeologists to change their field strategies, from digging simply to find artifacts to a more sensitive approach designed to recover relevant ecological and contextual information as well. Bones, pollen grains, fish scales, seeds, and **plant macrofossils** are critical to today's ecologically aware archaeology. Lewis Binford (1964) coined the unlovely term *ecofact* to emphasize the importance of nonartifactual remains contained in archaeological sites. Contemporary archaeology is largely involved with the recovery and subsequent analysis of artifacts and ecofacts and their interrelationships.

Although the identification of ecofacts is largely a biological endeavor, sorting and classifying artifacts is the primary province of the archaeologist. In this chapter, we shall examine the basis for *temporal artifact classification.* Later, we shall address alternative schemes for classifying and understanding material culture.

Types of Types

Archaeology's basic unit of classification is termed a type. Be careful here because **type**, like *culture* and *personality,* is an everyday word appropriated by anthropology and reassigned a specific, nonintuitive meaning. Artifact types are abstract, ideal constructs artificially created by the archaeologist to make sense of past material culture.

Although archaeologists excavate specimens, they analyze types. Rather than pouring over each of the thousands of individual items recovered on a dig, archaeologists usually abstract them into a few (dozen) carefully selected typological categories. Artifact types come in all shapes and varieties, and the naked word *type* must never be applied without an appropriate modifier. One must always describe precisely which type of type one is discussing. The word *type* is naughty when caught unmodified.

The same objects can, of course, be classified in many ways. Think about a familiar set of modern artifacts, say, a workshop of woodworking tools. Carpenters classify their tools by function—hammers, saws, planes, files, drills, and spokeshaves. But when insuring a carpenter's workshop, the insurance agent uses another set of classifications, sorting these same tools into new categories such as "flammable" and "nonflammable" or perhaps according to replacement value: "under $10," "between $10 and $25," and so on. Should the carpenter relocate, the furniture movers will group these same tools into another set of divisions such as "heavy" or "light," "bulky" or "compact," or perhaps (if you're lucky) "fragile" and "nonbreakable."

The point here—and the crux of archaeological classification in general—is this: Each classification must be formulated with a specific purpose in mind. Archaeology has no general, all-purpose classification; the more classifications the better. Irving Rouse (1970) urged archaeologists to ask continually, "Classification—for what?"

WHERE TO GO FROM HERE?

Classification in Archaeology: Some Classics: Brew (1946, pp. 44–66): "The Use and Abuse of Taxonomy," Ford (1954): "The Type Concept Revisited," Krieger (1944): "The Typological Method," Rouse (1960): "The Classification of Artifacts in Archaeology,"

Spaulding (1953): "Statistical Techniques for the Discovery of Artifact Types," Steward (1954): "Types of Types."

More Contemporary Views of Archaeological Typology: Adams (1988): "Archaeological Classification: Theory *Versus* Practice"; Binford (1965): "Archaeological Systematics and the Study of Cultural Process"; Binford and Sabloff (1982): "Paradigms, Systematics, and Archaeology"; Dunnell (1971): *Systematics in Prehistory;* (1986b): "Methodological Issues in Americanist Artifact Classification"; Hill and Evans (1972): "A Model for Classification and Typology"; Klejn (1982): "Archeological Typology"; Rice (1982): "Pottery Production, Pottery Classification, and the Role of Physicochemical Analyses"; Spaulding (1977): "On Growth and Form in Archaeology: Multivariate Analysis"; Thomas (1981): "How to Classify the Projectile Points from Monitor Valley"; Whallon and Brown (1982): *Essays on Archaeological Typology.*

Morphological Types

Modern observers exploring the range of material remains left by an extinct group will encounter many unfamiliar, even meaningless, artifacts. To make sense of the past using these remains, the first analytical step is to describe the artifacts carefully and accurately by grouping them into **morphological types**.

Emil Haury, an eminent Southwestern archaeologist, drafted one such description in his report on Ventana Cave, Arizona:

> *Discs*—Of the twenty-four stone discs, twenty-two are centrally perforated. They were all made of schist, from 36 to 75 mm. in diameter and averaging 8 mm. in thickness. The customary way of producing them was by breaking and then smoothing the rough corners by abrasion. . . . Only one was well made. . . . Drill holes are bi-conical and not always centrally placed. Two were painted red. Next to nothing is known about these discs. . . . (Haury 1950, p. 329)

Haury did not even speculate what the disks were used for (Figure 10–1). But he did illustrate and describe them in enough detail so that contemporary and future colleagues can visualize the artifacts without having to view them firsthand. Such bald description is the primary function of a morphological type (often termed a *class* in archaeological literature).

Morphological types have a second basic property: They are abstract. Types are not artifacts but are composite descriptions of many similar artifacts. Accordingly, every morphological type must encompass a certain range of variability: Several colors may have been applied; the quality of manufacture might vary; absolute size usually fluctuates; and so forth. W. W. Taylor (1948, p. 118) called this abstract quality an **archetype** to emphasize the elusive "ideal form" implicit in every morphological type.

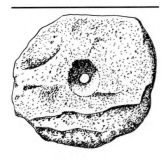

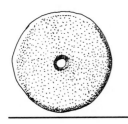

FIGURE 10–1   Two prehistoric stone discs excavated from Ventana Cave, Arizona (see Haury 1950, p. 29); the bottom disc is 35 mm. in diameter.

Tabletop Typology at San Cristobal

Archaeologists derive scant comfort from the fact that over and above the certainties of death and taxes, they are blessed with the additional constant of a seemingly limitless quantity of sherds to classify.
—Prudence M. Rice

To see how archaeologists create their types, we shall return to Nels Nelson's work at San Cristobal Pueblo in New Mexico. I stressed earlier that Nelson's method of stratigraphic excavation was a critical step in the history of archaeology. But Nelson also advanced archaeologists' thinking about how best to classify material culture. Remember that Nelson recovered over two thousand potsherds in his ten-foot controlled section at San Cristobal. In a previous chapter, I simply said that he sorted these sherds into five types and then plotted them stratigraphically (see Table 8–3). But I deliberately did not tell you how he arrived at these types (and I hope this bothered you). How did Nelson know there were five kinds of pottery at San Cristobal? Why not fifteen? Or fifty-five?

Put yourself in Nelson's boots. The date is 1914 and you have just invested several years excavating prehistoric pueblo ruins throughout the American Southwest. Because absolute dating techniques have not been invented yet and little relevant scientific literature exists, it all really boils down to your innate powers of observation. Approaching the trash heap at San Cristobal, you know certain basic facts about southwestern ceramics. In your travels through New Mexico and Arizona, you have seen some prehistoric pottery with ornamental indentations; other wares were painted, and still others were glazed. But these are merely impressions, more perceived than explicit. During your three days of excavating at San Cristobal, you accurately peeled off arbitrary one-foot sections, bagging the ceramics from each artificial horizon. Your workmen hauled these level bags into your rude field laboratory, washing the sherds and laying out the collections on a creaking makeshift table. What now?

What Nelson did was simple: He turned his senses loose, trying to absorb what he called "basic characteristics." Admitting that his procedures were "no doubt arbitrary," he just sorted things out on the table, trying to ignore frivolous differences and focusing on the major trends. One by one, he grouped similar sherds together into individual stacks.

Then he assigned a descriptive name to each pile. The first stack contained 649 pieces of unpainted pottery with rough surface corrugations. The "leading characteristics" were described in the following way:

> *1. Form, Size, etc.*—Normally a jar (olla), spherical body, short neck, flaring rim; occasional shoe or bird-shaped pots with knobs suggesting wings and tails; bowls uncertain. Sizes range from miniature to medium, approaching large.
> *2. Surface Finish*—Plain coil of primary and sometimes apparently secondary origin; indented coil (finger-nail or sharp implement being used) with occasional effort at ornamental effect. Coiling and indenting often obscured either by wear or by "wiping" during process of manufacture. Some specimens of later times show evidence of a micaceous wash.
> *3. Paste Composition*—Gray colored clay, more or less tempered with coarse sand or crushed rock of crystalline nature. In early times some crushed pumice stone may have been added, while in later times micaceous substance was occasionally mixed in. Vessel walls are thin and brittle, the latter fact being due probably to constant use over the fire. (Nelson 1916, p. 168)

Not great prose perhaps, but such baseline descriptions still form the foundation of archaeological classification, seven decades later.

Moving down the table, Nelson's second stack contained eighty-three sherds of so-called biscuit ware, a "peculiar kind of pottery, which can be detected even by the touch." One by one, Nelson worked his way through the piles of pottery until the "types" on Table 8–3 had been described and plotted.

Typology to Nelson was a matter of intuition, experience, and feel. Biscuit ware was "peculiar"; Type I pottery was "decidedly pleasing" (see Figure 10–2). In looking over the Type III sherds, he noted that "the new type of ceramics has gained in diversity of form and general adaptability, but it has lost not a little in decorative elegance." In more current terminology, Nelson defined a series of morphological types (Steward 1954). Also called "descriptive," these divisions are designed to reflect an artifact's overall, super-

FIGURE 10–2 Four types of ceramics recovered at San Cristobal
ruin (see Nelson 1916, Plate VII). (Courtesy the
American Museum of Natural History)

ficial appearance. Morphological types usually deal in broad generalities rather than specific traits, simultaneously embracing a wide range of properties—length, width, weight, material, color, shapes, and volume, just to name a few.

If You Can't Measure It, Is It Real?

The analyses by Nelson and Haury were grounded in what today we call the *modal concept of culture*. Establishing types at this level merely groups like with like. Nelson simply concentrated on the most flagrant differences among the stacked-up potsherds on the table. Even had he known about the cultural idiolect and the cultural system, Nelson would have declared both (temporarily) irrelevant. Forget for now the complex issues of why pottery changes, how the pottery was made, or what different kinds of pottery were used for. Interesting issues perhaps, but they can be resolved only during a later stage of analysis.

   To look more deeply into how the modal concept of culture works in archaeology, remove yourself from Nelson's boots and pretend to be me. You have just spent a good chunk of the 1970s enlisting more than three hundred people to help excavate a Nevada rock shelter that turned out to be forty feet deep. Literally tons of artifacts were recovered. Once washed and catalogued (to preserve contextual information), the artifacts lie mounded in your lab—just like Nels Nelson's San Cristobal potsherds? Where to now?

   Your first job, before anything else, is to describe what you found. Not only will such description form the basis of all further analysis, but it will provide your archaeological colleagues with the data necessary to ask their own questions of your artifacts.

   Archaeologists generally begin by creating morphological types and later incorporating these preliminary groups into special-purpose types. The initial sort is often fairly informal, sometimes just separating superficially similar artifacts into piles on the laboratory table. This is what Nelson did in 1914, and exactly what I did with the Gatecliff artifacts. Ignore the extraneous variables like stratigraphy, time depth, cultural affiliation, even provenience for now. The main concern here is to reduce the complexity by looking for homogeneity.

   The first sort is usually general, often conducted in the field. On most sites, excavators create separate "level bags" for each kind of artifact and ecofact recovered. Potsherds are bagged separately from the bones and stone tools. On historic-period sites, European ceramics are commonly separated from pottery of aboriginal manufacture. Kinds of stone tools are also distinguished: chipped stone artifacts in one bag, flaking debris in another, and broken grinding slabs in individual boxes to keep them from crushing everything else.

   Once the artifacts are catalogued, laboratory personnel dispatch selected artifacts, ecofacts, and field samples to specialists: artifacts needing first-aid and long-term stabilization to the conservation lab, bones to the zooarchaeologist, soil samples to the geoarchaeologist, plant remains to the ethnobotanist, and so forth. Everything else is sorted into rough categories for actual analysis.

Time will soon destroy the works of famous painters and sculptors, but the Indian arrowhead will balk his efforts and Eternity will have to come to his aid. They are not fossil bones, but, as it were, fossil thoughts, forever reminding me of the mind that shaped them. . . . Myriads of arrowpoints lie sleeping in the skin of the revolving earth. . . . The footprint, the mind-print of the oldest men.
—Henry David Thoreau

Figure 10–3 illustrates a fraction of the more than four hundred classifiable projectile points recovered at Gatecliff Shelter. (As an aside here, archaeologists term such artifacts *projectile points,* rather than *arrowheads,* because so many of them were actually hafted as darts and spears rather than arrows.) These projectile points were some of the most important artifacts recovered at Gatecliff, and we spent considerable time classifying them. Like Nelson with his San Cristobal sherds, we began by defining some morphological types. And like Nelson, we worried about just how many such morphological types there are in Figure 10–3. Two? Six? Twenty-five?

If you are looking for a fixed rule for how many types to make, forget it. Defining morphological types has progressed very little since the days of Nelson. Morphological types, I must repeat, are merely descriptive groupings, later to be tested for temporal and/or spatial and/or functional and/or technological significance. The point here is simple: Just get on with it, and then be explicit about what you have done.

Each point in Figure 10–3 is unique. But if you are any kind of observer at all, you should be able to distinguish some important similarities and differences among them. The points at the top of the page, for instance, are smaller than those at the bottom. Another difference is in how the points are notched for hafting.

- Some (like numbers 7, 8, and 9) are notched from the side.
- Numbers 14 and 15 are notched from the base.
- Points at the bottom are notched from the corner.
- Those in the upper left-hand side are not notched at all.

Differences like size and notch position are called **attributes** in archaeology, and they form the basis of morphological classification. Nelson looked at several different attributes on his San Cristobal sherds: the kind of paint, the surface texture, and the color and pattern of the design. There is no regulation governing the number of attributes people observe; use as many as seem appropriate. Morphological types are created in dozens of ways, based on as many criteria and attributes. How you do this rests solely on your best judgment as an archaeologist. One arrangement of the points in Figure 10–3 is shown in Figure 10–4.

I already mentioned two attributes for the Gatecliff points in Figure 10–3: size and notch position. These two attributes, as we shall see, are sufficient to create workable

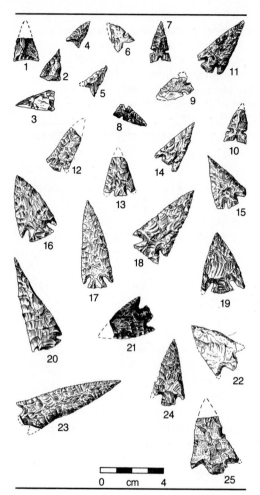

FIGURE 10–3 Assorted projectile points from Gatecliff Shelter. (Courtesy the American Museum of Natural History)

morphological types. But it is insufficient simply to say "size" and "notch position." To define adequate attributes, I must explain precisely what is meant by the terms, so that you can make identical observations.

Take size. We all know what size means, and it can be observed in several ways. Measure the length of a projectile point, and you know something about its size. The width measurement also reflects size. Or you can weigh something to find its size. You can even drop it in a cup of water; the amount of fluid displaced will tell you its volume. So what size are we talking about?

Over the years, I have found that *weight* is the best way to measure the size of a projectile point, although it is necessary to estimate the original weight of broken

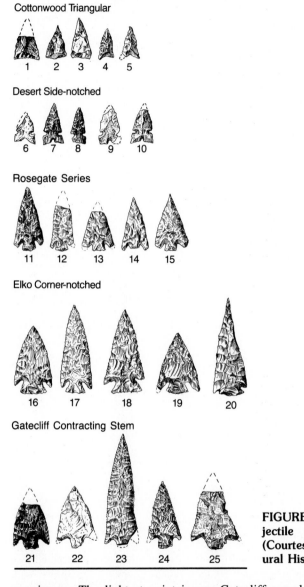

Cottonwood Triangular

1 2 3 4 5

Desert Side-notched

6 7 8 9 10

Rosegate Series

11 12 13 14 15

Elko Corner-notched

16 17 18 19 20

Gatecliff Contracting Stem

21 22 23 24 25

FIGURE 10–4 Typology of selected projectile points from Gatecliff Shelter. (Courtesy the American Museum of Natural History)

specimens. The lightest point in our Gatecliff sample weighs only 0.4 grams (Table 10–1), and the heaviest, more than five grams.

Weight was the first attribute I used to define my morphological types. If you look closely, you will see that the weights on Table 10–1 are patterned, with certain natural breaks in the distributions, defining three projectile point sizes in this collection:

TABLE 10–1—Attributes for Gatecliff Projectile Points

Specimen Number	Weight in Grams		Proximal Shoulder Angle
	Actual	Estimated Total	
1	0.8	(0.9)	—
2	0.8	0.8	—
3	0.9	0.9	—
4	0.4	0.4	—
5	0.8	(0.9)	—
6	0.3	(0.4)	200
7	0.8	0.8	180
8	0.5	(0.6)	180
9	0.6	0.7	180
10	0.7	(0.8)	190
11	2.3	2.3	100
12	1.1	(1.5)	100
13	1.2	(1.4)	95
14	1.5	1.5	85
15	2.5	2.5	80
16	4.1	4.1	110
17	3.5	3.5	120
18	3.9	3.9	130
19	3.5	3.5	120
20	4.1	(4.2)	150
21	2.3	(2.8)	80
22	3.3	(3.4)	85
23	5.2	(5.5)	80
24	2.7	2.7	100
25	4.4	(5.5)	60

Small points: weight less than 1.0 gram.

Medium points: weight between 1.0 and 2.5 grams.

Large points: weight over 2.5 grams.

Some variability arises naturally among projectile points because they are constructed by a **subtractive technology**. Flintknappers cannot fix their mistakes; they must simply work around errors, creating more variability in the finished product than is evident in, say, an **additive technology** like ceramic manufacture. Estimation of "total weight" in broken specimens introduces another source of unavoidable subjective error.

But by and large, the three size categories suitably reflect breaks in the distribution of weights. At least the weight groups are replicable; if you were to visit my laboratory, you would come up with the same weights and the same categories (within a small and definable measurement error). It is important that your "small points" are the same as mine.

The second attribute is notch position. Among the small points (numbers 1 to 10), some have notches and others do not. Two categories are hence apparent: small unnotched points and small side-notched points. I am hardly the first archaeologist to note this distinction, and the literature of Great Basin archaeology refers to these two morphological types in this way:

Cottonwood Triangular points (nos. 1–5)
 Weight: less than 1.0 gram
 Notching: absent

Desert Side-notched points (nos. 6–10)
 Weight: less than 1.0 gram
 Notching: present (and from the side)

In the Prologue, I noted that one of archaeology's small rewards is that we get to name our discoveries (but never after ourselves). Archaeological convention dictates that the point types receive first and last names. The first name generally refers to the site (or region) where they were first distinguished. The last name describes some obvious morphological characteristic. "Desert Side-notched" points were named in the late 1950s by M. A. Baumhoff and J. S. Byrne. "Desert" refers to their general distribution throughout the arid West, and "side-notched" tells us something about their appearance. Similarly, "Cottonwood Triangular" points were first recognized at the Cottonwood Creek site in Owens Valley, California (Riddell 1951). These points look triangular because they have no notches.

Points 11 through 15 are medium sized (weighing between 1.0 and 2.5 grams) and have notches creating a small base (or *stem*).

Rosegate series (nos. 11–15)
 Weight: between 1.0 and 2.5 grams
 Notching: present

The term *Rosegate* is an amalgam, a combination of "Rose Spring," a site in southeastern California (Lanning 1963), and "Eastgate," a small overhang near Eastgate, Nevada (Heizer and Baumhoff 1961). Originally, two different point types were defined, one named after each site, but during the investigation, we could find no significant difference between the two, and so we combined them. In this case, we modified the naming convention somewhat: The first term still denotes the place(s) of discovery, but because "Rosegate" combines two former types, it is termed a "series" (a higher-order category).

The larger points are more complicated. Numbers 16 through 25 weigh more than 2.5 grams, and Figure 10–3 shows that whereas some have expanding bases, others have contracting bases. But expanding and contracting are ambiguous terms, and on given points, archaeologists often disagree about just which stems expand and which contract.

Look at point 24: I call this stem *contracting,* but you might think that it is *expanding.* Who is right?

Who knows? Our types can be whatever we say, as long as each of us is consistent in defining the terms. Terminological difficulties like this are easily avoided with a little forethought.

I look at it this way: the *stem* is created by the notch, a slit added so that the point can be tied to a shaft. The edge of this notch forms an angle with the major axis of the point, and angles are interesting because they can be accurately measured: Draw an imaginary line along the notch of the point, and compute the angle between that line and the cross axis of the point. Sounds a bit complicated, but Figure 10–5 shows what I mean. Angles like this are usually measured using polar grid paper, with a measurement error of about ±5°. This is called the **proximal shoulder angle** because this side of the notch is nearest ("proximal to") the point shaft.

Table 10–1 lists the proximal shoulder angles for the ten large points from Gatecliff Shelter. Now the difference between expanding and contracting stems is apparent: Points 16 through 20 have angles greater than about 110°, and points 21 through 25 have angles smaller than that. On this basis, I define the following morphological types:

Elko Corner-notched points (nos. 16–20)
   Weight: greater than 2.5 grams
   Proximal shoulder angle: greater than (or equal
     to) 110°, and less than (or equal to) 150°.

Gatecliff Contracting Stem points (nos. 21–25)
   Weight: greater than 2.5 grams
   Proximal shoulder angle: less than 100°.

Elko points were initially recognized at sites in Elko County Nevada, and I first defined Gatecliff points—obviously—at Gatecliff Shelter. As morphological types, they differ only in basal form, as described by the angle measurements. All twenty-five points have been grouped by type in Figure 10–4. This example, while purposely simplified, demonstrates the first step in projectile point classification. Although a number of additional attributes were necessary in dealing with the more than four hundred points found at Gatecliff, the fundamental procedures are the same.

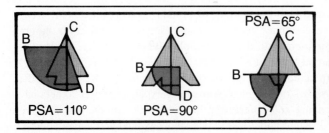

FIGURE 10–5 How to measure the proximal shoulder angle of a projectile point. (Courtesy the American Museum of Natural History)

To many, these names and measurements are mumbo jumbo. But such mumbo jumbo makes up the world of archaeological facts. Although it is boring to memorize endless names—and archaeologists are forever trying to rename everything—dealing with these five descriptive names is five times better than coping with twenty-five individual artifacts. And this is the function of morphological types.

Temporal Types in Prehistoric Archaeology

We need more rather than fewer classifications, different classifications, always new classifications, to meet new needs.
—J. O. Brew

Remember the caution under "Types of Types": "The word *type* is naughty when caught unmodified." I say this because archaeologists use this term in so many ways, and it is essential to distinguish which type of type is meant. So far, we have dealt strictly with morphological types, defined for baseline descriptive purposes. We now turn to a second, more important type, the **temporal type** (or **time-marker**). As the name implies, temporal types help archaeologists monitor change through time.

Perhaps without knowing it, you already took the first step toward defining a workable set of time-markers, by grouping the individual artifacts into morphological types. The next step is to see which of the morphological categories has significant temporal associatons. If morphological type B occurs only in strata dating between A.D. 500 and 1000, then this descriptive type can be elevated to the status of a temporal type. This promotion is useful because when artifacts belonging to temporal type B turn up in undated contexts, the dates A.D. 500 to 1000 become the most plausible hypothesis.

Temporal types are defined in accord with established scientific procedures (as set out in Chapter 2). Defining temporal types is a deductive process: Trial groupings are isolated according to form (as are morphological types). These abstract types are then tested for temporal significance against independent (usually stratigraphic) data.

Southwestern Ceramic Time-Markers

Nels Nelson's San Cristobal ceramic typology illustrates the process. Step 1 was to sort the 2300 sherds into five piles. After naming each category, he published concise descriptions so that other archaeologists could see how the classification was defined. Nelson then turned to the stratigraphic distribution of each morphological type (see Chapter 8). Two such types—corrugated and biscuit ware—were distributed throughout the ten-foot section. Nelson concluded that these categories were useless for chronological purposes, and so he put them aside. But the frequencies of three other types changed markedly through the stratigraphic profile at San Cristobal, and he devoted considerable time to discussing the temporal significance of his Types I, II, and III.

Procedures have changed little since 1914, but the terminology has. In the modern idiom, the five piles of potsherds were morphological types, basically descriptive hypotheses to be tested against the stratigraphic record. Only three morphological types (Types I, II, and III) passed the test. Because of their demonstrated stratigraphic significance, Nelson elevated them to the status of temporal types. When sherds of these three types were found in new, undated contexts, the San Cristobal stratigraphic associations suggested further temporal hypotheses for testing.

And these hypotheses have indeed been tested. Nelson's Type I, the early black-on-white pottery, is now known as Santa Fe Black-on-White (note the parallel conventions for naming ceramic and projectile point types: place name first, followed by key description). Tree-ring dating suggests that Santa Fe Black-on-White was first made about A.D. 1200, remaining popular until about A.D. 1350 (Breternitz 1966, p. 95). Nelson's Types II and III (the two-color and three-color glazed pottery) are now placed in a ceramic series called Rio Grande Glaze (a series is a higher-level category, grouping together several similar temporal types). Rio Grande Glaze ceramics show up in sites dating about A.D. 1300, the later types running into the historic period. In short, Nelson's temporal hypotheses have been wholly confirmed and refined by techniques not yet invented in 1914.

Gatecliff Projectile Points As Time-Markers

The Gatecliff Shelter point typology works in the same way. The morphological types that we derived are really just hypotheses waiting to be tested. Some may have temporal significance; others may reflect the different ways in which projectile points were broken and repaired; and some may even mirror divisions among social groups. But before behavioral life can be breathed into these formal categories, they must be comprehensively tested against independent data. To show how this works, we shall concentrate on temporal differences.

The stratigraphy of Gatecliff Shelter (discussed in Chapter 8) looks like a layer cake stacked forty feet high. Geology's law of superposition tells us that, all else being equal, the oldest artifacts will lie at the bottom, with later artifacts showing up progressively higher in the stratigraphic column. The Gatecliff deposits thus provide extraordinary temporal control over the past seven thousand years.

Figure 10–6 plots the vertical distribution of the more than four hundred classifiable projectile points from Gatecliff Shelter (note that additional types were required to classify the entire Gatecliff collection). Following archaeological convention, this temporal diagram is conditioned by the law of superposition, with the most recent archaeological divisions at the top and the most ancient at the bottom (just as they occur in the ground).

Look at the sharp stratigraphic differences evident on Figure 10–6. All the Desert Side-notched and Cottonwood Triangular points occurred in the uppermost part of Gatecliff Shelter. The Rosegate series points were found in slightly older strata; Elko

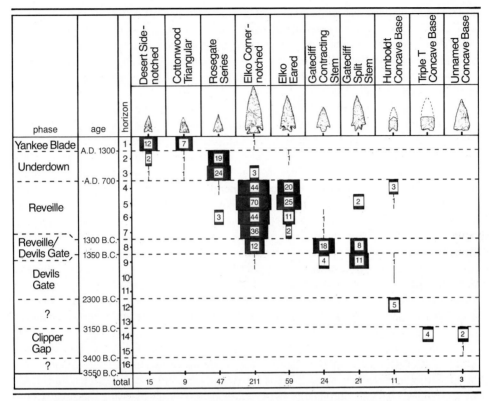

FIGURE 10–6 Relative proportions of selected projectile point types found at Gatecliff Shelter. Note that each stratum tends to be dominated by one or two extremely abundant time-sensitive types (see Thomas 1983b, Figure 66). (Courtesy the American Museum of Natural History)

points are older than this, and Gatecliff points older still. Because forty-seven radiocarbon dates were available to date the geological sequence at Gatecliff, it was possible to assign the following time ranges to each category:

Desert Side-notched: post A.D. 1300

Cottonwood Triangular: post A.D. 1300

Rosegate series: A.D. 500–A.D. 1300

Elko Corner-notched: 1500 B.C.–A.D. 500

Gatecliff Contracting Stem: 2500 B.C.–1500 B.C.

With this critical step, our morphological types have become temporal types. Each time similar points are found in undated contexts, we now have at least a clue (a hypothesis, really) to their time of manufacture.

Note carefully what happened here. (1) Individual artifacts were initially grouped strictly on formal criteria; all that mattered for morphological types was what the artifacts looked like. (2) These morphological categories were then tested against totally independent evidence, the layer-cake stratigraphy and the ladder of forty-seven radiocarbon dates available from Gatecliff Shelter. (3) All five morphological categories were significantly restricted in time, and so they were elevated to the status of temporal types. They effectively sort through time.

Not every morphological point type from Gatecliff made the grade. The frequencies of some morphological types (especially the larger, concave base points) did not change significantly through time, and these types flunked the test for graduating to the level of temporal type. Maybe somebody, eventually, will demonstrate that concave base points are indeed time-markers in the Great Basin; but until that demonstration, these types remain merely "morphological," without temporal significance.

A related issue emerges here. Throughout these pages, I stress the nature of archaeological data—data are not objects, data are observations made on objects—and the point typology from Gatecliff illustrates this principle. Using a series of formal attributes (weight, distal shoulder angle, and so forth), we grouped the individual Gatecliff artifacts into morphological types, each a hypothesis to be tested against independent temporal data. But note that our "independent" data—the datable context of each point inside Gatecliff Shelter—were merely another observation made on the same objects that we used to derive the initial hypothesis. Because formal attributes are autonomous relative to context, the criterion of independence holds, and so the test is valid.

This principle is critical to scientific inquiry in archaeology. Hypotheses (even simple ones like time-markers) need continual testing; as scientists, we should never become too comfortable with our "verified" hypotheses. Even without lifting a shovel, we can refine the Gatecliff chronology in several ways. Why not measure the microscopic hydration rim on each obsidian projectile point? This would give us an independent age estimate. Some points still have hafting sinew adhering to the base. Why not use the new accelerator technology to radiocarbon-date these fibers? Here would be another independent estimate of age. Both tests elicit more data without requiring more objects. This is one reason why well-curated museum collections are important research tools, enabling scientists of the future to generate new data from old objects.

Although critical to archaeology, time-markers have distinct limitations. In the Introduction to Part Three, I stressed that archaeology proceeds with its initial objective—establishing cultural chronologies—only by making an admittedly simplistic assumption. The deliberately simplified "modal" concept of culture focused attention on only shared aspects; the rest was temporarily ignored.

Now you can see why that simplifying assumption was necessary. Temporal types were defined for Gatecliff Shelter based on this modal definition. Never mind (for now) what the artifacts mean—we care only whether they change through time. As a result, some first rate time-markers were discovered at Gatecliff.

We have paid a price to find our time-markers. Although we now know that Desert Side-notched and Cottonwood Triangular points postdate A.D. 1300, much ignorance remains. Why should two morphological types exist simultaneously? Are two social groups living at Gatecliff in the post-1300 time period? Are Desert Side-notched points designed for hunting bighorn, whereas Cottonwood points are for rabbits? Are Cottonwood points really for "war arrows," left unnotched so that they cannot be pulled out once lodged? Or perhaps the difference is technological: Could the Cottonwood Triangular points be unfinished, simply blanks intended to be notched later?

These guesses are hypotheses at present untested. But you should recognize that such questions address issues more complex than just change through time. Answers may someday arrive, but only from archaeologists who transcend the restrictive modal concept of culture. When societal, technological, and functional variability is involved, we must build on a more comprehensive, systemic approach to culture (this approach is developed in detail in Part Four).

Temporal types are important stepping-stones, and the modal concept of culture is an appropriate tool for deriving them. But once the time-markers are suitably in hand, it is necessary to go beyond the specifics of stratigraphy and dating techniques to view culture in its full systemic context.

WHERE TO GO FROM HERE?

Recent Approaches to Ceramic Typology: Rice (1982) provides an impressive review relating traditional historical objectives and the newer physiochemical techniques in ceramic classification; see also Majewski and O'Brien (1987): "The Use and Misuse of Nineteenth-Century English and American Ceramics in Archaeological Analysis," Miller (1980): "Classification and Economic Scaling of 19th Century Ceramics," Plog (1980): *Stylistic Variation in Prehistoric Ceramics,* Rice (1976): "Rethinking the Ware Concept." Also, Rice's (1987) *Pottery Analysis: a Sourcebook* is a superb overview of current approaches to ceramic studies.

Background to Projectile Point Typology in the Great Basin: Baumhoff and Byrne (1959), Heizer and Baumhoff (1961), Heizer and Hester (1978), Lanning (1963), Thomas (1981, 1983b).

Seriation

Seriation is a deceptively simple technique, the unnecessarily abstruse discussion of which has become an embarrassment to quantitative archaeologists.
—William H. Marquardt

One powerful upshot of the typological concept is seriation, a technique that permits archaeologists to place stylistic periods into a relative chronological sequence. Unlike absolute dating procedures such as radiocarbon and dendrochronology, seriation works strictly with qualitative, relativistic ordering.

Seriation implicitly assumes that people are fickle: Sometimes styles change; sometimes new technologies arise. Most such new ideas are slow to catch on, with only a few pioneers participating in the fad. But fashions have a way of becoming chic in one group, eventually replacing earlier vogues, and then gradually falling into disuse.

Curves like that in Figure 10–7 often assume a characteristic form. In this case, new lighting technologies are gradually introduced, flourish for a while, and then slowly disappear. In the mid-nineteenth century, most houses in Pennsylvania were illuminated by candles and oil lamps; only a few households had gas lamps. But over the next fifty years, more and more families switched to gas lights. Those who could not afford such installations started using kerosene lamps (made possible by the growing petroleum industry in Pennsylvania and elsewhere). By the turn of the century, gas lights had virtually disappeared. Then along came another invention, electricity, and incandescent light bulbs started lighting the houses of Pennsylvania in increasing numbers. By 1940, "everybody" had electric lights, the gas and kerosene lamps fading into nostalgia.

The shape of such popularity curves, which struck Ford as somehow "battleship shaped," established the basis for seriation. By arranging the proportions of temporal types into lozenge-shaped curves, one can determine a relative chronological sequence. The classic example of such ordering was made by Sir Flinders Petrie (1899), who examined the contents of hundreds of Egyptian graves. After studying the ceramics, Petrie "seriated" the pottery styles in time simply by looking at the characteristics of the handles.

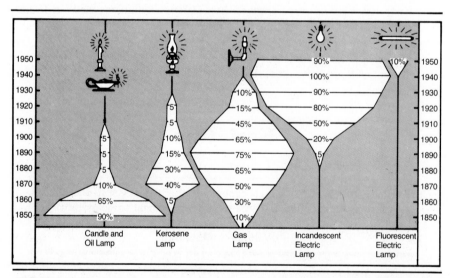

FIGURE 10–7   Seriation diagram showing how methods of artificial illumination changed in Pennsylvania between 1850 and 1950 (see Mayer-Oakes 1955, Figure 15). (Courtesy William J. Mayer-Oakes and the Carnegie Museum of Natural History)

This same phenomenon is evident in Nelson's sherd counts from San Cristobal Pueblo (Table 8–3). When San Cristobal was first built, ceramics were most commonly decorated with black-on-white painting. Moving up Nelson's stratigraphic column, two-color glaze rapidly takes over in popularity, with black-on-white embellishment fading out. Near the top of the column, three-color pottery comes into use. The town dump at San Cristobal faithfully preserved these ceramic fads to help archaeologists date the prehistoric sites of the American Southwest.

The sands and silts inside Gatecliff Shelter acted similarly, preserving such proportional patterning in the projectile points. Figure 10–6 shows that Elko Corner-notched points were vertically distributed across the strata at Gatecliff Shelter in near-perfect, "battleship-shaped" fashion. The other types are similarly distributed, but the smaller

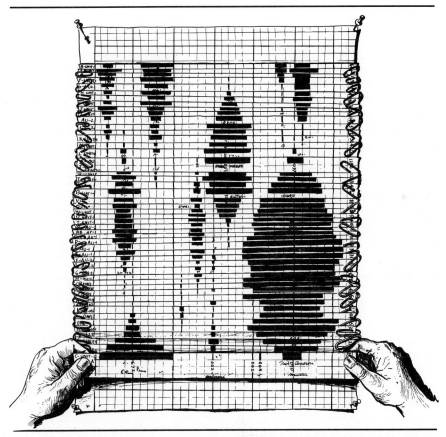

FIGURE 10–8 Constructing a seriation diagram literally by hand. Frequencies of types within each collection are drawn on individual slips and then moved along until the "battleship-shaped" curves become relatively smooth. Computer programs are currently available to do much of this tedious work (see Ford 1957, Figure 4). (Courtesy Nicholas Amorosi)

sample sizes tend to mask the battleships.

Artifacts tend to "seriate" in stratified deposits like San Cristobal and Gatecliff Shelter. This principle of seriation has been adapted by archaeologists to create a relative dating technique that works in the absence of stratified deposits.

In Chapter 1, we presented the percentage frequency chart (Figure 1–7) concocted by James Ford to demonstrate west-to-east changes in ceramic surface texture from many different sites across the American Southeast (Ford 1952, Figure 15). To do this, pottery is first washed, catalogued, and classified; then the percentages of each type are calculated across the relevant provenience units. The percentages are signified by horizontal bars on long, narrow stips of graph paper, "like slats of a venetian blind," and held together with paper clips. The strips are "arranged and rearranged in relation to one another until the clearest patterning appears" (Ford 1962, p. 42).

Figure 10–8 shows how the process works. In fact, the drawing has itself become an archaeological artifact. When researching the first edition of this book a decade ago, I discovered the original in an art file outside my office at the American Museum of Natural History. It was drawn more than thirty years ago by the late Nicholas Amorosi, who for decades illustrated artifacts at the American Museum. In fact, Nick drew the projectile points from Gatecliff Shelter. This "hands-on" demonstration of seriation has become a classic in the literature of archaeology. Those hands actually belonged to Nick. Virtually every elementary discussion of seriation includes it (including this one). The original piece-by-piece seriation diagram being illustrated was turned into a museum exhibit at Marksville, Lousiana—rusting paper clips and all!

Several assumptions are required to make this kind of seriation work. (1) Each artifact type is assumed to follow the unimodal (battleship-shaped) model: incipience, florescence, and decline. (2) Each archaeological provenience included is assumed to constitute a representative sample of the artifact types in use at the time. (3) Each provenience being seriated is assumed to represent a short interval and derive from a limited geographic area. The validity of these assumptions is addressed by Marquardt (1978) and McNutt (1973).

It should be obvious that seriation, like the other typological tools discussed in this chapter, rests squarely on the modal definition of culture. All seriation diagrams implicitly assume that the observed variability is due to temporal change; that is, only the shared aspects of culture (styles) are reflected in frequency change through time. Of course this assumption will be incorrect in many cases, because artifact frequencies often reflect functional, technological, and societal variability as well. When too much nontemporal variability is reflected, the collections simply do not seriate very well. But the fact that seriation diagrams do work so often indicates that the modal concept is once again useful, provided that one realizes the limitations.

WHERE TO GO FROM HERE?

Some Classics in Archaeological Seriation: Ascher (1959: "A Mathematical Rationale for Graphical Seriation"; Brainerd (1951): "The Place of Chronological Ordering in Archaelogical Analysis"; Dempsey and Baumhoff (1963): "The Statistical Use of Artifact

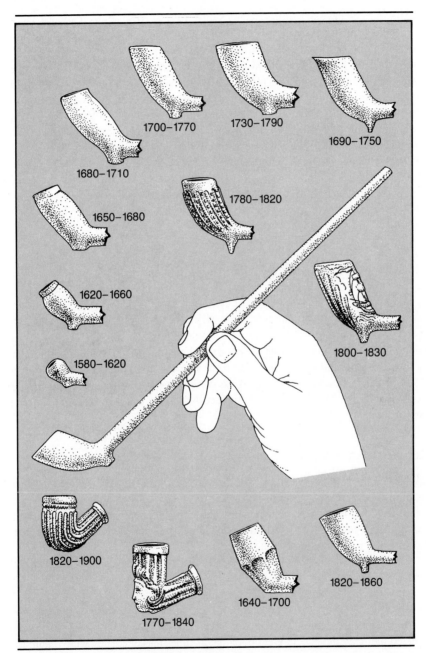

1700–1770

1730–1790

1690–1750

1680–1710

1780–1820

1650–1680

1800–1830

1620–1660

1580–1620

1820–1900

1770–1840

1640–1700

1820–1860

FIGURE 10–9 A simplified evolutionary sequence of English and American clay smoking pipes (adapted, in part, from Noël Hume 1976, Figure 97).

Distributions to Establish Chronological Sequence"; Ford (1949): "Cultural Dating of Prehistoric Sites in the Virú Valley, Peru"; (1952): "Measurements of Some Prehistoric Design Developments in the Southeastern States"; (1957): "A Quantitative Method for Deriving Cultural Chronology"; Rowe (1962): "Worsaae's Law and the Use of Grave Lots for Archaeological Dating"; Spier (1917): "An Outline for a Chronology of Zuñi Ruins."

Contemporary Approaches to Seriation: Braun (1985): "Absolute Seriation: A Time-Series Approach"; Dunnell (1970): "Seriation Method and Its Evaluation"; Hodson, Kendall, and Tautu (1971): *Mathematics in the Archaeological and Historical Sciences;* Kendall (1964): "A Statistical Approach to Flinders Petrie's Sequence Dating"; (1969): "Some Problems and Methods in Statistical Archaeology"; Marquardt (1978): "Advances in Archaeological Seriation"; McNutt (1973): "On the Methodological Validity of Frequency Seriation"; Rouse (1967): "Seriation in Archaeology."

Computer-assisted Methods for Seriation: Drennan (1976); Hole and Shaw (1967); L. Johnson (1968, 1972a); LeBlanc (1975).

Time-Markers in Historical Archaeology

Over the years, historical archaeologists have developed an impressive array of dating techniques suitable for historic-period artifacts. The same basic principles of classification apply to prehistoric and historic-period archaeological sites, but the specific procedures vary somewhat. For our purposes, it is sufficient to look at a handful of such dating methods (but you can easily pursue the subject by looking at some of the references listed at the end of this section).

Pipe Stem Dating

Changing technology has created a vast array of time-marker artifact types in historical archaeology: Before 1830, the fiber of the metal ran crosswise to the axis of a nail; after that, the fibers ran lengthwise. Nineteenth-century glass often had a purplish cast (caused by sunlight reacting with magnesium oxide, but magnesium was no longer added after World War I). Examples proliferate endlessly.

Historical archaeologists have been particularly clever in finding increasingly fine-grained ways to partition time on their sites. One classic way to date colonial-period American sites was developed by J. C. "Pinky" Harrington (1954). Clay tobacco pipes changed form markedly in the seventeenth and eigthteenth centuries, and broken fragments turn up by the hundreds on many archaeological sites of this period. Everybody recognized that clay pipes held great potential as time-markers: They were manufactured, imported, smoked, and thrown away, all within a year or so (Noël Hume 1976, p. 296). Some people studied changes in pipe bowl shape. Others observed that stem thickness also changed through time (Figure 10–9). Stem length bore a direct relationship to period of manufacture: Starting with six- to eight-inch pipes in the early seventeenth century and

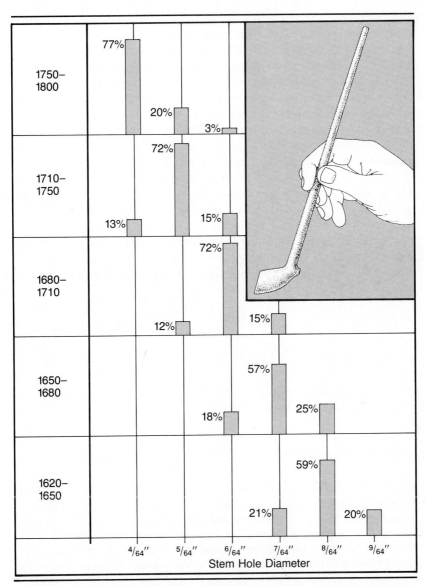

FIGURE 10–10 Harrington's diagram for estimating the age of English pipe stem fragments (adapted from Harrington 1954)

extending to the long "church warden" pipes of the early eighteenth century, the trend then reversed itself, ending in the short-stem pipes made during the nineteenth century.

Each method has merit, but the same problem plagued each one because the fragile clay pipes rarely survived in a condition sufficiently complete to allow fruitful analysis. While working with the pipe collection from Jamestown, including some fifty-thousand small chunks of broken stems, Harrington made a stimulating observation. The early pipe stems seemed to have relatively large bores which became smaller in the later specimens. Following up on this observation, Harrington measured the stem hole diameters for a series of 330 known-age pipes from Jamestown and Colonial Williamsburg (Virginia) and Fort Frederica (St. Simons Island, Georgia) (see Figure 10–10).

It turned out that inside diameter did change through time, and systematically at that. The resulting pipe stem chronology began in 1620 and lasted through 1800. Harrington divided this period into five cultural periods. Best of all, the technique was simple and cheap: "In making use of this dating device, the first requirement is a 39-cent set of drills; the second is common sense" (Harrington 1954, p. 8).

Fifteen years later, Lewis Binford (1962a) termed Harrington's method "clumsy" and reworked the original data to derive a statistical regression formula for estimating age from the size of pipe stem holes:

$$Y = 1931.85 - 38.26X$$

where X is the mean stem bore for a sample of pipe fragments and Y is the projected mean date. In effect, Binford moved the technique from a series of ordinal categories to the more precise (but not more accurate) metric estimates. Archaeologists have debated the pros and cons of pipe stem dating ever since, many investigators ignoring the cautions and "commonsense" stricture tendered by Harrington from the start.

Documentary Evidence to Define Time-Markers

Since so much research has been done on the history of the pottery industry in England and continental Europe, it is not unusual to know how the makers of this pottery classified, named, and traded their wares. To apply strictly formal classificatory methods to this material and ignore the historical data is like trying to reinvent the incandescent lamp by candlelight while ignoring the light switch at one's elbow.
—James Deetz

Nothing about the pipe stem example differs from procedures used in prehistoric archaeology. Harrington began with empirical observation, tested his notions against known-age controls, and then formulated his time-markers; Binford simply streamlined the estimates. But in many cases, those working on historic sites have a decided advantage over those

Figure 10–11 *The Last Supper* by Juan de Juanes (ca. 1550) showing bottle forms (see Deagan 1987, Figure 6.3). (Courtesy Museo del Prado, Madrid)

studying prehistoric remains because historical archaeologists also have access to documentary evidence that can help create even finer-grained temporal divisions.

One particularly handy method has been the study of period paintings to learn more about ancient artifact forms. When Kathleen Deagan was researching the shapes of Hispanic bottles used in the New World, for instance, she was dismayed to find that although green and clear glass littered sixteenth-century sites, not a single complete bottle from this period survived anywhere in Florida and the Caribbean (Deagan 1987, p. 130). But rather than simply give up, she temporarily turned art historian because bottles, it turns out, are frequently depicted in sixteenth-century Spanish art, such as *The Last Supper* by Juan de Juanes (Figure 10–11). Such paintings provided rare clues to unknown forms of Hispanic bottles, and Figure 10–12 is a chronological sequence of bottle forms abstracted largely from such paintings.

Noël Hume (1976, pp. 38–44) considered the role that paintings can play in reconstructing British colonial artifact forms. One particularly illuminating source is William Hogarth, an eighteenth-century English artist whose paintings, drawings, and engravings are littered with a vast spectrum of everyday, domestic artifacts of the time. Figure 10–13 shows Hogarth's well-known tavern orgy scene from his series *The Rake's Progress,* painted in 1735. Here, our roving rake sprawls in Rose Tavern, charmed and robbed by an obliging cadre of trollops, awash in artifacts of their day: chairs, clothes, caps, a watch, drinking glasses, plates, a sword, candlesticks, and so

FIGURE 10–12   Sixteenth-century Hispanic bottle forms found in archaeological sites throughout the the Caribbean (see Deagan 1987, Figure 6.2). (Reprinted by permission of the Smithsonian Institution Press from *Artifacts of the Spanish Colonies of Florida and the Caribbean, 1500–1800,* vol. 1, *Ceramics,* Kathleen Deagan, p. 131, fig. 6.2. © 1987 Smithsonian Institution, Washington, D.C.)

forth. Working from an enlargement of this print, the observant historical archaeologist should be able to learn plenty about artifact styles typical of the first third of the eighteenth century, right?

Perhaps, but historical archaeologists have learned to be cautious in evaluating the historical accuracy of surviving documents and commentary. Some paintings are as good as photographs. Historical archaeologists have concluded, for instance, that most artists in the Dutch and Flemish traditions can be trusted to render faithfully both people and objects. These artists sat directly across from the subjects they painted.

But Hogarth is a problem because his own writings suggest that most of his creations came from memory, often assembled from sketches squirreled away in his files. Sure enough, when specialists study the orgy scene, they find his rendering of everyday items is suspect: The brickwork is unrealistic; the scimitar-shaped knife wielded by the young lady is all wrong; and the bottles are about thirty years too early for the period of the drawing. Hogarth had learned how to draw a bottle during his early life, and kept on drawing that type, ignoring the changes that had taken place in the intervening years. Noël Hume (1976, p. 41) concluded that "in all probability, therefore, having drawn, say, a rat trap two or three times, Hogarth knew what a rat trap looked like and thenceforth extracted it from his memory 'prop room' whenever he needed it. Consequently, every trap he drew looked more or less the same, no matter whether it had been outmoded by new and better rat traps developed later on in his life" (Noël Hume 1976, p. 41). This case underscores the general point that historical archaeologists must be discriminating when dealing with documentary evidence.

FIGURE 10–13   The orgy scene from *An Evening at the Rose Tavern: The Rake's Progress, Scene III,* painted around 1732 to 1734 by William Hogarth. (Courtesy the Nelson-Atkins Museum of Art).

TABLE 10–2—Date Ranges for Hispanic Ceramics in Spanish Colonial Sites

I. Coarse Earthenware

A. Unglazed Coarse Earthenware

Olive Jar, early	1490–1570
Olive Jar, middle	1560–1800
Olive Jar, late	1800–1900
Bizcocho	1500–1550
Redware	1500–1750
Storage Jar	1500–1800
Feldspar Inlaid, redware	1530–1600
Orange Micaceous	1550–1650
Hidroceramo, tan or red paste	1700–1800
Hidroceramo, greyware	1780–1820
Greyware	1750–1850

B. Burnished, Painted, or Slipped Coarse Earthenware

Mexican Red Painted	1550–1750
Yucatán Colonial	1570–1650
Pisan slipware	1600–1650
Guadalajara Polychrome	1650–1800

C. Lead-glazed Coarse Earthenware

Melado	1490–1550
Green Bacin/Green Lebrillo	1490–1600
El Morro ware	1550–1770
Black Lead-glazed Coarse Earthenware	1700–1770
Rey ware	1725–1825

II. Majolica

A. Old World Majolica: Spanish

1. Moorish-influenced Spanish Majolica

Lusterware	1490–1550
Cuerda seca ware	1490–1550
Sevilla Blue on White	1530–1650
Sevilla Blue on Blue	1550–1630

4. Talaveran-Style Spanish Majolica

Type	Date
2. "Morisco ware"	
Isabela Polychrome	1490–1580
Yayal Blue on White	1490–1625
Columbia Plain	1490–1650
Santo Domingo Blue on White	1550–1630
3. Italianate Spanish Majolica	
Caparra Blue	1490–1600
Sevilla White	1530–1650
B. Old World Majolica: Italian	
Montelupo Polychrome	1500–1560
Ligurian Blue on Blue	1550–1600
C. New World Majolica: Mexico City	
1. Fine-grade wares	
Mexico City White	1580*–1650
Fig Springs/San Juan Polychrome	
San Luís Blue on White	1580*–1650
	1580*–1650

Type	Date
Talavera Polychrome	1550–1600
Talavera Blue on White	1600–1650
Ichtucknee Blue on White	1600–1650
5. Catalonian Spanish Majolica	
Catalonia Blue on White	1760–1820
Faenza White	1550–1600
Faenza Compendiaro	1550–1600
2. Common-grade wares	
Mexico City Blue on Cream	1600–1650
Mexico City Green on Cream	1600–1650
Aucilla Polychrome	1650–1700
San Luís Polychrome	1650–1750
Santa Maria Polychrome	1650–1760

Source: Used by permission of the author and the Smithsonian Institution Press from *Artifacts of the Spanish Colonies of Florida and the Caribbean, 1500–1800, vol. 1, Ceramics,* by Kathleen Deagan, p. 28, table 2. © 1987 Smithsonian Institution Washington, D.C..
*1575 in Mexico.

TPQ Dating

Regardless of how they are established, such date ranges (ceramics and otherwise) form the backbone of chronology in historical archaeology (see Table 10–2). They are used in two basic ways: to define a temporal cutoff point or to estimate a central temporal tendency. Let me explain how each works.

Kathleen Deagan and Joan Koch excavated an important cemetery named Nuestra Señora de la Soledad in downtown St. Augustine (Koch 1980, 1983). Because the deliberate inclusion of grave goods was rare, the excavators were forced to rely heavily on archaeology's two primary stratigraphic dating techniques (Chapter 8). Invoking the law of superposition, excavators attempted to work out grave-by-grave sequences of interment. Although superposition is no help on isolated graves, an early-to-late relative sequence can be worked out by detailed stratigraphic comparisons of which grave pits cut into which others.

The index fossil concept was also applied at Soledad. The first step is to classify the sherds into the various ceramic types commonly found on Spanish-American sites (Table 10–2). One such type is named Ichtucknee Blue on White. The last part describes the surface decoration, but "Ichtucknee" comes from the Ichtucknee River, where John Goggin first recognized the type based on specimens salvaged from Fig Springs (on the Ichtucknee River, in north central Florida). The estimated age of Ichtucknee Blue on White ceramics ranges between 1600 and 1650.

Each grave pit can then be dated according to the associational concept of **terminus post quem** (or TPQ), defined as "a date after which the object must have found its way into the ground" (Noël Hume 1970, p. 8). At Soledad, the TPQ indicates the first possible date that the latest-occurring artifact could have been deposited in that grave pit. So when a sherd of Ichtucknee Blue on White turned up in the grave fill at Soledad, excavators knew that this grave could not have been dug before 1600 (the date after which the sherd must have found its way into the ground). Had the same grave pit contained a sherd of, say, San Luís Polychrome (with an associated age range from 1650 to 1750), then the TPQ date would have to have been revised to 1650. This is how TPQ dating works.

In practice, the TPQ dating at Soledad was not that precise. But when combined with the correlative data from superposition (and documentary evidence about site usage), the TPQ estimates enabled Deagan and Koch to group the Soledad burials into three culture period classifications: seventeenth-century Spanish (TPQ: pre–1700), eighteenth-century Spanish (TPQ: pre–1762), and eighteenth-century British (TPQ: post–1762). Once this classification was established, they could look for cultural differences and similarities among burial assemblages. The Spanish-period burials were mostly shroud wrapped, whereas the British used coffins. The Spanish crossed the arms across the chest, whereas the British were interred with arms along the side. Spanish burials were oriented toward the east, British toward the west, and so forth.

TPQ estimates the date after which the grave must have been dug (or, technically, after which it was filled in). This estimate is the earliest possible date, given the accuracy of the known date range. The opposite estimate is (naturally) the **terminus ante quem**, the date before which a stratum or feature must have been deposited.

Mean Ceramic Dates

There is some disagreement about the utility of *terminus post quem* ceramic dating in historical archaeology. Many, such as Deagan (e.g., 1983, Chapter 10), find the concept to be useful in providing a valid baseline for site chronology. Noël Hume (1970, p. 11) has even declared that *terminus post quem* procedures provide the "the cornerstone of all archaeological reasoning."

Other archaeologists are less sanguine about TPQ dating. They point up a number of complicating factors (see South 1977a, pp. 202–204): Seventeenth-century Anglo-American sites are relatively rare, and less is known about the ceramic associations; status differences influence relative ceramic frequencies; and so forth. Some archaeologists argued that there is such a slight connection between the date of manufacture and the date of deposition of a ceramic type on historic sites that any attempt to date a site on the basis of pottery-manufacturing dates is subject to gross error (e.g., Dollar 1968, pp. 41–45).

Stanley South (1972, 1977a) has derived a provocative (and currently widespread) method to minimize these perceived problems (Figure 10–14). South's **mean ceramic date** approach shifts the emphasis away from beginning and end dates for ceramic wares, emphasizing instead the mid-range, *median* date. Working from information in *A Guide to Artifacts in Colonial America* (Noël Hume 1970), South constructed a model based on

FIGURE 10–14   Stanley South. (Courtesy Stanley South)

selected ceramic types, defined by attitutes of form, decoration, surface finish, and hardness *plus* the temporal dates assigned by Noël Hume for each type (South 1977a, Table 31).

Seventy-eight specific ceramic types were included in South's formulation (see Table 10–3). Canton porcelain, for instance, has a known range of dates between 1800 and 1830. The median date for this type is thus 1815. Bellarmine, brown, salt-glazed stoneware with a well-molded human face ranges in age from 1550 through 1625; the median date is 1587.

The mean ceramic date pools this information across a feature (or an entire site) by using Table 10–3 to determine the median date of manufacture for each time-sensitive sherd and then averaging these dates to arrive at the mean occupation date implied by the entire collection. Table 10–4 shows how the mean ceramic date is computed for the cellar fill in the Hepburn-Reonalds Ruin in Brunswick, North Carolina (South 1977a, p. 220, Table 32). Available historic records revealed that the building was probably still standing in 1734 and burned in 1776; the **median historic date** is thus $(1734 + 1776) / 2 = 1755$. South's mean ceramic date came out to be $Y = 1758.4$, only 3.4 years later than the median historic date. Moreover, the pipe stem date for this site is 1756, and so there is substantial agreement among all three sources. In fact, South has found that the mean ceramic dates seldom deviate from a range of ±4 years from the known median historic date. Such agreement is nothing short of remarkable.

The mean ceramic date relies on two central assumptions (Majewski and O'Brien 1987, p. 170): (1) that ceramic types are roughly contemporary at all sites at which they occur and (2) that the mid-range date of manufacture approximates the modal date of popularity.

Mean ceramic estimates are not limited to British colonial sites. South (1977a) expanded it to Spanish-American sites throughout the New World. Other investigators have tinkered with the mean ceramic dating procedure, attempting to apply it to nineteenth-century Anglo-American assemblages, English wine bottles, and even Native American pottery. Others have tried to take this research one step further by looking for the factors responsible for creating discrepancies between mean ceramic dates and their documentary equivalents.

Stan used to come up to Colonial Williamsburg with boxes full of sherds. He wanted to know about the types and dates of all kinds of ceramics, and I did my best to help him. I think that was when he was working on that formula. You know, the one that gives you a date you already know.
—Attributed to Ivor Noël Hume

WHERE TO GO FROM HERE?

Pipe Stem Dating in Historical Archaeology: The initial definition was provided by Harrington (1954); Binford's regression version was first published in 1962. The most comprehensive discussion of the evolution and use of pipe stem dating is found in Volume

TABLE 10–3—Some Ceramic Types Used to Construct Mean Ceramic Dates in Seventeenth Century Anglo-American Sites

Type Number	Date Range	Median Date	Ceramic Type Name and Page Reference
			Porcelain
5.	c.1800–1830	1815	Canton porcelain (262).
7.	c.1790–1825	1808	Overglaze enamelled China trade porcelain (258, 261).
26.	c.1660–1800	1730	Overglaze enamelled Chinese export porcelain (261).
31.	c.1745–1795	1770	English porcelain (137).
39.	c.1660–1800	1730	Underglaze blue Chinese porcelain (257).
41.	c.1750–1765	1758	"Littler's Blue" (119–23) (on white salt-glazed stoneware, porcelain, and creamware).
69.	c.1574–1644	1609	Chinese porcelain, underglaze blue, Late Ming (257, 264).
			Stoneware
Brown			
1.	c.1820–1900+	1860	Brown stoneware bottles for ink, beer, etc. (78–79).
46.	c.1700–1810	1755	Nottingham stoneware (Lustered) (114).
52.	c.1700–1775	1738	Burslem "crouch" pale brown stoneware mugs.
53.	c.1690–1775	1733	Brown salt-glazed mugs (Fulham) (111–13).
54.	c.1690–1775	1733	British brown stoneware (excluding 1, 52, 53) (112–114).
66.	c.1620–1700	1660	Deteriorated Bellarmine face bottles (one dated example to the 1760s) (56–57).
74.	c.1550–1625	1588	Bellarmine, brown salt-glazed stoneware, well-molded human face (55–57).
75.	c.1540–1600	1570	Rhenish brown-glazed sprigged, mould-decorated, Cologne-type stoneware (277–79).
Blue, gray			
44.	c.1700–1775	1738	Westerwald, stamped blue floral devices, geometric designs (284–85).
58.	c.1650–1725	1668	Sprig molding, combed lines, blue and manganese decorated Rhenish stoneware (280–81).
59.	c.1690–1710	1700	Embellished Hohr gray Rhenish stoneware (284).
77.	c.1700–1775	1738	Westerwald chamber pots (148, 281).
White			
16.	c.1740–1765	1753	Moulded white salt-glazed stoneware (115).
24.	c.1765–1795	1780	Debased "Scratch blue" white salt-glazed stoneware (118).
30.	c.1755–1765	1760	Transfer printed white salt-glazed stoneware (128).
34.	c.1744–1775	1760	"Scratch blue" white salt-glazed stoneware (117).
40.	c.1720–1805	1763	White salt-glazed stoneware (excluding plates and moulded) (115–17).
41.	c.1750–1765	1758	"Littler's blue" (119–23) (on white salt-glazed stoneware, porcelain, and creamware).

Source: South 1977a, Table 31, p. 210.
Used by permission of the author.

TABLE 10–4—Using the Formula with Ceramics from the Brunswick Hepburn–Reonalds Ruin (S7)

Ceramic Type	Type Median (X_i)	Sherd Count (f_i)	Product
22	1791	483	865,053
33	1767	25	44,175
34	1760	32	56,320
36	1755	55	96,525
37	1733	40	69,320
43	1758	327	574,866
49	(1750)	583	1,020,250
44	1738	40	69,520
47	1748	28	48,944
53,54	1733	52	90,116
56	1733	286	495,638
29	1760	9	15,840
		1960	3,446,567 ÷ 1960 = 1758.4

The mean ceramic date formula
$$Y = \frac{\sum\limits_{i=1}^{n} X_i \cdot f_i}{\sum\limits_{i=1}^{n} f_i} \qquad Y = \frac{3,446,567}{1960} = 1758.4$$

Source: South 1977a, Table 32, p. 220.
Used by permission of the author and Academic Press.

6 of the *The Conference on Historic Site Archaeology Papers,* especially the papers by Binford (1972b), Hanson (1972), Heighton and Deagan (1972). See also Hanson (1971) and Noël Hume (1976, pp. 296–301).

    Mean Ceramic Dating: The mean ceramic date was introduced in Volume 6 of *The Conference on Historic Site Archaeology Papers 1971* by Stanley South (1972) and was discussed by several others, including D. South (1972). See also Lofstrom, Tordoff, and George (1982); Majewski and O'Brien (1987, pp. 170–172); Salwen and Bridges (1977); South (1977a, Chapter 7); Turnbaugh and Turnbaugh (1977); Waselkov (1979).

Basic Archaeological Units

This chapter concludes the discussion of how archaeologists construct their cultural chronologies. But before moving on to more advanced archaeological objectives, we must still consider how these temporal types are synthesized into chronologies extending beyond the individual site. In effect, time-markers are the first building blocks laid down to create the foundations of regional chronology.

Americanist archaeology has adopted a relatively standardized framework for integrating chronological information on a large scale. This regional infrastructure was initially set out by Harvard archaeologists Gordon Willey and Phillip Phillips in their influential book entitled *Method and Theory in American Archaeology,* published in 1958. Although nomenclature still varies somewhat from region to region, the Willey–Phillips framework remains the most generally accepted system in the Americas.

Remember how temporal types are defined: You group individual artifacts into relatively homogeneous categories (morphological types), and then test them against independent data (such as site stratigraphy, correlation with other known sites, and direct artifact dating). Morphological types found to change systematically are elevated to the status of time-markers.

The next analytical step is to determine how temporal types themselves cluster to reflect site chronology. The first critical unit in supratype of synthesis is called a **component**, a culturally homogeneous stratigraphic unit within a single site. "Culturally homogeneous" is the buzzword here, the line separating homogeneous and heterogeneous often existing only in the excavator's mind. Many archaeological sites contain only a single component; that is, the artifact assemblage is essentially homogeneous (with respect to time) throughout the entire site. Most archaeological sites contain more than one component.

Because defining archaeological components rests on the intangible factor of cultural homogeneity, there can be no firm rules. At sites like Gatecliff Shelter, the strata are strikingly obvious from the stratigraphic profile (see Figure 8–4). Throughout most of the site, distinct lenses of sterile, noncultural silts separate the deposits into discrete living floors. These various surfaces can then be kept distinct (as individual components) or grouped together on the basis of shared time-markers or absolute dates. Gatecliff contained five distinct cultural components, each incorporating one to six living surfaces. Elsewhere, at places like Pueblo San Cristobal, the trash heaps had been churned and mixed. Although components still existed, they bled stratigraphically one into another without visible breaks. In such cases, components must be isolated analytically, without the assistance of obvious physical stratigraphy.

Components are thus site specific. But the components from several sites must usually be analytically combined to define the master regional chronology. The next analytical step is the **phase**: similar components as manifested at more than one site. Willey and Phillips (1958, p. 22) call a phase the "practicable and intelligible unit of archaeological study," defining it as "an archaeological unit possessing traits sufficiently characteristic to distinguish it from all other units similarly conceived . . . spatially limited to the order of magnitude of a locality or region and chronologically limited to a relatively brief interval of time."

Like the component, the phase concept is encumbered by weasel words like "sufficiently characteristic," "similarly conceived," and "relatively brief interval." No matter how hard archaeologists try, some degree of wishy-washy subjectivity lingers, and decisions still rely heavily on simple familiarity with the archaeological data at hand.

Gatecliff Shelter shows how the phase concept works in archaeology. Table 10–5 summarizes the cultural chronology of this site. We recognized five components at Gatecliff, each defined by shared time-markers and radiocarbon dates. The uppermost component was characterized by Desert Side-notched and Cottonwood Triangular projectile points, and Shoshone Brownware ceramics. It began in about A.D. 1300 and lasted until Anglo-American contact, about 1850 in central Nevada. The other components are similarly defined, each composed of different temporal types and spanning other episodes of time.

When talking only about Gatecliff, the analytical unit remains the component. But actually we excavated nearly a dozen sites in Monitor Valley (Thomas 1988b), and several of these sites contained a late assemblage similar to that recognized at Gatecliff. At the site level, these assemblages comprise a component. At a regional level, similar components are synthesized into a phase, which we named Yankee Blade after a nineteenth-century silver mine in nearby Austin.

Figure 10–15 diagrams the relationship between component and phase. Three archaeological sites have been tested within a region, and as is often the case, no single site contains the complete cultural sequence: The first site has Components A and B; the second site contains a new component called C; and the third site has Components A and C but lacks Component B. By analyzing the temporal types shared among the components and comparing the absolute dates, a regional sequence of phases can be constructed from evidence at these three sites.

TABLE 10–5—Cultural Occupations at Gatecliff Shelter

Horizon	Component	Stratum	Field Designation	Age (B.P.)	Date
1	Yankee Blade	1	GU Upper 14	650–450 B.P.	A.D. 1300–A.D. 1500
2	Underdown	1	Bone Bed	650 B.P.	A.D. 1300
3	Underdown	1	GU Lower 14	1250–650 B.P.	A.D. 700–A.D. 1300
4	Reveille	3,5	GU Upper 12		
5	Reveille	3,5	GU Lower 12	3200–1250 B.P.	1250 B.C.–A.D. 700
6	Reveille	3,5	GU 12 Living Floor		
7	Reveille	6,7	GU 11	3250–3200 B.P.	1300 B.C.–1250 B.C.
8	Reveille/Devils Gate	9	GU 9	3300–3250 B.P.	1350 B.C.–1300 B.C.
9	Devils Gate	11	GU 7	3400–3300 B.P.	1450 B.C.–1350 B.C.
10	Devils Gate (?)	13	GU 6	4050–3400 B.P.	2100 B.C.–1450 B.C.
11	Devils Gate (?)	17	GU 4	4250–4100 B.P.	2300 B.C.–2150 B.C.
12	?	19	GU 2	5000–4250 B.P.	3050 B.C.–2300 B.C.
13	Clipper Gap	20	GU 1A	5100–5000 B.P.	3150 B.C.–3050 B.C.
14	Clipper Gap	22	GU 6-74	5250–5100 B.P.	3300 B.C.–3150 B.C.
15	Clipper Gap	24	GU 4-74	5350–5250 B.P.	3400 B.C.–3300 B.C.
16	Clipper Gap	26	Square Beta, 685–700 cm	5500–5350 B.P.	3550 B.C.–3400 B.C.

Source: Thomas 1983b, Table 40.

The component is site specific, whereas the phase spans an entire region. So defined, the phase becomes archaeology's basic unit of areal synthesis. To ensure that the phase concept remains viable in practice, the definition is left purposely vague. Phases can be as short as a few generations, especially in areas where the chronology is based on dendrochronologically controlled painted ceramics. Phases can also last a long time period, like the Reveille phase of central Nevada, which begins about 1500 B.C. and continues until A.D. 500. The length of the phase depends in part on the kind of archaeological remains involved and also on our contemporary knowledge of these remains. Well-studied areas tend to have shorter phases.

The phase concept allows archaeologists to treat time, actually a continuous variable, as if it were a discrete set of points. The overall Gatecliff Shelter sequence lasted for about seven thousand years, and "years" are a perfectly viable way to think of time. But "years" can create difficulties in archaeological sites. We found it better to view Gatecliff in terms of five components, one stacked on another.

Each component has an associated array of dates and a set of characteristic artifacts. Gatecliff components can be compared with components at other nearby sites, and a regional chronology can be constructed. Using the phase as our smallest unit, we can establish regional contemporaneity. Strictly speaking, two events can never be truly "contemporary," even if we measure time in millimicroseconds. Time has no intrinsic units, and the smallest subdivision can always (at least in theory) be subdivided.

The job of archaeology's phase concept is to impose a set of minimal units on time, and the phase is that minimal unit. When we discuss the Yankee Blade phase, we are treating the time span from A.D. 1300 to A.D. 1850 as if it were an instant. By definition, two components of the Yankee Blade phase are simultaneous, provided that "simultaneous" is understood to last 550 years. As knowledge of the Yankee Blade phase expands, we may be able to distinguish divisions within the phase. It might be possible, for instance, to distinguish an early Yankee Blade component from a late Yankee Blade component. When this happens, the initial phase is segmented into *subphases*. This

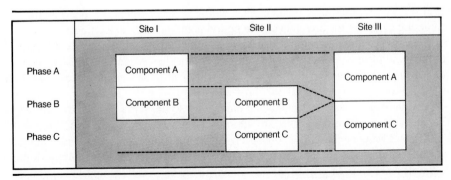

FIGURE 10–15   Relationships of the concepts of site, component, and phase.

increasing subdivision reflects the amount of research accomplished on each phase and underscores the degree to which our knowledge of the archaeological record is a contemporary phenomenon.

Summary

Archaeologists recover two kinds of things in their excavations: artifacts and ecofacts. Artifacts are the material cultural remains of human activity. Archaeology was once almost exclusively artifact oriented, but in the past few decades, archaeology has used more sensitive field techniques designed to recover relevant ecological information as well. The term ecofact describes the nonartifactual remains found in archaeological sites: bones, pollen grains, fish scales, seeds, and plant macrofossils (analysis of ecofacts is considered in detail in Chapter 11).

The type is the basic unit of artifact analysis, an ideal construct that allows archaeologists to transcend individual artifacts to consider more generalized categories. The morphological type reflects the overall appearance of a set of artifacts, emphasizing broad similarities rather than focusing on specific traits. Morphological types are descriptive, enabling the archaeologist to summarize large sets of individual artifacts into a few ideal categories.

The temporal type serves a more specific function, to monitor how artifacts change through time. Temporal types are best defined through stratigraphic analysis, by using the index fossil concept (introduced in Chapter 5).

Seriation is a relative chronological method that also enables archaeologists to monitor systematic artifact change through time. Seriation operates on the implicit assumption that stylistic change tends to begin gradually and then to pick up speed as the style catches on. After this peak of popularity, the frequency of the style tapers off gradually, until it disappears from the archaeological record entirely. Thus relative popularity takes on a characteristic "battleship-shaped" curve. Traditionally accomplished by graphic means, seriation can now be achieved through computer-assisted methods.

Historical archaeologists have been particularly clever in finding increasingly detailed ways to partition time on their sites: dating small fragments of tobacco pipe stems, evaluating evidence for time-markers in period paintings, and extracting a mean occupation date by averaging ceramic dates of manufacture across entire assemblages. But despite such differences—and the fine-grained results they produce—the basic procedures and assumptions behind artifact classification differ little between historical archaeology and archaeology in general.

A number of basic archaeological units apply to the supra-artifact level of analysis. The archaeological component is a culturally homogeneous stratigraphic unit within a single site: Components are thus site specific. Similar components at different sites can be synthesized into phases that are archaeological units of internal homogeneity, limited in both time and space. In general, phases comprise the basic archaeological building blocks for regional synthesis.

*Excavation of slave dwellings built during Jefferson's lifetime
at Monticello (Virginia): the remains of building "l," the storehouse (foreground),
building "m," the smokehouse-dairy (center), and the rebuilt walls of an 1809
stone house (background) (see Kelso 1986, Figure 6). (Courtesy William
M. Kelso and the Archaeological Institute of America)*

	BAND	TRIBE	CHIEFDOM	STATE	TYPE OF SOCIETY

LOCAL GROUP AUTONOMY

EGALITARIAN STATUS

EPHEMERAL, INFORMAL LEADERSHIP

UNSCHEDULED AD HOC RITUAL

RECIPROCAL OR BARTER ECONOMY

UNRANKED DESCENT GROUPS

PAN-TRIBAL ASSOCIATIONS, FRATERNAL ORDERS

CALENDRIC REGULARLY SCHEDULED RITUALS

RANKED DESCENT GROUPS

CENTRAL ACCUMULATION AND REDISTRIBUTIVE ECONOMY

HEREDITARY LEADERSHIP

ELITE ENDOGAMY

FULL-TIME CRAFT SPECIALIZATION

STRATIFICATION

KINGSHIP

TRUE LAW

BUREAUCRACY

MILITARY DRAFT

TAXATION

(Right margin label: SOME INSTITUTIONS, IN ORDER OF APPEARANCE)

BAND		TRIBE	CHIEFDOM	STATE	PRESENT-DAY AND RECENT EXAMPLE
KALAHARI BUSHMAN	SOUTH AFRICA	NEW GUINEA HIGHLANDERS	HAWAII	FRANCE	
AUSTRALIAN ABORIGINES		SOUTHWESTERN PUEBLOS, U.S.A.	TLINGIT INDIANS	ENGLAND	
ESKIMOS SHOSHONI	U.S.A.		NORTHWEST PACIFIC COAST	INDIA	
HADZA	EAST AFRICA			U.S.A.	

BAND	TRIBE	CHIEFDOM	STATE	ARCHEOLOGICAL EXAMPLES
EARLY INDIANS OF U.S.A. AND MEXICO	VALLEY OF OAXACA, MEXICO	GULF COAST OLMEC OF MEXICO (1000 B.C.)	CLASSIC MESO-AMERICA	
(10,000-6000 B.C.)	(1500-1000 B.C.)	Near East (5300 B.C.)	SUMER	
Near East (10,000 B.C.)	Near East (8000-6000 B.C.)	MISSISSIPPIAN OF MID-WEST U.S.A. (1200 A.D.)	SHANG CHINA	
			IMPERIAL ROME	

FIGURE IV–1. Levels of sociopolitical complexity (modified from Flannery 1972, figure 1; courtesy of Kent V. Flannery and Annual Reviews, Inc.)

PART FOUR

Archaeology's Intermediate Objective: Reconstruct Extinct Lifeways

Some of the methods, assumptions, and procedures by which archaeologists manufacture culture chronologies were presented in Part Three, as "Archaeology's Initial Objective." Constructing chronology is indeed one of archaeology's goals, but only the initial one. Of course it is true that many archaeologists have spent their entire careers working out the nuances of one regional sequence or another. But chronology must not be allowed to become an end in itself; rather, chronology is an absolutely necessary first step in setting up more sophisticated inquiries.

What are these "more sophisticated inquiries" you might ask. Archaeologists tend to subsume the various intermediate-level reconstructions under the general rubric of lifeway. To an archaeologist, the term *lifeway* describes the multifarious aspects of human existence: population density, settlement pattern, cultural ecology, technology, economy, social organization, kinship, legal systems, social stratification, ritual, sanctity, art. Year by year, archaeologists are expanding the horizons of what is known as lifeway.

The study of extinct lifeways–called **paleoethnography**—proceeds quite differently from the construction of cultural chronologies. As we saw in Chapters 6 and 7, one shift is in field technique. When constructing chronology, one seeks the largest, deepest, most clearly stratified site. It does not really matter where the artifacts come from within a level, as long as the mixture between the levels is minimized. In the past, many archaeological sites have been mined for time-sensitive artifacts; in these cases, horizontal provenience was simply not relevant to the temporal objectives. But in so doing, data potentially important to future problems were lost forever.

This field strategy must change when one begins to reconstruct a lifeway. Archaeologists must pay close attention to where artifacts come from within the stratigraphic units, that is, to their contexts. For example, a pottery vessel containing the bones of an infant tells us something quite different from what a vessel containing piñon meal does.

The focus must also shift from a site orientation to a regional orientation when reconstructing past lifeways. Single sites may be sufficient to define the relevant time-markers in a region, but no isolated site can be expected to exhibit the entire range of variability operative in a region. One site might be a major ceremonial or administrative center, and others might serve as outliers, or satellite sites, subordinate to the structure of the region.

Paleoethnography also requires the archaeologist to pay more attention to the nonartifactual contents of a site. The archaeologist concerned only with cultural chronology will view a fire hearth as a means of obtaining radiocarbon dates. But the fire hearth is a wealth of additional information to the paleoethnographer. Hearths often contain the remains of tiny seeds and hulls, which provide clues to which wild or domestic crops were harvested. Burned bones in a hearth can indicate not only which animals were eaten but also during which season the campsite was occupied. Even the structure of the charcoal itself can be important, telling the observant archaeologist where the people may have gathered their firewood and also something about past environments of the surrounding area.

Underlying these procedural shifts is the most critical difference between constructing chronology and reconstructing the lifeways of those now dead. At the root of the issue is one's definition of culture. When isolating temporal types one could simply follow a modal definition: Culture is what people share. Styles of making projectile points and decorating ceramics change because people's shared concept of what is proper changes through time. Culture, at this level, encompasses the beliefs that a society holds in common.

When analyzing extinct lifeways, contemporary archaeology transcends the shared, modal concept of culture. Cultural systems have evolved through time so that societies are equipped to adapt to their social and natural environments. It is this adaptation that comprises a society's lifeway. As we proceed through the subsequent chapters, be certain to note specific instances in which the systemic conception of culture leads archaeologists to study individuals' participation in culture, rather than merely their sharing in it.

The chapters in Part Four present the methods and techniques that contemporary archaeologists use to reconstruct past lifeways. As before, we shall proceed largely by example, so that you can see how these techniques work in actual cases of archaeological inference. But my examples are chosen not only to illustrate techniques; they also serve to introduce the broad nature of lifeways with which archaeologists work. Although each case is unique, it is possible to categorize the various lifeways in terms of their relative sociopolitical complexity. Figure IV–1 presents one such classification. Some of the societies listed in this figure will be used as examples of archaeological technique and method (for a critique of this "transformation, progressive" framework, see Leonard and Jones 1987).

In addition, the following chapters use some key terms that define the various levels of social and political organization. These terms will be introduced here so that the subsequent examples can be viewed in their proper evolutionary sequence:

Bands are the simplest of human societies. They are **egalitarian societies** integrated largely on the basis of kinship and marriage. Their leadership is informal and temporary, and labor is divided generally by sex and age. The Great Basin Shoshone are an excellent example of band structure, and we will frequently have occasion to discuss them.

Tribes are also egalitarian societies but are organized into much larger political units. Kinship is more complex and formalized than in band society, and the economy is often based on agriculture rather than foraging. The Pueblo Indians are one well-known example of tribal structure, and these groups are discussed in Chapters 13 and 14.

Chiefdoms have a basically unequal or ranked sociopolitical organization; that is, people are born into their cultural stations. The chief is a person of noble birth and is often held to be divine. Chiefdoms occur in the prehistoric and ethnographic American Southeast.

States are characterized by a strong and centralized government with a professional bureaucratic ruling class. The society lacks the kinship bonds evident in the less evolved political forms, and the structure is highly stratified by class. States maintain their authority through true law and have the power to wage war, levy taxes, and draft soldiers. States generally have populations numbering (at least) in the hundreds of thousands, and the urban centers generally exhibit a high level of artistic and architectural achievement. A state religion is generally practiced, even in areas of linguistic and ethnic diversity. The Classic Maya and the Aztecs are examples of state-level organization, and the evolution of the state is considered in some detail in Chapter 15.

These four categories provide a broad evolutionary framework within which individual societies can be categorized. In each of the subsequent chapters, you should be sure to understand into which level of sociopolitical complexity each society falls. Part Four considers how archaeologists go about reconstructing various aspects of each lifeway: subsistence, settlement pattern, social organization, religion, and ideology. Then Part Five will examine the process of evolution from simpler to more complex lifeways.

CHAPTER 11

How People Get Their Groceries: Reconstructing Human Subsistence and Ecology

Undoubtedly the desire for food has been, and still is,
one of the main causes of great political events.
—Bertrand Russell

Down in the valley the little stream flowed gently southward. Pleasant groves of trees were heavy with their new burden of early summer leaves. . . . To the north, a small herd of 200 to 300 long-horned bison—cows, bulls, yearlings, and young calves—were grazing in the small valley. A gentle breeze was blowing from the south.

As the bison grazed, a party of hunters approached from the north. Quietly, under cover of the low divide to the west and the steep slope to east, the hunters began to surround the grazing herd. Moving slowly and cautiously, keeping the breeze in their faces so as not to disturb the keen-nosed animals, they closed in on the herd from the east, north and west. Escape to the south was blocked by the arroyo. Now the trap was set.

Suddenly the pastoral scene was shattered. At a signal, the hunters rose from their concealment, shouting and yelling, and waving robes to frighten the herd. Spears began to fall among the animals, and at once the bison began a wild stampede toward the south. Too late, the old cows leading the herd saw the arroyo and tried to turn back, but it was impossible. Animal after animal pressed from behind, spurred on by the shower of spears and the shouts of the Indians now in full pursuit. The bison, impeded by the calves, tried to jump the gully, but many fell short and landed in the bottom of it. Others fell kicking, twisting and turning on top of them, pressing them below even tighter into the confines of the arroyo. In a matter of seconds, the arroyo was filled to overflowing with a writhing, bellowing mass of bison, forming a living bridge over which a few animals escaped. Now the hunters moved in and began to give the coup de grace to those animals on top, while underneath, the first trapped animals kept up the bellows and groans and their struggle to free themselves, until finally the heavy burden of slain bison above crushed out their lives. In minutes the struggle was over.

FIGURE 11–1 The "river of bones" excavated at the Olsen–Chubbock site, Colorado (see Wheat 1972, Figure 1). (Courtesy Joe Ben Wheat and the University of Colorado Museum)

One hundred ninety bison lay dead in and around the arroyo. Tons of meat awaited the knives of the hunters—meat enough for feasting, and plenty to dry for the months ahead—more meat, in fact, than they could use. Immediately, the hunters began to butcher their kill. . . . As it was cut off, some of the flesh was eaten raw, but most of the meat was laid on the skin to keep it clean. . . . Some carcasses were wedged well down in the arroyo, and these were too heavy for the hunters to move. The beautifully flaked spear points which had killed these animals went unretrieved. Wherever a leg jutted up, it was cut off, and other accessible parts were butchered; but much remained which could not be cut up.

For many days, the butchering, feasting, preparation of hides, and meat drying went on. In time, however, the meat remaining on the carcasses became too "high" for use, and the hunters had dried as much meat as they could carry; so finally they moved on, leaving the gully filled with bones and rotting flesh. . . .

Several thousand years passed before this last remnant of the arroyo was filled. . . . By 1880, there were no bison left, and the last Indians began to be replaced by White cattlemen. In 1957, the sod was broken for planting; shortly thereafter, the combination of drought and fierce winds that marked the early 1950s began to erode away the upper deposits that had covered the gully. . . . By 1957, the bones that filled the one-time arroyo were once again exposed on the surface. (Wheat 1972, p. 1-2)

This account was written by Joe Ben Wheat, the archaeologist who excavated the Olsen–Chubbuck site in eastern Colorado. During his excavations, Wheat studied the jumble of bones on bones, the scanty stone tools, and the bone-dry sands and silts that formed the ancient arroyo. But Wheat was fortunate to possess the vision to look beyond the bones and rocks: To him, Olsen–Chubbuck was "a picture so complete within itself, whose action was so brief and self-contained, that, except for minor details, one could almost visualize the dust and tumult of the hunt, the joy of feasting, the satisfaction born of a surplus of food, and finally, almost smell the stench of rotting corpses of the slain bison as the Indians left the kill scene" (Wheat 1972, p. 2). We shall be examining the Olsen–Chubbuck excavation in some detail. Not only does this site contain the remains of a remarkably well preserved Paleo-Indian bison kill, but the efforts of Joe Ben Wheat show us a great deal about how archaeologists reconstruct extinct subsistence patterns.

Figure 11–2 shows Richard MacNeish's (1967) reconstruction of various subsistence activities in the Tehuacán Valley of Mexico, based on archaeological excavation and analysis (see also Chapters 2 and 13). About nine thousand years ago the earliest inhabitants of the Tehuacán Valley secured their food through a variety of hunting and trapping techniques, combined with the collection of wild plant leaves, stems, fruits, pods, and seeds. Individual hunting patterns continued to change until about 4000 B.C., when hunting became a less important subsistence activity.

Figure 11–2 also indicates how plant cultivation gradually grew in importance in the Tehuacán subsistence system. People began growing hardy squash plants in the *barrancas* (steep-sided gulleys) near their cave sites as early as 6500 B.C. About this time, people also planted avocado trees and chili plants near springs, or along the banks of the Rio Salado, where the plants received a steady year-round supply of water. These minor subsistence activities accounted for only about 2.5 percent of the total diet in 6500 B.C. But later in time this rudimentary horticulture was supplemented by full-blown *barranca*

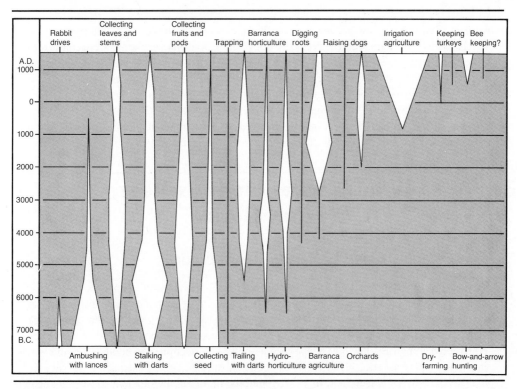

FIGURE 11–2 Estimates of the relative importance of various subsistence practices in the Tehuacán Valley, Mexico (see MacNeish 1967, Figure 188). (Courtesy Richard S. MacNeish and the University of Texas Press)

agriculture, the planting of grains such as corn and amaranth in fields, in the gulley bottoms, or on terraces where they would receive moisture from runoff during the rainy season. As agriculture became more important, the overall contribution of hunting and wild-plant collecting declined. At about 800 B.C., the advent of irrigation agriculture drastically changed the subsistence pattern in the Tehuacán Valley, corresponding with the increasing social and religious complexity.

What assumptions are involved in MacNeish's reconstruction of various subsistence practices from the archaeological record of the Tehuacán Valley? How did Joe Ben Wheat reconstruct the exact mode of bison hunting and butchering at the Olsen–Chubbuck site?

Archaeologists have a well-stocked arsenal of methods and techniques available for reconstructing the subsistence activities of the past. In this chapter we shall discuss three of the major techniques in some detail. The Olsen–Chubbuck site provides an excellent example of faunal analysis, illustrating how the archaeologist studies past hunting and dietary practices. Bones also provide a way of reconstructing the environment in which people do their shopping. Analysis of plant macrofossils is another important tool by which archaeologists determine what wild and domesticated plant foods were utilized in the past. **Palynology**, for instance, is a technique by which the fossil pollen grains from archaeological sites are studied. Not only does pollen analysis enable the archaeologist to reconstruct past vegetation, but several studies show how the analysis of fossil pollen can directly contribute to the study of past dietary practices. We also examine some additional, holistic approaches for reconstructing past diets, including computer simulation, **stable isotope analysis** of human bone, and various paleopathological indicators of "stress" in the human body. Finally, we look at the "man the hunter" myth which continues to cloud our attempts to reconstruct the human past.

What Archaeologists Learn From Bones

The Special Case of Olsen–Chubbuck

In 1957, Jerry Chubbuck, an amateur archaeologist, was driving through a ranch near Cheyenne Wells, Colorado. Chubbuck noticed an eroded area with a discontinuous outcropping of large bones protruding from the surface. Upon investigation, Chubbuck found a Paleo-Indian projectile point and an endscraper. Chubbuck wrote to Joe Ben Wheat describing his find, but Wheat was momentarily occupied on another dig and was unable to inspect the site. Meanwhile, Chubbuck also told Sigurd Olsen about the site. By an odd coincidence, Olsen had, in 1937, found the tip of another ancient spear point near the same spot. At the suggestion of curators at the Denver Museum of Natural History, Olsen and Chubbuck began to dig test pits into the site. On the basis of their test findings, Olsen and Chubbuck became convinced of the importance of their site. Once again they contacted Wheat, who first visited the site in April 1958. Olsen and Chubbuck refrained from further excavation so that Wheat could field a crew from the University of Colorado Museum. The summers of 1958 and 1960 were spent excavating at the site. The site was named, incidentally, after the toss of a coin established the sequence of names.

When Wheat first visited the Olsen–Chubbuck site, a deep furrow had been plowed lengthwise through the outcropping of bones. This furrow, coupled with the pits excavated by Olsen and Chubbuck, revealed a "river of bones" lying in a filled-in gulley, or arroyo. Wheat established a baseline to the south side of the bones and then divided the baseline into two-meter sections, providing the basic units of excavation. Wheat's crew began digging the odd-numbered sections, starting from the western end of the site. In this manner they determined the margins of the site and also created profiles of the arroyo and bone bed every two meters. Once the profiles had been drawn and photographed, the even-numbered sections could be excavated, exposing the entire bone bed. Trowels, various small knives, dental tools, and brushes were used to excavate the bones and artifacts. Shovels were used only to move backdirt and to trim the sides of the trenches. Each bone and carcass was wholly exposed in place and recorded.

The major problem at Olsen–Chubbuck was how to analyze the roughly 190 bison that had been killed there. Wheat devised a series of terms to assist in the task. Completely articulated individuals (those so deep in the arroyo as to preclude butchering) were catalogued as animal units. Partially butchered skeletons were treated similarly: pelvic-girdle units, rear-leg units, front-leg units, and so on. All animal units were drawn and photographed, and the associated artifacts (if any) were also photographed *in situ*. In addition to the animal units, over four thousand unarticulated, disassociated bones were present at Olsen–Chubbuck.

The animals ambushed at Olsen–Chubbuck are an extinct form of bison. Modern bison is characterized by short, curving horns and is known as *Bison bison*. The animals at Olsen–Chubbuck have been identified as *Bison antiquus* (Joe Ben Wheat, personal communication). Not only does *Bison antiquus* have nearly straight horns, but the Olsen–Chubbuck individuals are an average 25 percent larger than *B. bison*. This means that the adult males at Olsen-Chubbuck weighed about 2250 pounds, as compared with 1800 pounds for the modern bison bull. The females probably weighed up to 1000 pounds.

Because the bones were meticulously plotted and catalogued, Wheat could make certain inferences regarding the herd composition at Olsen–Chubbuck. Both sexes and all ages were represented in the single bison kill. About 6 percent of the bison were juveniles. Most of the young bison appeared to be a month or two old, although a couple of animals could not have been more than a few days old. Reasoning from figures for modern American bison, Wheat estimated that the kill could have occurred as early as April or as late as August, but the evidence points to a time fairly late in the calving season, probably late May or early June. Although he could not count the ones that got away, Wheat estimated that nearly all of the herd was ambushed, as two hundred is near the optimal modern herd size.

Careful analysis revealed even more details about that late spring day some ten thousand years ago. Wheat's description of the bottommost animals bellowing and ultimately suffocating is supported by the physical data. The lower half of the arroyo contained skeletons of forty whole or nearly whole animals who were virtually inaccessible. Of these, fifteen had been violently twisted on or around the axis of the vertebral column. Many bison had backs broken just behind the rib cage, and the forepart of the animal had rotated up to forty-five degrees. Three animals had been completely doubled up into a *U* shape, wedged against the sides of the arroyo. The herd had obviously been stampeded from north to south, based on orientations of the unbutchered carcasses.

A very limited array of cultural items was found associated with the Olsen–Chubbuck bones. As you might expect, these were artifacts directly involved in the killing and subsequent butchering of the bison: projectile points, scrapers, knives. Most striking were the two dozen beautifully flaked spear points found that were directly associated with the bison carcasses. Wheat used this evidence to infer that the hunters had been stationed along the path to the arroyo. Noting that projectile points were found lodged in the bodies of the lowermost animals in the arroyo, Wheat concluded that the very first animals to the arroyo had been ambushed. These animals were inaccessible to later butchers and could only have been speared as they were charged by the waiting hunters. Spears were probably heaved at the flanks of the moving herd, striking the lead animals and coercing the herd toward the arroyo. These animals would have tumbled into the arroyo first, precisely where Wheat found them.

The Olsen–Chubbuck site is an excellent illustration of the principles behind the reconstruction of extinct lifeways and stands as a vivid counterpoint to the chronologically oriented excavations considered in Part Three. We know that Joe Ben Wheat excavated Olsen–Chubbuck in order to reconstruct the lifeways of those ancient bison hunters. But suppose he had been interested only in chronology. How would his strategy have changed?

Although no contemporary archaeologist would do so, the Olsen–Chubbuck site could have been excavated for strictly chronological purposes. The scenario would go something like this. Chronological analysis is grounded in shared, modal behavior. Thus, any part of the site is as useful as any other. A trench would probably have quickly been sunk through the bones, in order to determine the stratigraphy. Then lateral trenches could be extended through the densest concentration of bone. Two aspects are important to chronology: Obtain a decent sample of cultural items, and then satisfactorily date these artifacts. In effect, the site could have been mined for projectile points, of which several were obtained. Then the bones themselves could be dated by the radiocarbon method. The results would be the statement "Firstview projectile points date roughly 8200 ± 500 B.C." In addition, the archaeologist concerned with chronology would surely note the presence of the extinct *Bison antiquus,* the bones of which are themselves time-markers.

When one is concerned strictly with chronology, it makes little difference where the artifacts come from in a site. Nelson established the relative chronology and stratigraphy at San Cristobal by digging in arbitrary one-foot units; it mattered not at all where the individual potsherds occurred within each of the ten levels. Similarly, had Olsen–Chubbuck been excavated merely for chronology, one could have rapidly trenched the site, collecting bones for radiocarbon dating, and begun building a decent sample of cultural items.

Of course there is not a qualified contemporary archaeologist around who would approach Olsen–Chubbuck in this manner. Reconstructing aspects of extinct lifeways is *de rigueur* in today's archaeology—everyone is a paleoethnographer. I merely wish to emphasize that the techniques of chronology building permit certain shortcuts, in both excavation and analysis. These shortcuts—especially applying the modal concept of culture and ignoring horizontal stratigraphy—are justified only in the extremely rare case when a regional chronology is wholly unknown. In truth, a paleoethnographic strategy can (and does) encompass all of the objectives of chronology building and yet preserves the contextual information necessary for reconstructing the details of lifeways long since past.

What Is an Archaeofauna?

Faunal materials are found in two contexts in archaeological sites. Sometimes archaeologists discover bones and shells resting precisely where they were butchered or eaten. Called **primary refuse** (Schiffer 1972), these deposits offer archaeologists an opportunity to reconstruct the sequence of events preceding the abandonment of the site. A kill site, such as Olsen–Chubbuck, is an excellent example of bones being discovered in their primary contexts. In many cases, the butchered carcasses can be carefully exposed and mapped *in situ*. Analysis is facilitated in such cases because the animal units are often intact and the archaeologists can readily infer the activities that occurred.

Bones also occur as **secondary refuse**, discarded away from their immediate area of use. For example, although Nelson saved only the ceramics from the San Cristobal trash heap, literally hundreds of bone scraps were also present. Today's more ecologically aware archaeologist would attempt to recover and analyze these faunal materials, in addition to the ubiquitous potsherds. At Gatecliff Shelter, we recovered more than sixty thousand animal bones (mostly bighorn sheep, rabbits, and rodents). But the depositional contexts were complex. In some places, we found bones exactly where they had been dropped after butchery; but most of the bones had been tossed into secondary discard areas near the drip line of the site, away from where people actually lived.

The contexts of the faunal materials condition, in large measure, the recovery techniques used in excavating archaeological sites. Primary refuse is commonly mapped in place and then removed to the laboratory for further study. The isolation of living floors enables analysts to determine rather accurately the nature and composition of archaeological faunal assemblages. Secondary refuse creates more difficulties because it consists of reworked trash heaps, whose primary contexts have been destroyed. In Chapter 6, we considered various ways of recovering faunal materials from sites. Obviously, recovering fish bones requires a digging strategy different from that for bison bones.

Once the faunal materials have been removed from the ground, the archaeologist is faced with the task of identification and analysis. Many graduate programs in archaeology offer courses in the identification of faunal remains, and a number of field archaeologists are also highly qualified in the identification of mammal, bird, mollusk, and even fish bones. In addition, there are specialists who are experts in the analysis of **archaeofauna**.

Identifying archaeological fauna is a complex procedure. One must first assign the specimen to a particular part of the body. Is it a rib splinter, part of the pelvis, or a skull fragment? Doing this requires a working knowledge of comparative anatomy. Next the specimens must be identified as accurately as the condition of the specimen (and the expertise of the analyst) permits. In many cases, the elements are so fragmentary that they cannot be identified as to species, but only to higher-order groups like family or even class. When possible, the bones are then identified by sex and age of the animal; sometimes the individual specimens are also measured and/or weighed (depending on the objective of the analysis). Many departments of anthropology have assembled their own comparative faunal collections, so that archaeological specimens can be readily and routinely identified. Often, archaeologists must do a "first sort" before consulting a faunal expert to deal with the more problematical and fragmentary specimens.

Analysis to this point is fairly routine and really concerned only with the zoological nuances of the material recovered. But analysis beyond the mere identification stage requires a serious archaeological input. Were these bones found in primary or secondary context? Have the specimens been butchered? Or worked into tools? Has the deposit been disturbed by erosion, or predators, or by later scavenging? Questions such as these can be answered only by a careful, step-by-step consideration of the archaeological contexts.

Getting Blood from the Stone

Until very recently, nobody could even guess what Neanderthal blood looked like: Museum cases are full of Mousterian (**Neanderthal**) artifacts; Ralph Solecki discovered pollen grains suggesting to him that Neanderthals were buried with flower bouquets; and Neanderthal cranial morphology has been debated for years. But how could archaeologists get a sample of Neanderthal blood?

A decade ago, Thomas Loy (then of the British Columbia Provincial Museum) developed a technique for crystallizing the hemoglobin in blood adhering to prehistoric knives and stone tools. These crystals vary according to the species of animal they came from (Loy 1983). It turns out that after a stone tool is used, the blood dries fairly quickly, and—if the combination of temperature, moisture, and soil acidity is just right—the hemoglobin can survive for millennia. Loy began his work by looking at stone tools from British Columbia, and he found hemoglobin from moose, caribou, grizzly bear, sea lion, and snowshoe hare. Not only that, but by measuring differences in the blood's oxygen isotopes, he can occasionally infer which drainage basin the animal lived in. And with a mass spectrometer, he can figure out the temperature during the month the animal died.

After revising and perfecting his extraction technique, Loy now finds that hemoglobin can survive more than 100,000 years. Analyzing blood residues on stone tools from Barda Balka (northeast Iraq), he found mammal red blood cells in the thinner deposits of blood (Bahn 1987). Given the estimated geological age of the site and *if* that blood is human (a big *if*), then Neanderthal is the only possibility—they were the only game in town.

Regardless of whether any Neanderthal blood ever turns up, Thomas Loy has singlehandedly scared archaeologists out of washing their artifacts—who knows what might be stuck onto them.

> Most of the time when I talk to groups, their first conclusion is: "Oh, gee, we'd better stop washing these things." My advice is: Right. *Don't* wash them; simply air-dry them; and if you have to have a smooth surface, brush them with a soft camel-hair brush. . . . I think that we have to develop a slightly different standard for what we think of as a quality artifact: it can no longer be one that's squeaky clean. We don't really *need* absolutely clean artifacts." (Loy quoted in Dolzani 1987, p. 8)

WHERE TO GO FROM HERE?

Recovering Blood Residues from Stone Tools: Thomas Loy's innovative research (1983, 1985) is not yet completely published; see also Bahn (1987). Brieur (1976) discussed additional techniques for recovering plant and animal residues.

The Basic Problem: What to Count?

Jumping from bones to lifeway requires a large leap. How do we proceed beyond mere identification of archaeological bones? Olsen–Chubbuck was a special case. The bones themselves were distributed stratigraphically in still-articulated skeletal portions (Wheat's "animal units"), such as forelimbs, hindlimbs, and vertebral columns. Animal units can often be recognized during excavation, assigned to taxon and often sex and age. At sites such as Olsen–Chubbuck, one can readily determine the number of animals involved (about 190), the sex distribution (about 57 percent were female), and even the season of the kill (late May or early June). The stacks of butchering units at Olsen–Chubbuck eventually allowed Joe Ben Wheat to reconstruct the order of the steps in the butchery process by invoking the law of superposition.

But sites like Olsen–Chubbuck are extremely rare, and in most cases, the task facing the faunal analyst is considerably more difficult. Bones found articulated *in situ* are relatively unusual; most sites require archaeologists to draw inferences directly from hundreds, often thousands, of isolated bone fragments. More commonly, the archaeologist is forced to work with the thousands of disarticulated bones that lie strewn throughout habitation sites.

To illustrate some of the problems posed by such sites, let me trot out my M.A. thesis research (Thomas 1969) as a cautionary example. My thesis project included the analysis of the food bones recovered from Smoky Creek Cave, a small site located in northern Nevada. Here the bones clearly represented several species, and no two bones articulated with each other. After the excavated bones had been identified to species, I wanted to construct the overall faunal food intake represented at Smoky Creek Cave. It was clear to me that a mouse bone represented somewhat less available meat than did an antelope bone. To "correct" for this vast size difference, I multiplied the total raw fragment counts by the meat potentially available from each species. After butchering several experimental animals and working my way through the available literature, I estimated that the average deer provided about one hundred pounds of usable flesh per animal. Because jackrabbits contribute only about three pounds per individual, one must kill more than thirty rabbits in order to obtain as much meat as is available from a single deer carcass. These cost–benefit relationships seemed to have important implications for prehistoric hunting practices, and I combined the size-corrected bone frequencies into a chart to provide a rough idea of the relative importance of food animals hunted in the Smoky Creek Cave vicinity.

Figure 11–3 indicates that bighorn sheep *(Ovis)* declined in overall dietary importance during the occupation of Smoky Creek Cave but that the cottontail rabbit *(Sylvilagus)* increased markedly in significance. The bottom of the site, about 150 centimeters, dates to about 1000 B.C.; the site was abandoned about A.D. 600; and Figure 11–3 suggests that mountain sheep decreased in importance after about A.D. 1. Whether this change is due primarily to environmental shifts or different hunting patterns, I did not speculate.

Figure 11–3 differed from Wheat's (1972) estimates in an important way. At Olsen–Chubbuck, Wheat dealt with actual individuals (the 190 *Bison antiquus*), whereas the Smoky Creek Cave data are relative. When dealing with isolated bones, one has no way to tell how many individuals were involved. A single bone could represent an entire animal or only one small part, which was perhaps scavenged and brought into the cave. The Olsen–Chubbuck estimates provided data about the probable number of calories consumed, whereas the Smoky Creek Cave estimates were viewed only relative to one another and were not translated into an absolute figure.

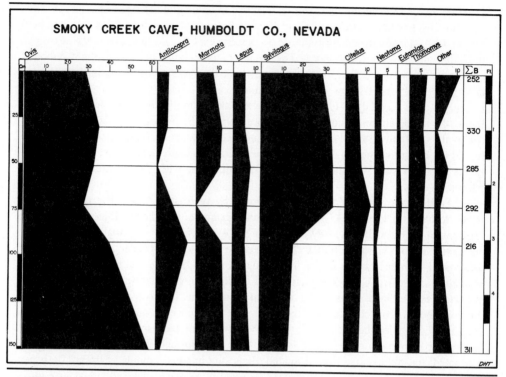

FIGURE 11–3   Estimates of the relative meat intake at Smoky Creek Cave, Nevada (see Thomas 1969, Figure 1).

My approach seemed perfectly reasonable (even inventive) at the time. But virtually everything I said about the Smoky Creek fauna is incorrect. Inadvertently I made a number of hidden assumptions, which we now know are untenable. I bring up the Smoky Creek Cave research only to highlight how far the analysis of bones from archaeological sites has come in the last two decades.

Note first what I was counting (and what was plotted on Figure 11–3). Lacking such obvious analytical units as at Olsen–Chubbuck, the most tempting way to proceed was simply to use raw bone counts as an indicator of relative frequency: If you dig up a hundred bighorn bones and only five antelope bones, then bighorn must have been twenty times more important than antelope, right? The **number of identified specimens (NISP)** formed the standard measure of archaeological fauna twenty years ago, but we now realize that many problems arise with such simple counts (Grayson 1973; 1984, p. 17).

First of all, one can never be certain whether all the various bone fragments are independent of one another. What if the hundred bighorn (*Ovis*) bones from the bottom of Smoky Creek Cave came from a single animal, whereas each antelope (*Antilocapra*) bone belonged to a different individual? In that case, antelope would be five times more abundant than the bighorn. The animals may also have been butchered differently, so that some bones were highly fragmented (and hence have disappeared from the archaeological record) or else identifiable elements, such as teeth, became dispersed and inflated the overall count.

I assumed that each bone recovered from Smoky Creek Cave could be considered as independent. Today, nobody familiar with the formation processes at archaeological sites would accept that assumption. In *Quantitative Zooarchaeology,* Donald Grayson enumerates eleven additional problems with the use of NISP as a basic counting unit (and many of these apply to the Smoky Creek Cave example).

Because of such difficulties, some archaeologists have turned to another technique of comparing animal frequencies, called the **minimum number of individuals (MNI)** method. Long used in paleontology, this method determines "that number of individuals which are necessary to account for all of the skeletal elements of a particular species found in the site" (Shotwell 1955, p. 272). That is, if you dig up one hundred fragments of bighorn bone, what will be the minimum number of individual bighorn required to account for the bones? To figure this out, you tabulate bone frequency by element (left femur, right tibia, hyoid . . .), looking for the most common skeletal element. If the proximal end of four right femurs shows up in the hundred bone fragments, then you will know that at least four bighorn "stand behind" the fragments. In this way, archaeologists have reduced large collections of bone fragments into the minimum number of individuals required to account for the bones and also to minimize the problem of interdependence among bones.

Unfortunately, several problems have also arisen in the minimum number of individuals approach. When the bones are highly fragmented, it is entirely possible that the four right femurs are represented by only fragments of one whole bone. Then it is necessary to see whether two fragments could have come from a single animal. If so, then only a minimum of three individuals are represented.

Moreover, the results depend on what one takes as a sampling universe. At a place like Smoky Creek Cave, with poorly stratified deposits, occupied over a long period of time, it would certainly be possible to have computed a minimum number of individuals over the entire occupation. But this approach has the unfortunate consequence of reducing hundreds of bone fragments to a minimum of one or two individuals, obviously a poor choice. Sometimes investigators choose to calculate their minimum numbers based on stratigraphic breaks observed during excavation. But once again, the minimum number per species depends on how fine one wishes to draw the stratigraphic boundaries. Grayson (1973, 1984) has analyzed these measuring problems in great detail.

The minimum number of individuals is known to be a direct function of the sample size of the stratigraphic units involved. Because of this difficulty, the results may not be comparable, as the minimum number has been computed in different ways. In general, the minimum number approach functions best when fine stratigraphic divisions are involved, containing bones that are not overly fragmented.

Yet another problem surfaces with the Smoky Creek Cave analysis. Note the hidden assumption that all bones recovered in our archaeological excavations must have resulted from human activities. Today, few archaeologists would be willing to so assume. If you spent tonight in Smoky Creek Cave, you would probably hear the scurrying pack rats that still live there. You probably would not see them, but coyotes, bobcats, and owls also occasionally stop by. By dragging in food bones, by leaving scats or owl pellets, or simply by dying there, each species may have contributed to the faunal remains we encountered in Smoky Creek Cave.

We realized at the time some difficulties in separating "natural" from "cultural" bone, and I even tried to figure out a way to correct for the problem (Thomas 1971). But the truth is that the depositional contexts are so complex in such caves and rock shelters that the natural and cultural assemblages may be hopelessly intermixed. Given our knowledge of the processes involved in the formation of the archaeological record in places like Smoky Creek Cave, no simple chart relying on *Number of Specimens Identified* can hope to reflect anything close to behavioral reality. The newer taphonomic approaches and the advent of stable isotope analysis point to more fruitful lines of inquiry.

WHERE TO GO FROM HERE?

General Sources on the Analysis of Faunal Remains from Archaeological Sites: Grayson (1984) has reviewed the basic assumptions, procedures, and analytical techniques of zooarchaeology in detail; Parmalee (1985) provides an important overview of current practices of identification and interpretation in zooarchaeology; Reitz and Scarry (1985) present an impressive introduction to the analysis of bones from historic-period sites; Wing and Brown (1979) provide a useful summary of diverse ways of reconstructing nutrition (including the use of animals bones); see also Carbone and Keel (1985).

Manuals to Help Archaeologists Identify Nonhuman Bones: Casteel (1977), Chaplin (1971), Cornwall (1956), Gilbert (1980), Olsen (1960, 1964, 1968, 1973), Ryder (1969).

Minimum Number of Individuals: Discussion and refinements on the minimum of individuals approach can be found in Flannery (1967b, p. 157), Ziegler (1973), and especially Grayson (1973, 1978, 1979, 1984).

Taphonomy

Taphonomy is a synthetic term coined by a Russian paleontologist, I. A. Efremov, combining the Greek words for tomb or burial *(taphos)* with that for law *(nomos)*. Generally considered a subdiscipline of paleontology, taphonomy is the study of the processes that operate on organic remains after death to form fossil deposits. As Diane Gifford (1981) pointed out, taphonomy embraces two distinct but necessarily related lines of investigation. The first focus is basic middle-range, actualistic research: documenting the observable, contemporary processes involved in the transition from behavioral to systemic contexts (observing so-called fossils in the making). The second analyzes the archaeological evidence in light of what is learned through the middle-range studies.

When an archaeologist encounters bones in a site, the first question is usually, Was this animal eaten by people? The answer is sometimes obvious. Joe Ben Wheat knew immediately that Olsen–Chubbuck's "river of bones" resulted from a prehistoric bison drive. And excavators working in the privies and dumps of historic Sacramento had no question that sawed beef bones reflected nineteenth-century meals at taverns and hotels. But sometimes, as at Smoky Creek Cave, both natural and cultural agents are doubtless responsible for depositing bones in the archaeological record. The picture becomes considerably more complex when dealing with late Pliocene/early Pleistocene sites. In many cases, documenting the presence of hominids depends on faunal evidence, and considerable research has been conducted in the attempt to find whether distinctly human patterns of bone butchery exist.

Butchering patterns at Olsen–Chubbuck were distinct. Not only were cut marks evident on individual bones, but still-articulated butchering units such as forelimbs, hindlimbs, and vertebral columns could still be identified in the field. These stacks of anatomically articulated butchering units at Olsen–Chubbuck allowed excavators to reconstruct the order of steps in the butchery process by invoking the law of superposition. Although such "signature" bone piles have some chance of preservation at such kill sites, it is rare that they survive in camps or village sites (Lyman 1987, p. 256). Archaeologists cannot simply assume that bone distribution is indicative of butchering techniques or that they are necessarily reflective of social organization.

Recent taphonomic studies by Andrew Hill and Anna Behrensmeyer suggest that there may be a pattern in the sequence of natural skeletal disarticulation. They studied sequences of skeletal disarticulation across a broad range of African mammals in a tropical savanna environment. The first joint to disarticulate is the forelimb-to-body, followed by caudal vertebrae-to-sacrum and scapula-proximal humerus (Hill 1979a, 1979b). The last joints to disarticulate tend to be various vertebrae from one another. Basically, these findings confirm the commonsense perception that more work is required to cut apart tighter joints than looser ones (Lyman 1987, p. 283).

Hill and Behrensmeyer (1984, p. 375) suggest that these documented sequences of "natural" disarticulation provide a "baseline" against which to judge the distinctiveness of human butchering practices. By comparing "natural" sequences of disarticulation with the clear-cut cases of butchery by humans at Olsen–Chubbuck, they found profound similarities between the two, regardless of the agent of disarticulation. In other words, they found that simple frequencies of disarticulation and articulation of joints in a bone assemblage did not permit archaeologists to infer that hominids had butchered the carcasses.

Despite their critical importance, relatively few studies involving human butchery have actually been conducted. In one recent assessment, Gifford-Gonzalez (in press) found fewer than a dozen relevant studies in the entire world.

WHERE TO GO FROM HERE?

General Sources on Taphonomy: Diane Gifford (1981) has reviewed specific contributions to archaeology; Lyman (1987) has written a thoughtful and in-depth review of recent butchering studies; Behrensmeyer and Kidwell (1985) have reviewed the contribution of taphonomy to the wider paleobiological context.

Paleobiology, a quarterly journal of the Paleontological Society, publishes technical papers dealing with paleobotany and paleozoology. Although still heavily slanted toward paleontology, many contributions now deal with archaeologically relevant topics.

Subscription information: c/o Department of Biological Sciences, University of Chicago, 5734 S. Ellis Avenue, Chicago Ill. 60637.

Dietary Reconstructions from Animal Bones

With these procedures in mind, we can take a brief look at the objectives and potential of faunal materials from archaeological sites. This discussion covers only the highlights, and ongoing studies will doubtless point up new directions for the analysis of faunal remains.

The Olsen–Chubbuck site was discussed in some detail at the beginning of this chapter. A major objective of the analysis was to determine the quantity of meat consumed by the Paleo-Indian hunting party. Wheat estimated that 190 bison were killed at Olsen–Chubbuck (1972, p. 114); of these animals, about 10 percent were not butchered in any way. Over 6000 pounds of usable meat were thus wasted. Taking into account the sex and age distribution of the herd, the degree of butchering, and the amount of usable meat per individual, Wheat estimated that the hunters at Olsen–Chubbuck obtained almost thirty tons of usable meat from this single kill. Moreover, roughly 4400 pounds of tallow and nearly 1000 pounds of marrow grease would have been available.

How long did this butchering take? Relying on relevant ethnographic sources, Wheat estimated that approximately 210 labor hours were required for the heavy butchering, and another 15 hours or so for the partly butchered animals. In other words, one hundred people could have completed the butchering in about 2.5 hours, or a party of ten could have butchered the entire herd in less than three days.

Some additional clues emerge from the Olsen–Chubbuck bone bed. The distribution of the hyoid bones (from near the throat) suggests that many tongues were removed—and presumably eaten—before or during the early stages of the butchering. Similarly, the distribution of shoulder blades suggests that some of the animals were butchered early to get at the internal organs, the hump, and the ribs. Judging from the distribution of the ribs, these choice pieces were probably cooked immediately and consumed while the remainder of the herd was being butchered. Feasting was a common occurrence among historic Plains Indians, and the evidence suggests that a victory feast was indeed held at Olsen–Chubbuck. Wheat goes on to note that even the heftiest bull was wholly butchered. Because the neck meat from these massive animals was generally so tough as to defy chewing even when dried, he suggests that the Olsen–Chubbuck Indians must have been making pemmican, which was the only really effective way of using neck meat from bulls.

Faunal Analysis in Historical Archaeology

Archaeologists have begun making important contributions to our understanding of faunal remains from historic period sites. As we have seen, historical archaeologists have the advantage of independent documentation which, though often biased, opens up the possibility of building middle-range bridges between the bones themselves and the behaviors they represent (Chapter 5).

Extensive documentation is available, for instance, to chronicle the subsistence practices in sixteenth-century Spanish Florida. Accounts from St. Augustine and elsewhere emphasize the chronic shortages of some traditional Iberian foods, and the substitution of less-valued New World resources (see Reitz and Scarry 1985). But significant biases and gaps are known to exist in the documentary base. For example, many important records were lost to deterioration, fire, and storms at sea. Other letters are known to have deliberately exaggerated (or even falsified) the situation to elicit greater support from the Spanish crown, and contradictions in eyewitness accounts are not uncommon.

But the main problem with the historic record for Spanish Florida is that it rarely contains the mundane details that archaeologists need. Whereas the contemporary accounts leave little doubt that the Spanish were displeased with their new diet, there is simply no substitute for the physical evidence obtained through archaeological excavation. Elizabeth Reitz and C. Margaret Scarry (1985) have recently synthesized the floral and faunal evidence from food remains recovered in excavations at St. Augustine (Florida) and Santa Elena (South Carolina). These results amply demonstrate the importance of dietary reconstruction in historical archaeology.

As in many such colonial situations, relying on traditional Old World subsistence practices did not work in the new environment. Many key Iberian food crops failed miserably in the coastal Florida environment, and the Spanish settlers were forced to alter their husbandry techniques to incorporate foods that could prosper in the coastal setting.

Lacking any sophisticated ecological knowledge, the settlers had to pass through an early period of adjustment and experimentation. The earliest shipments of livestock to St. Augustine and Santa Elena reflected Iberian food preferences. There was an initial attempt to cater to the traditional preference for mutton, for instance, but sheep raising was unsuccessful in Spanish Florida, primarily because the sheep were unable to defend themselves against wild dogs and wolves, and because they would not reproduce freely. At first, several marine species, especially marine fishes, filled the gap left by mutton; however, eventually, the meat supply of Spanish Florida shifted to beef and especially pork.

Shortly after their arrival in the New World, the colonists of Spanish Florida attempted to raise their favorite Old World crops, particularly wheat and grapes. But they were quick to note how successfully the Native Americans were growing their own indigenous crops, and soon the Spaniards began to supplement their harvests with maize, beans, and squash. Wild plants were never very important, presumably because the colonists rapidly substituted indigenous crops for traditional ones.

In effect, the Spanish strategy shifted toward an essentially aboriginal subsistence pattern, complemented by those European domesticates that could survive and prosper. Considerably more than half of the meat consumed in St. Augustine and Santa Elena by both Spanish settlers and aborigines derived from wild species, especially deer, sharks, sea catfishes, drums, and mullet. Spaniards also hunted and ate small mammals such as opossums, squirrels, and raccoons—which they disparagingly termed "the scum and vermin."

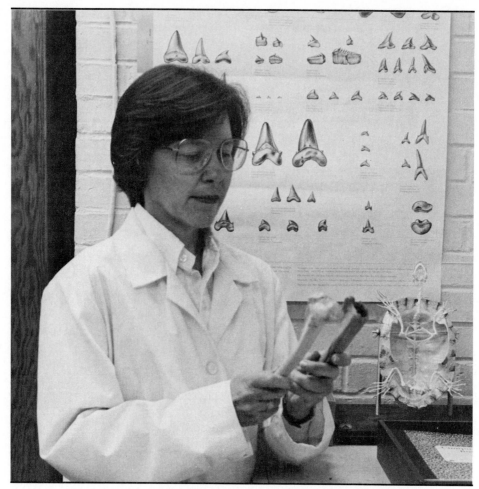

FIGURE 11–4   Betsy Reitz in the Laboratory of Zooarchaeology,
University of Georgia. (Courtesy Elizabeth Reitz)

The subsistence pattern that emerged at St. Augustine reflected a fusion of the
various elements available to the Spanish colonists. Whereas they continued to use Old
World livestock, the dietary importance of the various animals shifted significantly. And
although they continued to raise some Old World cultigens, these were mostly fruits and
vegetables that supplemented a diet based on domesticated New World plants. Thus
despite adopting many aboriginal items, the St. Augustine diet remained distinctly
Spanish. Several Old World plants and animals were still maintained; some of them were
even adopted by the Indians, and these food items were still processed through unmistakable Spanish institutions of the slaughterhouse, and the marketplace. Occasionally, the

rare supply ship from home would provide European delicacies such as olives, walnuts, and hazelnuts.

St. Augustine was established seventy years after the Spaniards began colonizing the New World, and some valuable lessons had been learned in this interval. Nevertheless, Reitz and Scarry found that significant dietary adaptations were still necessary to cope with the conditions of coastal Florida. These important dietary adjustments took place within the first forty years of the colonization of Spanish Florida. But once established, the balance remained virtually unchanged for the next two centuries.

The recent investigation by Reitz and Scarry—what one reviewer termed "an ethnobiological classic" (Ford 1987)—emphasizes the important shifts in archaeological approaches to diet and subsistence in the past decade. Now that field strategies in historical archaeology routinely consider the details of screen size, volumetric sampling, water screening, and flotation, investigators are generating an enormously valuable data base of fine-grained subsistence data that allow a detailed reconstruction of human adaptations to frontier environments.

The Gold Rush frontier in California offered a different set of challenges. The decades following the Civil War saw unprecedented differentiation in life-styles between the rich and poor. In the remote outpost of Sacramento, established in 1848, considerable economic wealth was channeled into the hands of the already well-to-do. Although the historical archaeologist has numerous techniques for studying this process of sociocultural differentiation, faunal remains are particularly useful because they are abundant, little subject to "curation" before being discarded, relatively unaffected by looting, and potentially informative about the daily life across a broad social spectrum.

Peter Schulz and Sherri Gust (1983a, 1983b) demonstrated the usefulness of combining historical documentation with faunal data derived from archaeological excavation in their analysis of four late-nineteenth-century sites in Sacramento (California):

> *The City Jail:* Minutes of the City Council indicated that meals were brought to the prisoners already prepared; an 1866 food contract allowed $.30 per chain gang worker and $.18 for other prisoners. Since nearly half of this went for bread, they suspected that only the cheaper cuts of meat were purchased.
>
> *Hannan's Saloon:* Judging from the complete lack of newspaper advertising for this saloon, and the fact that owner Owen Hannan lived in his bar, and was never mentioned in the numerous county histories, Schulz and Gust suspected this to have been a low-level establishment.
>
> *Klebitz and Green's Saloon:* The prosperous owners advertised daily in local papers and later expanded their interests to include real estate holdings and a sheep ranch. They paid to have biographies appear in local county histories; moreover, their saloon served as the Sacramento depot for the Bavarian Lager Beer Brewery.
>
> *Golden Eagle Hotel:* This hotel and oyster bar was one of the most highly regarded in the state, advertising in commercial, literary, and travel periodicals throughout the Pacific coast area and announcing well-to-do guests in the local papers. This establishment occasionally hosted dinners honoring millionaire railroad barons and touring American presidents.

From cheap, assembly-line meals dished out to city prisoners to sumptuous repasts served to California's powerful at the Golden Eagle, these four sites span the range of status in post–Gold Rush Sacramento. Hannan's Saloon was a cut above the jail, but well below the Klebitz and Green saloon.

These inferences derive strictly from historical documentation available for each site: local newspaper accounts, city directories, tax assessment rolls, census schedules, and business license registers. But remember that Rathje and his colleagues found huge discrepancies between such self-reports and actual out-the-back-door evidence (Chapter 5). How do we know that such documents accurately portray nineteenth-century reality?

These four sites were excavated between 1976 and 1980, as part of urban renewal of the original mercantile district of Sacramento. More than fifteen hundred beef bones were recovered during these excavations. Contemporary accounts indicate that shortly after California's famous "Gold Rush," Anglo-American settlers in Sacramento found beef to be more abundant than any other meat. But throughout this period, beef prices varied from extremely expensive for the choicest steaks to relatively cheap for the less desirable shanks and neck.

Using contemporary advertising from the late nineteenth century, Schulz and Gust (1983b) established retail prices for the various cuts of beef (Figure 11–5). Although prices were expressed at the time in dollars and cents, the available nineteenth-century documentation is not sufficiently precise to allow an exact price to be assigned to each cut. Instead, Schulz and Gust rank-ordered their data, reflecting a price scale from cheap (shanks and necks) through expensive (steaks cut from the short loin).

In effect, they determined the nineteenth-century "relative cost" of each cut, and these results can be displayed as cumulative curves for each site. The cumulative curve technique is becoming an increasingly popular way of statistically demonstrating trends in nonmetric data. If a faunal assemblage contained an "equal mix" of all beef bones, then a straight line would result on Figure 11–5. Expensive cuts cause the curve to bow outward; cheap cuts make the curves sag.

Figure 11–5 also shows some interesting relationships among the four target sites. The faunal assemblage from the Golden Eagle Hotel contains a disproportionate number of expensive cuts; more than 50 percent of the sample consists of T-bone cuts (derived from the short loin, the most costly portion of the beef carcass). By contrast, the bones from the Sacramento jail are mostly soup bones. Saloons of the day served free lunches to draw customers into the bar. Judging from the bone distributions, the saloon owners used mostly roasts—easy to cook, available in quantity, and ready throughout the day to be sliced by the bartender.

This innovative study demonstrates how food bones can be used to examine dietary differences by social status, at a time before any dietary surveys were taken in the United States. Whereas most archaeological data from the historical period relate to individual households, this study suggests a potential for understanding more about the nature of Victorian urban life by providing quantitative measures not available through documentary evidence alone.

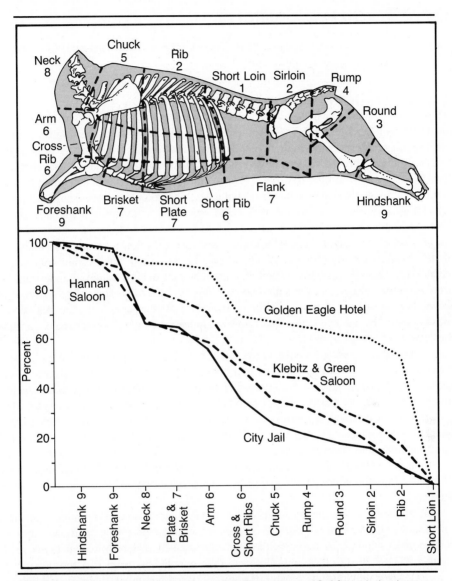

FIGURE 11–5 Faunal remains from Old Sacramento (California): (top) secondary cuts of beef, ranked according to late-nineteenth-century retail values; (bottom) beef cut frequencies from four archaeological deposits, plotted as cumulative frequency curves, with cuts ranked in ascending value (adapted from Schulz and Gust 1983a, figures 1 and 2). (Reprinted by permission of the Society for Historical Archaeology from *Historical Archaeology* 17[1]:48, 50)

*WHERE TO GO FROM HERE?*_____

Additional Sources on Faunal Remains in Historic-Period Sites: Brose (1967), Fradkin (1980), Mudar (1978), Reitz and Scarry (1985).

Going Beyond the Archaeological Record

Much archaeological research has become interdisciplinary, with archaeologists working closely with scientists from other fields. This relationship has traditionally been highly asymmetrical, the archaeologist drawing heavily on methods and theories developed in "harder" sciences, with little to offer in return. But increasingly, scientists in all fields—such as chemists, physicists, geologists, botanists, and zoologists—are learning that the archaeological record can provide well-dated specimens relevant to nonarchaeological questions.

Consider the case of **biogeography**, a discipline that studies and attempts to explain the distribution of modern plant and animal populations. Such inquiries are important to archaeology because they provide potential baseline data against which to understand the effect of human groups on nonhuman species. In one such biogeographical study, J. H. Brown once noted the curious "island" distribution of thirteen small mammal species (mostly squirrels, packrats, marmots, shrews, mice, and hares) in seventeen isolated Great Basin mountain ranges.

How, Brown asked, could these diverse species establish themselves in such isolated mountains when they are unable to survive in the "vast sea of sagebrush desert" that separated the far-flung ranges (Brown 1971, p. 467)? Only two explanations seemed possible for this spotty distribution: Either (1) the small mammals are somehow able today to cross these expansive sagebrush stretches and selectively migrate into such isolated mountain environments, or (2) the patchy modern distribution results from initial colonization across the entire area during the Pleistocene—more than twelve thousand years ago when the valley floor environment was more "hospitable" to such boreal creatures—followed by the extinction of geographically intermediate populations when the climate changed.

A zoologist by training, Brown was limited to data provided by modern mammal distributions. Lacking any evidence of the in-migration of boreal mammals into the isolated ranges today, Brown hypothesized that these boreal mammalian fauna in the seventeen Great Basin ranges must be true relic populations from Pleistocene times.

Enter Donald Grayson, zooarchaeologist. Trained not only to identify and interpret small animal bones, Grayson also had access to voluminous data deriving from archaeological excavations throughout the Desert West. He was in the enviable position of testing Brown's biogeographical model—an inference about the past derived strictly from contemporary distributions—against the growing body of relevant evidence available from the archaeological record.

Using procedures basic to the scientific cycle (outlined in Chapter 2), Grayson (1983b, p. 119) set about deriving the logical implications of Brown's hypothesis. *If*

Brown were correct—and the thirteen isolated species existed as relic populations from a widespread distribution during the Pleistocene—*then* the following implications should be true:

1. Boreal mammals present on only some of the mountains today should have been present in the past on those ranges from which they currently are absent.
2. No colonization by boreal mammals can have occurred during the post-Pleistocene interval.
3. The boreal mammals involved must have been present in the intervening lowlands where today they are absent (because Brown's model suggested that the lowlands had provided the corridor for access to the mountains during the Pleistocene).
4. There were species of boreal mammals on isolated mountains in the past where there are none in the mountains today.

These four test implications in hand, Grayson turned to evidence from the archaeological record at Gatecliff Shelter and elsewhere. In part because we used fine-grained screening throughout the decade of digging at Gatecliff (see Chapter 6), a huge collection of small mammal bones was available for study. Virtually all the bones recovered were those of species found in the nearby Toquima Range today. But Grayson located a dainty tooth and jawbone from a heather vole *(Phenacomys),* excavated from a stratum at Gatecliff dating about 5300 B.P. This was an extremely consequential find because, although widely distributed throughout the Sierra Nevada and Cascade Ranges, *Phenacomys* is today totally absent from the Gatecliff area; in fact, the nearest modern distribution is more than two hundred miles away.

The two tiny fragments, extracted from a collection of nearly fifteen thousand bones identified from Gatecliff Shelter, provided strong support for the fourth test implication of Brown's model—a boreal mammal on a Great Basin mountain range that is extinct from all these ranges today. On the basis of this evidence, Grayson (1983b, p. 121) speculated that heather voles were once widespread throughout the Great Basin (a proposition that can itself readily be tested in subsequent excavations).

Grayson then moved on to look at the faunal materials recovered from Danger Cave (Utah), an important site excavated by Jesse Jennings between 1949 and 1953 (Figure 11–6). By reanalyzing the museum collection of 3500 identifiable bones, Grayson found bones of yellow-bellied marmots and bushy-tailed wood rats (Grayson 1988). Because both species are today extinct in the vicinity of Danger Cave, Brown's model received further endorsement: Both critters must have once been present in the intervening lowlands, as this was the only access to the mountain isolates during the Pleistocene (see also Grayson 1987). Thus evidence from the archaeological record provided robust support for Brown's biogeographic model, previously derived only from contemporary mammal distributions. Biogeographers can now use this archaeological evidence to extend Brown's model to other contexts.

Grayson's study illustrates how archaelogical data are being incorporated into the broader world of science. Later in this chapter, we shall examine how human bones are providing unique data on the diseases and population pressures that acted on past

FIGURE 11–6 Donald Grayson excavating in the Pleistocene gravels at Danger Cave (Utah). (Courtesy Donald K. Grayson; photograph by David Rhode)

populations. Elsewhere, we noted how lessons learned from flintknapping experiments are being applied to modern eye surgery (Chapter 5). Even more exciting, eight-thousand-year old DNA (deoxyribonucleic acid) has recently been extracted from human brain tissue recovered archaeologically in Florida, suggesting that geneticists might soon be able to project their findings significantly back in time. Perhaps it will not be long before archaeologists can pay back the debts incurred in years of one-way interdisciplinary research.

What Archaeologists Learn from Plants

Paleoethnobotany (or **archaeobotany**) is the analysis and interpretation of interrelationships between people and plants from evidence in the archaeological record:

> Its objective is the elucidation of cultural adaptation to the plant world and the impact of plants upon a prehistoric human population, not simply the recognition of useful

plants, and its subject is all archaeological known cultures, including so-called civilizations. Perhaps more than any other class of archaeological data, including artifacts, plant evidence expresses most aspects of past societies and their involvement with both external, social, and natural environments (Ford 1979, pp. 286–287).

The formal study of plant remains from archaeological sites goes back at least to dynastic Egypt, when people began looking at the "mummified" cereals, fruits, and seeds found in royal tombs. Particularly in the past two decades, the study of such plant remains has become a major focus in Americanist archaeology. Although the analysis of plant remains in archaeological sites traditionally lagged far behind their faunal counterparts, the current vigor of paleoethnobotanists has closed the gap in rapid order.

Throughout these pages, we have stressed the selective nature of the archaeological record. Plant remains are particularly vulnerable to the biases of archaeological preservation. Archaeological sites in arid climates have a good chance of providing plant macrofossils for study. The fill of Danger Cave (Harper and Alder 1972, Jennings 1957) and Hogup Cave, Utah (Harper and Adler 1970), was almost entirely plant seeds, hulls, and chaff. In places, virtually no dirt was present inside these sites, even though the deposits were deeper than ten feet. From column samples of the fill, Harper and Alder (1970, 1972) reconstructed the vegetational history and climatic change in the vicinity of both Danger and Hogup caves. Particularly important over the last ten thousand years was the ubiquitous pickleweed *(Allenrolfea)*. Their study highlighted the degree to which present plant distributions may be misleading when analyzing the cultural ecology of even the recent past (see Mehringer 1977).

Unfortunately for the archaeologist, such plant macrofossils are hard to come by; the Great Basin samples are preserved only because of the general aridity of the environment. In more humid climates, plant remains generally are preserved only when they have been burned and hence carbonized. The most common method of recovering plant remains is flotation, a technique that has become almost standard procedure within the last decade or so (see Chapter 6). Plant remains are also sometimes preserved in waterlogged contexts (such as shipwrecks, mudslides, and wells), sun-dried adobe bricks, wattle-and-daub walls, and ceramics.

In the following sections, we shall examine a few of the diverse ways in which plant remains are utilized in current Americanist archaeology.

WHERE TO GO FROM HERE?

Miksicek (1987) has written an excellent overview of formation process of the archaeobotanical record; Carbone and Keel (1985) review the preservation factors in paleobiology (see also Hally 1981); Reitz and Scarry (1985) contribute an outstanding overview of how plant remains are recovered and analyzed from historic-period sites; Richard I. Ford (1979) prepared a more general, if now slightly dated review of paleoethnobotanical research; see also Adams and Gasser (1980), Asch, Ford, and Asch (1972), Minnis (1981), Renfrew (1973), Smith (1985), Yarnell (1982).

Journal of Ethnobiology contains original research papers in the fields of ethnotaxonomy, folk classification, ethnobotany, ethnozoology, cultural ecology, plant domestication, zooarchaeology, archaeobotany, palynology, dendrochronology, and ethnomedicine; first published in 1981.

Subscription information: Cecil H. Brown, *Journal of Ethnobiology,* Department of Anthropology, Northern Illinois University, DeKalb, Ill. 60115.

Applications of Palynology to Archaeology

The analysis of ancient plant pollen and spores, known as **palynology**, has recently become one of archaeology's more informative methods for examining prehistoric ecological adaptations. Most plants shed their pollen into the atmosphere, where it is rapidly dispersed by wind action. Pollen grains—microscopic single-celled organisms produced during plant reproduction—are present in most of the earth's atmosphere, including, of course, archaeological sites. Small wonder, for a single pine branch produces as many as 350 million individual pollen grains.

Although the interpretation of pollen concentrations is quite difficult, the initial steps in extracting and identifying pollen are rather simple (Bryant and Holloway 1983, pp. 198–202). Pollen samples are generally taken from the sidewall of test pits or trenches, special care being taken to prevent contaminating the sample with foreign pollen. The outer surface of the excavation profile is first cleaned with a *clean* trowel, and 0.5 to 1.0 liter of material is placed in a sterile, uncontaminated container. Samples are often taken at five- or ten-centimeter intervals—working from the bottom of the column to the top—to provide a continuous record of the pollen rain throughout the period of deposition. Careful stratigraphic drawings are made to facilitate correlation between the pollen record and the archaeological remains. Pollen samples can also be taken from the architectural features and artifact surfaces.

The pollen grains are isolated in the laboratory through the use of acid baths and centrifuging. Microscope slides containing the fossil pollen grains are then scanned at magnifications between 400X and 1000X, and the grains are counted until a statistically significant number has been recorded. Although sample sizes vary, most palynologists feel that at least two hundred pollen grains must be enumerated from each slide. These figures are converted to percentages and integrated into a pollen spectrum, indicating the proportional shift between stratigraphic levels within the site. The pollen profiles are then correlated with the known absolute and relative dates for each stratum.

The pollen diagrams provide several different kinds of data. One of the most important applications of palynology is the reconstruction of past environments. Pollen percentages that fluctuate through time indicate changes in prehistoric habitats. The postglacial climatic sequence in Europe, well known from hundreds of pollen samples, contains notable fluctuations in the forest cover, as indicated by the frequencies of hazel, oak, birch, and grass pollen. Once a regional sequence has been developed (often from noncultural deposits), archaeological samples can be statistically compared with the pollen rain from known extant plant communities. The ratio of tree (**arboreal**) to nontree pollen, for example, generally indicates the degree of forestation.

Palynology has been applied to Star Carr, a **Mesolithic** site in northern England, occupied about 7500 B.C. (Clark 1954, 1972). Figure 11–7, the major pollen diagram from Star Carr, reflects pollen frequencies determined from small uncontaminated samples of peats or lake muds. These samples were arranged in stratigraphic order, with the oldest at the bottom. Pollen was then extracted from each sample, and the various pollen grains identified and counted. The stratigraphic profile is divided into seven zones, with the human occupation of Star Carr spanning the transition from Zone IV to Zone V. Figure 11–7 expresses pollen frequencies as percentages of the total tree pollen. Note that the tree pollen frequencies are black and that the herbaceous vegetation is represented by white polygons.

Figure 11–7 is only one of several pollen profiles available from the Star Carr vicinity. These profiles, coupled with the identification of preserved plant macrofossils, enabled Clark's collaborators, D. Walker and H. Godwin, to reconstruct the ecological

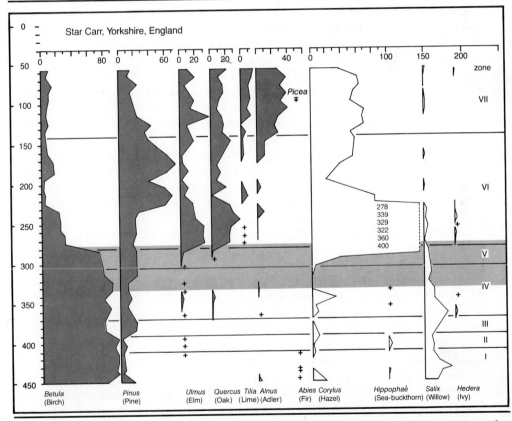

FIGURE 11–7 **Pollen diagram from alluvial deposits near Star Carr. The occupation of the Star Carr site is denoted by the shaded horizontal band (see Clark 1954, Figure 2). (Courtesy Cambridge University Press)**

development of the Star Carr area (see Clark 1954, pp. 38–69). Zones I, II, and III represent the late glacial period. The vegetation was apparently a park tundra dominated by herbaceous communities, with dense stands of birch or pine trees. This vegetation lasted until the occupation of Star Carr, roughly 7500 B.C. About this time the vegetation shifted to birch and pine forest, the park tundra disappearing altogether. Note in Figure 11–7 how the increasing abundance of hazel pollen suggests a shift to woodland conditions. Pollen diagrams from nearby localities also reflect the presence of species that attest to a warming climate during this time. In Zone VI, after the human abandonment of Star Carr, hazel achieved dominance in the forest, and elm and oak also became more abundant. This shift reflects the transition from birch woodland to mixed oak forest. Later pollen profiles from this area document the extension of herbaceous plant communities, which resulted from human deforestation.

The pollen evidence provides a clear picture of what the Star Carr landscape must have looked like during Mesolithic times. It is particularly interesting to note that the pollen diagrams show absolutely no indication of any large-scale deforestation during the early occupation of Star Carr. The abundant faunal remains indicate that although the Mesolithic people took advantage of the rich forest fauna, they left the forest itself virtually untouched.

Figure 11–8 presents another pollen diagram, this time from the Lehner site in southern Arizona (Mehringer and Haynes 1965). Excavations at Lehner in 1955 and 1956 yielded several Clovis fluted points, butchering tools, and charcoal in association with mammoth, horse, bison, and tapir remains (Haury et al. 1959). Four radiocarbon dates are available from the Lehner site, averaging about 11,200 radiocarbon years ago.

Beginning in 1962, palynologist Peter Mehringer set out to determine the nature of the environment of the early big-game hunters and their prey. Pollen analysis at Lehner is complicated by the repeated cut-and-fill sequences during prehistoric times, and it is difficult to find a single locality at Lehner that contains a continuous and unbroken pollen record.

Figure 11–8 shows the results of three different pollen profiles, each of which partially overlaps the others. The form of the Lehner pollen diagram differs from the Star Carr profile. The pollen spectrum at Lehner Ranch is dominated by high frequencies of pollen from **composites** (herbs such as ragweed and sagebrush) and **cheno-am** (plants of the goosefoot family and amaranth). This dominance is common in postglacial pollen profiles of this area and creates a problem because it masks the presence of the less common (yet more ecologically sensitive) indicators. In order to counter the high frequency of composite and cheno-am pollen, Mehringer applied the technique known as the **double fixed sum** (Mehringer and Haynes 1965, p. 19). The black profiles in Figure 11–8 are based on a standard two-hundred-grain summary for all pollen types. That is, exactly two hundred grains from each sample were counted, and the percentages were computed. A total of twenty-five individual two-hundred-grain samples are represented in Figure 11–8. Although the dominant cheno-am and composite pollen undoubtedly represents locally occurring species, they are insufficient by themselves for interpreting regional

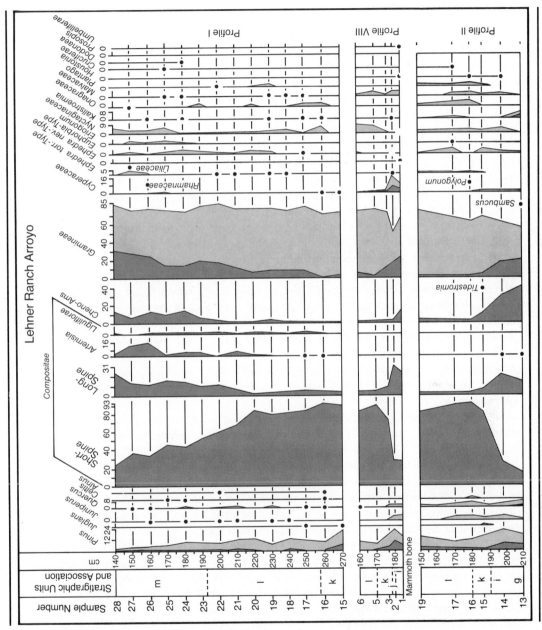

FIGURE 11–8 Pollen diagram from the Lehner Ranch site, Arizona (see Mehringer and Haynes 1965, Figure 8). (Courtesy Peter J. Mehringer)

385

vegetation or climate. For this reason, a second, one-hundred-grain, count was instituted, which is represented by the hatched area in Figure 11–8. The percentages for the second count were computed by ignoring the high abundance of cheno-am and composite pollen, counting only the other, rarer pollen types. By comparing the results of both counts, one can study both the gross frequencies of the dominants and the presence of the rarer species, which are in fact the most sensitive ecological indicators.

The pollen from stratigraphic units *i, j,* and *k* reflects the climatic conditions that prevailed during the mammoth-killing episode. The frequencies during this period are quite similar to modern samples collected nearby. The slightly greater abundance of pine, oak, and juniper pollen may indicate somewhat more moist or cool conditions before and during the deposition of the lower part of unit *k.* Somewhat later, in unit *l,* one sees a gradual shift in the composite categories. In all, the vegetation represented by the pollen spectra shown in Figure 11–8 is most probably a desert grassland, which today occupies more favored sites near the Lehner site. Mehringer and Haynes (1965, p. 23) "do not believe that the climate at the Lehner site 11,000 years ago could have differed from the present by more than a 3- to 4-inch increase in mean annual rainfall . . . and a 3 to 4 [degree] decrease in mean annual temperature."

Peter Mehringer analyzed the pollen content of the Mount Mazama volcanic ash (Mehringer, Blinman, and Peterson 1977). Remember from Chapter 6 that when Mount Mazama (Oregon) erupted nearly seven thousand years ago, it spewed volcanic ash throughout the western United States, even near the bottom of Gatecliff Shelter.

Lost Trail Pass Bog (Montana) was selected for a closer look at ash from the Mazama eruption. Using a sediment core 10 centimeters in diameter, Mehringer and his team extracted a sample of Mazama ash from a depth of 5.1 meters below the surface. Lake sediment on either side of the ash was radiocarbon dated at 6700 ± 100 and 6720 ± 120 years ago.

Mehringer then applied the **pollen influx** method to extract specific information about the Mazama eruption. "Pollen influx" estimates the number of pollen grains incorporated into a fixed volume of sediments over a particular time. If, for instance, one cubic centimeter of lake sediment containing 100,000 pollen grains was deposited in twenty-five years, then an average of 4000 pollen grains were deposited on a one-centimeter square surface during each of the twenty-five years represented by the sediments. Or, viewed in the other way, if the pollen influx is known, the number of years contained in a certain volume of sediment can be estimated.

For the Lost Trail Pass Bog, the rate of deposition was determined from sixteen radiocarbon determinations, and the total pollen influx was estimated by adding 100,000 tracers (*Lycopodium* spores) to each two-cubic centimeter sample before pollen extraction. The ratio of the artificially introduced tracers to the fossil pollen grains permitted the calculation of population estimates for each zone. The actual pollen influx for each stratigraphic zone could be estimated from the average pollen content. Figure 11–9 shows that a one-cubic centimeter column of the Mazama ash, containing 11,485 pollen grains, must have been deposited in about 2.8 years.

From this fine-grained calculation, Mehringer and his colleagues made several

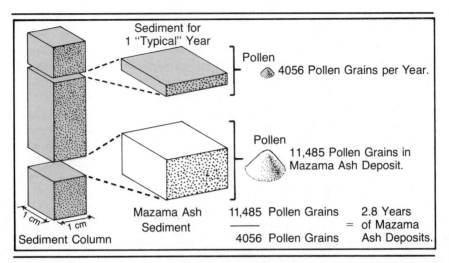

FIGURE 11–9 Diagram illustrating how ashfall duration is computed from pollen influx in a one-cubic centimeter column of Mazama ash (see Mehringer, Blinman, and Peterson 1977, Figure 3). (With permission of Peter J. Mehringer and *Science.* © 1977 by the American Association for the Advancement of Science)

inferences about the conditions under which the Mazama ash fell. Using pine and sagebrush pollen as seasonal indicators, they concluded that volcanic ash from a major eruption of Mount Mazama first fell in the autumn, about 6700 years radiocarbon years ago. Ash continued to fall over the next three years. This massive quantity of volcanic ash lowered the lake's productivity but, perhaps through a "mulching" effect, produced increased vigor and pollen production in some sagebrush steppe plants. Based on the pollen records for both aquatic and terrestrial species, these effects were relatively short term in both ecosystems.

One of the most dramatic palynological studies in archaeology used sediments recovered from Shanidar Cave, Iraq (Leroi-Gourhan 1975). Shanidar Cave had been occupied sporadically over about 100,000 years, with cultural remains spanning the Middle Paleolithic to fairly recent times. During his fourth season at Shanidar, Ralph Solecki and his crew discovered a Neanderthal skeleton that appeared to have been intentionally buried, roughly 60,000 years ago. The bones were extremely fragile, and the entire block was removed in a plaster jacket, earth and all. The box containing Shanidar IV was transported to the Iraq Museum where it remained unopened for two years. It was later discovered that the Shanidar IV grave actually contained four individuals—three adults and an infant.

Following routine field procedures, Solecki took soil samples from around and within the area of Shanidar IV. Although he had no specific purpose for collecting the samples, Solecki had learned in previous work on Native American burial mounds in Ohio that soil samples can provide unexpected dividends (Solecki 1971, p. 245). Some eight years later, these soil samples would provide "significant, if not startling results."

Project palynologist Arlette Leroi-Gourhan tested the Shanidar IV samples for pollen and—to everyone's surprise—pollen was preserved in great quantities in the Neanderthal grave site. Microscopic examination of the pollen spores indicated that the matrix around Shanidar IV contained dense concentrations of at least eight species of brightly colored wildflowers, including grape hyacinth, bachelor's button, and hollyhock. Leroi-Gourhan (1975) suggested that the flowers had been woven into the branches of a pinelike shrub, which apparently grew nearby on the Ice Age hillside. She also concluded that the individuals found in the Shanidar IV grave were laid to rest sometime between late May and early July. This interpretation had a profound effect on our understanding of Neanderthal ritual and belief (see chapter 14).

But once again, one must look more closely at the formation processes involved (Miksicek 1987, p. 227). Unfortunately, the pollen grains were extracted as an afterthought, and it remains quite possible that the flower pollen grains had nothing to do with the skeletons but were simply contained in the cave sediments, introduced by either natural or other cultural agencies. It is certainly possible that the pollen grains were in the Shanidar Cave before the grave pit was dug. If so, then the secondary botanical remains inside the burial pits have little relationship to the bones (and actually predate them). Because the samples were analyzed without adequate controls from elsewhere in the surrounding deposits and without consideration of the formation processes involved, it is impossible for us to understand what the Shanidar Cave pollen really means.

At any rate, once several pollen diagrams from an area have been analyzed and integrated, a regional sequence can be constructed. At this point, pollen analysis can even function as a relative dating technique. That is, an undated site can be placed in proper temporal sequence simply by matching the unknown pollen frequencies with the dated regional frequencies, just as in dendrochronology. In eastern Arizona, pollen analysis has even assisted in the reconstruction of the sequence of pueblo room construction (Hill and Hevly 1968). The regional pollen profile indicates that during the occupation of the Broken K pueblo, from A.D. 1100 to 1300, the relative frequency of tree pollen was decreasing. Through careful excavation, the floors of about fifty rooms were located and pollen samples taken. Samples from room floors are assumed to represent the pollen rain during site occupation. Each room was placed in temporal sequence by measuring the relative frequency of tree pollen (because earlier rooms have higher arboreal pollen counts than do the later rooms). The sequence of room construction compiled in this fashion corresponded precisely to the sequence based on architectural superposition and soil stratigraphy.

Broken K pueblo provides another application of palynology (see also Chapter 13). Hill and Hevly isolated room functions through the analysis of the fossil pollen spectrum. During excavation, they knew that several different sorts of rooms were represented. Many of the rooms contained fire hearths and stone slabs for grinding corn; these were interpreted as habitation rooms, in which daily activities generally were carried out. A second type of room, considered to be a storage facility was not only smaller than the habitation rooms but also lacking in the artifacts and features involved in food processing. A third type of room, markedly different from the others, was round and completely sunken below the ground surface. Both context and artifact yield convinced the excavators that these rare rooms must have been ceremonial, analogous to the modern pueblo kivas. On the basis of conventional archaeological reasoning, Hill and Hevly discerned three sorts of rooms: habitation, storage, and ceremonial.

What did the pollen from these rooms indicate? Pollen counts from Broken K pueblo were divided into "natural" and "economic" categories, the latter dominated by domestic maize (corn), squash, prickly pear cactus, and other edibles. The economic varieties were assumed to be largely introduced into the deposits by humans, whereas the natural pollen was probably windblown. As expected, the economic pollen was most common in the storage rooms, as the stored crops probably dropped their pollen as they were stacked in the room. Habitation and ceremonial rooms had some economic pollen grains, but in lower frequencies than in the storage rooms. Two kinds of pollen, Mormon tea *(Ephedra)* and buckwheat, were particularly abundant in the ceremonial rooms. It seems likely that because both species are considered sacred by modern Hopi and Zuni Indians, these species served a similar function in prehistoric ceremonies. Although this example is somewhat trivial, in that we already knew the room functions on the basis of other evidence, the Broken K pollen analysis provides a useful, scientifically valid method for reconstructing the nature of subsistence (and even ceremonial) activities in archaeological sites.

WHERE TO GO FROM HERE?

Some General Sources on Palynology in Archaeology: Bryant and Holloway (1983) provide an excellent overview of the ways of collecting pollen samples and the various ways in which pollen data are useful in archaeology; Stanley and Linskens (1974) and Tschudy and Scott (1969) provide general overviews of palynological method and theory.

Analysis of Plant Phytoliths

One extremely important method of learning about both wild and domesticated plants is through the analysis of microscopic plant opal phytoliths, literally, "plant stones." Phytoliths are formed when the silica ordinarily dissolved in groundwater is carried through plant roots and deposited in mineral form inside the plant, in places where water is used or lost through transpiration. When dead plant material decays, the almost indestructible opal phytoliths are deposited in the ground. Phytoliths have been found in sediments older than 60 million years. Distinctive phytoliths occur in members of the grass family and are also found in groups such as rushes, sedges, palm, conifers, and deciduous trees.

Phytolith analysis is superficially similar to pollen analysis. Both deal with plant remains at a microscopic level; samples for each are collected in the same way; and the same laboratory can be used for both analyses (in fact, the same sample can be used for both).

But there are differences. Some plants produce pollen but not phytoliths, and vice versa. Different taxa are commonly analyzed by each technique (Rovner 1983, p. 226). Although pollen is produced in a single form, phytoliths vary considerably within a single species. Phytoliths are preserved under a wider range of soil conditions than pollen. These critical differences render the methods complementary, and when taken together, they provide independent sources of data for the ethnobiologist.

Although phytoliths have been recognized in archaeological sites for decades, only occasionally before 1970 were archaeological deposits analyzed for phytoliths. Since then, interest in this unusual technique has exploded, and today, the identification and analysis of phytoliths recovered from archaeological sites hold great promise for reconstructing paleoenvironments and for tracking the process of plant domestication. Difficulties of taxonomy still plague phytolith analysis and hamper its widespread utilization in archaeological research.

Considerable progress has been made recently on these taxonomic issues, particularly in the grasses. Phytoliths are being used to study rice, millet, barley, and wheat. Particularly important to Americanist archaeology is Pearsall's (1978) "breakthrough" in the identification of corn *(Zea mays)* phytoliths, which allowed the introduction date of maize to be pushed back in Ecuador by several millennia. But to truly make a contribution to our understanding of how maize was domesticated, criteria for identifying the phytoliths of *teosinte* – the probable wild ancestor of maize – must be developed. Recent work using computer-assisted image analysis shows promise for distinguishing wild varieties of teosinte from cultivated primitive maize; similar diagnostics have now been defined for beans and squash (Bozarth 1987).

Phytolith analysis was successfully employed on samples we recovered in the high-altitude excavations at Alta Toquima Village (Nevada). Less than five miles south of Gatecliff Shelter, Alta Toquima is located in what is today a cold, wind-swept tabletop, at an elevation of eleven thousand feet (Thomas 1982). About A.D. 1000, a seasonally permanent base camp was established at Alta Toquima. The large number of grinding stones suggested that people were gathering summer-ripening seeds. But the area today supports no grassland; perhaps it never has, or maybe the serious overgrazing by sheep during the historic period eradicated this biotic community.

Flotation analysis did not produce sufficient carbonized plant remains, so we submitted to Irwin Rovner a series of 48 soil samples from the features, interior house floors, cultural middens, and exterior sterile zones at Alta Toquima. We were hoping that the phytoliths, if present, could tell us whether suitable grasslands existed during prehistoric times in the Alta Toquima area.

Rovner found pine phytoliths in every sample (no great surprise, since Alta Toquima is perched on the upper margin of the limber pine treeline). The exterior samples contained the most abundant amount of pine phytoliths, with considerably less on the interior floors, and very little occurred in feature samples. High altitude festucoid grass phytoliths did occur at Alta Toquima, but in inverse relationship to the pine distribution.

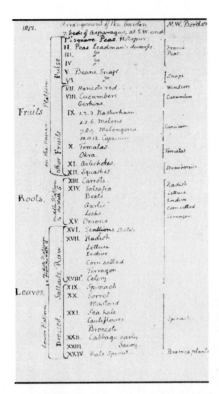

FIGURE 11–10   Thomas Jefferson's notes listing the vegetables planted in his garden helped archaeologist William Kelso determine the exact layout of that garden. (Courtesy Massachusetts Historical Society)

Most of the grass phytoliths occurred in the archaeological features, with little grass outside or inside the prehistoric houses. Rovner concluded that during the late prehistoric period, Alta Toquima was inside a pine grove, with the grasses introduced to the site through human transport. This grass must not have been used for flooring, bedding, or roofing. Rovner (1988) thinks that the Alta Toquima residents harvested now-extinct grasses, and phytoliths from these foodstuffs ended up in the refuse deposits.

Phytolith analysis has also assisted historical archaeologists in reconstructing the once-elaborate plantings of Thomas Jefferson. Among his other achievements, Jefferson was an avid and astute gardener, employing part of his Monticello (Virginia) plantation as a natural laboratory. One of Jefferson's objectives was to experiment with different kinds of livestock fodder – grasses, clover, alfalfa, and so forth. But whereas Jefferson left numerous drawings, plans, and accounts of the decorative portions of his garden, only a single sketch survives showing these more mundane aspects of Jefferson's garden. The Monticello Foundation has been reconstructing this garden, but will only restore those features whose existence can be confirmed independent of the surviving documentation.

Deciding whether Jefferson really planted fodder fields at Monticello seemed a suitable test for phytolith analysis. Irwin Rovner knew that the site of Monticello was predominantly woodland before Jefferson established his plantation there. If fodder fields

FIGURE 11–11 Aerial photograph showing the archaeology of Thomas Jefferson's huge garden at Monticello (upper right), one of the most extensive experimental vegetable gardens of its time in the United States. Note particularly the original orchard planting holes (white dots left center) and the western section of the 1809 garden fence postholes (dots extreme left) (see Kelso 1984, Figure 31). (Courtesy Thomas Jefferson Memorial Foundation and William Kelso)

actually existed, they should produce phytolith assemblages distinct from the woodland and natural grasses surrounding the plantation (Rovner 1988).

Archaeologist Scott Shumate collected a series of nineteen "blind" samples from various locations in and around Jefferson's garden, some from the projected fodder plots. Rovner, who processed these samples without any knowledge of their provenience, strongly indicated that such discrimination is possible. With the exception of only four individual particles found in scattered samples, all diagnostic grass phytoliths belonged to the projected fodder species. Almost no native grasses turned up in the samples either. If this initial sampling proves representative of the rest of Monticello, the procedure can provide significant clues for landscape architects reconstructing the eighteenth-century home of Thomas Jefferson.

WHERE TO GO FROM HERE?

Piperno's new book (1988) is an outstanding statement summarizing phytolith research at the moment and unquestionably the best source of information and guidance regarding methods and applications; Irwin Rovner (1983) provides a critical review of early progress on plant phytolith analysis (but considerable advances have been made since that time); another important overview is provided by Pearsall (1982); more recent research is reported in Bozarth (1987), Pearsall (1982), Pearsall and Trimble (1984), Piperno (1979, 1984, 1985a), Roosevelt (1984b), Rovner (1987, 1988), Rovner and Russ (in press).

The Phytolitharien is a newsletter dealing with recent developments in the analysis of phytolith research in archaeology.

Subscription information: Irwin Rovner, Editor, *The Phytolitharien Newsletter,* 1902 Alexander Rd., Raleigh, N.C. 27608.

Fossil Pack Rat Nests

One increasingly important, if somewhat surprising, source of macrofossils is in the ancient nests of wood rats *(Neotoma)* throughout the arid Desert West. These animals dragged home extensive quantities of food and nest materials; actualistic studies have demonstrated that pack rats do not usually travel more than one hundred meters from their nest (Bleich and Schwartz 1975). Throughout arid North America, these pack rat assemblages are commonly incorporated into rock-hard, urine-impregnated "middens." Because the plants contained in the middens must have come from the immediate vicinity of the nest itself, researchers have used pack rat midden analysis to reconstruct detailed environmental chronologies of Pleistocene and Holocene vegetational change throughout the greater American Southwest.

In one study, Wells and Berger (1967) excavated and radiocarbon-dated a number of fossil wood rat nests from the Nevada Test Site (scene of the recent nuclear explosions). Their study showed conclusively that the junipers, common throughout southern Nevada, grew as much as three thousand feet below their present range within the last twelve thousand years.

More recently, Robert Thompson and Eugene Hattori analyzed pack rat materials collected in stratigraphic segments from the rear wall of Gatecliff Shelter and from two small shelters in the nearby Gatecliff formation (Thompson and Hattori 1983). These midden units were soaked in the laboratory until the pack rat urine was dissolved and then were poured through geological screens, dried, and hand sorted. Selected specimens of juniper twigs, piñon pine needles, twigs and winter buds of quaking aspen, and wild rose twigs were submitted for radiocarbon dating. The dates, ranging from 9520 ± 480 B.P. to essentially modern, allowed Thompson and Hattori to devise a chronology of the changing plant communities in the immediate vicinity of Gatecliff Shelter for the past ten thousand years.

The most important finding was that the piñon pine was absent from Gatecliff area until about 6000 B.P. (and this was confirmed by macrofossils found in flotation samples processed on the Gatecliff hearths and also counts of fossil pollen grains in the Gatecliff sediments). This finding is extremely important because it indicates that people arrived in the Gatecliff area well in advance of the piñon pine. Clearly the people visiting Gatecliff before 6000 B.P. relied on plant foods other than the piñon pine, so critical to the economy of the historic Western Shoshone populations of the area.

WHERE TO GO FROM HERE?

Analysis of Pack Rat Nest Contents for Reconstructing Past Environments: In addition to their analysis of Gatecliff Shelter pack rat middens, Thompson and Hattori (1983) provide an excellent overview of both technique and the current state of knowledge; see also Madsen (1976), Mehringer and Ferguson (1969), Thompson and Mead (1972), Van Devender (1977), Van Devender and Spaulding (1979), Wells and Berger (1967), Wells and Jorgensen (1964).

Some Attempts to Reconstruct Prehistoric Diet

To this point, we have dealt separately with faunal and floral remains (and in truth, this is often the way such research begins). But analyzing and reconstructing past human diets require a more holistic outlook. Next, we shall discuss a range of methods dealing with the more general topic of paleonutrition.

Estimating Seasonality of Occupation

We have already seen how Joe Ben Wheat determined that the Olsen–Chubbuck bison kill must have occurred fairly late in the calving season, probably in late May or early June. **Seasonality** studies are particularly important to the study of nonsedentary people, who might have actually lived in several different base camps throughout the year.

Plant remains can also be useful for estimating the duration of human occupation. Figure 11–12 shows Kent Flannery's (1986) listing of the seasonal availability of important plant foods in the environment of the eastern Valley of Oaxaca (Mexico). Consider-

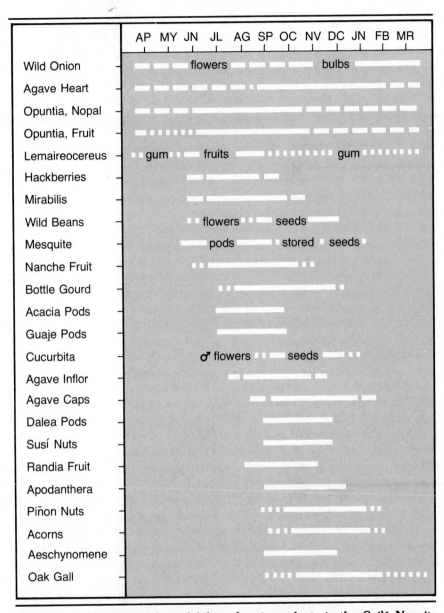

FIGURE 11–12 Seasonal availability of various plants in the Guilá Naquitz area, Oaxaca (Mexico). Solid lines indicate periods of peak availability; dashed or dotted lines indicate periods of occasional availability (see Flannery 1986, Figure 18.1). (By permission of Kent V. Flannery and Academic Press)

able seasonal variability is evident in this ecosystem, with some plants becoming available at the beginning of the rainy season (beginning in June), others toward the end of this period (around November), and still others during the dry season (in about April). By looking at deliberate caches of these wild plant foods, Flannery and his colleagues could tell something about the human utilization of Guilá Naquitz Cave.

Estimating site seasonality is hardly new in archaeology. In a classic study, Hildegarde Howard (1929) demonstrated the potential of such noncultural remains for reconstructing lifeways by identifying the avifauna (birds) from the Emeryville Shell-mound on San Francisco Bay. Howard identified several of the bones as those of cormorants, birds that breed on offshore islands in the early summer. After about a month, the nestlings moved onshore, where they were killed by prehistoric hunters. Because the bones found in the mound were those of relatively immature birds, Howard reasoned that the prehistoric hunts must have taken place between the middle of June and the end of July. Cormorants were found throughout the midden, leading Howard to infer that the site was occupied at least during the summer months. Howard also noted the presence of a foot bone from a young great blue heron and took it as evidence of a May occupation.

This single bone was used to extend the summer occupation of the site backward to include part of the spring, an example of what is now termed the *presence–absence* method of inferring seasonality (Monks 1981). Though certainly not in conflict with the cormorant data, Howard's adding a spring component on the basis of a single bone is nevertheless risky inference. Even if one could be certain that this bone had been introduced by humans, it seems more reasonable to require the presence of several different indicators for a given season as a basis for advancing a seasonality estimate.

Several other techniques have been used to estimate the season of use in archaeological sites. J. D. G. Clark, for instance, used antlers to derive seasonal information at Star Carr, a major Mesolithic site in northern England, occupied in about 7500 B.C. (Clark 1954, 1972). The major food animals at Star Carr were roe deer, red deer, and a few elk. Red deer remains were the most abundant, and virtually every red deer stag had been killed while he still carried his antlers. Based on populations of red deer, Clark knew that modern red deer carry their antlers from mid-October until late April (see Figure 11-13). Assuming that red deer of 9500 years ago behaved similarly, Clark inferred that Star Carr must have been occupied at least during the winter months. A great number of shed red deer antlers were also found at the site; Clark suggested that these must have been retrieved almost immediately after they had been shed; otherwise the deer themselves would have devoured them. This piece of information was taken to mean that Star Carr must have been occupied until at least early April, when red deer normally discard their antlers. The high frequency of unshed roe deer antlers also suggested an April occupation (see Figure 11–15). Just when the occupation began at Star Carr was problematical. Nearly half of the elk stags had antlers, indicating that they were killed sometime before December and perhaps as early as October.

In Clark's view, Star Carr was a settlement consisting of several families who occupied their site during midwinter and spring, returning to it at least once. Clark's excavation and interpretation of Star Carr is an archaeological "classic," a pioneering

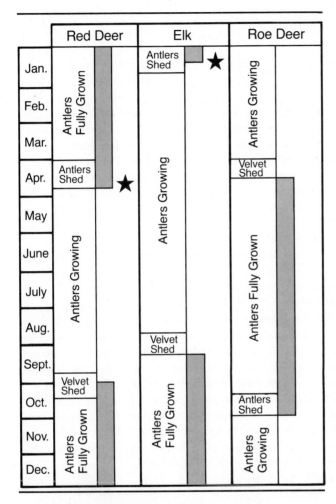

FIGURE 11–13 Inferred seasonal occupation at Star Carr, Yorkshire, England (see Clark 1954, Figure 5). (Courtesy Cambridge University Press)

★ **Indicates times at which site must have been occupied.**

☐ **Indicates period during which animals could have been obtained.**

achievement in the application of ecological approaches to archaeology. But perhaps because of the importance of Star Carr in the archaeological literature, several have questioned Clark's assessment, particularly his use of seasonal indicators.

Pitts (1979) rejects the interpretation of Star Carr as a complete Mesolithic settlement, suggesting instead that the area exposed was a specialized industrial activity zone where deer antlers were worked and animal hides were processed. Critical to the argument is his rejection of red deer as dominant based on antler counts. Pitts suggests that all the deer antlers were collected specifically for the manufacture of barbed points and, rather than computing frequency based on antlers as Clark had done, that mandibles instead be used for MNI counts. Viewed in this way, red deer do not seem to be the "key animal," and this underscores the problems with the minimum number of individuals approach.

More important, if red deer antlers were being collected throughout the year for tool manufacture, then they should not be used for seasonal estimates; if so, then Figure 11-13 must be incorrect.

Clark's inferences about Star Carr have also been questioned by Andresen and colleagues (1981). Relying on experimental and ethnoarchaeological studies (such as presented in Chapter 5), they reason that site formation processes label Star Carr as a hunting and butchering site, visited for very short periods at various times in the year (see also Jacobi 1978). They also question the use of red deer antlers as a seasonal indicator, best collected when shed in April: Fewer than 40 percent of the antlers recovered had actually been shed, and even these could easily have been stored. The unshed antlers could have been acquired any time between late summer and April. Clark had argued that in order for antlers to be worked into tools, they must have been collected shortly after they dropped; otherwise, they would not have been compact enough to be worked into tools. Andresen and his colleagues question this technological assumption, noting that shed antlers were not worked with any greater frequency than were their unshed counterparts. They also emphasized that two elk skulls lacked antlers, indicating they were collected in January or later.

Several other seasonality studies rely on growth lines in marine shells (Clark 1979, Coutts 1970, 1975; Coutts and Higham 1971; Koike 1975). Season of death can be estimated from thin sections of these teeth (e.g., Bourque, Morris, and Spiess 1978). Fish remains are also highly sensitive seasonal indicators, especially the vertebrae, otoliths (ear bones), and scales (Casteel 1972a, 1976b). But a note of caution is required here. Each technique can tell the archaeologist only when one or more animals died. The fact that some cormorants died at Emeryville in June or July is, by itself, archaeologically uninteresting. Archaeologists must be continually aware of the arguments of relevance involved to demonstrate that the death of a clam or a bighorn is somehow contemporaneous with (and relevant to) a specific behavioral event of interest (see also the warning in Chapter 9). Without the demonstration of such relevance, the seasonal dates might tell us something about red deer or cormorant archaeology, but nothing about people.

Letting the Archaeological Data Speak for Themselves

The Tehuacán project was in large part concerned with reconstructing the ancient subsistence patterns played out over the millennia of human prehistory, documenting, among other things, the development of agriculture in the Tehuacán Valley (MacNeish 1967). The diverse excavations uncovered vast amounts of material relevant to these problems— nearly 11,000 bones and other zoological specimens, 100,000 plant remains, and more than 200 human feces. Although these objects came from only five caves, they are critical to the issue of subsistence in this limited ecosystem and also may help us understand the origin and dispersion of plant domestication throughout the New World.

Richard MacNeish directed the excavations and analysis of this huge collection of objects in archaeological contexts. A dozen specialists—zoologists, botanists, geneticists, geologists—analyzed specific aspects of the Tehuacán Valley materials, describing, generalizing, speculating, and, at times, disagreeing. But this is always the price one pays when taking on interdisciplinary research projects.

Another risk in such broad-based inquiries is that the results will remain fragmented and analytically independent. In effect, archaeologists are torn between simply "contracting out" the specialized analyses and having to learn each specialty themselves. Neither alternative is particularly attractive, and archaeologists running a truly interdisciplinary project constantly straddle the fence between a superficial understanding of what the specialists are actually doing, and analytical anomie.

In the Tehuacán Valley Project, Richard MacNeish took the unprecedented step of attempting to draw together the diverse data into a single quantitative summary statement that reconstructed the overall subsistence network. He did so by computing bulk estimates of the food derived from all discarded plant and animal remains recovered in the Tehuacán cave excavations, an exercise "fraught with difficulties" (MacNeish 1967, p. 296). Although recognizing the hazards, Scotty MacNeish was never one to waste much time bemoaning the shortcomings in his data. He simply jumped in.

Kent Flannery (1967b) had analyzed the animal bones using the minimum number of individuals (MNI) concept. That is, of the 11,000 skeletal elements recovered, 4713 could be identified by type of animal and part of skeleton; they represented at least 1013 animals. Although some of the bones probably came from owl pellets and some were brought on-site through natural causes, Flannery felt that most bones were the remains of what had been eaten by people (see the earlier discussion of this assumption).

MacNeish translated Flannery's MNI counts into estimates of meat actually consumed prehistorically. If two right deer femurs were found on a given floor, he figured that at least two deer had been eaten during this occupation. In the Tehuacán Valley, deer yield about 20 liters of meat, and so the people living on that floor had consumed at least 40 liters of deer meat. Similar procedures were used for all other animal bones in the Tehuacán Caves, with meat estimates ranging from 10 liters for puma, 1.0 liter for rabbit, to less than 0.25 liter of meat for mice, snakes, lizards, and small birds.

Because MNI counts are not applicable to vegetal remains, MacNeish figured out another way to handle the masses of dried plant materials. Using a liter can (courtesy of Pemex Oil Company), he measured the volumes of fruits and vegetables—some bought in the Tehuacán marketplace, others collected in the field, corn kernels representing the various races from storage bins of the Rockefeller Foundation, and some actual archaeological specimens. After the rinds were removed, for instance, various gourds, squash, and pumpkins from the market were mashed up in the liter can, and MacNeish found that they averaged about one liter of flesh apiece. Every archaeological fragment was then tallied as representing one liter of food. The flesh of avocados, guavas, and prickly pears averaged about thirty examples "per smelly, sticky liter." About four hundred peanuts (from the Hotel Peñfiel Bar) filled MacNeish's liter container. Wild avocados were estimated as being about sixty fruits per liter, and so forth.

Because maize evolved during the human occupation of the Tehuacán Valley, scoring the corn was more difficult. Agricultural studies demonstrated that wild corn averaged eight rows of almost seven kernels each, and so using kernels of small green ears of that size, they estimated that about ten thousand kernels filled a liter can. Other races of corn varied between eight thousand and two thousand kernels per liter.

Another problem was the differential preservation of plant remains. Although some floors were sufficiently dry to preserve organics throughout, others allowed preservation only here or there. MacNeish derived a "PF" ("preservation factor") to balance out the differential preservation. On Zone A of Tecorral Cave, plant remains showed up in only two of the ten meter squares excavated; the total number of plant remains recovered were multiplied by a PF of five.

MacNeish attempted to derive the amount of food for each floor by combining three sets of data: Liters of meat estimated from the MNI determined by Flannery's study of the bones, liters of plant food estimated from a study of the actual remains and estimates from bulk yields of modern plants, and a calculation of the amount of plants that would have been there had the preservation been constant over the entire floor.

MacNeish was the first to admit that "there is probably a large margin of error in each calculation," and there is no escaping the rough nature of the estimates. Still, MacNeish maintained that because the degree of error was consistent through time, his computations should satisfactorily reveal food or subsistence changes throughout the Tehuacán Valley occupation.

The end result was a series of percentage graphs showing the changing importance of food through the nine-thousand-year-long Tehuacán Valley sequence (Figures 11–2 and 11–14). These are truly remarkable diagrams, the uneven calculations notwithstanding. Other archaeological sequences in **Mesoamerica** were considerably more fragmented, and few places provided conditions that preserved food remains in such quantity.

Paleopathology and Skeletal Analysis

The distinction was made in Chapter 3 between physical and cultural anthropology, stressing that archaeology deals with cultural phenomena. Like most black-and-white criteria, this distinction is not really as clear-cut as I have led you to believe. But in books like this it is necessary to begin somewhere, and so I excluded physical anthropology from our immediate domain of interest. Now it is time to redress the balance. In truth, archaeologists have been guilty of rather badly mistreating their colleagues in physical anthropology. All too often archaeologists excavating mortuary sites have called in a physical anthropologist (or osteologist) primarily as a technician whose job it is to produce some tables and figures regarding the bones. Before 1970 or so it was rare for the archaeologists even to invite the osteologists to the site, much less to solicit advice about the best way to go about testing the site and removing the human burials.

But recently one branch of physical anthropology has indeed worked closely with field archaeologists for the express purpose of studying the prehistoric biological system (Figure 11–15). Called **biocultural anthropology**, this new subdiscipline recognizes the

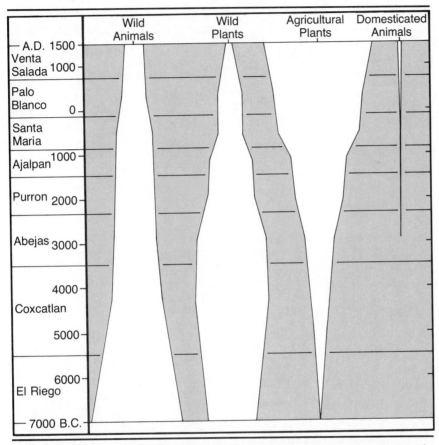

FIGURE 11–14   Changing trends in the importance of principal sources of food in the Tehuacán Valley, Mexico (see MacNeish 1967, Figure 186). (By permission of Richard MacNeish and University of Texas Press; © 1967)

need for cooperation between archaeologist and biologist in working toward a common goal. Of particular interest in the past decade or so has been the study of prehistoric health and demography.

For years, the field of **paleopathology** plugged along as the stepchild of clinical orthopedics. But the tension between medicine and anthropology has lessened. Although paleopathologists must often be satisfied with identifying a "disease cluster" rather than naming a specific pathogen, the fact that research is limited to dry bony tissues has not precluded the development of alternative stategies of inquiry (Buikstra and Cook 1980, p. 435).

The past two decades have seen significant progress in five directions. First has been the progress toward identifying specific diseases (and disease complexes), from both

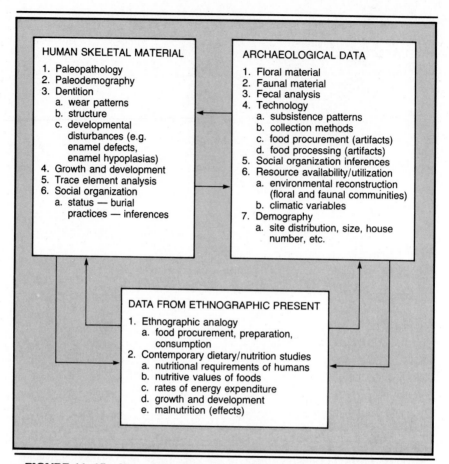

FIGURE 11–15 Interrelationships among human skeletal, archaeological, and ethnographic data (see Gilbert and Mielke 1985, p. xiii). (By permission of R. I. Gilbert and Academic Press)

the diagnosis of skeletal materials and the development of paleoepidemiological models for specific regions. Considerable progress has also been made in **paleodemography**, the study of mortality patterns in antiquity. Although this "life table" approach is subject to criticism, the potential for reconstructing differential reproduction and survival in the past remains great. Another important research direction has been the investigation of "nonspecific" indicators of stress, particularly as caused by nutritional deficiencies and/or infectious disease. Paleopathological researchers have succeeded relatively recently in developing chemical techniques for reconstructing ancient nutritional patterns. Finally, important progress has been made linking physical behavior to skeletal form.

We shall touch briefly on these major directions, stressing the potential role in enabling archaeologists to work with a broad range of specialists to derive a more complete picture of ancient diet, health, and demography.

WHERE TO GO FROM HERE?

Some General Sources on Paleopathology: The overview by Buikstra and Cook (1980) defines the sweep of paleopathology as a field of inquiry; Clark Spencer Larsen (1987) provides a comprehensive, up-to-date report on what human skeletal remains can tell archaeologists about nutrition, diet, health and physical behavior; other important review papers by Martin, Goodman, and Armelagos (1985) and Huss-Ashmore, Goodman, and Armelagos (1982) deal with nutritional inference from paleopathological research; papers in Cohen and Armelagos (1984) provide first-rate examples of how these new ideas are being put into practice; see also various papers in Gilbert and Mielke (1985). Ortner and Putschar (1981) is an important sourcebook on paleopathological diagnosis; see also Zimmerman and Kelley (1982).

Physical Anthropology News (PAN) is an excellent source for keeping up with current research in physical anthropology.

Subscription information: Department of Anthropology, Queens College, 65–30 Kissena Blvd, Flushing, N.Y. (11367)

Isolating the Diseases of the Past

The search for diseases of the past is hardly a new enterprise, but some disorders can now be placed in a more reliable biocultural matrix: for instance, the impact of malaria and hyperostosis in the eastern Mediterranean (Angel 1967, 1978), the problem of iron deficiency anemia in early-historic New World populations (Cybulski 1977, El-Najjar and Robertson 1976), and the relationship between malnutrition and infectious disease (e.g., Lallo, Armelagos, and Rose 1978, Taylor 1983).

One particularly important application has been the study of how increased population density is reflected in the proliferation of specific diseases. Jane Buikstra and Della Cook reported on a pattern of disease in western Illinois fully consistent with a diagnosis of tuberculosis. Although the presence of tubercular-like skeletal lesions is well documented in these mortuary samples, Buikstra (1981b) suggests that the responsible pathogen may no longer exist. That is, we are seeing archaeological evidence of a disease that has become extinct.

Reconstructing Diet by Analyzing Stable Isotopes in Human Bones

We already encountered the concept of isotopes when talking about radiocarbon dating (Chapter 9). Carbon, you will remember, has both stable and unstable isotopes, essentially the same molecule but with differing numbers of neutrons in the nucleus. One stable form, C-12, makes up about 99 percent of the world's carbon; C-13 is also stable but accounts for only about 1 percent. The unstable isotope, C-14, most familiar to archaeologists because of its important implications for dating technology, is extremely rare.

Over the past decade, researchers have established that owing to differing photosynthetic pathways, some kinds of plants differentially absorb these carbon isotopes. The first known pathway, discovered in experiments with algae, spinach, and barley, converts atmospheric carbon dioxide into a compound with three carbon atoms. This so-called C-3 pathway is characteristic of sugar beet, radish, pea, and wheat. A second pathway converts carbon dioxide from the air into a complex compound with four carbon atoms. This C-4 pathway includes many plants from arid and semiarid regions, such as maize, sorghum, and millet, the cereal staples of the Americas and Africa. A third CAM pathway (an acronym for "crassulacean acid metabolism") is found in succulents such as cactus.

These findings proved to be critical to reconstructing past diets because we now know that human bone reflects the isotopic ratios of the various plants ingested. Thus, by determining the ratios of carbon (and sometimes nitrogen) isotopes contained in bone collagen, archaeologists can reconstruct the dietary importance of various kinds of plants and animals. Although this relatively new research tool remains in the developmental stage, stable isotope analysis has already revolutionized the way in which archaeologists reconstruct prehistoric diets.

The methods and implications of the stable isotope method can be illustrated by returning to the Tehuacán Valley of Mexico. We outlined how Richard MacNeish used direct archaeological methods to reconstruct dietary change throughout the seven-thousand-year occupation of this highland Mexican valley. Now, with the help of stable isotope analysis, archaeologists have an unusual opportunity to double-check MacNeish's innovative and pioneering work.

Let us phrase this discussion in terms of the steps in the scientific cycle, introduced in Chapter 2. MacNeish's percentage diagrams (Figures 11–2 and 11–14) represent a theory synthesizing the dietary "facts" recovered in the Tehuacán Valley excavations. In one sense, this theory is the end product of MacNeish's scientific cycle. But because theories always require further testing, another cycle has already begun.

Remember that a theory is never actually tested; rather, it is the logical consequences of theories that are tested. When Michael DeNiro and Samuel Epstein began their analysis of stable isotopes in samples of human bone from the Tehuacán Valley, they were first required to develop bridging arguments, the logical implications of MacNeish's theory, expressed in terms compatible with the independent test. Because they were exploring the potential of stable isotope analysis, their first step was to convert Mac-Neish's theory—expressed as changing dietary proportions of plants and animals—into expectations phrased in terms of stable carbon and nitrogen isotope ratios. Basically, this meant that DeNiro and Epstein were required to derive isotope ratios for the various foods that MacNeish recovered archaeologically; this is middle-range research.

They began with the plants, classifying each according to the appropriate photosynthetic pathway used by modern specimens to fix carbon dioxide. Several species used a C-3 pathway; maize is a C-4 plant; and cacti belong to the CAM category. Similar assignments were made for the nitrogen isotopes. Because living plants displayed a range of isotopic ratios, average values were used as estimates.

But the prehistoric Tehuacános also ate meat, and so isotope ratios were required for the various meat sources as well. These results were less satisfactory because DeNiro and

Epstein did not know the percentage of C-3 and C-4 plants that these long-dead animals had consumed. It would, presumably, be possible to derive these values precisely using mass spectrometry on the actual animal bones recovered archaeologically; but instead, they used a complex, and less satisfactory, "mass balance equation" to derive the animal bone estimates and then combined the plant and animal ratios mathematically by phase.

Figure 11–16 illustrates this stable isotope conversion of MacNeish's dietary reconstruction as the solid line. This curve is, in effect, a summary of the "logical implications" of MacNeish's initial theory, as expressed in stable isotope terminology. (Actually, because of the primitive state of middle-range research linking MacNeish's theory to its isotopic correlates, three different conversions were attempted [see Farnsworth et al. 1985], but only the simplest is discussed here).

The next step in the scientific cycle, verification, requires that these logical consequences be compared with some new, independent data. DeNiro and Epstein (1981) obtained samples of the human bones recovered by MacNeish and his team at Tehuacán.

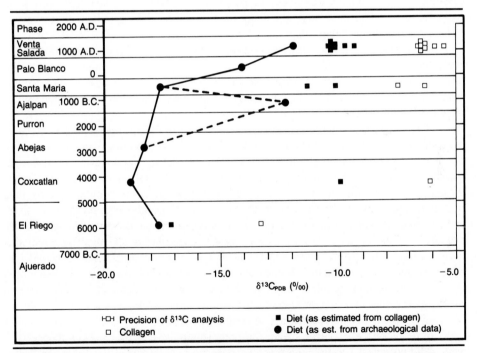

FIGURE 11–16 C-13 values of the diets of people living in the Tehuacán Valley, as derived from analysis of bone collagen. The solid line shows the major trend; the dashed line indicates periods for which data are unreliable (adapted from Farnsworth et al. 1985, Figure 1). (Reproduced by permission of Paul Farnsworth and the Society for American Archaeology)

This sample was relatively small—only twelve burials—because several samples no longer contained enough bone collagen to allow computation of carbon and nitrogen isotope ratios. The bone isotopic ratios were then obtained using mass spectrometry analysis.

Figure 11–16 compares the new carbon isotope data with expectations from Mac-Neish's reconstructions. The isotopic findings for the El Riego phase match closely MacNeish's interpretation. At this early phase, the Tehuacános subsisted strictly by hunting and by gathering wild plants—mostly C-3 food—with meat making up slightly over half of the diet.

Moving further on in time, MacNeish's reconstruction suggested that between the El Riego and Santa María phases, hunting and wild plant gathering slowly declined in importance as domesticated plant foods assumed greater importance. This process accelerated rapidly during the Palo Blanco and Venta Salada phases as maize became the staple. Specifically, MacNeish thought that during the Coxcatlán and Abejas phases, wild plants comprised about half the diet, domesticated plant materials being of minor but increasing importance (about 20 percent); meat sources remained significant but were proportionately declining (to about 30 percent). MacNeish believed that wild plant consumption continued through the Palo Blanco phase, ending only with the maize farming of the Venta Salada phase.

But isotopic evidence suggests otherwise. Rather than a gradual introduction of maize agriculture, the isotope ratios in the human bone suggest a dramatic dietary shift toward maize much earlier, between the El Riego and Coxcatlán phases. The isotope ranges suggest that most of the diet during Coxcatlán times and later was supplied by C-4 plants, probably maize.

This discrepancy has important ramifications for our understanding of plant domestication in the New World, but both dietary reconstructions are plagued with problems. One difficulty is the translation of MacNeish's proportional diagram into its isotopic correlates, a shortcoming of middle-range research that can be overcome only by a better understanding of isotopic fractionation in living plant populations. Another biasing factor is that MacNeish's reconstruction is based entirely on data from five caves, as these are the best places to find preserved animal bones and plant remains. But the occupation of the Tehuacán caves was only seasonal, and one wonders how representative these data are of the overall picture of Tehuacán subsistence. After all, sedentary villages were established elsewhere in the valley during the later phases, the cave sites being used in only marginal and specialized ways. In the next chapter, we shall analyze the fallacy of the "typical" site, demonstrating how the results from a single kind of site can be misleading when used to reconstruct the overall patterns.

In terms of the scientific cycle, the bone isotope test of MacNeish's theory verified—"did not reject," to be more precise—only the earliest part of the Tehuacán Valley sequence (the El Riego phase). For the last six thousand years, there remains a discrepancy between MacNeish's archaeological reconstruction and isotopic analysis of human bone. The current evidence does not permit an informed choice between the two alternatives. Perhaps MacNeish underestimated the importance of early agriculture in the

Tehuacán Valley. Or perhaps the small sample size and premature assumptions involved in the bone isotope technique make these results suspect. In either case, it is clear that stable isotope determinations will provide an important tool for archaeologists attempting to reconstruct prehistoric diet.

Farnsworth and his colleagues are quite right when they ask:

> How many times in the past has an archaeologist, after identifying and quantifying all the floral and faunal remains, sat pondering how best to weight the data or to compensate for possible sources of bias in order to arrive at a reasonably accurate dietary reconstruction? The stable isotope approach by itself does not identify the prehistoric diet, but it does provide a beacon that can tell the archaeologist the general direction in which to move. Anyone who has confronted the problem will recognize that this is no small aid (1985, p. 114).

Despite such positive beginnings, some problems exist for isotope analysis and reconstruction of diet. It is not clear, for instance, whether only arid climate animals are affected, but nitrogen isotope studies have to be closely questioned in the future.

On the other hand, certain "heavy" isotope ratios, such as lead and strontium, may provide evidence—from a comparison of teeth and bones—that will allow paleopathologists to determine whether an individual was buried in the same locale (that is, the same geochemical environment) in which he or she grew up. The horizon remains bright indeed for those using isotopic data to reconstruct human diet.

WHERE TO GO FROM HERE?

General Sources on the Use of Bone Isotope Ratios to Reconstruct Diet: Nikolaas J. van der Merwe pioneered the application of stable isotope analysis on human bone, and his lucid account in *American Scientist* is excellent reading (van der Merwe 1982); Schoeninger, DeNiro, and Tauber (1983) demonstrate how stable nitrogen isotopes can be used to determine relative proportions of marine and terrestrial diets; see also Chisolm, Nelson and Schwarez (1982), DeNiro and Schoeninger (1983), Gilbert (1985), Klepinger (1984).

Dietary Reconstruction of Prehistoric Tehuacán Valley: MacNeish's (1967) initial volume on the Tehuacán report contains the early dietary reconstruction; the bone isotope data are presented by Farnsworth et al. (1985); see also DeNiro and Epstein (1981). Anderson (1965) reports on analysis from tooth wear patterns on the Tehuacán skeletons.

Additional Applications of Stable Isotope Ratios for Reconstructing Prehistoric Diet: Middle United States: Bender, Baerris, and Steventon (1981); Northeastern United States: van der Merwe and Vogel (1978); Venezuela: van der Merwe, Roosevelt, and Vogel (1981); Lynott et al. (1986).

Looking for Indicators of Stress

Although the human skeleton was long overlooked as a source of potential information about human diet (Wing and Brown 1979), the balance shifted in the last decade. One focus has been the documentation of generalized stress responses in human hard tissue.

But both the causes and the effects of malnutrition are complex and can rarely be traced precisely. Instead, paleopathologists prefer to study the effects of **stress**, defined as any environmental factor that forces the individual or population out of equilibrium (Martin, Goodman, and Armelagos 1985, p. 228).

Stress is a behavioral impact that cannot be observed directly in archaeological skeletal populations. To overcome this problem, Alan Goodman modeled the effects of generalized stress. Past nutritional deficiencies can be inferred from the pattern and severity of the effects of stress on individuals, as well as the distribution of that stress on the contemporary population. This model views the degree of physiological disruption as dependent on both the severity of environmental stressors and the adequacy of host response (Figure 11–17).

A range of cultural factors—technological, social, and even ideological—can dampen the effect of stress on human populations. A particular nutritional constraint can, for instance, be overcome by (1) changes in technology that broaden (or intensify) the subsistence base, (2) social modifications that effectively distribute food to those in need, or (3) an ideology rewarding and reifying a sharing ethic. Culture likewise can increase stress: Intensifying agricultural production is known to increase the potential for nutritional deficiencies and infectious disease, and relying on monocropping makes populations vulnerable to drought-induced crop failure and protein inadequacies. When insufficiently buffered, stress creates physiological havoc by disrupting growth, decreasing fertility and fecundity, triggering (or intensifying) disease, and, in some cases, causing death (Figure 11–17).

The human skeleton retains evidence of stress in several ways: "In a sense, bone provides a 'memory' of past events and the behavior of its cells up to the point of the individual's death" (Martin, Goodman, and Armelagos 1985, p. 237). Numerous methods

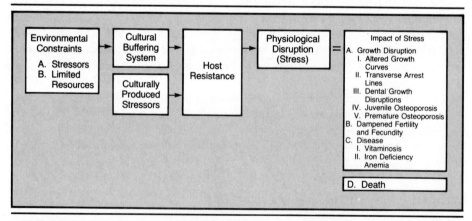

FIGURE 11–17 The interaction of environmental, cultural, and biological factors that can inhibit or enhance nutritional adaptation (see Martin, Goodman, and Armelagos 1985, Figure 8.1). (By permission of D. L. Martin and Academic Press)

exist for evaluating the way in which environmental stress affects the growth, maintenance, and repair of the long bones.

Harris lines, for instance, are bands of increased bone density—observable on
X-rays of human long bones. They are often caused by a variety of nutritional stressors,
especially severe and short-run dietary deprivation. Harris lines, which generally show up
between birth and eighteen years, have been observed on dozens of archaeological
samples and are consistently associated with decreased longevity.

Another common technique for monitoring physiological stress is the analysis of
dental hypoplasias, growth arrest lines formed from birth through six years (see Figure
11–18). Hypoplasias are often evident from gross examination, although some investigators also look at enamel cross sections. Not only does the presence of hypoplasias
betray the presence of environmental stress, but their size also can be measured, allowing
estimates of the duration of metabolic stress. Dale Hutchinson and Clark Larsen (1988)

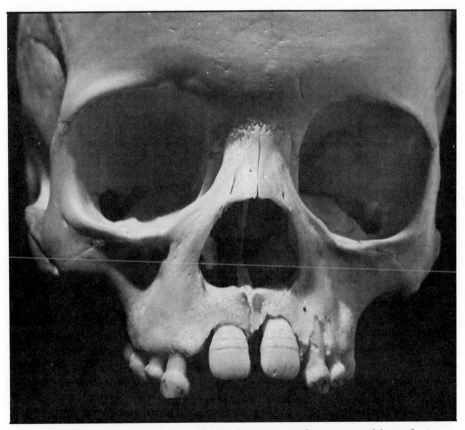

**FIGURE 11–18   Juvenile cranium showing significant enamel hypoplasias
in incompletely erupted central incisors. (Courtesy Clark Spencer Larsen;
photograph by Barry Stark)**

examined dental defects on a large sample of human skeletal materials from St. Catherines Island, ranging from prehistoric burial-mound populations through the seventeenth-century Christianized Guale Indians buried in the cemetery at Mission Santa Catalina. They found that the historic-period hypoplasias were wider than those during the pre-contact period. This pattern strongly suggested that the duration of stress was longer after the European contact, probably reflecting the long-term metabolic stresses associated with the arrival of the Europeans, through the introduction of Old World epidemic diseases and increased health risks overall.

These techniques, when applied to skeletal remains from meaningful archaeological contexts, can be extraordinarily helpful for understanding the effects of nutritional stress among human populations of the past.

WHERE TO GO FROM HERE?

Assessing "Stress" in the Archaeological Record: Martin, Goodman, and Armelagos (1985) review various skeletal pathologies as indicators of nutrition; see also Huss-Ashmore, Goodman, and Armelagos (1982), Powell (1985), Turner (1979).

Paleodemography

As with all other archaeological samples, the corpus of human skeletal materials available in the archaeological record contains great potential for understanding the past. But by the same token, such skeletal populations can carry with them several sources of biases. Extreme caution thus is required when skeletal populations are taken as representative of the behavioral populations from which they derive. One problem is the differential preservation of human skeletal samples. For example, older bones tend be more badly decomposed, and earlier burials in cemeteries are often disturbed by later interments. Despite such distortions, important conclusions can be drawn about prehistoric population profiles, provided that there are sufficient controls (Buikstra and Konigsberg 1985).

A particularly significant skeletal series was recovered by A. V. Kidder when he dug at Pecos Pueblo (see Chapter 1). More than two thousand human burials were recovered, ranging in age from A.D. 1300 to the historic period. When initially analyzed, T. W. Todd (1927, p. 493) crowed that "no other collection . . . surpasses this one for completeness of skeletons, precision of data, and thoroughness of care." The skeletal material from Pecos has been reanalyzed several times, and the changing nature of these analyses reflect the maturation of biocultural analysis.

Charles Mobley (1980) attempted to reconstruct the human demography at Pecos by using the raw age data initially published in 1930 and adding earlier prehistoric material from nearby Forked Lightning Ruin. Mortality, survivorship, and life expectancy curves for the Native American samples from Pecos were grouped across the seven chronological periods. Using the mortality curve as an example (Figure 11–19), we find that the earliest samples—Forked Lightning (A.D. 1150–1300), Pecos Black-on-White (1300–1375) and Glaze I (1375–1425)—exhibit the highest young-child mortality in the Pecos area and the

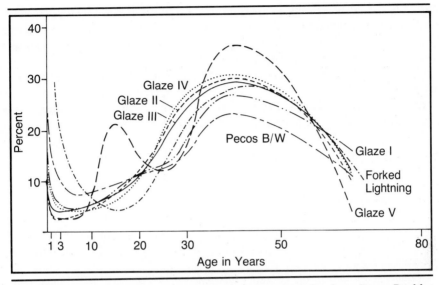

FIGURE 11–19 Mortality curves for the various samples from Pecos Pueblo (see Mobley 1980, Figure 1). (Reproduced by permission of the Society for American Archaeology)

lowest percentage of deaths in the thirty- to fifty-year age interval. By contrast, the Glaze II, III, and IV (A.D. 1425–1600) samples show relatively fewer child deaths and a higher percentage of deaths in the thirty- to fifty-year interval (the aberrance of the Glaze V sample was attributed to the small sample size). When compared with other available North American Indian population profiles, this demographic structure suggested to Mobley that the Pecos populations probably enjoyed better-than-average nutrition and superior hygiene, or perhaps both.

Mobley's study—like all those involving the archaeological record—was grounded in middle-range assumptions. When reanalyzing the same skeletal series from Pecos, Christopher Ruff (1981) found that Hooton had consistently overestimated the ages of the adult sample because of the limited criteria available in the 1920s to estimate age of death from skeletal material. Hooton's criteria also apparently contained systematic biases in the sexing of the Pecos skeletons, resulting in a suggested sixty-to-forty male–female adult sex ratio. Ruff (1981) thinks that Hooton and Todd were unprepared for the striking robustness encountered at Pecos, and hence they classified some females as males (a worry also voiced by Hooton in 1930). Using modern criteria, Ruff reconstructed a sex ratio much closer to fifty-fifty.

Ann Palkovich (1983) has pointed up an additional problem with Mobley's analysis. Only about 30 percent of the Pecos skeletal sample could be assigned to the temporal periods on Figure 11-19. Palkovich's statistical analysis shows that this one-third sample does not represent an unbiased sample of the entire archaeological population.

It turns out that infant remains are underrepresented in the ceramically dated samples—perhaps because of cultural preferences at Pecos or a bias in excavation. But in any case, this unrepresentative sample strongly suggests that the demographic profiles (such as that in Figure 11–19) may be seriously biased.

We dissect this example not to pick on Mobley but, rather, to underscore a general problem: Even relatively rarefied archaeological interpretations—though potentially informative for reconstructing past lifeways and population dynamics—still depend heavily on the fundamentals of sampling and reliable chronology.

WHERE TO GO FROM HERE?

Sources on Paleodemography: For a critical view of paleodemographic methods, see "Farewell to Paleodemography" (Bocquet-Appel and Masset 1982). Buikstra and Konigsberg (1985) responded to this criticism, concluding that imprecision in age indicators applied to older adults and interobserver error remains a problem. See also Angel (1969), Buikstra and Mielke (1985), Larsen (1987), Ramenofsky (1987), Van Gerven and Armelagos (1983).

Paleodemography of the Pecos Population: Primary data and initial interpretations are presented by Hooton (1930); Mobley (1980) and Ruff (1981) conducted relatively recent reanalyses of the sample; see also Howells (1960).

A Computer Simulation Approach

> Comprehensive models are built, if at all,
> by many hands over many decades.
> —James Doran

As research progresses in archaeology—or in any science—the level of inquiry becomes increasingly more complex. That is, as our quest for understanding progresses, so do the tools we use to answer these questions: Physicists hardly needed their cyclotrons before they knew about the atom. In archaeology, we see a similar relationship between research progress and analytical complexity. As long as cultural chronology held the attention of archaeology, analytical methods were relatively simple and easy to understand. But as archaeologists have begun to take seriously their role as social scientists, we find the difficulties of meaningful reconstruction require increasingly advanced techniques.

One such complex tool is **computer simulation**. By simulation, we mean the "dynamic representation achieved by building an explicit model and moving it through time" (McMillan and Gonzalez 1968, p. 26). Simulation is thus a problem-solving device, to be used when the system under consideration defies analysis through more direct means.

Several archaeologists have turned to computer simulation because their research problems had become sufficiently complex to warrant the added complexity in analysis. Next, we shall present two examples of computer simulation used as deductive devices to help understand problems of prehistoric subsistence. The first instance, my own work on the BASIN I model, was published over fifteen years ago and is presented here as an extremely simple example illustrating the general workings of subsistence-based simulation studies. A second, more complex example was derived by Robert Reynolds and points the direction toward future simulation studies in archaeology.

The BASIN I Computer Simulation Model

During prehistoric and protohistoric times, the semiarid steppe environment of the Great Basin was inhabited by groups of Northern Paiute, Western Shoshone, and Southern Paiute (or Ute), divisions based largely on linguistic boundaries. The ecological adaptation of these Shoshonean speakers depended on a meticulous, exacting exploitation of Great Basin **microenvironments**. Because they practiced no true agriculture, they traveled from one habitat to another to harvest the local wild crops as they became available. Nuts of the piñon tree, a staple Shoshonean resource, ripened in the late fall and often provided enough food for the winter. Buffalo berries and currants also became available in the low foothills about this time. Indian ricegrass seeds were usually ripe during the summer months, and so camp was moved from the piñon forest to the flat valley floor in late spring (see Figures 11-20 and 11–21). Many other local foods were utilized in the same cyclical fashion. Because of their intimate relationship with the natural environment, the Shoshoneans were able to fashion isolated native foodstuffs into a solid economic subsistence cycle.

This seasonal round required the aboriginal groups to schedule their itinerary in such a way as to exploit local productivity. But the relatively high mobility created an archaeological record that was extensive by nature—mostly concentrated as surface materials rather than as buried, stratified deposits. Before we could take to the field, it was necessary to consider more closely how such an archaeological record was formed and what it should look like when encountered, and to do this, we developed a computer simulation predicting the archaeological record of this area. This simulation projected a series of archaeological expectations for the Reese River Valley. Then, instead of looking for a couple of sites to excavate, we developed a way to sample the archaeological record for the entire region (see the next chapter for a discussion of the archaeological follow-up).

Predicting artifact frequencies in the archaeological record is tricky business. Rather than attempt to control all the variability involved, we programmed a relatively primitive computer to take the ethnographic data, monitor projected environmental variations, and then predict attendant artifact frequencies across the landscape. This simulation model was called *BASIN I*, an acronym for Basin Algorithmic SImulation of Numic (Numic being the generalized linguistic designation for Shoshonean speakers).

BASIN I is a function-specific model, designed to simulate deposition of archae-

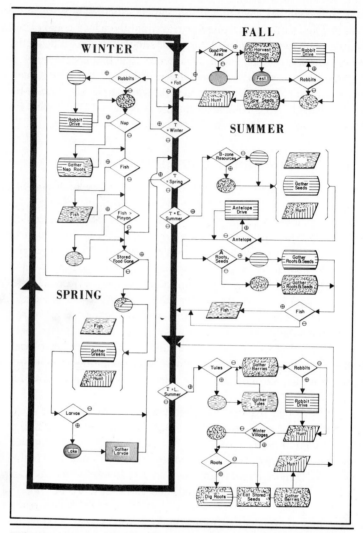

FIGURE 11–20   System flowchart from the BASIN I computer simulation designed to mimic the Western Shoshone economic cycle for the target year of 1840 (see Thomas 1972b, Figure 17.3).

ological artifacts resulting from a specific ethnographic pattern. The concern here is not to chart a cultural trajectory but, rather, to establish the "equilibrium basin" for the BASIN I intrastructural system. The simulation model does not use time in the conventional sense. That is, the one-thousand-year simulation run did not attempt to array systemic behavior over one thousand continuous years. Rather, the computer run simulated the same year, one thousand times. For BASIN I, the target year was 1840, a

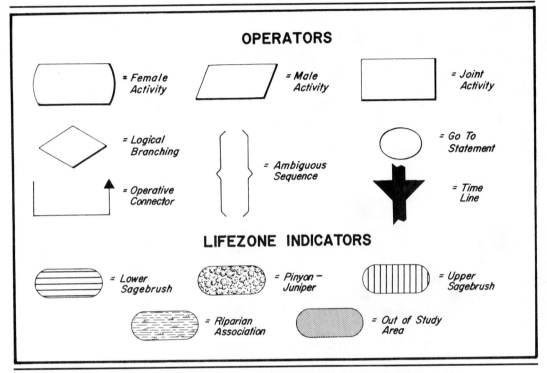

FIGURE 11–21   Key to FORTRAN symbols used in Figure 11–20
(see Thomas 1972b, Figure 17.4).

period suitably antedating the first documented Anglo-American contact in 1859. There is no assumption of environmental stability, as the simulation repeats the same year— 1840—over and over (1000 times).

Figure 11–20 shows how this computer model worked. Our research in the Reese River Valley began with a computer simulation of known Shoshonean settlement patterns, based strictly on the ethnographic research of Julian Steward in the 1920s and 1930s. The purpose of BASIN I was to translate mid-nineteenth-century Shoshonean seasonal movements into a body of concrete, testable archaeological expectations.

Figure 11–20 is the system flowchart for the computer simulation model; Figure 11–21 is the key to the symbols, which generally follow conventional FORTRAN IV computer language. The white diamonds represent logical decision points, that is, those in which the proposition can be answered yes or no. The upper diamond in Figure 11–20, for example, is read, "Is local piñon area good?" These various operators are conditioned by special subroutines, each simulating the behavior of the natural environment: piñon nut productivity, jackrabbit populations, availability of roots and tules, and so forth. The flowchart is roughly quartered by the four seasons of the year, the time line flowing clockwise through the seasons, with logical branchings shunting movement into the proper seasonal activities.

Progression through the flowchart is also determined by the truth of each logical decision. There are three kinds of "activity" boxes: The rectangle with excurvate sides denotes "female activities"; the parallelogram indicates "male activities"; and the rectangle represents activities in which both sexes participate. Inside each box is the activity involved—fish, gather greens, drive rabbits, and so forth—most activities involving distinctive tool kits. Activities are also coded by microenvironment.

To see how this coding works, look at the symbol in the upper right of Figure 11–20, which is read as "rabbit drive involving both sexes and taking place in the lower sagebrush-grass microenvironment." The activity immediately to the left of this is read as "piñon harvest involving only females and taking place in the piñon-juniper lifezone."

By stipulating relevant-use areas, tool kits, and discards, we simulated the archaeological record for each biotic community. BASIN I was basically a series of if . . . then statements: If the historic Shoshonean system had operated in prehistoric Reese River, then the archaeological patterning in lifezone X should appear like this.

In constructing this simulation, we confronted dozens of problems requiring more precise knowledge of the site formation processes: How many lithic flakes are discarded when a bighorn sheep is butchered? How many grinding stones enter the record in a single winter village? How often are points recycled? In retrospect, the weakest part of the BASIN I simulation was this "stipulation" of tool kits and by-products. We now term such stipulation an exercise in bridging argumentation, establishing reasonable archaeological correlates for postulated behavioral activities. Although archaeology over the past two decades has explicitly recognized these issues, discussion has served mostly to highlight the problems; considerably less has emerged in the way of solutions.

The BASIN I simulation model provided a way of projecting the archaeological record on a regional scale. The regional perspective, not at all uncommon in contemporary Americanist archaeology, carries with it a huge burden of methodological and theoretical assumptions. We shall discuss these developments later.

Reynolds's Simulation of Preagricultural Foraging in Eastern Oaxaca

A considerably more sophisticated computer simulation was developed by Robert Reynolds (1986) working with Kent Flannery to understand excavations at the Guilá Naquitz Cave in Oaxaca, Mexico. Among other questions, the research team was asking: What strategy led the occupants of Guilá Naquitz to select the mix of plants recovered on the preagricultural living floors?

As with most computer simulations, the specifics are laden with mathematical symbols and computerese, theorems, and formal definitions. Although this is an advantage in the simulation exercise—to define concepts in firm and unambiguous terms—it does make for rather tedious reading. We will avoid the mathematical specifics and concentrate on what Reynolds was trying to do and how he did it.

In Reynolds's model, a hypothetical group of five foragers, starting from a position of total ignorance, "learned" how to schedule their collection of the eleven major plant foods found at Guilá Naquitz, working by trial and error over an extensive period of time. The imaginary foragers kept trying to improve their efficiency by capturing more calories and protein per area searched. They were confronted with an unpredictable sequence of wet, dry, and average years, which in turn changed the plants' productivity. Information on past performance gradually accumulated in the memory of the cultural system. When a similar situation came up again, the deliberation on whether or not to modify the strategy was better informed with every successive decision.

Each such subsistence strategy evaluates the lifezone being searched, the rank order in which the plants are searched for in each zone, and the size of the harvest area for each. As time goes by, more experience is available to inform the group, until their performance becomes so efficient that additional modification does not have much chance of being an improvement. Figure 11–22 shows the decision-making strategy in such "learning."

At this point, Reynolds compared his computer-generated foraging strategies with those evident in the archaeological record of Zones D and E at Guilá Naquitz, the preagricultural levels dating earlier than 7500 B.C. (see Figure 11–23). The computerized foragers had learned several things in their trek through the mathematical Oaxacan landscape. Starting from a position of complete ignorance, they achieved a strategy similar to that of Guilá Naquitz Zone D within five hundred "time steps."

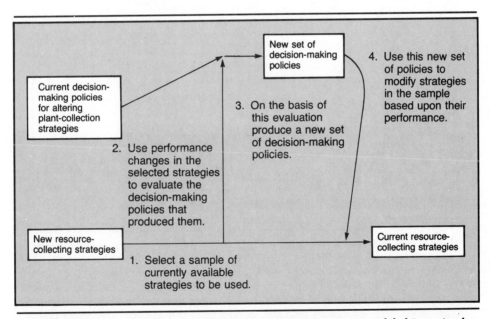

FIGURE 11–22 Interaction between the two adaptive systems modeled in a simulation of behavior at Guilá Naquitz (see Reynolds 1986, Figure 31.1). (By permission of Kent V. Flannery and Academic Press)

First, the group tended to make scheduling shifts in wet years, when overall yields were higher than normal. So when shifts were made, they occurred under relatively favorable circumstances. Even if the change reduced performance, there would be less to lose. The end result was that wet-year strategies tended to be more variable, more likely to include less-productive species. In effect, the hypothetical group came up with a two-part strategy, one for dry and average years and the other for wet years. In dry years, the group worked harder, in wet years, less hard.

Reynolds's model differs from my earlier BASIN I simulation in a number of ways. Whereas BASIN I modeled a single year, Reynolds's simulation attempted to develop

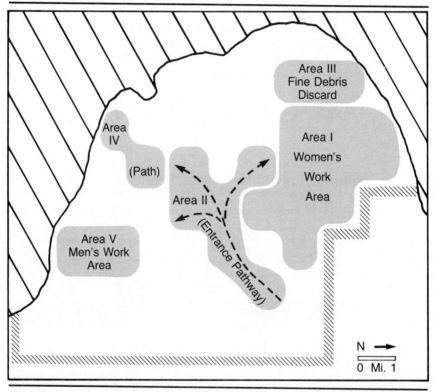

FIGURE 11–23   Interpretive drawing of Zone E at Guilá Naquitz, showing pathways and activity areas (across groups of one-meter squares). Area I is interpreted as a zone where one or two persons (probably women) processed and cooked seasonally restricted plants and discarded some fine-fraction plant and bone refuse into Area III. Area V is interpreted as an area where at least one person (probably male) processed animals, worked flint, and ate *susi* and piñon nuts. Area II is interpeted as a Y-shaped pathway leading into the cave and branching toward Areas I and V. Area IV is considered the terminus of one of these branches, containing less varied debris than does Area II (see Reynolds 1986, Figure 28.10).
(By permission of Kent V. Flannery and Academic Press)

systemic change through time. BASIN I also kept the various procurement subsystems independent from one another; Reynolds went much further by exploring the interaction among components, a necessary step to model daily decision making and resource scheduling.

Such computer simulations offer an alternative to the optimal foraging and linear programming approaches mentioned elsewhere. Each such analysis tends to be parochial and reflect the investigator's inherent biases. The more such approaches are taken, the better balanced will be our overall picture of human ecology.

WHERE TO GO FROM HERE?

Applications of Computer Simulation to Archaeology: Thomas (1972a, 1973), Wobst (1974), Wright and Zeder (1977), Zubrow (1971). The edited volume by Hodder (1978a) contains a broad variety of projects, from Pawnee site development, through simulation of population expansion on Polynesian outliers, through Neolithic axe distributions in Britain. See also Cribb (1987), Sabloff (1981).

The Myth of "Man the Hunter"

The BASIN I simulation model provided a way of projecting the archaeological record on a regional scale. The regional perspective, often used in contemporary Americanist archaeology, carries with it a huge load of methodological and theoretical assumptions. We shall discuss these developments in the next chapter. But for now, let me raise another increasingly important issue, that of gender bias in projecting our ethnocentric notions of the present into the past.

In the BASIN I simulation model, we were on firm ethnographic and ethnohistorical ground when we assigned various gender-specific activities. Keep in mind that the BASIN I computer simulation was designed to emulate behavior from a known group of people (the Western Shoshone) in a known spot (the Reese River Valley) for a known period of time (the year 1840). We thought that women harvested piñon pine nuts during the fall months because several eyewitness accounts from a few decades later supplied the bridging argumentation. We thought that all-male hunting parties stalked bighorn sheep for the same reason. We believed that entire family units participated in communal jackrabbit drives because this is what eyewitness accounts told us.

But how do we project these gender-specific roles into the past? As Spector and Whelan (1988) forcefully pointed out, most archaeologists—when making assertions or incorporating assumptions about the activities, capabilities, social roles, and relative positions of men and women in the past—rarely attempt to identify the sources for their assumptions and seem never to confirm or validate them. The problem arises when archaeologists begin "gendering" the past by applying stereotypical notions about men and women to specific kinds of artifacts and activities: Men always make the projectile points. Women always make the pottery. Women who are found buried with a grinding stone are assumed to have used this artifact in life. If a man was buried with the same grinding stone, it was because he manufactured it.

This is the myth of "man the hunter" (see inset). In many current archaeological discussions, such androcentric assumptions about human nature and society have either ignored women's activities altogether or characterized them in secondary, subservient terms. Only within the past few years have archaeologists begun to develop methods and concepts for looking at gender (Spector and Whelan 1988, p. 7). Contemporary Americanist archaeologists usually assume the existence of "knowable" correlations between the world of material remains and particular activities, behaviors, and beliefs. It makes good operational sense to define the linkages between the archaeological record and the behavior that produced it, and there is every reason to assume that gender is variously encoded in material remains and their spatial arrangements.

Some have addressed the so-called invisibility of women in the archaeological record: "As long as we do not correct for the imbalance created by the durability of bone as compared with that of plant residues, studies of human evolution will always have a male bias" (Isaac 1978, p. 102). This is the embedded notion that men always hunt and women always collect plant foods. More recently, when analyzing the artifacts from Gatecliff Shelter, I took up the same issue, speaking of "The Amazingly Invisible Woman":

> There is also an important correlation between the sexual division of labor and the productive modes in hunter-gatherer society. . . . Males tend to be highly visible in the archaeological record because many male fabrication activities involve subtractive technology [particularly stone tool manufacture]. Conversely, females make few artifacts subtractively, and their archaeological visibility suffers accordingly.
>
> Although both males and females employ additive technology, female fabrication is dominated by this self-corrective, centripetal mode of production, particularly basket making, fiber clothing manufacture, weaving, sewing, and, in some cases, pottery making. . . .
>
> Neither technology is sex specific, but there is an obvious association between the mode of technology and the sexual division of labor. Male tool kits are simply more archaeologically visible than female tool kits. . . . This bias must be kept in mind when reconstructing the activity structure of the various Gatecliff occupational surfaces. (Thomas 1983b, pp. 439–440)

When this was written, Glynn Isaac and I both felt that the archaeological record of hunter-gatherers was intrinsically biased against recognizing female activities.

Conkey and Spector identify the same problem—the invisibility of women in the archaeological record—but attribute the problem to androcentric bias and unquestioned assumptions: It is "more the result of a false notion of objectivity and of the gender paradigms archaeologists employ than an inherent invisibility of such data. . . . One can claim that female-related data in the archaeological record is invisible only if one makes some clearly questionable assumptions, such as the existence of an exclusive sexual division of labor" (Conkey and Spector 1984, p. 6). But whether the problem lies in perception or preservation (or, I suspect, both), the basic quandary remains, and these are not simple problems to solve.

Conkey and Spector (1984) called for an explicit framework for the archaeological study of gender. It does not exist today. There are no publications with titles like "Method for Examining Gender Through the Archaeological Record" or "Gender Arrangements and the Emergence of Food Production." But the lack of explicit discussion certainly does not mean that archaeologists have been silent regarding the gender behavior of the past. Contemporary archaeological inquiry is permeated with assumptions, assertions, and statements of "fact" about gender. Consciously or not, archaeologists are propagating culturally prescribed ideas about gender in their interpretations and reconstructions of the past.

"Tain't what a man don't know that hurts him,
it's what he knows that just ain't so."
—Frank McKinney Hubbard

When Hooton and Todd "sexed" the skeletons from Pecos, they did so by observing certain universal characteristics of the bones, and then attributing biological femaleness and maleness. As we have seen, the operational definitions of biological "male" and "female" skeletons have not remained static through time: What to Hooton were "females" are today considered to be "males." This is because of the evolving nature of the middle-range biological research linking the static skeletal remains of the past with their biological correlates.

If biologists have trouble projecting gender into the past, consider the difficulties faced by anthropologists. After all, there are fundamental differences between biological and cultural correlates. When physical anthropologists "sex" skeletons, they are working from biology. But in examining the material dimensions of gender, archaeologists are approaching culturally conditioned and culturally variable behavior. When archaeologists explore the location of male and female remains in a burial mound, when they observe gender-specific "status" differences in grave goods, and when they infer male and female activity areas in archaeological sites, they are looking at culturally determined, variable aspects of gender as it is expressed in the archaeological record. These are not biological givens to be assumed; they are cultural variables to be explored.

WHERE TO GO FROM HERE?

Some References Dealing with Archaeology and the Study of Gender: The best single overview is provided by Margaret Conkey and Janet Spector (1984); Joan Gero (1985) has written a splendid analysis of the issue (her work is also considered in Chapter 4 of this volume); Spector and Mary Whelan (1988) have prepared an innovative curriculum guide for incorporating gender analysis into archaeology courses. See also Gero (1983), Gibbs (1987), Marshall (1985), Spector (1983).

Specific Critiques of "Man-the-Hunter" Mythology: Dahlberg (1981), Fedigan (1986), Tanner (1981), Zihlman (1981), Zihlman and Tanner (1978).

Margaret Conkey and Janet Spector on the Man-the-Hunter Myth

The Man-the-Hunter model . . . includes a set of assumptions about males and females—their activities, their capabilities, their relations to one another, their social position and value relative to one another, and their contributions to human evolution—that epitomize the problems of androcentrism. . . . Among ourselves, to students enrolled in our introductory classes, and to the lay public . . . we present a picture of continuity in gender arrangements and ideology from early humans to the present, a continuity that suggests an inevitability, if not the immutability of this sphere of social life. . . .

[The] major issues include: (1) the prevalence of gender-specific models that result in gender-exclusive rather than gender-inclusive reconstructions of past human behavior; (2) the common assumption of a relatively rigid sexual division of labor that results in the sex linking of activities with one sex or the other, which in archaeology is often compounded by assuming sex linkages artifactually (e.g., projectile points as male, ceramics as female); and (3) the differential values placed on the different (and usually sex-linked) activities, such that there is a prevailing overemphasis on those activities or roles presumed to be male associated.

There is also another issue that is not—as are the above three issues—androcentrism or a component of male bias, and this issue is perhaps the most important archaeological issue lurking behind this review. What we find lacking in the Man-the-Hunter model is an explicit theory of human social life and, by implication,

the lack of a specific paradigm for the study of gender. Without such theory it is precisely in the attempts to reconstruct prehistoric social life that culturally derived (from our own culture), implicit notions about gender serve as the basis for reconstruction. . . .

We are not advocating that archaeologists abandon their currently preferred research objectives and replace them with those that elucidate gender organization, although we do believe that the methodological and theoretical restructuring that this would entail would lead to a much more compelling archaeology. We are not demanding that archaeology try to elucidate whether a male or a female made a certain tool or performed a certain task. . . .

One thing we *are* saying is that there are certain assumptions about these behaviors that underlie archaeological research and it is these assumptions that must be evaluated and reworked in light of recent feminist research. The organization of gender behavior relates to and is intimately a part of most other aspects of past cultural systems in which archaeologists have always been interested. Archaeologists will have to understand gender dynamics at some level if we are to continue to pursue some research objectives that we have set out for ourselves: site functions and uses, subsistence systems that are, of course, based on task differentiation; inter- and intrasite spatial phenomena; the power and role of material culture; mechanisms of cultural solidarity and integration; extradomestic trade and exchange system; and above all, the course of culture change. (Conkey and Spector 1984, pp. 7–8, 28)

Reprinted by permission of M. W. Conkey and J. Spector and Academic Press.

Summary

For the archaeologist, the study of subsistence generally focuses on the way in which people go about feeding themselves. A wide variety of techniques is now available to assist the archaeologist in such subsistence reconstructions. Faunal analysis—the study of animal remains in archaeological sites—can be directed toward a number of relevant objectives. In some cases, the faunal remains provide direct evidence of which species were hunted (or collected) for food, how these animals were captured, and the butchering methods employed. Some sites can provide clues as to exactly how many animals were killed at a time and how much meat was subsequently consumed (or wasted). Sometimes the reconstruction of hunting practices implies the presence of correlated patterns of social organization, as, for instance, the coordinated bison hunts that occurred on the American Plains. Bones and shells can also provide data regarding seasonality, the time of year during which sites were inhabited.

Plant remains, as well, are powerful sources of data regarding past subsistence practices. Macrofossils (intact plant parts) have been important not only to paleoclimatic reconstruction but also as direct evidence of which plant species were exploited, the season during which these plants were collected, and exactly how the various plant parts were cooked. Flotation is the most commonly used method for recovering plant macrofossils from archaeological sites. Plant microfossils—pollen grains, phytoliths, and spores—are also of interest to archaeologists. Fossil pollen grains can be systematically recovered from archaeological deposits and used to construct a pollen diagram, which plots the changing frequency of pollen throughout the occupational history of the site. Coupled with relevant data on modern plant biogeography, the pollen diagram enables the archaeologist to reconstruct the distribution of prehistoric plant communities and to document how these floral associations have changed through time. A regional pollen analysis can be used as a relative dating technique. The frequencies of economic pollen types can also serve as clues to the economic functions of specific intrasite areas, such as storage rooms and ceremonial areas.

Recently, sciences in one branch of physical anthropology have worked closely with field archaeologists for the express purpose of studying the prehistoric biological system. Called biocultural anthropology, this new subdiscipline recognizes the need for cooperation between archaeologist and biologist in working toward a common goal. Of particular interest in the past decade or so has been the study of prehistoric health and demography.

Significant progress has been achieved in several directions: the identification of specific diseases (and disease complexes), in both the diagnosis of skeletal materials and the development of paleoepidemiological models for specific regions; paleodemography (the study of mortality patterns in antiquity); the investigation of "nonspecific" indicators of stress (particularly as caused by nutritional deficiencies and/or infectious disease); and isolating chemical techniques for the reconstruction of ancient nutritional patterns.

CHAPTER 12

Why People Live Where They Live: Reconstructing Settlement Patterns

After the doldrums of World War II, archaeological fieldwork underwent a resurgence of sorts. Many archaeologists were seeking a new direction. One group of Latin American archaeologists working at Columbia University observed, quite rightly, that there had never been a big dig along the Pacific coast of Peru. Although a great deal of earth had been moved in this region, most of the archaeology had been restricted to test pit excavation, designed only to provide a workable temporal-spatial framework.

Among this group was Gordon Willey, who assembled a team of archaeologists to undertake a major excavation in coastal Peru. Willey and his team eventually decided that they should attempt the large-scale regional survey of one of the several valley systems that line the Peruvian coast. The Virú Valley was selected for a number of reasons: Some of the Columbia faculty had previously worked there; the valley itself was relatively small and could be surveyed by a small crew; and a regional chronology already existed that could be used to date sites on the basis of pottery found on the surface. In 1946, Willey and his team traveled to the Virú Valley to begin their big dig along the Peruvian coast.

Willey's Virú Valley Project received inspiration and guidance from a number of sources, but nobody was more important than Julian Steward, then of the Columbia University faculty. Although technically a social anthropologist, Steward had conducted a number of his own archaeological excavations in the Great Basin during the 1930s, and he maintained a keen interest in the evolution of civilizations throughout the world. As Willey firmed up his plans for the Virú Valley, Steward urged him to look beyond traditional spatial-temporal aims toward problems of more general anthropological significance. Specifically, Steward argued that Willey should be concerned with the forms, settings, and spatial relationships of the sites themselves and what these relationships might imply about the societies that constructed them. As Willey put it nearly thirty years later: "Steward began to convince me that archaeology should be something more than potsherd chronicle, and his settlement pattern suggestion showed me a way in which it might be done" (Willey 1974, p. 157). Steward's own research among the Pueblo societies of the American Southwest (Steward 1937b) had demonstrated how environmental-cultural-social relationships could be revealed in settlement distributions over the wider landscape, as well as how societal patterning could be revealed by settlement arrangements within individual communities.

The objectives of the Virú Valley Project were clearly modeled after Steward's concern with context and function: How did the different communities of the prehistoric Virú Valley interrelate and function during the various periods of human occupation? To implement his strategy, Willey defined a settlement pattern as the way in which people distributed themselves across the landscape.

> It refers to dwellings, to their arrangement, and to the nature and disposition of other buildings pertaining to community life. These settlements reflect the natural environment, the level of technology on which the builders operated, and the various institutions of social interaction and control which the culture maintained. Because settlement patterns are, to a large extent, directly shaped by widely held cultural needs, they offer a strategic starting point for the functional interpretation of archaeological cultures. (Willey 1953, p. 1)

In the course of the Virú Valley survey the research team visited and collected pottery from over three hundred site locations. The sites were characterized according to their inferred function into categories such as dwelling sites, pyramid mounds, cemeteries, and fortifications. The ceramic typology for the area allowed Willey to determine the time of occupation for most sites, and then he synthesized the dated site types into a series of overall community patterns. To do this, he prepared a number of valley site maps, with different symbols for the different functional classes of sites. Operating on the basis of site proximities, Willey attempted to define sustaining areas in order to determine which villages were aligned with which ceremonial center. At the conclusion of his Virú Valley monograph, Willey offered some cautious speculations regarding the meaning of settlement pattern in terms of population size and sociopolitical organization.

The Virú Valley Project stimulated a great deal of settlement pattern research during the 1950s. Willey himself edited a seminal volume entitled *Prehistoric Settlement Patterns in the New World* (Willey 1956). The overall importance of the regional approach was highlighted by the Society for American Archaeology's 1955 seminar entitled "Functional and Evolutionary Implications of Community Patterning" (Meggers 1956). This seminar marked a turning point in the history of American archaeology because it signaled archaeology's attempt to reach far beyond matters of mere chronology and typology. The focus was clearly comparative, as the participants attempted to define the various kinds of community patterning by combining ethnographic and archaeological data from throughout the world. A series of community patterns were defined—such as "free wandering," "central-based wandering," and "advanced nuclear centered"—and the presentation concluded with a discussion of the functional and evolutionary implications of the overall scheme (Meggers 1956, pp. 150–153).

Settlement pattern archaeology has flourished since the days of the Virú Valley

Project, and there have been major research efforts throughout the Old and New Worlds. In Mesoamerica alone, a number of significant surveys have been conducted. MacNeish directed the monumental Tehuacán Valley Project, which located 370 sites and excavated over two dozen of them. Major settlement pattern surveys have also been conducted in the Valley of Mexico, the Oaxaca Valley, and at some major Maya ceremonial centers such as Tikal.

Probably the greatest change in settlement pattern archaeology has been the reliance on established sampling theory in the design of such regional surveys. The early projects such as that by Willey in the Virú Valley were conducted on a largely hit-or-miss basis: "Survey was pursued to some extent by convenience and to some extent with an eye to covering all portions of the valley, all types of terrain, and all of the functional categories which began to emerge in the course of the work" (Willey 1974, p. 161). Modern archaeologists have since come to regard archaeological site sampling as simply a special case of the general survey sampling theory. A number of theoretical and statistical considerations are now generally applied to the issue of regional site sampling in archaeology (and some of these considerations are discussed briefly in this chapter).

WHERE TO GO FROM HERE?

The Virú Valley Project: Willey (1953): "Prehistoric Settlement Patterns in the Virú Valley, Peru"; also, Ford (1949): "Cultural dating of prehistoric sites in Virú Valley, Peru." See also Bennett (1950), Strong and Evans (1952), Willey (1974).

Other Classics in the Settlement Pattern Approach in Americanist Archaeology: Meggers (1956): "Functional and Evolutionary Implications of Community Patterning"; Willey (1956): *Prehistoric Settlement Patterns in the New World*. See also Blanton (1978), Chang (1968), Cowgill (1968), Flannery (1976a), Haviland (1965, 1970), Mac-Neish (1964, 1978), MacNeish, Peterson, and Neely (1972), Millon (1973), Parsons (1971), Sanders (1965).

The Fallacy of the "Typical" Site

We have seen the various ways in which culture can be viewed (Chapter 3). Although "shared culture" is useful for defining time-markers, the modal definition of culture is unacceptable for studying past lifeways. The "typical" can no longer be the focus of study. Instead, culture must be viewed as an adaptive system, and no single representative—be it artifact, component, or site—can be taken as typical or **normative.**

Nowhere is contemporary archaeology's concern with cultural variability more apparent than in regional archaeology. Look at Figure 12–1, which is a graphic rendering of the seasonal round of the Western Shoshone. Ethnographer Julian Steward attempted to reconstruct, where possible, the seasonal movement of aboriginal groups, based on

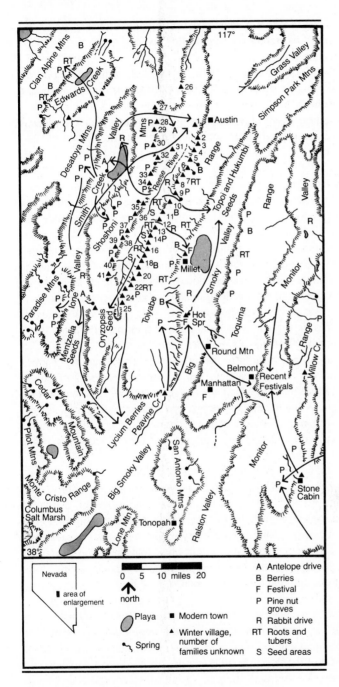

FIGURE 12–1 Seasonal round of the Western Shoshone and Northern Paiute in the central Great Basin (see Steward 1938, Figure 8). (Courtesy the Smithsonian Institution Press).

informant testimony collected between 1925 and 1936. A nonagricultural people, the Western Shoshone based their subsistence on seasonally ripening plant foods, supplemented to some degree by hunting.

Look closely at the pattern for the Reese River Valley, in the northwestern portion of Figure 12–1. The numbered village sites in the Toiyabe and Shoshone ranges are winter villages, sites established seasonally to exploit the ripening piñon nuts. Sites exist along the Reese River, and these localities were established in the summer to gather seeds and roots and to collect rabbits and occasionally hunt antelope. Other satellite sites were also established for ceremonial purposes, and in the upland areas to gather berries and hunt bighorn sheep.

Figure 12–1 was constructed from informant testimony, and these informants were often recalling events that had not occurred for fifty years. Yet despite the large amount of information that was irretrievably lost, a staggering amount of complexity remained, and the figure demonstrates how intricate and complex a seasonal round the Western Shoshone actually practiced. Figure 12–1 also illustrates the *fallacy of the typical site*. Suppose that an archaeologist had the opportunity to locate and excavate just one of Steward's Western Shoshone sites. Which one to choose? Winter village sites are of interest because they represent the lengthiest occupation and probably contain remains of a great variety of activities. But winter village sites are almost always located on windswept ridges, and all that is preserved are stone tools and ceramics. Perhaps, then, one should seek out one of the small upland shelters where hunters briefly camped while pursuing bighorn sheep. The preservation in these shelters is often good, and the chances are excellent of finding remains of sandals, snares, and perhaps even pieces of bows, arrows, and fire-making apparatus. But these small shelters represent only a minor portion of the overall Shoshone pattern. Women were not included in such small hunting parties, and the men were concerned with only a limited range of activities. Or perhaps one might choose to excavate a seed-gathering camp, an antelope drive, or a women's camp established to gather lycium berries.

One difficulty is clear: No matter which site is selected, a great deal will be missed. No single Shoshone site is sufficient to manifest the total range of cultural variability. One cannot just sample here or there, because there is no typical site. Let us take this difficulty one step further. Suppose that Archaeologist Alpha excavated a piñon-gathering station in the Toiyabe Range. Alpha's reconstruction of the lifeway might (correctly) suggest that the economy of that site was based on harvesting piñon nuts, that the camp contained between one and two dozen people, that the men were engaged in manufacturing stone tools and repairing their weapons, and that the women spent a great deal of time preparing piñon meal and sewing skin clothes. This is all correct, as far as it goes. But now suppose that Archaeologist Beta elected to excavate the scene of a *fandango*. Beta's reconstruction would suggest a grouping of two hundred to three hundred people who subsisted on communal hunting of jackrabbit and antelope and who spent a great deal of time dancing, gambling, and "living off the fat of the land." In other words, Archaeologist Alpha would reconstruct a hardworking society composed of small social groupings (extended families), whereas Beta would see a more festive society that lived in large aggregations and was particularly concerned with rite, ritual, and feasting. Yet in truth, both sites are involved in the seasonal round of the Western Shoshone, and so neither site can be taken as typical.

This is not just a hypothetical difficulty. Instances of precisely this misinterpretation have occurred in archaeological literature. Consider the case of the prehistoric **Fremont** and **Promontory** cultures of Utah.

The Fremont culture was initially recognized by Morss (1931) as a fairly sedentary society that subsisted mainly on maize–beans–squash horticulture. It flourished from about A.D. 500 to 1400 (Aikens 1966) and extended throughout much of the state of Utah. Fremont people lived in pit-house villages and aboveground pueblos, manufactured a distinctive black-on-gray and corrugated pottery, occasionally hunted bighorn sheep and deer, and painted characteristic pictographs on cave walls. To most archaeologists, the Fremont seemed to be a northern extension of the well-established Puebloan cultures found throughout the American Southwest.

The Promontory culture was defined by Julian Steward (1937a)—yes, the same Steward who conducted the ethnographic fieldwork mentioned earlier—on the basis of excavations in the Promontory Caves, located north of Salt Lake City. Steward "guess-dated" the Promontory manifestations at about A.D. 1000. Unlike the horticultural Fremont, the Promontory people seemed to be more Plains-like, subsisting mainly by means of bison hunting. No signs of agriculture were found in their sites, and pure Promontory sites never contained architectural remains, such as pit houses or pueblos. Promontory pottery consisted of a poorly made black plainware, and sites contained distinctive moccasins made of bison hide and other well-made leather items such as bags, pouches, and mittens.

The distinction seemed clear. About A.D. 500, Utah was occupied by a group of Fremont horticulturalists, who exhibited obvious ties to the Puebloan peoples of the American Southwest. Then, in about A.D. 1000, these agricultural peoples were displaced by the bison-hunting, cave-dwelling Promontory peoples, who had probably moved out from the Great Plains. Not only were the economies quite different, but so was the pottery, the architecture, the settlement pattern, and indeed most of the artifact inventory.

A great deal of archaeological evidence has been assembled since the 1930s regarding the Fremont and Promontory cultures, which rendered the traditional model untenable. Of greatest importance is the Fremont-Promontory chronology. Excavations by Aikens (1966) have shown Fremont and Promontory pottery, once thought to be distinct, to be in "complete association" in a number of sites. Moreover, radiocarbon dates seem to show that Fremont and Promontory materials existed together for a considerable span of time in northern Utah (Aikens 1966, p. 74). In addition, hundreds of Fremont sites have been found throughout the eastern Great Basin, but Promontory manifestations are now known to be limited to the Salt Lake region of northern Utah. The once distinctive Promontory moccasins and pottery now seem to be little more than northern variants of the overall Fremont pattern.

The two-culture model simply did not work. The newer interpretation is explained by Aikens (1966, p. 74): "Promontory does not in fact represent a cultural grouping distinct from the Fremont, and . . . the 'Promontory culture' is an artifact of archaeological misinterpretation of a few variant items of material culture from seasonal Fremont hunting camps." It is not surprising that little overlap exists between sites of the so-called Promontory and Fremont cultures. The classic Fremont sites were more or less permanent habitation sites, areas where horticulture was conducted and substantial dwellings were built. The Promontory occupations were simply seasonal bison-hunting stations, inhabited only sporadically and used for special, limited purposes. It is small wonder there is little overlap between the material culture of the two manifestations: One site represented a year-round, full-scale village, and the other was only a short-term seasonal stopover.

The Fremont-Promontory problem is but one example of how archaeologists are becoming aware of the intracultural variability inherent in archaeological sites. The Fremont-Promontory confusion occurred because Steward applied the modal concept of culture to problems of reconstructing lifeways, and as long as artifacts and sites were taken as "typical" of their cultures, the confusion lasted. But once archaeologists, such as Aikens, began viewing cultural remains in systemic contexts, the misinterpretation became clear. The remainder of this chapter will discuss the modern methods by which contemporary archaeologists deal with the variability involved in regional archaeological systems.

The Importance of Surface Archaeology

The probability of making surface finds decreases in inverse ratio to the square of the distance between the ground and the end of the searcher's nose.
—Louis Brennan

Traditionally, archaeologists anxious to examine past adaptations have attempted to find deep, stratified sites with a high degree of preservation. Caves and grottos such as Gatecliff Shelter are particularly fruitful in this regard. Plant and animal remains can be carefully excavated and analyzed using methods discussed in the preceding chapter. Recently, however, archaeologists have come to recognize the finite nature of their data. Many rivers have been dammed, flooding once-heavily occupied river bottoms; subdivisions are rapidly encroaching on wilderness areas where sites formerly remained untouched; and some misguided amateur collectors, eager to obtain artifacts and unmindful of scientific purposes, have wantonly destroyed some of the richest sites. Archaeologists are running out of sites. It has been estimated that in California alone, over one thousand sites are destroyed annually. Although this situation is distressing, the worst is yet to come. It is only a matter of time until archaeologists can no longer rely on stratified deposits for keys to the past, for most such sites will be gone.

Contemporary archaeologists are mindful of this problem and are looking for new avenues of prehistoric research. One relevant resource is the surface site, an area in which archaeological remains have simply lain on stable ground surfaces rather than becoming buried by sand, silt, and gravel. In regions that have been spared the plow, archaeologists have the unparalleled opportunity of collecting artifacts literally where they were dropped, often thousands of years ago.

Not only do those surfaces offer a laboratory for studying prehistoric remains, but they also represent adaptations different from the more traditionally excavated midden sites. Until recently, surface sites had been largely ignored, as they lacked the contextual relations (stratigraphy) necessary for establishing cultural chronologies. But current archaeology is examining more than merely time–space sequences, and surface sites provide unique data regarding past human–land relationships. This section considers one such area, the Reese River Valley of central Nevada. This project is presented as an illustration of some of the modern techniques used to reconstruct past lifeways.

The Surface Archaeology of the Reese River Valley

In Chapter 11, we examined BASIN I, the computer simulation model developed to mirror the subsistence and settlement patterns of the protohistoric Western Shoshone. Basically, the computer developed a series of projections for the archaeological record of Reese River Valley. The question then became how best to look in the field to generate meaningful archaeological data.

Some Minimal Requirements for Relevant Archaeological Data

To be relevant to such questions, our prehistoric data must satisfy three criteria. First, all facets of the seasonal round must be represented; it is not enough to generalize from a single site. Because these people moved from place to place every year, information from any single site (such as Gatecliff Shelter) can tell only a small part of the story.

Our data must also be unbiased: Capricious sampling techniques can lead the archaeologist astray in assessing the relative importance of the various sites. The single best way to ensure unbiased results in such situations is through judicious use of *probability sampling theory*. To conduct such a probability sample, one first chooses the **sampling elements** that are the objects of study. In many cases, these elements are archaeological sites, in the traditional sense. All of these elements taken together form a set of all possible elements, the **sampling universe**. Each element is assigned a consecutive number from 1 to N, and the numbers are randomly selected so that each has an equal probability of selection, 1/N. In this manner, a subset, called the **sample**, of the N elements is chosen, so that each member of the universe has an equal chance of inclusion.

In addition to providing relatively unbiased samples, random procedures have the added benefit of providing data amenable to further statistical manipulation. Moreover, because statistical analysis generally requires a random sample, archaeologists who accept a biased sampling design will immediately and unnecessarily tie their own hands.

Finally, the research design must provide for meaningful *negative evidence*. In addition to telling archaeologists what activities took place, such data must likewise indicate which activities did not occur in a particular area or lifezone. The requirement for negative evidence, only recently recognized as relevant to archaeological research, imposes severe yet necessary qualifications on fieldwork.

An Appropriate Archaeological Research Design

The upper Reese River Valley of central Nevada was chosen as the area that best satisfied the preceding prerequisites. The Reese River is a lazy little stream less than fifteen feet wide, which originates about forty miles south of Austin, Nevada. Flowing northward between the Shoshone and Toiyabe mountain ranges, the Reese finally empties into the Humboldt River. The valley itself is about fifteen miles wide and more than one hundred miles long. For survey purposes, a cross section was selected to provide a suitable universe, which, you will remember, should enclose roughly the area of an annual seasonal round of the historic Shoshoneans. The overall study area comprised a tract of land about fifteen miles wide by about twenty miles long.

The valley floor in this area lies about 6500 feet above sea level and is at present dominated by sagebrush shrubs. The piñon–juniper belt, so critical to winter forage, reaches between about 7000 and 8500 feet, covering the low flanks of the mountains. Thick stands of buffalo berries, currants, wild rice, and a host of other native foods also grace the montane forest belt. Above 8500 feet, trees yield again to low sagebrush. The mountain peaks, some of which tower over 11,000 feet, are tundralike, practically devoid of vegetation. A riparian zone consisting of willow, aspen, and cottonwood is found along all montane streams, as they gradually wind their way toward the Reese River.

These lifezones of the Reese River Valley were clearly defined and easily discerned in the field. Four lifezones were isolated for study: lower sagebrush–grass, piñon–juniper, upper sagebrush–grass, and the riparian zone, including both upland stream margins and the immediate vicinity of the Reese River.

The real challenge was to design a field strategy fitting these minimum requirements. Note first that BASIN I avoided the site concept entirely, expressing Shoshonean cultural geography in terms of the regional density and distribution of archaeological objects. This computer design quite literally forced us into a nonsite archaeological sampling strategy, and so this nonsite imperative became the first major requirement of the early research design (see Chapter 7). At the outset, we had some problems with logistics, figuring out exactly how to go about the actual sampling. We had been heavily influenced by Lewis Binford's (1964) seminal paper, which thoroughly demonstrated the advisability of probability sampling at the regional level, but feasibility was quite another matter. At the time (1968), I knew of no substantive application of such regionwide sampling that actually put Binford's ideas into practice. After considerable experimentation in a barley field near Davis, California, we found that five-hundred-meter quadrats were relatively easy to plot on the ground and then to search for archaeological remains. Thus the five-hundred-meter square formed the observational sampling unit of the Reese River survey. This turned out to be a fortunate choice and has proved to be relatively useful throughout much of the Desert West and elsewhere. In areas of higher artifact density, the size of the quadrat can often be reduced.

These considerations in the early phases of the Reese River research led us to devise a *nonsite stratified quadrat* approach to sample design. The study area (termed the *universe*) is selected to include an entire seasonal round. In the central Great Basin, this universe is a single valley system, situated between the north-south trending mountain ranges. The universe is then gridded into a series of large squares (**tracts**), which are each considered as a sample element. Every tract will be completely searched for all visible remains of prehistoric subsistence activities. In this case, archaeological sites per se cannot serve as elements, because before the survey one does not know how many of what kinds of sites are involved in the particular valley. This universe was circumscribed on aerial photographs and divided into about fourteen hundred tracts, each of them five hundred meters (about one-third of a mile) on a side. Each tract was numbered, and a 10 percent random sample was selected. Each tract was considered as a sampling element in this study (see Figure 12–2). Economic vicissitudes—time and money available, scope of the project, estimated unit variability, and so forth—determine how many tracts can be selected. The sampling fraction is expressed as n/N.

The actual fieldwork consisted of locating each of the 140 tracts of the sample on the ground and then surveying the entire five-hundred-meter square for signs of human occupation. All artifacts and waste chippage, whether an isolated find or part of a dense concentration, were mapped, catalogued, and collected. The most efficient survey unit was a team of six archaeologists, mainly instructors and students from the Universities of California (Davis) and Nevada. Each crew could survey one or two such tracts daily, depending on accessibility and local terrain. This sampling design attempted to minimize bias by forcing archaeologists to look in *every* topographic locale, even those unlikely to have habitation residue. It is not enough to say that people could not possibly have lived in a particular situation, for such statements are highly colored by the archaeologist's preconceived ideas and are unacceptable in scientific research. The random survey established (within statistical sampling error) precisely which types of localities were or were not occupied, with little bias or ethnocentrism involved. Artifacts recovered were then analyzed to determine prehistoric ecological relations.

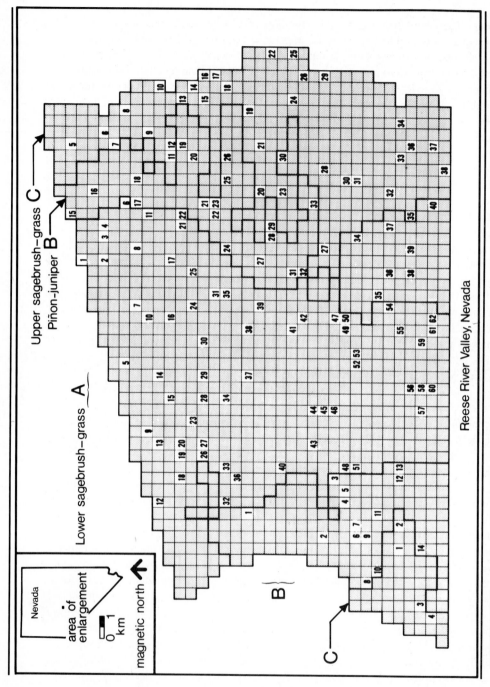

FIGURE 12–2 Grid sampling scheme used at Reese River. Each square is five hundred meters on a side, and a 10 percent sample was randomly selected for intensive survey. Note the three major "strata," which correspond to modern environmental zones (see Thomas 1973, Figure 6)

Reese River Valley, Nevada

Upper sagebrush–grass **C**

Piñon–juniper **B**

Lower sagebrush–grass **A**

Nevada

area of enlargement

0 1 km

magnetic north

Generating the Data

The Reese River fieldwork took about four months to complete, with a field crew varying in size from twenty-three to forty-five people. Approximately 3500 artifacts were recovered from the surface of the 140 tracts. But we still had amassed no data. This was done by observing a large series of attributes on each artifact and preparing an IBM card for each specimen. The initial computer output was in terms of temporal types, which ranged from roughly 5000 B.C. to historic times. After the temporal range of the samples had been determined, the temporal categories were combined in favor of more useful *functional types,* divisions based on distinctive attribute modes such as cutting-edge angle and degree of blade curvature.

The primary aim of the analysis was to evaluate the presence of consistent artifact assemblages that corresponded to the prehistoric exploitation of the lifezones. Areas of extensive hunting, for example, were expected to exhibit a distinctive assemblage: spent projectile points, butchering tools, and flaking debris resulting from resharpening rather than from primary artifact manufacture. Habitation areas, on the other hand, ought to reflect residential activities such as tool manufacture, clothing preparation and repair, and cooking and show remnants of house foundations, campfires, ritual paraphernalia, and the like. As discussed in Chapter 11, these projections were based on solid ethnographic and historic documentation, but the middle-range linkages were tentative and not well defined. Still, we used the BASIN I simulation to project the relative frequencies of each artifact within each lifezone. The principal objective of the fieldwork at Reese River was to examine the credibility of these projections from theory and, by implication, the overall model of Shoshonean adaptation.

Results at Reese River

Based on the fieldwork and analysis, we attempted a first-order synthesis of the archaeology of the Reese River Valley for the past seven thousand years. In a strict sense, the Reese River ecological pattern holds only for the Reese River locality, but further research at Gatecliff Shelter and elsewhere in central Nevada confirmed that these patterns existed well beyond the survey area.

The Reese River settlement pattern contained two major areas of residence. The *shoreline settlement* consisted of a series of large sites located on permanent water sources within the lower sagebrush–grass zones. The artifact assemblage suggested that the economic focus was on the wild grass and root crops that ripen in the late spring and early summer. These shoreline settlements consisted of massive linear scatters of artifacts— often a couple of miles long—that lie parallel to the flowing water. In this context, the "site" was anywhere along the river or stream, for no specific village areas were consistently reoccupied. These campsites were probably situated near scattered caches of harvested summer seeds, and the only structures were mere brush windbreaks and sunshades. The waste chippage indicates that much of the stone tool manufacture took place in the summer camps. The seed diet was doubtless supplemented by rodents and rabbits, both of which could be easily hunted on the nearby flats.

The other primary focus of habitation, the *piñon ecotone settlement,* was located in the dense stands of piñon and juniper trees, generally on long, low ridges that finger onto the valley floor. This "edge effect" is a rather common ecological adaptation that allows exploitation of dual lifezones, in this case, the piñon belt and the nearby valley floor. These sites are also linear scatters of artifacts and chippage, but unlike the shoreline settlements, the piñon ecotone sites consisted of more densely concentrated artifact clusters. The potential areas of habitation were more limited than those along the river, because there are only few suitable flat-topped ridges in the area. The piñon sites were occupied just after the fall pinecone harvest and only when the nut crop of the immediate area had been successful. In other years, the winter village had to be relocated in some more distant portion of the forest where the piñon nuts were available. The artifact inventory of these sites indicates that most hide preparation and clothing manufacture took place during the winter encampments. Deer and mountain sheep probably supplemented the diet of piñon nuts. Houses consisted of domed **wickiups**, sometimes surrounded by stone circles and covered with piñon tree bark or juniper boughs. These houses were often placed in shallow pits up to eighteen inches deep. Although only about five families could live on each ridge top, there might be several such villages within a one-mile radius.

In addition to the habitation sites, the remains of several special-purpose localities were mapped. On the flat valley floor several butchering assemblages were recovered (knives, scrapers, and resharpening flakes), apparently resulting from communal hunting of both jackrabbits and antelopes. Scattered about in the same area were additional artifacts (knives and grinding stones) that resulted from the women's seed-gathering forays. Evidence was also recovered that suggests that deer and mountain sheep were hunted in the piñon belt and also in the high, more barren mountains that flank the Reese River. All of these *task-group assemblages* represent short-term, ancillary subsistence activities undertaken by small groups of relatives working out of the more permanent habitation sites.

Some Implications

This extended example has been presented as a case study to show how archaeologists, working at a regional level, attempt to reconstruct an extinct lifeway. The initial step was to establish a local cultural chronology and then to impose the chronological controls necessary for further investigation. Some specific research objectives were then outlined and an archaeological strategy framed to gather the relevant data. In the Reese River case, the more conventional approach of excavating a few large stratified sites such as Gatecliff Shelter would not answer the questions under consideration. A research design based on the systematic random sampling of an entire valley was therefore devised. As archaeological research progresses in its anthropological endeavors, the archaeologist will have to adapt more and more nontraditional techniques.

In light of nearly two decades of hindsight, we must make several points about our research design at Reese River. First, we spent an inordinate amount of time fussing over irrelevant details. Randomized sampling on a regional scale was then still a largely untested procedure in archaeology. Although archaeology had begun to embrace the theory, archaeologists were still groping for pragmatic field techniques.

We spent far too much time, for instance, trying to ensure that our five-hundred-meter squares were perfectly square. We established a datum corner using a Brunton compass mounted on a photographer's tripod and then chained the quad boundaries using one-hundred-meter ropes. This system was not only cumbersome and time-consuming, but it was also misleading. We lost much of our alleged accuracy when transferring distance from the aerial photographs to the uneven ground surface. The Reese River Valley is an extremely vertical place, and some of the five hundred meter grids contained nearly a kilometer in elevation. When conducting such surveys, after all, were we talking about five hundred meters measured along the actual ground surface or five hundred meters as measured on an aerial photograph?

There were also minor problems with our grid system. We created a unique five-hundred meter network, using a centrally located butte as the horizontal datum. Today, we use the standard *Universal Transverse Mercator Grid,* printed on most field maps. This system creates ready-made grids, and the sampling units are already defined on the easily available U.S. Geological Survey quad sheets, making our sample more repeatable. In short, the early work at Reese River was hampered by the common problem of not knowing which bridges to cross and which ones to burn.

Given the opportunity, I would change a few nonpragmatic aspects of the Reese River survey as well. We should have defined four sampling strata instead of the original three. As it was, we "poststratified" in order to give the riverine area proper emphasis. We also should have used disproportionate sampling fractions between the strata. There is, to be sure, something almost seductive about a 10 percent sample, the fraction we applied throughout.

We probably should also have conducted a small pilot project, and then reevaluated on that basis (as suggested by Redman 1973). Our preoccupation with a magic 10 percent required that we invest an additional year of fieldwork at Reese River.

These second thoughts aside, the regional approach did indeed shed light on the prehistoric cultural ecology of the Reese River Valley. But as happens with all such fieldwork, many additional questions were raised. We began by assuming that the prevailing cultural and environmental chronologies were essentially correct. Although this assumption was generally true, the Reese River work highlighted the need for finer-grained chronological studies, based on stratified site excavation. This is why we dug Gatecliff Shelter. The settlement patterning observed in Reese River also raised the question of regional variability. And throughout the 1970s, we conducted a considerably more comprehensive program of regional archaeology in the vicinity of Monitor Valley and Gatecliff Shelter. Also because of lessons learned in Reese River, we realized the importance of erecting a middle-range research framework, to understand the processes through which the archaeological record of such areas is created. Considerable effort was spent looking at formation processes and middle-range research in the next stage at Monitor Valley.

*WHERE TO GO FROM HERE?*_____

Surface Archaeology of the Reese River Valley: The best overall summary of this research is given in Thomas (1973 and 1988b); see also Thomas (1972a, 1972b); Thomas and Bettinger (1976); Williams, Thomas, and Bettinger (1973).

Some Important Sources Dealing with Regional Archaeology and Sampling: Ammerman (1981), Bettinger (1977), Binford (1964), Dunnell and Dancey (1983), Hodder and Orton (1976), Judge, Ebert, and Hitchcock (1975), Lipe and Matson (1971), Mueller (1974, 1975), Nance (1983), Plog, Plog, and Wait (1978), Thomas (1978, 1986).

Some Sampling Considerations

The archaeological fieldwork at Reese River depended heavily on the theory of random error, and so we should now look at it in more detail. Archaeologists are becoming more and more aware of how important it is to think through their sampling procedures. They have always dealt with samples, of course, but the recent trend has been toward drawing samples in accordance with the accepted principles of probability. Several sources discuss archaeological sampling procedures, and the discussion here is intended only to highlight some of the more important aspects.

The first key sampling concept is that of population. In general usage, *population* refers to a group of living organisms of a single species that is found in a circumscribed area at a given time; this is a **biological population**. Cultural anthropologists also commonly use the term **cultural population** to denote a specific society, and archaeologists are often heard speaking of "prehistoric Pueblo III populations" or the "Shoshone-speaking population." Proper sampling, however, requires us to adopt a more restricted statistical usage for the term population.

Statisticians use the term *population* to refer not to physical objects (people, lemurs, or microbes) but, rather, to observations made on these subjects. The difference is both subtle and important. Shoshone Indians could comprise a biological or sociocultural population, but they could never be a **statistical population**. Only a set of related variates—such as stature, body weight, daily caloric intake, or presence of the Rh blood factor among Shoshone Indians—could comprise a statistical population. A statistical population is a set of variates (counts, measurements, or characteristics) about which relevant inquiries are to be made. Statistical populations thus differ from "populations" in the common usage; statistical populations are arbitrary and so must be carefully defined.

Some populations may consist of a finite number of variates, such as the stature of all living Shoshone Indians. But population can also be defined to include not only the stature of all living Shoshone but also of all Shoshone who lived in the past, and even of those who will live in the future. So populations can also be infinite. It would be troublesome indeed for an anthropologist to attempt to interrogate, measure, observe, or photograph the entire physical population of living Shoshone. And if the statistical population were defined to include Shoshone of all times and all places, complete

The Pros and Cons of Random Sampling

The role of random sampling remains confusing in Americanist archaeology. Some archaeologists swear by it; others only swear at it. In the following dialogue, Kent Flannery creates the traditional Real Mesoamerican Archaeologist (R.M.A.) and the methodologically oriented Skeptical Graduate Student as foils to illustrate both sides of the sampling question:

The Real Mesoamerican Archeologist doesn't like probability sampling. He regards it as (1) a waste of energy, (2) too time-consuming, (3) not as reliable as his intuition, and (4) not applicable to complex societies. He even has reservations about applying it to such "simple" political units as Formative villages. He and I have had acrimonious debates on the subject, neither of us backed up by very much data or mathematical expertise and each of us continually harassed by the Skeptical Graduate Student, who claims to have both.

The argument began in the Quinta Las Rosas, a now-defunct "nocturnal center" on the outskirts of Veracruz.

While the waiter filled our order, R.M.A. drew on a paper napkin the outline of the Rio San Jacinto drainage and the pattern of sites he had found so far. Reaching the end of the paper, he concluded, "and to the south, it looks as if there were no more Formative sites—just Early Classic, and some small Post-Classic sites."

Near his elbow, the Skeptical Graduate Student quickly added, "but we can't be sure of that, because our sample of sites is inadequate and our survey so far has been very haphazard and unsystematic."

Reprinted by permission of K. V. Flannery and Academic Press.

Now, short of calling attention to a whole projectile point on his backdirt pile, there is probably no easier way to make a Real Mesoamerican Archaeologist angry than by telling him that his survey techniques are inadequate. In fact, R.M.A. is still overheated from having read Binford's 1964 article "A consideration of archaeological research design." Fortunately, he believes that he saw Binford subjected to the ultimate put-down. He tells the story often. In fact, he tells it every time his Skeptical Graduate Student brings up the subject of sampling.

"It was at the 1964 meetings of the American Anthropological Association, held in Detroit," he says. Everybody was talking about Binford's article. Well, Bill Mayer-Oakes and Ronald Nash had tried out some of his techniques on Bill Sanders' Teotihuacán survey area, and they presented a critique . . ." (Mayer-Oakes and Nash 1964).

At this point, the Skeptical Graduate Student always rolls his eyes straight up at the ceiling and shakes his head in disbelief. The action was not lost on R.M.A., but he was interrupted by the waiter, who had just brought three rum-and-cokes. Three young ladies followed the waiter, circling our table with little attempt at subterfuge. One was clearly trying to see if R.M.A.'s lap would support her full body weight; I doubted it, but I've been wrong before.

"What Mayer-Oakes and Nash did was to take Bill Sanders' survey map of the Teotihuacán Valley, showing the location of all 500-odd sites he had found," R.M.A. went on. "To this, they applied the 'stratified random sampling program' that Binford had recommended. First, the 750-sq km valley was divided into seven 'strata' or environmental zones: the Rio San Juan delta, the Patlachique Range, Cerro Gordo, the lower valley, middle valley, upper valley, and northern valley. They then gridded the whole map with squares .6 km on a side, and selected a 20% sample of those squares at random. The sample was allocated so that various 'strata' received squares in proportion to their area—more squares in the biggest areas, and so on. Finally, they placed their grid with its sample areas over the map of Sanders' sites, to see how many they would have found." He smiled triumphantly. "And you know what they found? Do you know?"

"I can't imagine."

"They missed Teotihuacán. For God's sake, the largest Pre-Columbian city in the New World, 20 sq km. an estimated 125,000 population, and they missed it. Now why, for God's sake, should I use a technique that won't even find Teotihuacán? I could find it with my eyes shut and my hands tied behind my back."

"Yeah, it is hard to miss," I admitted.

"Well, they did it. And what's more, as Mayer-Oakes and Nash pointed out, the 20% stratified random sample recovered *none* of Sanders' 'Proto-Classic urban sites', *none* of his 'Cuanalan phase large villages', and only *one* of his 'Zacatenco phase hamlets'."

"Not too good, I guess."

R.M.A. adjusted his position slightly to accommodate the ample young lady who now occupied his left knee. "And do you know what Mayer-Oakes and Nash concluded?"

"Lay it on me."

"They said, and here I am going to quote them exactly to the best of my memory, 'given the same amount of time, we believe that an archeologist working by instinct (parenthesis)

i.e., expertise (close parenthesis) could certainly locate a greater number of sites' (Mayer-Oakes and Nash 1965, p. 16). Now, isn't that what I do every day? Hell, I found 33 sites last week without a table of random numbers."

The Real Mesoamerican Archeologist sat back in satisfaction while we finished our rum-and-cokes and ordered a round for our newly arrived companions. We hadn't heard from the Skeptical Graduate Student yet, which was unusual, but I figured he was too smothered under the weight of the young lady in his lap to reply. I was wrong, of course; he's never that out of breath.

"I have never," said S.G.S., "heard such a gross distortion of what went on at that session of the meeting."

"How would you know? You weren't even born yet."

"I was there," said S.G.S. "That was back when I was a Skeptical *Under*graduate Student. As I remember, Mayer-Oakes and Nash were rather temperate in their criticism, and even said, 'it seems clear that Binford's theoretical framework and specific sampling techniques offer much of interest and value to archaeologists working anywhere' (Mayer-Oakes and Nash 1965, p. 21).

"It seems to me," S.G.S. went on, "that you and several others who heard that talk have a complete misconception of what a 20% random sample is supposed to do. Somehow you seem to think that its purpose is to find a lot of sites—more than Sanders could find in his total survey, or more than I could find in a comparable period by racing around the Teotihuacán Valley with a bag over my head, picking up sherds."

"That isn't what it's supposed to do at all."

"And you, and many others, missed Binford's most important comment, since it came at the end of the conference session during a three-way conversation between Mayer-Oakes, Deetz, and Ascher."

"I don't remember a thing," said R.M.A.

"Mayer-Oakes had, in the interests of impartial scholarship, provided Binford with a copy of his results before the talk. It showed the following recovery of sites by the 20% sample (Mayer-Oakes and Nash 1965, p. 13):

Aztec sites
  (i) Urban—4
  (ii) Rural—61

Toltec sites
  (i) Urban—2
  (ii) Rural—30

Classic Teotihuacán sites
  (i) Urban—1
  (ii) Rural—23
  (iii) Traces of occupation—11

Proto-Classic hamlets—5
    Cuanalan hamlets—1
    Zacatenco hamlets—1

Pre-Classic hamlets—1

Preceramic sites—1

These Binford communicated to the assembled crowd."

"What a memory," I marveled.

"Then Binford compared these with the totals for each type of site found by Sanders. And do you know what?"

"I can already guess."

"Virtually *every* type of site recovered by the 20% stratified random sample—'rural Toltec sites', 'rural Aztec sites', and so on—was recovered in approximately the proportion it contributed to the whole site universe. If one type of site made up, say, 40% of the total 500-odd sites, it also made up about 40% of

the sites recovered by the sample. As Binford put it: 'the results are an excellent confirmation of the value of stratified random sampling'."

"Fantastic."

"You see," S.G.S. went on, "what the critics misunderstood was that probability sampling is not a discovery technique. It isn't a better way to find lots of sites. As Mayer-Oakes and Nash themselves said, 'we are not saying that Sanders has done a better survey, because . . . he has sampled more than 20% of the area, and it is not as if we can pit one approach against the other . . . this is about what we would find with 20% areal coverage' (Mayer-Oakes and Nash 1965, p. 14). Surveying the entire area is always preferable to surveying only 20% of it. But what you and most other people do is survey about 20% in a haphazard fashion. We can never know if you have recovered each site type in the same frequency with which it occurs in the total universe of sites. On the other hand, if you took a 20% sample according to probability sampling techniques, you could multiply each type of site by 5 and have some confidence —*in fact, a mathematically definable confidence*— that the results would approximate the real site universe."

R.M.A. sighed impatiently.

"A 20% random sample isn't designed to find Teotihuacán," S.G.S. continued, "or any other type of site that is unique or represented by only a few examples. If, in a universe of 500 sites, there are only five 'Zacatenco phase hamlets', then such sites make up only 1% of the universe; the chances are that, in a 20% sample, you would recover only one of them. In the case of Cuanalan phase large villages, there are only two in the whole universe; small wonder the sample didn't recover any at all. Probability sampling isn't the best way to find sites— it's just the best way to get a *representa-*

tive sample of sites, if you can't go for the whole universe as Sanders did."

"It's too complicated and it takes too long," R.M.A. replied. "And as Mayer-Oakes and Nash pointed out, 'increasing the areal coverage to find the rarer types of sites is a waste of time and resources' " (Mayer-Oakes and Nash 1965, p. 14).

"Why would it take any longer than your techniques?" asked S.G.S. "We spend most of our time pushing the Jeep out of the mud anyway."

Sitting in the slowly moving shadow of the ceiling fan, listening to Sonia prattle in one ear and S.G.S. in the other, I realized that opinions would always differ on what had happened in Detroit. Some people had gone away feeling vindicated, pleased to hear that traditional survey techniques would recover more sites, that probability sampling wouldn't find unique features like Cuanalan phase large villages or the Pyramid of the Sun. Others had gone away convinced that only probability sampling would produce reliable, statistically valid samples whose confidence levels could be defined in mathematical terms. There was no hope of rapprochement. (Flannery 1976b, pp. 132–135)

observation would be impossible. Because of this, most statistical populations are incompletely observable: Physical anthropologists can never hope to measure the cranial capacity of *Australopithecus robustus,* and archaeologists can never measure the length of every Clovis point.

This is why archaeologists nearly always deal with samples. A sample is defined as any subset of a statistical population, whether randomly, haphazardly, or capriciously selected. The objective behind probability sampling is to obtain samples that were selected from the statistical population with a known probability.

There is no single best way to select a sample, as too many practical and logistical matters enter into the decision. In the Reese River example, the physical population included fourteen hundred tracts of land, each which was five hundred meters on a side. Each tract contained archaeological objects, and each of the archaeological objects could be observed in a number (an infinite number) of ways. Thus in the single physical population, we could define an infinite number of statistical populations. This is why it is important to specify the research objective before taking the sample.

One objective at Reese River was to find the density of archaeological objects, say, projectile points, such as were discussed in Chapter 7. Because it was impractical to find the density of points in each of the 1400 squares, we elected to measure that density in only 140 of them and then to extrapolate to the entire statistical population. The only way that such an estimate can be unbiased is from a sample in which every element had an equal probability of selection. In this case, the probability of selecting any individual tract was exactly 1 to 1400.

Squares, Rectangles, or Circles: Which Is the Best Research Design?

There are literally dozens of strategies to enable archaeologists to select their samples. When we gridded the Reese River area into five-hundred-meter squares (see Figure 12–2), we were using a **quadrat sample** technique. This method, derived from quantitative sampling in plant ecology, has been used in several archaeological applications.

When describing our search for Mission Santa Catalina (Chapter 7), we briefly mentioned another popular method of archaeological sampling, the transect technique. Instead of using square sampling units, the **transect sample** defines long linear units. Teams of archaeologists can thus survey in long, straight lines. Transect sampling is often easier than quadrat sampling because access time is minimized; the team simply walks from point A to point B without having to travel throughout the region in a checkerboard fashion. There also is some evidence that transect samples tend to be statistically more efficient than are quadrat samples.

Figure 12–3 shows how transect sampling works. In this case, we wanted to find out how archaeological sites are distributed along the margins of Pleistocene Lake Tonopah, about one hundred miles south of Reese River, Nevada. Some twelve thousand years ago the lake was full, and the shoreline stood at about 4800 feet above sea level. Presumably,

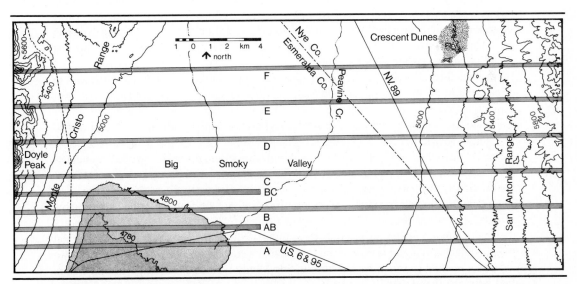

FIGURE 12–3   Transect sampling method used at Pleistocene Lake Tonopah, Nevada. Each transect is 150 meters wide, and the shaded portions indicate approximate lake levels during the late Pleistocene. An adaptation of this survey strategy was used in the search for Mission Santa Catalina (see Figure 7–2).

the early Paleo-Indians in this valley would have lived near the beach line. But as the climate became hotter and drier, Pleistocene Lake Tonopah began to shrink. One thing we wanted to learn at Lake Tonopah was how later Paleo-Indian groups changed their settlement pattern in response to the receding beach levels.

Lake Tonopah is now completely dry, and the area could have been gridded and sampled in a manner like Reese River. But because we were mainly concerned with the relationship of cultural materials to fossil beach terraces, it made more sense to run a series of east-west transects across the dry lake, laid out so as to intersect the known beach terraces in a perpendicular manner (see Figure 12–3).

The Lake Tonopah example differs in another important way from the Reese River sampling design. You will remember that at Reese River the fourteen hundred sampling tracts were divided into homogeneous strata (based on modern lifezones), and a 10 percent sample was selected within each stratum. Technically speaking, the Reese River design was a *stratified random quadrat sample*. At Lake Tonopah the climate had changed so drastically that environmental strata were less important, and so they were not included in the sampling strategy.

Look at Figure 12–3. The universe of transects is really a large series of 150-meter-wide strips running across dry Lake Tonopah because we wanted to obtain an overall picture. For reasons of time and budget we decided to select a systematic sample. A random method of selection would have us number every strip and then select random numbers to define which strips would become transects in the sample. In a **systematic sample selection**, only the first sampling unit is selected at random, and the remaining transects are chosen at intervals to complete the predetermined sampling fraction. There are statistical advantages and disadvantages to both sampling schemes. At Lake Tonopah we selected a systematic transect sample because we thought it would give us the best overall coverage of the zones in question.

Several other options exist for sampling designs in archaeology. In fact, it is easy to be led astray by the theoretical and statistical advantages of one sample design over another. At least as important as the abstract statistical characteristics of each design are the practical archaeological considerations, and archaeologists should never feel tied to any single sampling strategy. Random quadrats were used at Reese River because I wanted to know the distributions of artifacts and sites within discrete lifezones. Systematic transect sampling was employed at Lake Tonopah in order to provide clear-cut data on the relationships between archaeological sites and the Pleistocene beach terraces.

One final example should underscore the point that archaeologists must be flexible in designing their samples. While digging Gatecliff Shelter we needed to conduct a regional sampling operation in order to examine additional components of the seasonal round; Gatecliff represents only a fraction of the overall pattern of transhumance. So we devised a method of sampling the surrounding Monitor Valley. One key question was to find how the sites related to water.

Water can occur on the landscape in a number of ways. In the Reese River Valley, water was a *linear* resource, concentrated in streams that flowed year-round out of the mountains and into the Reese River, which ran south to north. At Pleistocene Lake Tonopah, water was a *circular* resource contained in a massive lake basin.

Monitor Valley presented yet a third option for distribution of water. With a few exceptions, Monitor Valley lacked the permanent streams of the Reese River area, and the dry lake in Monitor Valley was never an important Pleistocene lake. Water occurred primarily in springs that bubbled forth, flowed a short distance, and then disappeared. That is, water at Monitor Valley was neither circular nor linear—it was a *point* resource.

In order to compare how water-determined settlement patterns vary among valleys, we needed to sample the archaeological sites of Monitor Valley. Our survey area (Figure 12–4) contained a total of thirty permanent springs, each of which seemed to hold potential for prehistoric exploitation. From other work at Reese River we knew that prehistoric inhabitants tended to camp about 450 meters from their water source. At Reese River, we examined this distribution by walking linear strips along stream courses. But the Monitor Valley water was concentrated at single points, small springs scattered throughout the Toquima Mountains.

So we designed a sampling design to look at the relationship of sites to these springs. Neither quadrats nor transects seemed appropriate for sampling these springs. We elected to use a circular sampling unit in Monitor Valley: Each spring was considered a point, and so we surveyed the surrounding area using a radius of one-thousand meters. That is, we looked for all sites within one thousand meters of water. But we did not have time enough to survey all thirty springs, and so we numbered them one through thirty and selected a 50 percent random sample (see Figure 12–4). These one-thousand-meter-radius circles were then completely surveyed in order to locate, map, and collect all of the associated sites. The Monitor Valley survey was also concerned with sites located away from water (that is, more than one thousand meters from a spring). We thought there would be few such sites, but as a control, we overlaid a five-hundred-meter grid system (like that used at Reese River) and drew another random sample for survey. In this way we were forced to look even where we thought there would be no sites.

These three examples point out the importance of fitting the sampling scheme to the topography and the questions being asked. The basic sampling unit at Reese River was the 500-meter-square quadrat; the unit at Pleistocene Lake Tonopah was a 150-meter-wide transect; and the sampling unit in Monitor Valley was a 1000-meter circle. The Reese River and Monitor Valley samples were selected randomly, and the Lake Tonopah sample was determined systematically. The sampling fractions also differed: Reese River, a 10 percent sample; Monitor Valley, a 50 percent sample; and Lake Tonopah, a 7.5 percent sample. Do not be misled into thinking there is a single best sampling scheme. There is not.

Strategies in Regional Archaeology

This book has a number of common threads. An important one is the notion of strategy. There is no single strategy in modern archaeology, but several. This is why we spent so much time discussing the major anthropological mainstreams in Chapter 3, in order to see how differing approaches and assumptions can be applied to the same cultural phenomena.

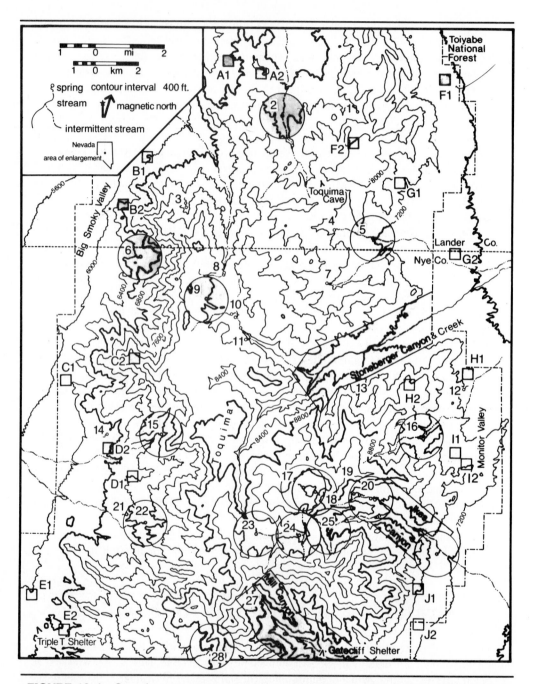

FIGURE 12–4 Sampling strategy used in the upland survey of the Toquima Range, near Gatecliff Shelter (see Thomas 1988b, Figure 2). Note that randomized circular and square sampling units were involved here. (Courtesy the American Museum of Natural History)

The four following sections also illustrate the multiple strategy concept. We shall consider four individual cases of regional archaeology and discuss the underlying rationale and motivation for each. Although the ultimate objectives are similar, the means for obtaining them vary considerably. There is no conflict here. In fact, it seems to be a healthy sign that contemporary archaeology is capable of mustering so many diverse approaches to tackle the fundamental issues.

An Ecological Determinants Approach: Reese River Piñon Ecotone Settlements

The first of four settlement models to be discussed explains the patterning of human settlements by examining relevant ecological parameters. Not to be confused with environmental determinism, the **ecological determinants approach** recognizes simply that human settlements are often located in response to a specific set of environmentally determined factors. As a model, the ecological determinants approach assumes that all else being equal, a particular constellation of environmental parameters will strongly condition the placement of habitation sites. The approach will be illustrated by further research in the Reese River Valley of central Nevada; other applications are listed at the end of this section.

We have already discussed in some detail the initial archaeological survey of the Reese River Valley. The upshot of the computer modeling and subsequent fieldwork was to test one theory—Julian Steward's theory regarding the ethnographic Shoshone Indians—and then to propose another—the prehistoric Reese River settlement pattern. The scientific cycle had taken a single turn, and it became time, once again, to test the new theory. Basically, the synthesis of the Reese River fieldwork suggested that a bimodal settlement pattern operated prehistorically in this region: Winters were spent in piñon camps located in the low foothills, and summer camps were established on the banks of the Reese River. The preliminary survey results indicated that these riverine summer settlements were simply long, linear scatters of artifacts that paralleled the Reese River. The test of this pattern would involve little more than walking the banks of the Reese River. This would be an interesting project because the sites seem to be distributed nonrandomly along the river, but that fieldwork has not yet been done.

More complex was the structuring of the winter camp locations, those small and nucleated settlements that can be found scattered throughout the foothills of the ranges in central Nevada. Particularly intriguing was the high degree of predictability of these sites' placement. After two years of working in the area, my crew and I came to the point at which we could predict the presence (and absence) of sites in places we had never been. This was fun, and to see why these predictions worked so well, we listed all the environmental criteria we could think of that related to these sites. That is, we knew we could find the sites intuitively, and so we tried to pin down our hunches in the form of objective criteria. Then we invested another year of fieldwork to test our set of site determinants.

We called each of these predicted site localities a **locus**, to distinguish it from the location of actual, known sites. We found that seven criteria were sufficient to predict the presence of known piñon ecotone settlements at Reese River:

1. The locus should be on a ridge or saddle.
2. The ground should be relatively flat (less than 5 percent slope).
3. The locus should be in the low foothills (less than 250 meters above the valley floor).
4. The locus should be within the extant piñon-juniper lifezone.
5. The locus should be near the piñon-juniper ecotone (within 1000 meters).
6. The locus should be near a semipermanent water source (within 1000 meters).
7. The locus should be some minimal distance from this source (greater than or equal to 100 meters).

We settled on these seven criteria based on our previous fieldwork in the area. After seeing many piñon ecotone sites, we were fairly sure that they were the best predictors of site location.

But no single criterion was sufficient in itself to predict sites. That is, not all sites were on ridges or saddles, but most were. Similarly, although the ground was usually flat (less than 5 percent slope), we did find sites from time to time that had more than a 5 percent slope. No single criterion was perfect, and so we decided that a combination of criteria might be the best predictor. We framed a **polythetic definition** of site location: If at least five of the seven environmental criteria are met, then we can expect to find a piñon site.

Note that the predictors are based strictly on noncultural, environmental parameters. We decided to test our predictions on a twelve-mile strip of mountains to the east of the Reese River. We obtained aerial photographs of the area and studied them closely, trying to find spots that satisfied at least five of the seven critical determinants. These archaeological sites are invisible from the air, and so the site predictions were based strictly on environmental criteria.

Seventy-four potential site locations were spotted on the aerial photographs. Then we took to the field to see whether there actually were sites in the seventy-four locations and also whether there were any sites that were not on the predicted spots.

The survey took about a month, with a crew of twenty archaeologists and students. We found archaeological sites on sixty-three of the seventy-four predicted locations, and so our polythetic predictions were about 85 percent accurate. We also found only two sites that were not located on the potential loci (97 percent accuracy). This fieldwork not only verified the fact that one can predict archaeological site locations on strictly environmental grounds but also proved that the initial random survey of the Reese River provided a satisfactory picture of where the piñon ecotone settlements were located.

Of the polythetic criteria, it was found that four factors (distance to water, distance to ecotone, elevation above valley floor, and percentage of slope) were sufficient to account for most of the observed variability in site location. Parameters were determined for each variable, and it was found—to our surprise—that the Reese River sites fell into almost perfect normal-curve distributions. In no case was the observed distribution statistically different from the expected normal frequencies.

These determinants can be summarized even further in terms of two simple probabilistic models. The first such model is the familiar bell-shaped curve, projected into three dimensions (Figure 12–5). This model applies to three of the four settlement pattern determinants: percentage of slope, distance to piñon ecotone, and elevation above the valley floor (transformed to square roots). All three variables truncate at zero and increase in a single direction ("steeper," "farther from the ecotone," and "higher"). The ridge along the top of the curve represents the maximum probability and corresponds to the parametric mean of the three-dimensional distribution.

A second model is presented in Figure 12–6, which applies to distance from the campsites to water. Previously (Figure 12–5), the two distance variables ("from ecotone" and "above valley floor") logically progressed in a single direction: up. This was specified in the polythetic definitions of site location. But the distance to water is different because the direction is unspecified. By considering a stream flowing out of the Toiyabes as a perfectly straight line, the bell-shaped probability curves must extend on both sides of that stream (Figure 12–6). Let us stand at a water source (zero distance) and then walk away at right angles. As the distance increases, so does the probability of finding an archaeological site. The most probable spot is located at the parametric mean (in this case estimated to be 450 meters). Once past this point, the probability of finding a campsite diminishes and ultimately approaches zero. Had we chosen to walk in the other direction from the stream (180 degrees away), exactly the same probability distribution would have held. In other words, because the water sources at Reese River tend to flow in a line (as ephemeral streams), the sites are predicted by two bands of probability, each running parallel to the water source.

We find these two probabilistic models to be useful descriptions of our Reese River data. The piñon ecotone camps can be viewed as a sample of $n = 65$ sites, drawn at

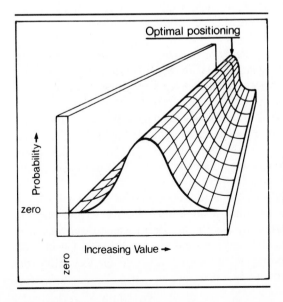

FIGURE 12–5 Three-dimensional probability model describing how archaeological sites in Reese River could be predicted from a knowledge of percentage land slope, distance to the piñon–juniper ecotone, and elevation above the valley floor (adapted from Thomas and Bettinger 1976, Figure 64). (Courtesy the American Museum of Natural History)

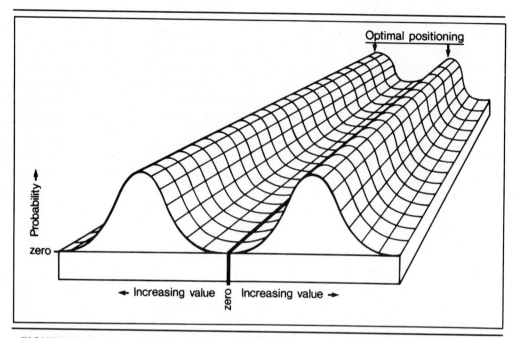

FIGURE 12–6   Three-dimensional probability model showing how the distance to water can be used to predict the presence of archaeological sites in the Reese River Valley (adapted from Thomas and Bettinger 1976, Figure 65). (Courtesy the American Museum of Natural History)

random from a hypothetical universe of all possible samples that exist under similar conditions. The probabilistic models in Figures 12–5 and 12–6 are theories, to be tested in other localities.

Archaeologists wishing to explore patterns of prehistoric cultural geography must do more than merely document where the sites are. To understand positioning criteria, it is necessary to consider where the sites are not, and the locus concept allowed us to do this at Reese River.

Since then, we have used this approach extensively elsewhere. We were wondering, for instance, how far the positioning criteria at Reese River really apply. Do these same site predictors operate similarly in other valleys? Does Monitor Valley contain equivalent piñon ecotone sites? Will site and assemblage distributions be both symmetrical and parallel to the water sources?

Between 1973 and 1975, we conducted a large-scale survey of Monitor Valley to find out. Comparative study of the site–locus interrelationship can provide a powerful tool for exploring the overall settlement fabric because we can learn where residential sites could and should be. Nearly all sites at Reese River were situated on loci, and fully 93 percent of the comparable sites in Monitor Valley also occurred on loci. Even the exceptions proved to be informative (Thomas 1988b).

Of course, the best-five-of-seven threshold definition is hardly a universal of hunter–gatherer residential behavior. This woodland-specific definition did not even hold for the uplands in Monitor Valley. Topographic site–positioning factors vary with the level of technology, the organizational structure of the adaptation, and the population density. These criteria vary across time and space. But finding site predictors that work is a first step toward understanding the processes that conditioned where the residential settlements were established.

WHERE TO GO FROM HERE?

The Ecological Determinants Approach in the Great Basin: Thomas (1983a, 1988b); Thomas and Bettinger (1976); Williams, Thomas, and Bettinger (1973).

   The Polythetic Concept in Anthropology: Carr (1984; 1985, Chapter 13); Clarke (1968, p. 668); Needham (1975); Solheim (1976); Williams, Thomas, and Bettinger (1973, pp. 227–228).

   Applications of the Ecological Determinants Approach: Baumhoff (1963), Gumerman (1971), Judge (1973), Schalk (1977).

A Locational Analysis Approach: Classic Maya Settlements

The preceding example from Reese River followed in the basic tradition of cultural materialism: Relevant environmental factors were isolated, and these in turn were used to predict prehistoric patterns of human settlement. The assumption was that people tend to live in places that best satisfy primary technological and ecological requirements. As it turned out, these environmental factors did predict the Reese River settlement pattern to a remarkable degree.

   But Chapter 3 demonstrated that modern anthropology contains several mainstreams, each of which suggests a particular method and perspective for approaching the same cultural phenomena. Though pervasive, cultural materialism by no means has an exclusive hold on current archaeological thinking. In the following example we will demonstrate how a more humanistic approach can be brought to bear on the issue of settlement patterns.

   One of America's most intensively studied civilizations is that of the Classic Maya, which flourished in the lowland forests of northern Guatemala and the surrounding regions from about A.D. 250 to 900. The bare outlines of the Maya settlement pattern are known. The ancient Maya constructed immense cities (that seem to have been densely populated) throughout the southern lowlands. These sites are typified by monumental pyramids that support temples, grand palaces, stone monuments with hieroglyphic texts, and lavish tombs that include the remains of royalty. There were also many lower-order centers of religious and political importance, and scattered around these lesser sites were the hamlets of the lower-status Maya.

   Interpreting settlement patterns requires an explicit theoretical framework, and this is where significant differences exist among archaeologists. For example, the archaeologist William Rathje—now better known for his work with the Garbage Project (discussed in Chapter 5)—argued that because the transportation of goods was difficult and irrigating agriculture impractical, the environment of the Maya provided an unlikely setting for the development of such a high-level civilization (Rathje 1971, p. 275). In particular, he contended that the southern Maya lowlands are uniformly deficient in resources essential at the individual household level: mineral salt, obsidian for tools, and volcanic stone for grinding slabs. Rathje suggested that the southern lowlands were divided into an outer buffer zone that bordered the highlands (where resources were in greater supply) and an inner core or central area "landlocked" and secluded from the highland resources by the buffer zone. Many archaeologists have discarded this model because we now know that the southern lowlands displayed significant environmental heterogeneity with regard to local resources; salt sources are known within the lowlands; early and equally impressive chiefdoms appeared in much of Rathje's "buffer zone"; and local, as well as long-distance, exchange seems to have been important throughout the archaeological sequence.

Many Maya archaeologists agree that two of the major determinants of the initial settlement location in the Formative or Preclassic periods were land and water. Which of these two factors is to be considered preeminent depends on the predispositions of the investigators, the environmental setting of their favorite sites, and their belief as to whether slash-and-burn agriculture or intensive agriculture was more important. Those who favor slash-and-burn agriculture see soil type as crucial and consider low-lying areas (**aguadas** or *bajos*) to be a liability; those who favor intensive agriculture view swampy terrain as a crucial source of water and a locus for raised fields and fish farming. Other archaeologists have argued that both factors were important (Marcus 1983, p. 462).

Although soil and water are considered critical to the initial establishment of sites, Joyce Marcus does not feel they fully explain the pattern of growth and spacing that Classic Maya cities later displayed. She argues that a complex set of sociopolitical factors, such as tribute demands, control of labor power, ritual and administrative services, and proximity to neighboring sites all came into play once those sites had been founded. Others also believe that environmental and sociopolitical factors should not be regarded as mutually exclusive (e.g., Rice and Rice 1980, p. 452).

Regional surveys have produced evidence that despite highly variable topography, there is a remarkable degree of regularity in the spacing of secondary centers around regional capitals (e.g., Flannery 1972; Harrison 1981, p. 274; Marcus 1973, 1974, 1976, 1983). Marcus would argue that such regularities of spacing suggest that the interplay of social, political, and economic factors came to override strictly environmental ones in determining the spacing between major centers. She contends that it is unlikely that any explanation of site locations and developmental trajectory that takes into account only soil and water will be fully satisfactory.

Still lacking in the Maya area is a field program designed to test the relative importance of all these factors through time, thereby assessing the dynamic interplay among them that led to such regularity in spacing between A.D. 500 and 800. Let us suppose that the southern Maya lowlands were dotted by one hundred sites during the Formative period. The initial selection of location was probably affected by a variety of environmental factors, for example, the presence of natural wells, soil quality, rainfall pattern, high ground, and so forth. Some type of catchment analysis (as discussed in the next section) might aid us in determining the relative weights of these initial factors. Once these one hundred sites were established, what were the factors that made some of them grow and others stay the same size or diminish? From the regularity in spacing, it is clear that some centers grew at the expense of others. Only extensive and systematic regional surveys will detect such patterns.

Because all states are characterized by administrative hierarchies, some archaeologists have attempted to establish these by calculating site area, extent of monumental architectural remains, or number of stone monuments (e.g., Morley 1920, 1938). However, there are dangers in assuming that size and political importance are isomorphic (e.g., Albany, Sacramento, and Springfield are capitals but are not the largest cities in the states of New York, California, and Illinois). Therefore, as an independent test, Marcus decided to use "emblem glyphs" or "place names" (Berlin 1958). The hieroglyphic texts on monuments at lower-order centers mentioned the "site names" of higher-order centers to which they owed allegiance. Marcus had been interested in finding a method to discover how the Maya themselves ranked their centers, so that she could compare their hierarchy with that generated by Western scholars.

Marcus discovered that (1) the site hierarchy changed over time; (2) at any one time, the Maya listed four centers as being "on high" or "regional capitals"; (3) the Maya view of which sites were secondary, tertiary, and quaternary did not always conform to site size differences; (4) there was only one "regional capital" per region; (5) the Maya envisioned their realm as divided into four administrative quadrants; and (6) sites could rise in the hierarchy by establishing their independence (sometimes following a battle) and then display their own "site name" and set up their own hieroglyphic monuments.

Marcus concludes there are two ways of viewing ancient Maya settlement patterns, as well as two distinct levels. As discussed in Chapter 3, these two ways can be labeled *etic* (how we, as archaeologists, rank centers) and *emic* (how each Maya center perceived itself, either subordinate or dominant).

The two levels are (1) a cosmological plane, which divides the world into four quarters, each with a capital; and (2) a "real-world" level, which has to do with the equidistant spacing of the secondary centers around those capitals and which presumably results from the services and functions of primary and secondary centers (see Marcus 1974, p. 877). Cosmology is brought into the picture only by the Maya themselves, who viewed their four most important centers as reigning over the four quadrants of the world. Other civilizations also envisioned their realm as divided into quadrants (e.g., the Sumerians and the Inka) or into five regions, with the capital at the center, surrounded by four districts named for the cardinal points of the compass (e.g. Shang China).

Marcus (1973, 1974, 1976) also utilized the basic tenets of **central place theory** to understand the equidistant spacing of secondary centers around regional capitals. A variant of locational analysis, central place theory was initially proposed as a series of models designed to explain how settlement hierarchies function and to determine demography within a modern market economy. Briefly stated, the location theory suggests that a hexagon is the most efficient geometric form for the equal division of an area among a number of points. Using the hexagon as the fundamental building block, the locational theory explains the spacing of towns and cities that act as centers for the distribution of goods and services to smaller towns and the rural hinterland. Several assumptions are made: (1) Population and purchasing powers, are uniformly distributed; (2) terrain and resources are uniformly distributed; (3) transport facilities are equal in all directions; and (4) all central places perform the same functions and serve areas of the same size. In theory, the most economic arrangement of service centers results in a hexagonal network or lattice.

Figure 12–7 shows the idealized lattice for the Classic Maya. The smallest unit of settlement is the village hamlet, probably little more than a cluster of thatched huts occupied by groups of related families (marked by the "3" in Figure 12–7). These tertiary centers were spaced around the secondary ceremonial-civic centers, which contained pyramids, carved monuments (**stelae**), and palacelike residences for the local priesthood. The secondary centers were in turn spaced in hexagon fashion around major Maya capitals. Capitals such as Copán and Tikal contained acropolises, multiple ceremonial plazas, and a great number of monuments. Linking the secondary centers of the various hexagons were marriage alliances between members of royal dynasties.

Marcus finds support for this "quadripartite" organization of regional capitals in an A.D. 731 Maya hieroglyphic text (Stela A, Copán) that gives three clauses stating (1) "four on high," (2) the names of four capitals (Copán, Tikal, Calakmul?, and Palenque), and (3) the four world quadrants (east, west, south, and north). Moreover, an A.D. 849 text (Stela 10, Seibal) gives the names of the four capitals at that time. From ethnohistoric data she knew that the sixteenth-century Maya divided their world into quadrants.

In accordance with their cosmology, four of these capitals were associated with the four world quadrants, regardless of their physical location. According to Marcus (1973, p. 915), "So strong was the cognized model that, despite the rise and fall of individual centers, there seem always to have been four capitals, each associated with a direction and, presumably, with a color."

All of this, of course, is only conjecture awaiting detailed confirmation. The crux of

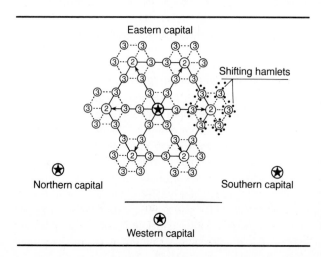

FIGURE 12–7 Joyce Marcus's hypothesis suggesting how the Lowland Classic Maya organized their territory from regional capitals to outlying hamlets. Circled stars indicate the four regional capitals; circled 2's represent the secondary centers; and circled 3's represent the tertiary centers. The small dots represent shifting hamlets around the tertiary centers (see Marcus 1976, Figure 1.12). (Courtesy Joyce Marcus and Dumbarton Oaks Research Library)

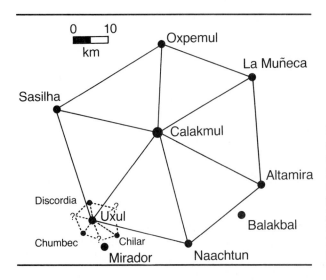

FIGURE 12–8 Calakmul, one of the four regional capitals in Figure 12–7. Note that the six secondary centers are almost exactly the same distance from Calakmul (see Marcus 1976, Figure 1–15). (Courtesy Joyce Marcus and Dumbarton Oaks Research Library)

the issue is how well the actual Maya settlement pattern corresponds to the Marcus model. The answer is that the sites fit the hexagonal distribution remarkably well. Consider the case of Calakmul, in the Petén of Guatemala (see Figure 12–8). Marcus identified Calakmul as one of the four major Maya regional centers. Surrounding Calakmul are five to eight virtually equidistant secondary centers. The Marcus model suggests that between A.D. 600 and 900 Calakmul was the "central place" of a hexagon consisting of Naachtun, Altamira, La Muñeca, Oxpemul, Sasilha, and Uxul. Some of the stelae at these secondary centers mention the emblem glyph (or site name) of the major center, Calakmul. Other central places such as Tikal and Naranjo display similar hexagonal arrangements of secondary centers.

Moreover, the secondary centers themselves seem to be at the center of smaller hexagonal lattices of tertiary sites. Uxul, for example, is encircled by Discordia, Chilar, and Chumbec (Figure 12–8). Analysis at the tertiary level is hampered by incomplete archaeological surveys of the lowlands, but the available data seem fairly consistent with the hexagonal model.

Aside from presenting the specifics of Maya cosmological principles and settlement, this example points up an important scientific principle. Some archaeologists are obviously participating in more than one anthropological mainstream. Archaeologists such as Rathje have presented largely ecological explanations for the patterning of Maya sites. Marcus has synthesized data from cosmology, epigraphy, and central place theory to propose an alternative theory for Maya settlement pattern. Other models could presumably be generated, grounded in other a priori assumptions.

What sets archaeology apart from religion is that each model—regardless of how it was derived—must then be tested against the independent archaeological data. As described in Chapter 2, some theories may survive the initial testing, and others will fail outright. Then it is time to revise the surviving theory and to test once again. It seems to be too early in the scientific cycle to see which of the competing Maya theories will prove victorious. Particularly important in the future will be systematic archaeological surveys designed to locate the small village hamlets, so often overlooked in previous archaeological surveys of the lowland rain forest.

WHERE TO GO FROM HERE?

Other Applications of Central Place Theory in Archaeology: Clarke (1968), Crumley (1976), Flannery (1972), G. Johnson (1972, 1975).

A Site Catchment Approach: Formative Villages in Oaxaca

The site catchment approach was introduced to archaeology by C. Vita-Finzi and Eric Higgs (1970, p. 5), who defined the objective as "the study of the relationships between technology and those natural resources lying within the economic range of individual sites." The **catchment principle** is quite simple: All else being equal, the farther away it is from the site, the less attractive a resource will be. That is, the longer one must travel to exploit a particular resource, the less rewarding that exploitation will be. Ultimately, there is a certain distance beyond which resources are probably not exploited at all—it simply is easier to move and establish a new site closer to the resource in question. !Kung women, for instance, almost never forage farther than ten kilometers from their base camp. Small groups of men may occasionally travel farther while hunting, but they generally make a separate overnight camp to avoid excessive travel (Lee 1969).

Vita-Finzi and Higgs applied their catchment concept to late Paleolithic and early Neolithic sites in the eastern Mediterranean. They drew circles of five-kilometer radius around the sites in question, reasoning that most resources used at these sites would come from within the circle. That is, the 7900-hectare area surrounding a site forms a catchment. Vita-Finzi and Higgs then analyzed the land within the catchments in terms of potential for agriculture. Sites with low percentages of arable land (less than 20 percent) were thought to have been unlikely spots for agriculture.

The pioneering effort of Vita-Finzi and Higgs was followed by other archaeologists anxious to explore the potential of catchment analysis. The original method is not without its defects, however, and several modifications have been made in the analysis of site catchments by other archaeologists. To see how catchment analysis works, let us examine an application by Flannery (1976a).

The site of San José Mogote is an Early Formative village located in the Etla region of the Valley of Oaxaca, Mexico. During the San José phase (1150–850 B.C.) the village covered an estimated seventy hectares and may have had up to seven hundred inhabitants. The site itself was excavated during nine field seasons by local workmen under the direction of Kent Flannery and Joyce Marcus of the University of Michigan. The preservation of archaeological remains at San José Mogote was exceptional, and samples of carbonized seeds, wood charcoal, pollen, and animal bones were recovered. On the basis of these excavated samples, Flannery attempted to reconstruct the site catchment. His method differs from the original Vita-Finzi and Higgs catchment analysis in that Flannery began with the actual resources exploited and then tried to reconstruct the necessary catchment, rather than taking the catchment radii as given.

Figure 12–9 summarizes the catchment areas operative at San José Mogote. They consist of a series of ever-widening concentric circles. Flannery concluded that San José Mogote needed a circle of less than a two-and-a-half-kilometer radius to satisfy all the basic agricultural requirements. Within a few hundred meters of the village were domestic dogs, which were eaten, and several wild plants such as prickly pear and hackberry. The Atoyac River flowed less than one kilometer from the site, and villagers could obtain mud turtles, opossum, and raccoon, in addition to necessary building materials such as reeds and sand for making adobe. Most important, of course, is that within a two-and-one-half-

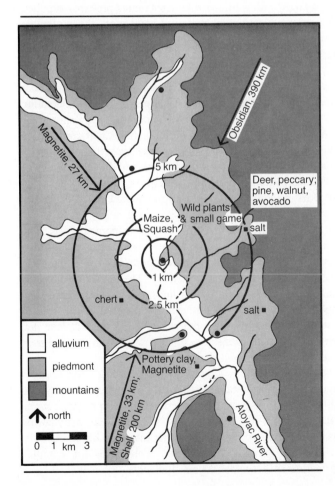

FIGURE 12–9 Site catchments for the village of San José Mogote, Oaxaca (see Flannery 1976a, Figure 4–6). (Courtesy Kent V. Flannery and Academic Press)

kilometer radius, the San José Mogote villagers had available to them more than fourteen hundred hectares of arable alluvium, and Flannery estimated that this land had an agricultural potential of over four hundred metric tons of maize. Flotation samples from house floors at San José Mogote indicate that teosinte also grew in the nearby cornfields. In essence, the two-and-one-half-kilometer catchment had the basic agricultural potential for supporting the estimated seven hundred persons at San José Mogote.

But a catchment of five-kilometers radius was required to satisfy the mineral resource requirements and also to provide some important wild seasonal plants, such as agave, prickly pear stem, rabbits (both jackrabbit and cottontail), and birds like quail, dove, and pigeon. An excellent source of chert for making stone tools was available only three kilometers to the southwest, and a salt source was also available within the five-kilometer radius. The five-kilometer radius is probably the threshold beyond which agricultural activity would yield decreasing returns.

Moving even farther out, a circle with a fifteen-kilometer radius probably supplied the necessary deer meat, other house construction materials, and pine, the preferable wood for cooking fires. Several other long-distance requirements can be noted in Figure 12–9, such as magnetite (used to make small iron-ore mirrors) and obsidian (used for utilitarian and ritual purposes).

Flannery then juxtaposed the San José Mogote catchment with those of similar Early Formative villages scattered along the Atoyac River (Figure 12–10). It is interesting to note that circles of two-and-one-half kilometers in radius do not overlap; each village was able approximately to satisfy its basic agricultural requirements without competition from neighbors. The five-kilometer circle for San José Mogote overlaps with neighbors on both sides, and the seven-and-one-half-kilometer radius intersects with the catchments of the four nearest neighbors. The fifty-kilometer radius overlaps with all villages, and exclusivity to resources disappears, producing a single large catchment for the entire Valley of Oaxaca.

Flannery interpreted the San José Mogote catchment areas in human terms. The innermost catchment circle consists of a small area of river bottomland and an upland area where the village site is located. Most of the agriculture occurs here, and this is the place of burial. This inner circle was probably aggressively defended. The five-kilometer area contains the area where people foraged for wild plants and animals and where they expected to encounter neighbors from nearby villages. Still farther out is the area of overlapping utility, where women did not venture but where men hunted deer and attended to mountaintop shrines. This outer zone was shared with even more distant strangers, probably even those speaking different dialects.

Thus a catchment analysis of the resources actually used at San José Mogote gives clues to how these early agricultural peoples related to the surrounding territories and to neighboring groups. The realities of site catchment areas, combined with relevant social factors, determined the actual location of villages and the spacing between neighboring communities. As Flannery stated (1976a, p. 117), "It is this interplay between social distance, subsistence needs, and the geometry of location that makes the complex settlement systems of the Formative such an interesting challenge."

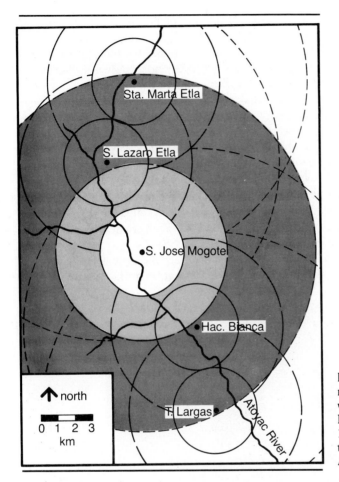

FIGURE 12–10 Catchments for Early Formative villages along the Atoyac River, Oaxaca (see Flannery 1976a, Figure 4–7). (Courtesy Kent V. Flannery and Academic Press)

WHERE TO GO FROM HERE?

Flannery's Work on the Mesoamerican Formative: Flannery (1976a).

Other Applications of Catchment Analysis in Archaeology: O'Connell (1975), Peebles (1978), Rossman (1976), Vita-Finzi and Higgs (1970), Zarky (1976).

A Biocultural Approach: Woodland Mortuary Practices

> De mortuis nil nisi bonum [say nothing but good of the dead]
> —Kurt Vonnegut Jr.

Archaeologists have traditionally focused on problems of prehistoric settlement patterns and cultural ecology by studying the density and distribution of cultural debris. Biocultural specialists study similar questions, but they examine instead the biological remains. That is, whereas archaeologists gravitate toward potsherds and arrowheads, biocultural anthropologists look among bones for their answers.

In Chapter 11, we examined how biocultural anthropologists were rapidly expanding our understanding of paleodemography. This biocultural approach has been taken to a regional scale by Jane Buikstra and her colleagues, who applied the regional perspective to issues of human biological variability in the lower Illinois Valley (Figure 12–11). Buikstra limited her study to the period between about 150 B.C. and A.D. 1000. The initial part of this sequence is known as the **Middle Woodland period**, which lasted until about A.D. 400. The well-known **Hopewell** burial mounds are a product of the Middle Woodland period. Following the Middle Woodland is a period conventionally defined by the absence of elaborate Hopewellian artifacts and structures. The period from A.D. 400 to A.D. 1000 is known as **Late Woodland period**.

The transition from Middle to Late Woodland has been the topic of discussion for decades. Basing their arguments largely on changing elements of artifact style and burial

FIGURE 12–11 Jane Buikstra excavating human skeletal remains. (Courtesy Jane Buikstra; photograph by Keith Swinden)

disposition, investigators have often depicted the Late Woodland period as a "dark age" or a period of "cultural decline." The transition period has been variously ascribed to migration, climatic change, disease, stress, and cultural fatigue. Buikstra mounted an integrated program of biocultural research to look beyond the specifics of artifact style and mortuary pattern to examine the complex interdependence between biological and cultural systems during Woodland times.

Buikstra's research combines the traditional human osteological studies with the more recent advances in archaeological field technique. The study of biological and cultural variability requires a large, unbiased mortuary sample from both periods, called a *paleoseries*. Significant error can be introduced by generalizing from a few, unrepresentative skeletons. At the Archaic-period Koster site, for instance, several Archaic-period individuals were buried in the central midden of Horizon VI. But these were only old and abnormally diseased individuals; obviously the remainder of the population had been buried elsewhere. For the purpose of examining the influence of disease and diet, this kind of sample is clearly inadequate.

The problems faced by Buikstra are similar to those faced by other archaeologists looking at settlement patterns. Realizing this, she initiated her program of *regional sampling* for mortuary sites in the lower Illinois Valley and found that the burial sites in this area are far more numerous than the published archaeological literature would suggest. Previous work had centered on a few spectacular sites and had overlooked dozens of less flashy or less accessible sites. Another advantage of the mortuary site survey is that the archaeological resources can be effectively conserved, minimizing both expense and damage to the archaeological sites. Buikstra's survey provided a mass of high-quality observational data. She systematically collected data, for instance, that indicated the soil attributes of each site, which further defined the areas that would preserve human bones and those that had soil conditions deleterious to the osseous material. Combined with data on site location and appearance, the decision of where to dig could be made intelligently, rather than in haphazard fashion.

Buikstra, as a biocultural anthropologist, combines the attributes of both osteologist and archaeologist. Not content to act merely as a technician, she designed a regional archaeological site survey to locate the mortuary sites she needed. Then, once the sites had been delimited, certain special areas were selected for detailed excavation, which she directed. In so doing, she has been able to obtain data that heretofore had escaped the attention of the prehistorian.

Specifically, Buikstra and her colleagues developed contrasting biocultural models for the Middle and Late Woodland periods. The Middle Woodland model can be summarized as follows:

1. Mounds comprise the major mortuary facility during Middle Woodland times.
2. Middle Woodland communities lived in evenly spaced villages along watercourses.
3. A system of social ranking can be identified within Middle Woodland communities.
4. Individuals of paramount rank within Middle Woodland communities controlled the redistribution of key economic resources (see Buikstra 1977, pp. 73–74).

By contrast, the Late Woodland period used mortuary areas other than burial mounds, and so the skeletal series is sometimes skewed. As a result of Buikstra's site survey and excavation techniques, Late Woodland cemeteries adjacent to burial mounds have been identified and studied for the first time, suggesting that previous samples from Late Woodland mounds were seriously biased. Buikstra and her colleagues systematically carried out reconnaissance, rather than relying on simple, intuitive methods.

A number of general points regarding the Middle-Late Woodland transition emerged. Although Late Woodland burials lack the exotic and spectacular burial goods noted for Middle Woodland Hopewell sites, the social organization reflected by these burials does not appear to have become less complex through time. That is, despite discontinuities at the artifact level, the underlying system of ranking appears to be relatively stable. In fact, more social change seems apparent during the Late Woodland period than between the Middle and the Late Woodland.

The patterning of genetic traits also supports the Middle-Late Woodland continuity. Buikstra analyzed the minute cranial and postcranial characteristics on eight Woodland paleoseries and found that the hypothesis of a population movement between Middle and Late times is extremely unlikely. But she did find evidence of another interesting discontinuity. During Middle Woodland times, the gene pool extended in an almost linear fashion up and down the major rivers of the area. This finding is completely consistent with the suggestion (based on cultural and environmental evidence) that Middle Woodland populations spaced themselves along the rivers and oriented to them as their primary means of interaction. But during Late Woodland times the genetic interaction appears to be more circular than linear, suggesting an orientation that included the surrounding upland regions. There seems to have been a marked population increase during Late Woodland times, leading to a circumscription of plant-collecting territories and a relative localization of gene pools. Of course, these suggestions are based on a preliminary assessment of the skeletal evidence and must be tested against other relevant biological and cultural data.

Going even further, Buikstra and her colleagues used the site survey data to estimate overall population densities during Late and Middle Woodland times. As expected, the population density did increase between 150 B.C. and A.D. 1000. But rather surprisingly, there was no striking increase associated with any particular segment of the Late Woodland period. Instead, the population gradually increased, perhaps associated with some shift in subsistence practices in areas that had minimal access to arable land.

Coupled with this population increase was a suggestion that life during Late Woodland times was "more biologically stressful" than during the Middle Woodland period. The life expectancy at age fifteen was a full five years less in Late Woodland times than in Middle Woodland. The suggestion of increased dependence on agriculture is strengthened by patterns of dentition. From combined studies on the amount of stable strontium in the bone, the number of cavities, and the attrition rates, the emerging conclusion is that carbohydrate intake increased markedly in the later Late Woodland sites.

It is clear that the findings integrate a holistic concern with prehistoric ecology, stressing relationships among variables relevant to prehistoric social organization, subsistence strategy, and biological (that is, genetic) factors. Not only do the biocultural data provide a new avenue of research per se, but they also open significantly new possibilities for further archaeological testing.

WHERE TO GO FROM HERE?

Buikstra's Research on Late Woodland Mortuary Practices: Buikstra (1976, 1977, 1981a); Charles, Buikstra, and Konigsberg (1986).

Summary

The regional approach has become a major theme in American archaeology in the last four decades or so. Focusing on the relationships between people and the land, settlement pattern archaeology transcends the single site in order to determine the overarching relationships among the various contemporary site types used by societies. The regional approach thus precludes assuming single sites as somehow typical or normative for a culture. Instead, the emphasis is on variability among sites within the settlement pattern. Nonstratified—or surface—sites are often critical to the regional approach, and a number of probability-based sampling designs are currently being used to minimize bias in recovering settlement pattern data.

Four strategies are highlighted to illustrate the regional approach to archaeology. The ecological determinants approach emphasizes the key underlying environmental and technological factors that condition the placement of archaeological sites. In some cases, strictly environmental criteria can be used to predict the locations of undiscovered archaeological sites. The locational analysis approach examines the relationship of key regional centers to outlying secondary sites. These organizational principles are sometimes manifested as a hexagonal lattice arrangement, in which the settlement pattern minimizes the transport of goods and services between major population centers and the outlying rural hinterland. The site catchment approach also focuses on the mode of procurement of subsistence items but stresses the strategic placement of major habitation areas. Such analyses assume that people tend to minimize travel between their places of residence and the location of key resources. Catchment areas thus contain a series of concentric circles that radiate from the major habitation sites. When a critical resource distance is exceeded, new habitation sites will be established in a more centrally located spot. The biocultural approach represents an important synthesis between strictly archaeological and physical anthropological research. This relatively new subdiscipline focuses on mortuary patterns and attempts to explore ways in which biological factors (such as rates of mortality, disease, and genetic distance) are related to sociocultural phenomena such as site placement, systems of social ranking, and redistribution of key economic resources. All four of these approaches are currently being applied to problems of regional patterning of archaeological sites.

CHAPTER 13

How People Relate to One Another: Reconstructing Extinct Social Systems

Not long ago, archaeologists believed that they could learn very little about the social organization of extinct societies. As an undergraduate, I was counseled by my sociocultural professors, "Nobody ever excavated a kinship system. . . . Just keep gluing your potsherds together. That's where the real culture is!"

Despite such sage counsel, archaeologists have made some significant progress toward understanding the social systems of the past. Throughout this book I have emphasized that as long as chronology remained the main objective, it was possible to apply a simplified modal definition of culture. But this shared, modal view of culture cannot be applied to the problems of lifeway, and particularly to reconstructing aspects of extinct social organization. The systemic view of culture was discussed earlier, the major point being the variability inherent in the archaeological record. From the systemic point of view, archaeological sites are not homogeneous, and strategies of excavation must be carefully tailored toward understanding intrasite and intraregional variability.

Cultural systems are internally heterogeneous, made up of a number of distributions that directly reflect the social system that produced them. Pueblo San Cristobal contained more than potsherds that can serve as time-markers (Chapters 5 and 7); the site also contained the physical residues left by families, specialized activity groups, and political organizations, as well as evidence about the social status of the individuals who produced the debris.

Pueblo San Cristobal contained the right objects, but the sociocultural data—relevant observations made on these objects—were not recovered. These data do not exist because Nels Nelson was not asking such questions when he dug the site. Any archaeological site can produce either chronological or sociocultural data—or both—depending on the objectives of the investigating archaeologist: San Cristobal is no exception.

The same is true at the artifact level. The same artifact might have functioned in several different spheres: Our interpretation depends on (1) how that artifact functioned when it entered the archaeological record and (2) which questions the archaeologist wishes to answer. In the terminology of Lewis Binford (1962b), we can recognize a technomic function in artifacts that operate in strictly utilitarian fashion, directly connecting people with their immediate environment. A candle becomes a technomic artifact when you need some light (Deetz 1977a, p. 51). If we were to judge such candles, we might look at qualities such as cost, availability, and candlepower. But when you light candles at a formal dinner—and dim the electrical ("technomic") lights—candles, as artifacts, shift to a sociotechnic function. At a candlelight dinner, the candlepower is secondary to the ambience created. What's a birthday cake without its candles? The votive candles in a Catholic church and lighted tapers in a Jewish menorah take this division one step further by serving an ideotechnic function, signifying and reinforcing our ideological rationalizations for life and providing the symbolic milieu into which individuals are enculturated. In addition, each candle has its stylistic dimension, crosscutting its function within the social matrix.

Next, we shall consider how archaeologists reconstruct past sociocultural behavior. Although studying extinct social systems is hardly new in archaeology, such research was propelled into the mainstream less than three decades ago. Our tools for monitoring social systems remain relatively crude, and our accomplishments are still modest. But archaeologists are taking social systems seriously, and more significant progress is bound to come in the years to follow.

What Is a Social System?

We will follow Walter Goldschmidt's (1960, p. 266) definition of **social organization**: "The structure of a society involves two things: first, there is a division into smaller social units, which we call groups; and second, there are recognized social positions (statuses) and appropriate behavior patterns to such positions (roles)." This will be our primary distinction: the *group* is a social subdivision, distinct from the network of *statuses* that define and influence the conduct of interpersonal relations.

Social groups are either residential or nonresidential in character. **Residential groups** consist of domestic families or households, territorial bands, or community-level villages. Consisting of relatively permanent aggregations of people, the residential group is spatial, local, and territorial (Service 1971, p. 12). By contrast, the **nonresidential group** (or **sodality**) consists of associations formed to regulate some specific aspect of society. Residential and nonresidential groups have quite different origins and courses of development. Residential groups are physical agglomerations of people; they are truly residential. But nonresidential groups are groups only in the abstract sense, and as such, they do not necessarily ever convene. The group spirit of nonresidential groups is usually maintained through the use of symbols such as names, ceremonies, mythologies, or insignias of membership. Although such groups might never convene, their boundaries can be fixed and recognized in the archaeological record. In a sense, the residential group functions to regulate discrete spatial matters, whereas the nonresidential group binds these territorial units together.

Many human societies are also integrated along status lines. Sometimes these statuses correspond closely to residential or nonresidential groups, but more commonly the status divisions crosscut conventional social groups. The statuses *male* and *female* might, for instance, comprise two separate residential groups, but usually they do not (Service 1971, p. 15). Similarly, membership in a specific nonresidential group might confer some degree of high status, or it might not.

Ethnographers commonly study social organization through the **kinship** network. The kinship "group" is an organized association of people who are somehow related to one another. Kinship statuses are really just special cases of a society's overall status framework. That is, kinship terms are really just familistic and egocentric status terms (Service 1971, p. 16). As we shall see, archaeologists have at times become concerned with reconstructing such kin groups, but that direction of study is today important mostly for historical reasons.

Joining such a social group requires a series of culturally prescribed guidelines for "appropriate behavior." For example, such rules generally govern where a couple lives after they are married and how they are to behave toward particular categories of people. Social organization thus embraces the structure and functions of the groups within a society, including how individual statuses relate to one another. Kinship, marital residence, and descent reckoning all are part of a society's internal organization. With this general orientation, let us see how archaeology goes about reconstructing social organizations that functioned in the past.

The Archaeology of Social Space

We begin by reconstructing some spatial correlates of human social behavior. To do so, we must make certain statements about past behavior that vanished long ago, that lies beyond our powers of direct observation. Our task as archaeologists is to examine the residues of this extinct social deportment—the garbage, the sites, the structures—because we assume that material culture reflects past behavior in some systematic fashion. We shall consider four levels of social behavior, with—fortunately for the archaeologist—each behavioral level corresponding to a distinctive kind of archaeological patterning.

Individual space: Individual behavior is often reflected at the *attribute* level of the archaeological record. The attribute (you will remember from Chapter 10) is a distinctive feature of an artifact, a characteristic that cannot be divided into smaller constituent units. Of course, a great deal of cultural behavior is shared by a large number of individuals, but it is the individual alone who actually combines the culturally prescribed attributes into a concrete, material culture. It is the individual who decided to put side notches (an attribute) on the small (another attribute) projectile points illustrated in Figure 10–3. Similarly, it is the individual who decided to combine a cord-impressed surface with a flared rim on a pot. Deetz (1968, p. 42) suggests that this patterning of attributes at the individual level is "archaeology's only case of perfect association." No amount of rodent activity, sloppy excavation, or miscataloguing in the laboratory can destroy the primary association between a cord-marked surface impression and a flared rim on a potsherd. Absolutely perfect patterning does not occur at any of the higher levels of archaeological patterning.

Small-group space: Material residues patterned at this second level results directly from action by members of minimal groups of interacting individuals: the hunting troop, the plant-collecting group, the war party. Such minimal group behavior is reflected in the archaeological record as the patterned combinations of artifacts that are called tool kits. Tool kits are identified only by their contexts, rather than by groupings of attributes. Hence the tool kit is extremely vulnerable to preexcavation disturbance, as well as actual blunders in excavation technique. In some cases, archaeologists fail to recognize the presence of a tool kit during excavation, and the items are analyzed as isolated artifacts. In this event, the second level of patterning may be missed altogether.

Household space: Another level of spatial patterning occurs at the community level, and the archaeological correlate is the household. Households, in turn, are commonly arranged into larger-order units, several of which constitute a community.

Finally, behavior at the society level is reflected in the overall settlement pattern, as in the case of the Reese River camps or the Classic Maya hierarchical network. This settlement pattern level of behavior was considered earlier in Chapter 9, and those examples are relevant to the reconstruction of social organization as well as to the analysis of settlement pattern.

Some Archaeological Precursors: The Ceramic Sociologists

One nearly universal requirement in human societies throughout the world is that married couples should live together. Because incest taboos prohibit marriage between people of the same family, an inevitable consequence of marriage is that a new household must be established. The bride and groom cannot remain living with their respective parents. One or the other—or both—must move. The possible alternatives for this shift in residence are few, and all societies express one or more culturally preferred modes of residence.

Ethnographers have defined five major patterns of postmarital residence among the world's population:

Matrilocal residence: A man may live with his wife and her mother.

Patrilocal residence: A woman may live with her husband and his father.

Avunculocal residence: A woman may live with her husband and his maternal uncle.

Bilocal residence: The couple may be permitted to live with either set of parents, depending on economic and personal factors.

Neolocal residence: The newly wedded couple may establish a home independent of both sets of parents (see Murdock 1949, p. 16).

Why do contemporary societies and those of the historic period practice such different kinds of residence patterns? Murdock suggests an economic explanation. Matrilocal residence occurs in societies (e.g., horticultural societies) in which cooperation among women is crucial to subsistence. Patrilocal residence is common in societies heavily dependent on pastoralism. Male cooperation is assured in this case by having the men bring their wives home in order to keep the male herding group intact. Neolocal residence often occurs in societies emphasizing the integrity of the nuclear family. The bilocal residence pattern is found among relatively unstable bands such as the Shoshone, for which economic and ecological necessity favors a flexible pattern of postmarital residence. Avunculocal residence is rare, generally developing as an evolved (and replacement) form of matrilocal residence.

Intoxicated with the potential of the new archaeology, many archaeologists in the early 1960s jumped into the study of prehistoric social organization. The energy directed at the detailed analysis of design elements on ceramics, for instance, produced three instantly classic studies.

William Longacre, then a graduate student working with Lewis Binford, began fieldwork at the Carter Ranch pueblo in eastern Arizona. Longacre set out to reconstruct the postmarital residence patterns by looking at 175 design elements on a sample of more than six thousand sherds. A second, related project was carried out by James Hill (1968, 1970a), another Binford student, who excavated the Broken K pueblo. Among other things, Hill was concerned with extending Longacre's work on matrilocal residence patterns. Because Broken K is almost three times as large as the Carter Ranch site, Hill thought that Broken K must have contained a larger number of residential units, perhaps of an equivalent nature. Using a combination of computer-related statistical techniques and detailed stylistic analysis, Hill became "reasonably certain" that matrilocal residence groups existed at Broken K in about A.D. 1300. Both studies are important today for historical reasons, and they were variously praised and criticized in the archaeological literature of the early 1970s.

The third such classic study of residential pattern was conducted by James Deetz (1965), who examined change in the social organization of eighteenth-century Arikara Indians in South Dakota. A number of social and environmental factors influenced the Arikara between A.D. 1600 and 1800, producing a profound change in their economy and social organization. For a variety of reasons, their strongly matrilineal, matrilocal social system broke down, becoming more flexible as it adapted to new physical and social environments. The residence pattern was influenced particularly by the rapid decline in population, and by rising male prestige due to trading and the resulting accumulation of wealth. The overall effect was the destruction of the aboriginal matricentered social organization and its replacement by a more mobile, if amorphous, system.

Deetz analyzed 2500 rim sherds from the Medicine Crow site in order to document the social change. As did Longacre and Hill, Deetz began with the explicit assumptions relating the material and nonmaterial aspects of culture (1965, p. 1): (1) The pottery was manufactured by women. (2) Because ceramic designs are handed down from mother to daughter, a matrilocal form of postmarital residence should result in a more consistent set of ceramic designs than would follow from a patrilocal pattern. And (3) each matrilocal group would tend to have its own distinctive kinds of ceramic decoration. Deetz selected twenty-four primary ceramic characteristics for study, including observations of the surface finish, the overall profile, the lip profile, and decoration.

To this point, Deetz had demonstrated two things. Based on ethnohistorical sources, he first established that the eighteenth-century Arikara underwent a change in social organization characterized primarily by their abandonment of the matrilocal pattern of residence. Then he found that the ceramics produced by Arikara women changed, showing a reduction in the degree of association among traditional design attributes. Deetz (1965, p. 86) then wondered: "To what extent, if any, are these two phenomena of change and transformation related?"

He considered three possibilities: (1) There is no relationship between change in social organization and change in ceramic patterning. (2) Some outside, unrecognized factor might be responsible for the coincidental change in eighteenth-century Arikara social organization and ceramics. (3) The changes in ceramic attribute patterning and social organization are indeed directly (and causally) related. Rejecting the first two possibilities, Deetz cautiously concluded that "the possibility of a functional and real connection between kinship change and pottery design is very high" (Deetz 1965, p. 98).

Deetz's Arikara study is an archaeological classic, a pioneering effort in the study of social change. As such, literally dozens of critics have analyzed his methods, his assumptions, and his conclusions. Critics faulted his statistics, his oversimplification of descent and residence patterns, and his failure to consider the influence of ongoing acculturation on pottery styles.

But the heaviest criticism was directed at the Deetz–Longacre–Hill model relating matricentered social organization to the specifics of ceramic design. Stanislawski (1972) had conducted ethnographic research among modern Hopi potters and reached markedly different conclusions, noting at least four contemporary methods for teaching ceramic manufacture, each crosscutting villages, settlement areas, and even tribal and linguistic groups. Modern potters make up to twenty different pottery types during their lifetime, and individual women make pottery quite different from that of their mothers. Women learn throughout their careers and feel free to apply any designs and styles they wish. Similarly, Friedrich (1970, p. 332) argued that the Deetz, Hill, and Longacre studies "have often rested on a naive view of culture as consisting of sets of objective elements correlated with one another in a limited and mechanical fashion." Based on a study of contemporary potters in a Tarascan village, Friedrich noted that design structure is more relevant than design elements. Stanislawski and Friedrich also scored Deetz and company for assuming that the spatial patterning of artifactual debris will reflect prehistoric social organization in such a straightforward manner.

The Longacre, Hill, and Deetz design studies are important—though not their conclusions (which have been discarded)—because they began pushing at the frontiers of archaeological knowledge. Archaeologists can, they argued, find out about extinct social systems. The limiting factor is not the archaeological record; the signficant limitations exist only in our perception of that record.

*Where To Go From Here?*_____

Mainstreams of Ceramic Sociology: Cronin (1962), Deetz (1965), Freeman (1962), Longacre (1968, 1970), Whallon (1968). See also Freeman and Brown (1964), Hill (1968, 1970a).

   Some Criticisms: Allen and Richardson (1971); Binford (1977, pp. 3–4); Clarke (1968, pp. 255–258, 595–601); Dumond (1977); Friedrich (1970); L. Johnson (1972a); S. Plog (1976); Stanislawski (1972); Watson, LeBlanc, and Redman (1971, pp. 34–45); Whallon (1968).

For additional research on design and attribute analysis, see LeBlanc and Watson (1973), Pyne (1976), Washburn (1976); also see the excellent review article on this subject by Watson (1977).

Tool Kits and Activity Areas

The next level of archaeological patterning is the tool kit, a related scattering of artifacts, waste products, and/or raw materials found in a spatially discrete assemblage (see Whallon 1973, p. 226). Tool kits are by no means ubiquitous in the archaeological record. In fact, for a tool kit to come down to the archaeologist "in one piece," the tools must be discarded nearly simultaneously, and the association must not have been destroyed by postdepositional factors.

Burial Assemblages As Tool Kits

Archaeologists have been aided in their study of prehistoric tool kits by the practice of burying individuals with items that presumably functioned together in a systemic context. Such grave associations provide singular clues to the composition of diverse prehistoric tool kits. One such discovery was made in the Valley of Mexico by George Valliant. While excavating at Ticoman, Valliant found two human burials accompanied by tool kits used for working hides into finished leather. Burial 17 at Ticoman was an elderly male, buried with the tools of his trade. Amidst these tools were found two spongy horn grainers or chisels (probably for detaching flesh from hide), three small obsidian scrapers, three large deer bone awls (for hide piercing), two bodkins (for sewing with thread or sinew), and a small shovel-tipped bone tool of no explicable use, except perhaps for fine work in preparing the hide or as an implement for weaving mats and baskets (Valliant 1931, p. 313). Also included were sixteen pocket gopher mandibles, each containing a sharp, chisel-ended incisor (see Figure 13–1). Burial 34 was uncovered nearby with a kit of fifteen stone and eleven bone tools, which Valliant suggested were for "finer work, like perhaps the tailoring of a hide." Beyond the specifics of leather-working technology, these two burials—both elderly men—suggest a high degree of craft specialization. Traditionally, archaeologists would often read such evidence as inferring that leather working at Ticoman was a "male" activity, but contemporary archaeologists are increasingly reluctant to assign such gender-specific roles without considerably more documentation.

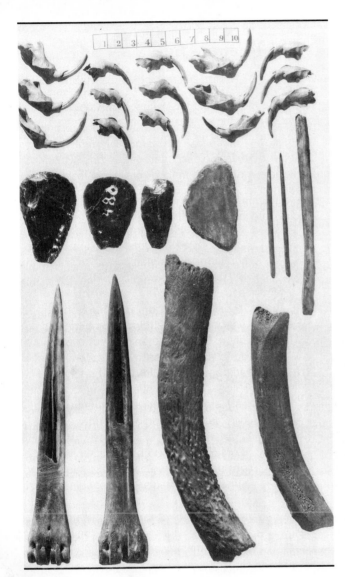

FIGURE 13–1 "Leather-worker's kit" associated with Skeleton 17 at Tico-man, Valley of Mexico. Top three rows: fifteen gopher mandibles; fourth row (left to right): three obsidian scrapers, one fragment of a pottery disc, two small bone bodkins, bone chisel. Bottom row (left to right): two deer metapodial awls, two hide grainers of deer antler (see Valliant 1931, Plate CI). (Courtesy the American Museum of Natural History)

Tool kits also may be found in archaeological contexts as **caches**. Dozens of such "cache pits" have been excavated throughout the Desert West and wherever arid climatic conditions favor the preservation of perishables. In Chapter 9, we discussed the cache of duck decoys from Lovelock Cave (Nevada). At the same site, a prehistoric basket-manufacturing kit was recovered (Ambro 1970) consisting of an outer cover of Canada goose skin and an inner folded pouch of red fox pelt. Inside were two completed bone awls and a bone awl blank, a coil of willow splints, and a small chert flake. The wad of willows had been carefully cut and shaped. Based on its stratigraphic associations, Ambro (1970, p. 76) suggested that the cache is more than five hundred years old.

This unremarkable bundle of hide, stone, bone, and wood provides some unusual clues. One bone awl is much larger than the others, suggesting that different tools were used for various stages of basket manufacture. These bone awls exhibit minute yet unmistakable microscopic striations along the tip. And the willow splints obviously had been prepared for use in a coiled basket. Hence, the wear patterns on the bone tools almost certainly result from coiled basket manufacture, and the patterns can be used in the future to determine the function of bone awls not found in such tight association with coiled baskets. Moreover, ethnographic accounts suggest that willow splints were probably gathered in the winter, when the leaves were absent from the bushes (Wheat 1967, p. 92). Although the association is less firm, a comparison with modern and historic Shoshone indicates that basket making was exclusively the activity of females (Wheat 1967, p. 91).

The caches of basket-making apparatus and the duck decoys suggests that Lovelock Cave must have been only one stopover during the year, but the fact that these bundles were there indicates the intention to return in the near future. This suggests a rather stable pattern of seasonal movement, necessitated, no doubt, by various wild crops available throughout the band's territory.

In both cases, these tool kits provide reasonably intact archaeological assemblages that can be correlated with the behavior that produced them. Inferences derived from the tool kits, of course, still remain open to question.

Activity Areas at Coxcatlán Cave

Grave associations and cache pits are relatively rare, and most archaeologists must rely on other analytical techniques to infer the composition of prehistoric tool kits. To see an early example of the tool-kit concept being used to infer intrasite activity areas, we return to MacNeish's excavations at Coxcatlán Cave in the Tehuacán Valley of Puebla, Mexico. Initially occupied in approximately 10,000 B.C., Coxcatlán Cave continued to accumulate debris until about A.D. 1300 or so.

The physical stratigraphy of Coxcatlán Cave was quite clear, and excavators easily separated the zones of occupation. Twenty-eight living surfaces were isolated, with a total of forty-two actual "occupations." During the excavation, concentrations of the artifacts, ecofacts, and features from each occupation were carefully mapped. These field data were then computer coded, and a series of "living floor maps" were plotted by a Cal. Comp. line plotter. Figure 13–2 shows one of the living-floor maps produced by the Tehuacán Valley study, representing Zone XXIII of the Coxcatlán Shelter, with a key to the ecofacts and artifacts. Zone XXIII, with radiocarbon dates ranging between approximately 7200 and 6700 B.C., was occupied during the Ajuereado Phase. The thickness of the floor was about fifteen centimeters, and it covered almost forty square meters.

After analyzing the artifacts, bones, and plant remains in Zone XXIII, the excavators defined three separate activity areas (Figure 13–2). Activity Area A contained a variety of stone, bone, and antler artifacts. MacNeish took the presence of a fully developed deer antler to identify a winter occupation. The abundance of bones

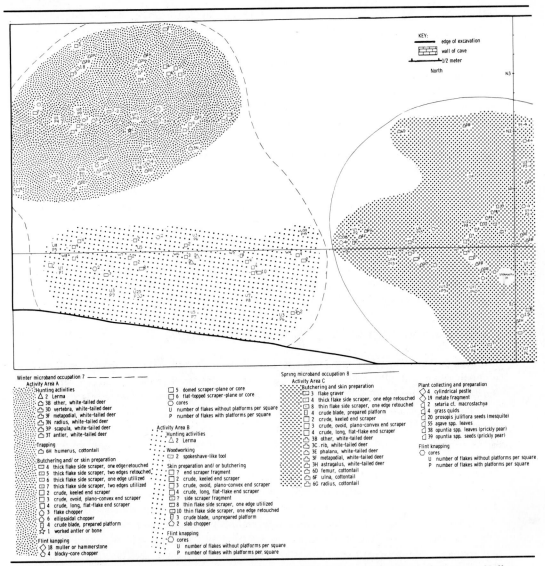

FIGURE 13–2   Presumed activity areas in Zone XXIII at Coxcatlán Cave, Tehuacán Valley, Mexico (see Fowler and MacNeish 1972, Figure 104). (Courtesy Richard S. MacNeish and the University of Texas Press)

and associated projectile points suggested that hunting was a major activity of the people who occupied Area A. The excavators suggest that butchering, skin preparation, and flintknapping may also have taken place during the brief winter visit.

Activity Area C was to the east of A. The artifacts include sidescrapers and endscrapers, a metate, other grinding stones, and a variety of deer and cottontail bones.

Perhaps most important, however, is the storage pit (labeled Feature 35). Found in this basin-shaped depression were the leaves and seeds of *Setaria,* mesquite, and *Opuntia* (cactus). These plant remains indicate not only the food preferences of the Ajuereado occupants but also the seasonality, as this particular selection of seeds would have been available only during the spring. The associated artifacts in Area C were interpreted as a relatively short occupation by a few individuals who came to Coxcatlán Cave to perform specific tasks. The seeds and grinding stones, along with the thin scattering of animal bones and the absence of projectile points, were taken as an indication that seed collecting was the major activity. Scraping and graving tools suggest hide preparation, and the core and flakes may denote some flintknapping during the spring occupation of Area C.

Spatially intermediate between A and C is Activity Area B. No animal or plant remains were found, and seed-grinding tools were also absent. Area B was tentatively interpreted as similar to A, involving hunting, skin preparation, and/or butchering, woodworking, and flintknapping.

Zone XXIII of Coxcatlán Cave is only a small part of the living floor analysis conducted for the Tehuacán Valley. MacNeish and his colleagues isolated over seventy-five occupations from about a dozen sites. Taken together, these data allow reconstruction of the subsistence pattern, ecology, and social organization of this area over the past twelve thousand years (as discussed in Chapter 11).

Archaeology Outgrows Its Age of Aquarius

Over the past two decades, archaeologists have looked more closely at the tacit assumptions that underpin unfettered reconstructions such as that for Coxcatlán Cave. Consider the issue of seasonality: In Chapter 11, we discussed the difficulties in seasonal estimates based on the presence/absence of "diagnostic" elements. Today, few archaeologists would accept the assignment of Activity Area A to winter simply because a fully developed deer antler was found there. Such conclusions ignore the formation processes involved. Remember the discussion of red deer bones at Star Carr? How do we know that the Tehuacános collected antlers only in the "hardened, October–February" condition? Such a linkage requires that we understand the processes of prehistoric antler working (and we presently lack such an understanding). And how did such a seasonally specific ecofact end up in Zone XXIII? Must humans have brought it in? How do we eliminate the pack rats and coyotes who live in the area today? In short, we lack the necessary bridging argumentation relating the shedding of a deer antler to human behavior at Coxcatlán Cave.

The assignment of Feature 35 is more satisfactory: Multiple plant indicators (available only during the spring) were deliberately deposited by humans into a storage pit. But few contemporary archaeologists would accept the extension of this single-feature spring estimate to the entire living surface.

The MacNeish reconstruction also attempts to explain artifact and ecofact distributions as inextricably related to time-specific activity areas. He and his colleagues expended much effort on piece-plotting artifacts to define clear-cut activity areas; more than six dozen living floor maps (like that in Figure 13–2) were published from the Tehuacán research, each one guided by three fundamental (and explicit) assumptions (spelled out in MacNeish et al. 1972, p. 7):

1. ecofacts found on a given surface are sufficient to define season of occupation;
2. artifacts and ecofacts found on the same surface define synchronous events;
3. intrasite spatial patterning is sufficient to define specific activity sets.

Today, not one of these assumptions is acceptable in light of available middle-range research.

This conclusion in no way belittles the achievements of MacNeish and his colleagues. The Tehuacán Valley project was the epitome of the 1960s' hyperreconstructionist archaeology, the standard-bearer of the interdisciplinary revolution. It typifies an enthusiastic era during which archaeologists boldly penetrated new areas of ecological and anthropological interest. This research will always retain an important place in the history of Americanist archaeology. But archaeology—like American culture itself—outgrew its Age of Aquarius. Our present understanding of site formation processes renders many of these 1960s assumptions simplistic or downright wrong.

The Archaeology of Individual Life Space

> Just as the bony skeleton provides the framework for the body around which the muscles and organs operate, so the arrangement of *facilities* on a site provides the skeleton around which activities are organized; the flow of persons and goods is accommodated to the facilities within a site.
> —Lewis Binford

In questioning the straightforward tool-kit/activity area association, archaeologists have begun to appreciate the scores of factors that conspire in the archaeological record to muddy seemingly clear-cut distinctions: differential preservation, variable "use lives" of artifacts, artifact curation, periodic episodes of site cleaning, recycling, and caching, to say nothing of a host of postdepositional processes. Archaeologists, in short, have begun the tedious process of building the middle-range bridges necessary to understanding spatial patterning in the archaeological record.

The Mask Site Model

To see how this bridge building progresses, let us look at debris-level patterning using Binford's Mask site as an example (Binford 1978a). Although the details of spatial use are specific to this single example, the underlying depositional processes can be seen operating in a wider range of sites and site types.

The Mask site is situated atop a north-south–oriented glacial moraine, 2.4 kilometers southwest of the present village of Anaktuvuk (Alaska). It is a hunting stand, an area where men congregate to watch for game and to plan hunting strategies once game is spotted. The site covers about 65 square meters, in the center of a cluster of five fire hearths. The differential use of the individual hearths depends on wind direction and herd movements. Figure 13–3 shows this classic hearth-centered seating arrangement. The distribution of tiny bone chips created while breaking open bones to get at the marrow, are concentrated around each hearth, the *drop zone*. Similar distributions are deposited by people sitting around a hearth chipping stone tools. Both flakes and bone chips were left in place by the Nunamiut Eskimo at the location where the stone working and marrow cracking took place.

Such drop zones contain primary refuse—bone chips and splinters, wood shavings, and the occasional item fumbled and forgotten during the activities. John Yellen (1976) saw the same kind of disposal when he was working among the !Kung. The primary refuse area there contained largely vegetable remains (nutshells and fruit and melon skins), bone fragments, and waste products of manufacturing activities (such as bits of ostrich eggshell, bone and wood shavings). Richard Gould (1968, p. 110; 1980, Chapter 5) and James O'Connell (1987) saw the same thing among Australian aborigines. Several formation processes condition what actually ends up in the drop zone. Light or small

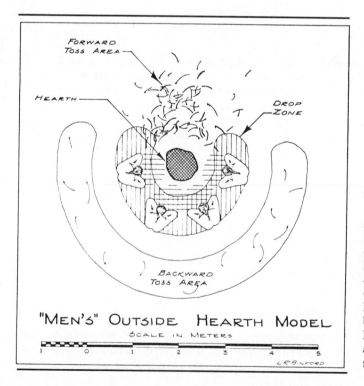

FIGURE 13–3 Models of drop and toss zones developed by Lewis Binford from observations at the Mask site in Anaktuvuk Pass, Alaska (see Binford 1983b, Figure 89). (Reprinted by permission of Lewis Binford and Thames and Hudson. Copyright © 1983)

objects are less visible and are incorporated into the archaeological record more readily, as they are less likely to be removed during cleanup.

But the spatial distribution of larger pieces of bone is quite different because these larger bones were tossed or placed beyond the hearth area, away from where the men were working and sitting. This *toss zone* results from a kind of "preventive maintenance" of the seating area; it contains relatively large items, generally in a secondary context. The Nunamiut disposed of their debris in two different ways: They simply dropped and forgot the small things and tossed away the larger items. At the Mask site, the residents threw sardine and pop cans away from the immediate hearth area after the contents were consumed. When Binford asked them why they disposed of their refuse in two different ways, they responded simply, "Who wants to sit down on a large bone?"

The most obvious consequence of such behavior is that debris becomes size sorted in the process of discard. This size-sorting effect has been shown to operate in diverse settings, and it can be a critical factor in the site formation process. Contrary to what one expects from a rigid tool-kit/activity area concept, item distribution can be patterned in the archaeological record strictly on the basis of size, without regard to function or derivation. Toss zones, in effect, can create zones of spurious intrasite association, and an uncritical use of the tool-kit and activity area concepts can mistakenly interpret such patterning.

The spatial configuration of the Mask site (Figure 13–4) is the result of several distinct disposal modes: dropping, tossing, resting, placing, and dumping. The configuration of the drop and toss zones varies from site to site, but similar underlying factors may be operative in a wide variety of situations.

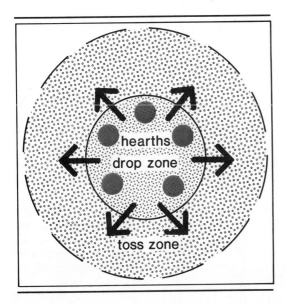

FIGURE 13–4 The Mask site refuse disposal model (see Binford 1987 and Thomas 1983b, Figure 221).

Drop Zone/Toss Zone Patterning at Gatecliff Shelter

We used Binford's Mask site model as a general framework for examining the spatial distribution of materials at Gatecliff Shelter. A toss zone can be created in any direction, and the Mask site model operates along a full 360° front. But in many cases, directionality can be determined by cultural or natural factors. The construction of summer houses or windbreaks, for instance, has a marked effect on refuse disposal practices. At Gatecliff, the immovable rear wall tightly structures debris discard, providing a natural backdrop for all activities conducted inside the shelter.

Despite such constraints, the same depositional processes might be expected to occur at Gatecliff as at the Mask site, creating predictable intrasite disposal areas. The hearths still provide the focus of cooking, eating, sleeping, tool manufacture, and repair. Similarly, a drop zone could be presumed to exist around the hearth area. But the configuration of Gatecliff Shelter might also be expected to influence the direction and configuration of the toss zone, as debris cannot be "tossed" through the rear of the cave. Toss zones should occur in this case outside the shelter drip line, on the apron of the cave.

Figure 13–5 shows how the Mask site model can be transposed to a setting in which the hearths are constructed within a restricted space. This derivative model provided a departure point for analyzing both the hearth positioning and the potential size sorting of debris at Gatcliff Shelter.

We plotted thirty-six hearths at Gatecliff and found the placement of these hearths to be tightly patterned according to the 180° Mask site model. In effect, each horizon was

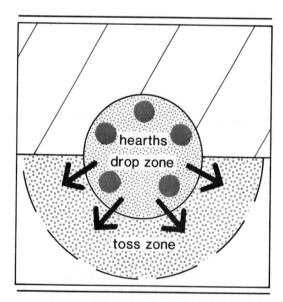

FIGURE 13–5   Drop zone/toss zone patterning, extrapolated from the Mask site model to a 180° version suitable for sites like Gatecliff Shelter (see Thomas 1983b, Figure 222).

characterized by a distinctive "hearth line," a band of fire hearths running across the mouth of Gatecliff Shelter. These parallels are particularly striking because each horizon is capped with a layer of compact calcareous silt, varying in thickness from six inches to two feet. These silt lenses effectively sandwich living surfaces between sterile layers, totally isolating the intrasite patterning from earlier horizons. That is, the internal structure of each living surface is separate from every other horizon.

The distance between these hearth lines and the rear wall was almost constant at four meters. So positioned, the hearths offered several distinct advantages: A distinct work area was defined between the hearth line and the rear wall. Placement somewhat inside the drip line protected the fires from rain, snow, and wind, venting the smoke outside. In effect, each hearth created a relatively warm and smoke-free rear room, a heated work and sleep area. The rear wall served as a heat sink, warming the inner part of the shelter with a small fire.

The sixteen cultural horizons were also analyzed to determine how debris size sorting was manifested in the archaeological record at Gatecliff. It turned out that the Gatecliff debris is indeed heavily size sorted. With the exception of Horizon 2—where bighorn sheep were butchered inside the cave—all the horizons clearly indicated that the artifacts, debitage, and ecofacts at the rear of the site were significantly smaller than those deposited near the drip line.

We found that debris size is the single most important factor influencing intrasite spatial patterning at Gatecliff. This means that if one wanted to predict where certain items would turn up inside Gatecliff Shelter, weight would be the most significant variable. Regardless of raw material, stage of manufacture, potential use-life, edge attrition, and typological or functional category, the internal positioning of debris is best predicted by a single variable: weight. This finding was important because it mandates considerable caution when using the tool-kit/activity area concept as an explanatory principle for understanding the human use of space.

Rethinking Activity Areas and Tool Kits

Archaeologists have been actively concerned with the reconstruction of activity areas and tool kits for only the past couple of decades. Our examples are somewhat ideal cases, instances in which the tool-kit associations seem to jump out at the archaeologist. More commonly, the field archaeologist will come upon a living surface that can be identified stratigraphically but not directly partitioned spatially. That is, although the vertical separation might be excellent, the horizontal, contextual nature of the floor is often obscure. A number of investigators have suggested statistical means for analyzing activity areas in such cases.

Before we leave the topic of tool kits, I must stress the recent difficulties with the tool-kit concept. Specifically as a result of ethnoarchaeological observations, investigators have pointed out that the "living floor" is an assumption that simply does not hold for many modern societies. Based on his recent work among the !Kung, for example,

Yellen (1977, p. 97) cautions archaeologists against assuming that tools found on living surfaces must be related to a single task or must form part of a single tool kit. At !Kung campsites, for instance, stone hammers and anvils are used to crack mongongo nuts, and these tools are often found in nuclear camp areas, which are also commonly littered with high concentrations of bone. But the stones have no relationship to the faunal remains. Both are physical remains of very different activities, and they occur together only fortuitously (see also Chapter 12). It thus should be apparent that inferring only a single tool kit could drastically influence the interpretation of, say, Coxcatlán Zone XXIII.

Binford (1973, pp. 242–243) also cautioned archaeologists about similar dangers regarding living floor analysis. Binford's work among the Nunamiut Eskimo suggested to him that the Nunamiut have an almost exclusively curated technology. That is, the Nunamiut hunters carry their artifacts about to such a degree that the tool inventories of their sites have precious little to do with the original activities that took place there. The problem for archaeologists dealing with Nunamiut sites is that there may be little relationship between the activities performed and the artifacts discarded.

These and other problems were addressed in Chapter 11, but it is important to emphasize the issue once again. Note the difference in interpretation between Coxcatlán Cave and Gatecliff Shelter. At Coxcatlán, the investigators assumed (1) that artifacts and ecofacts found on the same surface were deposited at the same time and (2) that intrasite spatial patterning corresponded to specific activity sets. In our analysis of patterning at Gatecliff, we could not justify these assumptions, and for good reason. Instead, we found that size sorting was sufficient to account for nearly all the patterning present.

In looking over the Coxcatlán Cave maps, we suspect that similar size sorting operated there. Viewed from the perspective of the Mask site model, one expects that areas in the rear of the cave should be the drop zone, whereas things found along the apron of the cave should be the toss zone debris. To conduct an adequate reanalysis, it would be necessary to consider the size of the various bones, plant parts, and artifacts. But the living floor map (Figure 13–2) certainly suggests that such is the case.

Activity Area B, adjacent to the rear wall of Coxcatlán Cave, contains only relatively small artifacts (mostly flakes and stone tool fragments), and no animal bones at all, just what one expects in a drop zone. Both Activity Areas A and C contain relatively large stone tools (including a hammerstone, a metate fragment, and a pestle), plus an assortment of white-tailed deer and cottontail rabbit bones, exactly the kind of debris to be tossed away from the sheltered work area at the rear of the site. Although we cannot be certain of this interpretation, it surely indicates that caution is in order when charting tool-kit/activity area correlates across site surfaces.

Where To Go From Here?

The Tool-Kit and Activity Areas Concepts in Archaeology: The papers in Kent (1987) provide an extraordinarily well balanced and diversified approach to activity areas. See also Fletcher (1977), Speth and Johnson (1976), Whallon (1973, 1974a).

Spatial Patterning of Hunter-Gatherer Households

Family and community social patterning is reflected in the archaeological record largely at the household level. One rudimentary example is the simple brush structure. The Shoshone, for example, built brush or bark structures called *wickiups* (see Figure 13–6). Often these temporary structures were surrounded by a ring of stones; such "house rings" are common in the archaeological record of the Desert West. Robert Bettinger and I excavated one structure on a ridge overlooking the Reese River, in Nevada. While making a surface collection of the area, we discovered dozens of small glass trade beads and a flat (clothes) iron cached beneath a grinding slab; apparently they used the flat iron in lieu of a hand stone (or mano). We named the site Flat Iron Ridge, and thinking that the site was a historic Shoshone house, we decided to excavate the well-preserved rock ring. The house floor surface was littered with historic artifacts (Figure 13–6), and from the square nails recovered, we estimated the duration of occupation to have been from about 1870 to 1890 (Thomas and Bettinger 1976, p. 323–324).

Because the interior had probably been swept, precise relationships among individual artifacts could be misleading, but an examination of the features within the structure is instructive (Figure 13–6). From the placement of the hearth, it seems clear that food was prepared in the eastern half of the house, near the doorway (which allowed smoke to escape outside). Artifacts found inside are generally small and probably contained within a drop zone (the toss zone being outside the shelter). The concentration of nails in the ashy area suggests that boards were probably salvaged from other settlements nearby and used for firewood. Across from the fire was a continuation of the drop zone, with relatively little ash, probably where the inhabitants slept.

Such simple household patterning is precisely what one expects for Shoshone houses of the early contact period. As discussed earlier, Shoshone social organization centered on the nuclear family, and according to Steward (1938, p. 239), "among Western Shoshone the household was very nearly a self-sufficient economic unit and as such an independent social and political unit." The house on Flat Iron Ridge probably sheltered just such an independent household. In aboriginal times this area was used extensively for piñon harvesting in the late fall, and perhaps this is also why the historic house was built. But there is ample evidence of lumbering in the vicinity, and it could well be that the Flat Iron Ridge household was engaged in cutting timber for the nearby ranches and mines.

Households in the Transition from Forager to Settled Villager

The Western Shoshone household is an excellent example of what the archaeological record of an egalitarian system looks like. More complex households have been encountered in Oaxaca (Mexico), constructed at a time when people were "settling down" into

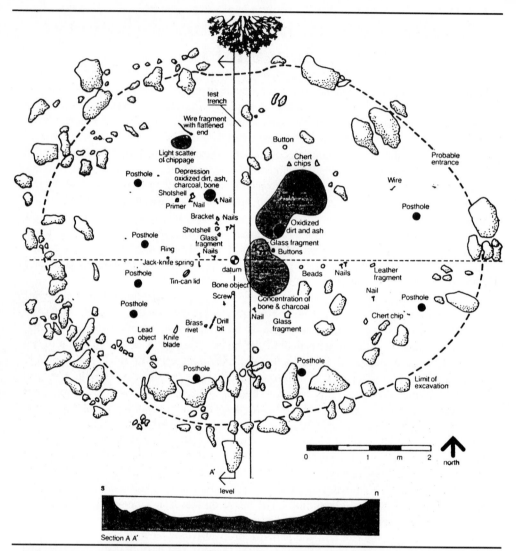

FIGURE 13–6   Distribution of historic artifacts in House A at the Flat Iron Ridge site, Reese River Valley (see Thomas and Bettinger 1976, Figure 36). (Courtesy the American Museum of Natural History)

villages. Kent Flannery and Marcus Winter (1976, p. 44) summarize evidence from a sample of twenty-two carefully excavated houses at several Oaxacan sites (see Figure 13–7). In every house they found evidence of grinding stones (for preparing corn), storage pits (generally filled with corn kernels and prickly pear seeds), large storage jars, bones of cottontail rabbits, fragments of pottery, and charcoal braziers, leading them to conclude

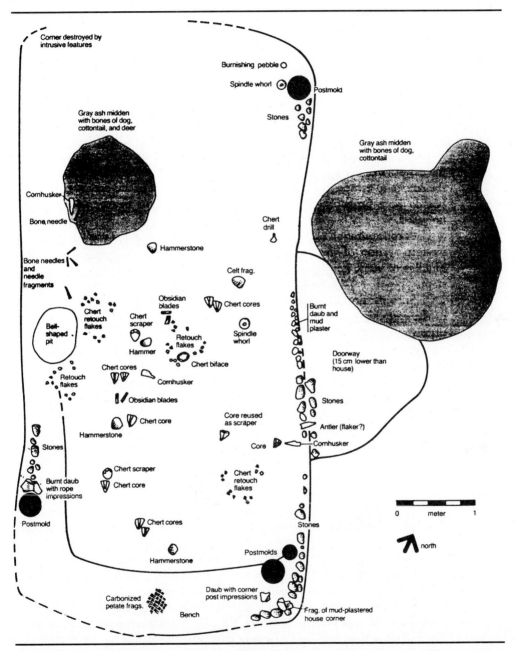

Corner destroyed by intrusive features

Burnishing pebble ○
Spindle whorl ◉ Postmold
Stones

Gray ash midden with bones of dog, cottontail, and deer

Gray ash midden with bones of dog, cottontail

Cornhusker
Bone needle

Chert drill ⚥

Bone needles and needle fragments

Hammerstone

Celt frag.

Obsidian blades
Chert cores
Chert scraper

Chert retouch flakes

Retouch flakes

Spindle whorl ◉

Bell-shaped pit
Hammer
Chert biface

Chert cores
Cornhusker

Retouch flakes

Obsidian blades

Core reused as scraper

Chert core

Hammerstone

Core
Antler (flaker?)
Cornhusker

Stones

Chert scraper
Chert core

Chert retouch flakes

Burnt daub with rope impressions

Postmold

Chert cores

Hammerstone

Postmolds

Burnt daub and mud plaster

Doorway (15 cm lower than house)

Stones

Stones

Carbonized petate frags.

Daub with corner post impressions

Bench

Frag. of mud-plastered house corner

0   meter   1

↗ north

FIGURE 13–7 Distribution of selected artifacts in House 1, Area A, at the Tierras Largas site, Oaxaca (see Flannery and Winter 1976, Figure 2–17). (Courtesy Kent V. Flannery and Academic Press)

that food was procured, prepared, and stored by each individual household between 1500 and 500 B.C. This pattern may also suggest that households were virtually autonomous in terms of their food supply, regardless of any additional specialization.

Each household also contains evidence of tool preparation: chert cores and core fragments, broken stone tools, and waste debris. The smaller items were probably contained in specific drop zones. Outside is the toss zone, the gray ash midden with dog and cottontail bones. Each household seems to have had access to local stone, and every household produced its own cutting and scraping implements.

There was some evidence for household specialization. One house, for instance, contained a bell-shaped pit, that contained a cache of chert flakes. The excavators interpreted this as the workshop of a part-time toolmaker who probably made the more refined stone implements for the village. Another house contained a storage pit with a cache of deer bones, some of which were unmodified, whereas others had been cut to produce socket-type handles and bone rings. Once again, although all households used bone tools, this single individual seems to have done a great deal of the tool manufacture for his (or her) neighbors. These tool kits seem analogous to the leather-working and basket-making kits discussed earlier. The inference about specialization depends largely on the placement and context of the tool kits in the community.

Another common analytical tool in studying residential patterns has been to characterize artifacts as either male or female. The leather-working kits are found, for example, only with males, and our analogy to the Western Shoshone of the last century suggests that the basket-making pouch belonged to a female. Using a similar ethnographic analogy from the highland Chiapas, Flannery and Winter (1976, pp. 42–45) made some suggestions about intrahousehold patterning in Oaxaca. They think that women's tools included grinding stones, pottery charcoal braziers, pots showing a crust where maize had been soaked in lime, some hammerstones for preparing food, special deer-bone tools for husking corn, spindle whorls for weaving, and needles for sewing. Most of the flint working seems to have been done by men using antler flakers; projectile points, chert knives, and scrapers also seem to have been men's tools. Men also used bone hide-working tools (like those found in the leather-working kits), celts for clearing land, and tools for making other tools, such as shaft smoothers and burins.

The Oaxaca houses seem to be divided along the midline, with the women's area on one side and the men's on the other. Figure 13–7, for instance, seems to have all the "male" artifacts—chert cores, scrapers, retouched flakes, and a biface—lying to the left of the door as one enters. To the right are the bone needles, deer-bone cornhuskers, and pierced pottery disks that probably function as spindle whorls. Moreover, the gray ash indicates that the cooking also occurred on the right or women's half of the house.

There are, of course, many potential problems with such gender-specific analogies. We know from ethnohistoric records that the first Navajo rug weavers were men who had learned the craft from Hopi and Zuni weavers. Then, about a century ago, women took over the basket weaving. Today, male Navajos have begun to weave rugs again. In this case, rug weaving is not exclusively a male or female activity, and more important, the gender linkage changes according to specific circumstances. This is a case in which a direct analogy to the present would actually hinder our understanding of the past. Archaeologists thus are becoming increasingly wary of such gender-specific analogies in reconstructing archaeological settlement and activity patterns.

The Oaxaca houses do not stand in total isolation. Associated with each is a cluster of related activity areas, including outside storage pits, a trash midden, a burial area, and an oven. These household clusters are then grouped into the total community. The village of San José Mogote is estimated to have contained several of these discrete yet related household clusters.

A different case of social space is evident at Betatakin, the Tsegi Phase cliff ruin in northeastern Arizona (Figure 13–8). Chapter 9 discussed how Jeffrey Dean (1970) used tree-ring data, with almost year-to-year accuracy, from nearly three hundred trees to determine the construction sequence of rooms, from initial occupation in 1250 to abandonment shortly after 1286. But Dean's objectives went far beyond mere architectural dating. He used this tight dendrochronological sequence to infer something about Tsegi Phase spatial organization at the Betatakin ruin.

FIGURE 13–8 Betatakin, a cliff dwelling in Tsegi Canyon (Arizona). (Courtesy Jeffrey S. Dean and the Laboratory of Tree-Ring Research, University of Arizona)

Dean recognized several functionally different room types at Betatakin:

Living rooms: Features that typify living rooms are one or more jacal walls, low-silled doorways, leveled and plastered floor, fire pits, mealing bins, interior wall plaster, and interior smoke blackening.

Courtyards: These are unroofed, irregularly shaped areas, which generally have plastered floors, fire pits, mealing bins, and storage pits that are generally surrounded by living and storage rooms.

Granaries: These rooms are designed to keep out insects, rodents, and weather. They have high-silled doorways, stone slab doors, and finely finished and chinked masonry.

Storerooms: These small rooms lack the distinctive features of dwellings and granaries and were probably used to store nonperishable items such as tools, ceremonial paraphernalia, and pottery.

Grinding rooms: These rooms have a battery of two to four stone slab bins, which held a series of graded metates.

Ceremonial chambers: These kivas are quite variable, ranging from completely subterranean to completely aboveground, from circular to rectangular in shape.

These various types of rooms are grouped into what Dean calls room clusters: at least one living room, one to six storage chambers (granaries and storerooms), occasionally a grinding room, and, in all but a few cases, a courtyard. The rooms in a cluster open directly into the courtyard or are connected with other rooms that do. The room cluster seems to be the basic architectural unit of Tsegi Phase villages such as Betatakin: Such sites are not merely agglomerations of individual rooms but, rather, agglomerations of room clusters.

Dean's detailed analysis of Betatakin architecture also suggests that the room cluster not only was the basic unit of residence but that it also provided a more or less exclusive territory for the resident social unit. Each room cluster was occupied by a household, the basic local unit of modern Pueblo society. Room clusters with a single living room were probably occupied by nuclear families, whereas clusters with more than one living room must have been the home of multifamily households (Dean 1970, p. 163).

Although in modern western Pueblo groups the extended families always occur within the larger lineage, there is no architectural unit that could correspond to a lineage at Betatakin. Therefore, if lineages once existed at Betatakin, they were nonlocalized and hence not visible in the archaeological record.

Beyond the room cluster complex, the only architectural unit that can be isolated during the Tsegi Phase is the village itself. Communities such as Betatakin possessed all the necessary mechanisms for mobilizing and directing the cooperation of the villagers in community projects. There is no firm correspondence between kivas and subvillage residence units, suggesting that the kivas must have functioned in conjunction with nonlocalized social units made up of members of several households. These social units could have been the nonlocalized clans or, alternatively, ceremonial sodalities whose membership cut across clan lines (or both). It is also interesting to note that dual organization (such as the moieties at Mesa Verde or Chaco Canyon) is lacking at Betatakin.

Betatakin provides evidence of how the Tsegi Phase villagers coordinated labor for community projects. Dendrochronology shows that tree cutting at Betatakin was a communal rather than an individual or household activity: A group of perhaps twenty people felled a number of trees, cut them to standardized primary and secondary beam length, and stockpiled them for future use, perhaps by later immigrants to the village. This occurred in 1269 and again in 1272, but the beams were not used until 1275 when a three-year period of immigration resulted in the construction of more than ten room clusters and one or more kivas.

Dean thinks that Betatakin was settled by a group of people who already constituted the functioning community. That is, "Betatakin, *as a social unit,* existed somewhere else prior to the founding of the village known by that name" (Dean 1970, p. 159). The overhang was carefully planned for habitation—probably by community decision—and the society had sufficient sanctions to carry out the task. A preplanned move such as this would require a strong leadership structure. The first settlement of Betatakin took the form of three or four spatially isolated room clusters, and subsequently the village grew by adding individual room clusters, presumably as more families arrived.

To summarize, the exceptionally well dated ruin of Betatakin was probably occupied by (matrilocal?) extended family households, each of which occupied a room cluster. Households were probably grouped into sodalities, and the village itself had a tight sociopolitical structure able to amass a labor force necessary for community work programs. It seems likely that there was also a formalized intervillage social structure.

Reconstructing Social Status

Success is counted sweetest
By those who ne'er succeed.
—Emily Dickinson

Status consists of the rights, duties, privileges, powers, liabilities, and immunities that accrue to a recognized and named social position (see Goldschmidt 1960, p. 266 and Goodenough 1965, p. 2). A single social status is a collection of rights and duties. In our own society, the status of "father" is determined by a series of duties owed to his son and the reciprocal responsibilities he can legitimately demand of his son. Similarly, the son owes certain obligations to his father and can expect certain privileges in return.

Social status is apportioned through a number of culturally determined criteria. Nearly all societies categorize their members in terms of their age and their consequent position in the cycle of life. Bohannan (1965, p. 149) notes that for African societies the

What Happens to Women When Foragers Settle Down?

Janet Spector and Mary Whelan emphasize how little we know about the changing roles of women in prehistory. Although we can find little enlightenment from studies of the archaeological record, some clues exist from recent ethnohistorical research. The following relies on Spector's and Whelan's (1988) excellent discussion (see also Binford and Chasko 1976).

Patricia Draper (1975) has explored gender relationships among foraging and settled agricultural !Kung of the Kalahari. Specifically, she examined how a shift in food production affected the status of the women involved. Draper showed that the egalitarian association between men and women dwindled rapidly in the sedentary contexts, in which women's influence and autonomy was drastically reduced. Draper charted the locations of gender-specific activities in both settings, documenting community layout, architecture, and household equipment. She found that in the agricultural setting, "gendered" divisions sprang up, creating a public–domestic dichotomy that was absent among the foragers.

A constellation of factors seemed to create a higher degree of gender asymmetry. There were significant differences in the mobility patterns and subsistence contributions between men and women. As foragers, both men and women were absent from the base camps for about the same amount of time, with women contributing at least as much to the diet as did their male counterparts (and they directly controlled the resources they collected). Moreover, among the foraging !Kung, Draper observed an absence of rigid gender typing of adult activities. Boys and girls played together,

with little pressure to conform to any specific set of gender roles. Child care, shared equally by the sexes, was taken for granted and was not a major time-consumer, given the average birth interval of about four years between children. The foragers spent an average of three days per week on subsistence-related activities, and at any given time, roughly one-third or more of the adult population remained in camp to supervise children whose parents were absent.

In the sedentary contexts, women participated very differently. Because the nonmobile !Kung women spent so much time processing domesticated foodstuffs, their contribution to overall group subsistence dropped significantly. The more substantial houses and increased material goods associated with sedentism also placed added burdens on women, increasingly limiting them to a definable domestic sphere. Men, on the other hand, became more peripherally involved in household activities, spending more time away from home, planting crops, tending fields, and herding animals.

Fieldwork by Gina Kolata (1974) sheds some light on why women become confined to the domestic sphere with the advent of sedentism. She showed that the shift to sedentary life was accompanied by increased fertility and birthrates, probably related to dietary change and differences in infant nursing practices. In effect, the sedentary !Kung lost a "natural check" on their fertility rates. Whereas the foragers enjoyed a relatively well balanced diet, the sedentary !Kung were generally taller and heavier, owing to the increased consumption of cow's milk and grain. Sedentary !Kung women began to menstruate earlier than their nomadic counterparts. The foraging girls often married at puberty (about 15.5 years of age); they had their first children at age 19, nursing them for three to four years (during which time they rarely conceived). In effect, late menarche and lengthy birth intervals kept population size in check (for a different view, see Blurton Jones 1986, 1987).

But as population size soared among sedentary !Kung, children were weaned much earlier and nursing was supplemented by processed grains and cow's milk. The fertility rates of sedentary women may be higher because of the effect of diet on the age of menarche and birth intervals. When the relatively well nourished (but thin) !Kung foragers nurse their children, they may have too little body fat to ovulate. Thus the increased body fat of sedentary women combined with their ability to wean children earlier may have increased fertility and births.

The roles of mother/father, man/woman were dramatically redefined as people became less mobile, and children were socialized differently in the process. Among sedentary !Kung, adult gender roles became rigidly defined and differentially valued. Children were at times viewed as potential members of the work force, and their gender roles were programmed at an early age. Boys often accompanied their fathers in excursions outside the village, to help with the herds. Girls were kept at home to assist with child care and domestic chores, duties at this point clearly identified with women.

Of perhaps greatest relevance to archaeology is the contrast between the material characteristics and spatial arrangements under the two different technoeconomic regimes. Draper (1975, pp. 104–108) noted that in the "small, circular, open and highly intimate" !Kung foraging camps, there were cultural sanctions against authoritarianism, physical aggression, and hoarding of material goods. Interactions between households were minimized in the agricultural villages because the households were spaced farther apart and fences had been erected to keep out the domestic animals. The degree of privacy increased, and people started hoarding material wealth. Property was more commonly assigned to men rather than women.

Spector and Whelan (1988, p. 25) argue that whereas archaeologists have been aware of such demographic variables when considering the effects of food production, this research has not been conducted from the differing perspectives of the men and women involved. Although the !Kung do not represent a universal cultural pattern, their case does vividly point up how the study of gender can contribute to our understanding of human evolution and cultural change.

list of male age categories generally runs like this: newly born infant, child on the lap, uninitiated boy, initiated bachelor, married man, elder, and retired elder. The specifics vary from culture to culture, of course, but the underlying principle of age almost always influences one's social standing in the society at large.

Gender is another ubiquitous status category. It is true, of course, that people are inescapably male or female, a biological fact obvious to all. As Robert Lowie noted dryly in *Social Organization,* "Sex . . . is an effective social sorter" (1948, p. 6). But rarely do societies assign status strictly along sexual lines, into two antithetical halves. Sexual links are more commonly merged with other principles of alignment in the definition of status.

Another related conditioner of status is kinship. As with sex and age, kinship in a sociocultural sense depends on a biological counterpart but is rarely identical with it (Lowie 1948, p. 7). Kinship terms provide cultural labels for the social positions that determine how interpersonal relations are conducted.

An obvious yet important point to be made here is that each individual simultaneously possesses several different social statuses, or what Goodenough (1965) terms *social identities*. For example, for a given adult male, "father" is only one of several statuses that are operative. That individual may also be a colonel in the air force, a captain of the bowling team, and a Harvard graduate. Each social position has its own collection of rights and duties. Which identity is currently operating depends on with whom the individual is interacting. The composite of the several identities maintained by a single individual is termed the *social persona* (Goodenough 1965, p. 7; also see Binford 1971, p. 17). As we shall see, it is this encompassing social persona that is reflected in the archaeological record, along with individual status categories such as sex and age.

Linton (1936, p. 115) observed that "most of the business of living can be conducted on the basis of habit, with little need for intelligence and none for special gifts." Societies have developed two rather different ways of assigning statuses, through ascription and through achievement. An **ascribed status** is assigned to individuals without regard to innate differences or abilities, determined at the moment of birth, with training for that status beginning immediately. Alternatively, a society can provide for statuses to be **achieved**, requiring special qualities of the individuals. Not assigned at birth, achieved statuses are left open until filled through competition and individual effort.

Egalitarian Societies: When We All Were Equal

The concept of status allows us to leap from the level of the individual to the level of the entire society. A society is termed *egalitarian* when the number of valued statuses is roughly equivalent to the number of persons with the ability to fill them (Fried 1967, p. 33). Such societies lack the means to fix or limit the number of persons capable of exerting power, and egalitarian societies are therefore characterized by generally equal access to important resources. The Great Basin Shoshone were generally egalitarian, with the leadership simply assumed by those best capable of leading others and authority restricted to a particular situation. A particularly good hunter might, for instance, assume a position of leadership when a group of men join to hunt bighorn. Or a particularly good dancer might take charge of *fandango* arrangements. A particularly good talker might keep the villagers informed about the ripening of plant foods in different areas and urge the people to cooperate for the group good (Steward 1938, p. 247). The key to leadership in an egalitarian society is experience and overall social standing.

A **ranked society**, on the other hand, is one in which "positions of valued status are somehow limited so that not all those of sufficient talent to occupy such statuses actually achieve them" (Fried 1967, p. 109). Such a social structure embodies an intrinsic hierarchy in which relatively permanent social stations are maintained, with people having unequal access to basic life-sustaining resources. Although the distribution of labor is determined by sex and age in both egalitarian and ranked societies, ranked societies tend to have economies that redistribute goods and services throughout the community. Many tribes of the American northwest coast (see Chapter 3) are ranked societies. The localized kin groups—not the individuals—control the resources, and the major economic goods flow in and out of a finite center (Fried 1967, p. 117).

The categories *egalitarian* and *ranked* define a social spectrum that can be traced archaeologically. Social status, as we have seen, is one aspect of the overall social system. And at times the ranking of social statuses can be reflected in the archaeological record.

Ranked Societies: How We Became Unequal

One common method that an archaeologist uses to examine the workings of extinct social systems is the analysis of mortuary practices. An important assumption comes into play here: that persons who are treated differentially in life will be treated differentially in death (Peebles 1971, p. 68). Death, in a sense, is a period of separation and reintegration for both the deceased and those left behind. The dead are separated from the living and must be properly integrated into the world of the dead. Social ties existed between the living and the once-living, and the ceremonial connections at death reflect in large measure these social relations. Peebles (1971, p. 69) emphasized the importance of studying human burials as the fossilized terminal statuses of individuals. Although these terminal statuses are often different from the statuses most commonly studied by ethnographers, those models defined archaeologically are every bit as real as those observable among ethnographic cultures (Harris 1968a, pp. 359–360).

Let us examine the ranking of social status evident at Moundville, one of the best-known and most intensively investigated ceremonial centers in the United States. Located on a bluff overlooking the Black Warrior River in Alabama, Moundville covers about three hundred acres and consists of twenty major ceremonial mounds surrounding a large plaza. Unlike simple burial mounds, Moundville consists largely of temple mounds, large flat-topped earthen structures designed to function as artificial mountains to elevate the temples above the landscape. Moundville was a major site in the Mississippian tradition, which reached its peak about two hundred to three hundred years before European colonization.

Initial archaeological investigations at Moundville were conducted by the ubiquitous C. B. Moore in 1905–1906 (see Chapter 1). Moore excavated both platform mounds and village areas and published his findings in two volumes (Moore 1905, 1907) (see Figure 13–9). As might be expected, Moore's work is not up to contemporary standards, but his data are still usable. The Alabama Museum of Natural History then excavated at Moundville from 1929 through 1941: Over half a million square feet of the village areas at Moundville were uncovered during this twelve-year period, in part by workers under the Civilian Conservation Corps.

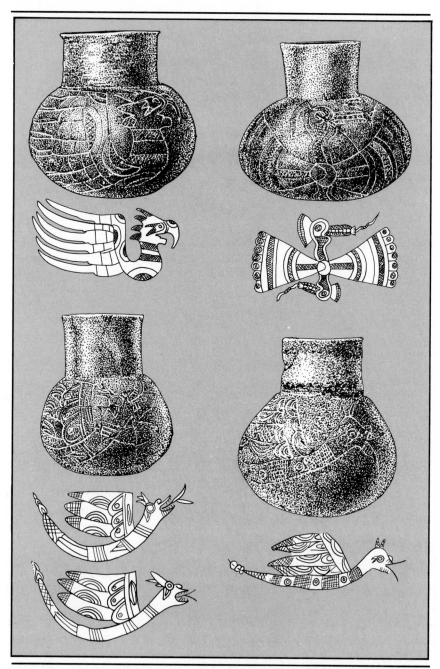

FIGURE 13–9   Ceramics recovered by C. B. Moore at Moundville (see Moore 1905, Figures 114, 115, 117, 118; Moore 1907, Figures 57 through 61)

More than three thousand burials have been excavated at Moundville, and they have provided an excellent database for studying Mississippian social structure. The task is complicated by the different methods of excavation employed, but recent work by Christopher Peebles, Susan Kus, and Vincas Steponaitis clearly indicate that a kind of "salvage archaeology"—salvaging museum collections excavated decades ago—can be fruitful indeed.

Peebles and Kus began their analysis by studying the abundant grave goods. Moundville is a major site in the *Southern cult* (also called the Southeastern Ceremonial complex), characterized by a series of distinctive motifs. Southern cult artifacts are termed *supralocal* because of their widespread distribution throughout the South; they are known from as far north as Georgia and as far west as Spiro (Oklahoma). Whatever the Southern cult really was—and archaeologists still debate the point (see J. A. Brown 1976)—the complex crosscut the boundaries of many distinctive local cultures.

Peebles and Kus recognized a second kind of distinctive grave goods, the *local symbols*. These artifacts are specially constructed animal effigy vessels, or parts of animals such as canine teeth, claws, and shells. Although the localized symbols are widely distributed in form, they have a distinctive and structured context within the Moundville area. The local symbols seem to have functioned as status items within a single site (that is, presumably within a single community), but the supralocal symbols designated the rank of individuals in the overall region.

Each mound at Moundville appears to contain a limited number of high-status adults. Grave goods include copper axes, copper gorgets, stone discs, various paints, and assorted exotic minerals such as galena and mica. Each mound also contains some less well accompanied (presumably lower-status) individuals, accompanied only by a few ceramic vessels. Because the Moundville mounds once supported ceremonial structures (temples), Peebles decided that the high-status burials from these mounds were associated with these temples. The lower-status burials—particularly the infant and skull burials—were probably ritual accompaniments to the high-status individuals.

The very highest status individuals in the mounds were accompanied by several supralocal symbols, including ceremonial axes and sheet copper plumes that depict the "eagle being" and the "dancing priest." Presumably these individuals had a status and a reputation that were recognized throughout the entire Moundville culture. By correlating the presence of higher- and lower-status symbols, Peebles then made some limited inferences about the mechanisms of ranking at Moundville. The very high prestige items tended to be buried with individuals of all ages and both sexes. This means that status at Moundville was probably assigned at birth. That is, one's social position was inherited and automatically assigned to all family members. This inference is reinforced by the fact that even infants and children—clearly too young to have accomplished anything very noteworthy in life—were buried with lavish grave goods. These individuals were important because of who they were, not what they did.

On the basis of comparison with ethnographic cases, Peebles and Kus (1977, p. 431) predicted that the Moundville burials should be divided into two major classes: the superordinate and subordinate dimensions. Subordinate ranking is a social ordering based on symbols and energy expenditure, a ranking determined exclusively by age and sex.

The older the individual is, the greater is the opportunity for accomplishment, and therefore the higher the rank will be. In the main, adult burials will be more complex than those of children, and child burials will be more complex than those of infants. In addition, men and women will not share all grave goods because some will be sex linked. The subordinate divisions consist of the "commoners" in a ranked society.

The superordinate division is a partial ordering based on criteria other than age and sex. In this case, class membership is determined by one's genealogy. Within the superordinate (that is, the ruling) dimension, some individuals will be infants, some children, and the rest adults. All groups will occur in every ranked category, except the paramount division. This supreme class will contain only adults, and generally only adult males.

In sum, Peebles and Kus predicted that the statuses should form a pyramid-shaped distribution. At the base of the pyramid are the commoners, whose statuses are determined strictly by sex and age. The next step up the social ladder consists of those few "special" individuals with ascribed (that is, inherited) status. Finally, at the top will be the paramount individuals, individuals on whom are lavished all the emblems of status and rank available in the society.

This model was tested by performing in-depth statistical analysis on 2053 of the best-documented burials from Moundville (see Figure 13–10). The supreme division (Cluster IA) is presumably the chief. The seven individuals in Cluster IA clearly represent the highest of statuses and the ultimate political authority. These individuals, probably all males, were buried in large truncated mounds and were accompanied by a lavish array of material culture, plus infants and human skulls presumably sacrificed for the occasion. The large copper axes found in the graves seem to be the material representations of the offices held by these individuals. Cluster IB individuals were also buried in or near the truncated mounds and have other Southern cult artifacts along with several mineral-based paints as part of their grave goods. These people were probably the second-order ritual or political officers whose duties included the ceremonial application of body paint or tattoos to others. This cluster contains both children and adult males. The final clustering of this superordinate dimension included adults and children who were buried in cemeteries near the mounds and in charnel houses near the main plaza; their grave goods include chest beads, copper gorgets, and galena cubes.

The important difference between the individuals of the superior Cluster A and those of subordinate Clusters B and C is that the latter are ascribed status strictly on the basis of sex and age. In Cluster III, for instance, stone ceremonial celts are found only with adult males, whereas infants and children have "toy" vessels, clay "playthings," and unworked freshwater shells. Unworked deer, bird claws, and turtle bones were found only with adults. The individuals in the lowest segment, C, were generally found away from the mounds and major ceremonial areas at Moundville.

This second set of data clarifies the nature of ranking in the Moundville society. The upper class of social elite were buried in a sacred area and accompanied by symbols of their exalted status. The Moundville elite apparently lived in larger, more complex dwellings than did the commoners. Elite membership was conditioned by genealogy, and

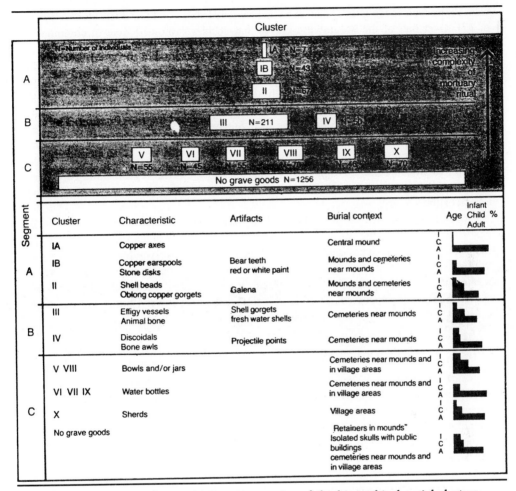

FIGURE 13–10 Diagrammatic representation of the hierarchical social clusters represented in burials at Moundville (see Peebles and Kus 1977, Figure 3). (Courtesy Christopher Peebles and the Society for American Archaeology)

because social position was inherited within the elite, even the children occupied such social positions.

Further down the ladder, the villagers' graves also reflected their social positions in life, positions conditioned largely by sex and age distinctions rather than inheritance. The less glamorous grave goods were distributed in a quite different manner. Graves contained pottery vessels, bone awls, flint projectile points, and stone pipes, which were distributed unevenly (mostly to older adults). Peebles infers that these individuals were required to achieve—rather than inherit—their social status. The prize artifacts in this social setting went to the "self-made individuals" who had achieved status on their own (Pfeiffer 1977, p. 97). Over half of the Moundville graves that Peebles examined were of commoners who were buried without any grave goods at all.

Peebles placed these studies of ranked status at Moundville into a regional framework. All the twenty-plus sites of the Moundville phase are part of a single polity. This cultural system was glued together by a common social organization and common ritual. Part of the production of this society as a whole was used to support a number of specialized politicoreligious offices (see also Steponaitis 1978). Most of these offices were physically associated with the major Moundville site itself, but others were part of the minor ceremonial centers and villages in the hinterlands. The recruitment to these high offices was probably limited to members at the apex of the social organization. Nevertheless, the bonds of clanship and reckoned genealogical relationship probably pervaded the whole of the society.

Peebles suggests that Moundville conformed to a chiefdom model (Fried 1967) characterized by a status framework containing fewer valued positions than there were individuals capable of handling them. The economy was probably redistributive, Moundville serving as a center of regional distribution of key goods. Since Peebles's work at Moundville, a ranked form of social organization has been recognized at other Mississippian sites in Tennessee, Georgia, Oklahoma, and the lower Illinois Valley. In all cases, burial populations served as the source of inference.

Where To Go From Here?

Important References on Moundville: Peebles and Kus (1977) provide the basic model distinguishing between ranked and egalitarian systems. Steponaitis (1983) redefines the ceramic chronology at Moundville by seriating the grave assemblages using modern quantitative methods. See also Peebles (1971, 1977, 1981, 1987).

The Southern Cult (or Southeastern Ceremonial Complex): Brown (1976), Waring and Holder (1945).

Social Status: The Archaeology of Slavery

Visitors motoring up the serpentine driveway to Thomas Jefferson's Monticello are first struck by the world-famous architecture, the vast gardens, and the glimpses of mountains in the sprawling Virginia countryside. Walking through Monticello, polite guides provide the visitor with ample (and at times, seemingly endless) details about the life of Jefferson—the third president, the architect, the statesman.

Until recently, you didn't hear much about Thomas Jefferson the slave owner. In the days when Thomas Jefferson lived at Monticello, the approach was called Mulberry Row, lined with nineteen buildings—the houses and workshops of Jefferson's slaves, hired laborers, artisans, and indentured servants. The mansion at Monticello still stands, capturing tourists by the thousands, but all but one of the structures at Mulberry Row have vanished.

Historical archaeologists working at Monticello have brought Mulberry Row back to life. Supported in part by the Thomas Jefferson Memorial Foundation, Inc., William Kelso and his crew have been excavating at Mulberry Row with the specific aim of understanding the patterns of slavery in the antebellum American South (see p. 354).

Jefferson had mixed feelings about slavery, once having remarked that life in a slaveholding society presented much the same problem as having "the wolf by the ears, and we can neither hold him nor safely let him go. Justice is in one scale, the self-preservation in the other" (cited in Kelso 1986, p. 5). Whereas he regarded the institution of slavery as preeminently brutal and immoral—and although he personally favored the abolition of all slavery—as a politician he realized that this solution would not be acceptable in the late-eighteenth-century United States. Jefferson had a plan to emancipate all slaves, but he also doubted whether the two races could successfully create a biracial society, and so he favored a plan to transport free blacks back to Africa or elsewhere.

His liberal sympathies notwithstanding, Jefferson owned a slave force sometimes numbering more than two hundred people. We know from surviving documents that unlike many slave owners of the time, Jefferson felt obligated to protect his slaves from ruthless treatment and to provide more than merely adequate clothing and housing. Jefferson claimed never to require more of his slaves than would be required of free laborers.

With this as background, Kelso and his crew began digging at Mulberry Row in 1980 to learn more about the living and working condition of Jefferson's slaves. Working from an insurance plat of 1796, Kelso suspected that Jefferson had done away with the "barracks" approach to slave housing, introducing single-family dwellings at Monticello. Although few ruins were visible, he soon found by exploratory excavation that the subsurface record of Mulberry Row was relatively undisturbed.

Kelso found not only that Jefferson seems to have improved the quality of slave housing at Monticello but also that a significant diversity in housing existed at any point in time. Whereas some slaves lived in a spartan, dirt-floored log cabin only twelve by fourteen feet, their neighbors lived in a comfortable and pleasing stone house twice that size, with a stone and brick fireplace, wooden flooring, and a neoclassical facade complete with elevated pediment.

It also seems likely that the residents of Mulberry Row were the house servants and artisans who enjoyed a considerably better standard of living than, say, the field hands, who lived in other settlements farther down the mountain. Even along Mulberry Row, there was probably a social hierarchy, with butlers and favorite cooks probably maintaining a better standard of living than maids or laundresses. The archaeological findings tend to confirm this pattern. Although the pig, cow, and deer bones recovered came mostly from poorer cuts of meat, more long bone fragments turned up at house "o" than at some other houses, such as "s," where bones from the less meaty parts were found; the "s" bones were often ground up, suggesting the use of meat in stews.

Excavations in building "o" also turned up a huge, high-quality ceramic assemblage dating around 1770–1800 (see Figure 13–11). Some 289 vessels were recovered, mostly representing thirty different forms and thirty-six different types. Although this tableware

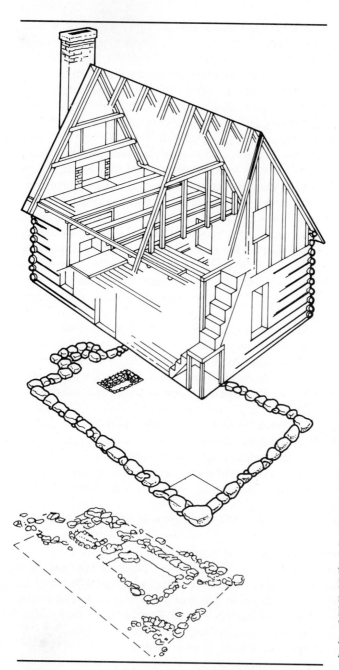

FIGURE 13–11 Artist's reconstruction of slave housing at Monticello. This figure shows a view of a slave quarter at Bremo Recess Plantation (Fluvanna County, Virginia) superimposed over the archaeological plan of a similar structure (servant's house "o") excavated at Monticello (see Kelso 1986, Figure 3). (Courtesy Thomas Jefferson Memorial Foundation, Anna Gruver, William M. Kelso and the Archaeological Institute of America)

might have been no longer suitable for use in the main house, the edges were now cracked or chipped, and the slaves living in house "o" may have dined and drunk from this rather elegant ware.

Historical archaeologists working along coastal Georgia and northern Florida have noted even greater diversity within the slave communities. Excavating at Cannon's Point Plantation, on St. Simons Island (Georgia), John Solomon Otto (1977, 1980, 1984) worked in several dwelling sites formerly occupied by people of three distinctly different racial and legal statuses. At the bottom of the social pyramid were the black slaves, essentially without legal status. In return for their labor in the fields, slaves received rations of food and clothing, gifts of some household articles, and housing. The overseers, free whites, supervised the fieldworkers and were paid modest salaries and provided with housing. Held in low esteem by the plantation employers, the overseers had minimal job security and dignity, whereas the plantation managers enjoyed considerably more social and economic success.

Otto excavated dwelling sites from each socioeconomic and racial category and found the status differences to be clear-cut. Perhaps as a symbol of racial solidarity, the oveseers lived in relatively comfortable houses, more closely resembling those of planters than slaves.

The food remains reflected a somewhat different racial and legal differentiation among these three groups. Although all groups supplemented their diet with wild mammals, fish, and turtles, the slave population was much more dependent on wild taxa than were either the white overseers or the planters.

Food preparation also varied by subordinate and elite status differences. The plantation owners, fed by domestic slaves, often enjoyed roasts and steaks served on transfer-printed platters, followed by seafood- and meat-based soups served in tureens. Food bones recovered from these contexts showed mostly saw marks on the scapulae, ribs, and vertebrae of large mammal bones, showing how the carcasses had been carefully butchered to produce regular cuts and joints for the planter's table.

But because they had less time for such elaborate food preparation, overseers and slaves commonly dined on one-pot meals that could be left simmering for hours. These meals were often served in bowls, and the ceramic inventory reflects this difference. Food bones recovered from slave and overseer quarters often have axe and knife marks because the bones were often cleaved open to increase nourishment; no saw marks are present because the bones were mostly used in stews.

Although archaeologists have had some success at reconstructing slave diets, the measurement of nutritional adequacy remains the subject of considerable debate. Few nutritional studies (of the kind discussed in Chapter 11) have been performed on slave skeletons, and so investigators have relied heavily on contemporary documentation that suggests that malnutrition was rampant in some places. The archaeological data confirm this, indicating that despite the opportunity to supplement their diet with wild foodstuff, slaves appear to have been consistently undernourished. The caloric intake from the core diet of slaves has been estimated to be about 2350 calories (Reitz, Gibbs, and Rathbun 1985, p. 185). By comparison, it has been estimated that adult males expend more than 6000 calories per day while performing moderate work.

Where To Go From Here? _____

The Archaeology of Slave and Plantation Life: Theresa Singleton's edited volume (1985) contains important papers dealing with settlement, artifact, and architectural patterning throughout the American Southeast; Orser's (1984) review paper is useful; Robert Schuyler's pioneering volume (1980a) was the first synthesis of archaeological projects dealing with black and Asian Americans. See also Ascher and Fairbanks (1971), Fairbanks (1977, 1984), Handler and Lange (1978, 1979), Lewis (1978), Otto (1977).

A Caution About "Status Studies" and Anglo-American Archaeology

Americanist archaeologists are increasingly studying "status," in the prehistoric and especially the historic contexts. The degree of social differentiation has variously been expressed in terms of Otto's racial/economic continuum of planter–overseer–slave (see also Miller and Stone 1970), in militaristic terms by using an officer–enlisted man dichotomy (South 1974, Ferguson 1975), or in more generic categories such as "adaptive success" (Hornerkamp 1982) and "ethnicity" (Schuyler 1980a).

It is important to keep in mind the cultural bases of such status categories. When we change cultural reference, we must also be willing to change the operational basis for status. Historical archaeology in the United States is still overwhelmingly oriented toward Anglo-American perspectives. For Deetz (1977a), for instance, the archaeology of colonial America has traditionally referred only to the archaeology of Anglo-America (including American blacks, as they are affiliated with Anglo-American society). But with the increasing interest in the early Hispanic presence in North America, several investigators have begun looking at what status meant in this rather different Euro-American context.

Status, or interpersonal differentiation, operated throughout Spanish Florida, for instance, but in a rather different manner than in Anglo-America. The rigid Spanish class hierarchy, emphasizing both wealth and social position, was transferred wholesale into St. Augustine and the rest of La Florida, where "people differentiated themselves wherever there are disparities of background or belongings to be envied or flaunted" (Bushnell 1981, p. 15). Relative social status in seventeenth-century St. Augustine was also heavily ascribed (conditioned by birthright): "*Criollos* [people of Hispanic descent born in the New World] were generally believed to be inferior both mentally and physically to *peninsulares* [those born in Spain] due to the enervating effects of New World climate" (Deagan 1983, p. 30).

Approaching mortuary variability within the sphere of St. Augustine requires an appreciation of the multiplicity of factors involved. In particular, the manifest inseparability of church and state within La Florida requires that we consider status in a religious light. One's perceived status relative to God unquestionably influenced where (and how) one encountered the afterlife. Some cemeteries were divided into districts for the holy and the unholy (Koch 1983, p. 220), and burial placement inside the church was conditioned at times by dichotomies such as clergy/lay person, blessed/unblessed, single/married, child/adult, and poor/affluent: "Even after death there were class distinctions. The

Hidalgo was buried in a private crypt, either in the sixteen-ducat or the ten-ducat section. Other plots of consecrated earth were priced at three or four ducats. A slave's final resting place cost one ducat, and a pauper was laid away free" (Bushnell 1981, p. 26). Such distinctions were variously reified in space. At times, the Gospel and Epistle sides of a church were differentially employed. Whereas parishioners were usually buried with their feet facing the altar, members of the priesthood were buried in the reverse position— "facing" their congregation.

There was great variability in mortuary practices at sixteenth- and seventeenth-century St. Augustine and its outliers, like Mission Santa Catalina. Thus, simply transferring such simplistic categories as "high status" and "low status" will obscure considerably more than they will clarify.

Summary

Contemporary archaeologists have been making important strides toward inferring the nature of prehistoric social organization from the archaeological record. Social organization encompasses two elements: the division of a society into smaller groups (or social units), and the allocation of a recognized set of social positions (statuses) that are accompanied by appropriate behavior patterns (roles). Archaeologists are currently examining both social groups and social statuses.

Extinct residential groups are reconstructed by analyzing the problem at four levels. Individual behavior is most commonly reflected in material culture at the attribute level of patterning. This is the initial level of analysis. The behavior of various minimal social groups—for example, families, hunting associations, and war parties—is most commonly reflected in the archaeological record at the tool-kit level. Community social patterning is generally evident in terms of individual households, which themselves are commonly arranged into larger-order subsistence units. Finally, behavior at the overall societal level is reflected in the regional settlement pattern, as discussed in some detail in the last chapter.

Archaeologists also attempt to reconstruct extinct patterns of social status and ranking. Status can be apportioned in one of two ways: An ascribed status is assigned to individuals at birth, without regard to innate differences or abilities. Status can also be achieved in those societies that prefer to allocate it as a reward for competition and group effort. Egalitarian societies are those in which the number of such valued social positions is roughly equivalent to the number of persons available to fill them. In ranked societies, the number of valued status positions is somehow limited, creating an intrinsic social hierarchy and unequal access to the basis of subsistence. Archaeologists are now capable of dealing with the mechanisms of status allocation, largely through the study of mortuary patterns. The critical assumption in such research is that persons who were treated differentially in life were also treated differentially in death. In other words, human burials represent the fossil terminal status of the individual, a basis on which the archaeologist can reconstruct patterns of ranking throughout societies.

CHAPTER 14

How People Relate to Their Cosmos: Religion and Ideology

An honest God is the noblest work of man.
—Robert Ingersoll

The religions and ideologies of the past have been of compelling interest to archaeologists since the very beginning of the discipline. We saw in Chapter 1 how Nabonidus, the sixth-century B.C. Babylonian king, searched among the ruins of his empire to pursue his worship of the ancient gods. The same was true of Petrarch, the early Renaissance scholar who turned to the religions of classical antiquity for moral guidance. In this chapter we shall discuss the major features of religious behavior and what clues remain for the archaeologist.

We begin by looking at religion. One basic premise common to every religion is a belief in the existence of souls, supernatural things, and supernatural forces. Religion, in effect, is a society's mechanism for relating these supernatural phenomena to the everyday world—a set of rituals, rationalized by myth, that mobilizes supernatural powers for the purpose of achieving or preventing transformations of state in humans and nature (see Wallace 1966, p. 107). Wallace's definition contains three operative elements—transformation of state, myth, and ritual—and we shall briefly examine each.

Transformation of State: Religion is universal because of the ubiquitous cultural desire to influence change in people and nature. Sometimes the objective is to effect the quickest possible transformation; sometimes the goal is to prevent an undesired change from occurring. The target of the transformation can be either a group or an individual, and the change itself can be minor or radical. Regardless, the prime objective of religious behavior is to influence the course of this change by appeal to a supernatural power, a power quite separate from that of the muscles, the brain, or the elements of nature (Wallace 1966, p. 107). It follows that if people were wholly satisfied with (or resigned to) the status quo, there would be no need for religion, and indeed, religious behavior itself would atrophy.

Myth: A major component of society's overall cosmology, myths identify and explain the nature of the relevant supernatural entities. Myths define how human beings interact with the supernatural and rationalize the various actions directed toward these supernatural structures. In many traditional societies, myths take the form of a narrative, describing events in the careers of the supernatural beings; more technologically advanced societies (with professional priesthoods) tend to codify their myths into an official mythology such as the Bible, the Koran, and other sacred texts.

Ritual: Religious beliefs are manifested in everyday life in a "program of ritual," a succession of discrete events such as prayer, music, feasting, sacrifice, and taboos. These stereotyped sequences are the cultural mechanisms by which individuals attempt to intercede with the activities of the supernatural.

It is thus fair to say that ritual comprises the fundamental aspect of religion. Myth becomes the secondary element, the cultural theory that rationalizes the ritual. Myth explains the nature of the powers involved, in setting forth the proper sequence of actions and in accounting for the observed successes and failures (Wallace 1966, pp. 106–107). In sum, religion consists of ritual, supported by myth, directed at a desired transformation of state.

Here, we shall examine briefly how past religions can be explored in the archaeological record. Wallace's anthropological definition of religion is particularly relevant to archaeology because of its emphasis on ritual and its de-emphasis of myth. Most rituals, after all, are closely related to material culture and, as such, are often represented in the archaeological record. Myth has few real-world correlates and is rarely preserved. The analysis of ritual behavior is thus archaeology's major contribution to the study of past religions.

Reconstructing Ritual Behavior

Religion: A daughter of Hope and Fear, explaining to Ignorance the nature of the Unknowable.
—Ambrose Bierce

A primary feature of religious behavior is ritual, or stereotyped, often obsessively repetitive behavioral sequences (Kluckhohn 1942, p. 78). Ritual sequences themselves consist of a number of individual acts, what Wallace termed "the smallest religious things" (1966, p. 67). Prayer, for example, is one part of many rituals, comprising a standardized, stylized manner of conveying one's feelings to the supernatural. Music— including dancing, singing, and instrument playing—is another component of ritual that is present in nearly every religion. Some rituals employ various artificial manipulations designed to produce the proper spiritual state, such as drugs and/or sensory or physical deprivation. Rituals are generally reinforced with a sacred oral or written literature, a set of sacred objects that often possess supernatural power (mana), a sequence of taboos, a variety of feasts and/or sacrifices, and, of course, a wealth of symbolism.

The primacy of ritual is instrumental: just as the blade of the knife has instrumental priority over the handle, and the barrel of a gun over the stock, so does ritual have instrumental priority over myth. It is ritual which accomplishes what religion sets out to do.
—Anthony Wallace

Wallace (1966, Chapter 3) distinguishes several categories of ritual: technology, therapy, social control, salvation, and revitalization. Of particular importance to archaeologists are technological rituals, as these aspects of religion are most often reflected in the archaeological record. Some technological rituals attempt to extract ecological information directly from nature (divination), and other such rituals attempt to control hunting success (through the availability and abundance of game), agricultural productivity, or the safety of flocks and herds. These so-called rites of intensification are directly aimed at protecting the technoeconomic base of the society.

We shall distinguish between calendrical and critical rituals (Titiev 1960). Because of their nature, rituals based on calendrical events can be scheduled and announced long in advance of their actual occurrence. The *calendrical ritual* has the advantage of giving its participants ample time to develop a sense of shared anticipation, and a chance to prepare for the big event. The gigantic Shalako figures appear in Zuni every December, just as the Western world celebrates Christmas annually on December 25. Both are examples of calendrical rituals.

But because the timing of calendrical rituals is so tightly circumscribed, these rites cannot possibly satisfy the immediate desires for supernatural assistance or divine comfort; this is the function of the *critical ritual*. Unlike the calendrical ritual (which is invariably communal), the critical ritual can be designed to benefit the entire society, a relatively small group, or even a single individual (Titiev 1960, p. 294). Sometimes critical rites are held to counteract a public emergency, but more often they are held when some important object has been stolen or somebody has become ill, and at such inevitable, yet noncalendrical, events as birth and death.

Critical Rituals of the Past

Mortuary Practices As Ritual Behavior

Archaeologists are most familiar with critical ritual behavior through evidence of human mortuary practices. In fact, cultural anthropologists rely heavily on burial practices in reconstructing the origins of religion. The argument goes like this: As early Paleolithic populations increased in size, people grew more accustomed to social living, and their universe became more culturally oriented and distinct from the natural environment. Families became more closely united. Archaeologists generally believe that an elaborate body of cosmological belief existed as early as Middle Paleolithic times, say, 75,000 years ago. Human burials are especially indicative of this ideological reification. "The mere fact of intentional burial implies that the living felt sufficient concern for the recently deceased that disposal of their body was a matter of group planning and execution. Intentional burial further implies that there existed beliefs concerned with an afterlife. Thus we have the beginnings of what may be termed religion" (Hester 1976, p. 146).

We have already encountered the sixty-thousand-year-old Neanderthal burials discovered by Ralph Solecki at Shanidar Cave (Chapter 11). The skeleton, called Shanidar IV, was encased in plaster, and when examined in the laboratory years later, it was discovered to be four individuals—three adults and an infant (Figure 14-1). When Leroi-Gourhan (1975) tested the Shanidar IV samples for pollen, she discovered pollen and interpreted the finds as indicating that Shanidar IV had been accompanied by a bouquet of brightly colored wildflowers, woven into the branches of a pinelike shrub. She concluded that the people found in the Shanidar IV grave were laid to rest sometime between late May and early July (see Chapter 11 for a discussion of potential site formation problems involved with the Shanidar burials).

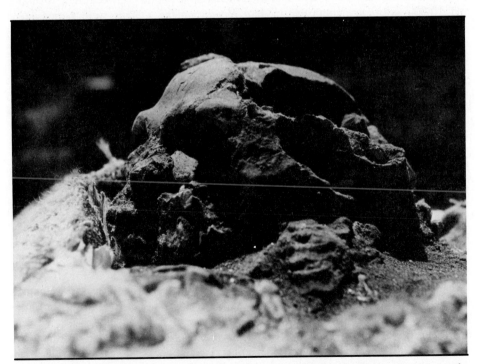

FIGURE 14-1 Skull of Neanderthal burial at Shanidar Cave; this person was probably killed by a roof fall inside the cave. (Courtesy Ralph Solecki)

On the basis of Shanidar IV, Solecki concluded:

> With the finding of flowers in association with Neanderthals we are brought suddenly
> to the realization that the universality of mankind and the love of beauty go beyond the
> boundary of our own species. No longer can we deny the early men the full range of
> human feelings and experience. (Solecki 1971, p. 250)

Although there are some problems with the specific interpretation, it is clear that the burial
was intentional, and many anthropologists interpret this behavior as signifying a belief in
the afterworld.

We have only a glimpse of what other Neanderthal burial practices were like during
the Middle Paleolithic in Eurasia. Harrold (1980) sees a trend toward differential treatment according to sex: Eight of the ten known Neanderthal males were accompanied by
grave furnishings—but not one of the seven females was so accompanied. These mortuary
practices have been considered the initial signs of purposeful and ritualized burial of the
dead. The grave furniture includes animal parts, often interpreted as offerings for use in
life after death. Such burials also suggest a conventionalized approach to death, a
disruptive event in all human societies. The very fact of establishing such a convention
suggests a cultural coding and externalizing of emotional reponses and a shared body of
ideas (R. White 1986, p. 19).

During the succeeding Eurasian Upper Paleolithic period (between roughly 35,000
and 10,000 B.P.), taxonomically modern *Homo sapiens sapiens* were buried in an
astonishing variety of positions. Burial practices also vary according to the nature and
quantity of grave goods, the number of people interred in the same grave, and the way in
which the body was decorated. Unlike the earlier Neanderthal burials, males and females
are treated comparably. Harrold (1980) interpreted this to mean that at least some females
in Upper Paleolithic society enjoyed social statuses as complex as those available to
males. Randall White (1986) also interprets this critical, noncalendrical ritual behavior as
suggesting the presence of age-graded social status during the Upper Paleolithic.

Public Architecture As Ritual Behavior

Evidence of critical rituals is also available to the archaeologist in architectural remains.
Kent Flannery and Joyce Marcus (1976) reconstructed the evolution of public spaces in
prehistoric Oaxaca, Mexico. The period from 2000 B.C. to A.D. 1 is particularly important
because this is when established village life evolved, bringing with it the origins of social
ranking and ultimately the rise of the Mesoamerican state. Flannery and Marcus demonstrated that in addition to the well-known ecological consequences of settled village life,
certain changes in social and religious structure also occurred. The physical development
of "public spaces" is interesting because it indirectly mirrors the ritual behavior during
these changing times.

During the preceramic era, architecture—public or otherwise—was virtually unknown. Dwellings were probably similar to the temporary structures noted earlier in the
discussion of the Reese River Shoshone. One site in Oaxaca, Gheo-Shih, provides some

clues. The site was occupied between about 5000 and 4000 B.C., probably by a macro-band during the rainy season of July and August.

The most interesting feature at Gheo-Shih consisted of two parallel lines of boulders, running for about twenty meters. The seven-meter space between them was swept clean, containing virtually no artifacts. Flannery and Marcus (1976, p. 207) suggest that this feature is analogous to the cleared "dance grounds" of the Great Basin Shoshone. Writing specifically about the Reese River Shoshone, Steward noted: "When visitors arrived [at the fall pine-nut festival] Tutuwa assigned each family a place in the camp circle which surrounded the dance ground . . . it had an opening on the eastern side, directly opposite which Tutuwa camped, and a pine-nut tree or post in the center. People merely erected temporary windbreaks for shelter" (1938, p. 107). Using the Shoshone analogue, Flannery and Marcus infer that the early Oaxacan hunter-gatherers placed their public structure near the heart of camp, and whatever activity occurred there was observed by everyone; it could not have been used for "secret rites" (such as take place in the kivas of the American Southwest). Moreover, such temporary features, requiring neither maintenance nor particular architectural skill, were probably used for ad hoc critical ritual. Similar areas persisted at San José Mogote until about 1600 B.C. in the form of small open areas, set apart from residential areas by a double line of staggered posts.

The first real public buildings at San José Mogote appear in about 1500 to 1300 B.C. In the western portion of the hamlet, a special area seems to have been set aside for the construction of a public area, the structures being rectangular, one-room buildings, each with an altar built against the southern wall. Directly north of this altar was a storage pit. The entire floor and pit were plastered with white stucco.

Construction continued with the erection of an impressive acropolis atop Mound I at San José Mogote. Faced with roughly cut limestone blocks (often weighing over a ton), the acropolis contained the remains of an adult sacrificial victim, buried beneath one retaining wall. The acropolis is the earliest example of a complex public building "removed from the heart of the village and raised to a new position some fifteen meters above" (Flannery and Marcus 1976, p. 215). Although visible from some distance, the buildings had only limited access by members of the community.

This trend culminated in about 500 B.C. in the founding of Monte Albán, located on a mountaintop some 400 meters above the valley. The plaza, about 300 meters by 150 meters, is located on one of the least accessible spots in the Valley of Oaxaca. Somewhat later (about A.D. 1), an entirely new kind of public building appeared, the royal residence (or palace). The ceremonial ball court also appeared about this time.

Architectural details aside, the evolution of public buildings tells a great deal about the evolution of ritual behavior. Even during the initial hunting-gathering period, a portion of the village had been set aside for "public" purposes; the space was accessible to all; and the rituals were observable by everyone. Somewhat later, ritual precincts were removed from ordinary habitation areas, but the citizens still had full access to the area. Flannery and Marcus refer to these structures as "generalized public buildings" (1976, p. 220). Two new trends occurred during the Middle Formative period. Ceremonial buildings were grouped by threes or fours facing inward to a common patio, rather than toward the domestic structures. These structures were also placed on low hills, elevated over the community.

The Flannery–Marcus architectural study spans the transition from the time of seminomadic hunting-gathering bands to that of sedentary village farmers. We also presume that ritual life underwent some profound changes. The early foragers seem to have engaged primarily in unscheduled critical rituals, such as initiation ceremonies, gambling, dancing, and athletic competition. These ad hoc rituals gradually were transformed into the more scheduled calendrical rituals that are more characteristic of sedentary agricultural villages. Often, such time-structured ceremonies were closely related to the predictable harvest and planting cycles. In later times carved monuments were erected, pertaining to the typical Mesoamerican 260-day calendar. Finally, by A.D. 1, a lavish set of public institutions was headquartered at Monte Albán atop the mountain dominating the Oaxacan landscape. By this time the agricultural village had evolved into a full-scale state organization.

Archaeoastronomy: Reconstructing Calendrical Ritual

The fault, dear Brutus, is not in our stars but in ourselves.
—William Shakespeare

The endless shifting of the sun, the moon, and the stars is one constant that must have influenced—in one way or another—every society on earth. Michael Coe suggested, for instance, that "if any one trait can be said to be distinctive of native cultures of prehispanic Mesoamerica, it is a deep concern with the heavenly bodies and the passage of time as marked by the apparent movements of these objects" (Coe 1975, p. 3). And yet, until the last couple of decades, Americanist archaeology has almost totally ignored the field of **archaeoastronomy**. Because of this avoidance, the study of past astronomical practices has been the subject of feverish speculation, some of it by the "crackpot fringe" that haunts the archaeological profession: If it wasn't visiting aliens, it must have been survivors from Atlantis.

The situation has changed recently as legitimate archaeological and ethnographic inquiries are being made into the relationship of religion and cosmology to astronomical phenomena. Before turning to these strictly archaeological assessments, let us introduce astronomical phenomena as ritual by introducing the notion of the *horizon calendar*. The Hopi Indians of Arizona began their agricultural season in February by clearing the fields, and the cycle ends in the final days of September when the last maize (corn) and beans were gathered. Although the precise time of each agricultural operation is determined by weather conditions, the entire cycle can be anticipated by a horizon calendar. That is, both the ritual and the actual agricultural practices are regulated by the daily shift in the position of the sunrise on the horizon. The slightest irregularities on the skyline were known to the Hopi, and reference points are established to pinpoint each change in the sun's position (see Figure 14–2). Many such horizon points are in turn associated with rituals or agricultural operations, due to commence when the sun rises behind the designated spot. "For a well-educated Hopi such terms as *neverktcomo* and *lohalin* have as precise a significance as have for us May 3rd and June 21st with which they correspond" (Forde 1963, p. 227). The daily observation of these solar positions was the responsibility of the "sun watcher," a religious official whose duty was to forewarn the people of upcoming important dates; he also kept a tally on a notched stick. The Hopi solar observations are perfect examples of what Titiev (1960) referred to as calendrical rituals.

But it is one thing to discuss the significance of solar ritual in a documented ethnographic case such as the Hopi, and quite another matter to establish such behavior prehistorically. The emerging field of archaeoastronomy still, quite frankly, meets with considerable skepticism by many archaeologists. In the following examples we shall see how scholars are attempting to study cosmology and ideology through astronomic indicators. Many cases introduce methods and techniques alien to many conventional archaeologists, and these innovations only add to the controversial nature of the findings.

The Caracol: Ancient Astronomical Observatory?

Chichén Itzá was an important Maya ceremonial center in Late Classic times, built in the *Puuc* style. Late in the tenth century A.D., it was invaded by Toltecs from Highland Mexico. In fact, this invasion legend has been correlated with the migration legends of Topiltzin Quetzalcoatl from Tula, the Toltec capital. The art and architecture at Chichén

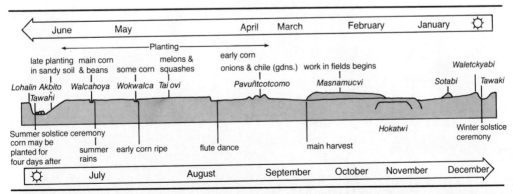

FIGURE 14–2 Horizon calendar used by the Hopi at the First Mesa Pueblo of Shimopovi. Indicating appropriate dates for agricultural operations and ceremonies, this calendar works because of the daily shifts in position of the sunrise on the horizon (see Forde 1963, Figure 75). (Courtesy Methuen & Co., Ltd.)

Itzá is similar in many details to that at Tula, and some reliefs and paintings at Chichén depict Mexican warriors defeating, capturing, and receiving tribute from the defeated Mayas.

The Caracol is considered to be the first important building of Toltec (or "Mexican") influence built at Chichén Itzá (Figure 14–3). It has always been something of a puzzle: a peculiarly shaped building, with a round tower set on a squared base. In fact, its non-Maya, non-Toltec configuration has sparked some strong feelings from Maya scholars. In a classic burst of indignation, J. E. S. Thompson wrote:

> Every city sooner or later erects some atrocious building that turns the stomach: London has its Albert Hall; New York, its Grant's Tomb; and Harvard, its Memorial Hall. If one can free oneself of the enchantment which antiquity is likely to induce and contemplate this building in all its horror from a strictly aesthetic point of view, one will find none of these is quite so hideous as the Caracol at Chichén Itzá. . . . It stands like a two-decker wedding cake on the square carton in which it came. Something was pretty clearly wrong with the taste of the architects who built it. . . .(1945, p. 10)

Thompson was not alone in his dismay at the architecture of the Caracol. Some have suggested it may have functioned as a *gnomon,* its vertical column casting a shadow and thereby providing a huge sundial for those living at Chichén Itzá. Others thought the

FIGURE 14–3 The Caracol at Chichén Itzá as it appeared when Frederick Catherwood, English artist and architect, visited the site in 1841. (Courtesy the American Museum of Natural History)

Caracol might have been a civic or military watchtower. And more than a century ago, some scholars remarked that the Caracol may have functioned as an observatory, and several others simply passed along that suggestion, without either serious investigation or critical comment. In fact, nobody bothered to make systematic astronomical observations until 1973–1974, when Anthony Aveni, Sharon Gibbs, and Horst Hartung took an engineer's transit and collected an impressive array of alignments and distances at Chichén Itzá.

Based on these findings, Aveni (1981, p. 39) claims that the Caracol is "the real stone calendar of the Mesoamerican world." The measurements by Aveni and his colleagues revealed a number of significant astronomical events coinciding with many projected alignments, and several others appeared to have astronomical matches that they could recognize. Aveni and his colleagues proposed no "grand cosmic scheme" to account for the astronomical design of the Caracol, but they believe strongly that the tower was erected specifically for astronomical purposes. The directions of the lower and upper platforms seem to have been laid out deliberately to point to major horizon events involving both the sun and the planet Venus. The circular building itself symbolizes both the Maya and Toltec God of Venus (Quetzalcoatl/Kukulcan).

The window complex provides for numerous sight lines, which these researchers think are for the Venus setting points because of the observed accuracy of fit and also because of the historical evidence regarding the importance of that planet in Mesoamerican cosmology. They further suggest that astronomical observations made throughout the year in different parts of the building by an astronomer-priest could have been used to inform the population of impending events of religious, civil, or agricultural significance.

Situated on the flat landscape of Yucatán, Chichén Itzá lacked natural horizon markers for charting the course of the setting sun, moon, and stars. And yet, the cyclical motions in the heavens were thought to be too obvious for the Maya-Toltecs—"so addicted to the keeping of a calendar"—to neglect. So they built the Caracol to create the artificial sight lines necessary to keep their calendar accurate and operating.

Alexander Thom's Archaeoastronomy

Another influential astroarchaeologist is Alexander Thom, emeritus professor of engineering science at Oxford University. Shunning most of the publicity that invariably accompanies this spectacular brand of prehistoric research, Thom plugged away for decades, surveying and interpreting a staggering number of prehistoric British and French sites.

Thom concentrated on **megalithic** sites consisting largely of tombs and sacred monuments of the middle Neolithic period (roughly the second millennium B.C.). He personally mapped 450 megalithic sites, meticulously recording the positions of the remaining stones and features (see Thom 1967, 1971). He also paid special attention to horizon features (not unlike the Hopi horizon calendar) that could have been used as engineering "foresights" and "backsights" during the construction phase.

Deeply impressed with the skill displayed in constructing such ritual alignments,

Thom believes that the builders of these monuments employed standard units of measurement: the megalithic yard (2.72 feet) and the megalithic fathom (5.44 feet). Although Thom interpreted the spread of the megalithic yard in terms of large-scale prehistoric migrations, it seems more plausible that the megalithic yard closely approximated the human pace and that the megalithic fathom was close to a double pace (which were used in Roman times).

Thom also tried to determine exactly how the hundreds of megalithic ritual circles were planned and built. Although many had noted that the megalithic circles are slightly out of round and lopsided, most simply wrote off the distortion to crude or sloppy construction methods. Although the geometry is too complicated to consider here, Thom finally decided that the circles were distorted because megalithic people simply refused to accept the actual value of pi as 3.1416. Instead, these builders simply rounded off pi to the nearest whole number, and Thom notes that repeatedly many of the smaller circles tended to have a diameter of about twenty-two feet—exactly eight megalithic yards—and were built on a pi value of roughly three. On the basis of sophisticated mathematical reasoning, Thom postulated (1) that the circle dimensions conform to integral numbers and (2) the builders must also have discovered the principle of Pythagorean triangles.

Thom was also deeply impressed with the accuracy of megalithic construction. The sprawling site of Avebury, in Wiltshire, England, for instance, was constructed with an accuracy approaching one in one thousand (accuracy that can be achieved today only by experienced surveyors with excellent optical equipment). Thom proposed that an elaborate construction technique was used at Avebury based on complex geometrics and the megalithic yard. He also cites a list of over 250 alleged alignments with the stars, the sun, and the moon. Thom argues that the stars were harnessed as timekeepers and even postulates how the megalithic calendar operated: At least sixteen equal divisions ("months"), each made up of twenty-two- to twenty-three-day periods, were used. Thom concluded: "One can only surmise that, having no pen and paper, [the megalithic architect] was building in stone a record of his achievements in geometry and perhaps also in arithmetic" (Thom 1966, p. 126).

The work of Alexander Thom directly places in question much of the traditional archaeological interpretation. Should he be correct, then the megalithic builders and priests possessed sophisticated astronomical and arithmetic capabilities, far greater than we have given them credit for. Although archaeological opinion changes slowly, Thom's meticulous and sophisticated research has already convinced many that he is correct (e.g., Atkinson 1966b and Renfrew 1973, pp. 337–339). The statement by Atkinson is enlightening in this regard:

> It is hardly surprising that many prehistorians either ignore the implications of Thom's work, because they do not understand them, or resist them because it is more comfortable to do so. I have myself gone through the latter process: but I have come to the conclusion that to reject Thom's thesis because it does not conform to the model of prehistory on which I was brought up involves also the acceptance of improbabilities of an even higher order. I am prepared, in other words, to believe that my model of European prehistory is wrong, rather than that the results presented by Thom are due to nothing but chance. (1975, p. 51)

Alexander Marshack's Archaeoastronomy

Another controversial investigator of prehistoric calendrical rituals is Alexander Marshack, who for the last quarter-century has been studying the nature of Upper Paleolithic engraving from throughout the Old World. In *The Roots of Civilization* (1972a), Marshack discusses how his research began as a relatively straightforward search for the origins of scientific thought. To his surprise, Marshack found that scientific thinking could be traced back only to the Greeks, and then the trail disappeared. Largely because he felt that "something was missing," Marshack has personally studied almost the entire body of the engraved, symbolic materials from the Upper Paleolithic.

Marshack's approach can be demonstrated by his analysis of an incised bone artifact from the Upper Paleolithic site of La Marche in central France (Marshack 1972b). Several hundred stone and bone artifacts were excavated at La Marche in 1937 and 1938, the majority of them coming from Magdalenian levels, approximately 12,000 to 13,000 B.C. One of the visually less exciting pieces is a discolored, deteriorated bone fragment, which has been engraved with a series of faint marks and lines (see Figure 14–4).

Marshack analyzed the La Marche bone over a three-year period, and his results reveal an unsuspected complexity. The bone had apparently been a shaft straightener, once broken and then reshaped into a pressure flaker for making stone tools. Of interest here are the intricate engravings, barely visible on the surface. Figure 14–5 shows a schematic rendition of the La Marche bone. Note particularly the two horses carved near the bottom. The unbroken horse was added second and seems to represent a pregnant mare with a rounded belly. Careful line-by-line analysis indicates that this mare in fact has three eyes, three ears, a second mane, and two backs.

Marshack's microscopic technique is similar to the ballistic analysis used in law enforcement. Each minute scratch is examined to determine the nature of the tool that performed the carving: Some tools are relatively flat and blunt, and others make a deeper, more V-shaped groove. Such analysis revealed that each of the mare's three ears was carved by a different stone point, presumably at different times.

A series of tiny marks covering the rest of the La Marche bone comprise a tangled sequence of engraving that Marshack thinks is neither random nor decorative but, rather, a complex form of notation. The marks appear in blocks (or sets), each quite distinct when closely examined. Row H, for instance, has been inscribed by a cutting edge that flares near the top, creating an irregular angle in cross section. The marks are created by a turning or twisting stroke, set at an angle of about fifteen degrees to the baseline of the bone. By contrast, the engravings above Row H are perpendicular to the axis of the bone and required only a single downward stroke.

Marshack's microscopic analysis indicates that at least six different tool tips were used to engrave the various sets of dots and lines. The internal complexity of the marking sequence suggests that the marks were accumulated through time. The two surfaces were probably carved at different times yet almost certainly within the same cultural contexts.

But what do these tiny marks mean? A number of hypotheses have been considered to explain engravings such as those on the La Marche bone. One investigator suggested

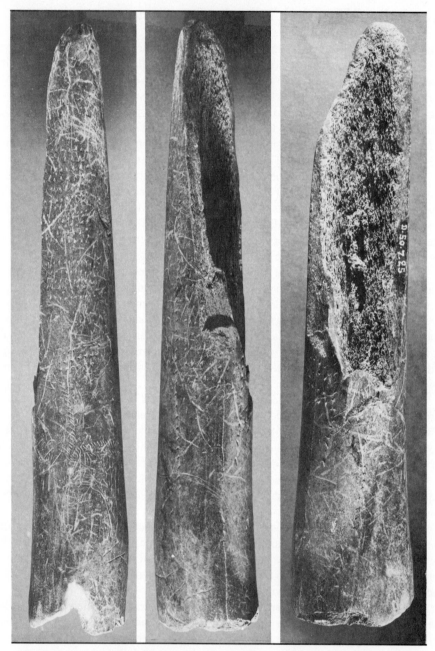

FIGURE 14–4   Three views of the La Marche bone. Note the faint, yet distinctive engravings on all sides. (Courtesy Alexander Marshack and the American Association for the Advancement of Science)

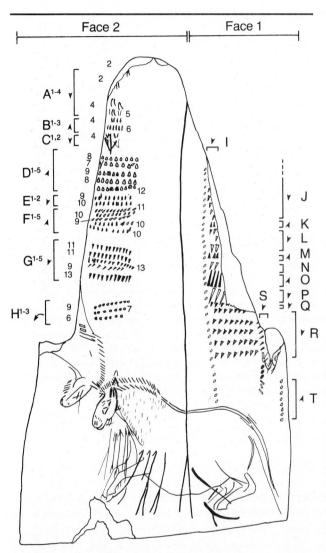

FIGURE 14–5 Marshack's schematic analysis of all intentional marks on both faces of the La Marche bone. Note that the engravings are broken down into sets, that several different engraving points were used, and also the sum of marks in each set. Also shown are the two horses, with later engraved additions. (Courtesy Alexander Marshack and the American Association for the Advancement of Science)

that the marks are hunting tallies, and another sees a recurrent use of the number seven, perhaps a ritual number.

Marshack proposes that the marks could be intentionally accumulated sets expressing observed phases of the moon, and he tested the La Marche bone against a lunar model (Figure 14–6). Beginning with Block A in the upper right corner, the counts are arranged sequentially, as indicated by microscopic analysis, with an overlay of modern astronomic

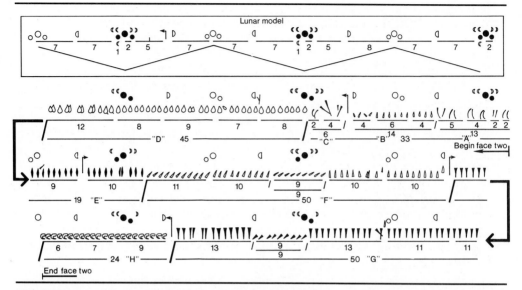

FIGURE 14–6 Marshack's lunar "test" of the La Marche engravings. This chart begins at the upper right and proceeds sequentially in alternative directions along each line, ending at the bottom left. One space in each two months (the right-angle arrow) represents zero, providing the proper total of fifty-nine marks for two months in a model scaled to sixty. The lettered sets, subsets, and cue marks are indicated, along with the astronomically correct observation point. The differences in the engraved points are schematically rendered. (Courtesy Alexander Marshack and the American Association for the Advancement of Science)

observations placed atop the counts. The darkened circles represent invisibility, and the white circles represent the full moon.

The fit with the lunar model is surprisingly close. Of twenty-three subsets of marks observable on the single face of the La Marche bone, only four (E^2, F^2, $G^{1,2}$) fail to begin or end at normal phases of the moon. Of these, three subsets correspond to the difficult period of the crescents and new moon, when precise observation is difficult. According to this interpretation, the marks cover a span of seven-and-a-half months.

But why were Magdalenian hunter-gatherers concerned some fourteen thousand years ago with recording the phases of the moon? Looking at ethnographic data from a range of Native American cultures, Marshack notes that in almost all cases, shamans maintained lunar counts in one form or another: Months were named according to their seasonal and regional significance, triggering appropriate ritual or economic responses. Marshack believes that the Upper Paleolithic notations, such as those on the La Marche bone, were also maintained by ritual specialists. If the La Marche count began with the late March thaw, then the notation would have ended in mid-November, approximately the time of the first snow. Such a sequence depends only on sequential marking and can be maintained even without named or recognized months or complex arithmetic. Marshack suggests that both the counting ritual and the reuse of animals on the La Marche bone strongly argue for a "scheduled," "time-factored" cultural year, even in Upper Paleolithic times.

To Marshack, the cognitive strategies used in the La Marche (and many other) notations differ from those employed by later record keepers living in settled farming villages. He thinks that the Upper Paleolithic engravings were made and used by the engraver alone. As later cultural and ecological pressures changed, notational systems of necessity became more stable and interpersonal, leading finally to the development of true writing.

Marshack's research remains "pioneering," and reactions to it are characteristically mixed. Many archaeologists are skeptical, suggesting that Marshack has "gone beyond the data," ignored "all likely alternative explanations," and failed to present the data necessary to support his hypotheses. But other archaeologists have lauded Marshack's analytical approach, using terms such as "significant breakthrough" and "breaking new ground." One investigator raves that Marshack "has come as close as any archaeologist ever to reading the mind of ancient man."

Although some skepticism remains about the interpretations, many recognize the potential of Marshack's analytical technique. One interesting follow-up study was conducted by Randall White (1982), who undertook experiments with *burins,* chisel-ended stone tools common in both European and North American assemblages. White manufactured a sample of twenty-five burins, then conducted use–wear experimentation on fresh bone and sandstone cobbles. After examining the edge damage incurred on the burins—the main reason for the experiment—White made a curious discovery. Quite by accident, when preparing some of the worked bone surfaces for photography, he discovered that the various burin experiments had produced some characteristic incisions on the bone. When used for scraping, the burins produced a flat, shallow, U-shaped groove; when the corner of the burin was offset and used for scraping, a characteristic V-shaped groove resulted; "graving" produced a symmetrical V-shaped cross section.

Thinking that this three-part subdivision of incisions "was too good to be true," White compared his results with the excellent microscopic photographs published by Marshack, to see how closely the experimental incisions compared with examples from Paleolithic portable art (like the La Marche bone). The fit was precise: Unknown to White, Marshack had identified precisely the same incision types on Paleolithic materials. In one sense, White's experiments contradict Marshack's hypothesis that different incision cross sections must have been produced by different tools: White produced three characteristic cross sections with the same burin, simply held three different ways. If upheld in subsequent experimentation, this finding would suggest that such artifacts might have been produced in a single "sitting" rather than over the course of a longer period, with different tools. Whether or not the La Marche bone is a lunar counting device is, however, a different question.

The archaeological community still does not know what to do with Marshack's research. Like Thom, he has begun asking new questions, generating new data, and offering new interpretations.

WHERE TO GO FROM HERE?

General References on Archaeoastronomy: Aveni (1981) provides the best overview of field; see also Baity (1973) for a dated summary of archaeoastronomical studies throughout the world. P. Brown (1976) provides an excellent nontechnical summary of the European megalithic research; see also Renfrew (1973). Aveni (1975, 1977) provides a great deal of material regarding New World astroarchaeology; and for specific studies see Aveni (1972), Aveni and Gibbs (1976), Dow (1967), Eddy (1974), Fuson (1969), Nuttall (1906), Thompson (1974), and Wedel (1967). For a less sympathetic view, see Mulholland (1978) and Rowe (1979).

    The Hopi Horizon Calendar: Fewkes (1893, 1898), Ellis (1975), Forde (1963), and Parsons (1925) discuss Pueblo observatories in detail, emphasizing their recognition in the archaeological record; see also Zeilik (1985).

    Alexander Thom's Research on Megalithic Alignments: Thom (1966, 1967, 1971); for a good synthesis, see Aveni (1981). Some favorable comment: Atkinson (1966b; 1975, p. 51), MacKie (1977), Renfrew (1973, pp. 337–339), Wood (1978). Some skeptical opinions: Burl (1979), Patrick (1979).

    Marshack on Paleolithic Calendrical Rituals: Marshack's major early publication is *Roots of Civilization* (1972a); see also (1972b). Some positive responses: Hester (1976, p. 181), Kessler (1972), Kurten (1972), Sieveking (1972). Some conflicting interpretations: Absolon (1957), Frolov (1970, 1971). Some skeptical reactions: Brose (1972), Lynch (1972), Rosenfeld (1972).

    Archaeoastronomy, published once a year as a supplement to the *Journal for the History of Astronomy,* carries articles relevant to the interdisciplinary study of astronomical practices; first published in 1979.

    Subscription information: Center for Archaeoastronomy, Space Sciences Building, University of Maryland, College Park, Md. 20742.

    Archaeoastronomy Bulletin is also published by the Center for Archaeoastronomy at the University of Maryland.

Analyzing the Functions of Ritual and Ideology

When people perform rituals, their intentions are explicit: They want to control nature, make people well, make people sick, save souls, or revitalize their society. But a related issue invariably arises: How successful is religious ritual in achieving these goals? The problem, of course, is how to deal with adaptation in the ritual context. To most anthropologists the "function" of a cultural element is its contribution to the survival of the society (see Wallace 1966, p. 169). Archaeologists have relatively little difficulty in determining the function of a particular hunting strategy, the function of a Clovis point, or even the function of a burial mound. All of these activities are closely linked to the society's technological, ecological, and demographic adaptation, and the linkages are not difficult to make even in the archaeological record.

But to determine the function of expressly religious behavior is more difficult, precisely because the obvious technological and ecological linkages are lacking. Vogt (1952), for instance, conducted a classic study of water witches (or dowsers). Even today, thousands of rural American farmers and ranchers use water witches to help them find the best location to drill for water. Despite the lack of well-documented empirical support, these farmers steadfastly hold on to the custom of dowsing for water. Why?

Or consider the case of voodoo death. Throughout Latin America, Africa, Australia, and New Zealand, deaths due to voodoo curses have been repeatedly reported by competent observers (e.g., Cannon 1942). Both American water witching and voodoo are examples of contemporary ritual behavior. But what is the function of these rituals? Does water witching really find water? Why is the custom still practiced so widely today? Does voodoo really kill people? If not, why is the ritual practiced in so many contemporary cultures?

In one sense, these functional interpretations depend on the empirical evidence alone. How well do dowsers really perform in predicting the location of underground water? Not very well, according to Vogt (1952). Or what about voodoo? Can black magic really cause death (yes, by literally frightening the victim to death, according to Cannon (1942)?

The facts rarely speak for themselves. As explained in Chapter 3, anthropological interpretation really depends on one's theoretical perspective. Some mainstreams of anthropological thought assign strategic priority to matters of technology and ecology; other approaches emphasize symbolic, structural, or cognitive components.

Archaeological thinking follows similar lines. In the remainder of this chapter we shall examine how one's theoretical perspective colors one's interpretations of the actual data. Although we are specifically concerned with the function of past ritual, we shall also consider how some current schools of thought operate within contemporary archaeology.

Some Adaptive Approaches to World View

Several examples were presented in Chapter 3 to suggest adaptive functions for ethnographic religious practices. The elaborate potlatch complex of the American northwest coast was one case in point. Adaptively oriented ethnologists suggested that the potlatch feasts were one way in which social status could be converted to material subsistence items (especially food) in times of ecological stress.

Why Some People Abhor Pigs

Archaeologists rely on adaptive perspectives to explain prehistoric religious practices. Why, for instance, was the pig domesticated as early as 6000 B.C. in parts of the Near East (like the Zagros Mountains) but apparently never in prehistoric times throughout other areas such as the Khuzistan steppe (Flannery 1965)?

An ideational perspective might argue that some religious taboo or dietary law must have been involved, probably the same religious tradition that today bans pork from the tables of Jews and Moslems. The Bible (both in the book of Genesis and again in Leviticus) denounces pigs as unclean beasts, forbidding tasting or even touching them. Somewhat later, Allah told Mohammed that followers of Islam should forever be forbidden to eat pigs. This perspective suggests to archaeologists that the absence of pig bones in many Near Eastern sites is due to religious prohibitions, which persist even today among millions of Jews and hundreds of millions of Moslems.

But there is an ecological alternative. The environment of the Khuzistan steppe is marked by erratic and unpredictable storms in the winter, followed by arid, scorching winds during the summer. The most successful human adaptation seems to have been transhumant herding, that is, moving flocks from plains to mountains. A mixed economy evolved about 7000 B.C.. The villagers grew crops of wheat and barley and tended flocks of domestic goats and a few sheep, a mixed economy that survived into late prehistoric times (Hole, Flannery, and Neely 1969, pp. 342–345).

Sheep and goats are ideal pastoral animals. Biologically adapted to arid environments, these beasts have digestive tracts that evolved to allow them to subsist on high cellulose diets, and the villagers of Khuzistan ran herds of goats as early as 7500 B.C.

But pigs are poorly suited to this lifeway because they are lowland creatures that evolved in forests and riverbank environments. Not equipped with a ruminant stomach, pigs are inefficient converters of the high-cellulose foods of the steppes. Wild pigs occur today on the Khuzistan steppe, but because they do best when fed foods such as nuts and fruits, pigs are found only near the lower reaches of river bottoms. Most importantly, pigs like grain and even invade modern grain fields in the spring, thereby placing them in direct competition with people.

Marvin Harris (1974) points out that pigs are "thermodynamically ill-adapted" to areas with hot, dry upland climates. Pigs cannot sweat to maintain their body temperature, and experiments show that pigs will die when exposed to even moderate amounts of direct sunlight. Wild pigs survive only in environments that permit them to keep their skin dampened, as they require external moisture to maintain body temperature. Pigs also refuse to flock in the way that sheep and goats do. Any transhumant society thus would find an attempt to herd their pigs simply not worth the effort. Moreover, because they have an extremely limited lung capacity and are winded easily, pigs cannot travel as tirelessly as sheep and goats can.

This combination of factors makes the pig a poor herd animal indeed. At 6000 B.C. there is a striking difference between archaeological sites in the oak–pistachio belt and those of the steppe. The relatively low site of Jarmo had permanent mud-walled houses, with courtyards and ovens, and the villagers raised goats, sheep, and domestic pigs, along with two strains of wheat and one of barley. But the contemporary sites on the upland steppes show only goats and sheep and probably reflect a seasonal pattern of herding.

Thus an adaptive interpretation looks beyond religious factors for ecological factors to explain the absence of domestic pigs in parts of the prehistoric Near East. The prehistoric Hebrews of 2000 B.C. were a society that subsisted on a mixed economy of herding and seasonal agriculture. Their herds of sheep, goats, and cattle provided the economic mainstay, and hence, from an adaptive standpoint, Jahweh rendered some sound ecological advice in prohibiting pork from the diet.

The Controversial Case of Aztec Cannibalism

Michael Harner (1977a, 1977b) has tendered a highly controversial interpretation of **Aztec** sacrifice and cannibalism (for a contrary view, see Ortiz 1978). Cannibalism is a topic that anthropologists encounter more commonly on TV talk shows than in their everyday research. Anthropologists Garn and Block (1970, p. 106) analyzed the nutritive value of cannibalism and concluded that "while human flesh may serve as an emergency source of both protein and calories, it is doubtful that regular people-eating ever had much nutritional meaning."

Not long ago, a highly publicized episode occurred when a plane carrying an amateur rugby team crashed in the remote Andes. Stranded in the wreckage for ten weeks, the surviving Uruguayans resorted to full-scale cannibalism of their dead teammates and friends. This case is probably unique in our own culture: The sixteen survivors were later assured by the archbishop of Montevideo that the Catholic church sanctioned cannibalism when undertaken for survival purposes (Read 1974).

Cannibalism is most commonly interpreted as no more than a bizarre custom or as a short-run survival method for a few desperate people. This conventional wisdom is also conveyed in almost all treatments of Aztec sacrifice and cannibalism. Estimates of the magnitude of Aztec sacrifice vary widely. The most commonly cited figure is twenty thousand victims per year (see Harner 1977a, p. 119). The account of the conquest by Bernal Diaz del Castillo (1956) describes human sacrifices in nearly every Aztec village he visited between 1519 and 1521. Here is one fairly typical episode:

> I remember that in the square where some of their *cues* stood were many piles of human skulls, so neatly arranged that we could count them, and I reckoned them at more than a hundred thousand. I repeat that there were more than a hundred thousand. And in another part of the square there were more piles made up of innumerable thigh-bones. . . . in this town of Tlascala we found wooden cages made of lattice-work in which men and women were imprisoned and fed until they were fat enough to be sacrificed and eaten . . . these prison cages existed throughout the country. (Diaz 1956, pp. 138, 183)

Structural anthropologist Levi-Strauss (discussed in Chapter 3) suggests that the Aztecs possessed a "maniacal obsession with blood and torture," a trait that is evident in all human cultures but reached its fullest expression only among the Aztecs (Levi-Strauss 1970, p. 388). Eric Wolf had another explanation, namely, that the Aztec constituted an extreme psychological type, "driven by imaginary and real indignities, cruel against himself and others . . . even engaged in fulfilling his prophecies of destruction by acting upon the assumption of imminent catastrophe" (1962, p. 145). Kroeber (1955, p. 199) concurs in the assessment of the Aztecs' cultural behavior as extreme. These conventional interpretations of Aztec sacrifice and cannibalism by Levi-Strauss, Kroeber, and others fall squarely in the ideational mainstream.

Michael Harner provides an interesting, if controversial, counterpoint within a wholly adaptive framework. Of concern here is not so much the number of people sacrificed—and recent evidence suggests as many as one-quarter million victims per year—as what happened to their bodies after the sacrifices. Harner documents case after case of ethnohistorical evidence to show that the Aztec victims provided not only a ritual outlet, but also a major source of protein and calories. According to Harner (1977a), the flesh of the victims was boiled, roasted, stewed with salt, peppers, and tomatoes; but rarely wasted. In fact, at a feast hosted by Montezuma, Diaz (1956, pp. 225–226) worried that he could not tell whether the dinner was human or something else, as they served fowls, turkeys, duck, venison, pigeons, and rabbits along with their human dishes.

Harner views sacrifice as a ritual response to increased population pressure. There was a meat shortage in the Mexican highlands during Aztec times, and ethnohistoric sources note that although the nobility had a rich diet, the commoners would eat almost anything; famine was not uncommon. Harner argues that as the population pressure of the central highlands increased, so did the incidence of cannibalism. During its peak, it reached as high as five victims per one hundred people.

The mode of Aztec warfare always puzzled the Spanish. Why did the Aztecs wage such aggressive warfare and then fail to consolidate the conquered territory? The Aztecs simply conquered and then withdrew. Harner believes that the Aztecs did not eat their own polity—this would have been socially and politically disruptive. Instead, they waged war to obtain captives, and so Harner named the Aztec state a "cannibal empire."

We must mention that Ortiz (1978) has vigorously challenged Harner's ecological interpretation of Aztec sacrifice. While admitting that the Aztecs obviously practiced human sacrifice and cannibalism on a large scale, Ortiz interprets the practice as a thanksgiving ritual, which operated on a strict calendrical base. Ortiz questions Harner's assertion that human flesh could have contributed a significant amount of protein and contends that the Aztecs' diet was entirely satisfactory without the inclusion of human protein. Ritual sacrifice was, according to Ortiz, an institutionalized means for Aztec warriors to achieve social status.

Harner's hypothesis of Aztec cannibalism and Harris's ideas on the sacred pig demonstrate how ecological, technological, and economic perspectives can be applied to religious strictures and ritual behavior. Of equal importance is the role of archaeology in such an explanation. Cultural anthropologists such as Harner and Harris cannot pursue their adaptive strategies in explaining cultural behavior without recourse to archaeology and archaeological data. Is there evidence to support their hypotheses?

The evidence must come from archaeology. But few Aztec sites have been excavated, partly because the Spaniards destroyed so much and partly because of the wealth of ethnohistoric documentation available. As Aztec studies proceed, archaeology will play a major role, especially because most of the Aztecs' own documents were destroyed and those of the Spaniards were drastically biased. Relevant archaeological data are still scanty and equivocal, and so hypotheses such as Harner's and Harris's remain only bold speculations until they can be adequately tested.

Some Ideational Approaches to World View

Humanists must cease thinking that ecology dehumanizes history, and ecologists must cease to regard art, religion, and ideology as mere "epiphenomena" without causal significance. In an ecosystem approach to the analysis of human societies, everything which transmits information is within the province of ecology.
—Kent Flannery

It is no secret that most archaeological research is adaptive, in that archaeologists first examine how societies function within their physical ecological framework. This emphasis is understandable, given the ecological, technological, demographic, and economic biases inherent in the archaeological record itself.

But since 1970, alternative explanations have appeared in the archaeological literature. A small but growing cadre of archaeologists has turned to an ideational emphasis in their research, examining the active role of ideology in shaping the ultimate social, and even technological, structure of societies. Chapter 12 introduced one example of this approach when discussing Joyce Marcus's innovative, if controversial, explanation of Classic Maya settlements. Rejecting a strictly ecological—that is, adaptive—model of Maya settlement patterns, Marcus emphasized the importance of cosmology and world view in determining the location of Classic Maya sites. Marcus is only one of several archaeologists who have recently expressed a dissatisfaction with a strictly ecological mode of archaeological explanation.

This point of view has probably been best expressed by Kent Flannery (1972), who contends that modern cultural ecological approaches are simply too narrow. Human ecosystems are characterized by exchanges of matter, energy, and information. Flannery accuses traditional paleoecologists of focusing strictly on the matter–energy exchange and ignoring altogether the informational aspect (art, religion, ritual, writing systems, and so on).

Flannery further argues that cultural ecologists and cultural materialists have focused too heavily on what Harris (1968b) calls technoenvironmental factors. "To read what the 'ecologists' write, one would often think that civilized people only ate, excreted and reproduced" (Flannery 1972, p. 400).

Flannery proposes an encompassing "ecosystem approach" that would include all information-processing mechanisms as part of the ecological whole. The problem here, of course, is that ritual, religion, cosmology, and iconography have traditionally been considered almost the exclusive province of the ethnographer, and archaeology lacks established analytical procedures for dealing with such "intangible phenomena" (Flannery and Marcus 1976).

The Peace Pipe As Ritual Weapon

Flannery and Marcus are not alone in their increased emphasis on the ideological aspects of extinct ecosystems. Robert L. Hall (1977) once accused modern archaeology of *econothink,* of placing undue emphasis on the changing tactics of technological adaptation and ignoring "what it may have been that prehistoric peoples found worthwhile to live for." Hall urged archaeologists to put as much effort into the study of the "cognitive core" of societies as they have in assessing the technoenvironmental, technoecological core. To illustrate his point, Hall used the calumet—or peace pipe—as an example of how his cognitive archaeology can broaden the horizons of archaeological investigations.

Hall went back to the Hopewell period of eastern United States prehistory. Probably the most famous Hopewell artifact is the platform pipe (see Figure 14–7), often found as grave goods in the burial mounds of the Hopewell. Hall argued that contemporary archaeology has concentrated strictly on the economic aspect of the Hopewellian exchange network and has ignored the symbolic and "affective" possibilities implied by ceremonial Hopewellian artifacts. Hall cites Michael Coe's indictment of most adaptively oriented eastern archaeologists:

> Those pipes, for instance, which have come to us from Hopewell and Mississippian cultures of the southeastern and eastern United States, are usually explained away in the following terms: well, these Indians had access to some rare stones, and they grew

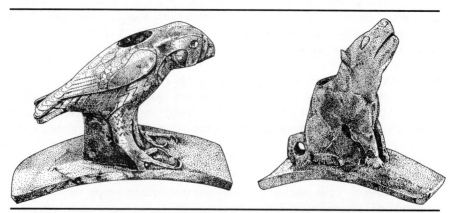

FIGURE 14–7   Sculptured bird-and-animal-effigy Hopewell pipes, from the Tremper Mound (Ohio). (Courtesy the American Museum of Natural History)

some tobacco, and they stuffed it in these pipes, and this was part of their leisure time, especially if they were high up in a well-stratified society, and they must have been so since they had such and such an economy. (Coe 1975, p. 195)

Coe and Hall argued that archaeologists spent so much time emphasizing economy and ecology that they entirely overlooked the symbolic importance of the very artifacts they dug up. Hall asks, for instance, why the long stem of a ceremonial pipe should symbolize anything more important than the pipe bowl, why the peace pipe used historically to establish friendly contact is almost always in the form of a weapon, or why the famous Hopewellian pipes take the form they do.

Hall (1977, pp. 502–503) began with a model familiar to all. Everyone engages in certain culturally dictated customs, whose exact meaning and origin may be lost. For example, the rite of "toasting" originally was the sloshing and spilling together of two persons' drinks to reduce the possibility that one planned to poison the other. But how many of us who have toasted friends realize the origin of the custom? Or saluting: Did you know that it originally represented the act of raising visors on armored helmets in order to expose the faces of the two persons encountering each other? Hall suggests that although the original function of the gestures lost their practical significance, the acts survive as elements of etiquette or protocol.

Hall applied similar reasoning to the Hopewell platform pipes. Throughout historic times in the eastern United States, Indian tribes observed the custom of smoking a sacred tribal pipe: When the pipe was present, violence was absolutely ruled out. Moreover, the calumet (or peace pipe) was generally manufactured in the form of a weapon. Among the Pawnee, for instance, the pipe was fashioned in the form of an arrow, and the Osage word for calumet means "arrowshaft" (Hall 1977, p. 503). Hall argued that the weaponlike appearance is the result of a specific ceremonial custom: The peace pipe was a *ritual weapon*.

This notion is then extended to the prehistoric Hopewell, who manufactured these pipes between 1600 and 2100 years ago. These pipes were also ritual weapons, but they were made before the introduction of the bow and arrow. The common Hopewell weapon was the **atlatl**, or spear thrower (see Figure 14–8). Hall suggested that the common Hopewell platform pipe symbolically represented a flat atlatl with an effigy spur. The animal on the bowl was almost invariably carved precisely where an atlatl spur would be needed on a spear thrower, and the curvature of the platform corresponds to the curvature on the atlatl. Hall concluded: "I see the Hopewell platform pipe as the archaeologically visible part of a transformed ritual atlatl, a symbolic weapon which in Middle Woodland times probably had some of the same functions as the calumet of historic times, itself a ritual arrow" (1977, pp. 504–505).

The importance of the Hopewell pipe goes beyond mere symbolism. Hall suggests that the platform pipe was not merely one of many items exchanged between groups: "It may have been part of the very mechanism of exchange." And here is the potential contribution of Hall's work.

Adaptively oriented research on eastern United States prehistory has defined the

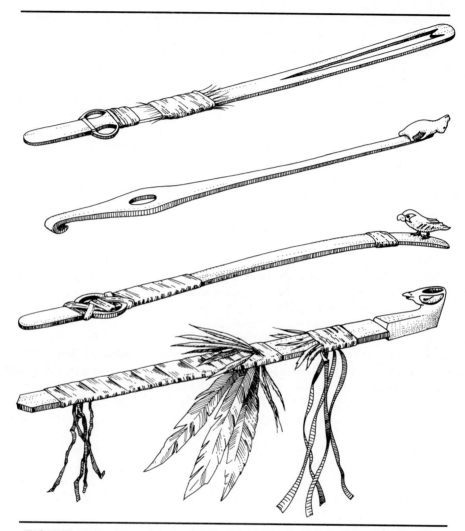

FIGURE 14–8   Some representations of atlatls in aboriginal North American
art (see Hall 1977, Figure 2). (Courtesy Robert Hall and the Society for
American Archaeology)

Hopewellian Interaction Sphere primarily in economic and environmental terms. Hall
suggested that the cognitive archaeology approach can add a larger understanding of the
Hopewell lifeway. Reasoning from historic Native American analogies, Hall contends
that peace pipe ceremonialism served to mediate interaction over a vast central portion of
the United States and Canada. Though one cannot ignore the economic and political

ramifications of such interaction, Hall urged archaeologists also to consider the symbolic details of Hopewellian exchange and mortuary practice. He argued that through "peace pipe diplomacy," the Hopewellian interaction sphere tended to reduce regional differences and promote friendly contact and communication between discrete groups.

Archaeologists have speculated about ritual and religion for decades, but the blending of the ecological with the ideological is a relatively new development. The work of Flannery, Marcus, Hall, Lathrap, Marshack, and others is currently being extended by the British school of symbolic archaeology (discussed in Chapter 3). Although these efforts cannot yet be termed "mainstream" Americanist archaeology, such ideational approaches are clearly on the rise.

Henry Glassie on Anglo-America's Georgian World View

> They left no writing, but they did leave all those houses.
> —Henry Glassie

We now turn to another trailblazing, if still controversial, approach also using an ideational perspective on culture. Folklorist Henry Glassie adopted the work of structural anthropology in an attempt to understand late-eighteenth- and nineteenth-century houses in Virginia. As you will remember (from Chapter 3), structuralism approaches culture as a system of shared cognitive structures, the cumulative creations of the mind, in particular looking for "structural" oppositions. Glassie looked at one hundred superficially similar farmhouses in Louisa and Goochland counties, an area termed "Middle" Virginia because it is wedged between the Tidewater area of Chesapeake Bay and the Appalachian Mountains. He began by asking how alike these houses really were and, more important, why?

Glassie found that the culture, as reified in these hundred houses was patterned to the extent that he could generate a "grammar," a detailing of how Middle Virginia houses were thought of *by the people who built them*. This explicit set of rules defined the various ways of combining architectural elements (doors, windows, latches, and chimneys) with variations in size, shape, and room arrangements. In effect, Glassie's grammar attempted to reflect the decisions made by a builder in planning and erecting any given house (see Figure 14–9).

With these *emic* rules in hand, Glassie discovered a trend toward privacy, stressing the "look" of the house's exterior. In about 1760, the basic structural layout of houses shifted from an organic to a geometric symmetry, from an "intensive" to an "extensive" form. Glassie concluded that at this time, there was an increase in the need for privacy, repetition, and control. This increasingly individual expression was:

accompanied by a contraction of the culture: the dominance of fewer house types, less variation within types once the fully symmetrical design had been achieved, and a diminishing of the inventory of detail and decoration. Houses once red, yellow and white became white. . . . Windows once had twelve, fifteen or eighteen lights; they came to have only twelve. (Glassie 1975, pp. 182–184)

Henry Glassie on the Importance of Artifacts

There are documents, government reports, and small books from which a little can be learned, but there is not enough to allow a historian to write about this area [Middle Virginia]—or about the many other areas that are like it primarily in being unknown. If this land and the people who made it have no place in the historical record, then the worth of the study of history must be called sharply into question. The written primary sources are too scanty, but there are fences in the forest and silent old houses set back from the roads. They are decaying and difficult to decipher, they demand tiring work in the field and complicated analysis, but they can be made to reveal the information upon which a strengthened historiography could be based. With brave exceptions, though, historians pass by such sources without a look. History moves on, leaving this land, like almost everywhere else, and these people, like almost everyone else, out of account. . . .

Two diseases have crippled and nearly killed the silent artifact as a source for history. Most historians, it seems, continue to view the artifact as only an illustrative adjunctive to the literary narrative. Perhaps when the elite is studied, this is not an unintelligent course of research. A knowledge of Thomas Jefferson might be based on his writings and only supple-

mented by a study of Monticello, but for most people, such as the folks who were chopping farms out of the woods a few miles to the east while Jefferson was writing at his desk, the procedure must be reversed. Their own statements, though made in wood or mud rather than ink, must take precedence over someone else's possibly prejudiced, probably wrong, and certainly superficial comments about them. The historian's benign neglect of silent artifacts and their people is a reasonable, if shallowly reasoned, response to the way that artifacts have most often been studied—obsessively, that is, as ends in themselves. Some archaeologists stop work when their findings are listed in site reports, and some connoisseurs not only persist in treating the artifact as a unique wonder rather than as a material manifestation of culture, they even eliminate from scrutiny the things that do not measure up to their own taste. Maybe some of these things are "bad," but most of them are "good" things that the connoisseur has failed to understand. The decision to eliminate some artworks from study makes as much sense as would the choice by the historian to read only books with pretty bindings or to study only old documents calligraphed in a lovely hand. Any artifact that can be provided with association in space and time, either by being accompanied by a document or better—as with gravestones or buildings—by being set into the land, is a valuable source of a great quantity of information. (Glassie 1975, pp. 7, 12)

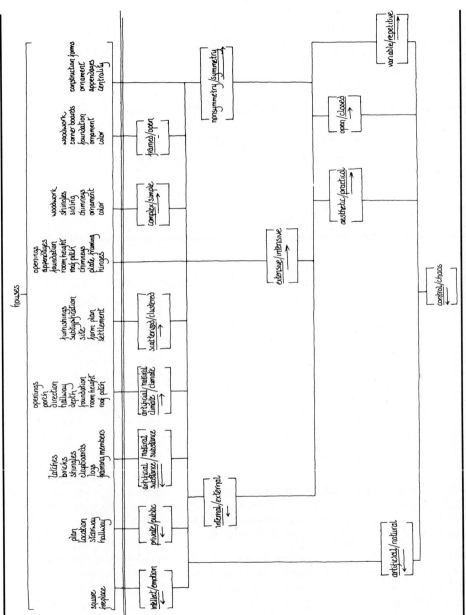

FIGURE 14-9 Glassie's "architecture of design" for understanding Middle Virginia houses. Above the double line are listed the observable phenomena that exhibit patterning. Below the line is a diagram of Glassie's structuralist interpretation of the mind of the architect—a guide to past decision making. The underlined term in the binary opposition is the one that was dominant at the earliest time. Arrows indicate the direction of change from about 1760 on. (Reprinted by permission of the University of Tennessee Press. From Henry Glassie's *Folk Housing in Middle Virginia.* Copyright © 1975 by the University of Tennessee Press)

529

To Glassie, the trend toward eighteenth-century individualism led to freedom for only a few, and increasing fear for most. This change in world view occurred during a mid-eighteenth-century economic crisis, a depression in the tobacco market. All except the most wealthy farmers were strained, and social stratification developed among rural white farmers. As people struggled to increase their individualism—to achieve "control"—they increasingly withdrew behind identical facades, suggesting to Glassie a retreat to impersonal stability.

Individual vigor was withdrawn from community-spirited projects and invested into abstract ideas like "racial superiority, nationalism or artificial symmetrical order" (Glassie 1975, p. 190). He concluded that the houses expressed and allowed greater *control* over post-Revolutionary circumstances in Middle Virginia, an environment that appeared to be chaotic, or out of control.

Individualism signals the point at which the face-to-face community dies.
—Henry Glassie

James Deetz Takes Glassie's Structuralism on the Road

Heavily influenced by Glassie's study of Middle Virginia architecture, James Deetz set out to see whether the same cognitive pattern could be found in colonial New England. Using a much broader range of data over a considerably longer time span, Deetz found that the earlier group-oriented lifeway had been replaced by the spirit of individualism, just as happened in Virginia.

Both Deetz (the archaeologist) and Glassie (the folklorist) tried to reconstruct the rules (or *cognitive patterns*) behind expressions of material culture, and both drew heavily on structuralist methods. Deetz's vision for historical archaeology was to transcend behavioral and environmental factors in order to view material culture in terms of its original cognitive state.

> The tiny ship that dropped anchor in Plymouth harbor in the December cold of 1620 carried a precious cargo. Its 102 passengers, Englishmen who had come to the New World for a variety of reasons, brought with them a blueprint—in their minds—for recreating the culture they had left behind. (Deetz 1977a, p.36)

The early British colonists to New England arrived with what Deetz termed a *medieval mind-set* that encouraged a group-oriented, corporate, and relatively undifferentiated life-style.

But in about 1660, another mind-set—the *Georgian order*—came to dominate the Anglo-American colonial and post-Revolutionary times. As cultural conservatism set in, people gradually drifted away from mother England to form more regionally differentiated folk cultures. Then, in about 1760, as the re-Anglification process began, the American populace left their Georgian order behind.

But during this key century, Deetz argued, Georgian attitudes created material culture correlates, patterns that became increasingly individualistic, often differentiated through symmetry and tripartite divisions.

Architecture: Medieval architecture, for instance, decreed only one or two rooms, arranged along asymmetrical floor plans. In these rooms took place all domestic activities, from sleeping and eating, to working and socializing. But with the Georgian world view, houses became functionally structured, and compartmentalized, with more balanced floor plans (Deetz 1977a, pp. 92–117).

Ceramics: Pottery also reflected the shift in early American "foodways." The medieval mind-set was characterized by plain, utilitarian earthenware, reflecting the dependence on dairying. Food was served directly from the cooking pot and consumed from "trenchers," unlovely wooden trays that were usually shared with one or more "trencher mates" (1977a, p. 52). During this period, ceramics held a small role in food consumption.

The Georgian world view provided a stark contrast. Not only did creamware and pearlware—products of the Industrial Revolution—become common, but they also were purchased as a matched set of plates and teacups. This "new Georgian order" established a one plate–one person commonality, reflecting greater discipline around the family table.

Whereas the medieval world view emphasized the natural, the Georgian mind-set became increasingly artificial. Before the Industrial Revolution, people relied on natural colored earthenwares, reflecting their earthy origins. But Georgian ceramics became progressively whiter as technology improved.

Mortuary Art: Gravestones also became white, instead of the greens, blacks, and blues and reds of the earlier markers. They also had backs sculpted smooth like the fronts, "denying their origin in the native stone" (Deetz 1983, p. 31). The messages written on these gravestones offered Deetz his most eloquent *entrée* into the shifting mind-sets of early America. Death during medieval times reminded colonists of their own mortality, and accordingly, gravestones displayed the "death's head," and the stones said simply "Here lies . . ." or "Here lies buried. . . ." But during the "Great Awakening," the typical inscription was "In memory of . . .," and the urn and willow motif became a "symbol of commemoration" instead of just a graphic representation of the individual's mortal or immortal components. Such "depersonalization" is also reflected in the epitaphs, which began to praise the worldly achievements of individuals. "These changes seem to indicate a secularization of the religion" (Deetz 1977a, p. 72).

Food Preparation: Medieval diners usually attacked their meat in joints, "showing in part at least the vestiges of the anatomy of the beast from which they came" (Deetz 1983, p. 31). But structured Georgian "foodways" were dominated by artificially segmented cuts of meat. Archaeologically, this shift is seen as the shift from chopping bones to sawing them.

Refuse Disposal: These shifting mind-sets can also be inferred through the development of trash disposal. During the early medieval days, trash was simply tossed out of doors and windows, creating a sheet of refuse that allowed domestic animals like pigs and chickens to scavenge for leftovers.

But by the mid-eighteenth century, the Georgian New Englander's mind-set dictated a more orderly method for disposing of trash, and people began digging square pits up to seven feet deep. The frequency of chamber pots also skyrocketed with this transition, reflecting a desire for increased privacy.

Summarizing the conceptual linkages between Glassie's Middle Virginia and New England, Deetz argues that

> shrinking chimneys, lowering ceilings and roofs, and tucking behind of ells and sheds in Virginia appears in New England not only in similar architectural changes but also in the disappearance of shared seating at meals, shared utensils, and the appearance of the very impersonal, private urn and willow design, which is profoundly different from both the earlier death's heads and cherubs, both of which extensively related the individual to the community by portraying a part of him or her as it passed by. Simple forms replace complex forms in the rapid change from multicolored ceramics to those predominantly white and blue. In foodways, complex pottages and stews give way to discrete foodstuffs, served separated one from another. . . . The disappearance of borders on louvres, doors and windows in houses is paralleled by the reduction in size and complexity on borders on gravestones, and at least a change in the average width and decorative elaboration of the marleys (edges) of plates and saucers toward less framed, more open forms. And the shift to symmetry reflected in central hall houses—tripartite and severely symmetrical—in all of the Anglo-American world is paralleled by the emergence of a symmetrical relationship between the individual and his or her material culture, utensils, foodstuffs, and burial pits. (Deetz 1983, p. 33) (Reprinted by permission of J. Deetz and *Geoscience and Man*)

To arrive at his synthesis of these conceptual changes in New England, Deetz used the same oppositions employed by Glassie in describing Middle Virginia housing (Figure 14–9): intellect/emotion, private/public, artificial/natural substance, scattered/clustered, extensive/intensive, complex/simple, framed/open, and nonsymmetry/symmetry. All of these fall under Levi-Strauss's larger opposition, order/chaos or culture/nature (Leone 1986, p. 426).

As you can see, Deetz has taken the work of Glassie one step further. In the next chapter, we shall examine how Mark Leone did Deetz one better, by examining not only the operation of the Georgian world view but also how and why it came to be.

Ideational or Adaptive: Where Is Americanist Archaeology Going?

Some of the statements in this chapter might seem to be outright contradictions, particularly when archaeologists attempt to determine the nature and function of past ideology and world view. This is because we peeked on both sides of the fence, by looking at both ideational and adaptive views. These examples show how competing strategies operate in archaeology. Traditionally, Americanist archaeologists have felt more comfortable working within the adaptive framework of research, and for good reason. Not only does the adaptive explanation seem to explain the distribution of animal bones in Near Eastern sites, but it also proposes how different lifeways operated in this area.

What about the ideational strategies? Anthropologists working with contemporary cultures, or with societies and their historic documentation, are free to examine ideational alternatives, such as religious dictates that prohibited the eating of pork. But problems can arise with the introduction of archaeological evidence, particularly in the absence of written records. There are no informants to interrogate, and the actual legal sanctions seem unretrievable. This is why ideational strategies have not fared well so far in prehistoric archaeology. It is also why historical archaeologists have taken the lead in developing ideational approaches.

Chapter 2 emphasized that within the framework of established scientific methods, it is irrelevant where one's hypotheses come from. Hypotheses can come from day-dreams, computers, textbooks, or geniuses. Explanations are never judged on their points of origin; they are judged only on their ability to explain phenomena. Thus, strategies of research are neither right nor wrong. Either research strategies open up useful avenues for research, or they do not.

Adaptive explanations have prospered in archaeology because they are relatively easy to test; that is, traditional ecological explanations do indeed open useful avenues of research. Ideational explanations in archaeology are more difficult to translate into concrete, testable propositions. Some ideational approaches follow in the same vein, proceeding according to the canons of acceptable scientific methods; other ideational strategies reject this method of explanation altogether. Whether these ideational approaches will ultimately prove fruitful remains to be seen. But one thing is clear: Archaeologists can ill afford to ignore any potential source of understanding, whether it is ecological, technological, societal, religious, or cosmological. No anthropological main-stream has an exclusive pipeline to the truth.

Summary

Religion consists of three interrelated aspects: a set of rituals, rationalized by myth, designed to mobilize supernatural powers for the purpose of achieving (or presenting) transformations of state in humans and nature. Of these three elements—ritual, myth, and transformations of state—ritual emerges as the primary factor. This is an important fact for archaeology, as ritual is most closely related to material culture and, as such, is the most conspicuously represented element in the archaeological record.

Rituals are either calendrical or critical. Calendrical rituals are always scheduled in advance and are publicly announced long before their actual occurrence. Archaeologists are currently attempting to recognize such calendrical practices in the archaeological record and to relate this time-factored behavior to the evolution of ritual activity. But because the calendrical rituals are, by nature, planned beforehand, they cannot meet all of a society's religious requirements. That is, the calendrical ritual is insufficient to cope with emergency requests to the supernatural: This instead is the function of the critical (noncalendrical) ritual. Certain life crises (such as birth, death, and marriage) are simply not calendrically determined, and so societies also have a mechanism for invoking supernatural aid at infrequent intervals.

It is assumed that ritual behavior—and in a larger sense, religious behavior in general—functions for the good of society. That is, religion probably has some sort of long-term survival value. But functional explanations invariably arise from implicit research strategies. Archaeologists are currently studying the function of religious behavior from both adaptive and ideational perspectives. Some investigators emphasize ecological and demographic functions, and others stress more ideational factors to explain religious phenonema. As discussed in detail in Chapter 3, such strategies of research are neither "right" nor "wrong"; either research strategies open up useful avenues of explanation, or they do not. Archaeology is currently exploring several possibilities.

Temple 1 at Tikal (Guatemala). (Courtesy the American Museum of Natural History).

PART FIVE

Processual Studies in Archaeology

Science is facts; just as houses are made of stone, so is science made of facts; but a pile of stones is not a house and a collection of facts is not necessarily science.
—Henri Poincaré

In the last section, we considered how archaeologists reconstruct past lifeways. The focus of these studies—regardless of whether the subject is ecology, social organization, or ideology—is on specifics. A lifeway is firmly bound in both time and space: the Maya subsistence–settlement pattern, the bison kill at Olsen–Chubbuck, and the alleged periodicity of the La Marche bone.

As discussed in Chapter 4, the ultimate objective of archaeology is to define the processes that underlie human behavior. A lifeway must be distinguished from a process. The term *lifeway* is used to refer to a single cultural system at a fixed point in time and space. By contrast, a *process* exists at a much more basic level, quietly directing the overall evolution and operation of the cultural system.

The interest in cultural processes is an indirect call for more attention to archaeological theory. *Theory* is a term we have used very little so far, but it is important nevertheless. Social scientists use the word *theory* in a number of different ways. In one usage, theory is an untested explanation, which would probably be false if ever properly tested. We might speak of Von Däniken's "Chariots of the Gods theory," which argues that the major cultural advances on earth have resulted from visitations by extraterrestrial beings (Von Däniken 1971). Many archaeologists would call this "theory" an improbable and untested generalization. In this sense, theory is almost a dirty word.

Theory is also used to refer to a general set of untested principles or propositions. In this sense, one deals with theory as opposed to practice. Thus a new invention to harness solar energy might work in theory (that is, on paper) but would require extensive field testing before one could decide whether it was a successful design. If the solar device functioned as expected, the theory would be valid; if the device failed, the theory would be held invalid.

Although both usages are common, they are of little interest in a discussion of general archaeological theory. In this case, it is more useful to distinguish between research strategies and the theories they produce. The anthropological mainstreams introduced in Chapter 3 are research strategies, each setting forth a series of assumptions and terms that define the direction of inquiry. Structuralists, you will remember, concentrate on myth and religion because these aspects are less constrained by external, material considerations. Cultural materialists, on the other hand, concentrate on precisely those material conditions, because cultural materialistic theory holds that the variables of economy, ecology, technology, and demography will ultimately prove to be causal. That is, the basic theoretical orientation leads structuralists to concentrate on the ideational sphere, whereas cultural materialists focus on the external conditions of the mundane world. These principles do not comprise a theory; they comprise a research strategy that, each mainstream believes, best conforms to the canons of acceptable explanation (which vary according to each school of thought). Because these are strategic principles (rather than theoretical beliefs), they cannot be disproved.

General theory attempts to explain cultural variability: the origin and evolution of sex and gender roles, why warfare is so prevalent, the origins of dietary patterns and food avoidance, the impact of natural selection on human behavior, the reasons for settlement and demographic trends, the workings of the Georgian mind-set. Such theories can be disproved in light of data that suggest the existence of better, more acceptable theories. The ultimate test of all such theoretical frameworks is in their ability to explain and predict cultural phenomena.

There is one final usage of the term theory to be considered. One frequently hears that the social sciences lack formal theory. The critic in this case is lamenting that the social sciences have been unable, to date, to come up with the elegant theoretical structures common in the physical sciences. A formal theory in this sense begins with a set of axioms that are assumed to be true. A series of theorems are then deduced from the axioms, and it is these axioms that make testable predictions about the real world. Anyone who has ever taken a college course in physics, chemistry, or mathematics is well aware of how such formal theories operate.

Formal theory in the social sciences is another matter entirely. First, one should not expect to find such a creature as a formal archaeological theory. Remember the point made in Chapter 4, that the ultimate goal of archaeologists must be to stop doing archaeology. This is because the archaeologist is after timeless and spaceless generalizations, and such generalizations cannot be made without recourse to data from ethnography, history, and the study of contemporary, functioning societies. Thus, at this level, archaeology cannot have a unique body of theory; that theory must be shared with the rest of social science.

It is a mistake to believe that a science consists of nothing but conclusively proven propositions, and it is unjust to demand that it should. It is a demand only made by those who feel a craving for authority in some form and a need to replace the religious catechism by something else, even if it be a scientific one.
—Sigmund Freud

The truth is that with the exception of economics, social science has made very little progress at establishing formal theory. Part of this difficulty has to do with the nebulous kinds of data with which social scientists must work. Social scientists lack the "intuitively evident quantities" with which Newton began: length as measured by sticks, time as measured by clocks, force as felt in the muscles (Rapaport 1959, p. 351). Social scientists must spend a great deal of time and effort on defining even the most elementary units of observation (as discussed in Chapter 10).

Beyond the methodological problems, others contend that as a matter of basic principle, it will be impossible for the social sciences to become truly "scientific." We are told that inanimate objects do not obey strict laws, that free will makes human behavior unpredictable. The fact that social science has so little formal theory rests more in pragmatics than in principle. The laws of social science are more difficult to isolate because of the ambiguous measures used by social scientists and because of the emotive involvement between subject and scientist. Predictions are difficult to make because of the difficult mathematics implied by many social science problems. And even when predictions are made, social scientists have difficulty carrying out precise experiments to determine whether the propositions have been verified. Moreover, the nature of social science is such that progress must be made in much smaller steps than occurs in the physical sciences. For all of these reasons, it is not surprising that the social sciences have lagged far behind.

Given the primitive nature of general theory in the social sciences, we shall concentrate in this final section on how archaeologists study theory, and we shall de-emphasize the actual theories and processes involved. In this context it is most important to understand how a processual study works in archaeology; the actual theories and processes used are really incidental to our purposes.

In Chapter 5, we examined the processes of forming the archaeological record. More and more, archaeologists have come to realize how little is actually known about how our archaeological sites are formed. Also called middle-range research (or, at times, middle-range theory), such processual studies provide archaeologists with the bridging arguments necessary for adequate interpretation. This is how ethnoarchaeology and experimental archaeology help in the theory-building process.

In the last chapter, we shall consider the study of more general evolutionary processes. The focus of our discussion will purposely be limited, considering particularly the origins of agriculture, the origin of the state, and some recent investigations into the ideational processes reflected in the archaeological record.

Processual archaeology has its dreamers, its missionaries and its prophets. For the most effective pursuit of laws of culture process that directed past human behavior, everyone must get into the act.
—Stanley South

CHAPTER 15

General Theory in Archaeology

If you, like Jack London, are seeking to gaze on the face of truth, you will find little in this chapter. Although my intention is to discuss general theory in archaeology, I must confess at the outset that archaeologists are still groping. Truth, I fear, has yet to be located. But let me tell you something about the search.

In this chapter, I shall present some examples of how archaeologists are working to define the processes that underlie (and explain) cultural behavior. You will remember that back in Chapter 3 we examined how Leslie White divided cultural phenomena into three interrelated spheres: technology, sociology, and ideology. We shall be considering an example from each of these spheres of human behavior in order to see how social scientists deal with matters of process. But be sure not to confuse the upcoming discussion with truth. The following processual explanations are bound to change, and I have deliberately chosen several examples for their overall historical significance. It is more important right now to concentrate on how the questions are framed. More satisfying answers will come later.

Understanding Hunter-Gatherers

"Hunter-Gatherer As Primitive" Theories

The first humans on earth were hunter-gatherers, and some vestige of this lifeway persisted for 99 percent of the human past (Lee and DeVore 1968, p. 3). Anthropologists—many of them archaeologists—have conducted in-depth projects aimed at defining the processes that underlie this hunting-gathering existence, and we already mentioned several in Chapters 5 and 13. As the title of this section—pilfered from Robert Bettinger's (1987) compelling review—implies, the anthropological perception, before the mid-1960s, of hunter-gatherer existence focused largely on negatives, and accordingly, hunter-gatherers were viewed as occupying the bottom rung of the evolutionary ladder.

One notable classification scheme was devised by Lewis Henry Morgan, a Rochester lawyer who later turned to ethnography. Morgan has been called "the most important social scientist in nineteenth-century America" (Fenton 1962, p. viii). In *Ancient Society* (1877), Morgan divided the progress of human achievement into three major "ethnical periods"—savagery, barbarism, and civilization—which were scaled to seven categories according to status, as follows:

1. *Lower status of savagery:* Commenced with the infancy of the human race in restricted habitats, subsistence on fruits and nuts. No such tribes remained into the historical period.
2. *Middle status of savagery:* Commenced with the acquisition of fish and the use of fire. Humankind spread over greater portion of the earth's surface. Exemplified by Australian aborigines and Polynesians.
3. *Upper status of savagery:* Commenced with the invention of the bow and arrow. Exemplified by the Athapascan tribes of Hudson's Bay Territory.
4. *Lower status of barbarism:* Commenced with the invention or practice of pottery. Exemplified by the Native American tribes of the United States east of the Missouri River.
5. *Middle status of barbarism:* Commenced with the domestication of animals in the Eastern Hemisphere, and in the Western with cultivation by irrigation and the use of adobe brick and stone in architecture. Exemplified by villages in New Mexico and Mexico.
6. *Upper status of barbarism:* Commenced with the manufacture of iron. Exemplified by Grecian tribes of the Homeric Age and Germanic tribes of the time of Caesar.
7. *Status of civilization:* Commenced with the use of a phonetic alphabet and the production of literary records; divided into ancient and modern.

Although many other evolutionary schemes have been proffered, they all shared, with Morgan's stages, the perception of the hunter-gatherer as exemplifying "savagery" in one way or another, basically primeval, rudimentary, and primitive. Morgan's evolutionary stages are no longer used in Americanist archaeology (although they were until recently, providing the principal model for archaeologists reconstructing prehistoric social life and customs in the People's Republic of China; see Freeman 1977, p. 93).

"Hunter-Gatherer As Lay Ecologist" Theories

A flurry of ethnographic studies, mostly conducted in Australia and Africa during the 1960s, suggested that hunter-gatherers may not have been so primitive after all. Contrary to widespread belief, hunter-gatherers were not huddled on the brink of extinction. And surprisingly, their lives were not nasty, not brutish, not short. Bettinger (1987, p. 123) terms this the awakening to the "hunter-gatherer as lay ecologist."

Richard Lee (1969), for instance, found that water management was the single most important resource in determining the settlement pattern and human demography of the !Kung people he studied. Because flowing water is practically unknown on the Kalahari Desert, the !Kung anchor their camps to a few well-known springs. Throughout the 2500 square miles of the Dobe and Nye Nye regions, only five water holes are "permanent," and of these, three are known to have failed. According to Lee, the seasonal movements of the !Kung "must be continually revised in light of the unfolding rainfall situation throughout the growing season and beyond." In years of relatively abundant rainfall, camp location was dictated by availability of food and known locations of neighboring groups. In moderately dry winters, the !Kung, by necessity established themselves near the five best water sources. But in drought years, Lee found as many as seven normally autonomous groups coexisting at a single water hole. This is how the availability of water structured the !Kung settlement pattern.

The studies by Lee (and also those by Yellen, see Chapter 5) show how ethnographers and ethnoarchaeologists were looking at the ecological adaptation of hunter-gatherers, always with an eye to the past. As Hawkes (1987, p. 341) points out, this view of hunter-gatherers arises largely because of the rich ethnographic descriptions available for the !Kung. Not only were important scientific papers written and widely distributed (e.g., Lee 1968, 1979), but the films of John Marshall brought the !Kung into classroom and living rooms throughout the world. The !Kung have come to be viewed as what Hawkes terms "prototypical" hunter-gatherers: well-nourished foragers working short hours, relying on plant foods collected by women, and maintaining low birthrates, thereby keeping their population within sufficiently low limits to minimize threats to local resources (for a contrary view, see Blurton Jones and Sibley 1978; Blurton Jones 1986, 1987). According to Lee (1979, p. 158) "the !Kung are superb botanists and naturalists, with an intimate knowledge of their natural environment." Exhilarated in large measure by such descriptions of the !Kung, Marshall Sahlins (1972) crowed that hunter-gatherers were the "original affluent society."

"Hunter-Gatherer As Optimal Forager" Theories

Over the past few decades, archaeologists and ethnoarchaeologists have begun approaching hunter-gatherers from another perspective. Some researchers took a second look at the !Kung, concluding that these foragers may not have been "affluent" after all. Other researchers branched out and studied other foraging groups and found that the !Kung are not very "typical."

Several investigators believe that a processual understanding of hunter-gatherers can be obtained from the larger body of developing theory in evolutionary biology. One relatively early effort was by Edwin Wilmsen (1973), who proposed a generalized model of hunter–gatherer spatial organization. Beginning with the perspective of locational geography, Wilmsen borrowed a theory initially derived from observations on Brewer's blackbirds (but intended to apply to the relationship between the distribution of resources and consumers in general). This biogeographic model suggested that blackbirds tend to space themselves throughout their territories according to a precise mathematical formula. Wilmsen then examined how well the model seemed to account for known hunter-gatherer patterns and suggested that the revised model could be tested against archaeological evidence.

Since then, several others have followed Wilmsen's lead, looking to evolutionary biology for general theoretical guidance. One increasingly popular method of inquiry involves the use of the **optimal foraging theory**, a broad-based theoretical perspective that attempts to develop a set of models general enough to apply to a wide range of animal species, yet rigorous and precise enough to explain the details of behavior exhibited by a particular forager (Eric Smith 1983, p. 626).

James O'Connell proposes that the underlying logic behind the application of optimal foraging theory to archaeology may go something like this: Because archaeologists embrace such a huge empirical domain, a general theory of behavior may be required. Much of the relatively recent archaeological record was created under conditions similar to those observed ethnographically. Provided that one exercises the cautions implicit in good archaeological practice, there is every likelihood of success in accounting for the general structure of the archaeological record in behavioral terms. Middle-range research is critical to this endeavor; mature general theory may not be.

The temporally more remote segments of the archaeological record lack adequate analogies. The patterns of behavior in the remote past are simply too dissimilar to those of the present to allow any acceptable linkage between the two. Optimal foraging theory may offer a partial solution to this problem. Although the patterns of behavior may then be vastly different from the present, a _uniformitarian_ assumption holds that the principles that shape the behavior of modern _Homo sapiens_—and in fact, all organisms—are constant and unchanging in time and space. Evolutionary ecologists have embodied theory at a general level, anchored in assumptions derived from basic postulates of natural selection theory. This approach uses mathematical and graphic representations for the rigorous deduction of testable hypotheses (in the mode of Chapter 2).

The stock of evolutionary ecology is clearly rising—as is evident in the pages of major scientific journals like _Science_ and _Nature_—with both generality and testability capable of drawing adherents who are desperately seeking a way to understand and explain human variability (in both the present and the past). Although neither whole nor unified, optimal foraging models are general and offer some degree of explanatory power. Specific applications remain today provisional and directed at limited aspects of cultural systems, but because optimal foraging models are grounded in the general theory of natural selection, such models do indeed hold the promise of moving toward a general, more unified understanding of human behavior—provided that the assumptions hold for the archaeological record, and provided that the applications hold up under empirical scrutiny.

Perhaps the greatest appeal of optimal foraging models is their ability to bring specific testable projections of human behavior to bear on real data. Although most such "testing" has been conducted by biologists, applications to human populations have appeared in the past decade. As one proponent readily acknowledges, "Rigorous tests assume that most variables are under experimental control—a condition that few ethnographers, and no paleoanthropologists, are capable of meeting" (Eric Smith 1983, p. 648). But whereas optimal foraging theory does not provide lawful statements about reality, it does offer a structured method of inquiry, perhaps "more interesting to stalk than to live by" (Winterhalder 1987, p. 313).

One problem in foraging theory concerns prey choice and diet breadth: Out of the array of available things to eat, which ones should an efficient forager attempt to harvest? To answer this question, optimal foraging theorists have developed the *diet–breadth model,* and to see how foraging theory works in practice, let us consider this model in detail. We begin with a hypothetical predator seeking prey scattered randomly throughout the environment. The idea is to specify which and how many resources this forager should pursue in order to achieve the highest net rate of energy intake while foraging. Seven assumptions are necessary in the diet–breadth model (see Winterhalder 1987, p. 316):

Currency

1. Some optimal foraging models assume that the hypothetical organism attempts to maximize its net rate of energy intake while foraging; other approaches use different currencies.

Constraints

2. Prey is encountered randomly (that is, the next kind of prey encountered is independent of the last kind encountered).
3. For a particular diet breadth, either the hypothetical organism takes a prey item, or it does not (there are no "partial" preferences).
4. The "quality" of a prey type can be evaluated independently of the others in terms of its stable ranking (defined as net energy value per unit of pursuit and handling costs).
5. "Foraging" consists of two independent phases. Predators first "search" all prey jointly but "pursue" the target prey singly.
6. The density of prey remains constant throughout the foraging interval.
7. Costs and benefits associated with resources are treated as firm expectations (without considering statistical variability).

As Winterhalder (1987, p. 316) noted wryly, "Despite its appearance, this is not a paralyzing list."

O'Connell suggests that these "assumptions" can also be perceived as hypotheses, themselves subject to testing. Viewed in this way, applications of foraging models routinely use a set of hypotheses regarding (1) the goals of foraging, (2) the alternative methods of achieving these goals, (3) the costs and benefits associated with these alternative means, (4) the currencies in which these costs and benefits are to be measured, and (5) the time frame in which the goals are to be met. *If* the forager is behaving "optimally" with respect to the specified goals and *if* the currencies and so forth are correct, *then* certain predictions about behavior will follow. But if these predictions are not met, then one or more of the various hypotheses will be judged to be incorrect. Optimal foraging models, as such, are never actually tested, nor is the question of optimality (which is assumed).

Figure 15–1 illustrates the diet–breadth model in a graph. The baseline contains the "ranked" number of resource types in the diet of our hypothetical forager, scaled according to the "currency" we mentioned. As each prey type is added to the diet, the "search" curve (i.e., the average search costs) decreases, and the "pursuit" curve (the average pursuit costs) increases. In other words, the more one searches, the more one will find; but because the prey types are rank ordered, these new additions are more difficult to capture (or less rewarding when secured). The *optimal diet breadth* occurs at the intersection of the two curves. This general format allows the investigator to project hypothetical changes when any of the environmental parameters are shifted.

When converted to its algebraic format, this model provides a set of predictions (*X*) about how foragers should behave under circumstances *Y*. The animal ecologist can determine the explanatory power of such projections by observing and recording behavior

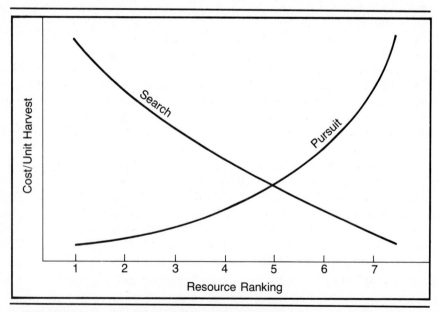

FIGURE 15–1 The MacArthur and Pianka diet–breadth model (see Winterhalder 1987, Figure 2.2)

in a quantitative manner; ecologists working on living animal populations can simultaneously measure the state of the environment to see whether X and Y covaried as the theory predicts.

This model was used to study human populations by James O'Connell (an archaeologist) and Kristen Hawkes (an ethnographer), who applied the diet–breadth model to examine plant use by the modern Alyawara (of Australia). They began by asking why the Alyawara had effectively stopped eating native grass and tree seeds, foods that had been staples in the "traditional" diet and remain available today.

An optimal diet model (similar to the one in Figure 15–1) provides a series of predictions X: If Alyawara collectors forage optimally, then the resources taken in each "patch" will depend on the relative energy return per unit of handling time and the average return from collecting in that patch. Resources yielding a return higher than the average for a patch should be included in the diet, but resources with lower returns should not. Stating their expectations in formal algebraic terms, these propositions generated specific expectations expressed in kilocalories per forager hour (O'Connell and Hawkes 1981, p. 108).

Situation Y in this case reflects the state of the environment: degree of rainfall, relative temperature, and, most importantly, geographic distribution and condition of available plant communities, all in one place at a single point in time—that is, near Bendaijerum between 1974 and 1975. The covariation between Y and X was monitored across a series of Alyawara foraging events observed by O'Connell. On eleven visits to sandhills, energy returns were indeed well above average for the patch, and although several species of ripe seeds were available in these patches, they were never harvested because the returns from other higher-ranked resources (roots and fruit) never fell low enough. The seeds were collected only during a brief period after they had reached maximum size and before they had hardened (when handling time was relatively low and energy returns were correspondingly high; Figure 15–2).

The predictions based on the model passed the test for plant collection in the sandhills: "Foraging behavior in this habitat is clearly consistent with the predictions of the optimal diet model" (O'Connell and Hawkes 1981, p. 109). Foraging in the mulga woodland produced different results, with Alyawara foraging behavior not fitting the optimal diet prediction about the threshold at which lower-ranked resources will be added. O'Connell and Hawkes believe that future modeling must include cost–benefit analyses of manufacturing and maintaining processing gear. Another reason for the lack of fit between behavior and predictions in the mulga woodland could be that the returns were not accurately observed or that the average foraging returns from the mulga patch were initially underestimated (see O'Connell and Hawkes 1984, p. 512–516 and footnote 3).

Using an array of such optimal foraging models, O'Connell and Hawkes effectively answered their initial research question: The Alyawara stopped eating native grass and tree seeds—even when available—because they were "too expensive" in cost–benefit terms. They also were able to figure out why such food was so important in traditional times: Before the introduction of European foods, pressure on native plant resources must

FIGURE 15–2   Bessie Ngwarriya, an Alyawara-speaking Aborigine, winnows *Acacia coriacea* seeds in a wooden tray at Bendaijerum (central Australia) in late 1974. (Courtesy James F. O'Connell)

have been much greater, with collectors depleting certain high-ranked resources even in a good year.

Although the potential of foraging theory for archaeology was somewhat overstated by early proponents, more recent studies, such as that by O'Connell and Hawkes, present more balanced views of both costs and benefits. Today, applications of optimal foraging theory to modern human populations command the serious attention of the anthropological community.

Numerous applications of optimal foraging models to strictly archaeological data have been attempted (see Where to Go from Here?). Shifting empirical referents from the ethnographic present to the archaeological past means that neither behavior or environment can be directly observed. But before optimal foraging theory—or any other general theory—can be brought to bear on archaeological data, it is necessary to infer past behavior from the archaeological record and also to infer past environmental states from the paleoenvironmental record. Both records are static, and all dynamics must be inferred through middle-range linkages.

We might also point out that the process of reconstructing (or inferring) past behavior is itself often a theory-dependent endeavor. If, for instance, one reconstructs the behavior of *Homo erectus* (an extinct species), a theoretical framework is necessary to define the possible alternative behavioral models that could be tested archaeologically. Theory is implicated at every stage because it sets the direction of research and anticipates the range of plausible results. We cannot simply dig a number of sites, reconstruct behavior, and then seek an explanation in general theoretical terms.

As you can appreciate from our example, optimal foraging projections require comprehensive cultural and paleoenvironmental chronologies, an accurate picture of (1) who lived where (and when) and (2) what plants and animals were (or were not) available for inclusion in the diet. In Chapter 11, we noted that archaeology has emerged from its Age of Aquarius, and we now require better-reasoned associations to establish reliable estimates of seasonality and annual round. We no longer live in the if-wishing-would-make-it-so euphoria of the new archaeology of the 1960s and 1970s.

Grinding stones were once considered to be isomorphic with (1) women and (2) seed collection, but we no longer assume such a relationship. Projectile points once meant "men went hunting," but we now realize that the relationship between gender and technology is considerably more complex. We must keep in mind that the mere presence of bones and seeds at an archaeological site is no longer considered to be valid evidence of human consumption. Rather, we must adequately document the procurement and processing strategies applied to these resources: how the seeds are processed and how such processing shows up in the archaeological record.

While recent middle-range research on seasonality, size sorting and intrasite patterning, tool kits and activity areas, regional variability, taphonomy, and postdepositional modifications proceeds apace—as documented in earlier chapters—such progress carries with it the sober realization that archaeological data are more intractable than was appreciated during the first decades of the new archaeology. Generating such fine-grained data is, granted, a tall order, but technological advances in archaeology—such as accelerator C-14 and stable isotope analysis of human skeletal remains—may eventually be able to fill the bill.

These are not shortcomings in optimal foraging theory but uniquely archaeological problems emerging from the specifics of the past and the immaturity of our middle-range methods of understanding. Optimal foraging models may prove to be an effective bridge for archaeologists to use to pass into the realm of general theory. But such a passage should not require that archaeologists retrogress into another 1960s Age of Aquarius, when we relied on middle-range assumptions now known to be incorrect.

If successfully applied, the perspective of evolutionary biology may provide a way to understand long-term human dietary change and land use patterns: "The value of such theory lies in its role as a reference dimension, as a source of testable hypotheses about the organization of subsistence-related behavior in a wide range of environmental, technological, and social circumstances (O'Connell and Hawkes 1981, p. 116).

There is some danger here, of course, because archaeologists are, from time to time, seduced and sidetracked by slick techniques. Some unfortunately think that any general theory is preferable to no theory at all, and archaeologists remain in constant peril of simply buying their theory straight off the rack.

But there can be no question that optimal foraging models do indeed open up potentially fruitful lines of inquiry: Either the foraging models stand up to observable behavior, or they do not. When models fail to fit behavioral reality, they can be refined or discarded. This is perhaps the greatest strength of the optimal foraging effort in anthropology.

WHERE TO GO FROM HERE?

On the Current State of General Theory in Americanist Archaeology: For a fairly critical view, see Binford (1977, pp. 1–10), Dunnell (1980a, 1983), Meltzer (1979), Salmon (1982, p. 140), Thomas (1986). For a bleak opinion, see Trigger (1984).

On the Relevance of Optimal Foraging Theory to Archaeology: Robert Bettinger (1980) provides an early, programmatic statement for archaeologists (see also Bettinger 1987); Eric Alden Smith (1983) wrote a balanced, discriminating piece on the same topic; see also Durham (1981), O'Connell and Hawkes (1984), Smith and Winterhalder (1981, 1985), Winterhalder (1981). *Foraging Theory* by D. W. Stephens and J. R. Krebs (1986) is a superlative general treatment of the subject; for a discussion of the concept of optimization, see Maynard Smith (1978).

Some Specific Applications of Optimal Foraging Theory to Ethnographic People: Winterhalder (1980, 1981) on the Boreal Forest Cree. Hawkes, Hill, and O'Connell (1982), Hill and Hawkes (1983), and Hill et al. (1987) for research on the Aché of Paraguay. Hames and Vickers (1982) on Amazonian groups. O'Connell and colleagues on the Alyawara of Australia. Hawkes and O'Connell (1981), O'Connell and Hawkes (1981), and Smith (1981) on the Inuit. For criticisms of the O'Connell and Hawkes (1981) application, see Balme (1983), Durham (1981, p. 225), Martin (1985, pp. 615–616), and especially the exchange between Sih and Milton (1985) and O'Connell and Hawkes (1985).

Some Specific Applications of Optimal Foraging Theory to Archaeology: Bayham (1979); Bettinger and Baumhoff (1982); K. T. Jones (1984); O'Connell and Hawkes (1981); O'Connell, Jones, and Sims (1982); Perlman (1980); Smith (1983, p. 633); Winterhalder (1981); Yesner (1981).

Some Theories on the Domestication of Plants and Animals

Regardless of how one views hunter-gatherers—as primitives, as lay ecologists, or as optimal foragers—such adaptations provide a baseline from which to explore the evolution of more advanced technology, such as agriculture and pastoralism.

Countless theories have been constructed to account for the initial efforts at domesticating plants and animals. Anthropologists of the eighteenth and nineteenth centuries were concerned largely with devising worldwide evolutionary schemes, yet lacked the relevant archaeological data. The cultural evolutionists relied instead on analogies with contemporary primitive societies and linguistic evidence. As we saw, Lewis Henry Morgan in *Ancient Society* (1877) suggested that animal domestication (pastoralism) must have preceded agricultural villages throughout the Eastern Hemisphere. His evidence? Read this: "That the discovery and cultivation of cereals by the Aryan family was subsequent to the domestication of animals is shown by the fact that there are common terms for these animals in the several dialects of the Aryan language, and no common terms for the cereals or cultivated plants" (Morgan 1877, p. 23). Morgan viewed plant domestication mostly as an expedient means for providing food for the already domesticated herds.

Childe's Oasis Theory

Through the years, a number of other theories appeared, and their evolution is instructive, indicating major avenues of thought. One of the more pervasive explanations—termed the *oasis theory*—was offered in the 1940s by British archaeologist V. Gordon Childe. Briefly stated, Childe's theory held that as the Pleistocene (Ice Age) glaciers melted, the world's climate became warmer and generally more arid. In the desert areas, especially those of the Near East, the acquisition of water became a major problem for survival. As both people and animals flocked to the oases and rare desert streams in the difficult search for nourishment, the forced association between people and animals eventually produced a symbiotic relationship. In time, this situation modulated from mutual benefit to mutual dependence. Childe explained the mechanisms (processes) for the beginnings of animal domestication in rather simple terms:

> The huntsman and his prey thus find themselves united in an effort to circumvent the dreadful power of drought. But if the hunter is also a cultivator, he will have something to offer the famished beasts: the stubble of his freshly reaped fields will afford the best grazing in the oasis. Once the grains are garnered, the cultivator can tolerate half-starved mouflons or wild oxen trespassing upon his garden plots. Such will be too weak to run away, too thin to be worth killing for food. Instead, man can study their habits, drive off the lions and wolves that would prey upon them, and perhaps offer them some surplus grains from his stores. The beasts, for their part, will grow tame and accustomed to man's proximity. (1951a, pp. 67–68)

The domestication of animals was possible in Childe's scheme only after people had become successful cultivators of plants. In order to find the roots of floral domestication, one needed to look no further than the nearby Nile Valley. The "nobler grasses"—ancient ancestors of modern wheat and barley—apparently grew in abundance on the banks of the Nile, where they were subjected to annual flooding and enrichment by the fertile alluvial soil. Childe felt that the plants of the Nile Valley were controlled by nature's perfect irrigation cycle and that it remained only for "some genius" to produce similar artificial irrigation conditions elsewhere.

The Natural Habitat Zone Model

Although Childe and others felt that the Egyptian area held the key to early domestication, a second, competing hypothesis (named by Gary Wright 1971, p. 455) was proposed by Harold Peake and H. J. Fleure (1927). The Peake–Fleure model highlighted a number of preconditions that they felt were critical to the origin of domestication:

1. The natural area must have hosted a regular and reliable harvest each year.
2. The geography must have been rather restricting, and so many people were required to stay put and change rather than simply move elsewhere with an old adaptation.

Thomas Malthus: Starvation and Misery Are Inevitable

Thomas Robert Malthus (1766–1834) was born into a wealthy eighteenth-century English family (see Figure 15–3). Thomas's father, Daniel, was the embodiment of the Age of Reason, well connected in intellectual and philosophical circles. To this entire generation, the world was on the threshold of paradise: the laws of reason would eventually eradicate all poverty, misery, and suffering.

Despite this rosy, British, establishment outlook, difficulties lurked only a few miles away. These were the years that Charles Dickens called "the best of times, the worst of times," and revolution was sweeping France. Being gentlemen of leisure, the Malthus family debated the significance of the French Revolution. Father Daniel remained enthusiastic, still arguing that "reason" would be sufficient to lift humanity from darkness, superstition, and cruelty.

Young Malthus disagreed, and he brooded about the future of civilized humanity. How could society be perfected when population growth was so obviously outstripping the available resources? Their British country manor rocked as father and son debated their positions. Finally, young Malthus prepared a treatise so that he could more effectively marshal his arguments against his father. Daniel Malthus was so impressed with the document that he encouraged his son to publish it, which he did (anonymously) as *An Essay on the Principle of Population As It Affects the Future Improvement of Society* (1798). Five years later, Malthus published a second essay, documenting his speculations and answering his numerous critics.

The Malthusian essays explore the relationship between the human population and the resource base available to support it. The Malthusian argument holds that because human fertility is essentially constant, the human population will be governed only by a changing mortality rate. Population size will grow unchecked until something dramatic happens. Population size can be reduced only by what Malthus termed "vice and misery," by catastrophes such as war, epidemic, or disaster.

The basic Malthusian position remains an important force in contemporary economics, although neo-Malthusians (such as Kenneth Boulding) reject Malthus's assumption that people's capabilities for production and redistribution cannot exceed population. The neo-Malthusian premise is that population growth is a dependent variable, determined by preceding changes in subsistence potential.

FIGURE 15–3 Thomas Robert Malthus. (Courtesy the American Museum of Natural History)

3. The area could not have been forested or swampy, because early technology did not allow for clearing fields or filling swamps.
4. The area could not have been isolated, for contact with other cultures was necessary to facilitate the breakdown of custom and taboo that could have inhibited change.

Peake and Fleure examined a number of candidates, eventually concluding that only Southwestern Asia met their requirements. Essential to their theory was the natural distribution of wild plants suitable for domestication (particularly wild wheat, emmer, and einkorn); wild cattle and goats would also have been available. The Peake–Fleure argument held that climatic change led to the domestication of plants and animals, but only in areas of their natural occurrence.

Braidwood's "Hilly Flanks" Theory

Shortly after World War II, Robert Braidwood of the University of Chicago traveled to the foothills of Iraq to spearhead a series of strategic excavations designed to test the competing hypotheses regarding the origins of domestication. Braidwood's excavations employed a bevy of natural scientists, and the results questioned the very existence of significant post-Pleistocene climatic shifts in the Near East. Instead, Braidwood and his team found that the climate had been essentially stable during the period of animal and plant domestication. In light of these data, Childe's oasis theory was rejected. Braidwood proposed a new explanation, which came to be known as the "hilly flanks theory." Rather than calling on environmental processes to explain the origins of agriculture, Braidwood and his colleagues suggested that because the climate had been essentially constant, a post-Pleistocene readaptation (the Mesolithic) would have been unnecessary in the Near East.

Braidwood concluded instead that agriculture had arisen in the Near East as a "logical outcome" of culture elaboration and specialization. The hunters and gatherers simply "settled in" during the post-Pleistocene, becoming intimately familiar with their plant and animal neighbors. As culture evolved further, so did more efficient means of exploitation and agriculture, which formed another quite natural link in the long evolutionary chain. The hilly flanks theory is thus an elaboration of the earlier Peake–Fleure model, yet without the climatic elements and environmental deterioration.

Although the Childe, Peake–Fleure, and Braidwood theories use different data and reach conflicting conclusions, they do agree on the fundamental processes that triggered the initial domestication of Old World plants and animals. All three theories make the implicit assumption that humanity continually seeks to improve its technology and subsistence. Whenever the proper conditions come along, it is "logical" that plants and animals will be domesticated, because domestication provides a more technologically advanced economic base.

This assumption is fundamental. Childe, Braidwood, and the others were basically Malthusians; that is, they shared the basic economic premises set forth almost two hundred years ago by Thomas R. Malthus. The Malthusian position stresses that population will grow until checked by changing mortality, Malthus's "vice and misery."

You can see why the Childe and Braidwood theories are fundamentally Malthusian in nature. Why were plants and animals domesticated? The Malthusian argument suggests that domestication occurred simply as a natural consequence of people's continual struggle to improve technology. Because growing crops and keeping flocks are more advanced means of subsistence, people quite naturally stopped foraging to become full-time farmers and herdsmen. Once agriculture was adopted, the human population was free to increase dramatically. The wholesale shift to domestication came to be known as the Neolithic Revolution.

Population-based Theories Deriving from Ester Boserup

In the past few decades, anthropologists have begun to turn away from Malthusian explanations. Particularly difficult to accept is the economic and ecological determinism implied by the neo-Malthusian position (see Zubrow 1976). Childe argued that when the climate changed, people would readily turn to domestication. Braidwood rejected Childe's notion, arguing instead that domestication arose as an evolutionary elaboration of the "settling-in" process.

An important alternative was provided by Ester Boserup. Whereas the Malthusian argument is essentially pessimistic, with starvation and misery increasing as the human population increases toward the carrying capacity, the Boserup model is a more optimistic one, suggesting that technological responses will become available "when they are needed." The fact remains, of course, that the population increases exponentially, whereas resources do not; food production cannot be intensified infinitely. And there are implied limits even under the Boserup model. Many contemporary theories of plant and animal domestication tend to focus on population growth as a key factor, although other investigators retain the more traditional Malthusian perspective. Several have actively applied the ideas of Boserup to the prehistoric evidence. The perspectives differ on their view of population growth: Is it a cause or an effect?

Binford's "Explanatory Sketch"

As Lewis Binford (1968b, p. 327) points out, the Malthusian perspective implies that people will continuously attempt to increase their food supply, and this is why the Childe, Peake–Fleure, and Braidwood explanations of domestication are fundamentally Malthusian. Yet despite these arguments, the archaeological record clearly shows long periods of technological and economic stability. How can such stability be explained in the face of Malthusian progress?

Binford uses the **niche** and **habitat** concepts. Habitat refers to the environmental setting in which an organism lives, and a niche is the way in which it exploits that habitat. An animal's habitat is its "address," and its niche is its "profession." Binford views plant domestication as merely another one of humans' possible ecological niches. We know of many ethnographic and archaeological cases in which well-developed hunting-gathering societies (such as the California Indians and groups on the northwest Pacific coast) never grew crops at all; yet they lived in rather large, settled villages. Why, they might have asked, adopt the risks of some new method when the old one seems to work well enough?

Why, indeed? Binford prefers Boserup's theoretical position, in which people adapt to new energy sources (such as domesticated plants) only when forced to do so. Binford thus rejects Braidwood's notion that agriculture developed because "culture was ready for it." On this point, Binford agrees with Childe's earlier argument that domestication constitutes a new niche, one imposed by changing conditions. But whereas Childe named climatic and environmental changes as the initiating factors, Binford proposed that the true stress on these groups was pressure from other human populations.

Specifically, population pressure was exerted by groups of people with an extremely successful Mesolithic adaptation who were occupying the same habitat, such as within the Fertile Crescent. The post-Pleistocene emphasis on riverine and lacustrine food sources (fish, shellfish, sea mammals) permitted a more sedentary and comparatively lavish existence than that of the more traditional hunter-gatherer modes of subsistence. The competitive pressure on the nonsedentary, non-Mesolithic peoples must have been severe, and it is in these marginal areas, Binford suggests, that people first turned to domestication for survival.

Binford's hypothesis attempts not only to explain most of the known facts but also

Ester Boserup: Technology Will Respond When Needed

In her influential book, *The Conditions of Agricultural Growth: The Economics of Agrarian Change Under Population Pressure* (1965), Danish economist **Ester Boserup** reversed the classic Malthusian equation (Figure 15–4). Instead of regarding population growth as a response to changing economic and ecological potential (as did Malthus), Boserup argued that population growth is itself the autonomous or independent variable. Population growth as such is held to be a major factor in determining agricultural development and productivity (Boserup 1965, p. 11).

Concerned primarily with contemporary agrarian societies, Boserup asked, What happens when the population increases? In low-density, primitive agricultural areas, excess land is available, and such societies practice slash-and-burn agriculture. People move from one plot to another, eventually coming back to the original plot. All of this occurs within a home territory. In such a system, the land is given sufficient time to replenish its resources through lengthy fallow periods. Slash-and-burn methods were common in Europe before World War I and today support some 200 million people in Africa, Latin America, and Asia.

But as population increases, the land must be used more intensively, and so the fallow periods become shorter and shorter. People must work harder as land becomes more scarce, and technology increases in the form of agricultural machinery, fertilizers, and pesticides. Boserup sees the frequency of cropping as a key variable and contends that economic systems can be viewed along a continuum. At one end is the society with excess uncultivated land; at the other extreme is the society with multicropped land, in which a second crop is sown as the first is reaped. Boserup believes that all forms of primitive land use can be viewed along this continuum, that population growth is the prime mover causing societies to evolve from one stage to another.

to provide directly testable implications for further archaeological fieldwork. Specifically, Binford's theory predicts:

1. There must have been a population increase owing to a new and efficient Mesolithic lifeway in the optimal zones before the first domestication.
2. The earliest evidence of domestication should come not from these optimal zones where the Mesolithic lifeway functioned but, rather, in the marginal, less favored areas (as the law of evolutionary potential would suggest).
3. The material culture of the earliest Neolithic populations should be essentially similar to that of their Mesolithic neighbors.
4. There should be no circumscribed center of domestication; the process should have occurred simultaneously in several areas under population pressure (see Wright 1971, p. 461).

FIGURE 15–4 Ester Boserup. (Courtesy Ester Boserup)

Kent Flannery (1969, 1973b) applied Binford's "density equilibrium" model to the archaeology of the Near East. Following Binford's arguments to their logical conclusion, Flannery suggests that the "optimal" habitats should have been the centers for population growth, with the marginal areas receiving the emigrant overflow. Flannery discusses a "broad-spectrum" revolution that began about 20,000 B.C. and amounted to a major broadening of the subsistence base from mostly hunting to include larger amounts of fish, crabs, water turtles, mollusks, and migratory waterfowl (Flannery 1969, p. 77). To Flannery, this change in subsistence was due less to post-Pleistocene climatic change than to a simple overuse of prime land. The demand for the previously ignored invertebrates, fish, waterfowl, and plant resources would have increased in precisely those "marginal" areas in which Binford believes that the initial domestication of plants occurred. Flannery, like Binford, contends that the population increase (á la Boserup) could have functioned as a major factor, encouraging hunting-gathering groups to begin cultivating plant crops. In both cases, population pressure becomes the major independent variable.

The processes that triggered plant and animal domestication remain poorly understood. The Flannery–Binford model was roundly criticized, and both subsequently recanted (Binford 1983a, pp. 198–202) or heavily modified (Flannery 1986, pp. 10–12) their earlier arguments. Meyers (1971) and Cohen (1977, pp. 7–8) were correct that this model lacked empirical support, as the archaeological record shows no evidence of inland migration near the early agricultural centers. Cohen also pointed out that the "broad-spectrum" adaptation was not restricted to seacoasts and that agriculture actually arose earlier and in areas other than those recognized by Flannery and Binford. Kent Flannery noted candidly:

> Although [the theory] has won an almost frightening acceptance among some of my colleagues, it is still unproven and highly speculative . . . our archaeological data (such as they are) do not show strong population increases in "optimum" areas like the Lebanese woodland, but the very opposite . . . the model comes too close to making population growth and climatic change into prime movers. (1973b, p. 284)

Cohen's Overt Population Pressure Theory

Although no longer a viable theoretical candidate, Binford's (1968b) discussion was a turning point in the archaeological literature because it tried to identify the stimuli that changed hunter-gatherer adaptations into agriculture-based lifeways. Mark Cohen's important (1977) book took matters one step further by suggesting that population growth was even more pervasive than Boserup thought. In *The Food Crisis in Prehistory: Overpopulation and the Origins of Agriculture,* Cohen asked two important questions: (1) Why would successful hunter-gatherers decide to become agricultural? and (2) Why do people around the world acquire agriculture at about the same time?

Cohen's answer is that by about fifteen thousand years ago in the Old World, and eight thousand to ten thousand years ago in the New, the human population had spread out across most of the globe, basically exhausting all available strategies for garnering a living through hunter-gatherer life-styles. The quality of life began to deteriorate as the larger population led people away from the desirable (but scarce) large fauna toward more plentiful, if less desirable, "secondary" recourses (such as grains and tubers). In light of a continually growing human population, no options remained except agriculture—and that's what people did, by increasingly intensifying their exploitation of the more productive plant species, some of which changed genetically in the process.

Cohen's heavy reliance on population pressure has been variously challenged. Some assert that population pressure could not have been such an important causal factor because people knew how to control population levels before they reached carrying capacity. Others see population pressure as a problem restricted to relatively recent times, the result of health advances made during the Industrial Revolution.

David Rindos and the Coevolutionary Model

The previous discussions in this section consider the relationship among human sedentism, population growth, and resource-selection strategies. This interest has suggested numerous scenarios in which one of these variables is assigned causal priority over the other two. Childe and Braidwood argued that sedentism must have come first, followed by domestication and population growth. Those favoring the Boserup school contended that population growth was primary, with the other two variables falling into a secondary role. Recent discussion of plant and animal domestication tends to minimize the importance of the neo-Malthusians and the Boserupians and, like the optimal foraging theoretical framework introduced earlier, moves toward an approach more specifically grounded in Darwinian selection (Dunnell 1980b, Leonard and Jones 1987). Although there is considerable diversity in the selectionist approaches, we present here the innovative evolutionary approach of David Rindos to the long-standing issue of plant domestication.

In contrast, some more recent studies have suggested that major changes in social systems tend to be **coevolutionary**, that there is mutual selection among components rather than a linear cause-and-effect sequence. David Rindos (1984), for instance, argued that the origins of agriculture can best be understood by exploring the evolutionary forces affecting the development of domestication systems. Viewed in this way, domestication is seen not as an evolutionary stage but, rather, as a process, "the result of coevolutionary interactions between humans and plants" (Rindos 1984, p. xiv).

Like the optimal foragers, Rindos relies heavily on our understanding of Darwinian principles developed in more than a century of research by geneticists, plant ecologists, and, more recently, molecular plant biologists. Specifically, Rindos asserts that the relationships between plants and people must be appreciated without recourse to either cultural adaptations or human intent (Rindos 1984, p. xiv). *Incidental domestication* occurs as the product of the dispersal and protection of wild plants by members of nonagricultural human societies, as the direct result of human feeding behavior. Eventually, this relationship will select for certain changes in the plants involved, "preadapting" them for further domestication. Initial domestication fosters a relationship that promotes and preserves a "conservative" interaction between people and plants: The size of human populations "carried" by the plant communities is limited, and in return, the rate change in the incidental domesticate is low (compared with what will develop later).

Specialized domestication occurs as new types of plant–people interactions develop. As humans come to be the dispersal agents for various species of plants, these plants are dispersed into the specific area of human habitation. In effect, a new brand of ecological succession takes place in which the plants being used as human food become increasingly more common in areas where people are living. This change is largely demographic, the effect of people's changing their environment so as to benefit indirectly the domesticated plant. That is, people become so dependent on the plant communities that the survival of both is interdependent. People also begin selectively destroying various plant species around their communities, in effect setting the stage for the development of complex agricultural systems. Full-blown *agricultural domestication* takes place when practices like weeding, irrigation, and plowing create new opportunities for plant evolution, thereby increasing the rate at which domesticated plants evolve.

Michael O'Brien (1987) applied the coevolutionary approach to the issue of plant domestication in the prehistoric midwestern United States. O'Brien thinks that "incidental domestication" (in the sense of Rindos) took place in the Woodland Midwest between about 3000 B.C. and 300 B.C.. (during the Late Archaic and Early Woodland periods). Intensive flotation of archaeological deposits, as considered in Chapter 7, revealed an increasing dependence on native-annual plant foods during this time. The organically rich deposits surrounding such seasonally occupied camps provided ideal habitats for colonization by wild plants and incidental domesticates—such as goosefoot and marsh elder—which in turn would have attracted further human attention. Considerable evidence from settlement pattern studies (such as discussed in Chapter 12) suggests that groups were reoccupying or reusing key locales over extended periods of time (Braun and Plog 1982, p. 515; O'Brien 1987, p. 186). Populations began to aggregate in the major valley trenches, with settlements adjacent to active major stream channels (Braun 1987).

Why would such changes occur at the same time? From the perspective of coevolutionary theory, the Late Archaic and Early Woodland periods saw the interactions between people and plants intensify to the point that human groups were reoccupying selected areas because of these favorable human–plant interactions. Braun (1987, p. 172) contends that by 200 B.C., horticultural experimentation had reached a critical threshold of productivity and flexibility. Sedentism had become a viable option for those groups participating in the plant interactions, although the risks of this strategy may have been high (due to periodic droughts or floods).

Whatever the population growth rates may have been at this time, they surely increased during the succeeding Middle Woodland and early Late Woodland periods (O'Brien 1987, pp. 186–187), perhaps presenting significant demographic problems by A.D. 400. The combination of increasing community size and probable in-migration from outside the valley effectively decreased the size of the resource catchments available to each village. Ceramics were made with thinner walls to allow more rapid heat conduction, perhaps a response to more efficient preparation of seed-based gruels and porridges. Braun and Plog (1982) propose that as populations in the river valleys increased during Middle Woodland times, the regions became more socially integrated, and selective mechanisms were created to buffer the potential problems of environmental risk. Human burial practices during this time became more elaborate, suggesting perhaps that Middle Woodland groups began to solidify use rights through more formal ancestral ties. Clearly, the Middle Woodland groups had moved past specialized domestication into a stage of full-blown agricultural domestication, in Rindos's sense.

The coevolutionary explanatory framework has the advantage of moving beyond single-factor, "prime mover" arguments. Cohen's population pressure argument, for instance, assigns causal priority to population growth. Under the coevolutionary approach, however, the question of which came first—population growth, plant domestication, or sedentism—becomes irrelevant.

The question of why humans entered into such a coevolutionary relationship with plants is, likewise, to Rindos (1984, p. 141) "a question without real meaning. We might as well ask why certain ants established coevolutionary relationships with fungi or certain birds with specific fruits." The changes occurred as a result of maximizing fitness at a particular time, in a particular place: "They were neither inevitable nor desirable, but merely happened." By using this evolutionary perspective, Rindos thus sidesteps thorny issues such as human intent, conscious selection, the "cultural factors" that give rise to domestication, and even the when and where of agricultural invention—focusing instead on the coevolutionary relationships that developed between and among plant and animal species.

There is no need to explore further the theories attempting to account for plant and animal domestication (and, believe me, dozens of additional explanations exist). The point is not to define the exact moment that somebody first planted a seed or monkeyed around with the genetics of penned animals but, rather, to illustrate how the search for processes proceeds.

Progress in archaeology (or any science) does not occur in a theoretical vacuum. Note that Braidwood made certain (Malthusian) assumptions about the nature of human evolution: Culture evolves on its own. Several more recent investigators followed Boserup by assuming that cultures change only when forced to do so, such as when the population increases. As these pages have emphasized over and over again, the facts in archaeology will never speak for themselves. We arrive at the truth only by framing theories that are then used to predict future finds in the archaeological record. Some processes predict the past successfully; others do not. This is how we judge the success of our theories.

WHERE TO GO FROM HERE?

Overviews of Domestication: Stark (1986) provides an up-to-date discussion of the models applied to food production in the Americas. Green (1980) discusses the primary economic and ecological approaches; see also Asch and Asch (1985), Bender (1975, 1985), Braun and Plog (1982), Roosevelt (1984a, 1984b), Wright (1971).

Some Studies Retaining Malthusian Perspectives: Cowgill (1975a, 1975b), Hassan (1974, 1975, 1981), Polgar (1972).

Some Models Deriving from Boserup's Work: Cohen (1977), Flannery (1969, 1973b, 1986), Harner (1970), D. Harris (1972), Patterson (1971), P. E. L. Smith (1976), P. E. L. Smith and Young (1972).

Criticisms of the Population Pressure Approach: Bender (1975), Cowgill (1975a), Dunnell (1979, 1982b), Hassan (1975, 1981), Hayden (1981a), Price and Brown (1985, p. 14), Roosevelt (1980).

Some Theories on Origins of the State

The first human being who hurled an insult instead
of a stone was the founder of civilization.
—Attributed to Sigmund Freud

In Chapter 3 we discussed in some detail how contemporary social scientists study the societal and political dynamics of cultural institutions. There were, you will remember, two basic research approaches. The synchronic procedure emphasizes the *in situ* analysis of functioning cultural systems. This is the basic concern of ethnographers, sociologists, economists, psychologists, and (as we saw in this chapter) ethnoarchaeologists. Synchronic studies provide a picture of the dynamics of a system that operates at a single point in time: now. Part Three discussed the ways in which archaeologists, too, can conduct synchronic studies of another time period: then. In effect, the general objective of reconstructing past lifeways is an attempt to unravel the specifics and dynamics of single societies.

Anthropology's second fundamental approach is diachronic, emphasizing the development of societies over a span of time. Although the ethnographer can justly point to the richness of the detail available in contemporary society, such studies invariably fall short in an evolutionary sense because the time factor is lacking. Of course, archaeological data lack great ethnographic detail, but archaeology can provide a chronicle of *in situ* cultural developments without which diachronic studies cannot proceed.

The previous section considered some theories of plant and animal domestication, one of the most important technoecological developments in the history of human evolution. We shall now turn to the evolution of sociopolitical institutions as another example of how archaeologists are working to construct general theories to account for stability and change.

What Is the State?

Some specifics of sociopolitical change were introduced briefly in Chapter 3, and various ethnographic and archaeological bands, tribes, chiefdoms, and states have been considered throughout the text. In Chapter 13, for instance, we examined how archaeologists distinguish a ranked, chiefdom-level society from an egalitarian band (such as the Shoshone), based strictly on the archaeological record. We also considered some mechanics of settlement patterning in a state-level society, the Classic Maya. But it remains for us to study how these various sociopolitical structures—the band, the tribe, the chiefdom, and the state—came to be. That is, we have considered some aspects of synchronic dynamics but have so far ignored the issue of diachronic evolution. We shall immediately rectify this situation by focusing on the most complex political structure, the state.

The state has been defined in a number of ways over the years, and to simplify this discussion, we will follow Kent Flannery's definition:

> The state is a type of very strong, usually highly centralized government, with a professional ruling class, largely divorced from the bonds of kinship which characterize simpler societies. It is highly stratified and extremely diversified internally, with residential patterns often based on occupational specialization rather than blood or affinal relationships. The state attempts to maintain a monopoly of force, and is characterized by true law. (1972, pp. 403–404)

States generally have powerful economic structures and often a true market system. The state economy is controlled by an elite, which maintains its authority by means of a combination of law and differential access to key goods and services. States generally have populations numbering at least in the hundreds of thousands, and this population is often concentrated in large cities. Much of the population consists of economic specialists, dependent on the labor of others for subsistence. States are also known for a high level of artistic achievement, monumental architecture, and an overall state religion.

The state is thus a complex form of sociopolitical organization, and any number of contemporary examples could be cited (such as modern France or England or the United States). Ethnographers and other social scientists have studied the modern state for decades, and its dynamics are relatively well understood. But it is clear that these contemporary states are the products of a long chain of sociopolitical evolution, and how they came to be remains an unanswered question. Archaeological states are evident throughout the world in such diverse places as Classic (or maybe Formative) Mesoamerica, the Near East, Shang China, Egypt, India, and Imperial Rome. Although contemporary ethnographic studies can satisfactorily unravel the synchronic dynamics of functioning state-level organization, no amount of study of modern states can explain their evolution. The state as we know it today is a worldwide phenomenon, with a long history preserved in the archaeological record. Only through a consideration of the archaeological evidence can an accurate diachronic study be made of societies as they developed to the state level.

Theories of the origin of the state go back to the nineteenth-century cultural evolutionists, discussed briefly in Chapter 3. A number of causal factors were suggested to account for the development of the state: irrigation, warfare, population growth, circumscription, trade, cooperation and competition, and the integrative power of great religions (see Flannery 1972, pp. 405–407, and Henry Wright 1977, 1986).

Wittfogel's "Irrigation" Hypothesis

In order to see how archaeologists, as social scientists, attempt to unravel the evolution of the state, we shall begin by looking at one of the historically important theories, Karl Wittfogel's **irrigation hypothesis**. As before, we are more concerned with the nature of the search than with providing the ultimate truth.

A particularly well known theory regarding the origin of the state was expressed by Karl A. Wittfogel in his influential book *Oriental Despotism* (1957). Wittfogel asserted that the mechanisms of large-scale irrigation are directly responsible for creating the state. He argued that the great oriental societies (China, India, Mesopotamia) followed a radically different evolutionary course than did the societies of Western Europe and elsewhere. The state evolved because of special conditions required by large-scale irrigation: the imposition of inordinately strong political controls to maintain the hydraulic works, the tendency for the ruling class to merge with the ruling bureaucracy, the close identification of the dominant religion with governmental offices, and the diminution of private property and economic initiative. Wittfogel contended that after a creative period in which the bureaucracy was begun, stagnation set in, corrupting power and creating a despotic and feudal system. Wittfogel saw the hydraulic society as an initial step to totalitarianism, and his theory of the state was clearly framed with twentieth-century perspectives in mind. In fact, "it was my belief in these values that put me behind the barbed wire of Hitler's concentration camps" (Wittfogel 1957, p. v).

Wittfogel's theory can be translated into a simple flow chart as shown in Figure 15–5. According to this interpretation, the state evolved in direct response to the demands of large-scale irrigation. The need for coordinated labor, massive construction, and so forth, led to increased wealth, military strength, and eventually to the powerful ruling bureaucracy that characterized state development.

Carneiro's "Warfare and Circumscription" Hypothesis

A second explanation for the origin of the state, offered by Robert Carneiro, rests on a different initial premise, that autonomous political units never willingly surrender their sovereignty. Carneiro terms Wittfogel's irrigation hypothesis a "voluntaristic" theory, one requiring that "at some point in their history, certain peoples spontaneously, rationally, and voluntarily gave up their individual sovereignties and united with other communities to form a larger political unit deserving to be called a state" (Carneiro 1970a, p. 733; see also Carneiro 1988). This is why he objects to the irrigation hypothesis of Wittfogel and others.

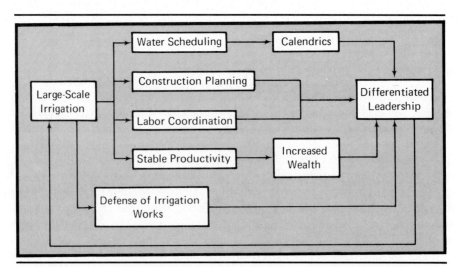

FIGURE 15–5 Schematic diagram of Wittfogel's irrigation hypothesis for the origin of the state (adapted from Wright 1977, Figure 7.1). (Courtesy Henry Wright and the School of American Research)

Carneiro argues, instead, that egalitarian settlements will be transformed into chiefdoms, and chiefdoms into kingdoms, only when coercive force is involved, and warfare is especially pertinent to this transformation. Of course, some tribes might agree to cooperate in times of stress, but such federations are temporary and voluntarily dissolved once the crisis has passed. Carneiro's initial premise stipulated that political change of lasting significance will come about only as result of coercive pressure. Warfare is the only mechanism powerful enough to impose bureaucratic authority on a large scale. Thus warfare—the world's main coercive device—plays an important role in the origin of the state.

But it is clear from the archaeological record that warfare is considerably older and more widespread than the state is. Because warfare does not invariably lead to state formation, Carneiro is quick to add that though necessary, warfare is insufficient in itself to account for the state. According to Carneiro, it is in areas where agricultural land is at a premium—areas that are environmentally "circumscribed"—that warfare predictably leads to state formation. Competition over land arose first where arable land was restricted by natural barriers such as mountains, deserts, or seas. The vanquished peoples had no place to flee and thus were required to submit to the expanding political units of the victors. Carneiro points out that the early states near the Nile, the Tigris-Euphrates, the Indus Valley, and the valleys of Mexico and Peru all evolved in areas of circumscribed agricultural land. Conversely, in areas where agricultural land was plentiful—such as in northern Europe, central Africa, and the eastern woodlands of North America—states were quite late in developing, if they did at all.

Figure 15–6 expresses Carneiro's circumscription theory as a flow diagram. The combination of population growth and circumscribed agricultural resources leads to increased warfare, which in turn leads to the centralized political organization characteristic of state-level complexity.

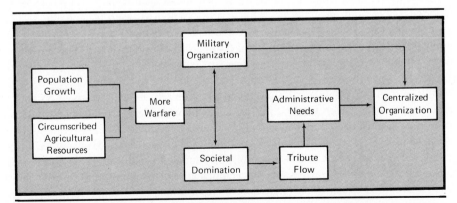

FIGURE 15–6 Schematic diagram of Carneiro's circumscription and warfare hypothesis for the origin of the state (adapted from Wright 1977, Figure 7.3). (Courtesy Henry Wright and the School of American Research)

Newer Directions in State Formation Theory

Both the irrigation and circumscription hypotheses are examples of general theory in anthropology. Each proponent would claim that all else being equal, this theory explains the origin of the state throughout the world, at any time. But more recently, in his review of the tremendous quantity of data now relating to state-level organization in Mesopotamia, the Indus Valley, Mesoamerica, and the central Andes, Henry Wright (1986) found that the regularities postulated by Wittfogel, Carneiro, and others cannot be sustained by the archaeological record, as it is now understood (see also Flannery 1972, Service 1975, Wright and Johnson 1975). Similarly, while granting that Wittfogel and Carneiro have stimulated considerable controversy and research, Cohen (1981, p. 106) asserts that their theories "have 'failed' as explanations to varying degrees because localized research has failed (1) to confirm the existence of the postulated common element in areas of state formation; (2) to demonstrate its absence in other areas; or (3) to confirm its postulated role in the evolutionary process."

In the discussion dealing with the origins of agriculture, you read a section entitled "Cohen's Overt Population Pressure Theory." At this point, you might think that perhaps Mark Cohen would have jumped into the particularistic breach, to suggest his own, population pressure–driven theory to explain the origin of the state. If you thought this, you would be wrong.

Cohen (1977) asked a compelling question: "Why did many independent human populations begin to organize themselves hierarchically at the same time after so many millennia of egalitarian structure?" The answer to this question, according to Cohen, lies in the consequences of the abandoning of a hunting-gathering lifeway in favor of an agricultural strategy. Although the number of calories increased with domestication, so did vulnerability to environmental fluctuations, and as such stress increases, so did the development of cultural buffering mechanisms: the development of storage systems, increased interregional trade (in both luxury and subsistence items), and the increasing importance of centralized authorities who became essential to ensuring economic security.

Well aware of the possibility of "alternative pathways" to civilization, Cohen proposed two hypotheses for the origin of the state: as (1) occurring in "special environments" and/or as (2) "epiphenomena." The first explanation suggests that if population pressure–driven vulnerability to environmental fluctuations is a major stimulus to political evolution, then one might expect the process of centralization to be most pronounced under conditions in which vulnerability was high, in which large populations would need "buffering" against environmental variability, in which populations were "circumscribed" (*sensu* Carneiro), or in which environments were sufficiently varied to encourage a single centralized political system. But admitting that such explanations are "problematical," Cohen decided that such environmental/ecological explanations might not explain the specific evolution of states, as "there appears to be ample justification for recognizing a common set of adaptive problems as underlying the more *general* emergence of centralized governments" (Cohen 1981, pp. 121–122).

Alternatively, if the earliest state developed as *epiphenomena*—as specific outcomes of more general selective pressures favoring centralization explainable only by historical factors—then the process may reflect more "random creative processes" rather than the result of more systematic selective processes. In short, whereas Carneiro's integrated theory relies on the potential territorial expanse of a social unit as the key factor in state formation, Cohen worries that no single "prime mover" may ever be found.

But lest we close on a note of anomie, let me mention one final theory regarding the evolution of the state, that constructed by Allen Johnson and Timothy Earle (1987). Drawing on three case studies—France and Japan (both during the Middle Ages) and the Inka of the Andes—they concluded that state formation can indeed be explained on the basis of a few universal factors.

Johnson and Earle found subsistence intensification to be a necessary, if not sufficient, cause of state formation. Without packing of the landscape, capital improvements, carefully regulated agricultural cycles, competition for prime lands, and populations sufficiently large to support a market economy, a society would not be economically tied closely enough together to lead toward this level of social complexity. Rather, state-level organization can develop only when two conditions are present: "high population density, with explicit needs for an overarching system of integration; and opportunities for sufficient economic control to permit the stable finance of regional institutions and to support a ruling class. Where these two sets of conditions occur together, we find the rapid expansion of the political economy and the beginning of the state" (Johnson and Earle 1987, p. 270). This newest synthesis has yet to receive the critical review it deserves (as did the Wittfogel and Carneiro theories it attempts to replace). While the jury remains out about the success of these newer theories, there is no question that further elaboration will be necessary. Do not believe, for a minute, that Johnson and Earle will have the final word on the origins of the state.

Some Theories on the Evolution of Ideology

In the last analysis magic, religion, and science
are nothing but theories of thought.
—Sir James Frazer

Searching for Ideology in the Archaeological Record

This part of the book deals with cultural processes and how archaeologists go about finding (and understanding) them. I made the point in Chapters 2 and 4 that these processual statements are really timeless and spaceless generalizations. Although a statement about lifeway must be firmly bound by the when and the where, processual statements presumably hold, independent of time and space.

Having said this, I must point out that this assertion can be challenged. Human beings are governed, as it were, by the laws of physics. Humanity is ultimately a pawn at the mercy of the immutable laws of the universe. Unfortunately, recognition of this fact does not lead to an explanation of cultural uniformity and diversity: Humans are not like electrons.

Unlike electrons, humans have the ability to perceive, to know, and to humanize themselves. It is said that although animals know, only humans know they know. Although the electron is oblivious to our measurement of it, the human mind is not. Because the human subject knows the object of his or her inquiry, the subject can reflect on behavior as both subject and object, able to change some aspects of both self and nature.

This human awareness may make impossible a prediction of future states of humanity. That is, if one follows this line of argument, the laws governing the form and pattern of human behavior may not be so immutable after all. Although the social sciences can to some degree explain the present and predict the past, one can be less sure about predicting the distant future, because of the human interaction. Once a prediction is made, human cognition may interact with that very prediction and alter the evolutionary course.

This may seem to be a picky philosophical point, but let me take the argument one step further. I contended earlier that cultural laws are independent of time and space. Stating that the laws of culture are timeless and spaceless implies an assumption that human cognition has remained a constant. How else could such laws be independent of time?

But cognition is not a constant. It is apparent that the cultural laws that governed human life some two million years ago will not explain the range of variability in human behavior today. Aside from the obvious taxonomic difficulties of classifying early hominid fossil remains, we are also faced with the problem of dealing with the emergence of human cognition. Did *Australopithecus africanus* have modern cognitive powers? Undoubtedly not. Did **Homo erectus** "think" in the same way we do? I doubt it. What about Neanderthal *(Homo sapiens neandertalensis)?* Did they think, talk, and communicate as we do? And what about the artists who painted the bulls on the walls of Lascaux some fifteen thousand years ago? What were they thinking about? All of these questions are germane to the original point: How far back in time are we entitled to generalize the laws of cultural behavior?

Archaeologists have been traditionally reticent to pursue such questions. This is partly due to the domination of archaeology by the cultural materialists, and also because of the difficulty of treating past systems of ideology and symbolism. As Lewis Binford (1967, p. 234) forcefully argued, "We would be paleopsychologists, and our training equips us poorly for this role." And yet, as archaeology pushes toward its processual objectives, it becomes clear that archaeologists are indeed becoming increasingly concerned with matters of cognition, symbolism, and ideation.

So little work has been done in this area that it is difficult even to discuss the relationship of cognitive processes, past and present. In truth, we are dealing with a highly controversial area that archaeologists have only begun to investigate. Some feel that contemporary archaeologists are afraid to ask "pertinent" questions; others think that all questions dealing with the archaeology of ideology are silly and unanswerable: There is not much agreement here.

A major theme of this book has been that archaeologists have three basic goals: chronology, lifeway, and process. Before we can successfully analyze these processes, we must thoroughly understand both the chronology and the specific lifeways involved. Chapter 14 discussed a number of investigations that are attempting to deal with cognition and ideation at the level of lifeway. Unfortunately, lifeway studies remain so tenuous that generalized conclusions at the processual level are currently premature. But let us examine what is being done in this important direction.

For example, Alexander Marshack's technique for analyzing Upper Paleolithic engravings was discussed in some detail in Chapter 14. Marshack contends that the La Marche bone could have been used as a notational device for keeping track of the phases of the moon. This "lunar hypothesis" has received a great deal of critical attention by archaeologists. But in one sense this is unfortunate, as it represents but a single aspect of Marshack's highly innovative research.

At a different level of abstraction, Marshack is also concerned with finding the cognitive processes and strategies implied by the Upper Paleolithic engravings and cave art. The lunar notations—if, in fact, that is what they are—represent a single symbolic system, a prewriting, prearithmetic mode of symbolization. But these notations were undoubtedly only one of many symbolic systems that operated during the Upper Paleolithic. The same cultures created an elaborate complex of cave paintings; yet these paintings involved a very different symbolic system. Doubtless, there were many other such systems of symbol use that simply have not been preserved in the archaeological record.

Thus, at the level of lifeway, Marshack is examining symbolic artifacts to determine their function within a specific cultural setting. But simultaneously, Marshack raises profound questions concerning the evolution of human cognitive and intellectual capacity. Surely an evolving notational system that spans some 25,000 years implies something about the developing cognitive powers of the people whom it symbolized. In another study, Marshack (1976) has examined artifacts made by Neanderthals to determine whether the level of symbolic complexity represented on the artifacts necessarily implies that the Neanderthals had language.

These are extremely complicated questions, and few answers are available at this time. Yet archaeologists are becoming increasingly aware of the need to deal with matters of ideology. Like Marshack's work, Alexander Thom's research raises issues that cannot be ignored. Should Thom be correct—and the current evidence seems to be on his side—then British archaeologists will be forced to grant an extremely high degree of cognitive ability to the Neolithic peoples responsible for Stonehenge and the megalithic tombs (Renfrew 1973, p. 239). The same is true of Glassie's structural analysis of the Georgian world view and Deetz's extension of the model to New England.

Significant research on the evolution of cognition has only begun. Binford was correct when he noted that archaeologists are poorly trained as paleopsychologists. Perhaps this is why some of the major advances seem to be made by scholars such as Marshack and Thom who began their research without the conventional archaeological training. One thing is certain: No matter what happens to the processual theories of Marshack, Thom, Glassie, and the others, the questions they raise are important, and we will undoubtedly see a florescence of research on such ideational matters in the next few years.

Why Did the Georgian Order Evolve?

Let us return to the Georgian order to explore the next step for ideational studies in archaeology. As you will remember, Deetz defined the emergence of the Georgian mind-set in New England culture as a movement characterized by intellect (rather than emotion), privacy, and refined substances, as oriented toward internal matters, and becoming increasingly subdivided to maintain control (Deetz 1977, pp. 37-43).

So far, so good, but as Mark Leone and his colleagues working at Historic Annapolis (Maryland) asked, control over what?

Leone approached the eighteenth-century Georgian order in terms of *critical theory* (introduced briefly in Chapter 3). James Deetz attempted to relate material culture in New England to the ideologies that produced it. But Deetz was largely concerned with description; according to Leone, he was not concerned with ultimate origins, not concerned as to why American patterns existed and why today is—or is not—their product (Leone 1986, p. 425).

Leone departs from Deetz by looking at the "recursive" or active dualities of material culture (Leone 1988a). In focusing on data from eighteenth-century Annapolis, Leone examines the spread of the Georgian order from a position grounded in "critical theory." Specifically, the Georgian order and its local adaptation are related to the penetration of merchant capitalism and the crises it created. In effect, the Annapolis group redefined capitalism, not as an economic system, but as a culture (Leone 1988a).

Merchant Capitalism As Time-factoring Behavior

Viewed from the perspective of critical theory, the changing pressures on the wealthy not only affected the ways in which the Georgian mind-set was manifested but in turn were caused by the redistribution of wealth associated with the establishment of a class structure. One material culture indicator of the profit-making motive is instruments that measure time and regulate work, and devices for measuring space (associated with land ownership, speculation, and sea travel for trade and profit). Clocks, watches, musical instruments, scientific instruments—globes, barometers, spy glasses, and sundials— divide time, space, and sound (Leone 1988a). Measured time is related to the regularization of work. Musical instruments are just one index of several that concern management in voice, speech, and song—all aspects of Georgian arts that are associated with the restructuring of wealth.

To Leone, such artifacts become important not as a function of people's having more money to spend nor as a mind-set, but as a way to justify the concentration of money in few hands. These items intensify social stratification and consolidate capital. The cognitive order is itself part of a single profit-making system, which can be detected archaeologically (Leone and Shackel 1987).

Landscape Archaeology As Ideology

Thomas Jefferson's garden was the focus of intensive archaeological investigation (Chapter 11), and Mark Leone also used landscape architecture to explore Glassie and Deetz's concept of the Georgian order. Leone's specific objective—once again from the perspective of critical theory—was to learn how landscape gardens were conceptualized and what role they played in eighteenth-century life in Maryland.

Consider the case of the formal gardens that existed in Annapolis during the late eighteenth century. Best known is the two-acre garden of William Paca, a signer of the Declaration of Independence (see Figure 15–7). The garden was originally built in the 1760s, behind a large, five-part Georgian mansion, with facade and floor plan exhibiting bilateral symmetry. Viewed from Deetz's perspective of the Georgian world view, this house could be taken as reflecting the ideas of person as individual, the afterlife as a specific reward for personal behavior in this one, privacy, the segregation of everyday life's different activities from one another, and the segregation of the members of the family—all examples of the Georgian life-style (Deetz 1977, Leone 1984, p. 29).

The garden likewise is Georgian, with a central axis, a straight, broad path descending through four sets of steps as one leaves the house, dividing into two parts. These steps lead one physically and visually down over a series of small terraces, creating the same effect as when looking at a Georgian facade or floor plan: bilaterally balanced symmetry.

The garden survived into the early twentieth century, when it was destroyed to make room for a two-hundred-room hotel. When the hotel was torn down in 1968, Historic Annapolis, Inc.—a well-known preservation organization with nearly four decades of history—commissioned Stanley South to excavate in and around the standing house. A sequence of historical archaeologists then moved into the garden area, first testing and then excavating large areas. Original wall footings were found, documenting the terraces (which could be seen in profile); thus the garden's basic topography became available. Trenching and examination of the profiles showed a canal and pond at the bottom of the garden, surrounded by a natural garden (or "wilderness") at the lowest third of the garden. Foundations for a central pavilion, spring house, and footings for a bridge over the ponds were discovered, and 125 paleobotanical samples were recovered from the wet fill. These archaeological data were combined with a few period descriptions, plus a contemporary portrait of William Paca with the garden as background: The pavilion, bath house, spring house, and Chinese Chippendale bridge all have been restored. Today, the Paca garden is open to the public as both an archaeologically based reconstruction and a horticultural experiment.

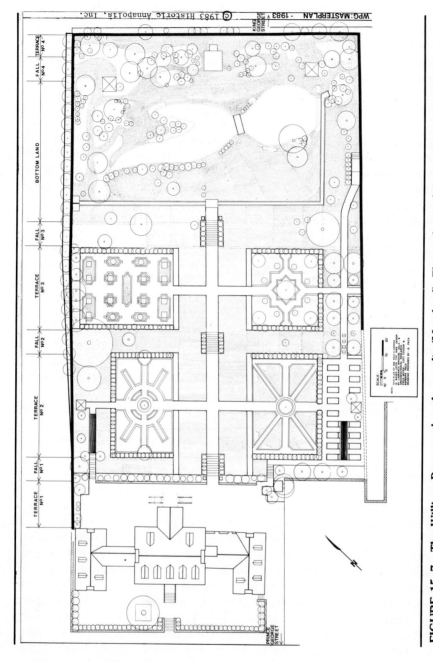

FIGURE 15–7   The William Paca garden, Annapolis (Maryland). The outlines of the garden, including the basic subdivisions and the shape of the pond are archaeologically derived, but the terraces are conjectural, as are the positions of most of the plantings. The Paca garden slopes from left to right for a total of 16.5 feet (see Leone 1984, Figure 1). (Courtesy Mark Leone and Historic Annapolis)

Mark Leone first visited the garden in the early 1980s, and his impressions remained the "touchstone" for his subsequent archaeological analyses: "As I began to walk through the garden from the top, which is sixteen feet higher than the bottom, which is 150 feet away, I found it difficult to tell distances; I felt I was being controlled, as paths, precise borders, openings, stairs, and objects that had to be stepped over operated everywhere to control me. This sensation was especially true regarding sight" (Leone 1988b: 31).

After studying two other large gardens in Annapolis, Leone synthesized the rules used. The Paca garden was constructed as a volume, following the laws of perspective and using baroque rules for creating optical illusions: Converging or diverging lines of sight (to make distances appear shorter or longer) were created, and rows of beds or shrubs were formed into trapezoids and focal points (rather than strictly parallel lines) to manipulate the view. "The gardens are three-dimensional spaces built consciously using rules which were well understood to create illusions for those who walked through them" (Leone 1988b:32).

But why the illusion? And why would such Anglo-American gardens proliferate just before the American Revolution and then disappear—like the rest of Georgian material culture—during the early nineteenth century?

For an answer, Leone turned to the general body of materialist theory and deduced a hypothesis that attempts to explain governance through ostentation. When money forms the only power base, those governing have little need to demonstrate their right or power to govern. They are in control and certainly intend to stay that way. But ostentatious display becomes important when it is necessary to convince the governed that those in power deserve to stay there. *Show* becomes important when those in authority do not necessarily control the purse strings or power structure.

The William Paca garden was built by a wealthy man, but one who lived in a time of contradictions. Although not born to particular affluence, he married into plenty of it. Although a slave owner, he argued for the Bill of Rights. Although descended from planters and tied to merchants, he grew up and lived in economic circumstances in which everyone around him was facing serious economic and political change.

Paca could have built his garden anytime during his lifetime, but he chose to do so when his power to protect his wealth was being diminished by Britain. Parliamentary restrictions on trade and local officeholding compromised profits and power in the 1760s. Paca was socially and economically isolated by a larger and even more difficult-to-control slave population, plus an increasing number of poor white farmers and day laborers, anxious to learn who their future allies would be.

Mark Leone believes that the formal Anglo-American gardens were built deliberately to demonstrate a knowledge of—and control over—the laws of nature. Paca was trying to create the illusion that either (1) he still retained the power over his own wealth or (2) he should be granted new, American-based political clout to do so. In this perspective, the garden was not a statement of what existed. The Paca garden was ideology, an "adjunct to power" at a time when his class's wealth and prestige were being undermined and diminished. Formal gardens were statements designed to stabilize prosperity and power, and not necessarily a reflection of either.

A Final Word About General Theory in Archaeology

Throughout this book I have stressed that contemporary archaeology embraces a number of sometimes complementary, often conflicting anthropological mainstreams. Although a number of archaeologists are currently turning to the ideational perspective for answers, the fact remains that the archaeology of the 1960s and 1970s was dominated by cultural materialistic, cultural evolutionary, and cultural ecological thought (see Part One of this book). As stated over and over again in Chapter 3, these mainstreams are really strategies that direct research. The materialistic perspective suggests merely that the variables of demography, technology, ecology, and environment will ultimately prove to be most successful in predicting cultural variability and change. These variables are obviously most readily inferred from the archaeological record.

We have examined how contemporary archaeologists study these technological, ecological, demographic, and environmental processes in contemporary archaeology. It is impossible, in a book of this scope, to consider the entire range and substance of theory available. Rather, I wished to focus on major areas of study—such as hunter-gatherer dynamics and the origins of agriculture—to demonstrate how archaeologists explore processes and to discuss briefly the nature of the processes themselves. Once again, let me caution you that my emphasis has been more on the search and less on the actual explanation offered.

Summary

The establishment of general theory in archaeology requires that archaeologists transcend the specifics of chronology and lifeway to examine the relevant processes that condition human behavior in general. Archaeological theory still remains to be defined, partly because data are lacking on so many key issues and also because archaeologists are only now beginning to search in earnest for explanations and processes.

The bulk of archaeological theory deals with matters of technoecological and sociopolitical change, and this emphasis reflects the recent domination of archaeology by cultural materialistic and cultural ecological thought. At one time, archaeologists phrased their theoretical arguments largely in Malthusian terms, viewing population growth as a dependent variable, generally preceded by technological innovation. In the Malthusian perspective, culture was seen as constantly struggling to improvise new and more efficient modes of production. The past decade has seen a fundamental shift in perspective, and many archaeologists have explicitly rejected the neo-Malthusian premise. In its stead are substituted the views of Ester Boserup, who argues that population growth is not merely a response to evolving technology but, rather, that population growth is itself the key *independent* variable. According to Boserup, technological innovation occurs largely as the result of an already increasing population density, not the Malthusian reverse. The conflicting theoretical viewpoints of both Malthus and Boserup are manifested in the many current attempts at explaining technological and sociopolitical evolution.

Several investigators suggest that a processual understanding of hunter-gatherers can be obtained from the larger body of developing theory in evolutionary biology. One particularly popular method of inquiry uses optimal foraging theory, a broad-based theoretical perspective that attempts to develop a set of models general enough to apply to a broad range of animal species, yet rigorous and precise enough to explain the details of behavior exhibited by a particular forager. Other recent studies have suggested that major changes in social systems may be coevolutionary, that there is mutual selection among components rather than a linear cause-and-effect sequence. David Rindos (1984), for instance, argued that the origins of agriculture can best be understood by exploring the evolutionary forces affecting the development of domestication systems. Viewed in this way, domestication is not seen as an evolutionary stage but, rather, as a process, "the result of coevolutionary interactions between humans and plants."

Contemporary archaeologists are much less well equipped to deal with the evolution of ideology and human cognition. In fact, this issue has been seriously raised only in the past decade or so. Progress along this line has been slow, partly because of the intrinsic difficulties in studying cognition through archaeological remains and partly because archaeologists have traditionally been reluctant to stray far from the relatively safe ground of technology, environment, ecology, and demography. The trend in contemporary Americanist archaeology seem to be away from a single monolithic school of thought, and several archaeologists seem perfectly willing to transcend the mainstreams of cultural ecological and cultural materialistic thought in order to examine the ideational perspectives available in general anthropology. Whether this diversification will actually lead to progress in the study of cognitive evolution remains to be seen.

BIBLIOGRAPHY

Aberle, David F., 1960. The influence of linguistics on early culture and personality theory. In *Essays in the Science of Culture*, Gertrude E. Dole and Robert L. Carneiro, eds. New York: T. Y. Crowell, pp. 1–29.

Abruzzi, William. Flux among the Mbuti Pygmies of the Ituri Forest: an ecological interpretation. In *Beyond the Myths of Culture: Essays in Cultural Materialism*, Eric B. Ross, ed. New York: Academic Press, pp. 3–31.

———, 1982. Ecological theory and ethnic differentiation among human populations. *Current Anthropology* 23(1):13–35.

Absolon, Karel, 1957. Dokumente und Beweise der Fähigkeiten des fossilen Menschen zu zählen im mahrischen Paläolithikum. *Artibus Asiae* 20:123–150.

Adams, Karen R., and Robert E. Gasser, 1980. Plant microfossils from archaeological sites: research considerations and sampling techniques and approaches. *The Kiva* 45(4):293–300.

Adams, Richard E. W., ed., 1977. *The Origins of Maya Civilization*. Albuquerque: University of New Mexico Press.

———, and T. Patrick Culbert, 1977. The origins of civilization in the Maya lowlands. In *The Origins of Maya Civilization*, Richard E. W. Adams, ed. Albuquerque: University of New Mexico Press, pp. 3–24.

———, W. E. Brown, Jr., and T. Patrick Culbert, 1981. Radar mapping, archaeology, and ancient Maya land use. *Science* 213(4515):1457–1463.

Adams, Richard N., 1981. Natural selection, energetics, and "cultural materialism." *Current Anthropology* 22(6):603–624.

Adams, William Y., 1988. Archaeological classification: theory *versus* practice. *Antiquity* 62(234):40–56.

Adovasio, J. M., and Ronald C. Carlisle, 1988. Some thoughts on cultural resource management archaeology in the United States. *Antiquity* 62(234):72–87.

————, and Joel Gunn, 1977. Style, basketry, and basketmakers. In *The Individual in Prehistory*, James N. Hill and Joel Gunn, eds. New York: Academic Press, pp. 137–154.

Aikens, C. Melvin, 1966. Fremont–Promontory–Plains relationships in northern Utah. Salt Lake City: *University of Utah Anthropological Papers*, no. 82.

Aitken, M. J., 1960. Magnetic dating. *Archaeometry* 3:41–44.

————, 1974. *Physics and Archaeology* [2nd ed.]. Oxford, England: Oxford University Press (Clarendon).

————, 1985. *Thermoluminescence Dating*. Orlando, Fla.: Academic Press, Inc.

Alekshin, V.A., 1983. Burial customs as an archaeological source. *Current Anthropology* 24(2):137–149.

Alexander, Herbert L., Jr., 1963. The Levi site: A Paleo-Indian campsite in central Texas. *American Antiquity* 28(4):510–528.

Allen, William L., and James B. Richardson, III, 1971. The reconstruction of kinship from archaeological data: the concepts, the methods, and the feasibility. *American Antiquity* 36(1):41–53.

Alsop, Joseph, 1964. *From the Silent Earth: A Report on the Greek Bronze Age*. New York: Harper & Row.

Ambro, Richard D., 1970. A basket maker's work kit from Lovelock Cave, Nevada. Berkeley: *Contributions of the University of California Archaeological Research Facility*, 7:73–79.

Ambrose, W. R., 1976. Intrinsic hydration rate dating of obsidian. In *Advances in Obsidian Glass Studies*, R. E. Taylor, ed., Park Ridge, N.J.: Noyes Press, pp. 81–105.

Ammerman, A. J., 1981. Surveys and archaeological research. *Annual Review of Anthropology* 10:63–88.

Anati, Emmanuel, 1972. Comment on *Upper Paleolithic Engraving* by Alexander Marshack. *Current Anthropology* 13(3-4):461.

Andersen, H. H., and S. T. Picraux, eds., 1987. *Nuclear instruments and methods in physics research: section B, beam interactions with materials and atoms*. Proceedings of the Fourth International Symposium on Accelerator Mass Spectronomy, B29:1–446. Ontario, Canada, 1987.

Anderson, James E., 1965. Human skeletons from Tehuacan. *Science* 148:496–497.

Anderson, James N., 1973. Ecological anthropology and anthropological ecology. In *Handbook of Social and Cultural Anthropology*, John J. Honigmann, ed. Chicago: Rand McNally and Co., pp. 179–240.

Andresen, John M., Brian F. Byrd, Mark D. Elson, Randall H. McGuire, Ruben G. Mendoza, Edward Staski, and J. Peter White, 1981. The deer hunters: Star Carr reconsidered. *World Archaeology* 13(1):31–46.

Angel, J. Lawrence, 1967. Porotic hyperostosis, anemias, malarias, and marshes in the prehistoric Eastern Mediterranean. *Science* 153:760–763.

————, 1969. The bases of paleodemography. *American Journal of Physical Anthropology* 30:427–437.

———, 1978. Porotic hyperostosis in the Eastern Mediterranean. *Medical College of Virginia Quarterly* 14:10–16.

Armelagos, George, 1987. Biocultural aspects of food choice. In *Food and Evolution: Toward a Theory of Human Food Habits,* Marvin Harris and Eric B. Ross, eds. Philadelphia: Temple University Press, pp. 579–594.

Arnold, J. R., and W. F. Libby, 1949. Age determinations by radiocarbon content: checks with samples of known age. *Science* 110:678–680.

Asch, David L., and Nancy E. Asch, 1985. Prehistoric plant cultivation in west-central Illinois. In Prehistoric food production in North America, Richard I. Ford, ed. *Anthropological Papers, Museum of Anthropology, University of Michigan* 75:149–203.

Asch, Nancy, Richard I. Ford, and David L. Asch, 1972. Paleoethnobotany of the Koster Site: the archaic horizons. *Illinois State Museum Reports of Investigations* no. 24.

Ascher, Marcia, 1959. A mathematical rationale for graphical seriation. *American Antiquity* 25:212–214.

Ascher, Maxine, 1974. Theories of intuitive perception applied to ancient anthropological inquiry. Ph.D. diss., Walden University, Naples, Fla.

Ascher, Robert, and Charles H. Fairbanks, 1971. Excavation of a slave cabin: Georgia, U.S.A. *Historical Archaeology* 5:3–17.

Atkinson, R. J. C., 1966a. Decoder misled? review of *Stonehenge Decoded* by Gerald S. Hawkins. *Nature* 210(5043):1302.

———, 1966b. Moonshine on Stonehenge. *Antiquity* 40(159):212–216.

———, 1975. Megalithic astronomy—a prehistorian's comments. *Journal for the History of Astronomy* 6(Pt. I, No. 15):42–52.

Aveni, Anthony F., 1972. Astronomical tables intended for use in astro-archaeological studies. *American Antiquity* 37(4):531–540.

———, ed., 1975. *Archaeoastronomy in Pre-Columbian America*. Austin: University of Texas Press.

———, ed., 1977. *Native American Astronomy*. Austin: University of Texas Press.

———, 1981. Archaeoastronomy. In *Advances in Archaeological Method and Theory,* vol. 4, Michael B. Schiffer, ed. New York: Academic Press, pp. 1–77.

———, and S. L. Gibbs, 1976. On the orientation of Pre-Columbian buildings in central Mexico. *American Antiquity* 41:510–517.

———, S. Gibbs, and H. Hartung, 1975. The caracol tower at Chichén Itzá: An ancient astronomical observatory? *Science* 188:977–985.

Avery, T. E., and T. R. Lyons, 1981. *Remote Sensing: Aerial and Terrestrial Photography for Archaeologists*. Washington, D.C.: National Park Service, Supplement 7.

Bada, Jeffrey L., Roy A. Schroeder, and George F. Carter, 1974. New evidence for the antiquity of man in North America deduced from aspartic acid racemization. *Science* 184:791–793.

———, Roy A. Schroeder, Reiner Protsch, and Rainer Berger, 1974. Concordance of collagen-based radiocarbon and aspartic-acid racemization ages. *Proceedings of the National Academy of Science* 71(3):914–917.

Bahn, Paul G., 1987. Getting blood from stone tools. *Nature* 330:14.

Baillie, M. G. L., 1982, *Tree-Ring Dating and Archaeology*. Chicago: University of Chicago Press.

Baity, Elizabeth Chesley, 1973. Archaeoastronomy and ethnoastronomy so far. *Current Anthropology* 14(4):389–449.

Balme, J., 1983. Review of *Hunter-Gatherer Foraging Strategies*, Bruce Winterhalder and E. A. Smith, eds. *Mankind* 13:438–440.

Bamforth, Douglas B., 1986. A comment on "functional variability in an assemblage of endscrapers." *Lithic Technology* 15:61–64.

———, and Albert C. Spaulding, 1982. Human behavior, explanation, archaeology, history, and science. *Journal of Anthropological Archaeology* 1(2):179–195.

Banning, E. B., and L. A. Pavlish, 1978. Direct detection in radiocarbon dating. *Journal of Field Archaeology* 5(4):480–483.

Bannister, Bryant, 1962. The interpretation of tree-ring dates. *American Antiquity* 27(4):508–514.

———, 1970. Dendrochronology. In *Science in Archaeology: a Survey of Progress and Research* [2nd ed.], Don Brothwell and Eric Higgs, eds. New York: Praeger Publishers, pp. 191–205.

———, and William J. Robinson, 1975. Tree-ring dating in archaeology. *World Archaeology* 7(2):210–225.

Barrera, William M., Jr., and Patrick Vinton Kirch, 1973. Basaltic-glass artefacts from Hawaii: their dating and prehistoric uses. *The Journal of the Polynesian Society* 82(2):176–187.

Barth, Fredrik, 1956. Ecologic relationships of ethnic groups in Swat, North Pakistan. *American Anthropologist* 58:1079–1089.

Baumhoff, Martin A., 1963. Ecological determinants of aboriginal California populations. *University of California Publications in American Archaeology and Ethnology* 49(2):155–236.

———, and J. S. Byrne, 1959. Desert Side-notched points as a time marker in California. Berkeley: *University of California Archaeological Survey Report* 48:32–65.

Bayard, Donn T., 1969. Science, theory, and reality in the "new archaeology." *American Antiquity* 34(4):376–384.

Bayham, Frank E., 1979. Factors influencing the Archaic pattern of animal exploitation. *The Kiva* 44(2-3):219–235.

Beadle, George W., 1977. The origin of *Zea mays*. In *Origins of Agriculture*, Charles A. Reed, ed. The Hague: Mouton, pp. 615–635.

Beardsley, Richard K., 1956. Functional and evolutionary implications of community patterning. *American Antiquity* 22(2, Pt. 2):129–157.

Behrensmeyer, Anna K., and Susan M. Kidwell, 1985. Taphonomy's contributions to paleobiology. *Paleobiology* 11(1):105–119.

Bell, Robert E., 1977. Obsidian hydration studies in highland Ecuador. *American Antiquity* 42(1):68–78.

Bender, Barbara, 1975. *Farming in Prehistory*. New York: St. Martin's Press.

———, 1985. Emergent tribal formations in the American Midcontinent. *American Antiquity* 50(1):52–62.

Bender, Margaret M., David A. Baerreis, and Raymond L. Steventon, 1981. Further light on carbon isotopes and Hopewell agriculture. *American Antiquity* 46(2):346–353.

Benedict, Ruth, 1934. *Patterns of Culture,* Boston: Houghton Mifflin.

Benner, S. M., and R. S. Brodkey, 1984. Underground detection using differential heat analysis. *Archaeometry* 26:21–36.

Bennett, C. L., R. P. Beukens, M. R. Clover, H. E. Gove, R. B. Liebert, A. E. Litherland, K. H. Purser, and W. E. Sondheim, 1977. Radiocarbon dating using electrostatic accelerators: negative ions provide the key. *Science* 198:508–510.

Bennett, Wendell C., 1950. The Gallinazo Group, Virú Valley, Peru. *Yale University Publications in Anthropology* no. 43.

Berenson, Bernhard, 1962. *Rudiments of Connoisseurship: Study and Criticism of Italian Art.* New York: Schocken.

Berger, R., 1979. Radiocarbon dating with accelerators. *Journal of Archaeological Science* 6:101–104.

Berlin, Heinrich, 1958. El glifo "emblema" en las inscripciones mayas. *Journal de la Société des Américanistes de Paris* 47:111–119.

Berrera, W. M., Jr., and P. V. Kirch, 1973. Basaltic-glass artifacts from Hawaii: their dating and prehistoric uses. *Journal of Polynesian Society* 82:176–187.

Bettinger, Robert L., 1977. Aboriginal human ecology in Owens Valley: prehistoric change in the Great Basin. *American Antiquity* 42(1):3–17.

———, 1980. Explanatory/predictive models of hunter-gatherer adaptation. *Advances in Archaeological Method and Theory*, vol. 3, Michael B. Schiffer, ed. New York: Academic Press, pp. 189–255.

———, 1987. Archaeological approaches to hunter-gatherers. *Annual Review of Anthropology* 16:121–142.

———, and M. A. Baumhoff, 1982. The Numic spread: Great Basin cultures in competition. *American Antiquity* 47(3):485–503.

Bevan, Bruce W., 1983. Electromagnetics for mapping buried earth features. *Journal of Field Archaeology* 10(1):47–54.

———, and J. Kenyon, 1975. Ground-penetrating radar for historical archaeology. *MASCA Newsletter* 11(2):2–7.

———, David G. Orr, and Brooke S. Blades, 1984. The discovery of the Taylor house at the Petersburg National Battlefield. *Historical Archaeology* 18(2):64–74.

Bigham Gary N., 1973. Zone of influence—inner continental shelf of Georgia. *Journal of Sedimentary Petrology* 43(1):207–214.

Binford, Lewis R., 1962a. A new method of calculating dates from kaolin pipe stem samples. *Southeastern Archaeological Conference Newsletter* 9(2):19–21.

———, 1962b. Archeology as anthropology. *American Antiquity* 28:217–225.

———, 1964. A consideration of archaeological research design. *American Antiquity* 29(4):425–441.

———, 1965. Archaeological systematics and the study of cultural process. *American Antiquity*. 31(2):203–210.

————, 1967. Smudge pits and hide smoking: the use of analogy in archaeological reasoning. *American Antiquity* 32(1):1–12.

————, 1968a. Archeological perspectives. In *New Perspectives in Archeology*. Sally R. Binford and Lewis R. Binford, eds., Chicago: Aldine, pp. 5–32.

————, 1968b. Post-Pleistocene adaptations. In *New Perspectives in Archeology,* Sally R. Binford and Lewis R. Binford, eds., Chicago: Aldine, pp. 313–341.

————, 1968c. Some comments on historical versus processual archaeology. *Southwestern Journal of Anthropology* 24(3):267–275.

————, 1969. Conceptual problems in dealing with units and rates of cultural evolution. *Anthropology UCLA* 1(1):27–35.

————, 1971. Mortuary practices: their study and their potential. In *Approaches to the Social Dimensions of Mortuary Practices,* James Brown, ed. *Society for American Archaeology Memoir,* 25:6–29.

————, 1972a. *An Archaeological Perspective.* New York: Seminar Press.

————, 1972b. The "Binford" pipe stem formula: a return from the grave. The *Conference on Historic Site Archaeology Papers,* 6:230–253.

————, 1973. Interassemblage variability—The Mousterian and the "functional" argument. In *The Explanation of Culture Change: Models in Prehistory,* Colin Renfrew, ed. London: Duckworth, pp. 227–254.

————, ed., 1977. *For Theory Building in Archaeology.* New York: Academic Press.

————, 1978a. Dimensional analysis of behavior and site structure: learning from an Eskimo hunting stand. *American Antiquity* 43(3):330–361.

————, 1978b. *Nunamiut Ethnoarchaeology.* New York: Academic Press.

————, 1980. Willow smoke and dogs' tails: hunter-gatherer settlement systems and archaeological site formation. *American Antiquity* 45(1):4–20.

————, 1981. *Bones: Ancient Men and Modern Myths.* New York: Academic Press.

————, 1982. The archaeology of place. *Journal of Anthropological Archaeology* 1(1):5–31.

————, 1983a. *In Pursuit of the Past: Decoding the Archaeological Record.* London: Thames and Hudson.

————, ed., 1983b. *Working at Archaeology.* New York: Academic Press.

————, 1984. *Faunal Remains from Klasies River Mouth.* Orlando, Fla.: Academic Press.

————, 1986. An Alyawara day: making men's knives and beyond. *American Antiquity* 51(3):547–562.

————, 1987. Researching ambiguity: Frames of reference and site structure. In *Method and Theory for Activity Area Research: an Ethnoarchaeolgical Approach,* Susan Kent, ed. New York: Columbia University Press, pp. 449–512.

————, and Jack B. Bertram, 1977. Bone frequencies—and attritional processes. In *For Theory Building in Archaeology,* Lewis R. Binford, ed., New York: Academic Press, pp. 77–156.

————, and W. J. Chasko, Jr., 1976. Nunamiut demographic history: a provocative case. In *Demographic Anthropology: Quantitative Approaches,* Ezra B. W. Zubrow, ed., Albuquerque: University of New Mexico Press, pp. 63–144.

————, and James F. O'Connell, 1984. An Alyawara day: the stone quarry. *Journal of Anthropological Research* 40(3):406–432.

————, arid J. A. Sabloff, 1982. Paradigms, systematics, and archaeology. *Journal of Anthropological Research* 38(2):137–153.

Binford, Sally R., and Lewis R. Binford, eds., 1968. *New Perspectives in Archeology*. Chicago: Aldine.

Bird, Junius, 1980. Comments on sifters, sifting, and sorting procedures. In *A Complete Manual of Field Archaeology*, Martha Joukowsky, Englewood Cliffs, N.J.: Prentice-Hall, Inc., pp. 165–170.

Birdsell, Joseph B., 1953. Some environmental and cultural factors influencing the structure of Australian aboriginal populations. *American Naturalist* 87(834):171–207.

————, 1972. *Human Evolution: an Introduction to the New Physical Anthropology*. Chicago: Rand McNally.

Blanton, Richard E., 1978. *Monte Albán: Settlement Patterns at the Ancient Zapotec Capital*. New York: Academic Press.

Blegen, Carl, 1963. *Troy and the Trojans*. London: Frederick A. Praeger.

Bleich, Vernon C., and Orlando A. Schwartz, 1975. Observations on the home range of the desert woodrat, *Neotoma lepida intermedia*. *Journal of Mammalogy* 56:518–519.

Blurton Jones, Nicholas, 1986. Bushman birth spacing: a test for optimal interbirth intervals. *Ethology and Sociobiology* 7(2):91–105.

————, 1987. Bushman birth spacing: direct tests of some simple predictions. *Ethology and Sociobiology* 8(3):183–203.

————, and R. M. Sibly, 1978. Testing adaptiveness of culturally determined behaviour: do Bushman women maximize their reproductive success by spacing births widely and foraging seldom? In *Human Behaviour and Adaptation*, N. Blurton Jones and V. Reynolds, eds. Symposia of the Society for the Study of Human Biology, vol. 18. London: Taylor & Francis, Ltd., pp. 135–157.

Bocquet-Appel, J., and C. Masset, 1982. Farewell to paleodemography. *Journal of Human Evolution* 11:321–333.

Bohannan, Paul, 1965. *Social Anthropology*. New York: Holt, Rinehart and Winston.

Bonath, Shawn, 1978. An evaluation of the mean ceramic date formula as applied to South's majolica model. *Historical Archaeology* 12:82–92.

Bonnichsen, Robson, 1977. *Models for Deriving Cultural Information from Stone Tools*. Ottawa: National Museum of Man, Mercury Series, Archaeological Survey of Canada Paper no. 60.

Boserup, Ester, 1965. *Conditions of Agricultural Growth, the Economics of Agrarian Change Under Population Pressure*. Chicago: Aldine.

Bostwick, John A., 1980. The Plaza II site excavation of a colonial Spanish well in St. Augustine, Florida. *Historical Archaeology* 14:73–81.

Bourque, Bruce J., Kenneth Morris, and Arthur Spiess, 1978. Determining the season of death of mammal teeth from archeological sites: a new sectioning technique. *Science* 199:530–531.

Boyd, William C., 1950. *Genetics and the Races of Man*. Boston: Little, Brown and Company.

Bozarth, Steven R., 1987. Diagnostic opal phytoliths from rinds of selected *Cucurbita* species. *American Antiquity* 52(3):607–615.

Braidwood, Robert J., 1959. Archeology and the evolutionary theory. In *Evolution and Anthropology: A Centennial Appraisal*. Washington, D. C.: Anthropological Society of Washington, pp. 76–89.

Brainerd, George W., 1951. The place of chronological ordering in archaeological analysis. *American Antiquity* 16:301–313.

Braun, David P., 1985. Absolute seriation: a time-series approach. In *For Concordance in Archaeological Analysis: Bridging Data Structure, Quantitative Technique, and Theory,* Christopher Carr, ed. Kansas City, Mo.: Westport Publishers, pp. 509–539.

———, 1987. Coevolution of sedentism, pottery technology, and horticulture in the central Midwest, 200 B.C.–A.D. 600. In *Emergent Horticultural Economies of the Eastern Woodlands,* William F. Keegan, ed. Southern Illinois University at Carbondale, Center for Archaeological Investigations Occasional Paper 7:153–181.

———, and Stephen Plog, 1982. Evolution of "tribal" social networks: theory and prehistoric North American evidence. *American Antiquity* 47(3):504–525.

Brennan, Louis A., 1973. *Beginner's Guide to Archaeology*. Harrisburg, Pa.: Stackpole Books.

Breternitz, David, A., 1966. An appraisal of tree-ring dated pottery in the Southwest. *Anthropological Papers of the University of Arizona,* no. 10.

Brew, John Otis, 1941. Preliminary report of the Peabody Museum Awatovi expedition of 1939. *Plateau* 13(3):37–48.

———, 1946. Archaeology of Alkali Ridge, Southeastern Utah. *Papers of the Peabody Museum of American Archaeology and Ethnology* no. 21.

———, 1961. Emergency archaeology: salvage in advance of technological progress. *American Philosophical Society Proceedings* 105(1):1–10.

Brieur, Frederick L., 1976. New clues to stone tool function: plant and animal residues. *American Antiquity* 41(4):478–484.

Brigham, Clarence S., 1937. Clarence Bloomfield Moore. *Proceedings of the American Antiquarian Society* (1936) 46:12–14.

Brose, David S., 1967. The Custer Road dump site: an exercise in Victorian archaeology. *Michigan Archaeologist* 13(2):1–128.

———, 1972. Comment on *Upper Paleolithic Engraving* by Alexander Marshack. *Current Anthropology* 13(3-4):462.

Brothwell, Don, and Eric Higgs, eds., 1970. *Science in Archaeology: a Survey of Progress and Research* [2nd ed.]. New York: Praeger Publishers.

Browman, David L., 1981. Isotopic discrimination and correction factors in radiocarbon dating. In *Advances in Archaeological Method and Theory,* vol. 6, Michael B. Schiffer, ed. New York: Academic Press, 241–295.

Brown, Ian W., 1978. James Alfred Ford: the man and his works. *Southeastern Archaeological Conference, Special Publication,* no. 4.

Brown, James A., 1976. The Southern cult reconsidered. *Midcontinental Journal of Archaeology* 1(2):115–135.

Brown, James H., 1971. Mammals on mountaintops: nonequilibrium insular biogeography. *American Naturalist* 105:467–478.

Brown, Peter Lancaster, 1976. *Megaliths, Myths and Men: an Introduction to Astroarchaeology.* New York: Harper & Row.

Brown, Robert, 1963. *Explanation in Social Science.* Chicago: Aldine.

Brown, Roger, 1965. *Social Psychology.* New York: Free Press.

Bryant, Vaughn M., Jr., and Richard G. Holloway, 1983. The role of palynology in archaeology. In *Advances in Archaeological Method and Theory,* vol. 6, Michael B. Schiffer, ed. New York: Academic Press, pp. 191–224.

Buchler, I. R., and H. A. Selby, 1968. *Kinship and Social Organization.* New York: Macmillan.

Buck, Bruce A., 1982. Ancient technology in contemporary surgery. *The Western Journal of Medicine* 136:265–269.

Buckley, Theodore Alois, 1873. *The Iliad—Homer.* Bell and Daldy.

Buikstra, Jane E., 1976. Hopewell in the lower Illinois Valley: a regional study of human biological variability and prehistoric mortuary behavior. *Northwestern Archeological Program Scientific Papers,* no. 2.

———, 1977. Biocultural dimensions of archeological study: a regional perspective. In *Biocultural Adaptation in Prehistoric America,* Robert L. Blakely, ed. *Proceedings of the Southern Anthropological Society,* no. 11. Athens: University of Georgia Press, pp. 67–84.

———, 1981a. Mortuary practices, palaeodemography, and palaeopathology: a case study from the Koster site (Illinois). In *The Archaeology of Death,* R. Chapman, I. Kinnes, and K. Randsborg, eds. Cambridge: Cambridge University Press, pp. 123–132.

———, ed., 1981b. *Prehistoric tuberculosis in the Americas.* [*Scientific Papers Series, no. 5*] Evanston: Northwestern University Center for American Archaeology.

———, and Della C. Cook, 1980. Paleopathology: an American account. *Annual Review of Anthropology* 9:433–470.

———, and L. Konigsberg, 1985. Paleodemography: critiques and controversies. *American Anthropologist* 87:316–333.

———, and James H. Mielke, 1985. Demography, diet, and health. In *The Analysis of Prehistoric Diets,* Robert I. Gilbert, Jr. and James H. Mielke, eds. New York: Academic Press, pp. 359–422.

Bullard, W. R., Jr., 1960. Maya settlement pattern in northeastern Petén, Guatemala. *American Antiquity* 25(3):355–372.

Bumsted, M. Pamela, in press. Past human behavior from bone chemical analysis—respects and prospects. *Journal of Human Evolution.*

Burgh, Robert F., 1950. Comment on Taylor's *A Study of Archeology. American Anthropologist* 52(1):114–117.

Burl, Aubrey, 1979. *Prehistoric Avebury,* New Haven, Conn.: Yale University Press.

Bushnell, Amy, 1981. *The King's Coffer: Proprietors of the Spanish Florida Treasury 1565–1702,* Gainesville: University Presses of Florida.

Butzer, K. W., 1982. *Archaeology as Human Ecology.* Cambridge, England: Cambridge University Press.

Calder, William M., III, and David A. Traill, 1986. *Myth, Scandal, and History: the Heinrich Schliemann Controversy and a First Edition of the Mycenaean Diary.* Detroit: Wayne State University Press.

Caldwell, Joseph, 1959. The new American archaeology. *Science* 129(3345):303–307.

Camilli, Eileen Lois, 1983. Site occupational history and lithic assemblage structure: an example from southeastern Utah. Ph.D. diss., University of New Mexico, Albuquerque.

Campbell, John M., 1968. Territoriality among ancient hunters: interpretations from ethnography and nature. In *Anthropological Archeology in the Americas,* Betty J. Meggers, ed. Washington, D. C.: The Anthropological Society of Washington, pp. 1–21.

Cannon, Walter B., 1942. "Voodoo" death. *American Anthropologist* 44(2):169–181.

Carbone, Victor A., and Bennie C. Keel, 1985. Preservation of plant and animal remains. In *The Analysis of Prehistoric Diets,* Robert I. Gilbert and James H. Mielke, eds. New York: Academic Press, pp. 1–19.

Carneiro, Robert L., 1962. Scale analysis as an instrument for the study of cultural evolution. *Southwestern Journal of Anthropology* 18(2):149–169.

———, 1968. Ascertaining, testing and interpreting sequences of cultural development. *Southwestern Journal of Anthropology* 24(4):354–374.

———, 1970a. A quantitative law in anthropology. *American Antiquity* 35(4):492–494.

———, 1970b. A theory of the origin of the state. *Science* 169:733–738.

———, 1972. From autonomous village to the state, a numerical estimation. In *Population Growth: Anthropological Implications,* Brian Spooner, ed. Cambridge, Mass.: MIT Press, pp. 64–77.

———, 1973a. Classical evolution. In *Main Currents in Cultural Anthropology,* Raoul Naroll and Frada Naroll, eds. Englewood Cliffs, N.J.: Prentice-Hall, Inc., pp. 57–121.

———, 1973b. The four faces of evolution: unilinear, universal, multilinear, and differential. In *Handbook of Social and Cultural Anthropology,* John J. Honigmann, ed. Chicago: Rand McNally.

———, 1977. Comment. *Current Anthropology* 18:222–223.

———, 1988. The circumscription theory: Challenge and response. *American Behavioral Scientist* 31(4):497–511.

Carr, Christopher, 1977. A new role and analytical design for the use of resistivity surveying in archaeology. *Mid-Continental Journal of Archaeology* 2(2):161–193.

———, 1982. *Handbook on Soil Resistivity Surveying: Interpretation of Data from Earthen Archaeological Sites.* Evanston, Ill.: Center for American Archeology Press.

———, 1984. The nature of organization of intrasite archaeological records and spatial analytical approaches to their investigation. In *Advances in Archaeological Method and Theory,* vol. 7, Michael B. Schiffer, ed. New York: Academic Press, pp. 103–222.

————, ed., 1985. *For Concordance in Archaeological Analysis: Bridging Data Structure, Quantitative Technique, and Theory*. Kansas City, Mo.: Westport Publishers, Inc.

Carrillo, Richard F., 1974. English wine bottles as revealed in a statistical study. *The Conference on Historic Site Archaeology Papers* 7:290–317.

Casteel, Richard, W., 1970. Core and column sampling. *American Antiquity* 35(4):465–467.

————, 1972a. Some archaeological uses of fish remains. *American Antiquity* 37(3):404–419.

————, 1972b. Two static maximum population-density models for hunter-gatherers: a first approximation. *World Archaeology* 4(1):19–40.

————, 1976a. Comparison of column with whole unit samples for recovering fish remains. *World Archaeology* 8(2):192–196.

————, 1976b. *Fish Remains in Archaeology and Paleoenvironmental Studies*. New York: Academic Press.

————, 1977. Characterization of faunal assemblages and the minimum number of individuals determined from paired elements: continuing problems in archaeology. *Journal of Archaeological Science* 4(2):125–134.

Chadwick, John, 1976. *The Mycenaean World*. Cambridge, England: Cambridge University Press.

————, 1987. *Linear B and Related Scripts*. Berkeley: University of California Press.

Chamberlin, T. C., 1890. The method of multiple working hypotheses. *Science* (old series) 15(366):92–96.

Champion, Timothy, Clive Gamble, Stephen Shennan, and Alasdair Whittle, 1984. *Prehistoric Europe*. Orlando, Fla.: Academic Press.

Chang, K. C., 1967. *Rethinking Archaeology*. New York: Random House, Inc.

————, ed., 1968. *Settlement Archaeology*, Palo Alto, Calif.: National Press Books.

Chaplin, R. E., 1971. *The Study of Animal Bones from Archaeological Sites*. London: Seminar Press.

Charles, Douglas K., Jane E. Buikstra, and Lyle W. Konigsberg, 1986. Behavioral implications of terminal Archaic and Early Woodland mortuary practices in the lower Illinois Valley. In *Early Woodland Archaeology*, Kenneth B. Farnsworth and Thomas E. Emerson, eds. Kampsville, Ill.: Center for American Archeology Press, pp. 458–474.

Childe, V. Gordon, 1951a. *Man Makes Himself*. New York: New American Library.

————, 1951b. *Social Evolution*. New York: Henry Schuman.

Chippindale, Christopher, 1983. *Stonehenge Complete*. Ithaca, N.Y.: Cornell University Press.

Chisolm, Brian S., D. Erle Nelson, and Henry P. Schwarez, 1982. Stable-carbon isotope ratios as a measure of marine versus terrestrial protein in ancient diets. *Science* 216:1131–1132.

Clark, Donavan L., 1964. Archaeological chronology in California and the obsidian hydration method: Part 1. Los Angeles: *University of California Archaeological Survey Annual Report*, pp. 139–225.

Clark, George R., II, 1979. Seasonal growth variations in the shells of recent and prehistoric specimens of *Mercenaria mercenaria* from St. Catherines Island. In The Anthropology of St. Catherines Island: the Refuge-Deptford Mortuary Complex, David Hurst Thomas and Clark Spencer Larsen, *Anthropological Papers of the American Museum of Natural History* 56(1):161–172.

Clark, Grahame, 1977. *World Prehistory in New Perspective* [3d ed.]. Cambridge, England: Cambridge University Press.

Clark, J. D. G., 1954. *Excavations at Star Carr, an Early Mesolithic Site at Seamer, near Scarborough, Yorkshire*. Cambridge, England: Cambridge University Press.

———, 1972. Star Carr: A case study in bioarchaeology. *McCaleb Module in Anthropology,* no. 10. Reading, Mass.: Addison-Wesley Modular Publications.

Clarke, David L., 1968. *Analytical Archaeology*. London: Methuen and Co., Ltd.

———, 1972. Archaeology: the loss of innocence. *Antiquity* 47:6–18.

Cleator, P. E., 1976. *Archaeology in the Making*. New York: St. Martin's Press.

Cleere, Henry, ed., 1984. *Approaches to the Archaeological Heritage: a Comparative Study of World Cultural Resource Management Systems*. Cambridge, England: Cambridge University Press.

Cleland, Charles, and James Fitting, 1968. The crisis in identity: theory in historic sites archaeology. In *The Conference on Historic Sites Archaeology Papers* 2(2):124–138.

Cochran, William G., 1963. *Sampling Techniques* [2nd ed.]. New York: Wiley.

Coe, Michael D., 1975. Native astronomy in Mesoamerica. In *Archaeoastronomy in Pre-Columbian America,* Anthony F. Aveni, ed. Austin: University of Texas Press, pp. 3–31.

Coggins, Clemens C. 1975. Painting and drawing styles at Tikal. Ph.D. diss., Harvard University, Cambridge, Mass.

Coghlan, H. H., 1940. Prehistoric copper and some experiments in smelting. *Transactions of the Newcomen Society* 20:49–65.

Cohen, Mark Nathan, 1977. *The Food Crisis in Prehistory: Overpopulation and the Origins of Agriculture*. New Haven, Conn.: Yale University Press.

———, 1981. The ecological basis of New World state formation: general and local model building. In *The Transition to Statehood in the New World,* Grant D. Jones and Robert R. Kautz, eds. Cambridge, England: Cambridge University Press, pp. 105–122.

———, 1987. The significance of long-term changes in human diet and food economy. In *Food and Evolution: Toward a Theory of Human Food Habits,* Marvin Harris and Eric B. Ross, eds. Philadelphia: Temple University Press, pp. 261–283.

Cohen, Mark Nathan, and George J. Armelagos, eds. 1984. *Paleopathology at the Origins of Agriculture*. Orlando, Fla.: Academic Press.

Coles, John M., 1967. Experimental archaeology. *Proceedings of the Society of Antiquaries of Scotland.*

———, 1973. *Archaeology by Experiment*. New York: Scribner's.

Collins, Paul W., 1965. Functional analysis in the symposium "Man, culture, and animals." In *Man, Culture, and Animals,* Anthony Leeds and Andrew P. Vayda, eds. Washington, D.C.: *American Association for the Advancement of Science,* no. 78, pp. 271–282.

Conard, Nicholas, David L. Asch, Nancy B. Asch, David Elmore, Garry Gove, Meyer Rubin, James A. Brown, Michael D. Wiant, Kenneth B. Farnsworth, and Thomas G. Cook, 1984. Accelerator radiocarbon dating of evidence for prehistoric horticulture in Illinois. *Nature* 308:443–446.

Conkey, Margaret W., 1980. The identification of prehistoric hunter-gatherer aggregation sites: the case of Altamira. *Current Anthropology* 21(5):609–630.

———, 1982. Boundedness in art and society. In *Symbolic and Structural Archaeology,* Ian Hodder, ed. Cambridge, England: Cambridge University Press, pp. 115–128.

———, and Janet Spector, 1984. Archaeology and the study of gender. In *Advances in Archaeological Method and Theory,* vol. 7, Michael B. Schiffer, ed. Orlando, Fla.: Academic Press, pp. 1–38,

Cook, S. F., and Robert F. Heizer, 1965. Studies on the chemical analysis of archaeological sites. *University of California Publications in Anthropology,* vol. 2.

Cordell, Linda S., 1986. Women archaeologists in the Southwest. Paper presented at Daughters of the Desert: Women Anthropologists and Students of the Native American Southwest. Wenner-Gren Foundation International Symposium, Oracle, Arizona.

Cornwall, I. W., 1956. *Bones for the Archaeologist.* London: Phoenix House.

———, 1969. Soil, stratification, and environment. In *Science in Archaeology* [rev. ed.], Don Brothwell and Eric Higgs, eds. London: Thames and Hudson Ltd., pp. 120–134.

Coutts, Peter J. F., 1970. Bivalve growth patterning as a method for seasonal dating in archaeology. *Nature* 226:874.

———, 1975. The seasonal perspective of marine-oriented prehistoric hunter gatherers. In *Growth Rhythms and the History of the Earth's Rotation,* G. D. Rosenberg and S. K. Runcorn, eds. London: Wiley, pp. 243–252.

———, and Charles Higham, 1971. The seasonal factor in prehistoric New Zealand. *World Archaeology* 2(3):266–277.

Cowan, Richard A., 1967. Lake margin ecological exploitation in the Great Basin as demonstrated by an analysis of coprolites from Lovelock Cave, Nevada. *University of California Archaeological Survey Reports* 70:21–35.

Cowgill, George L., 1968. Computer analysis of archeological data from Teotihuacan, Mexico. In *New Perspectives in Archeology,* Sally R. Binford and Lewis R. Binford, eds. Chicago: Aldine, pp. 143–150.

———, 1975a. On the causes and consequences of ancient and modern population changes. *American Anthropologist* 77:505–525.

———, 1975b. Population pressure as a non-explanation. In *Population Studies in Archaeology and Biological Anthropology: a Symposium,* A. Swelund, ed. *Society of American Archaeology Memoir,* no. 33, pp. 127–131.

Crabtree, Don E., 1966. A stoneworker's approach to analyzing and replicating the Lindenmeier Folsom. *Tebiwa* 9:3–39.

————, 1968. Mesoamerican polyhedral cores and prismatic blades. *American Antiquity* 33(4):446–478.

————, 1979. Interview. *Flintknappers' Exchange* 2(1):29–33.

Creer, Kenneth M., 1977. Geomagnetic secular variations during the last 25000 years: an interpretation of data obtained from rapidly deposited sediments. *Geophysical Journal of the Royal Astronomical Society* 48(1):91–109.

————, and John S. Kopper, 1974. Palaeomagnetic dating of cave paintings in Tito Bustillo Cave, Asturias, Spain. *Science* 186(4161):348–350.

Cressman, Luther S., 1977. *Prehistory of the Far West: Homes of Vanished Peoples*. Salt Lake City: University of Utah Press.

Cribb, Robert L. D., 1987. The logic of the herd: a computer simulation of archaeological herd structure. *Journal of Anthropological Archaeology* 6(4):376–415.

Cronin, C., 1962. An analysis of pottery design elements, indicating possible relationships between three decorated types. In *Chapters in the Prehistory of Eastern Arizona I*, Paul S. Martin and others, eds., *Fieldiana Anthropology* 53:105–114.

Cross, John R., 1983. Twigs, branches, trees, and forests: problems of scale in lithic analysis. In *Archaeological Hammers and Theories*, James A. Moore and Arthur S. Keene, eds. New York: Academic Press, pp. 87–106.

Crumley, Carole, 1976. Toward a locational definition of state systems of settlement. *American Anthropologist* 78(1):59–73.

Cybulski, Jerome S., 1977. Cribra orbitalia, a possible sign of anemia in early historic native populations of the British Columbia coast. *American Journal of Physical Anthropology* 47:31–40.

Dahlberg, Frances, ed., 1981. *Woman the Gatherer*. New Haven, Conn.: Yale University Press.

Dale, W. S. A., 1987. The shroud of Turin: relic or icon? In *Nuclear Instruments and Methods in Physics Research: Section B, Beam Interactions with Materials and Atoms*, H. H. Andersen and S. T. Picraux, eds. Proceedings of the Fourth International Symposium on Accelerator Mass Spectrometry B29:187–192.

Dancey, William S., 1976. Riverine period settlement and land use pattern in the Priest Rapids area, central Washington. *Northwest Anthropological Research Notes* 10(2):147–160.

————, 1981. *Archaeological Field Methods: an Introduction*. Minneapolis: Burgess Publishing Co.

Daniel, Glyn, 1962. *The Idea of Prehistory*. Baltimore: Penguin Books.

————, 1976. *A Hundred and Fifty Years of Archaeology*. Cambridge, Mass.: Harvard University Press.

————ed., 1981. *Towards a History of Archaeology*. New York: Thames and Hudson.

————, and Colin Renfrew, 1988. *The Idea of Prehistory*. Edinburgh: University of Edinburgh Press.

Davis, Hester A., 1972. The crisis in American archeology. *Science* 175:267–272.

Davis, Jonathan O., 1978. Quaternary tephrochronology of the Lake Lahontan *Nevada Archaeological Survey Research Paper*, no. 7.

————, 1983. Geology of Gatecliff Shelter: sedimentary facies and Holocene clim

The Archaeology of Monitor Valley: 2. Gatecliff Shelter, David Hurst Thomas. *Anthropological Papers of the American Museum of Natural History* 59(1):64–87.

———, Wilton N. Melhorn, Dennis T. Trexler, and David Hurst Thomas, 1983. Geology of Gatecliff Shelter: Physical stratigraphy. In The Archaeology of Monitor Valley: 2. Gatecliff Shelter, David Hurst Thomas, *Anthropological Papers of the American Museum of Natural History* 59(1):39–63.

Davis, Mary B., compiler, 1987. *Field Notes of Clarence B. Moore's Southeastern Archaeological Expeditions, 1891–1918: A Guide to the Microfilm Edition*. Bronx, N.Y.: Huntington Free Library, Museum of the American Indian.

Deagan, Kathleen, 1973. Mestizaje in colonial St. Augustine. *Ethnohistory* 20(1):55–65.

———, 1974. Sex, status and role in the *Mestizaje* of Spanish colonial Florida. Ph.D. diss., Department of Anthropology, University of Florida, Gainesville.

———, 1978a. Cultures in transition: fusion and assimilation among the Eastern Timucua. In *Tacachale: Essays on the Indians of Florida and Southeastern Georgia During the Historic Period*, Jerald Milanich and Samuel Proctor, eds. Gainesville: University Presses of Florida, pp. 89–119.

———, 1978b. The material assemblage of 16th century Spanish Florida. *Historical Archaeology* 12:25–50.

———, 1979. Self-awareness and coming of age in historical archeology: review of Schuyler's *Historical Archaeology: A Guide to Substantive and Theoretical Contributions. Reviews in Anthropology* 6(3):365–372.

———1980. Spanish St. Augustine: America's first "melting pot." *Archaeology* 33(5):22–30.

———, 1981. Downtown survey: the discovery of 16th century St. Augustine in an urban area. *American Antiquity* 46(3):626–634.

———, 1982. Avenues of inquiry in historical archaeology. In *Advances in Archaeological Method and Theory*, vol. 5, Michael B. Schiffer, ed. New York: Academic Press, pp. 151–177.

———, 1983. *Spanish St. Augustine: the Archaeology of a Colonial Creole Community*. New York: Academic Press.

———, 1987. *Artifacts of the Spanish Colonies of Florida and the Caribbean, 1500–1800*, Vol 1: *Ceramics, Glassware, and Beads*. Washington, D.C.: Smithsonian Institution Press.

Dean, Jeffrey S., 1970. Aspects of Tsegi phase social organization: a trial reconstruction. In *Reconstructing Prehistoric Pueblo Societies*, William A. Longacre, ed. Albuquerque: University of New Mexico Press, pp. 140–174.

———, 1978a. Independent dating in archaeological analysis. In *Advances in Archaeological Theory and Method*, vol. 1, Michael B. Schiffer, ed., New York: Academic Press, pp. 223–255.

———, 1978b. Tree-ring dating in archeology. *University of Utah Miscellaneous Anthropological Papers, Paper no. 24*. 99:129–163.

Deetz, James, 1965. The dynamics of stylistic change in Arikara ceramics. Urbana: *Illinois Studies in Anthropology*, no. 4.

———, 1967. *Invitation to Archaeology*. Garden City, N.Y.: Natural History Press.

————, 1968. The inference of residence and descent rules from archeological data. In *New Perspectives in Archeology*, Sally R. Binford and Lewis R. Binford, eds. Chicago: Aldine, pp. 41–48.

————, 1970. Archeology as a social science. *Bulletins of the American Anthropological Association* 3(3, pt. 2):115–125.

————, 1973. Ceramics from Plymouth, 1635–1855: The archaeological evidence. In *Ceramics in America*, I. M. G. Quimby, ed. Charlottesville: University of Virginia Press, pp. 15–40.

————, 1977a. *In Small Things Forgotten: The Archaeology of Early American Life*. Garden City, N.Y.: Anchor Books.

————, 1977b. Material culture and archaeology—what's the difference? In *Historical Archaeology and the Importance of Material Things*, Leland Ferguson, ed. Society for Historical Archaeology, Special Publication Series, no. 2, pp. 9–12.

————, 1983. Scientific humanism and humanistic science: a plea for paradigmatic pluralism in historical archaeology. *Geoscience and Man* 23 29:27–34.

————, 1988. Material culture and worldview in colonial Anglo-America. In *The Recovery of Meaning: Historical Archaeology in the Eastern United States*, Mark Leone and Parker Potter, eds. Washington, D. C.: Smithsonian Institution Press, pp. 219–233.

Dempsey, Paul, and Martin A. Baumhoff, 1963. The statistical use of artifact distributions to establish chronological sequence. *American Antiquity* 28:496–509.

DeNiro, M. J., and S. Epstein, 1981. Influence of diet on the distribution of nitrogen isotopes in animals. *Geochimica de Cosmochimica Acta* 45:341–351.

————, and Margaret J. Schoeniger, 1983. Stable carbon and nitrogen isotope ratios of bone collagen: variations within individuals, between sexes, and within populations raised on monotonous diets. *Journal of Archaeological Science* 10(3):199–203.

DePratter, Chester B., and James D. Howard, 1977. History of shoreline changes determined by archaeological dating: Georgia Coast, U.S.A. *Technical Papers and Abstracts, Gulf Coast Association of Geological Societies* 27:252–258.

Deuel, Leo, 1977. *Memoirs of Heinrich Schliemann*. New York: Harper & Row.

De Vries, H. L., 1958. Variation in concentration of radiocarbon with time and location on earth. Koninkl. Nederl. Akademie van Wetenschappen, Amsterdam: *Proceedings*, Series B 61(2):1–9.

Diaz Del Castillo, Bernal, 1956. *The Conquest of New Spain*. Albert Idell, ed. and trans. Garden City, N.Y.: Dolphin.

Dibble, Harold L., 1987. Measurement of artifact provenience with an electronic theodolite. *Journal of Field Archaeology* 14(2):249–254.

Diener, Paul, and Eugene E. Robkin, 1978. Ecology, evolution and the search for cultural origins: the question of Islamic pig prohibition. *Current Anthropology* 19(3):493–540.

Dimbleby, Geoffrey W., 1977. *Ecology and Archaeology*. London: Arnold.

Divale, William Tulio, 1972. Systemic population control in the Middle and Upper Palaeolithic: inferences based on contemporary hunter-gatherers. *World Archaeology* 4(2):222–243.

————, and Marvin Harris, 1976. Population, warfare, and the male supremacist complex. *American Anthropologist* 78(3):521–538.

Dixon, Keith A., 1971. Archaeological site preservation: the neglected alternative to destruction. *Pacific Coast Archaeological Society Quarterly* 7:51–70.

Dollar, Clyde D., 1968. Some thoughts on theory and method in historical archaeology. *The Conference on Historical Site Archaeology Papers* 2(2):2–30.

Dolzani, Michael, 1987. Blood from a stone. *Mammoth Trumpet* 3(4):1, 3, 8.

Donnan, Christopher B., 1971. Ancient Peruvian potters' marks and their interpretation through ethnographic analogy. *American Antiquity* 36(4):460–466.

Doran, James, 1970. Systems theory, computer simulations and archaeology. *World Archaeology* 1(3):289–298.

Douglass, Andrew Ellicott, 1929. The secret of the Southwest solved by talkative tree rings. *National Geographic* 56(6):736–770.

Dow, James W., 1967. Astronomical orientations at Teotihuacán: A case study in astroarchaeology. *American Antiquity* 32(3):326–334.

Draper, Patricia, 1975. !Kung women: Contrasts in sexual egalitarianism in foraging and sedentary contexts. In *Toward an Anthropology of Women*, R. Reiter, ed. New York: Monthly Review Press, pp. 77–109.

Drennan, Robert D., 1976. A refinement of chronological seriation using nonmetric multidimensional scaling. *American Antiquity* 41(3):290–302.

Dumond, Donald E., 1965. Population growth and cultural change. *Southwestern Journal of Anthropology* 21(4):302–324.

————, 1977. Science in archaeology: the saints go marching in. *American Antiquity* 42(3):330–349.

Dunn, Mary Eubanks, 1983. Phytolith analysis in archaeology. *Mid-Continental Journal of Archaeology* 8(2):287–301.

Dunnell, Robert C., 1970. Seriation method and its evaluation. *American Antiquity* 35(3):305–319.

————, 1971. *Systematics in Prehistory*. New York: Free Press.

————, 1979. Trends in current Americanist archaeology. *American Journal of Archaeology* 83(4):437–449.

————, 1980a. Americanist archaeology: the 1979 contribution. *American Journal of Archaeology* 84:463–478.

————, 1980b. Evolutionary theory and archaeology. In *Advances in Archaeological Method and Theory,* vol. 3, Michael B. Schiffer, ed. New York: Academic Press, pp. 35–99.

————, 1982a. Americanist archaeological literature: 1981. *American Journal of Archaeology* 86:509–529.

————, 1982b. Science, social science, and common sense: the agonizing dilemma of modern archaeology. *Journal of Anthropological Archaeology* 38:1–25.

————, 1983. A review of the Americanist literature for 1982. *American Journal of Archaeology* 87:521–544.

————, 1984. The Americanist literature for 1983: a year of contrasts and challenges. *American Journal of Archaeology* 88:489–513.

————, 1985. Americanist archaeology in 1984. *American Journal of Archaeology* 89:585–611.

————, 1986a. Five decades of American archaeology. In *American Archaeology Past and Future: a Celebration of the Society for American Archaeology 1935–1985,* David J. Meltzer, Don D. Fowler, and Jeremy A. Sabloff, eds. Washington D.C.: Smithsonian Institution Press, pp. 23–49.

————, 1986b. Methodological issues in Americanist artifact classification. In *Advances in Archaeological Method and Theory,* vol. 9, Michael B. Schiffer, ed. New York: Academic Press, pp. 149–207.

————, and William S. Dancey, 1983. The siteless survey: a regional scale data collection strategy. In *Advances in Archaeological Method and Theory,* vol. 6, Michael B. Schiffer, ed. New York: Academic Press, pp. 267–287.

Durham, William, 1981. Overview: optimal foraging analysis in human ecology. In *Hunter-Gatherer Foraging Strategies: Ethnographic and Archeological Analyses,* Bruce Winterhalder and Eric Alden Smith, eds. Chicago: University of Chicago Press, pp. 218–232.

Easton, Donald F., 1981. Schliemann's discovery of 'Priam's Treasure': two enigmas. *Antiquity* 55:179–183.

Ebert, James I., 1984. Remote sensing applications in archaeology. In *Advances in Archaeological Method and Theory,* vol. 7, Michael B. Schiffer, ed. New York: Academic Press, pp. 293–362.

Eddy, J. A., 1974. Astronomical alignment of the Big Horn medicine wheel. *Science* 184(4141):1035–1043.

Ehrenberg, Ralph E., 1987. *Scholars' Guide to Washington, D.C. for Cartography and Remote Sensing Imagery.* Washington, D.C.: Smithsonian Institution Press.

Eighmy, Jeffrey L., Robert S. Sternberg, and Robert F. Butler, 1980. Archaeomagnetic dating in the American Southwest. *American Antiquity* 45(3):507–517.

Eighmy, Jeffrey L., and David E. Doyel, 1987. A reanalysis of first reported archaeomagnetic dates from the Hohokam area, Southern Arizona. *Journal of Field Archaeology* 14(3):331–342.

Ellis, Florence Hawley, 1975. A thousand years of the Pueblo sun-moon-star calendar. In *Archaeoastronomy in Pre-Columbian America,* Anthony F. Aveni, ed. Austin: University of Texas Press, pp. 59–87.

El Najjar, Mahmoud Y., and Abel Robertson, Jr., 1976. Spongy bones in prehistoric America. *Science* 193:141–143.

Ericson, J. E., 1975. New results in obsidian hydration dating. *World Archaeology* 7(2):151–159.

Euler, Robert C., and George J. Gumerman, 1978. *Investigations of the Southwestern Anthropological Research Group: An Experiment in Archaeological Cooperation.* Flagstaff: Museum of Northern Arizona.

Evans, Clifford, 1968. (Obituary of) James A. Ford, 1911–1968. *American Anthropologist* 70(6):1161–1167.

Evans, J. A. S., 1977. Redating prehistory in Europe. *Archaeology* 30(2):76–85.

Fagan, Brian, 1985. *In the Beginning: an Introduction to Archaeology* [5th ed.]. Boston: Little, Brown and Company.

———, 1988. *In the Beginning: an Introduction to Archaeology* [6th ed.]. Glenview, Ill.: Scott, Foresman/Little Brown.

Fairbanks, Charles H., 1977. Backyard archaeology as research strategy. *The Conference on Historic Site Archaeology Papers* 11:133–139.

———, 1984. Plantation archaeology of the southeastern coast. *Historical Archaeology* 18:1–14.

Farnsworth, Paul, James E. Brady, Michael J. DeNiro, and Richard S. MacNeish, 1985. A re-evaluation of the isotopic and archaeological reconstructions of diet in the Tehuacan Valley. *American Antiquity* 50(1):102–116.

Faul, Henry, 1971. Potassium-argon dating. In *Dating Techniques for the Archaeologist*, Henry N. Michael and Elizabeth K. Ralph, eds. Cambridge, Mass.: MIT Press, pp. 157–163.

Fedigan, Linda Marie, 1986. The changing role of women in models of human evolution. *Annual Review of Anthropology* 15:25–66.

Feldman, Mark, 1977. *Archaeology for Everyone*. New York: Quadrangle.

Fenton, William N., 1962. Introduction to *League of the Iroquois* by Lewis Henry Morgan. New York: Corinth Books, pp. v–xviii.

Ferguson, Leland B., 1975. Analysis of ceramic materials from Fort Watson: December 1780–April 1781. *The Conference on Historic Site Archaeology Papers* 8:2–28.

Fewkes, Jesse Walter, 1893. Tusayan katchinas. Washington, D.C.: *Fifteenth Annual Report of the Bureau of Ethnology 1893–1894*, pp. 251–313.

———, 1898. The winter solstice ceremony at Walpi. *American Anthropologist* 11(3):65–87.

Findlow, Frank J., Victoria C. Bennett, Jonathon E. Ericson, and Suzanne P. De Atley, 1975. A new obsidian hydration rate for certain obsidians in the American Southwest. *American Antiquity* 40(3):344–348.

Fitting, James, E., ed., 1973. *The Development of North American Archaeology*. Garden City, N.Y.: Doubleday.

Fladmark, Knud R., 1978. *A Guide to Basic Archaeological Field Procedures*. Burnaby, British Columbia: Department of Archaeology, Simon Fraser University.

Flannery, Kent V., 1965. The ecology of early food production in Mesopotamia. *Science* 147(3663):1247–1255.

———, 1966. The postglacial "readaptation" as viewed from Mesoamerica. *American Antiquity* 31(6):800–805.

———, 1967a. Culture history vs. cultural process: a debate in American archaeology. *Scientific American* 217(2):119–121.

———, 1967b. Vertebrate fauna and hunting patterns. In *The Prehistory of the Tehuacan Valley*, vol. 1, Douglas S. Byers, ed. Austin: University of Texas Press, pp. 132–177.

———, 1968. Archeological systems theory and early Mesoamerica. In *Anthropological Archeology in the Americas*, Betty J. Meggers, ed., Washington, D.C.: Anthropological Society of Washington, pp. 67–87.

———, 1969. Origins and ecological effects of early domestication in Iran and the Near East. In *The Domestication and Exploitation of Plants and Animals,* P. J. Ucko and G. W. Dimbleby, eds. Chicago: Aldine, pp. 73–100.

———, 1972. The cultural evolution of civilizations. *Annual Review of Ecology and Systematics* 3:399–426.

———, 1973a. Archeology with a capital S. In *Research and Theory in Current Archeology,* Charles L. Redman, ed., New York: Wiley and Sons, pp. 47–53.

———, 1973b. The origins of agriculture, *Annual Review of Anthropology* 2:271–310.

———, 1976a. Empirical determination of site catchments in Oaxaca and Tehuacán. In *The Early Mesoamerican Village,* Kent V. Flannery, ed., New York: Academic Press, pp. 103–117.

———, 1976b. The trouble with regional sampling. In *The Early Mesoamerican Village,* Kent V. Flannery, ed., New York: Academic Press, pp. 159–160.

———, 1982. The golden Marshalltown: a parable for the archeology of the 1980s. *American Anthropologist* 84(2):265–278.

———, ed., 1986. *Guilá Naquitz: Archaic Foraging and Early Agriculture in Oaxaca, Mexico.* Orlando, Fla.: Academic Press.

———, and Joyce Marcus, 1976. Formative Oaxaca and the Zapotec cosmos. *American Scientist* 64(4):374–383.

———, Chris L. Moser, and Silvia Maranca, 1986. The excavation of Guilá Naquitz. In *Guilá Naquitz: Archaic Foraging and Early Agriculture in Oaxaca, Mexico,* Kent V. Flannery, ed., Orlando, Fla.: Academic Press, Inc., pp. 65–95.

———, and Marcus C. Winter, 1976. Analyzing household activities. In *The Early Mesoamerican Village,* Kent V. Flannery, ed., New York: Academic Press, pp. 34–44.

Fleming, Stuart, 1977. *Dating Techniques in Archaeology.* New York: St. Martin's Press.

———, 1979. *Thermoluminescence Techniques in Archaeology.* New York: Oxford University Press.

Flenniken, J. Jeffrey, 1978. Reevaluation of the Lindenmeier Folsom: a replication experiment in lithic technology. *American Antiquity* 43(3):473–480.

———, 1981. Replicative systems analysis: a model applied to the vein quartz artifacts from the Hoko River site. *Laboratory of Anthropology Reports of Investigations* no. 59. Pullman: Washington State University.

———, 1984. The past, present, and future of flintknapping: an anthropological perspective. *Annual Review of Anthropology* 13:187–203.

———, and J. Haggarty, 1979. Trampling as an agency in the formation of edge damage: an experiment in lithic technology. *Northwest Anthropological Research Notes* 13(2):208–214.

———, and Terry L. Ozbun, 1988. Experimental analysis of Plains grooved abraders. *Plains Anthropologist* 33(119):37–52.

———, and Anan W. Raymond, 1986. Morphological projectile point typology: replication experimentation and technological analysis. *American Antiquity* 51(3):603–614.

Fletcher, Roland, 1977. Settlement studies. In *Spatial Archaeology,* David L. Clarke, ed. New York: Academic Press, pp. 47–162.

Foley, Robert, 1981. Off-site archaeology: an alternative approach for the short-sited. In *Pattern of the Past: Studies in Honour of David Clarke,* Ian Hodder, Glynn Isaac, and Norman Hammond, eds. Cambridge, England: Cambridge University Press, pp. 157–183.

Ford, James Alfred, 1949. Cultural dating of prehistoric sites in the Virú Valley, Peru (Part 2 of James Alfred Ford and Gordon R. Willey, Surface survey of the Virú Valley, Peru). *Anthropological Papers of the American Museum of Natural History* 43(1).

————, 1952. Measurements of some prehistoric design developments in the southeastern states. *Anthropologial Papers of the American Museum of Natural History* 44(3).

————, 1954. The type concept revisited. *American Anthropologist* 56(1):42–54.

————, 1957. A quantitative method for deriving cultural chronology. *Pan American Union. Technical Manual,* no. 1. (Reprinted as *University of Missouri, Museum of Anthropology, Museum Brief,* no. 9.)

————, 1962. A *quantitative method for deriving cultural chronology.* Washington, D.C.: Pan American Union, Technical Manual, I.

————, 1969. A comparison of formative cultures in the Americas: diffusion or the psychic unity of man? *Smithsonian Contributions to Anthropology,* vol. 2.

————, and Clarence H. Webb, 1956. Poverty Point, a late Archaic site in Louisiana. *Anthropological Papers of the American Museum of Natural History* 46(1):1–140.

————, and Gordon R. Willey, 1941. An interpretation of the prehistory of the eastern United States. *American Anthropologist* 43(3):325–363.

Ford, Norman D., 1970. *How to Travel and Get Paid for It.* (12th revised edition.) Greenlawn, N.Y.: Harian Publications.

Ford, Richard I., 1979. Paleoethnobotany in American archaeology. In *Advances in Archaeological Method and Theory,* vol. 2, Michael B. Schiffer, ed., New York: Academic Press, pp. 285–336.

————, 1983. The evolution of corn revisited. *The Quarterly Review of Archaeology* 4(4):12–13, 16.

————, ed., 1985. Prehistoric food production in North America. *University of Michigan, Museum of Anthropology, Anthropological Papers,* no. 75.

————, 1987. Ethnobiology in historical archaeology. *The Quarterly Review of Archaeology* 18(2):10–11.

Forde, C. Daryll, 1963. *Habitat, Economy and Society: a Geographical Introduction to Ethnology.* New York: E.P. Dutton.

Fowler, Don D., 1977. Models and Great Basin prehistory—Introductory remarks. In *Models and Great Basin Prehistory: a Symposium,* Don D. Fowler, ed., *Desert Research Institute Publications in the Social Sciences,* no. 12, pp. 3–10.

————, 1982. Cultural resources management. In *Advances in Archaeological Method and Theory,* vol. 5, Michael B. Schiffer, ed. New York: Academic Press, pp. 1–50.

————, 1986. Conserving American archaeological resources. In *American Archaeology: Past and Future: a Celebration of the Society for American Archaeology 1935–1985,* David J. Meltzer, Don D. Fowler, and Jeremy A. Sabloff, eds. Washington D.C.: Smithsonian Institution Press, pp. 135–162.

———, and Catherine S. Fowler, eds., 1971. Anthropology of the Numa: John Wesley Powell's manuscripts on the Numic peoples of western North America, 1868–1880. *Smithsonian Contributions to Anthropology,* no. 14.

Fowler, John M., 1974. Protection of the cultural environment in federal law. In *Federal Environmental Law,* E. L. Dolgin and T. C. P. Guilbert. St. Paul: West Publishing Co., pp. 1466–1517.

Fowler, Melvin L., and Richard S. MacNeish, 1972. Excavations in the Coxcatlán locality in the alluvial slopes. In *The Prehistory of the Tehuacan Valley,* vol. 5, Richard S. MacNeish, Melvin L. Fowler, Angel Garcia Cook, Frederick A. Peterson, Antoinette Nelken-Terner, and James A. Neely, eds. Austin: University of Texas Press, pp. 219–340.

Fradkin, Arlene, 1980. Hog jowls and coon meat: an analysis of faunal remains from the Hampton Plantation, St. Simons Island, Georgia. *Southeastern Archaeological Conference Bulletin* 22:57–59.

Freeman, Leslie G., Jr., 1962. Statistical analysis of painted pottery types from Upper Little Colorado drainage. In *Chapters on the Prehistory of Eastern Arizona,* vol. 1, Paul S. Martin and others. *Fieldiana Anthropology* 53:87–104.

———, 1977. Paleolithic archeology and paleoanthropology in China. In *Paleoanthropology in the People's Republic of China,* W. W. Howells and Patricia Jones Tsuchitani, eds., *Committee on Scholarly Communication with the People's Republic of China,* no. 4. Washington, D.C.: National Academy of Sciences.

———, and James A. Brown, 1964. Statistical analysis of Carter Ranch pottery. In *Chapters in the Prehistory of Eastern Arizona,* vol. 2, Paul S. Martin and others. *Fieldiana Anthropology,* 55:126–154.

Fried, Morton H., 1967. *The Evolution of Political Society.* New York: Random House.

Friedman, Irving, and Robert L. Smith, 1960. A new dating method using obsidian, Part I: the development of the method. *American Antiquity* 25(4):476–522.

———, and Fred W. Trembour, 1978. Obsidian: the dating stone. *American Scientist* 66(1):44–51.

———, 1983. Obsidian hydration dating update. *American Antiquity* 48(3):544–547.

Friedman, Jonathan, 1974. Marxism, structuralism and vulgar materialism. *Man* 9(3):444–469.

Friedrich, Margaret Hardin, 1970. Design structure and social interaction: archaeological implications of an ethnographic analysis. *American Antiquity* 35(3):332–343.

Frison, George C., and Bruce A. Bradley, 1980. *Folsom Tools and Technology at the Hanson Site, Wyoming.* Albuquerque: University of New Mexico Press.

Fritts, H. C., 1976. *Tree Rings and Climate.* New York: Academic Press.

Fritz, John M., 1978. Paleopsychology today: ideational systems and human adaptation in prehistory. In *Social Archaeology: Beyond Subsistence and Dating,* Charles L. Redman, Mary Jane Berman, Edward V. Curtin, William T. Laughorne, Jr., Nina M. Versaggi, and Jeffrey C. Wanser, eds. New York: Academic Press, pp. 37–59.

———, and Fred J. Plog, 1970. The nature of archaeological explanation. *American Antiquity* 35(4):405–412.

Frolov, Boris A., 1970. Aspects mathématiques dans l'art préhistorique. *Valcamonica*

Symposium: Actes du Symposium International d'Art Préhistorique, E. Anati, ed. International Symposium on Prehistoric Art (Valcamonica), Capo di Ponte, pp. 475–478.

———, 1971. Die magische Sieben in der Altsteinzeit. In *Bild der Wissenschaft*, pp. 258–261.

Fuson, R. H., 1969. The orientation of Mayan ceremonial centers. *Annals of the Association of American Geographers* 59:494–511.

Garn, Stanley M., and Walter D. Block, 1970. The limited nutritional value of cannibalism. *American Anthropologist* 72:106.

Garrison, Ervan G., James G. Baker, and David Hurst Thomas, 1985. Magnetic prospection and the discovery of Mission Santa Catalina de Guale, Georgia. *Journal of Field Archaeology* 12(3):299–313.

Geertz, Clifford, 1966. Religion as a cultural system. In *Anthropological Approaches to the Study of Religion*, Michael Banton, ed. *ASA Monographs*, no. 3. New York: Frederick A. Praeger, pp. 1–46.

———, 1973. *The Interpretation of Cultures*. New York: Basic Books.

Gentner, W., and H. J. Lippolt, 1969. The potassium-argon dating of Upper Tertiary and Pleistocene deposits. In *Science in Archaeology*, Don Brothwell and Eric Higgs, eds. London: Thames and Hudson, pp. 88–100.

Gero, Joan M., 1981. Excavation bias and the woman-at-home ideology. Paper presented at the 21st annual meeting of the Northeastern Anthropological Association, Saratoga, New York.

———, 1983. Gender bias in archaeology: A cross-cultural perspective. In *The Socio-politics of Archaeology*, Joan Gero, David M. Lacy, and Michael L. Blakey, eds. University of Massachusetts Department of Anthropology Research Report, No. 23, pp. 51–57.

———, 1985. Socio-politics and the woman-at-home ideology. *American Antiquity* 50(2):342–350.

———, 1988. Gender bias in archaeology: here, then and now. In *Resistance of the Science & Health Care Professions to Feminism*, Sue V. Rosser, ed. Elmsford, N.Y.: Pergamon Press Inc., in press.

———, David M. Lacy, and Michael L. Blakely, eds., 1983. *The Socio-politics of Archaeology*. University of Massachusetts Amherst Department of Anthropology Research Report no. 23.

———, and Dolores Root, 1989. Public presentations and private concerns: Archaeology in the pages of *National Geographic*. In *Politics of the Past, Proceedings of the World Archaeological Congress, Southampton, England, September 1986*, Peter Gathercole and David Lowenthal, eds. London: Allen and Unwin Publishers, in press.

Gibbon, Guy, 1984. *Anthropological Archaeology*. New York: Columbia University Press.

Gibbs, Liv, 1987. Identifying gender representation in the archaeological record: contextual study. In *The Archaeology of contextual Meanings*, Ian Hodder, ed. Cambridge, England: Cambridge University Press, pp. 79–89.

Giddings, J. L., 1961. Cultural continuities of Eskimos. *American Antiquity* 27(2):155–173.

———, 1966. Cross-dating the archaeology of northwestern Alaska. *Science* 153(3732):127–135.

Gifford, Carol A., and Elizabeth A. Morris, 1985. Digging for credit: early archaeological field schools in the American Southwest. *American Antiquity* 50(2): 395–411.

Gifford, Diane P., 1981. Taphonomy and paleoecology: a critical review of archaeology's sister disciplines. In *Advances in Archaeological Method and Theory,* vol. 4, Michael B. Schiffer, ed., New York: Academic Press, pp. 365–438.

Gifford, James C., 1960. The type-variety method of ceramic classification as an indicator of cultural phenomena. *American Antiquity* 25(3):341–347.

Gifford-Gonzalez, Diane, n.d. Ethnographic analogues for interpreting modified bones: some cases from East Africa. In *Bone Modification,* R. Bonnichsen and M. Sorg, eds. Orono, Maine: Center for the Study of Early Man, in press.

Gilbert, B. Miles, 1980. *Mammalian Osteology.* Laramie, Wis.: Modern Printing.

Gilbert, Robert I., Jr., 1985. Stress, paleonutrition, and trace elements. In *The Analysis of Prehistoric Diets,* Robert I. Gilbert, Jr. and James H. Mielke, eds. Orlando, Fla.: Academic Press, pp. 339–360.

———, and James H. Mielke, eds. 1985. *The Analysis of Prehistoric Diets.* Orlando, Fla.: Academic Press.

Givens, David B., 1987. Doctor rate update: 1968 PhD survey results. *Anthropology Newsletter* 28(4):1, 12.

Glassie, Henry, 1975. *Folk Housing in Middle Virginia.* Knoxville: The University of Tennessee Press.

Goldschmidt, Walter, 1960. *Exploring the Ways of Mankind.* New York: Holt, Rinehart and Winston.

———, 1983. Review of *Beyond the Myths of Culture: Essays in Cultural Materialism,* Eric B. Ross, ed. *American Anthropologist* 85(3):695–698.

Goodenough, Ward H., 1965. Rethinking "status" and "role": Toward a general model of the cultural organization of social relationships. In *The Relevance of Models for Social Anthropology,* Michael Banton, ed. *ASA Monographs,* no. 1. New York: Frederick A. Praeger, pp. 1–24.

———, 1970. *Description and Comparison in Cultural Anthropology.* Chicago: Aldine.

———, 1971. Culture, language, and society. Reading, Mass.: *Addison-Wesley Module in Anthropology* 7:1–48.

Gorenstein, Shirley, 1977. History of American archaeology. In *Perspectives on Anthropology, 1976, Special Publication of the American Anthropological Association,* no. 10, pp. 86–100.

Gould, Richard A., 1966. Archaeology of the Point St. George site, and Tolowa prehistory. *University of California Publications in Anthropology,* vol. 4.

———, 1968. Living archaeology: the Ngatatjara of western Australia. *Southwestern Journal of Anthropology* 24(2):101–122.

———, 1980. *Living Archaeology.* Cambridge, England: Cambridge University Press.

————, 1985. The empiricist strikes back: a reply to Binford. *American Antiquity* 50(3):638–644.

————, and Patty Jo Watson, 1982. A dialogue on the meaning and use of analogy in ethnoarchaeological reasoning. *Journal of Anthropological Archaeology* 1(4):355–381.

Gould, Stephen Jay, 1980. Senseless signs of history. In *The Panda's Thumb,* by Stephen Jay Gould. New York: Norton.

Gove, H. E., 1987. Turin workshop on radiocarbon dating the Turin shroud. *Nuclear Instruments and Methods in Physics Research* B29(1,2):193–195.

Gowlett, J.A.J., and R.E.M. Hedges, 1986. *Archaeological Results from Accelerator Dating.* Oxford, England: Oxford University Committee for Archaeology.

Grange, Roger T., Jr., 1974. Pawnee potsherds revisited: formula dating of a Non-European ceramic tradition. *The Conference on Historic Site Archaeology Papers* 7:318–336.

Grayson, Donald K., 1973. On the methodology of faunal analysis. *American Antiquity* 38(4):432–439.

————, 1978. Minimum numbers and sample size in vertebrate faunal analysis. *American Antiquity* 43(1):53–65.

————, 1979. On the quantification of vertebrate archaeofaunas. In *Advances in Archaeological Method and Theory,* vol. 2, Michael B. Schiffer, ed. New York: Academic Press, pp. 199–237.

————, 1983a. *The Establishment of Human Antiquity.* New York: Academic Press.

————, 1983b. The paleontology of Gatecliff Shelter: small mammals. In *The Archaeology of Monitor Valley*: 2. *Gatecliff Shelter,* David Hurst Thomas. *Anthropological Papers of the American Museum of Natural History* 59(1):99–126.

————, 1984. *Quantitative Zooarchaeology: Topics in the Analysis of Archaeological Faunas.* Orlando, Fla.: Academic Press.

————, 1986. Eoliths, archaeological ambiguity, and the generation of "middle-range" research. In *American Archaeology Past and Future: a Celebration of the Society of American Archaeology 1935–1985,* David J. Meltzer, Don D. Fowler, and Jeremy A. Sabloff, eds. Washington, D.C.: Smithsonian Institution Press, pp. 77–133.

————, 1987. The biogeographic history of small mammals in the Great Basin: observations on the last 20,000 years. *Journal of Mammalogy* 68:359–375.

————, 1988. Danger Cave, Last Supper Cave, and Hanging Rock Shelter: the faunas. *Anthropological Papers of the American Museum of Natural History* 66(1):1–130.

————, and David Hurst Thomas, 1983. Seasonality at Gatecliff Shelter. In *The Archaeology of Monitor Valley: 2. Gatecliff Shelter,* David Hurst Thomas. *Anthropological Papers of the American Museum of Natural History* 59(1):434–438.

Green, Stanton W., 1980. Toward a general model of agricultural systems. *Advances in Archaeological Method and Theory,* vol. 3, Michael B. Schiffer, ed. New York: Academic Press, pp. 311–355.

Greiser, Sally T., and Payson D. Sheets, 1979. Raw material as a functional variable in use-wear studies. In *Lithic Use-wear Studies,* Brian Hayden, ed. New York: Academic Press, pp. 289–296.

Grew, Raymond, and Eric R. Wolf, eds., 1984. *Comparative Studies in Society and History* 26(1).

Griffin, James B., 1959. The pursuit of archaeology in the United States. *American Anthropologist* 61(3):379–389.

———, 1985. The formation of the Society for American Archaeology. *American Antiquity* 50(2):261–271.

Griffin, Martha M., and Vernon J. Henry, 1984. Historic changes in the mean high water shoreline of Georgia, 1857–1982. *Georgia Department of Natural Resources, Bulletin 98*.

Grootes, P. M., 1978. Carbon-14 time scale extended: comparison of chronologies. *Science* 200(4337):11–15.

Grosscup, Gordon L., 1960. The culture history of Lovelock Cave, Nevada. *Archaeological Survey Report*, no. 52.

Gryba, Eugene M., 1988. A Stone Age pressure method of Folsom fluting. *Plains Anthropologist* 33(119):53–66.

Gumerman, George J., ed., 1971. The distribution of prehistoric population aggregates. *Prescott College Anthropological Reports*, no. 1. Prescott, Arizona: Prescott College Press.

———, 1973. The reconciliation of theory and method in archeology. In *Research and Theory in Current Archeology*, Charles L. Redman, ed. New York: Wiley, pp. 287–299.

Gumerman, George J., and David A. Phillips Jr., 1978. Archaeology beyond anthropology. *American Antiquity* 43(2):184–191.

Gunn, Joel, 1975. Idiosyncratic behavior in chipping style: some hypotheses and preliminary analysis. In *Lithic Technology: Making and Using Stone Tools,* Earl Swanson, ed. The Hague: Mouton Publishers, pp. 35–62.

Haag, William G., 1959. The status of evolutionary theory in American archeology. In *Evolution and Anthropology: A Centennial Appraisal,* Washington, D.C.: Anthropological Society of Washington, pp. 90–105.

———, 1968. (Obituary of) James Alfred Ford, 1911–1968. *The Florida Anthropologist* 21(1):31–33.

———, 1985. Federal aid to archaeology in the Southeast, 1933-1942. *American Antiquity* 50(2):272–280.

———, 1986. Field methods in archaeology. In *American Archaeology Past and Future: a Celebration of The Society for American Archaeology 1935–1985,* David J. Meltzer, Don D. Fowler, and Jeremy A. Sabloff, eds. Washington D.C.: Smithsonian Institution Press, pp. 63–76.

Haggett, Peter, 1966. *Locational Analysis in Human Geography*. New York: St. Martin's Press.

Hall, Robert L., 1976. Ghosts, water barriers, corn, and sacred enclosures in the eastern Woodlands. *American Antiquity* 41:360–364.

———, 1977. An anthropocentric perspective for eastern United States prehistory. *American Antiquity* 42(4):499–518.

Hally, David J., 1981. Plant preservation and the content of paleobotanical samples: a case study. *American Antiquity* 46(4):723–742.

Hames, Raymond B., and William T. Vickers, 1982. Optimal diet breadth theory as a model to explain variability in Amazonian hunting. *American Ethnologist* 9(2):358-378.

Hammond, Norman, 1976. Introduction. In *Archaeology in Northern Belize: 1974–1975 Interim report of the British Museum–Cambridge University Corozal Project,* Norman Hammond, ed. Cambridge, England: Cambridge University, Center of Latin American Studies.

Hammond, Philip C., 1974. Archaeometry and time: a review. *Journal of Field Archaeology* 1(3/4):329–335.

Handler, Jerome, and Frederick Lange, 1978. *Plantation Slavery in Barbados: an Archaeological and Historical Investigation.* Cambridge, Mass.: Harvard University Press.

———, 1979. Plantation slavery on Barbados, West Indies. *Archaeology* 32(4):45–52.

Handsman, Russell, 1981. Early capitalism and the center village of Canaan, Connecticut: A study of transformations and separations. *Artifacts* 9:1–21.

———, 1982. The hot and cold of Goshen's history. *Artifacts* 3:11–20.

Hanson, Lee H., Jr., 1971. Kaolin pipe stems—boring in on a fallacy. *The Conference on Historic Site Archaeology Papers* 4(1):2–15.

———, 1972. A few cents more. *The Conference on Historic Site Archaeology Papers* 4(1):2–15.

Hardesty, Donald L., 1977. *Ecological Anthropology.* New York: Wiley.

Hardin, Margaret Ann, 1977. Individual style in San Jośe pottery painting: the role of deliberate choice. In *The Individual in Prehistory,* James N. Hill and Joel Gunn, eds. New York: Academic Press, pp. 109–136.

Harner, Michael J., 1970. Population pressure and the social evolution of agriculturalists. *Southwestern Journal of Anthropology* 26(1):67–86.

———, 1977a. The ecological basis for Aztec sacrifice. *American Ethnologist* 4(1):117–135.

———, 1977b. The enigma of Aztec sacrifice. *Natural History* 86(4):47–51.

Harp, Elmer, Jr., 1975. *Photography in Archaeological Research.* Albuquerque: University of New Mexico Press.

Harper, K. T., and G. M. Alder, 1970. Appendix I: The macroscopic plant remains of the deposits of Hogup Cave, Utah, and their paleoclimatic implications. In *Hogup Cave,* C. Melvin Aikens. *University of Utah Anthropological Papers,* no. 93, pp. 215–240.

———, 1972. Paleoclimatic inferences concerning the last 10,000 years from a resampling of Danger Cave, Utah. In *Great Basin Cultural Ecology: a Symposium,* Don D. Fowler, ed. *Desert Research Institute Publications in the Social Sciences,* no. 8, pp. 13–23.

Harrington, Jean C., 1954. Dating stem fragments of seventeenth and eighteenth century clay tobacco pipes. *Quarterly Bulletin: Archaeological Society of Virginia* 9:(1).

———, 1955. Archeology as an auxiliary science to American history. *American Anthropologist* 57(6):1121–1130.

Harris, D. R., 1972. The origins of agriculture in the tropics. *American Scientist* 60:180–193.

Harris, Jack S., 1940. The White Knife Shoshone of Nevada. In *Acculturation in Seven American Indian Tribes,* Ralph Linton, ed. New York: D. Appleton-Century Co., pp. 39–118.

Harris, Marvin, 1968a. Comments. In *New Perspectives in Archeology,* Sally R. Binford and Lewis R. Binford, eds. Chicago: Aldine, pp. 359–361.

———, 1968b. *The Rise of Anthropological Theory.* New York: T. Y. Crowell Co.

———, 1974. *Cows, Pigs, Wars and Witches: the Riddles of Culture.* New York: Random House.

———, 1979. *Cultural Materialism: the Struggle for a Science of Culture.* New York: Random House.

———, 1980. History and ideological significance of the separation of social and cultural anthropology. In *Beyond the Myths of Culture: Essays in Cultural Materialism,* Eric B. Ross, ed., New York: Academic Press, pp. 391–407.

———, 1985. *Good to Eat: Riddles of Food and Culture.* New York: Simon & Schuster.

———, 1987a. Cultural materialism: alarums and excursions. In *Waymarks: The Notre Dame Inaugural Lectures in Anthropology,* Kenneth Moore, ed. Notre Dame, Ind.: University of Notre Dame Press, pp. 107–126.

———, and Eric B. Ross, eds., 1987b. *Food and Evolution: Toward a Theory of Human Food Habits.* Philadelphia: Temple University Press.

———, 1988a. Anthropology: ships that crash in the night. *American Anthropologist,* in press.

———, 1988b. *Culture, People, Nature: an Introduction to General Anthropology.* New York: Harper & Row.

Harrison, Peter D., 1981. Some aspects of preconquest settlement in southern Quintana Roo, Mexico. In *Lowland Maya Settlement Patterns,* Wendy Ashmore, ed. Albuquerque: University of New Mexico Press, pp. 259–286.

———, and B. L. Turner II, 1978. *Pre-Hispanic Maya Agriculture.* Albuquerque: University of New Mexico Press.

Harrold, Francis B., 1980. A comparative analysis of Eurasian Palaeolithic burials. *World Archaeology* 12(2):195–211.

Hassan, Fekri A., 1974. Population growth and cultural evolution. *Reviews in Anthropology* 1:205–212.

———, 1975. Determination of the size, density and growth rate of hunting-gathering populations. In *Population, Ecology and Social Evolution,* S. Polgar, ed. The Hague: Mouton.

———, 1981. *Demographic Archaeology.* New York: Academic Press.

Haury, Emil W., 1950. *The Stratigraphy and Archaeology of Ventana Cave, Arizona.* Albuquerque: University of New Mexico Press, and Tucson: University of Arizona Press.

———, 1962. HH-39: recollections of a dramatic moment in Southwestern archaeology. *Tree-Ring Bulletin* 24(3–4):11–14.

————, E. B. Sayles, and William W. Wasley, 1959. The Lehner mammoth site, southeastern Arizona, *American Antiquity* 25:2–30.

Haviland, William A., 1965. Prehistoric settlement at Tikal, Guatemala. *Expedition* 7:14–23.

————, 1969. A new population estimate for Tikal, Guatemala. *American Antiquity* 34:429–433.

————, 1970. Tikal, Guatemala and Mesoamerican urbanism. *World Archaeology* 2(2):186–198.

————, 1974. *Anthropology.* New York: Holt, Rinehart and Winston.

————, 1978. On Price's presentation of data from Tikal. *Current Anthropology* 19(1):180–181.

Hawkes, Jaquetta, 1967. God in the machine. *Antiquity* 41(163):174–180.

Hawkes, Kristen, 1987. How much food do foragers need? In *Food and Evolution: Toward a Theory of Human Food Habits,* Marvin Harris and Eric B. Ross, eds. Philadelphia: Temple University Press, pp. 341–356.

————, Kim Hill, and James F. O'Connell, 1982. Why hunters gather: optimal foraging and the Aché of eastern Paraguay. *American Ethnologist* 9(2):379–398.

————, and James F. O'Connell, 1981. Affluent hunters? Some comments in light of the Alyawara case. *American Anthropologist* 83(3):622–626.

————, James F. O'Connell, and N. Blurton Jones, 1987. Hardworking Hadza grandmothers. In *Comparative Socioecology of Mammals and Man,* R. Foley and V. Standen, eds. London: Basil Blackwell.

Hawkins, Gerald S., 1963. Stonehenge decoded. *Nature* 200(4904):306–308.

————, 1964. Stonehenge: A Neolithic computer. *Nature* 202(4939):1258–1261.

————, 1965. *Stonehenge Decoded.* Garden City, N.Y.: Doubleday.

Hayden, Brian, 1979. *Palaeolithic Reflections: Lithic Technology and Ethnographic Excavation Among Australian Aborigines.* Atlantic Highlands, N.J.: Humanities Press.

————, 1981a. Research and development in the Stone Age: technological transitions among hunter-gatherers. *Current Anthropology* 22(5):519–548.

————, 1981b. Subsistence and ecological adaptations in modern hunter-gatherers. In *Omnivorous Primates,* Robert S. O. Harding and Geza Teleki, eds. New York: Columbia University Press, pp. 344–421.

————, 1987. *Lithic Studies Among the Contemporary Highland Maya.* Tucson: University of Arizona Press.

————, and Aubrey Cannon, 1984. The structure of material systems: ethnoarchaeology in the Maya highlands. *Society of American Archaeology Papers* no.3.

Hazard, Thomas, 1960. On the nature of Numaym and its counterparts elsewhere on the Northwest Coast. Paper presented to the 127th Annual Meeting of the American Association for the Advancement of Science, Denver.

Heat Moon, William Least (William Trogdan), 1982. *Blue Highways: a Journey into America.* Boston: Little Brown.

Hedges, R. E. M., and J. A. J. Gowlett, 1986. Radiocarbon dating by accelerator mass spectrometry. *Scientific American* 254(1):100–107.

Heighton, Robert F., and Kathleen A. Deagan, 1972. A new formula for dating kaolin clay pipestems. *The Conference on Historic Site Archaeology Papers* 6(2):220-229.

Heizer, Robert F., and Martin A. Baumhoff, 1961. Wagon Jack Shelter. In *The Archaeology of Two Sites at Eastgate, Churchill County, Nevada: Wagon Jack Shelter. University of California Anthropological Records* 20(4):119–138.

————, 1962. *Prehistoric Rock Art of Nevada and Eastern California,* University of California Press.

————, and C. W. Clewlow, Jr., 1968. Projectile points from site NV-Ch-15, Churchill County, Nevada. *University of California Archaeological Survey Reports,* 71: 59–88.

————, and John A. Graham, 1967. *A Guide to Field Methods in Archaeology: Approaches to the Anthropology of the Dead.* Palo Alto, Calif.: National Press.

————, and Thomas R. Hester, 1978. Great Basin. In *Chronologies in New World Archaeology,* R. E. Taylor and C. W. Meighan, eds. New York: Academic Press, pp. 147–199.

————, and Lewis K. Napton, 1970. Archaeology and the prehistoric Great Basin lacustrine subsistence regime as seen from Lovelock Cave, Nevada. *Contributions to the University of California Archaeological Research Facility,* no. 10.

Heller, F., and H. Markert, 1973. The age of viscous remnant magnetization of Hadrian's Wall (Northern England). *Geophysical Journal of the Royal Astronomical Society* 31:395–406.

Hempel, Carl G., 1959. The logic of functional analysis. In *Symposium on Sociological Theory,* L. Gross, ed. Evanston, Ill.: Row, Peterson, pp. 271–307.

————, 1965. *Aspects of Scientific Explanation: Other Essays in the Philosophy of Science.* New York: Free Press.

Hester, James J., 1976. *Introduction to Archaeology.* New York: Holt, Rinehart and Winston.

Hester, Thomas R., Robert F. Heizer, and John A. Graham, 1975. *Field Methods in Archaeology.* (6th ed.) Palo Alto, Calif.: Mayfield.

Heyerdahl, Thor, 1950. *The Kon-Tiki Expedition: by Raft Across the South Seas.* London: Allen & Unwin.

————, 1971. *The Ra Expeditions.* Garden City, N.Y.: Doubleday.

Hill, Andrew, 1979a. Butchery and natural disarticulation: an investigatory technique. *American Antiquity* 44:739–744.

————, 1979b. Disarticulation and scattering of mammal skeletons. *Paleobiology* 5(3):261–274.

————, and Anna Kay Behrensmeyer, 1984. Disarticulation patterns of some modern East African Mammals. *Paleobiology* 10(3):366–376.

————, 1985. Natural disarticulation and bison butchery. *American Antiquity* 50(1):141–145.

Hill, James N., 1968. Broken K Pueblo: patterns of form and function. In *New Perspectives in Archeology,* Sally R. Binford and Lewis R. Binford, eds. Chicago: Aldine, pp. 103–142.

————, 1970a. Broken K Pueblo: Prehistoric social organization in the American Southwest. Tucson: *Anthropological Papers of the University of Arizona,* no. 18.

————, 1970b. Prehistoric social organization in the American Southwest: theory and method. In *Reconstructing Prehistoric Pueblo Societies,* William A. Longacre, ed. Albuquerque: University of New Mexico Press, pp. 11–58.

————, 1977. Individual variability in ceramics and the study of prehistoric social organization. In *The Individual in Prehistory,* James N. Hill and Joel Gunn, eds. New York: Academic Press, pp. 55–108.

————, and R. K. Evans, 1972. A model for classification and typology. In *Models in Archaeology,* David L. Clarke, ed. London: Methuen, pp. 231–273.

————, and Joel Gunn, 1977. *The Individual in Prehistory: Studies of Variability in Style in Prehistoric Technologies.* New York: Academic Press.

————, and Richard H. Hevly, 1968. Pollen at Broken K Pueblo: some new interpretations. *American Antiquity* 33(2):200–210.

Hill, Kim, and Kristen Hawkes, 1983. Neotropical hunting among the Aché of eastern Paraguay. In *Adaptations of Native Amazonians,* R. Hames and W. Vickers, eds., New York: Academic Press, pp. 139–188.

————, Hillard Kaplan, Kristen Hawkes, and A. Magdalena Hurtado, 1987. Foraging decisions among Aché hunter-gatherers: new data and implications for optimal foraging models. *Ethnology and Sociobiology* 8:1–36.

Hodder, Ian, 1978a. *Simulation Studies in Archaeology.* Cambridge, England: Cambridge University Press.

————, ed., 1978b. *The Spatial Organisation of Culture.* Pittsburgh, Pa.: University of Pittsburgh Press.

————, 1982a. *Symbols in Action: Ethnoarchaeological Studies of Material Culture.* Cambridge, England: Cambridge University Press.

————, ed., 1982b. *Symbolic and Structural Archaeology.* Cambridge, England: Cambridge University Press.

————1985. Postprocessual archaeology. In *Advances in Archaeological Method and Theory,* vol. 8, Michael B. Schiffer, ed. Orlando, Fla.: Academic Press, pp. 1–26.

————, 1986. *Reading the Past: Current Approaches to Interpretation in Archaeology.* Cambridge, England: Cambridge University Press.

————, ed., 1987a. *Archaeology as Long-term History.* Cambridge, England: Cambridge University Press.

————, ed., 1987b. *The Archaeology of Contextual Meanings.* Cambridge, England: Cambridge University Press.

————, 1987c. The meaning of discard: ash and domestic space in Baringo. In *Method and Theory for Activity Area Research: an Ethnoarchaeological Approach,* Susan Kent, ed. New York: Columbia University Press, pp. 424–488.

Hodder, Ian, and Clive Orton, 1976. *Spatial Analysis in Archaeology.* Cambridge, England: Cambridge University Press.

Hodson, F. R., D. G. Kendall, and P. Tautu, eds., 1971. *Mathematics in the Archaeological and Historical Sciences.* Edinburgh: Edinburgh University Press.

Hole, Frank, Kent V. Flannery, and James A. Neely, 1969. Prehistory and human ecology of the Deh Luran Plain: an early village sequence from Khuzistan, Iran. *University of Michigan, Memoirs of the Museum of Anthropology,* no. 1.

———, and Robert F. Heizer, 1973. *An Introduction to Prehistoric Archeology* (3d ed). New York: Holt, Rinehart and Winston.

———, and Mary Shaw, 1967. Computer analysis of chronological seriation. *Rice University Studies,* vol. 53.

Holly, Gerald A., and Terry A. Del Bene, 1981. An evaluation of Keeley's Microwear approach. *Journal of Archaeological Science* 8:337–352.

Hooton, Earnest Albert, 1930. The Indians of Pecos Pueblo: A study of their skeletal remains. *Papers of the Phillips Academy Southwestern Expedition 4.* New Haven, Conn.: Yale University Press.

Hornerkamp, Nick, 1982. Social status as reflected in faunal remains from an eighteenth century British colonial site. *The Conference on Historic Site Archaeology Papers* 15:87–115.

Hosley, Edward, 1972. Comment on Cognitive aspects of Upper Paleolithic engraving by Alexander Marshack. *Current Anthropology* 13(3–4):465–466.

Howard, Hildegarde, 1929. The avifauna of Emeryville shellmound. *University of California Publications in Zoology* 32:301–394.

Howells, W. W., 1960. Estimating population numbers through archaeological and skeletal remains. In *The Application of Quantitative Methods in Archaeology,* R. F. Heizer and S. F. Cook, eds. Viking Fund Publications in Anthropology, No. 28. Chicago: Quadrangle, pp. 158–185.

Hoyle, Fred, 1966a. Stonehenge—an eclipse predictor. *Nature* 211(5048):454–456.

———, 1966b. Speculations on Stonehenge. *Antiquity* 40(160):262–276.

Hoyt, John H., and John R. Hails, 1967. Pleistocene shoreline sediments in coastal Georgia: deposition and modification. *Science* 155:1541–1543.

———, and Vernon J. Henry, Jr., 1971. Origin of capes and shoals along the southeastern coast of the United States. *Geological Society of America Bulletin* 82:59–66.

Huss-Ashmore, Rebecca, Alan H. Goodman, and George J. Armelagos, 1982. Nutritional inference from paleopathology. In *Advances in Archaeological Method and Theory,* vol. 5, Michael B. Schiffer, ed., New York: Academic Press, pp. 395–474.

Hutchinson, Dale, and Clark Spencer Larsen, 1988. Determination of stress episode duration from linear enamel hyoplasias: a case study from St. Catherines Island, Georgia. *Human Biology* 60(1): 93–110.

Huxley, Julian, ed., 1940. *The New Systematics.* Oxford, England: Oxford University Press (Clarendon).

Irwin, Henry T., 1968. The Itama: Early Late-Pleistocene Inhabitants of the Plains of the United States and Canada and the American Southwest. Ph.D. dissertation, Harvard University.

Irwin-Williams, Cynthia, n.d. Women in the field: pioneers in archaeology. *Women in Science: Righting the Record,* Gaby Kass-Simon, ed., Bloomington: University of Indiana Press, in press.

Isaac, Glynn L., 1978. The food-sharing behavior of protohuman hominids. *Scientific American* 238(4):90–108.

———, Richard E. Leakey, and Anna K. Behrensmeyer, 1971. Archaeological traces of early hominid activities, east of Lake Rudolph, Kenya. *Science,* 173:1129–1133.

Iversen, J., 1956. Forest clearance in the Stone Age. *Scientific American* 194:36–41.

Jacobi. R. M., 1978. Northern England in the eighth millennium BC: an essay. In *The Early Post-Glacial Settlement of Northern Europe,* Paul Mellars, ed. London: Duckworth, pp. 295–332.

Jarman, H. N., A. J. Legge, and J. A. Charles, 1972. Retrieval of plant remains from archaeological sites by froth flotation. In *Papers in Economic Prehistory,* E. S. Higgs, ed. Cambridge, England: Cambridge University Press, pp. 39–48.

Jefferson, Thomas, 1787. *Notes on the State of Virginia.* London: John Stockdale (reprinted Chapel Hill: University of North Carolina Press, 1954).

Jennings, Jesse D., 1957. *Danger Cave. University of Utah Anthropological Papers,* no. 27.

———, 1985. River basin surveys: origins, operations, and results. *American Antiquity* 50(2):281–296.

Jeppson, Lawrence, 1970. *The Fabulous Frauds, Fascinating Tales of Great Art Forgeries.* New York: Waybright and Talley.

Jochim, Michael A., 1983. Optimization models in context. In *Archaeological Hammers and Theories,* James A. Moore and Arthur S. Keene, eds. New York: Academic Press, pp. 157–172.

Johnson, Allen W., and Timothy Earle, 1987. *The Evolution of Human Societies: from Foraging Group to Agrarian State.* Stanford, Calif.: Stanford University Press.

Johnson, Gregory A., 1972. A test of the utility of central place theory in archaeology. In *Man, Settlement and Urbanism,* P. J. Ucko, R. Tringham, and G. W. Dimbleby, eds. London: Duckworth, pp. 769–785.

———, 1975. Locational analysis and Uruk local exchange systems. In *Ancient Civilization and Trade,* Jeremy A. Sabloff and C. C. Lamberg-Karlovsky, eds. Albuquerque: University of New Mexico Press, pp. 285–339.

Johnson, LeRoy, Jr., 1968. Item seriation as an aid for elementary scale and cluster analysis. *University of Oregon Museum of Natural History Bulletin,* no. 15.

———, 1969. Obsidian hydration rate for the Klamath Basin of California and Oregon. *Science* 165:1354–1356.

———, 1972a. Introduction to imaginary models for archaeological scaling and clustering. In *Models in Archaeology,* D.L. Clarke, ed. London: Methuen, pp. 309–379.

———, 1972b. Problems in "avant garde" archaeology. *American Anthropologist* 74:366–377.

Johnston, R. B., 1961. Archaeological application of the proton magnetometer in Indiana (U.S.A.). *Archaeometry* 4:71–72.

Jolly, Clifford J., and Fred Plog, 1987. *Physical Anthropology and Archeology* [4th ed.]. New York: Alfred A. Knopf.

Jones, Kevin T., 1984. Hunting and scavenging by early hominids: a study in archaeological method and theory. Ph.D. diss. University of Utah, Salt Lake City.

Jones, Olive, 1971. Glass bottle push-ups and pontil marks. *Historical Archaeology* 5:62–73.

Joukowsky, Martha, 1980. *A Complete Manual of Field Archaeology: Tools and Techniques of Field Work for Archaeologists*. Englewood Cliffs, N.J.: Prentice-Hall.

Judd, Neil M., 1929. The present status of archaeology in the United States. *American Anthropologist* 31(4):401–418.

Judge, W. James, 1973. *Paleoindian Occupation of the Central Rio Grande Valley in New Mexico*. Albuquerque: University of New Mexico Press.

———, James I. Ebert, and Robert K. Hitchcock, 1975. Sampling in regional archaeological survey. In *Sampling in Archaeology,* James W. Mueller, ed. Tucson: University of Arizona Press, pp. 82–123.

Kalin, Jeffrey, 1981. Stem point manufacture and debitage recovery. *Archaeology of Eastern North America* 9:134–175.

Keeley, H. C. M., 1978. The cost-effectiveness of certain methods of recovering macroscopic organic remains from archaeological deposits. *Journal of Archaeological Science* 5:179–183.

Keeley, Lawrence H., 1974. Technique and methodology in microwear studies: a critical review. *World Archaeology* 5(3):323–336.

———, 1980. *Experimental Determination of Stone Tool Uses: a Microwear Analysis*. Chicago: University of Chicago Press.

———, and M. H. Newcomer, 1977. Microwear analysis of experimental flint tools: a test case. *Journal of Archaeological Science* 4:29–62.

Keene, Arthur S., 1981. *Prehistoric Foraging in a Temperate Forest: a Linear Programming Model*. New York: Academic Press.

———, 1983. Biology, behavior, and borrowing: a critical examination of optimal foraging theory in archaeology. In *Archaeological Hammers and Theories,* James A. Moore and Arthur S. Keene, eds. New York: Academic Press, pp. 137–155.

———, 1985. Nutrition and economy: models for the study of prehistoric diet. In *The Analysis of Prehistoric Diets,* Robert I. Gilbert and James H. Mielke, eds. Orlando, Fla.: Academic Press, pp. 155–190.

Keesing, Roger M., 1974. Theories of culture. *Annual Review of Anthropology* 3:73–97.

———, 1976. *Cultural Anthropology: a Contemporary Perspective*. New York: Holt, Rinehart and Winston.

Kehoe, Alice B., and Thomas F. Kehoe, 1973. Cognitive models for archaeological interpretation. *American Antiquity* 38(2):150–154.

Kelley, Jane Holden, 1977. Comment on Schiffer and House. *Current Anthropology* 18(1):57.

———, and Marsha P. Hanen, 1988. *Archaeology and the Methodology of Science*. Albuquerque: University of New Mexico Press.

Kelly, Robert L., 1983. Hunter-gatherer mobility strategies. *Journal of Anthropological Research* 39(3):277–306.

————, 1985. Hunter-gatherer mobility and sedentism: a Great Basin study. Ph.D. diss. University of Michigan, Ann Arbor.

Kelso, William M., 1982. Jefferson's garden: landscape archaeology at Monticello, *Archaeology* 35(4):38–45.

————, 1984. Landscape archaeology: a key to Virginia's cultivated past. In *British and American Gardens in the Eighteenth Century,* Robert P. Maccubbin and Peter Martin, eds. Williamsburg, Va.: Colonial Williamsburg Foundation, pp. 159–169.

————, 1986. Mulberry Row: slave life at Thomas Jefferson's Monticello. *Archaeology* 39(5):28–35.

Kemeny, John G., 1959. *A Philosopher Looks at Science.* New York: Van Nostrand Reinhold.

Kendall, David G., 1964. A statistical approach to Flinders Petrie's sequence dating. *International Statistical Institute Bulletin (Proceedings of the 34th Session, 1963)* 40(2):657–680.

————, 1969. Some problems and methods in statistical archaeology. *World Archaeology* 1(1):68–76.

Kent, Susan, 1984. *Analyzing Activity Areas: an Ethnoarchaeological Study of the Use of Space.* Albuquerque: University of New Mexico Press.

————, 1987, Parts as wholes: a critique of theory in archaeology. In *Method and Theory for Activity Area Research: an Ethnoarchaeological Approach,* Susan Kent, ed. New York: Columbia University Press, pp. 513–546.

Kenyon, Jeff L., and Bruce Bevan, 1977. Ground-penetrating radar and its application to a historical archaeological site. *Historical Archaeology* 11:48–55.

Kessler, Evelyn S., 1972. Comment on Cognitive aspects of Upper Paleolithic engraving by Alexander Marshack. *Current Anthropology* 13(3–4):466.

Kidder, Alfred V., 1924. *An Introduction to the Study of Southwestern Archaeology.* New Haven, Conn.: Yale University Press.

————, 1928. The present state of knowledge of American history and civilization prior to 1492. Paris: *International Congress of History, Oslo, 1928, Compte Rendu,* pp. 749–753.

————, and Samuel J. Guernsey, 1921. Basket-maker caves of northeastern Arizona. *Papers of the Peabody Museum of American Archaeology and Ethnology* 8(2).

————, Jesse D. Jennings, and Edwin M. Shook, 1946. Excavations at Kaminaljuyu, Guatemala. *Carnegie Institution of Washington Publication* no. 561.

King, Thomas F., 1971. A conflict of values in American archaeology. *American Antiquity* 36(3):255–262.

————, 1976. Review of *Public Archaeology,* Charles McGimsey. *American Antiquity* 41(2):236–238.

————, 1977. Issues in contract archaeology. *Archaeology* 30(5):352–353.

————, Patricia Parker Hickman, and Gary Berg, 1977. *Anthropology in Historic Preservation: Caring for Culture's Clutter.* New York: Academic Press.

Kish, Leslie, 1965. *Survey Sampling.* New York: Wiley.

Klein, J., J. C. Lerman, P. E. Damon, and E. K. Ralph, 1982. Calibration of radiocarbon dates: tables based on the consensus data of the workshop on calibrating the radiocarbon time scale. *Radiocarbon* 24(2):103–150.

Klejn, L. S., 1982. Archeological typology, trans. P. Dole. *British Archaeological Reports, International Series* no. 153.

Klepinger, Linda L., 1984. Nutritional assessment from bone. *Annual Review of Anthropology* 13:75–96.

Kluckhohn, Clyde, 1942. Myths and rituals: a general theory. *Harvard Theological Review* 35:45–79.

Knuttson, K., and R. Hope, 1984. The application of acetate peels in lithic usewear analysis. *Archaeometry* 26:49–61.

Koch, Joan K., 1980. Nuestra Señora de la Soledad: a Study of a Church and Hospital Site in Colonial St. Augustine. Unpublished M. S. Thesis, Department of Anthropology, Florida State University, Tallahassee.

———, 1983. Mortuary behavior patterning and physical anthropology in colonial St. Augustine. In *Spanish St. Augustine: the Archaeology of a Colonial Creole Community,* Kathleen Deagan. New York: Academic Press, pp. 187–227.

Koike, Hiroko, 1975. The use of daily and annual growth lines of the clam *Meretrix lusoria* in estimating seasons of Jomon period shell gathering. In *Quaternary Studies,* R. P. Suggate and M. M. Cresswell, eds. Wellington: Royal Society of New Zealand, pp. 189–193.

Kolata, Gina Bari, 1974. !Kung hunter-gatherers: feminism, diet, and birth control. *Science* 185:932–934.

Kottak, Conrad P., 1977. The process of state formation in Madagascar. *American Ethnologist* 4(1):136–155.

Kraft, John C., Ilhan Kayan, and Oguz Erol, 1980. Geomorphic reconstructions in the environs of ancient Troy. *Science* 209(4458):776–782.

Krieger, Alex D., 1944. The typological concept. *American Antiquity* 9(3):271–288.

Kristiansen, Kristian, 1984. Ideology and material culture: An archaeological perspective. In *Marxist Perspectives in Archaeology,* Matthew Spriggs, ed. Cambridge, England: Cambridge University Press, pp. 72–100.

———, 1987. From stone to bronze—the evolution of social complexity in northern Europe, 2300–1200 BC. In *Specialization, Exchange, and Complex Societies,* Elizabeth M. Brumfield and Timothy K. Earle, eds. Cambridge, England: Cambridge University Press, pp. 30–51.

Kroeber, Alfred L., 1955. On human nature. *Southwestern Journal of Anthropology* 11(3):195–204.

———, and Clyde Kluckhohn, 1952. Culture: a critical review of concepts and definitions. *Papers of the Peabody Museum of American Archaeology and Ethnology,* no. 47(1).

Kurten, Bjorn, 1972. Comment on Cognitive aspects of Upper Paleolithic engraving by Alexander Marshack. *Current Anthropology* 13(3–4):466.

Kus, Susan, 1984. The spirit and its burden: archaeology and symbolic activity. In *Marxist Perspectives in Archaeology,* Matthew Spriggs, ed. Cambridge, England: Cambridge University Press, pp. 101–107.

Lallo, John W., George J. Armelagos, and Jerome C. Rose, 1978. Paleoepidemiology of infectious disease in the Dickson Mounds population. *Medical College of Virginia Quarterly* 14:17–23.

Lane, Rebecca A., and Audrey J. Sublett, 1972. Osteology of social organization: residence pattern. *American Antiquity* 37(2):186–201.

Lanford, W. A., 1977. Glass hydration: a method of dating glass objects. *Science* 196(4293):975–976.

Lange, Frederick W., and Jerome S. Handler, 1985. The ethnohistorical approach to slavery. In *The Archaeology of Slavery and Plantation Life*, Theresa A. Singleton, ed. Orlando, Fla.:Academic Press pp. 15–32.

Lanning, Edward P., 1963. Archaeology of the Rose Spring site Iny-372. *University of California Publications in American Archaeology and Ethnology* 49(3):237–336.

Larsen, Clark Spencer, 1982. The anthropology of St. Catherines Island: 3. prehistoric human biological adaptation. *Anthropological Papers of the American Museum of Natural History* 57(3):157–270.

———, 1987. Bioarchaeological interpretations of subsistence economy and behavior from human skeletal remains. In *Advances in Archaeological Method and Theory*, vol. 10. Michael B. Schiffer, ed. Orlando, Fla.: Academic Press, pp. 339–445.

———, and David Hurst Thomas, 1982. The anthropology of St. Catherines Island: 4. the St. Catherines period mortuary complex. *Anthropological Papers of the American Museum of Natural History* 57(4):271–342.

———, 1986. The archaeology of St. Catherines Island: 5. the South End mound complex. *Anthropological Papers of the American Museum of Natural History* 63(1):1–46.

Lathrap, Donald W., 1973. Gifts of the Cayman: some thoughts on the subsistence basis of Chavin. In *Variation in Anthropology*, Donald W. Lathrap and Jody Douglas, eds. Urbana: Illinois Archaeological Survey, pp. 91–105.

Layton, Thomas N., 1973. Temporal ordering of surface-collected obsidian artifacts by hydration measurement. *Archaeometry* 15(1):129–132.

LeBlanc, Steven A., 1975. Micro-seriation: a method for fine chronologic differentiation. *American Antiquity* 40(1):22–38.

LeBlanc, Steven A., and P. J. Watson, 1973. A comparative statistical analysis of painted pottery from seven Halafian sites. *Paleorient* 1:117–133.

Lee, Richard B., 1968. What hunters do for a living, or, how to make out on scarce resources. In *Man the Hunter*, Richard B. Lee and Irven DeVore, eds. Chicago: Aldine, pp. 30-48.

———, 1969. !Kung Bushman subsistence: an input-output analysis. In *Environmental and Cultural Behavior*, Andrew P. Vayda, ed. Garden City, N.Y.: Natural History Press, pp. 47–79.

———, 1979. *The !Kung San: Men, Women, and Work in a Foraging Society*. Cambridge, England: Cambridge University Press.

———, and Irvin DeVore, 1968. *Man the Hunter*. Chicago: Aldine.

Leonard, Robert D., and George T. Jones, 1987. Elements of an inclusive evolutionary model for archaeology. *Journal of Anthropological Archaeology* 6(3):199–219.

Leone, Mark P., 1972. Issues in anthropological archaeology. In *Contemporary Archaeology: a Guide to Theory and Contributions,* Mark P. Leone, ed. Carbondale: Southern Illinois University Press, pp. 14–27.

———1977. The new Mormon temple in Washington, D.C. In *Historical Archaeology and the Importance of Material Things,* Leland Ferguson, ed. *Society for Historical Archaeology, Special Publications Series* 2:43–61.

———1982. Some opinions about recovering mind. *American Antiquity* 47(4): 742–760.

———1983. Method as message. *Museum News* 62(1):35–41.

———, 1984. Interpreting ideology in historical archaeology: using the rules of perspective in the William Paca garden in Annapolis, Maryland, In *Ideology, Power, and Prehistory,* Daniel Miller and Christopher Tilley, eds. Cambridge, England: Cambridge University Press, pp. 25–36.

———, 1986. Symbolic, structural, and critical archaeology. In *American Archaeology Past and Future: A Celebration of the Society for American Archaeology 1935–1985,* David J. Meltzer, Don D. Fowler, and Jeremy A. Sabloff, eds., Washington, D.C.: Smithsonian Institution Press, pp. 415–438.

———, 1987. Rule by ostentation: the relationship between space and sight in eighteenth-century landscape architecture in the Chesapeake region of Maryland. In *Method and Theory for Activity Area Research: an Ethnoarchaeological Approach,* Susan Kent, ed. New York: Columbia University Press, pp. 604–633.

———, 1988a. The Georgian order as the order of merchant capitalism in Annapolis, Maryland. In *The Recovery of Meaning: Historical Archaeology in the Eastern United States.* Mark P. Leone and Parker B. Potter, eds., Washington D.C.: Smithsonian Institution Press, pp. 235–261.

———, 1988b. The relationship between archaeological data and the documentary record: eighteenth century gardens in Annapolis, Maryland. *Historical Archaeology* no. 22(1):29–35.

———, and Constance A. Crosby, 1987. Epilogue: middle-range theory in historical archaeology. In *Consumer Choice in Historical Archaeology,* Suzanne M. Spencer-Wood, ed. New York: Plenum Press, pp. 397-410.

———, and Parker B. Potter, 1988. Introduction: Issues in historical archaeology. In *The Recovery of Meaning: Historical Archaeology in the Eastern United States,* Mark P. Leone and Parker B. Potter, eds. Washington, D.C.: Smithsonian Institution Press, pp. 1–22.

———, Parker B. Potter, Jr., and Paul A. Shackel, 1987. Toward a critical archaeology. *Current Anthropology* 28(3):283–302.

———, and Paul A. Shackel, 1987. Forks, clocks and power. In *Mirror and Metaphor,* Daniel Ingersoll, ed. Latham, Md.: American University, in press.

Leroi-Gourhan, Arlette, 1975. The flowers found with Shanidar IV, a Neanderthal burial in Iraq. *Science* 190(4214):562–564.

Levi-Strauss, Claude, 1963a. Review of George G. Simpson's *Principles of Animal Taxonomy. L'homme* 3(1):140.

———, 1963b. *Structural Anthropology*, New York: Basic Books (reprinted in 1967 by Doubleday).

———, 1969a. *The Elementary Structures of Kinship* [2nd ed.]. Boston: Beacon Press.

———, 1969b. *The Raw and the Cooked*. New York: Harper.

———, 1970. *Tristes Tropiques: an Anthropological Study of Primitive Societies in Brazil*. New York: Atheneum.

Lewarch, Dennis E., and Michael J. O'Brien, 1981. The expanding role of surface assemblages in archaeological research. In *Advances in Archaeological Method and Theory*, vol. 4, Michael B. Schiffer, ed. New York: Academic Press, pp. 297–342.

Lewis, Lynne G., 1978. *Drayton Hall: Preliminary Archaeological Investigations at a Low Country Plantation*. Charlottesville: University of Virginia Press.

Libby, Willard F., 1955. *Radiocarbon Dating* [2nd ed.]. Chicago: University of Chicago Press.

Liebowitz, Harold, and Robert L. Folk, 1980. Archeological geology of Tel Yin'am, Galilee, Israel. *Journal of Field Archeology* 7(1):23–42.

Linton, Ralph, 1936. *The Study of Man: an Introduction*. New York: D. Appleton–Century.

Lipe, William D., 1974. A conservation model for American archaeology. *The Kiva* 39(3–4):214–245.

———, and Alexander J. Lindsay, eds. 1974. Proceedings of the 1974 cultural resource management conference. Flagstaff: *Museum of Northern Arizona Technical Series* no. 14.

———, and R. G. Matson, 1971. Human settlement and resources in the Cedar Mesa area, southeastern Utah. In *The Distribution of Prehistoric Population Aggregates*, George J. Gumerman, ed. Prescott, Arizona, Prescott College Press, pp. 126–151.

Little, Barbara J., 1988. Craft and culture change in the 18th-century Chesapeake. In *The Recovery of Meaning: Historical Archaeology in the Eastern United States*, Mark P. Leone and Parker B. Potter, eds. Washington, D.C.: Smithsonian Institution Press, pp. 263–292.

Loendorf, Lawrence L., 1973. Prehistoric settlement patterns in the Prior Mountains, Montana. Ph.D. diss., University of Missouri, Columbia.

Lofstrom, Ted, Jeffrey P. Tordoff, and Douglas C. George, 1982. A seriation of historic earthenwares in the Midwest, 1780-1870. *The Minnesota Archaeologist* 41(1):3–29.

Logan, Michael H., and William T. Sanders, 1976. The model. In *The Valley of Mexico*, Eric R. Wolf, ed. Albuquerque: University of New Mexico Press, pp. 31–58.

Lomax, Alan, and Conrad M. Arensberg, 1977. A worldwide evolutionary classification of cultures by subsistence systems. *Current Anthropology* 18(4):659–708.

Long, A., and Bruce Rippeteau, 1974. Testing contemporaneity and averaging radiocarbon dates. *American Antiquity* 39(2):205–215.

Longacre, William A., 1964. Archeology as anthropology: a case study. *Science* 144:1454–1455.

———, 1968. Some aspects of prehistoric society in east-central Arizona. In *New Perspectives in Archeology*, Sally R. Binford and Lewis R. Binford, eds. Chicago: Aldine, pp. 89–102.

————, 1970. Archaeology as anthropology: a case study. *University of Arizona Anthropological Papers,* no. 17.

Lorrain, Dessamae, 1968. An archaeologist's guide to nineteenth century American glass. *Historical Archaeology* 2:35–44.

Loud, Llewellyn L., and M.R. Harrington, 1929. Lovelock Cave. *University of California Publications in American Archaeology and Ethnology* 25(1):1–183.

Lowie, Robert H., 1948. *Social Organization.* New York: Holt, Rinehart and Winston.

Loy, Thomas H., 1983. Prehistoric blood residues: detection on tool surfaces and indentification of species of origin. *Science* 220(4603):1269–1271.

————, 1985. Recent advances in blood residue analysis. In *Proceedings of the Second Australian Conference on Archaeometry.* Canberra: Research School of Pacific Studies, Prehistory, Australian National University.

Lyman, R. Lee, 1987. Archaeofaunas and butchery studies: A taxonomic perspective. In *Advances in Archaeological Method and Theory,* vol. 10, Michael B. Schiffer, ed. New York: Academic Press, pp. 249–337.

Lynch, Thomas F. 1972. Comment on Cognitive Aspects of Upper Paleolithic engraving by Alexander Marshack. *Current Anthropology* 13(3–4):466–467.

Lynott, Mark J., Thomas W. Boutton, James E. Price, and Dwight E. Nelson, 1986. Stable carbon isotopic evidence for maize agriculture in southeast Missouri and northeast Arkansas. *American Antiquity* 51(1):51–65.

Lyons, T. R., and T. E. Avery, 1984. *Remote Sensing: a Handbook for Archaeologists and Cultural Resource Managers.* Washington, D.C.: National Park Service, U. S. Department of the Interior.

MacArthur, R. H., and E. R. Pianka, 1966. On optimal use of a patchy environment. *American Naturalist* 100:603–609.

MacKie, E. W., 1977. *Science and Society in Prehistoric Britain.* London: Paul Elek.

MacNeish, Richard S., 1964. Ancient Mesoamerican civilization. *Science* 143(3606): 531–537.

————, 1967. A summary of the subsistence. In *The Prehistory of the Tehuacan Valley,* vol. 1, Douglas S. Byers, ed. Austin: University of Texas Press, pp. 290–309.

————, 1972. Summary of the cultural sequence and its implications in the Tehuacan Valley. In *The Prehistory of the Tehuacan Valley, vol. 5: Excavations and Reconnaissance,* Richard S. MacNeish, Melvin L. Fowler, Angel Garcia Cook, Frederick A. Peterson, Antoinette Nelken-Terner, and James A. Neely, eds. Austin: University of Texas Press, pp. 496–504.

————, 1978. *The Science of Archaeology?* North Scituate, Mass.: Duxbury Press.

————, Frederick A. Peterson, and James A. Neely, 1972. The archaeological reconnaissance. In *The Prehistory of the Tehuacan Valley, vol. 5: Excavations and Reconnaisance,* Richard S. MacNeish, Melvin L. Fowler, Angel Garcia Cook, Frederick A. Peterson, Antoinette Nelken-Terner, and James A. Neely, eds. Austin: University of Texas Press, pp. 341–495.

————, Melvin L. Fowler, Angel Garcia Cook, Frederick A. Peterson, Antoinette Nelken-Terner, and James A. Neely, eds., 1972. *The Prehistory of the Tehuacan Valley, vol. 5: Excavations and Reconnaisance.* Austin: University of Texas Press.

Madsen, David B., 1976. Pluvial-post-pluvial vegetation changes in the southeastern Great Basin. In Holocene environmental change in the Great Basin. Robert Elston, ed. *Nevada Archaeological Survey Research Paper* 6:104–119.

Magne, Martin P. R., 1985. Lithics and livelihood: Stone tool technologies of central and southern Interior British Columbia. *National Museum of Man, Mercury Series Archaeological Survey of Canada Paper* no. 133.

Majewski, Teresita, and Michael J. O'Brien, 1987. The use and misuse of nineteenth-century English and American ceramics in archaeological analysis. In *Advances in Archaeological Method and Theory,* vol. 11, Michael B. Schiffer, ed. New York: Academic Press, pp. 97–210.

Malinowski, Bronislaw, 1961. *Argonauts of the Western Pacific.* New York: Dutton [first published in 1922].

Mangelsdorf, Paul C., 1974. *Corn, Its Origin, Evolution, and Improvement.* Cambridge, Mass.: Harvard University Press.

Mansfield, Victor N., 1980. The Bighorn Medicine Wheel as a site for the vision quest. *Archaeoastronomy Bulletin* 3(2):26–29.

Marcus, Joyce, 1973. Territorial organization of the lowland Classic Maya. *Science* 180(4089):911–916.

———, 1974. Reply to Romanov and Hammond. *Science* 183:876–877.

———, 1976. *Emblem and State in the Classic Maya Lowlands: an Epigraphic Approach to Territorial Organization.* Washington, D.C.: Dumbarton Oaks.

———, 1983. Lowland Maya archaeology at the crossroads. *American Antiquity* 48(3):454–488.

Marquardt, William H., 1978. Advances in archaeological seriation. In *Advances in Archaeological Method And Theory,* vol. 1, Michael B. Schiffer, ed. New York: Academic Press, pp. 257–314.

Marshack, Alexander, 1972a. *The Roots of Cizilization.* New York: McGraw-Hill.

———, 1972b. Upper Paleolithic notation and symbol. *Science* 178:817–828.

———, 1976. Implications of the Paleolithic symbolic evidence for the origin of language. *American Scientist* 64(2):136–145.

Marshall, Yvonne, 1985. Who made the Lapita pots? A case study in gender archaeology. *Journal of the Polynesian Society* 94(3):205–233.

Martin, Debra L., Alan H. Goodman, and George J. Armelagos, 1985. Skeletal pathologies as indicators of quality and quantity of diet. In *The Analysis of Prehistoric Diets,* Robert I. Gilbert and James H. Mielke, eds. Orlando: Academic Press, pp. 227–279.

Martin, John F., 1985. Optimal foraging theory: a review of some models and their applications. *American Anthropologist* 85:612–629.

Martin, Paul S., 1954. Comments on Southwestern archaeology: its history and theory, Walter W. Taylor. *American Anthropologist* 56:570–572.

Matson, Richard Ghia, 1971. Adaption and environment in the Cerbat Mountains, Arizona, Ph.D. diss. University of California, Davis.

Mayer-Oakes, William J., 1955. Prehistory of the upper Ohio Valley. *Annals of the Carnegie Museum,* vol. 34.

————, and Ronald J. Nash, 1964. Archaeological research design—a critique. Paper presented at the American Anthropological Association, 1964.

Mayes, P., 1962. The firing of a pottery kiln of Romano-British type at Boston, Lincs. *Archaeometry* 4:4–18.

Maynard Smith, J., 1978. Optimization theory in evolution. *Annual Review of Ecology and Systematics* 9:31–56.

Mazess, Richard B., and D. W. Zimmermann, 1966. Pottery dating from thermoluminescence. *Science* 152(3720):347–348.

McDonald, William A., 1967. *Progress into the Past: the Rediscovery of Mycenaean Civilization.* New York: Macmillan.

McEwan, Bonnie G., 1986. Domestic adaptation at Puerto Real, Haiti. *Historical Archaeology* 20(1):44–49.

McGimsey, Charles R., Ill, 1972. *Public Archeology.* New York: Seminar Press.

McHargue, Georges, and Michael Roberts, 1977. *A Field Guide to Conservation Archaeology in North America,* Philadelphia: Lippincott.

McIlrath, Sharon, 1984. Obsidian blades: tomorrow's surgical tools? *American Medical News,* 2:29–30.

McKinley, Robert, 1981. Review of *Cultural Materialism: the Struggle for a Science of Culture* by Marvin Harris. *American Ethnologist* 8(2):395–396.

McManamon, Francis P., 1984. Discovering sites unseen. In *Advances in Archaeological Method and Theory,* vol. 7, Michael B. Schiffer, ed. New York: Academic Press, pp. 223–292.

McMillan, Claude, and Richard F. Gonzalez, 1968. *Systems Analysis: a Computer Approach to Decision Models* [rev. ed.]. Homewood, Ill.: Irwin.

McNutt, Charles H., 1973. On the methodological validity of frequency seriation. *American Antiquity* 38:45–60.

Meggers, Betty J., 1955. The coming of age of American archeology. In *New Interpretations of Aboriginal American Culture History.* Washington, D.C.: Anthropological Society of Washington, D.C., pp. 116–129.

————, 1956. Functional and evolutionary implications of community patterning. In *Seminars in Archaeology, Society for American Archaeology Memoir,* no. 11, pp. 129–157.

————, ed., 1968. *Anthropological Archeology in the Americas,* Anthropological Society of Washington, D.C.

————, 1971. *Amazonia: Man and Nature in a Counterfeit Paradise.* Chicago: Aldine.

Mehringer, Peter J., 1977. Great Basin late-Quaternary environments and chronology. In *Models and Great Basin Prehistory: A Symposium,* Don D. Fowler, ed. *Desert Research Institute Publications in the Social Sciences* 12:113–167.

————, 1986. Prehistoric environments. In *Handbook of North American Indians,* vol. 11, Warren L. D'Azevedo, ed. Washington, D.C.: Smithsonian Institution, pp. 31-50.

————, Eric Blinman, and Kenneth L. Peterson, 1977. Pollen influx and volcanic ash. *Science* 198(4314):257–261.

————, and Charles W. Ferguson, 1969. Pluvial occurrence of Bristlecone pine (*Pinus aristata*) in a Mohave Desert mountain range. *Journal of the Arizona Academy of Science* 5(4):284–292.

————, and Vance Haynes, 1965. The pollen evidence for the environment of early man and extinct mammals at the Lehner mammoth site, southeastern Arizona. *American Antiquity* 31(1):17–23.

Meighan, Clement W., 1976. Empirical determination of obsidian hydration rates from archaeological evidence. In *Advances in Obsidian Glass Studies*, R. E. Taylor, ed. Park Ridge, N.J.: Noyes Press, pp. 106–119.

————, Leonard J. Foote, and Paul V. Aiello, 1968. Obsidian dating in west Mexican archeology. *Science* 160:1069–1075.

Meltzer, David J., 1979. Paradigms and the nature of change in American archaeology. *American Antiquity* 44(4):644–657.

————, Don D. Fowler, and Jeremy A. Sabloff, eds. 1986. *American Archaeology Past and Future: a Celebration of the Society for American Archaeology 1935-1985*. Washington, D.C.: Smithsonian Institution Press.

Meyers, J. T., 1971. The origins of agriculture: an evaluation of hypotheses. In *Prehistoric Agriculture*, S. Struever, ed. Garden City, N.Y.: Natural History Press, pp. 101–121.

Michael, H. N., 1984. Extending the calibration of radiocarbon dates: the search for ancient wood. *MASCA Journal* 3(1):17–19.

————, and Elizabeth K. Ralph, eds., 1971. *Dating Techniques for the Archaeologist*. Cambridge, Mass.: MIT Press.

Michels, Joseph W., 1973. *Dating Methods in Archaeology*. New York: Seminar Press.

————, and Carl A. Bebrich, 1971. Obsidian hydration dating. In *Dating Techniques for the Archaeologist*, Henry N. Michael and Elizabeth K. Ralph, eds. Cambridge, Mass.: MIT Press, pp. 164–221.

————, and Ignatius S. T. Tsong, 1980. Obsidian hydration dating: a coming of age. In *Advances in Archaeological Method and Theory*, vol. 3, Michael B. Schiffer, ed. New York: Academic Press, pp. 405–444.

Michener, James A., 1974. *Centennial*. New York: Random House.

Miksicek, Charles H., 1987. Formation processes of the archaeobotanical record. In *Advances in Archaeological Method and Theory*, vol. 10, Michael B. Schiffer, ed. New York: Academic Press, pp. 211–247.

Miller, Daniel, 1982. Artifacts as products of human categorisation processes. In *Symbolic and Structural Archaeology*, Ian Hodder, ed. Cambridge, England: Cambridge University Press, pp. 17–25.

————, and Christopher Tilley, 1984. *Ideology, Power and Prehistory*. Cambridge, England: Cambridge University Press.

Miller, George L., 1980. Classification and economic scaling of 19th century ceramics. *Historical Archaeology* 14:1–40.

Miller, J. A., 1969. Dating by the potassium-argon method—some advances in technique. In *Science in Archaeology*, Don Brothwell and Eric Higgs, eds. London: Thames and Hudson, pp. 101–105.

———, 1953. Evolution and process. In *Anthropology Today*, Alfred L. Kroeber, ed. Chicago: University of Chicago Press, pp. 313–326.

———, 1954. Types of types. *American Anthropologist* 56(1):54–57.

———, 1955. *Theory of Culture Change*. Urbana: University of Illinois Press.

Stewart, T. D., 1973. *The People of America*. New York: Scribners.

Stini, William A, 1985. Growth rates and sexual dimorphism in evolutionary perspective. In *The Analysis of Prehistoric Diets*, Robert I. Gilbert, Jr. and James H. Mielke, eds. Orlando, Fla.: Academic Press, pp. 191–226.

Stolt, Robert H., ed., 1986. Geophysics. *Special Issue: Geophysics in Archaeology*, J. C. Wynn, ed. pp. 533–633.

Stoltman, James B., 1966. New radiocarbon dates for southeastern fiber tempered pottery. *American Antiquity* 31(6):872–874.

———, 1973. The Southeastern United States, In *The Development of North American Archaeology: Essays in the History of Regional Traditions*, James E. Fitting, ed. University Park: The Pennsylvania State University Press, pp. 117–150.

Stone, Doris, ed., 1984. Pre-Columbian plant migrations. *Papers of the Peabody Museum of Archaeology and Ethnology* no. 76.

Stone, Irving, 1975. *The Greek Treasure*. Garden City, N.Y.: Doubleday.

Straus, Lawrence G., 1980. The role of raw materials in lithic assemblage variability. *Lithic Technology* 9(3):68–72.

Strong, William Duncan, and Clifford Evans,Jr., 1952. Cultural stratigraphy in the Virú Valley, Northern Peru. *Columbia University Studies in Archaeology and Ethnology* no. 4.

Struever, Stuart, 1964. The Hopewell interaction sphere in riverine-western Great Lakes cultural history. *Illinois State Museum Scientific Papers,* 12(3):85–106.

———, 1968a. Flotation techniques for the recovery of small-scale archaeological remains. *American Antiquity* 33(3):353–362.

———, 1968b. Woodland subsistence settlement systems in the lower Illinois valley. In *New Perspectives in Archeology*, Sally R. Binford and Lewis R. Binford, eds. Chicago: Aldine, pp. 285–312.

———, and John Carlson, 1977. Koster site: the new archaeology in action. *Archaeology* 30(2):93–101.

Stuckenrath, R., 1977. Radiocarbon: some notes from Merlin's diary. *Annals of the New York Academy of Science* 288:181–188.

Stuiver, Minze, 1982. A high-precision calibration of the A.D. radiocarbon time scale. *Radiocarbon* 24:1–26.

———, Calvin J. Heusser, and In Che Yang, 1978. North American glacial history extended to 75,000 years ago. *Science* 200(4337):16–21.

———, and Renee Kra, eds., 1986. Calibration Issue: 12th International Radiocarbon Conference. *Radiocarbon* 28(2B).

———, and Gordon W. Pearson, 1986. High-precision calibration of the radiocarbon time scale, AD 1950–500 BC. *Radiocarbon* 28(2B):805–838.

————, and Henry A. Polach, 1977. Discussions of reporting of 14C data. *Radiocarbon* 19(3):355–363.

————, and Paula J. Reimer, 1986. A computer program for radiocarbon age calibration. *Radiocarbon* 28(2B):1022–1030.

Sturtevant, William, 1964. Studies in ethnoscience. *American Anthropologist* 66(3):99–131.

Styles, Bonnie W., 1985. Reconstruction of availability and utilization of food resources. In *The Analysis of Prehistoric Diets,* Robert I. Gilbert, Jr. and James H. Mielke, eds. Orlando, Fla.: Academic Press, pp. 21–59.

Sussman, Carole, 1985. Microwear on quartz: fact or fiction? *World Archaeology* 17(1):101–111.

Suttles, Wayne, 1960. Affinal ties, subsistence and prestige among the coast Salish. *American Anthropologist* 62(2):296–305.

Swanson, Earl, ed., 1975. *Lithic Technology: Making and Using Stone Tools.* The Hague: Mouton.

Tainter, Joseph A., 1983. Settlement behavior and the archaeological record: concepts for the definition of "archaeological site." *Contract Abstracts and CRM Archaeology* 3(2):130–132.

Tanner, Nancy Makepeace, 1981. *On Becoming Human.* Cambridge, England.: Cambridge University Press.

Tarling, D. H., 1975. Archaeomagnetism: the dating of archaeological materials by their magnetic properties. *World Archaeology* 7:185–197.

————, 1983. *Palaeomagnetism: Principles and Applications in Geology, Geophysics and Archaeology.* London: Chapman & Hall.

————, 1985. Archaeomagnetism. In *Archaeological Geology,* George Rapp, Jr., and John A. Gifford, eds. New Haven, Conn.: Yale University Press, pp. 237–263.

Tatje, Terrance A., and Raoul Naroll, 1970. Two measures of societal complexity: an empirical cross-cultural comparison. In *A Handbook of Method in Cultural Anthropology,* Raoul Naroll and Ronald Cohen, eds. New York: Natural History Press, pp. 766–833.

Taylor, C.E., 1983. Synergy among mass infections, famines, and poverty. In *Hunter and History,* R. I. Rotberg and T. K. Rabb, eds. Cambridge, England: Cambridge University Press, pp. 285–303.

Taylor, R. E., 1985. The beginnings of radiocarbon dating in *American Antiquity:* a historical perspective. *American Antiquity* 50(2):309–325.

————, 1987a. AMS 14-C dating of critical bone samples: proposed protocol and criteria for evaluation. *Nuclear Instruments and Methods in Physics Research: Section B, Beam Interactions with Materials and Atoms*, H. H. Andersen and S. T. Picraux, eds. Proceedings of the Fourth International Symposium on Accelerator Mass Spectrometry, Ontario, Canada B29:159–163.

————, 1987b. *Radiocarbon Dating: an Archaeological Perspective.* New York: Academic Press.

———, and Ian Longworth, eds., 1975. Dating: new methods and new results. *World Archaeology* 7(2).

———, and Clement W. Meighan eds., 1978. *Chronologies in New World Archaeology*. New York: Academic Press.

———, L. A. Payen, C. A. Prior, P. J. Slota, Jr., R. Gillespie, J. A. J. Gowlett, R. E. M. Hedges, A. J. T. Jull, T. H. Zabel, D. J. Donahue, and R. Berger, 1985. Major revisions in the Pleistocene age assignments for North American skeletons by C-14 accelerator mass spectrometry: none older than 11,000 C-14 years B. P. *American Antiquity* 50(1):136–140.

Taylor, Walter W., 1948. A study of archeology. *American Anthropological Association, Memoir 69*.

———, 1954. Southwestern archaeology, its history and theory. *American Anthropologist* 56:561–570.

———, 1972. Old wine and new skins: a contemporary parable. In *Contemporary Archaeology*, Mark P. Leone, ed. Carbondale: Southern Illinois University Press, pp. 28–33.

Thom, Alexander, 1966. Megaliths and mathematics. *Antiquity* 40(158):121–128.

———, 1967. *Megalithic Sites in Britain*. Oxford, England: Oxford University Press (Clarendon).

———, 1971. *Megalithic Lunar Observations*. Oxford, England: Oxford University Press (Clarendon).

Thomas, David Hurst, 1969. Great Basin hunting patterns: a quantitative method for treating faunal remains. *American Antiquity* 34(4):392–401.

———, 1971. On the use of cumulative curves and numerical taxonomy. *American Antiquity* 36(2):206–209.

———, 1972a. A computer simulation model of Great Basin Shoshonean subsistence and settlement patterns. In *Models in Archaeology*, David L. Clarke, ed. London: Methuen, pp. 671–704.

———, 1972b. Western Shoshone ecology: Settlement patterns and beyond. In *Great Basin Cultural Ecology, a Symposium*, Don D. Fowler, ed. *Desert Research Institute Publications in the Social Sciences*, 8:135–153.

———, 1973. An empirical test for Steward's model of Great Basin settlement patterns. *American Antiquity* 38(2):155–176.

———, 1974. *Predicting the Past: an Introduction to Anthropological Archaeology*. New York: Holt, Rinehart and Winston.

———, 1975. Review of *Hogup Cave* by C. Melvin Aikens. *American Antiquity* 40(4):501–502.

———, 1976. *Figuring Anthropology: First Principles of Probability and Statistics*. New York: Holt, Rinehart and Winston.

———, 1978. The awful truth about statistics in archaeology. *American Antiquity* 43(2):231–244.

———, 1981. How to classify the projectile points from Monitor Valley, Nevada. *Journal of California and Great Basin Anthropology* 3(1):7–43.

———, 1982. The 1981 Alta Toquima Village project: a preliminary report. *Desert Research Institute Social Sciences Technical Report Series* no. 27.

———, 1983a. The archaeology of Monitor Valley: 1. epistemology. *Anthropological Papers of the American Museum of Natural History* 58(1):1–194.

———, 1983b. The archaeology of Monitor Valley: 2. Gatecliff Shelter. *Anthropological Papers of the American Museum of Natural History* 59(1):1–552.

———, 1986. Contemporary hunter-gatherer archaeology in America. In *American Archaeology Past and Future: a Celebration of the Society of American Archaeology 1935–1985,* David J. Meltzer, Don D. Fowler, and Jeremy A. Sabloff, eds. Washington D. C.: Smithsonian Institution Press, pp. 237–276.

———, 1987. The archaeology of Mission Santa Catalina de Guale: 1. search and discovery. *Anthropological Papers of the American Museum of Natural History* 63(2):47–161.

———, 1988a. Saints and soldiers at Santa Catalina: Hispanic designs for colonial America. In *The Recovery of Meaning in Historic Archaeology,* Mark P. Leone and Parker B. Potter, eds., Washington, D.C.: Smithsonian Institution Press, pp. 73–140.

———, 1988b. The archaeology of Monitor Valley: 3. survey and additional excavation. *Anthropological Papers of the American Museum of Natural History.* 66(2):131–633.

———, and Robert L. Bettinger, 1976. Prehistoric pinõn ecotone settlements of the upper Reese River Valley, central Nevada. *Anthropological Papers of the American Museum of Natural History* 53(3):263–366.

———, and Clark Spencer Larsen, 1979. The anthropology of St. Catherines Island: 2. the Refuge-Deptford mortuary complex. *Anthropological Papers of the American Museum of Natural History* 56(1):1–179.

———, Stanley South, and Clark Spencer Larsen, 1979. Rich man, poor men: observations on three antebellum burials from the Georgia Coast. *Anthropological Papers of the American Museum of Natural History* 54(3):393–420.

Thompson, F. O. H., 1975. Rescue archaeology: research or rubbish collection? *Antiquity* 49(193):43–45.

Thompson, J. Eric S., 1945, A survey of the northern Maya area. *American Antiquity* 11(1):2-24.

———. 1974. Maya astronomy. London: *Philosophical Transactions of the Royal Society* 276:83–98.

Thompson, Robert S., and Eugene M. Hattori, 1983. Packrat *(Neotoma)* middens from Gatecliff Shelter and Holocene migrations of woodland plants. In *The Archaeology of Monitor Valley: 2. Gatecliff Shelter,* David Hurst Thomas. *Anthropological Papers of the American Museum of Natural History* 59(1):157–167.

———, and J. I. Mead, 1982. Late Quaternary environments and biogeography in the Great Basin. *Quaternary Research* 17(1):39–55.

Tiger, Lionel, and Heather T. Fowler, eds., 1978. *Female Hierarchies.* Chicago: Beresford Book Service.

Tilley, Christopher, 1982. Social formation, social structures and social change. In

Symbolic and Structural Archaeology, Ian Hodder, ed. Cambridge, England: Cambridge University Press, pp. 26–38.

———, 1984. Ideology and the legitimation of power in the Middle Neolithic of southern Sweden. In *Ideology, Power, and Prehistory*, Daniel Miller and Christopher Tilley, eds. Cambridge, England: Cambridge University Press, pp. 111–146.

Tindale, Norman B., 1985. Australian aboriginal techniques of pressure-flaking stone implements: some personal observations. In *Stone Tool Analysis: Essays in Honor of Don E. Crabtree*, Mark G. Plew, James C. Woods, and Max G. Pavesic, eds. Albuquerque: University of New Mexico Press, pp. 1–33.

Titiev, Mischa, 1960. A fresh approach to the problem of magic and religion. *Southwestern Journal of Anthropology* 16:292–298.

Todd, T. Wingate, 1927. Skeletal records of mortality. *The Scientific Monthly* 24:481–496.

Tribbe, Frank C., 1983. *Portrait of Jesus? The Illustrated Story of the Shroud of Turin*. Briarcliff Manor, N.Y: Stein & Day.

Trigger, Bruce G., 1971. Archaeology and ecology. *World Archaeology* 2(3):321–336.

———, 1978. *Time and Traditions: Essays in Archaeological Interpretation*. New York: Columbia University Press.

———, 1981. Archaeology and the ethnographic present. *Anthropologica* 23(1):3-17.

———, 1984. Archaeology at the crossroads: what's new? *Annual Review of Anthropology* 13:275–300.

Tringham, Ruth, Glenn Cooper, George Odell, Barbra Voytek, and Anne Whitman, 1974. Experimentation in the formation of edge damage: a new approach to lithic analysis. *Journal of Field Archaeology* 1(1/2):171–196.

Tschudy, Robert H., and Richard A. Scott, eds., 1969. *Aspects of Palynology*. New York: Wiley.

Tunnell, C., 1977. Fluted projectile point production as revealed by lithic specimens from the Adair-Steadman site in northwest Texas. In *Paleoindian Lifeways*, Eileen Johnson, ed. *The Museum Journal* vol. 17, West Texas Museum Association, Texas Tech University, Lubbock, pp. 140–168.

Tuohy, Donald R., and L. Kyle Napton, 1986. Duck decoys from Lovelock Cave, Nevada, dated by 14-C accelerator mass spectrometry. *American Antiquity* 51(4):813–816.

Turnbaugh, William, and Sarah Peabody Turnbaugh, 1977. Alternative applications of the mean ceramic date concept for interpreting human behavior. *Historical Archaeology* 11:90–104.

Turner, Christy G. II, 1979. Dental anthropological indications of agriculture among the Jomon people of central Japan, pt. 10: Peopling of the Pacific. *American Journal of Physical Anthropology* 51(4):619–636.

Turner, Victor, 1967. *The Forest of Symbols: Aspects of Ndembu Ritual*. Ithaca, N.Y.: Cornell University Press.

———, 1987. Body, brain, and culture. In *Waymarks: The Notre Dame Inaugural*

Lectures in Anthropology, Kenneth Moore, ed. Notre Dame, Ind.: University of Notre Dame Press, pp. 71–105.

Tylor, Edward Burnett, 1871. *Primitive Culture,* vols. 1 and 2. London: Murray.

———, 1889. On a method of investigating the development of institutions, applied to laws of marriage and descent. *Journal of the Royal Anthropological Institute* 18:245–272.

Ulriksen, C.P., 1983. *Application of Impulse Radar to Civil Engineering.* Hudson, N.H.: Geophysical Survey Systems.

Upham, Steadman, 1982. *Politics and Power: An Economic and Political History of the Western Pueblo.* New York: Academic Press.

———, 1987. The tyranny of ethnographic analogy in Southwestern archaeology. In *Coasts, plains, and deserts: essays in honor of Reynold J. Ruppé,* S. Gaines, and G. A. Clark, eds. *Arizona State University Anthropological Research Papers,* 38: 265–279.

Valliant, G. C., 1931. Excavations at Ticoman. *Anthropological Papers of the American Museum of Natural History* 32(2).

van der Merwe, Nikolaas J., 1982. Carbon isotopes, photosynthesis, and archaeology. *American Scientist* 70:596–606.

———, Anna Curtenius Roosevelt, and J. C. Vogel, 1981. Isotopic evidence for prehistoric subsistence change at Parmana, Venezuela. *Nature* 292:536–538.

———, and J. C. Vogel, 1978. 13-C content of human collagen as a measure of prehistoric diet in Woodland North America. *Nature* 276:815–816.

Van Devender, Thomas R., 1977. Holocene woodlands in the southwestern deserts. *Science* 198:189–192.

———, and W. G. Spaulding, 1979. Development of vegetation and climate in the southwestern United States. *Science* 204:701–710.

Van Gerven, Dennis P., and George Armelagos, 1983. "Farewell to paleodemography?" Rumors of its death have been greatly exaggerated. *Journal of Human Evolution* 12:353–360.

Vaughan, Patrick C., 1985. *Use–Wear Analysis of Flaked Stone Tools.* Tucson: University of Arizona Press.

Vayda, Andrew P., and Bonnie J. McCay, 1975. New directions in ecology and ecological anthropology. *Annual Review of Anthropology* 4:293–306.

Vita-Finzi, C., and E. S. Higgs, 1970. Prehistoric economy in the Mount Carmel area of Palestine: site catchment analysis. *Proceedings of the Prehistoric Society* 36:1–37.

Vogt, Evon Z., 1952. Water witching: an interpretation of ritual pattern in a rural American community. *Scientific Monthly* 75:175–186.

Von Däniken, Erich, 1971. *Chariots of the Gods?* New York: Bantam Books.

von Frese, R. R. B., and V. E. Noble, 1984. Magnetometry for archaeological exploration of historical sites. *Historical Archaeology* 18(2):38–53.

Wagner, Gail E., 1982. Testing flotation recovery rates. *American Antiquity* 47(1):127–132.

Walker, Phillip L., 1985. Anemia among prehistoric Indians of the American Southwest. In Health and disease in the Prehistoric Southwest, Charles F. Merbs and Robert J. Miller, eds. *Arizona State University Anthropological Research Papers,* 34:139–164.

Wallace, Anthony F. C., 1966. *Religion: An Anthropological View.* New York: Random House.

Walter, W., 1954. Southwestern archaeology, its history and theory. *American Anthropologist* 56(4, pt. 1):561–570.

Wand, J. O., R. Gillespie, and R. E. M. Hedges, 1984. Sample preparation for accelerator-based radiocarbon dating. *Journal of Archaeological Science* 11(2):159–163.

Ward, R. G. W., ed., 1987. Applications of tree-ring studies: current research in dendrochronology and related subjects. *BAR International Series,* no. 333.

Wardle, H. Newell, 1929. Wreck of the archaeological department at the Academy of Natural Sciences of Philadelphia, *Science* 70(1805):119–121.

———, 1956. Clarence Bloomfield Moore (1852-1936). *Bulletin of the Philadelphia Anthropological Society* 9(2):9–11.

Waring, A. J., Jr., and Preston Holder, 1945. A prehistoric ceremonial complex in the Southeastern United States. *American Anthropologist* 47(1):1–34.

Waselkov, Gregory A., 1979. Zumwalt's Fort: an archaeological study of frontier process in Missouri. *The Missouri Archaeologist* 40:1–129.

Washburn, Dorothy K., 1976. Symmetry classification of Pueblo ceramic designs. In *The Structure of a Chacoan Society in the Northern Southwest: Investigations at the Salmon Site: 1974–1975,* Cynthia Irwin-Williams, ed. Portales: Eastern New Mexico University Press, pp. 91–120.

———, ed., 1983. *Structure and Cognition in Art.* Cambridge, England: Cambridge University Press.

Washburn, Sherwood L., 1951. The new physical anthropology. *Transactions of the New York Academy of Sciences,* series 2, 13:298–304.

Waterbolk, H. T., 1971. Working with radiocarbon dates. *Proceedings of the Prehistoric Society* 37(2):15–33.

Watson, Patty Jo, 1973. The future of archeology in anthropology: Cultural history and social science. In *Research and Theory in Current Archeology,* Charles L. Redman, ed. New York: Wiley pp. 113–124.

———, 1974. Flotation procedures used on Salts Cave sediments. In *Archeology of the Mammoth Cave Area,* Patty Jo Watson, ed. New York: Academic Press, pp. 107–108.

———, 1976. In pursuit of prehistoric subsistence: a comparative account of some contemporary flotation techniques. *Midcontinental Journal of Archaeology* 1(1):77–100.

———, 1977. Design analysis of painted pottery. *American Antiquity* 42(3):381–393.

———, 1985. The impact of early horticulture in the upland drainages of the Midwest and Midsouth. In Prehistoric food production in North America, Richard I. Ford, ed. *Anthropological Papers of Museum of Anthropology, University of Michigan,* 75:99–148.

————, 1986. Archaeological interpretation, 1985. In *American Archaeology Past and Future: a Celebration of the Society of American Archaeology 1935–1985,* David J. Meltzer, Don D. Fowler, and Jeremy A. Sabloff, eds. Washington D. C.: Smithsonian Institution Press, pp. 439–457.

————, Steven A. LeBlanc, and Charles L. Redman, 1971. *Explanation in Archeology: an Explicitly Scientific Approach.* New York: Columbia University Press.

————, 1984. *Archeological Explanation: the Scientific Method in Archeology.* New York: Columbia University Press.

Watson, Richard A., 1972. The "new archaeology" of the 1960s. *Antiquity* 46:210–215.

————, 1976a. Inference in archaeology. *American Antiquity* 41:58–66.

————, 1976b. Laws, systems, certainty, and particularities. *American Anthropologist* 78:341–344.

Wauchope, Robert, 1965. (Obituary of) Alfred Vincent Kidder, 1885-1963. *American Antiquity* 31(2, pt. 1):149–171.

————, 1966. Archaeological survey of northern Georgia with a test of some cultural hypotheses. *Society for American Archaeology,* Memoir no. 21 (*American Antiquity* 31[5]pt.2).

Webb, Clarence H., 1968. (Obituary of) James Alfred Ford, 1911–1968. *Texas Archaeological Society Bulletin* 38:135–146.

Webb, George Ernest, 1983. *Tree Rings and Telescopes: the Scientific Career of A. E. Douglass.* Tucson: University of Arizona Press.

Weberman, A. J., 1971. The art of garbage analysis. *Esquire* 5(456):113–117.

Webster, David L., 1977. Warfare and the evolution of Maya civilization. In *The Origins of Maya Civilization,* Richard E. W. Adams, ed. Albuquerque: University of New Mexico Press, pp. 335–372.

Wedel, Waldo R., 1967. The council circles of central Kansas: Were they solstice registers? *American Antiquity* 32(1):54–63.

Weide, Margaret L., 1969. Seasonality of Pismo clam collecting at Ora-82. *University of California Archaeological Survey Annual Report, 1968–1969,* 11:127–141.

Wells, Philip V., and Rainer Berger, 1967. Late Pleistocene history of coniferous woodland in the Mohave Desert. *Science* 155(3770):1640–1647.

Wells, Philip V., and Clive D. Jorgensen, 1964. Pleistocene wood rat middens and climatic change in Mohave Desert: A record of juniper woodlands. *Science* 143:1171–1174.

Wendorf, Fred, 1979. Changing values in archaeology. *American Antiquity* 44(4):641–643.

————, 1987. The advantages of AMS to field archaeologists. In *Nuclear Instruments and Methods in Physics Research: Section B, Beam Interactions with Materials and Atoms,* H. H. Andersen and S. T. Picraux, eds. Proceedings of the Fourth International Symposium on Accelerator Mass Spectrometry, Ontario, Canada B29:155–158.

Weymouth, John W., 1986. Geophysical methods of archaeological site surveying. In *Advances in Archaeological Method and Theory*, vol. 9, Michael B. Schiffer, ed. Orlando, Fla.: Academic Press, pp. 311–395.

———, and Robert Huggins, 1985. Geophysical surveying of archaeological sites. In *Archaeological Geology*, George R. Rapp, Jr., and J. Gifford, eds. New Haven, Conn.: Yale University Press, pp. 191–235.

Whallon, Robert E., Jr., 1968. Investigations of late prehistoric social organization in New York State. In *New Perspectives in Archeology*, Sally R. Binford and Lewis R. Binford, eds. Chicago: Aldine, pp. 223–244.

———, 1973. Spatial analysis of occupation floors I: application of dimensional analysis of variance. *American Antiquity* 38(3):266–278.

———, 1974a. Working with the "new paradigm". *Reviews in Anthropology* 1(1):25–33.

———, 1974b. Spatial analysis of occupation floors II: the application of nearest neighbor analysis. *American Antiquity* 39(1):16–34.

———, 1986. A spatial analysis of four occupation floors at Guilá Naquitz. In *Guilá Naquitz: Archaic Foraging and Early Agriculture in Oaxaca, Mexico*, Kent V. Flannery, ed. Orlando, Fla., Academic Press, pp. 369–384.

———, and James A. Brown, eds., 1982, *Essays on Archaeological Typology*. Evanston, Ill.: Center for American Archaeology Press.

Wheat, Joe Ben, 1972. The Olsen-Chubbuck site: a Paleo-Indian bison kill. *Society for American Archaeology Memoir* no. 26.

Wheat, Margaret M., 1967. *Survival Arts of the Primitive Paiutes*. Reno: University of Nevada Press.

Wheeler, Mortimer, 1954. *Archaeology from the Earth*. Oxford, England: Oxford University Press (Clarendon).

White, J. Peter, 1968. Fabricators, outils, écaillés or scalar cores? *Mankind* 6(12):658–666.

———, 1985. Digging out big-men? *Archaeology of Oceania* 20:57–60.

———, and H. Dibble, 1986. Stone tools: small-scale variability. In *Stone Age Prehistory*, G. N. Bailey and P. Callow, eds. Cambridge: Cambridge University Press, pp. 47–53.

———, and Nicholas Modjeska, 1978. Where do all the stone tools go? Some examples and problems in their social and spatial distribution in the Papua New Guinea Highlands. In *The Spatial Organisation of Culture*, Ian Hodder. ed., Pittsburgh: University of Pittsburgh Press, pp. 25–38.

———, Nicholas Modjeska, and Irari Hipuya, 1977. Group definitions and mental templates: an ethnographic experiment. In *Stone Tools as Cultural Markers: Change, Evolution and Complexity*, R. V. S. Wright, ed., Canberra: Australian Institute of Aboriginal Studies, Prehistory and Material Culture Series, no. 12, pp. 380–390.

———, and David Hurst Thomas, 1972. What mean these stones? Ethno-taxonomic models and archaeological interpretations in the New Guinea Highlands. In *Models in Archaeology,* David L. Clarke, ed. London: Methuen, pp. 275–308.

White, Leslie A., 1949. *The Science of Culture.* New York: Grove Press.

———, 1959. *The Evolution of Culture.* New York: McGraw-Hill.

———, 1975. *The Concept of Cultural Systems.* New York: Columbia University Press.

White, Randall, 1982. The manipulation of burins in incision and notation. *Canadian Journal of Anthropology* 2:129–135.

———, 1986. *Dark Caves, Bright Visions: Life in Ice Age Europe.* New York: American Museum of Natural History in association with W. W. Norton & Company.

White, Theodore E., 1953. A method of calculating the dietary percentage of various food animals utilized by aboriginal peoples. *American Antiquity* 18(4):396–398.

———, 1954. Observations on the butchering technique of some aboriginal peoples, nos. 3, 4, 5, and 6. *American Antiquity* 19(3):254–264.

Wildeson, Leslie E., 1979. Coming of age in applied archaeology. *Reviews in Anthropology* 6(3):373–385.

Wilk, Richard R., 1985. The ancient Maya and the political present. *Journal of Anthropological Research* 41(3):307–326.

Wilken, Gene C., 1971. Food-producing systems available to the ancient Maya. *American Antiquity* 36(4):432–448.

Willey, Gordon R., 1953. Prehistoric settlement patterns in the Virú Valley, Perú. *Bureau of American Ethnology,* bulletin 155.

———, ed., 1956. Prehistoric settlement patterns in the New World. *Viking Fund Publications in Anthropology,* no. 23.

———, 1967. (Obituary of) Alfred Vincent Kidder. *National Academy of Sciences Biographical Memoirs,* vol. 39, New York: Columbia University Press, pp. 292–322.

———, 1968. One hundred years of American archaeology. In *One Hundred Years of Anthropology,* J. O. Brew, ed. Cambridge, Mass.: Harvard University Press, pp. 29–53.

———, 1969. (Obituary of) James Alfred Ford, 1911–1968. *American Antiquity* 34(1):62–71.

———, 1974. The Virú Valley settlement pattern study. In *Archaeological Researches in Retrospect,* Gordon R. Willey, ed. Cambridge, Mass.: Winthrop, pp. 149–178.

———, 1976. Mesoamerican civilization and the idea of transcendence. *Antiquity* 50(199/200):205–215.

———, 1977. The rise of Maya civilization: a summary view. In *The Origins of Maya Civilization,* Richard E. W. Adams, ed. Albuquerque: University of New Mexico Press, pp. 383–423.

———, and Philip Phillips, 1958. *Method and Theory in American Archaeology.* Chicago: University of Chicago Press.

———, and Jeremy A. Sabloff, 1980. *A History of American Archaeology* [2nd ed.]. New York: Freeman.

Williams, Barbara, 1981. In *Breakthrough: Women in Archaeology,* New York: Walker.

Williams, J. Mark, 1984. A new resistivity device. *Journal of Field Archaeology* 11(1):110–114.

Williams, Leonard, David Hurst Thomas, and Robert Bettinger, 1973. Notions to numbers: Great Basin settlements as polythetic sets. In *Research and Theory in Current Archeology,* Charles L. Redman, ed. New York: Wiley, pp. 215–237.

Williamson, Ray A., Howard J. Fisher, and Donnel O' Flynn, 1977. Anasazi solar observations. In *Native American Astronomy,* Anthony F. Aveni, ed. Austin: University of Texas Press, pp. 203–218.

Willis, E. H. 1969. Radiocarbon dating. In *Science in Archaeology,* Don Brothwell and Eric Higgs, eds. London: Thames and Hudson, pp. 46–57.

Wilmsen, Edwin N., 1973. Interaction, spacing behavior, and the organization of hunting bands. *Journal of Anthropological Research* 29(1):1–31.

Wilson, David, 1974. *The New Archaeology.* New York: Knopf.

Wilson, Ian, 1986. *The Mysterious Shroud,* Garden City, N.Y.: Doubleday.

Wing, Elizabeth S., and Antoinette B. Brown, 1979. *Paleonutrition: Method and Theory in Prehistoric Foodways.* New York: Academic Press.

Winlock, H. E., 1942. *Excavations at Deir el Bahri, 1911–1931.* New York: Macmillan.

Winterhalder, Bruce, 1980. Environmental analysis in human evolution and adaptation research. *Human Ecology* 8(2):135–170.

———, 1981. Optimal foraging strategies and hunter-gatherer research in anthropology: Theory and models. In *Hunter-Gatherer Foraging Strategies,* Bruce Winterhalder and Eric Alden Smith, eds. Chicago: University of Chicago Press, pp. 13–35.

———, 1987. The analysis of hunter-gatherer diets: stalking an optimal foraging model. In *Food and Evolution: Toward a Theory of Human Food Habits,* Marvin Harris and Eric B. Ross, eds. Philadelphia: Temple University Press, pp. 311–339.

———, and Eric Alden Smith, eds., 1981. *Hunter-Gatherer Foraging Strategies: Ethnographic and Archaeological Analyses.* Chicago: University of Chicago Press.

Wissler, Clark, 1917. The new archaeology. *The American Museum Journal* 17(2):100–101.

Wittfogel, Karl A., 1957. *Oriental Despotism: a Comparative Study of Total Power.* New Haven, Conn.: Yale University Press.

Wobst, H. Martin, 1974. Boundary conditions for Paleolithic social systems: a simulation approach. *American Antiquity* 39(2):147–178.

Wolf, Eric R., 1962. *Sons of the Shaking Earth.* Chicago: University of Chicago Press.

———, ed., 1976. *The Valley of Mexico: Studies in Pre-Hispanic Ecology and Society.* Albuquerque: University of New Mexico Press.

Wolfman, D. 1984. Geomagnetic dating methods in archaeology. In *Advances in Archaeological Method and Theory,* vol. 7, Michael B. Schiffer, ed. New York: Academic Press, pp. 363–458.

Wood, John Edwin, 1978. *Sun, Moon and Standing Stones.* Oxford, England: Oxford University Press.

Woodall, J. Ned, and Philip J. Perricone, 1981. The archaeologist as cowboy: the consequence of professional stereotype. *Journal of Field Archaeology* 8:506–508.

Woodbury, Richard B., 1954. Review of *A Study of Archaeology* by Walter W. Taylor. *American Antiquity* 19:292–296.

————, 1960. Nels C. Nelson and chronological archaeology. *American Antiquity* 25(3):400–401.

————, 1973. *Alfred V. Kidder*. New York: Columbia University Press.

Wormington, H. M., 1981. Foreword. In *Breakthrough: Women in Archaeology,* Barbara Williams. New York: Walter.

Wright, Gary A., 1971. Origins of food production in southwestern Asia: a survey of ideas. *Current Anthropology* 12(4-5):447–477.

Wright, Henry T., 1977. Toward an explanation of the origin of the state. In *Explanation of Prehistoric Change,* James N. Hill, ed. Albuquerque: University of New Mexico Press, pp. 215–230.

————, 1986. The evolution of civilizations. In *American Archaeology Past and Future: a Celebration of the Society for American Archaeology 1935–1985,* David J. Meltzer, Don D. Fowler, and Jeremy A. Sabloff, eds., Washington D.C.: Smithsonian Institution Press, pp. 323–365

————, and Gregory A. Johnson, 1975. Population, exchange, and early state formation in southwestern Iran. *American Anthropologist* 77(2):267–289.

————, and Melinda Zeder, 1977. The simulation of a linear exchange system under equilibrium conditions. In *Exchange Systems in Prehistory,* Timothy K. Earle and Jonathon E. Ericson, eds. New York: Academic Press, pp. 233–253.

Wright, Herbert E. Jr., 1977. Environmental change and the origin of agriculture in the Old and New Worlds. In *Origins of Agriculture,* Charles A. Reed, ed. The Hague: Mouton, pp. 281–318.

Wylie, Alison, 1985. Putting Shakertown back together: critical theory in archaeology. *Journal of Anthropological Archaeology* 4:133–147.

Wynn, J. C., ed., 1986. Special issue: Geophysics in archaeology. *Geophysics* 51(3):533–639.

Wynne, E. J., and Tylecote, R. F., 1958. An experimental investigation into primitive iron-smelting technique. *Journal of Iron and Steel Institute* 190:339–348.

Yarnell, Richard A., 1974. Intestinal contents of the Salts Cave mummy and analysis of the initial Salts Cave flotation series. In *Archaeology of the Mammoth Cave Area,* Patty Jo Watson, ed. New York: Academic Press, pp. 109–112.

————, 1982. Problems of interpretation of archaeological plant remains of the Eastern Woodlands. *Southeastern Archaeology* 1(1):1–7.

Yellen, John E., 1976. Settlement patterns of the !Kung: an archaeological perspective. In *Kalahari Hunter-Gatherers,* R.B. Lee and I. DeVore, eds. Cambridge, Mass.: Harvard University Press, pp. 47–72.

————,1977. *Archaeological Approaches to the Present: Models for Reconstructing the Past.* New York: Academic Press.

————, 1983. Women, Archaeology and the National Science Foundation. In *The Socio-politics of Archaeology,* Joan M. Gero, David M. Lacy, and Michael L. Blakey, eds. Amherst: University of Massachusetts Department of Anthropology Research Report, no. 23, pp. 59–65.

Yesner, David, 1981. Archaeological applications of optimal foraging theory: harvest strategies of Aleut hunter-gatherers. In *Hunter-Gatherer Foraging Strategies Ethnographic and Archaeological Analyses,* Bruce Winterhalder and Eric A. Smith, eds. Chicago: University of Chicago Press, pp. 148–170.

Young, David E., 1976. The relevance of cognitive anthropology for the interpretation of archaeological data. In *Primitive Art and Technology,* J. S. Raymond, B. Loveseth, C. Arnold, and G. Reardon, eds. Calgary: Archaeological Association, University of Calgary, pp. 72–91.

Young, David E., and Robson Bonnichsen, 1985. Cognition, behavior, and material culture. In *Stone Tool Analysis: Essays in Honor of Don E. Crabtree,* Mark G. Plew, James C. Woods, and Max G. Pavesic, eds. Albuquerque: University of New Mexico Press, pp. 91–131.

Zarky, Alan, 1976. Statistical analysis of catchments at Ocós, Guatemala. In *The Early Mesoamerican Village,* Kent V. Flannery, ed. New York: Academic Press, pp. 117–130.

Zeilik, Michael, 1985. The ethnoastronomy of the historic Pueblos, I: calendrical sun watching. *Archaeoastronomy* 8:S1–S24.

Ziegler, Alan C., 1973. Inference from prehistoric faunal remains. *Addison-Wesley Module in Anthropology,* no. 43.

Zihlman, Adrienne, 1981. Women as shapers of the human adaptation. In *Woman the Gatherer,* Frances Dahlberg, ed. New Haven, Conn.: Yale University Press, pp. 75–120.

Zihlman, Adrienne, and Nancy Tanner, 1978. Gathering and the hominid adaptation. In *Female Hierarchies,* Lionel Tiger and Heather T. Fowler, eds. Chicago: Beresford Book Service, pp. 163–194.

Zimmerman, Larry J., 1977. Prehistoric locational behavior: a computer simulation. *Office of the State Archaeologist,* report no. 10. Iowa City: University of Iowa Press.

Zimmerman, Michael R., and Marc A. Kelley, 1982. *Atlas of Human Paleopathology.* New York: Praeger.

Zubrow, Ezra B. W., 1971. Carrying capacity and dynamic equilibrium in the prehistoric Southwest. *American Antiquity* 36(2):127–138.

———, 1976. Demographic anthropology: an introductory analysis. In *Demographic Anthropology: Quantitative Approaches,* Ezra B. W. Zubrow, ed. Albuquerque: University of New Mexico Press, pp. 1–25.

Zugibe, Frederick T., 1982. *The Cross and the Shroud: A Medical Examiner Investigates the Crucifixion.* Garnerville, N.Y.: Angelus Books.

GLOSSARY

Accelerator mass spectrometric (AMS) technique: A relatively new method of radiocarbon dating that counts the proportion of carbon isotopes directly (rather than using the indirect Geiger counter method), thereby drastically reducing the quantity of datable material required.

Acculturation: The adoption of a trait or traits by one culture from another; the influence of one culture on another.

Achieved status: See **Status, achieved**.

Adaptive strategy: Technology, ecology, demography, and economics that define human behavior, as seen from a research perspective.

Additive technology: Manufacturing processes in which artifacts take form by the addition of material to the original mass; ceramic production and basket making are additive technologies.

Aguada (Spanish): A large circular basin dug into the clay soil of a swampy area.

Alliance theory: A structural explanation for marriage, exchange, and exogamy.

Alluvium: Gravel, sand, and soil that are deposited by flowing water.

Americanist archaeology: The brand of archaeology that evolved in close association with anthropology in the Americas; practiced throughout the world.

Analogy: A means of reasoning based on the assumption that if two things are similar in some respects, then they must be similar in other respects.

Anthropological linguistics: The cross-cultural study of human language and its implications for cultural behavior.

Anthropology: The study of humankind, extant and extinct, from an all-encompassing holistic approach.

Anthropometry: A subdiscipline of physical anthropology that specifically examines the measurements of human morphology.

Antiquarian: A term used in the eighteenth and nineteenth centuries referring to someone who collected antiquities.

Anvil stone: A rough stone on which other lithics or food (such as nuts) are placed and smashed with a stone hammer.

Applied archaeology: The use of archaeological techniques to conserve sites and preserve information from sites to be destroyed.

Arbitrary level: The basic vertical subdivision of an excavation square; used only when easily recognizable "natural" stratification is lacking.

Arboreal: Pertaining to trees.

Archaeoastronomy: The study of the relationship between astronomical events and past cultural behavior.

Archaeobotany: See **Paleoethnobotany**.

Archaeofauna: An assemblage of animal remains recovered from a single archaeological context.

Archaeological context: See **Context, archaeological.**

Archaeological record: The surviving physical remains of past human activities.

Archaeological site: Any concentration of artifacts, features, or ecofacts manufactured or modified by humans.

Archaeology: The study of the human past. Americanist archaeology's initial objective is the construction of cultural chronology; its intermediate objective is the reconstruction of past lifeways; and its ultimate objective is the discovery of the processes that underlie and condition human behavior.

Archaeomagnetism: A dating technique based on the earth's changing magnetic configuration.

Archetype: An abstract classification that emphasizes the elusive "ideal form" implicit in all **morphological types**.

Aré: A term used by the Duna of the New Guinea highlands for both the initial core and the flakes broken off the core.

Aré kou: The tools used by the Duna of the New Guinea highlands; the term refers to flakes tied with orchid fibers into a cane or wooden handle that are used for shredding fibers or drilling holes.

Arrowhead: An informal term denoting the stone tips mounted on arrowshafts; the term **projectile point** is generally preferable because it avoids an inference regarding the method of hafting and propulsion.

Artifact: Any object used or manufactured by humans.

Artifact, sociotechnic: A tool that is used primarily in the social subsystem.

Artifact, technomic: A tool that is used primarily to cope with the physical environment; its variability is explicable largely in ecological terms.

Ascribed status: See **Status, ascribed**.

Atlatl: An Aztec term for spear thrower, a wooden shaft used to propel a spear or dart. The atlatl functions like an extension of the arm, providing more thrusting leverage.

Attribute: An individual characteristic that distinguishes one artifact from another by means of its size, surface texture, and design pattern.

Auger: A power or manual tool used for digging test holes; auger testing is generally restricted to the earliest stages of archaeological reconnaissance.

Australopithecus: The most ancient and most primitive human, dating back roughly five million years in South Africa.

Awl: A bone or stone tool tapered to a point and used to pierce holes, make decorations, or assist in basket weaving.

Aztec: The last major pre-Columbian civilization in Mesoamerica; its capital, Tenochtitlán, lies under the modern Mexico City.

Band: The simplest form of human society. It is egalitarian and based largely on kinship and marriage, and its division of labor is generally determined by age and sex.

Biface: A stone tool that has been flaked on both sides.

Binford, Lewis R.: (**1930–**): An influential contemporary Americanist archaeologist, considered by many to be the father of the new archaeology.

Biocultural anthropology: A research strategy that combines physical anthropology and archaeology to investigate prehistoric biological systems.

Biogeography: A subdiscipline of biology that studies, and attempts to explain, the distribution of modern plant and animal populations.

Biological population: See **Population, biological**.

Blank: An intermediate manufacturing stage in the production of stone tools.

Boserup, Ester (1910–): A Danish economist who devised an influential "optimistic" model that proposes that technological responses tend to be available whenever population pressure increases toward the carrying capacity.

Boucher de Perthes, Jacques (1788–1868): A controller of customs at Abbeville, France, who, in the early part of the nineteenth century, found the bones of now-extinct mammals associated with stone tools in the ancient gravels of the Somme River.

Bridging argument: Logical statements linking the static archaeological record to the past dynamics that produced it; **middle-range research**, using contemporary observations—mainly through ethnoarchaeology and experimental archaeology—is generally required to define these linkages.

Brongniart, Alexandre (1770–1847): A French botanist who recognized that distinctive fossils could be used to define geological strata; see also **Cuvier**.

Burial Mound Builders: The nineteenth-century term used to describe the prehistoric Native Americans who constructed the burial and temple mounds that are widespread east of the Mississippi.

Burin: A flaked stone artifact with a narrow chiseled edge, used for engraving stone and bone.

Burnarbashi: Ruins near Balli Dagh, Turkey, once thought to have been the site of ancient Troy.

Cache: A collection of artifacts and/or ecofacts that has been deliberately stored for future use.

Cairn: A memorial or landmark, generally consisting of piled stones and often indicating where something valuable was stored.

Campo santo: (Spanish) Cemetery associated with a church.

Catchment: The resource area around an archaeological site that is within convenient walking distance.

Central place theory: A series of theoretical models designed to explain how settlement hierarchies function and how they determine demography in modern market economies.

Chancel: The part of a church nearest the altar, reserved for the clergy's use and sometimes set off by a railing or screen.

Cheno-am: Plants of amaranth and the goosefoot family.

Chiefdom: A ranked sociopolitical organization in which people are born into their place in the society.

Chopper: A large, roughly formed stone tool.

Chronology: A sequential ordering that places cultural entities in temporal (and often spatial) distribution.

Circumscription theory: A hypothesis associated with Robert Carneiro that suggests that warfare, because of increasing population density and environmental (and social) circumscription, led to the development of the state.

Ciriaco (1391–ca. 1449): An Italian Renaissance scholar who helped establish the modern discipline of archaeology.

Clan: A unilineal kin group, usually exogamous, that provides security and social control.

Classical archaeology: The study of Old World Greek and Roman civilizations.

Clovis spear point: A spear point manufactured using percussion flaking by American Paleo-Indians, roughly twelve thousand years ago. Characterized by one or more fluting flakes, Clovis points are found throughout the United States and, to a lesser degree, Canada.

Cocina: (Spanish) Kitchen.

Coevolution: Recent theory in cultural evolution suggesting that changes in social systems are best understood as mutual selection among components rather than a linear cause-and-effect sequence. David Rindos (1984), for instance, has argued that the origins of agriculture can best be understood by exploring the evolutionary forces affecting the development of domestication systems. Viewed this way, domestication is not seen as an evolutionary stage, but rather as a process, "the result of coevolutionary interactions between humans and plants" (Rindos 1984:xiv).

Cognitive archaeology: The study of past mental processes as viewed through the archaeological record.

Component: A culturally homogeneous stratigraphic unit within an archaeological site.

Composites: Herbs such as ragweed and sagebrush.

Computer simulation: The use of a computer to imitate the dynamic behavior of an explicit model; particularly useful for examining how such systems respond to changing conditions.

Conjunctive approach: As defined by W. W. Taylor, the explicit connection of archaeological objects within their cultural contexts.

Conservation archaeology: A movement in contemporary archaeology that explicitly recognizes archaeological sites as nonrenewable resources.

Context, archaeological: Artifacts, features, and residues as found in the archaeological record.

Context, systemic: Artifacts, features, and residues as they functioned in the behavioral system that produced or used them.

Convento: (Spanish) A monastery, convent, or cloister that houses members of a religious order.

Coprolite: Dessicated remains of human or animal feces that can carry both dietary and climatic information.

Core: A piece of stone from which other pieces of stone are flaked off to make artifacts.

Cortex: The weathering evident on an unmodified stone cobble.

Crescent: A crescent-shaped bifacially flaked stone tool generally restricted to the Paleo-Indian period and almost always found in association with extinct Pleistocene lakes. Sometimes known as Great Basin Transverse points, these artifacts may have been used for hunting large shorebirds.

Critical theory: A series of attempts to adapt ideas from Karl Marx to an understanding of events and circumstances of twentieth-century life that Marx did not know. "Critical" in this sense means that the relations between the assumptions and discoveries of a scholarly discipline and its ties to modern life become a central concern and are subject to examination, automatically relating the questions, methods, and discoveries of a science like anthropology to those of the anthropologist's own culture.

Cross trenching: An extraordinarily destructive method sometimes used by architectural historians, in which parallel trenches are excavated to a shovel blade in width, with backdirt thrown on the unexcavated spaces between. This outmoded strategy was designed to disclose foundations for restoration but paid little attention to artifacts and stratigraphy.

Cultural anthropology: A subdiscipline of anthropology, emphasizing nonbiological aspects—the learned social, linguistic, technological, and familial behaviors of humans.

Cultural chronology: The ordering of past material culture into meaningful temporal segments.

Cultural ecology: The study of the relationship between human populations, other organisms, and their physical milieus, which together constitute integrated systems.

Cultural evolution: A subdiscipline of anthropology that emphasizes the systematic change of cultural systems through time.

Cultural materialism: A research strategy that assumes that technological, economic, and ecological processes—the modes of production and reproduction—lie at the causal heart of every sociocultural system; largely associated with the research of Marvin Harris.

Cultural population: See **Population, cultural**.

Cultural process: The cause-and-effect cultural relationships not bound by time and space; the why of culture and the ultimate aim of Americanist archaeology.

Cultural resource management (CRM): The conservation and carefully planned investigation of archaeological materials; generally refers to efforts to safeguard remains of the past through legislation and applied archaeology.

Cultural system: The nonbiological mechanism that relates the human organism to its physical and social environments; one shares cultural traits but participates in the overall cultural system.

Culture: The nonbiological mechanism of human adaptation.

Curated technology: Artifacts that are reused and transported so often that they are rarely deposited in contexts that reflect their actual manufacture and use.

Cuvier, Georges (1769–1832): The founder of comparative anatomy; used principles of anatomy to extend and perfect Linnaean classification by recognizing similarities between extant and fossil animals.

Darwin, Charles (1809–1882): Ninteenth-century scientist who developed a theory to explain the origin of plant and animal species through a process of natural selection that tends to perpetuate adaptive variations.

Data: Relevant observations made on objects that then serve as the basis for study and discussion.

Dating, absolute: Dates expressed as specific units of scientific measurement, such as days, years, centuries, or millennia; absolute determinations attempt to pinpoint a discrete, known interval in time; see also **Dating, relative**.

Dating, relative: Dates expressed through relativistic relationships, for example, earlier, later, more recent, after Noah's flood, and prehistoric.

Datum point: The zero point, a fixed reference used to keep vertical control on a dig. When combined with the grid system, archaeologists can plot any find in three dimensions.

Deagan, Kathleen (1948–): One of the leading contemporary Americanist archaeologists, specializing in the excavation and analysis of Spanish colonial–period sites in the American Southeast and Caribbean.

Declination: The difference between true and magnetic north.

Deduction: A means of reasoning from the general to the specific. In deductive arguments, the conclusions must be true, given that the premises are true.

Dendrochronology: Tree-ring dating.

Denticulate: An artifact with several small tool-like projections on the working edge.

Depositional process: The transformation of materials from a systemic to an archaeological context. Such processes are directly responsible for the accumulation of archaeological sites, and they constitute the dominant factor in forming the archaeological record.

Diachronic: A term referring to two or more reference points in time.

Differential heat analysis: Remote sensing technique in which the variability in heat absorption and dissemination is used to plot hidden archaeological features.

Direct percussion: A technique used to manufacture stone tools, in which flakes are produced by striking a core with a hammerstone or against a fixed anvil stone; see also **indirect percussion**.

Disturbance process: Changing the contexts of materials within the archaeological site itself. Examples include such diverse mechanisms as dam building, farming, and heavy construction, as well as noncultural activities such as freeze-thaw cycles, landslides, and simple erosion.

Doctrine of uniformitarianism: Asserts that the processes now operating to modify the earth's surface are the same processes that operated long ago in the geological past. This simple principle provided the cornerstone of modern geology.

Double fixed sum: A technique used in palynology that allows the analyst both to study the gross frequencies of the dominants and to monitor the presence of the rarer species (which tend to be the most sensitive ecological indicators).

Ecofact: The nonartifactual remains found in archaeological sites, such as seeds, bones, and plant pollen.

Ecological determinants approach: A research strategy in settlement archaeology that emphasizes the location of human settlements in response to specific ecological factors.

Ecology: The study of entire assemblages of living organisms and their physical milieus, which together constitute an integrated system.

Ecosystem: The living organisms and their nonliving environment. The flow of energy through an ecosystem leads to a clearly defined structure, biotic diversity, and system of exchange cycles between the living and nonliving parts of the ecosystem.

Effigy: An image or representation, usually depicting people or animals; often made of pottery or stone.

Egalitarian society: A society in which the number of valued statuses is roughly equivalent to the number of persons with the ability to fill them.

Egyptology: The study of dynastic Egypt and its relics.

Emic: A term referring to anthropological concepts and distinctions that are somehow meaningful, significant, accurate, or "appropriate" to the participants in a given culture (Harris 1968b, p. 571); see also **Etic**.

Empirical: Based on practical experience and physical evidence.

Endscraper: A stone tool with an acute edge used for flensing or softening hides.

Eolith: An extremely crude stone object, once thought to be the work of humans but now known to have been created through natural processes.

Epigraphy: The study of inscriptions.

Ethnoarchaeology: The study of contemporary peoples to determine processual relationships that will aid in unraveling the archaeological record.

Ethnocentrism: The belief that one's own ethnic group is superior to all others.

Ethnographer: One who performs a primarily descriptive study of contemporary or modern cultures.

Ethnohistory: The study of non-Western cultures using evidence from documentary sources and oral traditions.

Ethnology: The study of contemporary cultures; one of the four sub-disciplines of anthropology.

Etic: Applied to concepts and distinctions that are meaningful and appropriate to the community of scientific observers; see also **Emic**.

Evolution: A gradual, ongoing process that reflects adaptive change. Biological evolution involves significant changes in the gene frequencies of a species' gene pool.

Evolutionary potential, law of: See **Law of evolutionary potential**.

Evolution, general: The overall advance or progression stage by stage, as measured in absolute terms; the evolution from heterogeneity toward homogeneity.

Evolution, specific: The increasing adaptive specializations that improve the chances for survival of species, cultures, or individuals.

Exogamy: Marriage outside a particular social group or range of kinship.

Experimental archaeology: A means of studying archaeological process through experimental reconstructions of necessary conditions.

Faunal analysis: The study of animal remains from archaeological sites to illustrate past hunting and dietary practices.

Feature: The nonportable evidence of technology. Usually refers to fire hearths, architectural elements, artifact clusters, garbage pits, and soil stains.

Fetish: An inanimate object associated with a spiritual being or magical powers.

Field notes: The written record containing firsthand, on-the-spot observations; field notes are considered primary field data.

Firman: A permit issued by an oriental government or ruler.

Flake: Lithic fragment (usually debris) resulting from the manufacturing of stone tools. Sometimes the flakes are merely waste from a core; in other cases, flakes themselves can function as tools.

Flaker: An artifact, often made of antler, used for detaching flakes during flintknapping.

Flint: A kind of raw stone material commonly used to manufacture stone tools. The term is often used interchangeably with chert and also as a generic term denoting stone tools (generally restricted to the Old World).

Flintknapping: The art of manufacturing stone tools.

Flotation: The use of fluid suspension to recover tiny plant and bone fragments from archaeological sites.

Flute: Distinctive thinning flake or flakes evident on Folsom and Clovis projectile points.

Folsom culture: A Paleoindian manifestation, dating about 9000–7000 B.C., distributed throughout much of North America.

Folsom projectile point: A spear point characterized by a single flute on each face and fine pressure flaking. Folsom points were made from about 9000–7000 B.C. and are generally found only on the Great Plains and in the American Southwest.

Ford, James A. (1911–1968): An archaeologist who worked mainly in the American Southeast; his major theoretical contribution to archaeology was the development of the seriation technique of chronological ordering.

Foreshaft: A pointed stick, generally made of hardwood or bone, mounted at the distal end of an arrow, dart, or spear; often tipped with flaked stone.

Fremont culture: An agricultural, Puebloan people who lived throughout most of Utah from about A.D. 500 to 1400.

Gastrolith: Stones or pebbles found in the stomachs of fish, reptiles, and birds; used for grinding food.

Gatecliff Shelter: A prehistoric archaeological site in Monitor Valley (central Nevada); the deposits span the last seven thousand years.

General evolution: See **Evolution, general**.

Geoarchaeology: The investigation of the relationship between archaeological and geological processes.

Geomagnetism: The geological variant of **Archaeomagnetism**.

Graver: A stone tool with a protruding edge or point used for fine cutting.

Great Basin: The intermountain region of the American West bordered by the Sierra Nevada Range on the west and the Wasatch Range on the east.

Grid system: The two-dimensional intersecting network defining the squares in which archaeologists dig; usually laid in with strings, stakes, and a transit.

Grinding stone: Lithic artifact generally used to process plant foods.

Ground-penetrating radar: A **remote sensing** device that transmits a radar pulse into the soil. When a discontinuity is encountered, an echo returns to the radar receiving unit, where it can be interpreted.

Habitat: The physical environment in which an organism lives.

Half-life: The time required for half of the C-14 available in an organic sample to decay.

Haliotis: The genus of abalone used for manufacturing beads and ornaments.

Hammerstone: Generally unmodified river cobble used in flintknapping.

Hematite: A reddish mineral commonly used in body paint and for pictographs.

Hissarlik: The massive ruins above the Scamander Plain, Turkey, that **Schliemann** established to be the ruins of ancient Troy.

Historical archaeology: "The study of human behavior through material remains, for which written history in some way affects its interpretation" (Deagan 1982, p. 153).

Homer: A ninth-century B.C. Greek poet and author of the *Iliad* and *Odyssey,* as well as numerous other epics and hymns.

Homo erectus: The ancestor of modern humans who evolved from *Australopithecus,* contained a brain about two-thirds the size of contemporary humans', and established a number of flake tool traditions.

Hopewell: An archaeological culture associated with the Middle Woodland period in the American Midwest, from about 50 B.C. to A.D. 400. It is characterized by dome-shaped burial mounds, large earthen wall enclosures, and finely decorated pottery and clay pipes.

Horncore: The hard, bony inner portion of animal horn.

Humanism: An intellectual tradition that emphasizes the importance of the scholar's intuition and feelings in the acquisition of knowledge; sometimes used to denote antiscientific inquiry.

Hypothesis: A statement that goes beyond bare description; a suggestion that must be tested on independent evidence.

Hypotheticodeduction: A means of testing hypotheses by using deductive reasoning to find and verify the logical consequences.

Ideational strategy: The research perspective that defines ideas, symbols, and mental structures as driving forces in shaping human behavior; see **Adaptive strategy**.

Ideotechnic: The distinctive properties of an artifact that reflect most clearly the mental, cognitive component of culture.

Idiolect: The reflection of individual variation; the way in which an individual speaker pronounces his or her language or practices his or her culture.

Incised slate: A flat, unshaped stone tablet containing motifs inscribed by a human hand.

Index fossil concept: A theory that proposes that strata containing similar fossil assemblages will tend to be of similar age. In archaeology, this concept enables archaeologists to characterize and date strata within archaeological sites using diagnostic artifact forms.

Indirect percussion: A technique used to manufacture stone tools in which flakes are produced by striking a core with a punch made of bone, wood, or antler; see **Direct percussion**.

Induction: A means of reasoning from the particular to the general so that the conclusions contain more information than the premises do.

Infrastructural determinism, principle of: A research strategy used by cultural materialists, in which causal priority is assigned to the modes of production and reproduction. Technological, demographic, ecological, and economic processes become the independent variable, and the social system is the dependent variable. Domestic and political subsystems (the "structure") are considered to be secondary; values, aesthetics, rituals, religion, philosophy, rules, and symbols (the "superstructure") all are tertiary; see also **Infrastructure**.

Infrastructure: Those elements considered by cultural materialists to be the most important to satisfying basic human needs: the demographic, technological, economic, and ecological processes (the modes of production and reproduction) assumed to lie at the causal heart of every sociocultural system.

In situ: A term referring to the position in which an item is initially encountered during excavation or survey.

Irrigation hypothesis: A theory, largely associated with Karl Wittfogel, suggesting that the mechanisms of large-scale irrigation are directly responsible for the origins of the state.

Jasper: A high-quality chert often used as raw material for the manufacture of stone tools.

Jefferson, Thomas (1743–1826): The third president of the United States and considered by many to be the father of Americanist archaeology because of his meticulous excavation of a Virginia burial mound.

Kidder, Alfred V. (1885–1963): A prominent southwestern and middle-American archaeologist, known especially for his early stratigraphic excavations at Pecos Pueblo and his multidisciplinary approach to archaeology.

Kill site: The place where animals are dispatched and where primary disarticulation takes place.

Kinship: Socially recognized relationships based on real or imagined descent and marriage patterns.

Kiva: An underground circular chamber associated with the historic and prehistoric Pueblo Indians of Arizona, Colorado, and New Mexico; used primarily by men and for ceremonial purposes.

La Florida: The name that Spanish explorer Ponce de León gave to the land he discovered in the Easter season (*Pascua Florida* = Feast of Flowers) in 1513. The Spanish used the term to refer to the land they claimed in the North American Southeast.

Language: The overall manner of speaking that reflects general shared speech patterns.

Late Woodland period: The time period from about A.D. 400–A.D. 1000 in the American Midwest. It follows the Middle Woodland era but lacks the elaborate Hopewellian artifacts and structures.

Law of evolutionary potential: The group with the more generalized adaptation has greater evolutionary potential (potential for change) than does the group with the more highly specialized adaptation.

Law of superposition: The law that states that in any pile of sedimentary rocks that have not been disturbed by folding or overturning, the strata on the bottom will have been deposited first.

Laws: Universals in nature that state what has been, what is, and what will be.

Level bag: A paper sack containing archaeological objects from a single horizontal level within a single excavation square. Finds are usually grouped by type (various artifact classes, bones, plant remains, charcoal) and put into labeled baggies inside the level bag. Contemporary archaeologists stand in awe of predecessors who conducted fieldwork in the prebaggie era.

Levi-Strauss, Claude (1908–): A French anthropologist, and founder of the structuralist approach.

Libby, Willard F. (1908-1980): An American physicist who received the Nobel Prize for developing the radiocarbon-dating technique.

Lifeway: The what and who of culture: settlement pattern, population density, technology, economy, organization of domestic life, kinship, social stratification, ritual, art, and religion.

Lightfoot, Dr. John (1602–1675): The master of St. Catharine's and vice-chancellor of Cambridge University who in 1642 declared that humans, heaven, and earth all were created by the Trinity on October 23, 4004 B.C. at nine o'clock in the morning.

Line level: A small spirit-bubble designed for suspension from a string; often used to lay in horizontal lines across an archaeological site (but not as accurate as transit-defined vertical provenience).

Linguistics: A subdiscipline of anthropology that emphasizes the relationships between cultural behavior and language.

Living surface: A generic and imprecise term applied to an assumed level of human occupation within an archaeological site; a handy term to use in the field but tricky to defend after analysis.

Locus: A predicted archaeological site locality.

MacNeish, Richard "Scotty" (1918–): A New World archaeologist who pioneered research on the evolution of agriculture; also an important figure in regional archaeology and the study of the earliest human migrations into the New World.

Magnetometry: The use of a **magnetometer** for mapping subsurface anomalies.

Majolica: A distinctive kind of colorful, decorated earthenware that is tin enameled and glazed; usually of Italian, Spanish, or Mexican origin.

Malthus, Thomas Robert (1766–1834): The proponent of the theory that population growth will overrun available resources unless it is controlled by catastrophes such as war, epidemic, or natural disaster.

Mano: A smooth stone tool held in the hand and used to crush grain or seeds on a metate; see **Grinding stone**.

Manuport: An artifact transported, but not necessarily modified, by human agencies.

Marshalltown: The trowel-manufacturing mecca of America; located in Iowa, and the future site of the Archaeological Hall of Fame.

Material culture: The artifacts and ecofacts used by a group to cope with their physical and social environment.

Maya, Classic: Major precolumbian civilization in Middle America; the Classic Maya period, characterized by the use of the long-count calendar, extends from A.D. 300 to A.D. 900.

Mean ceramic date: A statistical technique devised by Stanley South for pooling the median age of manufacture for temporally significant pottery types.

Median historic date: The intermediate age of occupation for a known-age site.

Megalithic: Of or pertaining to the Middle Neolithic period; characterized by the presence of large stone monuments.

Mesoamerica: The area in Central America in which various Classic and Postclassic civilizations developed, including the Olmec, Teotihuacán, Aztec, and Maya.

Mesolithic: The Middle Stone Age; a period of transition from hunting and gathering to agriculture, featuring settlements based on broad-spectrum wild resource exploitation.

Mestizo: A person of mixed blood (particularly used to denote mixed European and Native American ancestry).

Metate: A stone on which grain or seeds are crushed with a **mano**; see also **Grinding stone**.

Microblade: A long, narrow flake ranging in length from about 15 mm to 45 mm and in width from about 5 mm to 11 mm.

Microenvironment: A characteristic biotic assemblage, often exploited as a distinctive ecological niche.

Microflaking: The minute edge flaking that occurs when stone tools are used.

Micropolish: Edge and surface abrasion and gloss that accrues from tool use; sometimes evident only when stone tools are studied under high-powered microscopy.

Microscarring: Minute patterns of edge damage on a stone tool, often suggesting how that tool was utilized.

Microwear: The patterns of edge damage on a stone tool providing archaeological evidence of the ways in which that tool was used.

Midden: Refuse deposit resulting from human activities, generally consisting of soil, food remains such as animal bone and shell, and discarded artifacts.

Middle Paleolithic: Generic grouping for those cultures that flourished between about 35,000 and 100,000 B.P.; the best-known such tradition is termed Mousterian, the culture carried by Neanderthals.

Middle-range research: Investigation aimed at linking the static data from the archaeological record with the dynamic processes that formed it.

Middle Woodland period: The time period during which the Hopewell culture flourished throughout the American Midwest, from roughly 50 B.C. to A.D. 400.

Milpa: The Mayan term for slash-and-burn agriculture.

Minimum number of individuals (MNI): The number of individual animals necessary to account for all the skeletal elements of a particular species found in a faunal assemblage.

Mission Santa Catalina de Guale: See **Santa Catalina de Guale.**

Mode: A cluster of artifact attributes that vary through time and space.

Moiety: A division of a society into two distinct social categories or groups, often on the basis of descent.

Monitor Valley: A high-altitude area in the central Great Basin (Nevada); the location of Gatecliff Shelter.

Moore, Clarence Bloomfield (1852–1936): Considered to be one of the forebears of Americanist archaeology, he traveled along the southeastern coast of North America in the *Gopher* excavating major sites along the way. Moore's major contributions to archaeology were his excavations at Moundville, Alabama, and Poverty Point, Louisiana.

Morphological type: A descriptive and abstract grouping of individual artifacts whose focus is on overall similarity rather than specific form or function.

Mortar: A stone or wooden receptacle with a cup-shaped depression, generally used for processing plant foods (such as acorns); usually used with a **pestle**.

Mound: An artificial construction commonly used for human burial or as a foundation for a temple or dwelling; see also **Temple mound**.

Mound Builder People: A mythical, non–Native American people, postulated in the nineteenth century as responsible for constructing the thousands of burial mounds in the eastern United States.

Mount Mazama ash: Volcanic ash (or **tephra**) originating from the eruption of Mount Mazama (Crater Lake, Oregon) nearly seven thousand years ago. Undisturbed beds of Mazama ash provide important contextual dates for archaeological sites throughout the northwestern United States.

Multivariate: A perspective that views several interacting variables simultaneously (rather than focusing on one variate at a time, as in *univariate* analysis).

Munsell Color Chart: A loose-leaf notebook containing hundreds of standardized color chips, graded along scales of value, hue, and color; a standard means of describing all color gradations.

Nabonidus (d. 538 B.C.): The last king of the Neo-Babylonian Empire; often considered to be the first archaeologist because he searched the ruined temples of ancient Babylon to answer questions about the remote past.

Nave: The central part of a church.

Neanderthal (*Homo sapiens neanderthalensis*): An extinct species existing about 100,000 to 50,000 years ago and predominantly associated with the Mousterian culture in the Stone Age.

Nelson, Nels (1875–1964): An archaeologist who moved from Denmark to the United States at an early age and had a profound effect on twentieth-century North American archaeology. Working primarily in the Southwest—though he traveled and excavated sites throughout the world—Nelson is best known for his contributions to the stratigraphic method of excavation.

Neolithic: The New Stone Age, during which self-sufficient agriculture developed; characterized by the use of polishing and grinding stones and the origin of ceramics.

New archaeology: A label commonly associated with Lewis R. Binford and his students, emphasizing the importance of understanding underlying cultural processes.

New World: The Western Hemisphere, North and South America, and the neighboring islands.

Niche: The functional role of an organism within a community; not only where that organism lives, but also what it does and eats and how it responds to the environment.

Nock: The groove into which the bowstring is inserted on an arrow.

Nomothetics: The search for general laws and theories.

Nonresidential group: See **Sodality**.

Nonsite archaeology: The recovery and analysis of unclustered physical remains produced by human activities. Nonsite (often called *off-site*) archaeology generally concentrates on remains recovered in a surface or plow zone context.

Normative: Describes a view of human culture stressing shared culture; important to defining cultural units in time and space.

Number of identified specimens (NISP): A largely outdated measure of sample size in archaeological fauna.

Objet d'art: An object of artistic value.

Obsidian: Volcanic glass often used as raw material for the manufacture of stone tools; see also **Obsidian hydration dating**.

Obsidian hydration dating: The technique of dating obsidian artifacts by measuring the microscopic amount of water absorbed on fresh surfaces.

Ocher (or **ochre**): An iron ore compound generally mixed with earth, clay, blood, or grease to be used as paint.

Olive jar: A kind of pottery vessel used to ship olives and wine (and many other commodities) from Spain; commonly found in Spanish colonial archaeological sites; a useful **time-marker**.

Olivella: A genus of shell commonly used as raw material for the manufacture of beads and ornaments.

Olla: A Spanish term for a ceramic vessel generally used to store and cool water.

Optimal foraging theory: A broad-based theoretical perspective used in evolutionary biology that attempts to develop a set of models general enough to apply to a broad range of animal species, yet rigorous and precise enough to explain the details of behavior exhibited by a particular forager.

Paleoautopsy: The technical analysis of a human burial by a trained physical anthropologist specializing in paleopathology.

Paleodemography: The study of mortality patterns in antiquity.

Paleoethnobotany: The analysis and interpretation of interrelationships between people and plants from evidence in the archaeological record; also called *archaeobotany*.

Paleoethnography: A fundamental focus in contemporary archaeology; the study of extinct lifeways.

Paleopathology: The analysis of the cause, nature, and distribution of disease using evidence recovered from archaeological sites.

Palynology: The technique through which the fossil pollen grains and spores from archaeological sites are studied.

Paradigm: An intellectual tradition that conditions the way in which its followers generate, perceive, and interpret empirical data.

Pecos Conference: A convention of southwestern archaeologists originally established in 1927 by A. V. Kidder to determine a uniform cultural chronology and a relatively consistent terminology; the conference is still held today.

Pedology: The study of soils and their structure.

Pestle: An oblong implement used for pounding or grinding in a **mortar**.

Petrarch (1304–1374): An Italian poet, often considered the first humanist and perhaps the most influential individual of the early Renaissance. He provided a strong impetus for archaeological research by looking to antiquity for moral philosophy. His humanism led to a rediscovery of the past.

Petrie, Sir Flinders (1853–1942): A British Egyptologist who developed the technique of sequence ordering known as **seriation**.

Petrographic: Having to do with the microscopic analysis of geological structures.

Phase: An archaeological construct possessing traits sufficiently characteristic to distinguish it from other units similarly conceived; spatially limited to roughly a locality or region and chronologically limited to a relatively brief interval of time.

pH test: A procedure to determine relative acidity or alkalinity.

Physical anthropology: A subdiscipline of anthropology that views humans as biological organisms.

Phytolith: The tiny silica particles contained in plants. Sometimes these fragments can be recovered from archaeological sites, even after the plants themselves have decayed.

Pictograph: A rendering, often painted on the walls of caves or cliffs, that represents a form of nonverbal communication used by nonliterate people.

Piltdown hoax: Bones were found at Piltdown, England, that supposedly provided the missing link between fossil and modern humans. Fluorine tests subsequently indicated that the Piltdown fossil was a clever and deliberate combination of a modern skull and the jaw of an orangutan.

Plant macrofossil: The preserved or carbonized plant parts recovered from archaeological sites.

Pleistocene: The geological period characterized by the advance and retreat of glaciers and the development of early humans.

Pollen analysis: The analysis of fossil pollen in order to reconstruct past vegetation and climate.

Pollen influx: The estimate of the number of pollen grains incorporated into a fixed volume of sediments over a particular time. If the pollen influx is known, the number of years contained in a certain volume of sediment can be estimated.

Polythetic definition: A class is polythetic if a large number of its members share most of the characteristics; there is no necessary or sufficient criterion of membership.

Population, biological: A group of organisms of a single species that at a given time are capable of interbreeding.

Population, cultural: A specific society, such as the Shoshone or Arikara.

Population, statistical: A set of variates (counts, measurements, or characteristics) about which relevant inquiries are to be made.

Postprocessual archaeology: A relatively new school of thinking that uses the **ideational strategy** and cautions against the shortcomings of scientific methods and the **new archaeology**.

Potassium–argon dating: An absolute dating technique that monitors the decay of potassium (K-40) into argon gas (A-40).

Pothunting: Illegal artifact collecting.

Potlatch: Among the nineteenth-century northwest coast Native Americans, a ceremonial giving away or destroying of property in order to enhance status.

Prehistoric: The time period before the appearance of written records.

Primary refuse: Archaeological debris in contexts where it was used and discarded.

Principal component analysis: A multivariate statistical technique designed to reduce redundancy in a body of data and to clarify underlying structural relations.

Processual archaeology: See **New archaeology**.

Profile: A section or exposure showing primary depositional or developmental strata within a buried archaeological site.

Projectile point: A chipped stone artifact used to tip an arrow or atlatl dart or spear.

Promontory culture: Once thought to be a bison-hunting, cave-dwelling people in northern Utah; now recognized as a seasonal variation of the Fremont culture.

Promontory peg: A carved wooden artifact, probably used as the trigger for a snare; first recognized at the Promontory Caves, northwest of Salt Lake City, Utah.

Protohistoric: The transition period between the prehistoric and the historic eras.

Proton precession magnetometer: An instrument used to measure the strength of magnetism between the earth's magnetic core and the sensor, used in **remote sensing**.

Provenience: In general, where an artifact came from. In the context of a specific site, it refers to the horizontal and vertical position of an object in relation to the established coordinate system.

Proximal shoulder angle: A metric attribute reflecting the shape of the base on a projectile point; based on angle formed by the hafting notch and the axis of the shaft.

Pueblo: A Spanish term meaning town or village and applied by sixteenth-century explorers to the village dwellings of the American Southwest. When capitalized, it generally refers to a specific group, culture, or site; uncapitalized, it is a nonspecific reference to certain archaeological sites in the Southwest.

Quadrat sampling: See **Sample, quadrat**.

Quid: The fibrous remains of rhyzomes that were chewed by many hunting-gathering peoples.

Radiocarbon dating: A physiochemical method of estimating the length of time since the death of an organism.

Random sample selection: See **Sample selection, random**.

Ranked society: A society in which there is unequal access to the higher-status categories, and thus many people who are qualified for high-status positions are unable to achieve them.

Reclamation process: The transition of cultural materials from the archaeological record back into the systemic context, such as the scavenging of archaeological artifacts for reuse by both nonindustrial and industrial peoples. The act of archaeological excavation is itself reclamation.

Reese River Valley: Upland valley in central Nevada where Thomas conducted extensive regional archaeology; occupied during the historic period by Western Shoshone people.

Remote sensing: The battery of nondestructive techniques used in geophysical prospection and to generate archaeological data without the need for excavation.

Research design: Programmatic statement outlining four key elements as a blueprint of archaeological research: statement of perspective, synthesis of the existing database, research domains, and relevant research strategy.

Residential group: Physical agglomerations of people at the domestic, territorial, or community level.

Resistivity: See **Soil resistivity**.

Reuse processes: The transformation of materials through successive states within the behavioral system. Potsherds, for example, are sometimes ground up to be used as **temper** in manufacturing new vessels.

Rock art: An inclusive term referring to both pictographs (designs painted on stone surfaces) and petroglyphs (designs pecked or incised into stone surfaces).

Rosetta stone: A black basalt stone found in 1799 that bears an inscription in hieroglyphics, demotic characters, and Greek. By working from the known to the unknown, scholars were able to decipher the ancient Egyptian hieroglyphs.

Roughout: An early stage in the manufacture of bifacially chipped stone tools. Roughouts are often manufactured in quarry areas and later reworked elsewhere into finished artifacts.

Sample: Any subset of a population.

Sample, quadrat: An archaeological research design in which the sampling element is a square or rectangular grid.

Sample selection, random: A method of selecting a sample in which every element has a known and equal probability of selection.

Sample selection, systematic: A method of selecting a sample in which the first element is drawn randomly and the others are selected at predetermined intervals.

Sample, transect: An archaeological research design in which the sampling element is a fairly long linear unit.

Sampling element: The object of study in a probability sample.

Sampling universe: The set of all possible elements to be considered in a probability sample.

Santa Catalina de Guale: Spanish mission site (ca. 1566–1680) located on St. Catherines Island (Georgia).

Scapula saw: An artifact manufactured from the shoulder blade of a bighorn sheep or antelope.

Schlepp effect: The result of butchering process in which the meat is piled on the skin and the lower limb bones are used to drag home the hide bearing the meat. When this is done, the upper limb bones are discarded at the kill site, and the lower limb bones are found more commonly at the habitation site.

Schliemann, Heinrich (1822–1890): A German businessman who retired to study Greek archaeology. Often considered the progenitor of contemporary archaeological method, he established scientific excavating procedures in an effort to prove the historic validity of Homer's city of Troy.

Science: The search for universals in nature by means of established **scientific methods** of inquiry.

Scientific method: An operational series of systematic procedures by which investigators examine empirical phenomena and reach reasoned conclusions.

Seasonality: An estimate of when during the year a particular archaeological site was occupied.

Secondary refuse: Artifacts, bone, shell, and other habitation debris discarded away from the immediate area of use.

Seriation: A temporal ordering of artifacts based on the assumption that cultural styles (fads) change and that the popularity of a particular style or decoration can be associated with a certain time period.

Settlement pattern: The distribution of human populations throughout their habitat.

Shaft straightener: An artifact manufactured from a coarse (often volcanic) stone, with a groove used as a rasp to finish spears and arrowshafts; see **Spokeshave**.

Shaman's bundle: A parcel of sacred objects, often used in magic and/or curing.

Shoshone: The Native American group that inhabited much of the Great Basin during both historic and prehistoric times.

Shroud of Turin: A sheet of twill-woven linen cloth on which appears a pale sepia-tone image of the front and back of a naked man about six feet tall; pale carmine stains of blood mark wounds to the head, side, hands, and feet. The shroud was alleged to be the actual cloth in which Christ's crucified body was wrapped.

Sidescraper: A stone tool with one sharpened edge and a blunt back side.

Sidewall: The vertical margin of an archaeological excavation. It is an important record of site stratigraphy and often provides the axis for measuring artifact provenience; experienced excavators step over sidewalls, never near the edge; it is considered very bad form to cave in somebody's sidewall.

Sinew: Thread made from uncured animal tendon.

Site datum: See **Datum point**.

Smith, William (1769–1839): A British surveyor who collected fossils from geological strata throughout England. Smith made the important discovery that different exposures of the same stratum contained comparable fossils, eventually leading to the formulation of the **index fossil concept**.

Social organization: The structural organization of a society. It is first divided into smaller social units, called *groups*. Second, it has recognized social positions, or *statuses,* and appropriate behavior patterns for these positions, or *roles*.

Society of Professional Archaeologists (SOPA): An organization incorporated in 1976, and created largely in response to the rapid growth of culture resource management in the United States and Canada. One of its major functions has been to compile and maintain an up-to-date listing of qualified professional archaeologists. Those accepting such certification must subscribe to SOPA's code of ethics, institutional standards, and standards of research performance.

Sociotechnic artifact: See **Artifact, sociotechnic**.

Sodality: A nonresidential social group based on a common interest or voluntary participation.

Soil horizon: The product of the natural weathering of geological and archaeological surfaces.

Soil resistivity: A **remote sensing** technique that monitors the degree of electrical resistance in soils—which often depends on the amount of moisture present—in a restricted volume near the surface. Buried features are usually detected by the differential retention of groundwater.

Sondage: An exploratory excavation designed to expose stratigraphy and determine whether a thorough excavation is warranted; a genteel term for **test pit**.

Southern cult: A ceremonial complex widely distributed throughout the American Southeast in Mississippian times, characterized by distinctive motifs such as the cross, the sun circle, the swastika, and the forked eye; also known as the Southeastern Ceremonial Complex.

Specific evolution: See **Evolution, specific**.

Spokeshave: A stone tool with a semicircular concavity used for smoothing spears or arrowshafts. See **Shaft straightener**.

Stable isotope analysis: A technique for reconstructing past diets by analyzing the isotopic ratios (particularly carbon and nitrogen) contained in human bone.

Stadia rod: A long, brightly colored rod, with accurate calibrations for obtaining elevations with a surveying instrument.

State: A society having a strong centralized government with a professional ruling class. Leadership is not based on kinship affiliation, though it may be, and the structure is highly stratified by class.

Statistical population: See **Population, statistical**.

Status: The rights and duties associated with a particular social position.

Status, achieved: The social rights and duties attributed to individuals according to achievement rather than inherited social position.

Status, ascribed: The social rights and duties attributed to an individual at birth, regardless of ability or achievement.

Stela: A freestanding carved stone monument (plural: *stelae*).

Sterile layer: A deposit lacking evidence of human occupation.

Stratigraphy: An analytical interpretation of the structure produced by the deposition of geological and/or cultural sediments into layers, or **strata**.

Stratum: More or less homogeneous or gradational material, visually separable from other levels by a discrete change in the character of the material being deposited or a sharp break in deposition (or both).

Stress: Any environmental factor that forces an individual or population out of equilibrium. Some effects of stress can be observed in human bone tissue.

Striation: Microscopic scratches on stone tools which often reveal the direction of force and the nature of tool use.

Structural anthropology: A research perspective that views culture as the shared symbolic structures that are cumulative creations of the mind. The objective of structural analysis is to discover the basic principles of the human mind as reflected in major cultural domains—myth, art, kinship, and language. A fundamental dualism is considered to be a universal, with binary contrasts operating in all cultures; generally associated with the seminal work of **Claude Levi-Strauss**.

Structure: A domestic and political system assumed by the cultural materialist to be causally conditioned by **infrastructure**.

Subtractive technology: A manufacturing process in which artifacts take form as material is removed from the original mass; **flintknapping** is a subtractive technology.

Superstructure: The values, aesthetics, rules, beliefs, religions, and symbols assumed by cultural materialists to be causally conditioned by **infrastructure**.

Surface archaeology: The recovery and analysis of unburied physical remains produced by human activities.

Surface site: An area in which archaeological remains can be found on stable ground surfaces.

Symbolic anthropology: The research perspective that views culture as embodied in symbols, through which members of a society communicate their world view and values—to one another and to anthropologists. In this view, culture is more than a private common denominator among individuals, becoming a public phenomenon transcending the cognitive realization of any single individual; closely linked with the work of Clifford Geertz.

Synchronic: Referring to a single period in time.

Systematic sample selection: See **Sample selection, systematic**.

Systemic context: See **Context, systemic**.

System of communication: The underlying rationale of language, to communicate information among individuals.

Talisman: A charm or fetish thought to produce unusual, extraordinary happenings.

Talus: A natural slope formed by the accumulation of rock debris.

Taphonomy: the study of processes that operate on organic remains after death to form fossil and archaeological deposits. The term combines the Greek word for tomb or burial *(taphos)* with that for law *(nomos)*.

Taylor, Walter W. (1913–): Considered a revolutionary figure in twentieth-century Americanist archaeology. Taylor proposed the conjunctive approach to archaeology, emphasizing the connection of objects to their cultural contexts.

Technomic artifact: See **Artifact, technomic**.

Temper: The foreign material introduced into clay to keep pottery from cracking when fired; also known as *grog*.

Temple mound: A large flat-topped earthen structure designed to function as an artificial mountain and to set the temple above the landscape.

Temple Mound Period: The time period from about A.D. 700 to European colonization when Native Americans of the Mississippian tradition built large flat-topped earthen structures designed to function as artificial mountains elevating their temples above the landscape.

Temporal type: A morphological type that has been shown to have temporal significance; also known as a **time-marker**.

Teotihuacán: A major urban center that flourished during the Classic period of Mexican prehistory, from roughly 300 B.C. to A.D. 900; located about twenty-five miles north of modern Mexico City.

Tephra: Volcanic ash.

Tephrachronology: The analysis of undisturbed beds of volcanic ash with the aim of constructing a temporal sequence.

Terminus ante quem: The date before which a stratum or feature must have been deposited.

Terminus post quem: The date after which a stratum or feature must have been deposited.

Test pit: A small exploratory sounding designed to determine a site's depth and stratigraphy, preparatory to full-scale excavation; see also **Sondage**.

Time-marker: A temporally significant class of artifacts defined by a consistent clustering of attributes; see also **Temporal type**.

Tool kit: A spatially or functionally patterned combination of artifacts.

Tract: The sampling element in a **quadrat sample** research design.

Transect sampling: See **Sample, transect**.

Transept: That part of a church built out at right angles to the **nave**.

Tree-ring dating: The use of annual growth rings in trees to date archaeological sites.

Tribe: An egalitarian society generally consisting of a group of bands. Its kinship is more complex than that of the **band**, and its economy is often agricultural rather than foraging.

Trojan War: A ten-year struggle during which, according to Homer's *Iliad,* the Greeks invaded Troy to recover Helen, the wife of the Spartan king Menelaus.

Troweling: Small-scale, controlled hand excavation, best accomplished with a sharpened **Marshalltown** trowel.

t-test: A univariate statistical test designed to discover differences among relatively small samples of variates.

Type: A class of archaeological artifacts defined by a consistent clustering of **attributes**.

Typology: The systematic arrangement of material culture into **types**.

Ungulate: A term referring to hoofed animals, including ruminants, swine, horses, tapirs, rhinoceroses, and elephants.

Uniface: A stone tool that has been flaked on only one side.

Utilized flake: A piece of stone debitage used for cutting or slicing. The edge may be damaged from use, but not from deliberate modification.

Varve: A stratified deposit of silt often caused by the annual melting of glaciers.

Virchow, Rudolph Ludwig (1821–1902): A German scientist and naturalist who conducted a broad-based ecological study of the Trojan plain in conjunction with Schliemann's excavations at Hissarlik.

Warp: In weaving, the foundation threads that run lengthwise over and through which the **weft** crosses at right angles.

Wattle-and-daub: A building technique using a wooden framework (the **wattle**) that has been plastered or **daubed** with a mixture of mud, sand, and plant fibers.

Weft: In weaving, the horizontal threads that interlace through the **warp**.

Whetstone: A hone stone used to sharpen other tools.

Wickerwork: Woven basketry that is composed of a flexible thin **weft** and a thick **warp**.

Wickiup: A domed hut used by the Shoshone, sometimes surrounded by circles of stone and covered with piñon tree bark or juniper boughs.

Xerophyte: A plant that grows in arid conditions.

Zoomorph: An animal form used as a symbol in art.

INDEX

NOTE: All terms in **bold** are defined in the Glossary (pp. 649-670)